THE

FRANCO-MOROCCAN CONFLICT

1943-1956

Published for the Carnegie Endowment for
International Peace

THE
FRANCO-MOROCCAN CONFLICT

1943-1956

by

STÉPHANE BERNARD

NEW HAVEN AND LONDON, YALE UNIVERSITY PRESS

1968

Copyright © 1968 by Yale University.
Translated by Marianna Oliver, Alexander Baden Harrison Jr.,
and Bernard Phillips from volumes 1 and 2 of *Le Conflit
Franco-Marocain, 1943–1956,* published by the
Institut de Sociologie Solvay of the Free University
of Brussels, 1963.
Designed by Marvin H. Simmons,
set in Granjon type,
and printed in the United States of America by
The Vail-Ballou Press, Inc., Binghamton, N.Y.
Distributed in Great Britain, Europe, Asia, and
Africa by Yale University Press Ltd., London; in
Canada by McGill University Press, Montreal; and
in Latin America by Centro Interamericano de Libros
Académicos, Mexico City.

Library of Congress catalog card number: 67-24490

To my wife, whose help and encouragement
were the true inspiration of this book.

FOREWORD

It is a truism that decolonization is one of the great factors shaping our day and age. The domestic policies of the former metropolitan countries, the foreign policies of the Great Powers, and the whole complex of international relations have been largely conditioned by the vast movement of emancipation that began with the end of World War II and now pursues its ineluctable course before our eyes. Some territories became independent after long and bitter struggle; others did so without violence. Rarely, however, has sovereignty been transferred without acute tensions or clashes between the colonial powers and youthful nationalist movements. The decision to include in a series devoted to international conflicts a study in depth of a characteristic case of decolonization is not, therefore, surprising.

The work that follows is not an isolated monograph. In 1956, the Carnegie Endowment for International Peace conceived a plan of studying a series of international disputes. Its purpose was not so much to describe certain aspects of contemporary history as to contribute to an understanding of the mechanism of the conflicts and of the nature of the tensions that mark our times. As Proudhon has put it, "Like everyone, when I saw the cannon take the place of the conference table, I longed to know more of this extradialectical method of settling international difficulties, to find out what makes governments and people act as they do when they reject persuasion and instead seek to encompass each other's destruction, and, since events themselves were doing the talking, to discover the meaning of these events."[1]

There were several possible approaches to the theme conflicts and tensions. We decided to analyze individual cases, and were

1. P.-J. Proudhon, *La Guerre et la paix, 1* (Paris, 1961), 4–5.

vii

faced at once with a problem of selection. At one extreme, we were limited by methodological considerations; since no satisfactory typology of international conflicts has been developed as yet, we had no criterion for scientific selection. Therefore, to keep all our studies in a single global political context—what Morton Kaplan calls the "international system"—we limited our choice to conflicts that developed after World War II. We discarded the minor conflicts unknown to the general public and solved, in most cases, without emotional commitment. At the other extreme, we did not consider it feasible to study the great conflicts, such as the cold war, because of insufficient information. In the intermediate area thus defined, where we decided to remain, there was still the problem of whether to concentrate on a single category of conflicts or to examine sharply differentiated cases. We chose the latter, for we believed that, at this stage in the evolution of political science, it was of primary importance that our field of investigation be as wide as possible. In fact, despite the recent development of political science and despite the increasingly large number of studies dedicated to international relations and to the systematic analysis of conflicts, we must still concede that little real progress has been made in this field. For this reason, the Endowment felt that, by the application of such a method, something useful might be achieved, thus contributing to the advancement of this branch of knowledge.

It must be added that the essential differences among the subjects and the particular preoccupations of each author made it impossible to ensure the perfect parallelism among the various studies that strict application of the case method would have required. Some of the studies in the series give greater importance to reconstruction of facts, while others concentrate on elaboration of theories. Methods of analysis, hypotheses advanced, general theoretical concepts—all are equally diverse. This was inevitable. Nevertheless, the Carnegie Endowment endeavored to secure some degree of homogeneity by arranging frequent meetings of those responsible for the four studies.

The study of the Franco-Moroccan conflict, the second in the series, was published in French in 1963. The first, published in 1959, dealt with the conflict between France and Germany over the Saar;[2] a study on the Trieste conflict appeared in a French edition in December 1966 and one on Cyprus is now in progress. Each study has an historical section and a theoretical section that seeks to reconstruct the mechanism of the conflict. Highly skilled research assistants assembled firsthand documentation, without which these studies could certainly never have been completed. An advisory committee of eminent persons, usually from the countries in question, met several times in the course of each study. The committee assisted the director of each investigation in order to facilitate the work and to contribute to a better understanding of the problems. Lastly, and this point should be stressed, each study was entrusted to a specialist who was not a national of any of the countries involved in the conflict.

We will not dwell here on the difficulties of contemporary historical research—a point fully discussed by the author in his preface—but these difficulties must be recognized as the major cause of the slow progress of the studies. The Carnegie Endowment's preparation of manuscripts, checking of documents, and verification of facts have also been complicated by the very nature of the sources used.

The first three studies in the series have been published in French as *Étude de cas de conflits internationaux* by the Institut de Sociologie Solvay of the Free University of Brussels, to which we extend our sincere gratitude.

Before concluding, we should like particularly to thank the members of the Advisory Committee on the Franco-Moroccan conflict for their valuable help in our research, and to convey our appreciation to the research assistants and to all those who contributed to the preparation of this study.

Lastly, we should like to express our deepest appreciation to Stéphane Bernard, of the Institut de Sociologie Solvay of the Free University, who agreed to carry out this difficult assignment. It proved a delicate piece of research indeed, whose scope and complexity inevitably involved problems that sometimes seemed insoluble. Though a sociologist by training, the author

2. Jacques Freymond, *Le Conflit sarrois, 1945–1955,* Études de cas de conflits internationaux, no. 1 (Brussels, Institut de Sociologie Solvay, 1959; Eng. trans. London, Stevens and Sons, 1960; German trans. Frankfurt, Forschungsinstitut der Deutschen Gesellschaft für Auswärtige Politik, 1961).

never minimized the historical aspects we brought to his attention, and we are grateful to him. His perseverance and sagacity
enabled him to clarify the main features of the conflict and to
formulate a theory of decolonization that will, we hope, contribute to the development of the systematic analysis of conflicts
and to the advancement of political science in general.

John Goormaghtigh
Director of the European Centre
of the Carnegie Endowment

Geneva
March 1966

CONTENTS

Volume 2

PREFACE

When the Carnegie Endowment asked the author, some years ago, to carry out a study of the Franco-Moroccan conflict, the idea of analyzing the nature and limits of political determinism on the basis of a specific, clearly defined case had been in his mind for some time. The present work is the result of this coincidence of interest.

Analysis of a decolonization conflict brings into play, under one guise or another, all the variables of the political system. It calls on the resources of the theory of power. It is concerned with the basic historical and sociological data characteristic of groups in conflict. In these circumstances, there are two equally valid methods of approach. One can concentrate on the history of the conflict with only brief complementary analyses of other facets of the problem. Or one can focus the investigation from the outset on the theory of a political system in the process of decolonization. In the latter case, however, as much attention must be given to the history of the conflict and the study of its socio-institutional basis as to the theoretical analysis.

As a sociologist, I inclined to the second formula. This study, in the original French edition, consists of three parts of equal importance.[1] The first is devoted to the history of the conflict. The second seeks to reconstruct its sociological mechanism. The third describes the institutions and social groups brought into play; it was put last to indicate that it was primarily for reference purposes, although the information it contains supplements the

---

1. Stéphane Bernard, *Le Conflit franco-marocain, 1943–1956* (Vol. 1, *Historique;* Vol. 2. *Mécanisme de la décolonisation du protectorat: Contribution à la théorie du système politique;* Vol. 3, *Institutions et groupes sociaux; Annexes*), Centre européen de la dotation Carnegie pour la paix internationale, Études de cas de conflits internationaux, No. 2 (Brussels, Institut de Sociologie Solvay of the Free University of Brussels, 1963), pp. 389, 286, 402.

historical part and, like the latter, provides the basis for the
theoretical part. The third volume is not included in the present
edition, since it is assumed that scholars interested in the supplementary information it contains can draw upon the French
text. However, comments on the third volume have been included here for the benefit of the reader who seeks further information.

The major problem in regard to the historical part was the
collection and utilization of material. Four principal sources
were used: bibliographic materials, archives in the public domain
at the time the investigation began, interviews, and restricted
archives to which access was obtained through the interviews.

During the early stages of research, the bibliographic materials
available were of limited interest. The conflict had just been resolved, and only a few memoirs and eyewitness accounts had
been published. Most of the supplementary periodical material
had been written when the conflict was at its height. A few more
general works gave a rough idea of what had happened and
served as guidelines until other material became available and
relegated most of them to the background.

Available documents—Moroccan, French, and international
summaries of events; diplomatic records; archives in the public
domain; and the press—painted an incomplete and superficial
picture of the conflict. Moreover, it was necessary to draw upon
the last with discretion; to try to compile a history of the present
day from newspaper clippings would be to drown in a sea of
paper. Press accounts were used only to round out the story of
certain sequences of events or to verify data impossible to check
otherwise.

Actually, the basic material for the study came from interviews
and unpublished archives. The use of interview techniques with
political figures presents obvious risks. When an expert con-
fidently undertakes an extensive series of interviews with the
personnel of a business firm, he is in full control of the situation
and generally obtains the information he needs to formulate his
conclusions. In a political investigation, which brings the researcher into contact with people who did not initiate the in-

vestigation and who are under no obligation to assist in it, the person interviewed has the upper hand, at least at the beginning. He reveals only what he wants to reveal. In addition, interviews are not as a rule definitive unless they can be held as often as necessary, and this is rarely the case. Interviews with Europeans in Morocco were, despite some refusals, numerous enough to constitute an acceptable sampling of the most important groups. Most of those interviewed—whether they came from the Residency, the settler groups, the Army, or the business world—submitted to questioning with good grace. It was necessary, however, to keep our interviews with the Muslims to an absolute minimum, since the new leaders of Morocco were too absorbed in the harassing tasks of building a new state to be able to participate usefully in exchanges of views directed toward the past. Nevertheless, various nationalist and some underground leaders were interviewed. In France, the investigators kept to political circles without exception: refusals were rare (certain right-wing leaders and one center minister). While eyewitness accounts offer an essential point of departure for political research, the information provided must be taken with a grain of salt. Intentionally false statements are rare and fairly easy to detect. But sins of omission are legion, and errors made in good faith are more numerous and tenacious. Certain mutually reinforcing statements reproduce errors of fact accepted as truths by an entire social group. Thus it is necessary to exercise caution in using these accounts, even if at first sight they seem sufficiently consistent.

Finally, the archives made it possible to put the history of the conflict on a solid documentary footing. Indeed, our investigation opened the gates of an almost inexhaustible reservoir of archives —although this certainly does not mean that every major respondent gave us access to his personal papers. The other side of the coin is that new documents were constantly being discovered, requiring continuous revision of the text until the most important archives had been explored. The result is that although the researcher is ultimately in a position to clear up many historical points, he can rarely identify his sources. I can only assure the reader that wherever in the account a fact is given without reservation, it can be considered as reasonably supported by authentic documents or by an adequate number of consistent reactions.

The correlation of documentary sources and interviews was only the first stage of the investigation. The second was a follow-up interview with the respondent once the manuscript was ready for his consideration. Such interviews were held only for the Grandval and, to a lesser extent, the Boyer de Latour periods. Most of the remaining problems were concentrated in those two periods, and the chapters concerned were largely rewritten after these additional inquiries. It seems clear, therefore, that a scholar wishing to attain maximum accuracy in writing contemporary political history must make two investigations—one before and one after the preliminary drafting of the manuscript. It should be noted, however, that the additional accuracy achieved by this method does not necessarily provide a better basis for embarking upon the sociological study of a phenomenon such as decolonization. We knew enough, before reviewing the Grandval period, to go on to the study of the mechanism of the conflict, insofar as that study depended on a knowledge of that period. The theory of a political system is seriously affected only by the major errors committed in writing the system's history. Fortunately, these are generally eliminated in the preliminary stages of the investigation.

Is the writing of contemporary history more fraught with error than writing about the past? That is not unlikely. What seems certain is that the historian of the present runs a greater risk of having his errors exposed than does the historian of the past. If Louis XIV returned to earth with all his records, many reputations would be shaken. For the contemporary historian, Louis XIV is always just outside the door. Moreover, the question is not whether an historical study, undertaken with a view to providing material for a sociological analysis, is or is not complete. It is generally recognized that history can achieve only an approximate and indefinitely perfectible reconstruction of the past. From our point of view, the only question is whether the gaps and errors that inevitably occur in the history of a recent colonial conflict are or are not likely to affect the theory of decolonization based upon it. It is our belief that the material gathered during our investigation reduces this risk to a minimum.

The problems posed by the history of the conflict are not merely technical; they also concern the author's attitude to his subject. I have departed from the canon of historical method on two points: first, by letting it be known that my scale of values inclined more toward nationalism than colonialism; second, by assuming that the possible alternatives to certain historical accidents had no retrospective significance because of the inevitable developments of which those accidents were a part. A brief explanation is called for on both these points to avoid possible misunderstanding.

Value judgments in political analysis are a source of debate. Some people think they tend to mar the objectivity of the account and the author should not intrude. Others maintain that few contemporary political historians are consciously or unconsciously without bias and that, since it is impossible to eliminate this bias, it is better to be frank about it. And so no secret has been made of the fact that the author is more favorably disposed toward peoples struggling for their emancipation than toward groups defending by force privileges that are contrary to the spirit of the times. It should be noted, however, that this scale of values is not mine alone. It belongs to the times. Even the most intransigent supporters of the colonial status quo respect it in their own fashion. When a colonial regime is attacked, it defends itself by reversing its relationship to history after history has ceased to be favorable to it. Generally, such a regime merely stands on its record and acts as though it were still an instrument of progress even when it is becoming incapable of dealing with the very problems it engenders. It does not go so far as to adopt a complete transmutation of values by holding that the oppressor is the equal of the oppressed and has equal rights. This distinction is important. Although there is little sense in judging someone by a scale of values other than his own, the undertaking regains its raison d'être once it becomes apparent that those who write history and those who make it are bound inextricably by the dominant values of the civilization to which they belong.

Moreover, it would be wrong to confuse detachment and objectivity. To the historian of contemporary political life, objectivity consists less in taking refuge in the calm indifference of an Olympian judgment than in going beyond his own value judgments to analyze without prejudice the mechanism of the human actions he is investigating. If some contradiction still lurks in this attitude, it is because man is held to be both responsible for his acts and the tool of circumstances. Furthermore, it does not seem to me that the historian's attitude toward his subject need necessarily distort his conception of the phenomena he analyzes. If, instead of a study of the decolonization of Morocco, the Endowment had sponsored a study of the colonization of Africa, I would have written without hesitation that colonization was as inevitable in the era that produced it as its disappearance is today.

The second point raises an equally delicate question. What might have been is of interest to both history and sociology. When a sociologist ponders an historical development other than what actually occurred, he merely renders unto history that which is history's—the accidental and the unforeseeable that characterize any chain of social events. When he concludes that this eventuality would not have appreciably altered the evolution of which it constitutes one of the conceivable accidents, the sociologist defines his own field of investigation by emphasizing the essential elements in the sociological process.

The historian's task is to reconstruct a meaningful past while pointing out that events might have transpired otherwise. The sociologist's task is to show to what extent social events are governed by necessity. To complicate matters, historians have always been interested in both kinds of problems: from earliest times many great historians have tried to be their own sociologists. Since there is a growing tendency for history and sociology to become further differentiated while providing mutual support in interdisciplinary research, some confusion has resulted as to the roles of the two disciplines. This is undoubtedly a passing phase that will fade as their relationship is readjusted.

The history of a conflict reveals what is intrinsic and what is accidental in the chain of events. What is more real than a human act? Yet, what is less necessary, since any human act is committed by one or more individuals who might have died the day before or never have been born? Obsessed as it is with the concrete, history does not go far enough to distinguish the fundamental categories of sociological analysis. Still, if the problem of inevitability in history arises at the level of historical research, it can only be satisfactorily analyzed in terms of general sociology or political economy. I could have made a clearer distinction between the history of the conflict and the study of its sociological mechanism. I preferred to outline, in the historical study, those concepts that would be proven in the theoretical section. This approach seemed most apt to demonstrate that, although the historian inevitably encounters sociological problems along his way, he can hope to solve them only on other than historical grounds.

There remains the theoretical, and to the author's mind the most important, part of the book—for the first volume, as well as the third volume of the French edition, are merely preparatory analyses. Three axioms guided this investigation. First, political science, taken as an autonomous discipline, offers no solid foundation upon which to build a construction of this kind. Second, sociologists, social psychologists, and specialists of underdevelopment have elaborated most of the material requisite to a tentative formulation of the basic elements of the theory of political systems. Third, a researcher should innovate only insofar as the disciplines concerned contain glaring omissions. Science is a collective task, and it is useless to hope that one day a satisfactory theory of the political phenomenon can be developed if every research worker thinks he has a right to start over again from scratch. In this study, decolonization has therefore been treated as a problem of general sociology, and the author's personal views have been incorporated only when it seemed impossible to do otherwise.

The theoretical section is based as closely as possible on this methodological approach. In general, the structural and functional theories of social systems have merely been adapted to the study of a complex political system, while as satisfactory a balance as possible has been maintained between analysis of the political variables considered in their mutual interactions and analysis of their functional correlatives. The only personal construction introduced into this common fund of knowledge and theories relates (apart from the formulation of certain general principles) to the specific relationship which, in the political system, links the potential authority of those who govern to the attitudes adopted toward them by the governed and to the means of coercion exercised by the authorities within the framework of a given governmental structure. It is generally accepted today that the theory of political systems must be based on a study of collective political attitudes considered in their relation to the social situations that condition them. Thus the only satisfactory method of rounding out the demonstration is to analyze, in a second stage, the complementary and no less basic relationship established at the upper level of the system between these attitudes and the decision-making capacity of the leaders. So far, specialists in political sociology do not appear to have given this relationship the attention it deserves. That omission needed repairing, and I have done my best to do so without disguising the fact that a great deal remains to be done in this direction.

This model, however, is related to a trend in modern research broad enough to eliminate any fear that it might be gratuitous. Apart from the fact that such research stems directly from a celebrated formula of Vilfredo Pareto, our thoughts on this point clearly relate to the theory of decision-making. The study of the authority of a political system as a function of collective attitudes and of force is an essential aspect of this theory. True, there are other conceptions of this phenomenon; but I had to discard them because in general they were evolved for purposes different from mine, and are, for the most part, useless for a large-scale study of fluctuations in the decision-making capacity of a system and, a fortiori, of several political systems.

The orientation of the author's research is, moreover, in line with the current preoccupations of theoreticians. Jean Meynaud wrote in his remarkable *Introduction à la science politique*:

> The most deplorable feature of contemporary political exegesis is its habit of appearing in bits and pieces. We are capable of grasping successively the various forces

that govern the process, but we are unable—or able only in an impressionist fashion—to establish their interrelations, to estimate their respective influences and, most important, to relate them in specific terms to a view of the whole. Analysis is limited to a juxtaposition of factors which we do not know how to integrate; it has not so far been able to provide an articulated configuration of the variables in the governmental process.[2]

The theoretical section may be regarded as a contribution to the creation of an integrated political theory as understood by Professor Meynaud. We hope, for example, to show that the concepts of *political system* and of *structure of authority* can be usefully associated at the present stage of theoretical formulation.[3]

The theoretical part in turn calls for some explanation: the theses it puts forward apply only to a clearly defined type of phenomena; they are determinist in nature and should be regarded as tentative rather than proved. They are based on information that is necessarily incomplete and often mediocre. Lastly, they are not, in the true sense of the word, demonstrable. Let us consider these points in greater detail.

The theory of the decolonization of Morocco relates, first of all, to a specific phenomenon; it is applicable only to colonial conflicts of the same type, although it undoubtedly contains certain elements pertinent to other types of colonial conflict. It is also based on certain generalizations valid for all political conflicts. But it is not applicable either to all domestic conflicts or to all international conflicts, not even to those of a quasi-colonial character—such as the Hungarian crisis, the revolt of the barbarians against the Roman Empire, or the innumerable situations in which the conflict between two groups occupying the same territory has been resolved either by a modus vivendi or by the slow assimilation of one group by the other.

It is also true that political determinism is not popular, particularly as regards dynamic interpretations. In some quarters, it is criticized as being in thrall to a mystique of revolution that tran-

2. Jean Meynaud, *Introduction à la science politique,* Cahiers de la fondation nationale des sciences politiques, no. 100 (Paris, 1959), pp. 221 ff.

3. See, inter alia, references made to the latter concept by J. Meynaud, ibid., pp. 220, 222.

scends rational argumentation; in others, it is held responsible
for an unduly mechanistic conception of life in society. Thus
attacked on two fronts, the determinist school is in an awkward
position. Its advocates explain, to little effect, that widely construed determinism is a matter of degree and that a comprehensive sociology must station itself halfway between absolute
determinism and unconditional spontaneity. As soon as the word
is spoken, its corrosive power appears to destroy the reservations
with which its use is meant to be surrounded. Yet there is nothing mysterious in the association of human spontaneity and
social necessity. Evolution is a primal reality in the life of societies. It is related to specific causes under the effect of which the
most solidly established social modes are constantly pushed into
the background by new forms better adapted than the old ones
to the problems facing societies. Political struggles graft themselves onto this phenomenon. Certain groups try to prevent the
evolutionary processes that others seek to promote. Those opposed to evolution find themselves ipso facto at a distinct disadvantage compared with those acting in accordance with it. If
at the dawn of the Machine Age in Europe there had been a
Steam Engine Party and a Muscular Energy Party, the former
would inevitably have won. The same is true whenever political
struggles are determined by a sufficiently clear-cut sociological
imbalance. There is only one important difference between this
imaginary model and decolonization. In the latter case, the
group opposing the political evolution of the system is also, in
certain respects, the most determined agent of its technological
development. The same group seeks paradoxically to promote
the evolution of the system at the base and to stifle it at the
summit. This contradiction introduces a special difficulty into the
analysis, but it does not change its nature.

In the present stage of political science, the theory of the decolonization of Morocco can be no more than an outline, a rapid
and elliptical reconnaissance of the problems posed by the study.
In the words of Frank A. Pinner:

> Theoretical models never emerge full-blown from the
> heads of their creators. In their nymphal state, they are
> rather formless images of the logical structures they are

to become. Such images bear to future theories the same relation as the painter's first sketch to the final painting: although vague in outline and gingerly drawn, they nevertheless exhibit a basic over-all design showing the chief dimensions and relationships. Inasmuch as such images are imprecise, arguments can easily arise over their potential worth; this in part explains the everlasting disputes of the methodologists.[4]

This is exactly the sense in which the word "outline" is understood here. The theoretical section does not contain a single point of view immune to objections or lengthy explanation. It is not a model that bears comparison with those in the most advanced social sciences. It is evident that the approach described in the methodological introduction to Volume 2 has been followed only very loosely in the body of the demonstration. This defect is easily explained: a discipline can only conform strictly to its methodological principles through the cumulative efforts of scholars in the field working toward the development of a common enterprise. Political science has not reached this point. The best a researcher can do for the time being is to bring his stone to the edifice in the hope that others will build upon it.

This emphasis on general ideas does not mean that present gaps in political theory are a sufficient explanation of the backwardness of this discipline as contrasted with the other social sciences. The inadequacy of the theoretical framework is only one of the obstacles to its development. Our ignorance of sociological data is another—perhaps of greater gravity for the future. Political theory certainly lags behind the facts. Statistical data so far assembled would appear, even now, to be adequate for a better knowledge of the political system than we now possess. Even when this lag has been overcome, however, new advances in theory will be possible only if our factual knowledge can be decisively improved in accuracy and in scope. Political science has described many phenomena in an imprecise and fragmentary fashion, and the analyses in this study are no exception. Only the improvement of investigating techniques and the

---

4. Frank A. Pinner, *Notes on Method in Social and Political Research* (East Lansing, Mich., Bureau of Social and Political Research, 1960), p. 189.

rationalization of political procedures will make it possible to make decisive advances.

There remains the question of proof, that source of innumerable misunderstandings. Except in well-defined areas, clearly experimental in character, the social sciences cannot, strictly speaking, provide proof for the theoretical views upon which they are built. One can establish the existence of a sociological fact. One can, to a certain extent, prove the falsity of a sociological prognostication by showing that it has not been borne out by the facts. It is generally impossible to establish the truth or falseness of a theoretical interpretation of the facts because no experimental criteria exist in social science to back up a judgment of this kind. Sociological phenomena are too ambiguous and too complex for the truth or falsehood of a theory to be demonstrated de plano, once that theory has been sufficiently elaborated to be removed from the facile charge of oversimplification. No one can prove whether Marx and Keynes were wrong or right in their basic doctrines. Thus they are still subjects of debate. Obviously, I make no pretensions to compare myself with such great minds as these, but the problem of proof is the same in my case as in theirs. In the social sciences, knowledge generally advances by side-stepping the problem of proof. By common consent, more comprehensive theories are substituted for less comprehensive ones, and there is no crucial test that can distinguish one from the other. In matters of theory, the more suitable system replaces the less suitable without undergoing trial by proof. We can only note this problem in passing; it warrants close study by experts in the theory of knowledge. Our reference was only intended to stress the futility of subjecting the exploration of social facts to demands of proof that are incompatible with research of this kind.

As Volume 3 of the French edition of this study has not been translated into English, it may be helpful to define, for English readers, its purpose and raison d'être. This volume, subtitled *Institutions and Social Groups: Annexes,* consists, aside from the annexes, of five parts: (1) "Moroccan Political Institutions and Social Groups," (2) "Metropolitan Institutions and Social Groups," (3) "The Franco-Moroccan Economic and Financial

Organization," (4) "Urban Terrorism and Guerrilla Warfare," and (5) "The International Context."

The purpose of the third volume was to round out the historical material analyzed in the first volume by as detailed an analysis as possible of the institutional, sociological, economic, and financial materials that had to be studied before the second volume could be written. In the French as well as in the English edition, Volume 2 is the heart of the work. Thus, Volumes 1 and 3 of the French edition had the characteristics of preparatory studies for the analysis of the mechanism of the conflict, which constitutes the purpose of Volume 2. The omission of Volume 3 in the English translation is justified not only by the fact that it is mainly composed of studies which can, in many cases, be considered as appendices but also because readers desiring to consult it may use the French edition.

However, three sections of this third volume which may be of particular interest to readers are briefly described below.

The first of these studies, Chapter 7 of the third part of Volume 3 of the French edition—concerned with the problem of economic and financial pressures—distinguishes between those pressures exerted in order to obtain a particular advantage and those exerted to influence the colonial policy of the regime. The consequences, in relation to each of these ends, of the intervention of large and small interests are studied successively. The second study, the fourth part of Volume 3 of the French edition, deals with the activities of the urban terrorists, the French police, the counter-terrorists, the guerrilla groups, and, finally, with those of the French army and its Moroccan auxiliaries. It contains a full statistical table of acts of terrorism and of urban victims. The third study, part five of Volume 3, presents the international context of the crisis. It consists of five chapters devoted respectively to: (1) "The Indochinese, Tunisian, and Algerian Crises," (2) "Political Support from Arab and Afro-Asian States," (3) "The Role of the United Nations," (4) "The Evolution of the Cold War," and (5) "The Attitudes of the United States, United Kingdom, and Spain."

It remains for me to describe how the work was organized, the contribution of our collaborators on the project, and the manner in which the historical data was checked.

As far as possible, the work was organized according to the guidelines laid down by the Carnegie Endowment for the series. Each study was conducted by a director with two full-time assistants who, under his direction, were responsible for the interviews, documentary research, analyses of press reports, and preliminary syntheses needed to carry on the investigation in a given country. Jean-Yves Goëau-Brissonière, *Chargé de conférences* at the Law School of the University of Paris, and at that time adviser to the Foreign Minister on North African Affairs, filled this essential role in France for more than two years. His task was rendered very difficult because Franco-Moroccan political ties had just been dissolved, and the archives and Residential staff had been dispersed. M. Goëau-Brissonière held interviews,[5] ferreted out and analyzed documentation, studied press reports, and drafted analyses. He was the mainspring of a joint research project that would inevitably have failed had he not overcome, with unflagging good humor, difficulties that at first seemed insurmountable.

Rabat presented a particular problem, since, ordinarily, the team would have consisted of a European and a Muslim consultant. But the multitude of tasks confronting the young Moroccan elite on the dissolution of the protectorate did not make it feasible to recruit a Moroccan assistant. Research in Morocco was carried out in Rabat by M. Patrice Blacque-Belair, who had all the necessary contacts through his close ties with various Muslim and European circles. It was obviously impossible to gather as much significant material in Rabat as was put together in Paris by M. Goëau-Brissonière. However, it was essential to undertake a certain number of interviews, in both Moroccan and European circles, to scrutinize archives, study the local press, and make analyses; the problems of documentation and interpretation posed by the Moroccan aspects of the crisis could not otherwise have been properly resolved. These various activities were suc-

5. The 76 interviews conducted in the course of the investigation were divided as follows: Europeans in Morocco and the Residential staff: 34, including 29 by Jean-Yves Goëau-Brissonière, and 5 by Patrice Blacque-Belair; Muslims: 11; metropolitan political circles: 31, including 24 by Goëau-Brissonière.

cessfully carried out by M. Blacque-Belair with an independence of judgment and a critical spirit not often encountered in such a politically charged atmosphere. I should add that despite two sojourns in Morocco, it would have been difficult for me to arrive at an adequate understanding of the Moroccan problem without the opportunity of engaging in detailed discussions with a consultant who was able to fill in the meager outlines of local situations that were all I possessed at the beginning of the study. It was equally important for me to be introduced to nationalist leaders and senior Residential officials who had stayed in Morocco by a person who enjoyed the confidence of both sides. The investigation thus owes much to M. Blacque-Belair.

In Brussels, through the good offices of the Endowment, the author was assisted for a year, with great intelligence and perseverance, by Mme. Jacqueline Simont-Bastenié, then *Chargée de recherches* at the Institut de sociologie Solvay. Mme. Simont-Bastenié's many contributions to the analysis of the material included a draft statistical study of terrorist activities based on the international press summaries of the Royal Institute of International Affairs and a detailed analysis of material relating to the section on social groups and institutions.

A number of researchers cooperated with this permanent team. M. Pierre Viansson-Ponté, head of the political section of the staff of *Le Monde,* undertook a study of the attitudes of economic and financial groups, interviewing a number of leading persons in the process. M. Claude Benoit, *Licencié ès lettres* and *Diplomé* of the Institut d'études politiques of the University of Paris, worked on the attitudes of political parties, workers' trade unions, and employers' organizations. He, too, did considerable interviewing, and collected a large amount of material. This documentation enabled him to give a clear picture of the way in which the bodies concerned reacted to Moroccan problems. M. Raymond Barrillon, at that time parliamentary reporter for *Le Monde,* engaged in a systematic analysis of the principal votes in the National Assembly on North African matters during the period under study. In each case, the significance of the votes and their political effect was brought out. Part of the task of reviewing the metropolitan press was entrusted to the journalist M.

Jean-Louis Guillaud, who also did research on various military matters and conducted a number of interviews. M. Michel Froment, *Docteur en droit* and *Diplomé* of the Institut d'études politiques of the University of Paris, analyzed parliamentary proceedings relating to Morocco. M. Gilbert Gantier studied certain aspects of the economic and financial organization. In Paris, Mme. France de la Rosière, then a secretary at the Ministry for Foreign Affairs, effectively carried out various tasks connected with the records of the individual protagonists, conducted a number of interviews, and drew up a list covering the composition and political hue of the successive French governments concerned. The maps were designed by Robert Winslow of New York. Lastly, M. Jean-Paul Trystram, *Maître de conférence* at the Faculté des lettres of the University of Aix-Marseille, kindly volunteered to organize, in Rabat, the first meetings devoted to the study of specifically Moroccan aspects of the crisis.

It will be apparent that on many occasions the author and his full-time associates ventured outside their special fields. I myself was not particularly well versed in North African sociology, nor particularly well informed on economic and financial matters, nor yet well qualified to act the part of historian. However, necessity is the mother of invention, and the conduct of an investigation of this kind soon forces one to enlarge his ordinary field. Initially, we tried to stay as close as possible to the ideal of entrusting all the studies to specialists in the different fields. A thousand material and human necessities soon led us all to trespass on each other's terrain.

This is one of the reasons the Endowment wanted the director of the project and his staff to be able to explain their difficulties to a group of international experts chosen for their experience and impartiality. It therefore set up an advisory committee, which met on several occasions in Geneva in the course of the investigation. The suggestions made by the members of the committee greatly assisted us in clarifying our concept of the conflict.

Since verifying facts and technical references turned out to be a more delicate problem than was at first expected, it may be well to specify here the procedure finally adopted. Too much material was collected to make it possible to envisage checking it for accuracy before the manuscript of the historical section was completed. When writing started on that part of the work, our files contained hundreds of dates, political statements, and references to events of all kinds. In most cases, this material came from interviews, official documents, or unpublished archives directly or indirectly relating to facts whose authenticity was obvious, but which could only be incorporated into the account subject to later verification. To have attempted to check all these data while the material was being collected would have been both wasteful and dangerous—wasteful because only some would be used in the manuscript and dangerous because if our regular staff had had to do the checking while working full-time on collecting material, the investigation might well have bogged down. The first draft of the historical section, therefore, referred only to the small number of works quoted or technical references stemming from the documentation used or from the preliminary analyses made by my fellow workers. I had hoped that the checking that remained could be done by them while I drafted the other two sections. It eventually became clear that this procedure was unsatisfactory and that the prolongation of the drafting period would make it impossible. In the circumstances, it became essential to call in someone who could do this work.

The important task of checking and verification was entrusted to Mme. Christiane Zuber-Bouvard, a member of the staff of the Endowment's European Office, who worked with the author and with M. Goëau-Brissonière. In the existing state of political chronologies, only rarely could a date or an event directly connected with the Franco-Moroccan conflict be immediately verified. All checking and every footnote posed a problem that could be solved only by referring to documentation available in Geneva or through an exchange of letters. Only the extracts from the Moroccan press sent from Rabat during the first two years of the investigation were published as they stood, on the basis of information transmitted by the consultant who supplied them. In fact, it was impossible to check the extracts a posteriori at the time the verification of sources was undertaken: the newspapers in question were unavailable in Europe and there was no longer a consultant in Morocco. Otherwise, all dates, quotations, and references in the text were checked and, where necessary, supplemented. Without the admirable pertinacity and accuracy of Mme. Zuber-Bouvard, the manuscript of the historical section would have been useless from the scholarly point of view.

At the time we began our work, the RAND Corporation had just completed a study of the decisions taken in Paris on Morocco in the last year of the conflict. This manuscript was still unpublished and could not, of course, be given to us, but various documents and interviews used in its preparation were kindly made available to us. Our passages drafted on the basis of these documents relate to the activities of the Centre d'études et de documentation,[6] the dealings of General Boyer de Latour with Présence française,[7] and the study of this pressure group in Volume 3 of the French edition. We were thus spared the necessity of engaging in research that might have duplicated the work of the RAND Corporation.

As is the rule in studies sponsored by the Carnegie Endowment, the book was written entirely by the author.[8] It goes without saying that the author assumes full responsibility for the interpretations of fact, judgments on the protagonists, and theories that are his own.

Since this book is really the work of a team, I should like to express my gratitude to all who helped in its execution and completion. First, my warmest thanks to my full-time colleagues, the researchers who helped them, and the editors who worked on the manuscript. The book owes them too much for me to regard this opportunity of working with them as other than a privilege. I want to add a note of appreciation for the fine English translation of Volumes 1 and 2 which was done by Mrs. Marianna Oliver and Messrs. Alexander B. Harrison, Jr., and Bernard B. Phillips. I should also like to thank the members of the Advisory

6. See pp. 342–43.
7. See p. 368 ff.
8. Vol. 3 of the French edition contains the few exceptions to this statement. Alfred Grosser wrote most of the chapter on the metropolitan press and Viansson-Ponté most of the chapter on the attitude of economic and financial interests. Three other passages are largely based on certain surveys made in Morocco for the purposes of the study. These are the notes on the French press in Morocco, the Muslim workers' unions, and the *paysannat*.

Committee, the directors of the other investigations, and the experts who read the manuscript, for their suggestions. Particularly helpful was the advice of Arnold Wolfers, director of the Washington Center of Foreign Policy Research; of Alfred Grosser, director of studies and research at the Fondation nationale des sciences politiques in Paris and professor at the University of Paris; and of H. E. Ahmed Taïbi Benhima, Permanent Representative of Morocco to the United Nations. M. Jean Lacouture, an expert on North African affairs, was kind enough to read the historical section of this work while completing his own illuminating study, *Cinq hommes et la France*. At the Free University of Brussels, I profited from the advice of, among others, M. Henri Neuman, professor of financial economics, who was good enough to read over certain passages. I am deeply grateful to him. Lastly, despite so much support, I should have found it very hard to devote to my task all the attention it demanded had not the director of our Institut, Professor Arthur Doucy, permitted me from the start to devote to it the attention I would ordinarily have spent on other research; I want to express my gratitude to him. I should not like to end this preface without thanking the Carnegie Endowment for the trust it bestowed on me in making me the director of this project. My thanks go particularly to the director of its European Centre, John Goormaghtigh. His breadth of vision, his grasp of scientific problems, and his steady encouragement were a source of constant and valuable support. Thanks to the Endowment, I was able to proceed from what began as an embryonic concept of decolonization to the mapping of many of its contours. I am well aware of the perils of the undertaking and of the long road still to be traveled if political science is one day to take its rightful place among the other social sciences. I believe, however, with the Endowment, that the most important thing, after measuring the obstacles that divide us from our goal, is to press boldly forward.

Stéphane Bernard
Director of the Centre de Théorie
Politique de l'Institut de Sociologie
de l'Université Libre de Bruxelles

ABBREVIATIONS

A.R.S.   Action républicaine et sociale (Republican and Social Movement)

D.S.T.   Direction de la surveillance du territoire (Security Department of the Territory)

M.R.P.   Mouvement républicain populaire (Popular Republican Movement)

N.L.F.   Front de libération nationale (National Liberation Front)

P.D.I.   Parti démocratique de l'indépendence (Democratic Independence Party)

R.G.R.   Rassemblement des gauches républicaines (Assembly of the Republican Left)

R.P.F.   Rassemblement du peuple français (Assembly of the French People)

S.F.I.O.   Section française de l'Internationale ouvrière (French Socialist Party)

U.D.S.R.   Union démocratique et socialiste de la résistance (Democratic and Socialist Resistance Union)

U.G.S.C.M. Union générale des syndicats confédérés du Maroc (General Union of Federated Trade Unions of Morocco)

VOLUME 1

Chapter 1

HISTORICAL BACKGROUND

The Franco-Moroccan conflict may be considered as having begun on January 22, 1943, with the meeting at Anfa between Sultan Sidi Mohammed ben Youssef and President Franklin D. Roosevelt. It is true that the thirteen-year period between that date and the liquidation of the French protectorate in the summer of 1956 covers only one particularly important phase in the history of relations between France and Morocco. Nevertheless, the phenomenon of decolonization which evolved over those thirteen years marks a sufficiently sharp break with what preceded and what followed to be considered independently. The choice of so recent a starting date is naturally somewhat arbitrary. The study of the conflict would be incomplete without reference to events prior to 1943. But to enter into details about them would be to err in the opposite direction and to confuse two different topics of research on the pretext that the first would throw some light on the second. It is hoped that this dual hazard has been avoided by reducing the background material to a brief summary highlighting the relevant aspects of the past.

Diplomatic Activities of the Powers

Morocco entered contemporary history with the conquest of Algeria. Shaken militarily, first by France at the battle of Isly on August 14, 1844, and then by the Spanish seizure of Tetuán in 1859–60, the Sharifian Empire was forced to sign with those two countries agreements [1] that served, in part, to sanction the advantages they had gained as a result of their military pressures on the empire.

1. Among others, the Treaty of Tangier, signed Sept. 10, 1844, under which the Sultan undertook to withdraw all assistance from the Algerian Emir, Abd el-Kader, who was fighting against France.

3

This first trial of strength might have brought about the weakening or complete loss of Moroccan sovereignty as early as the middle of the last century. It did not do so because Great Britain, anxious to prevent the establishment of a Great Power across the straits from Gibraltar, intervened diplomatically between the Sharifian Empire and the countries that were casting covetous eyes in its direction. France and Spain were forced for a time to accept the situation. Britain, whose position had been strengthened by her diplomatic aid to Morocco, obtained, under the Anglo-Moroccan treaties of December 1856, freedom of trade throughout the Sharifian Empire, tax exemption for British traders,[2] and a considerable expansion of consular privileges. The most-favored-nation clause automatically extended these benefits to all the Powers that had previously traded with Morocco, which thus became largely defenseless against European commercial enterprises.

Apart from the capitulary privileges she had been forced to grant, Morocco was subject to a system of diplomatic and consular protection that in some cases removed from the Sultan's authority Moroccan nationals employed by foreigners established in the country. Abuses connected with the right of protection soon became so flagrant that in 1880 the Sultan succeeded in having an international conference held at Madrid to regulate the system. The Madrid Convention limited and codified "protection" but at the same time extended the benefits of the most-favored-nation clause to all signatories and gave foreigners the right to acquire land in Morocco with the authorization of the Maghzen (the traditional administration headed by the Grand Vizier) while making them liable, in theory at least, to taxation. The economic motives which had led France to take an interest in Morocco were thus weakened to a certain extent, but the French position was strengthened a year later when the Third Republic established a protectorate over Tunisia.

French diplomatic activity thenceforth assumed a different guise: since the Powers could not be forced into a pure and simple recognition of the conquest of Morocco, the Paris government resorted to bargaining, using rights acquired in other

2. Except as regards customs duties.

regions of North Africa to obtain the gradual consent of European rivals to its establishment in the Sharifian Empire. Italian claims were waived by the agreement of 1902, whereby Italy surrendered her Moroccan ambitions in exchange for recognition of freedom of action in Tripolitania. British claims were renounced two years later under the Franco-British agreement of April 8, 1904, in which France abandoned Egypt to Britain in return for recognition of French freedom of action in Morocco. Spain fell into line on October 3 of the same year after obtaining recognition of her rights to a separate sphere of influence in the Sharifian Empire.

Only the Germany of Wilhelm II held out. The day was past when Bismarck sought to ease Franco-German relations by encouraging France's colonial ambitions. Cool to the idea of being left out of the earlier bargaining and anxious to develop her own colonial empire, Germany intervened. The crisis caused by Germany's entry onto the scene was temporarily ended on June 18, 1906, at the Conference of Algeciras. The policy of the dismemberment of Morocco sought by France and Spain was foiled and the principle of international assistance to an independent Morocco approved. Obviously, German intervention could be eliminated only by further bargaining: the Agadir incident, in July 1911 (a German warship arrived at that port to "protect" German firms in the area), was the determinant of French policy on this score. On November 4, 1911, as an outcome of negotiations with Germany, France acquired a free hand in Morocco in return for ceding part of her domain in the Congo to Germany. The following year, Morocco, now completely isolated, was forced to accept the French protectorate.

Internal Developments

This succession of treaties and diplomatic maneuvers cannot be studied apart from the internal situation in the Sharifian Empire. From the conquest of Algeria to the Treaty of Fez of March 30, 1912, there had been constant interaction between what went on inside Morocco and the moves planned around her on the diplomatic chessboard. From this point of view, there were three important reigns: that of Sultan Mulay Hassan (1873–94), his son Abd el-Aziz (1894–1908), and the latter's brother, Mulay Hafid (1908–12).

In the mid-nineteenth century, Mulay Hassan became the champion of Moroccan independence, centralization of the Sharifian state, and restoration of its finances. With the help of diplomatic backing from Britain, he succeeded in thwarting the annexationist ambitions of France and Spain, and was able to open Morocco to international trade while at the same time reducing to a minimum the sacrifices of sovereignty necessarily involved in such a change of status. Thus sheltered from foreign designs, he built up an army, sought, through frequent expeditions, to reestablish central authority over the four corners of the empire, and, what was most important, managed to reinstate financial order.

The accession to the throne of Mulay Hassan's son Abd el-Aziz did not at first prevent the new Sultan's Prime Minister, Grand Vizier Ba Ahmed, from successfully continuing the policy of the previous reign; the situation did not really begin to deteriorate until after Ba Ahmed's death in 1900. Abd el-Aziz was extravagant and eccentric and foolish enough to allow himself to be drawn into a bungling attempt at tax reform that turned his subjects against him. The treasury was soon empty and domestic anarchy, which had been restrained for a time by Mulay Hassan, erupted again on a wider scale. The Sultan's foreign advisers had not been without influence in these disconcerting events. At that period, a state like Morocco could hope to resist European pressure only as long as its finances remained sound. Once it was ruined and forced to borrow, the dismantling of its internal sovereignty became child's play. Abd el-Aziz had not sense enough to see through the maneuvers of foreign agents who encouraged his eccentricities solely in order to plunge him further into debt. This technique of penetration made it possible to hasten the end of a regime which, in any case, was by then at the end of its tether.[3]

In France, efforts were renewed to intensify the economic penetration of the country even before the death of Ba Ahmed.

3. For discussion of this controversial point, see Jean and Simonne Lacouture, *Le Maroc à l'épreuve* (Paris, 1958), p. 29.

An extremely dynamic committee of financiers had been set up with Eugène Étienne, deputy from Oran and vice-president of the Chamber of Deputies, as its leading light. In 1902, the Compagnie marocaine was established by the Société Schneider. During the next two years, the bankrupt Sultan was forced to negotiate two successive loans. The first, amounting to 22½ million francs, was floated in equal parts in England, France, and Spain. However, the Sultan received only half that sum,[4] the rest being withheld by the banks as commission. The second loan was granted by the Consortium of French Banks. Once again, the Sultan actually received only 48 million francs out of more than 62 million. Repayment of the debts absorbed most of the Moroccan tax receipts. The Sultan was forced to agree to go through the Consortium for any future loans and ultimately to authorize it to set up a state bank. After 1904, the collection of maritime customs was controlled by the Consortium. Abd el-Aziz was caught in a web with little hope of freeing himself.

Despite obstacles placed in its way by German diplomacy, French penetration took on new vigor in 1907 with the effective establishment of the state bank, constituted by the Act of Algeciras of April 7, 1906. The development of foreign enterprises inevitably provoked serious tension between France and the tribes. The Sultan, trapped between French business interests and the violent reactions of the Moroccan people, forfeited his throne. In August 1907, the announcement that work on the port of Casablanca was being started by the Compagnie marocaine touched off an uprising among the neighboring tribes, who descended on the town and were driven off. Within two years, the revolt against Abd el-Aziz had become general. Accused of abandoning Morocco to foreigners, overwhelmed on every side, he handed over the reins to his brother, Mulay Hafid.

Hardly had the new reign begun when the same causes started to produce the same effects. Spain seized the Rif after the Sultan refused to recognize the validity of concessions granted by local chieftains to Spanish nationals. In 1910, the Sultan had to negotiate a further loan of 100 million francs to pay off debts contracted in the previous reign, to cover work carried out by

4. Exactly 13,500,000.

French companies in Morocco, and to compensate Europeans in Casablanca for losses sustained in the disturbances of 1907. This time, the Moroccan treasury got nothing. By the next year, Mulay Hafid was in the same straits as his predecessor. He was besieged in Fez by the tribes and had to appeal for help to the French forces of General Charles-Émile Moinier. Spain immediately took advantage of this situation to extend her activities in the northern part of the country. This twofold intervention set off the Agadir crisis, which brought the final settlement of the German claim. Protected by French diplomacy, French investors now had a clear field. The Compagnie générale du Maroc was set up in 1912 by the Consortium of French Banks, while the Compagnie marocaine doubled its activities under the cloak of an association between the Société Schneider and the Banque de l'Union parisienne.

At Fez, on March 30, 1912, France and Morocco signed the Protectorate Treaty.

Establishment of the Protectorate and the Principal Stages in the Process of Pacification (1912–34)

Once the status of Morocco was settled, the politico-economic organization of the country went on apace together with the process of pacification. Actual colonization followed in the wake of military action, until finally the last outposts of resistance were dissolved and the French settlers could devote themselves exclusively to their work.

The stages of the undertaking succeeded one another in accordance with the normal pattern of growth in colonial economies. The essential infrastructure—roads, harbors, railways—was created simultaneously with the embryonic political, administrative, and financial superstructure necessary to the life of a colony. As this dual physical and institutional network developed, rural colonization forged ahead, mineral resources were exploited, and the commercial machinery for production and marketing increased and multiplied. The development of the European community, the growth of the modern townships in which it congregated, organization of Moroccan auxiliary forces, advances in public health, and, little by little, the complex inter-action of the positive and negative impact of colonization upon the traditional ways of life gradually rounded out the picture.

There is a striking contrast between the consummate ease with which the French administration solved the enormous problems of establishing the protectorate, and the ineptitude—or, more correctly, the impotence—manifested by the same administrative apparatus when it had to face the political and social problems raised by the conflict between the two communities after World War II.

Pacification was carried out in four main stages. First, between 1912 and 1914, came the subjugation of the *bled maghzen,* that part of the country traditionally under the Sultan's control be-cause it was by far the most accessible. Then followed the sub-jugation of the Moyen Atlas, which continued until 1920. The Rif war followed immediately, from 1921 to 1925; in order to conquer Abd el-Krim, France had to call on as many troops as the Fourth Republic was to send to Algeria twenty-five years later.[5] From 1930 to 1934, a final series of military operations made it possible to wipe out the last pockets of resistance in the Haut Atlas, the Anti-Atlas, and on the edges of the Sahara.

Despite the term, pacification meant neither more nor less than military conquest. At least the initial campaign, under the able and humane leadership of General Louis Lyautey, developed into war as soon as the thrust into the Atlas Massif began. This resistance to foreign conquest was quite different in principle from the combination of terrorism and guerrilla operations which shattered the protectorate thirty years later. The Moroccan campaign was a genuine war, waged by a modern army against armed tribesmen fighting until their means of resistance was exhausted. In such circumstances, the losing side always submits. The conquered people have no way open but submission, pro-vided they are quickly made to feel the advantages of such action and are not reduced to despair by a direct onslaught upon their way of life. Experience has shown that this consent to coloniza-tion remains only as long as the conquered community is not

5. See p. 367.

transformed by the very process of colonization into a different social body with new requirements, aspirations, and potentialities.

In contrast to this initial resistance to conquest, the terrorism and guerrilla activities of the last years of the protectorate seem to have been the revolt of a conquered community, changed by colonization, against a foreign power established on its soil. In this new context, in which the political determinants triumph over the military factors, the rules of the game are different. Western strength miscarries. We shall see later how and why this is so.[6] It is sufficient at this stage to have indicated in passing one of the major problems of decolonization.

Awakening of Moroccan Nationalism (1930–37)

Pre-1912 Morocco had not been without its elite: even before the establishment of the protectorate, there had been a group of great bourgeois families (particularly at Fez) who would have been able to provide political leadership for an independent Morocco. Frustrated in this ambition by the arrival of the French, this traditional elite did not rally to the new regime without mental reservations. The latent tension created by this feeling of frustration grew worse when, between 1925 and 1930, the young Moroccans who, thanks to the French, had received a western education, reached adulthood under an administration that had no thought of offering them a share in governing their country. These seeds of discontent soon found fertile soil when disaffection spread to the skilled craftsmen in the towns, who were increasingly feeling the effects of competition from manufactured goods introduced by the colonial regime, and of the shrinking purchasing power of their traditional clientele. The union of these three factors was to breed an urban nationalism, already clearly conditioned by the impact of colonization on certain components of the traditional environment.

Latent at first, the crisis broke out in 1930 during the so-called Berber *dahir* affair.[7] On May 16 of that year, a *dahir* (decree)

6. See p. 456.

7. Protectorat de la république française (empire chérifien), *Bulletin officiel*, May 30, 1930, p. 652; also Robert Montagne, *Révolution au Maroc* (Paris, 1953), pp. 180 ff.

was issued at Rabat setting up "customary tribunals" in Berber country to deal with civil cases; it also established a complete system of penal and criminal justice based on French law and deliberately removed both systems from the jurisdiction of the Maghzen. The reform was ostensibly justified as recognition of Berber customary law, a loose body of tribal rules conforming with, and supplementary to, Koranic law. This, however, was only a pretext. The real aim was to facilitate French control by creating a division between the Arabs and the Berbers and at the same time making it easier to win over the latter.

The promulgation of the *dahir* was immediately interpreted by the most perceptive and in many cases the most westernized elements of the population as a threat to their political and religious integrity. This protest movement, launched by the intellectuals —both traditionalist, like Mohammed Allal el-Fassi, and westernized, like Ahmed Balafredj—immediately succeeded in attracting to it the skilled craftsmen and shopkeepers of the towns. The affair took on international proportions when Emir Chekib Arslan, head of the Syro-Palestinian Committee's Delegation to the League of Nations, aroused the Arab world, after holding inquiries at Tangier and Tetuán, by proclaiming that the French were trying to Christianize Morocco. The sensitivity of Islam to this kind of appeal ensured the complete success of the campaign from Tangier to the Dutch East Indies.

The Berber *dahir* was later watered down and its most untenable provisions deleted. Nevertheless, the damage was done. Moroccan youth had become aware of its own mission and powers. It had formed an alliance with the townspeople in the north and had linked its activities with those of the pan-Arab agitators of the Middle East. Moreover, the idea of capitalizing upon what they called the "Arab-Berber division" had taken root in the minds of the French and was to reappear to play a major role between 1951 and 1955.

Once under way, the crisis gained momentum both in Morocco and France. In 1932, a number of young Moroccans living in Paris launched the periodical *Maghreb*. It enjoyed the patronage of Radical Socialist and Socialist leaders, was circulated clandestinely in Morocco, and soon had the support of educated

Moroccan youth. The next year, opponents of the 1930 Berber *dahir* brought out, this time at Fez, a nationalist weekly in French, *L'Action du peuple*. Supported by alumni associations of the Muslim schools, *L'Action du peuple* threw itself into a series of political campaigns which culminated, in 1934, in a public demonstration of nationalist feelings on the occasion of a visit to Fez by the Sultan.

The Residency reacted at once: *L'Action du peuple* was suspended and *Maghreb* was banned from Morocco. The founders of *L'Action du peuple* adopted a different course. An opposition party was created, the Comité d'action marocaine. On December 1, 1934, the new party brought out a plan of reforms which, without as yet questioning the protectorate, called for respect for the Treaty of Fez, the ending of direct administration, administrative and judicial unity for all Morocco, and the participation of Moroccans in the exercise of power. But the time was not yet ripe. Presented successively to the Maghzen, the Residency, and the Laval government, the plan failed.

The Comité d'action, which was at first encouraged by the Blum government, was soon rent by internal dissension that made it easy for the Residency to resume control over Moroccan nationalism. The Comité was, in fact, divided between a traditionalist wing represented by Allal el-Fassi and a modernist wing represented by Mohammed Hassan el-Ouazzani. Split by the effect of these centrifugal forces, it preserved, toward the end, only a facade of unity. In March 1937, the Residency took advantage of this situation and dissolved the Comité, thus hoping to put an end to its continual expansion.[8]

Two clandestine parties sprang from this proscription: the National Party for the Realization of the Plan of Reforms and the Popular Movement. The first, under Allal el-Fassi, Ahmed Balafredj, and Mohammed Lyazidi, was by far the larger. It represented the traditionalist movement (Islamist and monarchist), and was one day to become the Istiqlal. The second, led by el-Ouazzani, represented the modernist trend. It was republican in spirit and more democratic, remained confined to a small

8. Robert Rézette, *Les Partis politiques marocains* (Paris, 1955), pp. 87 ff.

circle in Casablanca, and was to give rise, after the war, to the P.D.I.

The National Party at once resumed on a wider scale the recruiting and organizing to which the Comité d'action had devoted itself a year earlier. These activities were restricted to the towns and were carried on underground until July 23, 1937, at which time the new party presented its demands to Paris. This approach was no more successful than the first. Despite this temporary check, the National Party was strengthened by the growth of its organization and decided to proceed to direct action and to appeal to Moroccan public opinion in the towns.

Meanwhile, the waters of a wadi that supplied the Moroccan quarters of Meknes were diverted to the benefit of the settlers, thus provoking an explosion of popular discontent which the National Party used to advantage in organizing a mass, large-scale movement. This crisis developed according to a pattern that foreshadowed the trials of strength of the postwar period: petitions demanding the withdrawal of the measure, the arrest of agitators, mass meetings, scuffles, the spread of the disturbance to other towns, and, finally, suppression. Troops had to occupy the *médina* of Fez "to prevent any popular reaction." [9] The leaders of the movement were arrested. Allal el-Fassi was deported to Gabon, where he remained for nine years. El-Ouazzani was put under house arrest. Ahmed Balafredj took refuge at Tangier. The incident ended in total defeat for Moroccan nationalism.

Nevertheless, it should be recognized that General Auguste Noguès, then Resident-General, made a real effort to modify the traditional attitude of the French administration toward the young educated Moroccans and to give them the opportunity to express their opinion. This attempt, as even Chekib Arslan admitted, was beginning to bear fruit [10] when the war put an end to the experiment.

This first outburst of agitation had been stifled by the regime without too much difficulty, but Moroccan nationalism had nevertheless revealed from the outset some of its characteristic

9. Ibid., p. 110.
10. Ibid., p. 112.

features: the coalition of the young traditionalists and westernized youth, alliance of youth with the common people in the
towns, the dualism of a nationalism torn between a mass party of
traditionalist views and a minority with republican leanings,
sensitivity of the Arab world to events in North Africa, indifference of the Métropole to those same events despite the support of
certain circles and committees, and, finally, in Morocco itself, the
extreme rigidity of a regime firmly resolved to yield none of its
privileges. Later, the involvement of the Palace and the growth
of nationalism among the urban neo-proletariat were to intensify
the drama. Nevertheless, the prewar skirmishes had largely foreshadowed this course of events.

Wartime Morocco up to the Landing of 1942

As soon as war was declared, Morocco took the side of France.
The National Party unequivocally affirmed Franco-Moroccan
solidarity. Mohammed V proclaimed his fidelity to France at the
outset and never wavered in the course of the ordeal.[11] This
demonstration of loyalty did not prevent him from keeping
himself informed about Germany when the collapse of France
seemed, for a time, to make an Axis victory inevitable. The
nationalist parties in the Spanish zone, freer and less bound by
ties of sentiment to France, did not hesitate to lean toward the
German alliance, but what was left of the political organizations
in the French zone remained quiet. Of equal importance for the
future was the fact that relations between the Moroccan population and the Vichy-controlled protectorate progressively deteriorated as a result of conditions created by the war-requisitioning
for the benefit of France, tax increases, and the unfair distribution of consumer goods. When the Allies landed in 1942, the
Moroccans were ready to renew the conflict in a world transformed by war.

11. Although Sultan Sidi Mohammed ben Youssef did not become King Mohammed
V until March 2, 1956, the latter title appears throughout this study in conformity
with general usage in Morocco and France.

Chapter 2

THE ANFA CONFERENCE AND
THE PUAUX PERIOD—
RESUMPTION OF CONTROL
(NOVEMBER 8, 1942–MARCH 2, 1946)

On November 8, 1942, Anglo-American forces landed in North Africa and swept Morocco into the war. Two months later, President Franklin D. Roosevelt and Prime Minister Winston Churchill held a secret conference at Anfa, a suburb of Casablanca, and announced to the world their determination to continue the war until the unconditional surrender of the enemy. On January 22, 1943, the President gave a dinner party in the Sultan's honor. The Prime Minister was present, as were the Crown Prince, Mulay Hassan, Elliott Roosevelt, one of the President's sons, and General Auguste Noguès, then Resident-General. Elliott Roosevelt has given a vivid account, not without humor, of the dinner conversation carried on that evening by an expansive Roosevelt, freeing all the colonies in advance in the euphoria of a successful dinner, a Sultan gradually won over by the glowing prospects which seemed to be opening before him, and a Churchill, half joking and half serious, who ended by losing his good humor altogether when he saw that his efforts to change the subject were in vain.[1]

The conversation turned upon the radical changes that would inevitably take place in the status of the colonies and protectorates after the war, on the need to devote Morocco's natural wealth to raising the standard of living of her population, and on the assistance the United States would be able to give, once peace returned, in training leaders and officials and in the exploitation of

1. Elliott Roosevelt, *As He Saw It* (New York, 1946), pp. 109–12, confirmed in Charles-André Julien, *L'Afrique du Nord en marche: nationalismes musulmans et souveraineté française* (Paris, 1952), p. 342.

15

the country's resources. The conversation made a lasting impression on the Sultan.

Not all critics agree with Elliott Roosevelt's version. But whether his testimony is accepted or rejected, the Anfa meeting is like one of those historical aphorisms which, true or false, sum up a character or a situation. The hope placed by the colonial peoples, at the end of the war, in the anticolonial liberalism of the United States and her President is an historical fact. If the conversation at Anfa has come down to us somewhat distorted, it is of little consequence to those who try to evaluate events that have become history.

What was the psychological and political context in which Moroccan nationalism was going to make its reappearance? How would that context evolve in the years to come? The France of 1940 had lost face. The colonizer's strength had been checked by a superior force. Morocco had seen her masters using devious tactics against the German conquerors or resigning themselves to their presence. The sacrifices accepted by the Moroccan soldier on the battlefields of France, the generosity with which he agreed in advance to further privations, gave rise to the feeling that Morocco had thereby acquired certain claims on France. In the throes of global war, the world outside was laying the groundwork for a new era.

The Allied landing suddenly brightened these still dim hopes. From the recall of General Noguès in June 1943 to the departure of Gabriel Puaux in March 1946, although nothing decisive took place, external conditions were to become more and more favorable to nationalism. This contrast between an international climate of opinion, gradually won over to the side of the colonial peoples, and the stubborn struggle against an inevitable process by a colonial regime that would not—or could not—relinquish its hold was to remain to the end one of the major themes of the conflict.

As matters stood, it seemed that the forces of change would soon defeat the forces of conservatism. Compromised by their support of the Vichy regime, the French community in Morocco and its representatives were outweighed in the political balance for the first time in the history of the protectorate. The principle of the right of self-determination, which the future victors had made part of their Charter for war and for peace, also seemed as though it must lead by one road or another to the emancipation of the colonies. Direct contact between Moroccans and Americans had suddenly brought these new ideas down from the realm of theory to that of a living reality. The Americans were arousing hope on every side. First, by their liberal and anticolonial traditions: had they not formerly sympathized with the Rif and with Ethiopia? Were they not architects of the Atlantic Charter? Second, by their words and deeds: Had their President not just renewed an ancient friendship? Was he not preparing to free Morocco from the chains of colonialism?

The illusion did not last. In Morocco itself, Puaux vigorously suppressed the initial mass manifestations of nationalist revival. The tone had been set before his arrival. As early as March 1943, Moroccans celebrating the Algerian decrees that reestablished the laws of the Republic had been brutally dispersed by a police force in which Gaullists and Vichyites had cooperated. Throughout North Africa, Gaullism was fast disappointing the hopes of the dependent peoples. Either because of wartime necessities or determination to be master of the situation in the face of allies whose intentions he suspected, the head of the Provisional Government let slip France's opportunity to welcome the aspirations of colonial peoples. The supporters of the status quo, although momentarily disconcerted by the fall of Vichy, sought to restore themselves to grace by supporting the Gaullists.

In this final phase of the war, when the international situation seemed auspicious, the Moroccan nationalist movement was still in almost the same embryonic state as in 1937. The environment was unquestionably more favorable in Morocco, and especially in the outside world. But the international setting was shortly to lose its flexibility, and any initiative would have to come from Morocco itself. Only the potentiality existed. The fusion of nationalism and a sense of national identity had not yet taken place. Some years were to pass before the neo-proletariat of the western towns entered the field, and still more before the *bled,* or countryside, began to stir.

In the middle of 1943, the conflict was still, in many respects, only beginning. The partnership between the Sultan and the Resident-General had not yet been dissolved. Apart from Ahmed Balafredj, the leaders of the National Reform Party were still in prison or in exile. Deprived of the spur of urban nationalism since 1937, the Moroccan people remained poised uncertainly between the forces of the past and those of the future. But it was already apparent that events were stronger than the men seeking to hold them back.

Despite the authority, humanitarianism, and liberalism he had displayed during his term of office, General Noguès was too deeply compromised by his attitude toward Vichy and the Allied landing for the Provisional Government to contemplate keeping him in his post.[2] The decision was not long delayed. On June 5, 1943, almost as soon as he reached Algiers, De Gaulle appointed a new Resident-General to Rabat. Gabriel Puaux was no stranger to the Arabs. A believer in strong measures, he had dissolved the Syrian and Lebanese parliaments at the beginning of the war and suspended the constitutions of both countries. His reputation as a strong man had preceded him to Rabat, where the satisfaction felt in some quarters was equalled only by the apprehension in others.

It may appear surprising today that the leader of Free France should have chosen as his representative in Morocco a man so far removed by temperament and past record from an understanding of the aspirations of Arab nationalism. But one must beware of hindsight. In June 1943, De Gaulle's sole thought was to bring North Africa into the war. He did not plan to deal with North African nationalism until after the war. In addition to this basic consideration, a whole series of ancillary factors—the untimeliness of the claims put forward, the mistrust inspired by a nationalist movement that had cooperated with the Germans at Tangier until 1943, and above all the feeling that "the Americans are behind this"—led the General to reject coldly and sternly, for the time being, Moroccan aspirations toward independence.

2. For General Noguès' attitude in 1940, see Vincent Monteil, *Les officiers* (Paris, 1958), pp. 104 ff., 131 ff.

Hence his determination to give the Resident-General a free rein. Puaux saw the situation from the point of view of a colonial official charged with reestablishing control over a turbulent protectorate. His one desire was to do away with the nationalists, and he made no secret of his intention to use force for this purpose.

Puaux's hostility to anything that might have been regarded as a concession to the hopes of the young Turks of the Protectorate, the discontent of educated Moroccan youth suddenly cut off from all contact with a Residency that again scorned their views, and the failure of the trial of strength attempted by the French in the Levant inevitably encouraged Moroccan nationalism to emerge from the obscurity in which it had lingered since 1937.

The former leaders of the National Party, once reassembled, founded the Istiqlal Party[3] at Rabat on December 10, 1943, with Ahmed Balafredj, who had returned from Tangier at the beginning of that year, as Secretary-General. It was obvious that the party was still nothing more than the expression of the traditional elite and the frustration of the young men deprived of the political role to which they aspired. In a sense, the organization had to start from scratch: training leaders, resuming control over the masses, canvassing key areas of the country. The Residency's uncompromising attitude helped the speedy realization of these tasks.

On January 11, 1944, just after the Istiqlal had been created, it issued a manifesto that was delivered on the same day to the Sultan, and to the French, British, and Americans.[4] The Soviet Union received it through its ambassador at Algiers. More than fifty signatures were appended to the manifesto.[5] Recalling that Morocco had always been a free and sovereign state, the Istiqlal based its claims on the blood shed by Moroccan soldiers on the field of battle, the changes that had taken place in the world,

3. The word "Istiqlal" means independence.
4. Istiqlal Party, "Proclamation of the Istiqlal Party," *Documents 1944–1946* (Eng. ed. Paris, 1946), pp. 1–5.
5. Especially by "8 businessmen or industrialists, 5 farmers or landowners, 6 Maghzen officials, 4 judges, 7 professional men, 10 ulamas, and 18 educators." Albert Ayache, *Le Maroc* (Paris, 1956), p. 346 n.

and the moral commitments assumed by the Allies in the Atlantic Charter. It demanded the reestablishment of Moroccan independence and the setting up of a democratic government.

A new and significant fact was that the nationalist movement, which had always been considered hostile to the Sultan, had on this occasion taken great care to let it be understood that its claims were identical with the wishes of the Sultan, his Maghzen, and the nation at large. One is tempted to wonder whether the Istiqlal, at the time, really believed in the possibility of speedy liberation for Morocco. Its representatives today say that they knew no serious steps could be taken before the end of the war, that they sought only to serve notice of their intentions, to give the new generation a goal, and to take the Allies at their word by linking, in effect, the principles for which they claimed to be fighting with the demands of the nationalists. It may well be that the wisdom acquired in later years serves as an alibi for the illusions of youth that were all the more understandable because the state of the world and recent precedents seemed to justify every hope.

In any event, the new party had taken care to protect itself on all fronts. The manifesto had not come out of a vacuum. A week before its publication, Ahmed Balafredj and Mohammed Lyazidi had been in touch with responsible American officials who had unofficially signified their agreement with the positions taken, provided that no disturbances ensued. There was a war going on, they pointed out, and while Morocco's rights would be recognized when peace came, in the event of disorder, American troops would support the French.

In the meantime, Balafredj had been in touch with Si Hadj Thami el-Glaoui, Pasha of Marrakesh, who had been informed of American support, or sensed it and raised no objection. As for the Sultan, he had read and approved the document even before it was officially handed to him, although it would be going too far to say he had inspired it.[6] As soon as the manifesto had been

6. According to the Istiqlal, there had been an understanding with the Sultan that the manifesto would be presented to him by a party delegation immediately preceding an audience granted by the Sultan to the Adviser for Sharifian Affairs, so that France would be seized of the document the same day the Allies received it.

delivered to the Palace, the Sultan convened his counselors, who endorsed the nationalist claims after approving their spirit if not all their terms. If apparently trustworthy reports are to be believed, el-Glaoui himself was present.

The event did not come as a surprise to the Residency. Puaux had been forewarned of these developments by the Commandant of the Region of Fez, General Louis Suffren. In addition, he did not believe that the Anglo-Americans had had a hand in it and attributed the nationalists' illusions in that respect to unofficial contacts between the Istiqlal and unauthorized British and American agents. The Resident-General's first act was to remind the Sultan of his responsibilities by declaring that he had placed himself in the camp of France's enemies. He then turned his attention to el-Glaoui and the notables, in order to drive a wedge between them and the Palace. An emissary was sent to the Pasha to explain that the manifesto did not have American support. In the light of this statement, el-Glaoui and his friends withdrew their support from the nationalists.

For his part, the Sultan had instructed three of his counselors, including the *Fqih* Si Mohammed ben Larbi el-Alaoui and Si Mohammed Mammeri, to establish regular contact with the Istiqlal, to negotiate the deletion of certain terms in the manifesto that were regarded as somewhat impolitic, to keep the Istiqlal informed of the Residency's reactions and the evolution of the situation. There can be no doubt that there was collusion between the Palace and the principal nationalist party. This was also a new phenomenon.

Although one of the aims of the manifesto was to confront France and her allies with a clear-cut policy, the success of the demonstration depended entirely upon its immediate impact. From the point of view of the nationalists, it was essential that the reverberations be powerful enough for the Istiqlal to appear from the beginning as spokesman for a clearly defined national policy. All necessary arrangements had therefore been made for an impressive flood of delegations and petitions to converge upon Rabat as soon as the manifesto was published. In Fez itself, the urban population had been stirred up. The intention was to urge the masses to demonstrate their feelings for the nationalist claims as defined by the Istiqlal, not to incite them to riot. The youth movement had been disorganized by the 1937 suppression and was exposed because of the state of war to crushing police retaliation in the event of any serious disturbance. It could not, for the time being, contemplate any real show of strength.

The reaction of the rank and file—still few in number—was at first just what the party wanted. Petitions piled up at Rabat, where delegations arrived one after the other, while at Fez a secret excitement—"almost mystic," as Robert Montagne was to say[7]—seized the people. The barely concealed hope that the Europeans would soon be driven out of Morocco, particularly evident among the shopkeepers and Moroccan servants in close contact with the French, plunged the town's French colony into a state of anxiety all the sharper because of the strength of its previous illusions regarding Morocco's stability.

Assuming that France would talk of reform and take refuge behind empty formulas in order to frustrate nationalist action, Balafredj and his friends took the initiative. On January 18, he sent a letter to the Sultan commenting on the manifesto in terms that made it quite clear the Istiqlal would not accept any reform as long as Moroccan sovereignty was curbed for the benefit of France. The letter specified that the Istiqlal would agree to negotiate with the Residency only if France first accepted the principle of Moroccan independence. The next day, as though to forestall any repressive action by the Residency, the party rounded out its policy with a declaration specifying that it had no intention whatever of realizing its aspirations by force.

The next move had to come from Algiers, from which Puaux himself had asked for orders, after dealing with the most pressing matters. De Gaulle was determined on no account to give in as long as the war continued. He dispatched his Commissioner for Foreign Affairs, René Massigli, to Rabat with instructions to call the Sultan to order and insist on strict observance of the Treaty of Fez, using as inducements promises of administrative, economic, and social improvements adapted to the needs, traditions, and condition of the country. No other policy was possible,

7. Montagne, *Révolution au Maroc*, p. 197.

in view of the state of war.[8] But the conduct of politics, like that of war, is an art, and these instructions could have been carried out in many different ways. In Rabat, as elsewhere, there was no lack of officials bent upon catching the youthful movement in the act of rebellion and stamping it out. This was only one step away from the deliberate provocation and crushing of riots. That step was certainly not in line with the official policy of the leader of Free France, but he could hardly prevent it in view of the firm position he had taken in directing the replacement of Noguès.

Massigli was received by the Sultan on January 28, and told him unequivocally that De Gaulle rejected any possibility of independence. Mohammed V was forced to repudiate the Istiqlal. In the presence of the Resident-General, he was obliged to declare to his viziers that "the word independence must disappear from our hearts and our lips." Matters were pushed so far that he was even forced to accuse the Istiqlal publicly of having stabbed the Allies in the back. Several members of his entourage who were compromised by the crisis, notably the Vizier of Justice, had to be dismissed by the Palace. The Sultan never forgave Puaux for these forced disavowals.

Mohammed V had promised the Istiqlal to do everything in his power to prevent arrests. It appears that he had guaranteed a state of calm provided no one was molested, and the Residency had agreed to his terms. Affairs would no doubt have rested there had not a move by Philippe Boniface, Director of the Interior and Contrôleur Civil, who controlled the security police, dramatically revived a political incident that was dying down. Boniface, who until the very end worked to make any peace between the nationalists and the government impossible, had in his files information which seemed to prove collusion between certain nationalist leaders—particularly Balafredj—and the Germans. This was not unlikely, although Robert Montagne himself recognized that the information in question did not constitute

8. The communists fell into line. Although, early in 1943, the Moroccan Communist newspaper, *Al Wattan*, had taken a stand in favor of Moroccan independence, the party vigorously opposed the nationalists' action after the 1944 disturbances. It then changed tactics and defended the nationalist militants then under arrest. Ayache, pp. 345 ff.

valid proof.[9] In other circumstances, no great importance would have been attached to such a charge in a French milieu that was just emerging from a long period of collaboration with the Axis.[10] The day after Massigli's audience with the Sultan, without even consulting the Resident-General, Boniface acted. Balafredj and Lyazidi were arrested by military security together with a sizable group of influential members of the Istiqlal.

When the news came out, quick as lightning despite censorship, riots broke out simultaneously in Rabat, Casablanca, and Salé. General Philippe Leclerc, then at Fedala, sent his tanks to Rabat. A policeman, two civilians, and a number of Moroccans were killed in Rabat in the course of clashes between the mob and Leclerc's soldiers. At Fez, the cradle of the movement, popular reaction was better grounded and more enduring. The nationalists took refuge in the mosques. The mob turned on the police, thirty of whom were killed in ten days of rioting. The ulama of Karaouyne University were arrested on February 1: this inaugurated a practice that was to widen the gulf between the Residency and the Palace. In Rabat and Salé, to use Montagne's expression, "the people were practically dragooned." [11]

The repression was deliberately brutal. Moroccans convicted of having lynched Europeans were shot under martial law without trial. Thousands of persons were interned near Ifrane. Balafredj was exiled to Corsica. Abderrahim Bouabid was arrested at Salé and kept in prison for two years. Once again, by methods strangely reminiscent of those employed in 1937, the movement was crushed. Although the riots were undoubtedly provoked by arrests ordered by the D.S.T., there are two opposing theories in this connection. The nationalists and the French liberals believed that the arrests were deliberately made by Boniface to arouse popular reaction which would make it possible, in view of the war, to crush the nationalist movement in its infancy. French supporters of the Residency, however, held that in the circumstances the arrests were the normal consequence of collusion between certain nationalist leaders and the Axis.

Two facts suffice to show that the Resident-General's policy in

9. Montagne, p. 198.
10. Rézette, Les Partis politiques marocains, p. 145.
11. Montagne, p. 199.

Morocco depended for support upon forces which were intent only on accomplishing their own ends by even more drastic means—if that were possible—than his own. It is a fact, first of all, that Boniface made the arrests on his own initiative and without instructions from the Residency. Confronted with a fait accompli, and outflanked by the D.S.T., which had escaped his control, the Resident-General could only back up his subordinate. It was also established that at the time of the riots, the Resident-General had to intervene in order to prevent General Suffren from shelling Fez, an incredible move that, in the middle of the war, might well have set the whole Arab world aflame. The fact that the arrests were made the day after Massigli's meeting with the Sultan, at a time when the crisis had been virtually settled to France's satisfaction, leads one to the unavoidable conclusion that the Director of the Interior employed a classic police maneuver and deliberately provoked the riots so as to crush resurgent nationalism more effectively.[12]

On March 15, 1944, Puaux set up four mixed commissions on reform with instructions to submit proposals for the modernization of general administration, education, justice, and agriculture. However halfhearted Puaux's spirit of reform, the initiative was a timely one. Although the crisis had ended in an indisputable victory for the Residency, at least for the time being, this was in fact a Pyrrhic victory for the protectorate system, as it brought the spirit of nationalism back into the northern towns. Despite the check on the Istiqlal, the political future of the protectorate remained dark. It was, therefore, most important to reduce tension and announce a liberalization of the regime. To mark the turning point, 387 prisoners were set free in Fez on July 14, 1944. Aware of the maneuver, the nationalists parried by spreading the report, true or false, that the clemency of the authorities was due to American intervention.

On October 14, the Resident-General presented to the Sultan the program of reforms proposed by the four commissions.[13] On

12. Analogous incidents initiated or utilized by the same protagonists recur repeatedly, although the historian obviously cannot produce concrete proof thereof. But if serious, precise, and consistent assumptions constitute proof in the technical sense of the term, the existence of provocation may be considered as established.

13. *Plan de réformes* (Rabat, 1945), special publication consisting of all documents concerning implementation of the reform program; see also Julien, pp. 350 ff.

November 26, Puaux announced to the Moroccans that the Sultan had given "his consent to a series of reforms which would be a landmark in the evolution of the country." [14] The commissions had made a laudable effort to consider the problems placed before them as fairly as possible in each case; nevertheless the remedies proposed were, without exception, mere palliatives. Even concessions of principle, in most cases, were of little consequence, as the initiators of these proposals recognized that the shortage of capital and raw materials caused by the war would preclude their implementation for a long time to come.

The Administrative Commission recommended certain modifications in the administrative distinctions between French and Muslim civil servants, while at the same time proposing equal pay for equal work for the two categories. It was not denied that the number of Muslims in the Sultan's administration was inadequate. According to the Commission, of 20,492 public posts on February 1, 1944, only 5,492 (or 26 percent) were occupied by Muslims, and of these only 771 civil servants held anything more than the most subordinate positions. [15] This state of affairs was attributed chiefly to competition from private business, to inadequate training of the candidates, and to certain inequities in salary. There was no mention of that insurmountable obstacle: the mentality of French civil servants of every grade who refused to share with Moroccans the task of governing their country. The possibility of liberalizing the regime and of apportioning administrative duties at the policy-making level between Moroccans and Frenchmen was nowhere envisaged.

The Commission on Education made no secret of the immensity of needs in its area. Of one million Moroccan children of school age, only 34,000 were attending Franco-Muslim primary schools or their equivalent, although an additional 100,000 or 200,000 were receiving the traditional Koranic teaching in Muslim schools in urban and rural areas. The progress made in recent years was no more encouraging. Only 2,500 additional pupils had been receiving a modern education each year for the

14. *Plan de réformes*, p. 2.
15. The figures vary considerably, according to whether one considers the notables and some of the auxiliary militia as officials. Actually, there was no high-ranking Moroccan official in the Neo-Sharifian administration.

past ten years. On the basis of these statistics the Commission recommended a program to enroll 100,000 new pupils in the next ten years, at an estimated cost of 110 million francs a year. It was also demanded that Muslims have access to French secondary schools and that all students have the opportunity to prepare for the French *baccalauréat* in the Franco-Muslim schools. Provision was made for a certain flexibility in the curriculum. Here again, the approach to the problem was remote and theoretical. There was no thought of providing education for all young Muslims either then (which could have been justified by the temporary lack of funds) or in the foreseeable future. The effect of population growth on the proposed measures was not even calculated. For all practical intents and purposes, reform was limited to the curriculum. The construction of school buildings could wait for better times. Only Franco-Moroccan education was considered: the traditional Muslim and French systems were ignored. Segregation of the two school populations was maintained. The vital problem of technical education was hardly touched upon. No adequate allocation of national income to Moroccan education was envisaged, even in principle: this basic shortcoming was sufficient to offset any positive aspects of the reform program.

In judicial matters, the measures proposed were equally superficial. Apart from preparatory studies for a Moroccan penal code and an attempt to modernize the civil and commercial tribunals —limited by a shortage of funds and of trained magistrates to a few pilot projects—there was no change in the status quo. The confusion as to the locus of responsibility which benefited the local officials of the Maghzen and their French supporters was maintained. The jurisdiction of the pashas and cadis in penal matters remained discretionary. Neither was there any change in the authority of the notables, upon which the system was based. To establish a modern legal and administrative organization would clearly have involved a complete overhaul of budgetary practices, an idea that did not seem to occur to the members of the Commission.

There remained the question of the rural areas and their economy. The plethora of sociological and technical difficulties which hindered the modernization of Moroccan agriculture was not disguised by the Commission's rapporteurs; nevertheless, the political aspects of the problem for the most part were passed over in silence. In any event, it was recognized that the war and its manifold consequences had greatly weakened the effect of the provisions the regime had previously adopted for the protection of the Moroccan peasants. An enormous effort was called for to modernize tools, methods, and the social system. In substance, the rapporteurs declared that to date, no unified, overall approach to the problems of Moroccan agriculture had been possible because of the lack of a central agency for coordination and study. To meet this need, the Commission recommended the creation of a Conseil supérieur du paysannat with powers sufficiently wide and general to control the drafting of reforms affecting Moroccan agriculture, as well as the coordination of the activities of the administrative services concerned. The Commission also recommended the establishment of Secteurs de modernisation du paysannat in the *bled* to speed up modernization of traditional farming methods. To this central proposal, designed, at that stage at least, merely to prepare an institutional framework that would subsequently be filled in, there were added a number of welfare measures, such as the creation of a family-property-holding system [16] and certain measures to improve the status of rural workers; the regularization of the status of the *khammessat;* the settlement of agricultural workers on farms; and the granting of a number of economic and social advantages to the Moroccan peasants. Here again, no sizable budgetary allocation was contemplated for the proposed reforms. A much more general and significant shortcoming was that no plans were made to improve the conditions of the urban proletariat, which remained the only possible outlet for the exodus from rural areas. There was no question of political reforms as such, or of any liberalization of the existing regime.[17]

To evaluate a reform program, it is not enough to study what has been proposed, or even enacted. It is also essential to give

16. Land-holding patrimony that can be neither transferred nor seized.
17. According to the Resident-General, this would have necessitated a series of further reforms which, for lack of time, could not be carried out.

careful study to the actual implementation of the decisions taken. Such further investigation would be meaningless in the present case. The Puaux reforms actually remained, as a whole, a dead letter. Most of the *dahirs* that would have made them law were never signed because of the growing tension between the Resident-General and the Sultan after the repressive measures of 1944. No one in Rabat had any serious thought of diminishing the role of the colonial authority in order to increase that of the Moroccans. The passivity displayed by the settlers and their organ, the Government Council, during Puaux's sojourn in Rabat is sufficient proof that the French colony did not feel its vested interests threatened by the Resident-General's activities.[18]

The Istiqlal immediately reacted. In a memorandum of December 1, the party described the Puaux proposals as no more than "a poultice on a wooden leg."[19] It alleged, not without reason, that they did not really deal with any of the defects in the system. In substance, the Istiqlal declared that the overall administration—the "crux of the present crisis"—remained unchanged: the proposed reforms in education would always lag behind the growth of the population; the penal powers of the pashas and the cadis, the bane of the whole system, were kept intact. As for peasant land reforms, the experiment was to cover only 2,000 hectares, and even this was to be distorted by the administrative controls supposed to set it in motion. All this was only too true, but it was also true that the prolongation of the war made the value of discussion doubtful.

The Algiers government could have fallen back upon its former intransigence and replied that it was unwise to change horses in midstream and that the necessary changes would be made after the war. Instead of creating disappointment by announcing reforms that were meaningless or that might conceivably have been justified ten years earlier, it would have been far better to reject any change in the status quo for the time

18. The reforms begun under Puaux were no real cause for alarm until his successor reactivated them in quite a different spirit; then came conflict between the Residency and the settlers, and Labonne's rapid downfall.

19. Istiqlal Party, "Memorandum on Moroccan Reforms," *Documents 1944–1946* (Eng. ed. Paris, 1946), p. 10.

being. At the same time the government could have pledged itself to give the North African nationalists a chance to try their hand at home rule immediately after the war.

The Brazzaville Conference, convened on January 30, 1944, on the initiative of General de Gaulle and René Pleven, had already proved disappointing. Of greater importance to Africa south of the Sahara than to North Africa, the meeting—at which all the participants were white except for Governor Félix Eboué—had been written off as a complete failure. The bold views of the participants who had called for a sort of French commonwealth or federation had been swept aside and the necessity of unconditional French supremacy had been recognized. In Morocco itself the repercussions were negligible. Subsequently, the event was blown up by propagandists to such a point that it took on retrospective importance quite out of proportion to its original significance.

In Algiers, De Gaulle alone had broader views, but he thought it premature to reveal them in public, and very probably he did not feel free or able to risk an authority that was still provisional for a question that was not of immediate concern.

At this time—thanks to the Istiqlal, which, although driven underground, was more active than ever—nationalism was gaining ground with the masses. The Sultan realized this during a visit to Marrakesh in the spring of 1945. The enthusiasm of the people under el-Glaoui's jurisdiction, the shouts of "Long live the King," "Long live the Nation," the banners demanding independence, the new intensity in the voice of the people, all revealed to him that public opinion was maturing and that the time was coming for him to draw close again to the party which he had disavowed grudgingly and only under compulsion. The Sultan took up the challenge and predicted great events auspicious for Islam and Morocco. He made it quite clear—in order to avoid any suspicion of siding with the Residency—that his hopes were identical with those of his people.[20] This message, delivered on the eve of the founding of the Arab League, at the very moment when there was awakening the vast longing for independence that was to bring the Muslim world into conflict with

20. Ibid., p. 352.

European colonial imperialism, could not fail to stir the Moroccan crowds profoundly.

While the Sultan responded with good grace to the nationalist appeals voiced by the masses, relations between the Residency and the Palace reached a deadlock. Mohammed V had not forgiven Puaux for forcing him to disavow the Istiqlal in public. Distressed by the brutality of the 1944 repression and by the Resident-General's disdainful attitude toward the Maghzen, the Sultan had reached a point where he was unwilling to sign anything. This right was the only weapon which the Treaty of Fez had left him, and he meant to use it. All legislation in the protectorate was paralyzed, thus forcing France to choose between a Sultan whom it had undertaken to protect and a Resident-General who was, after all, only a temporarily appointed high official.

The Sultan had De Gaulle's ear and knew it. For some time he had been thinking of taking advantage of the government's move to Paris and the approaching end of the war to request Puaux's recall. De Gaulle, for his part, had been devoting considerable thought to the modus vivendi that France would have to establish with her overseas territories, especially Morocco, once peace was restored. As far as the protectorate was concerned, he had come to the conclusion that his best course, as head of the French government, would be to reach a personal understanding with the Sultan. The mutual esteem of the two chiefs of state, the feeling they both had of being more than mere politicians, made matters easier.

The head of the Provisional Government was not unaware that the Sultan had allowed certain nationalist leaders to establish contact with the Germans during the war, but he did not emphasize the fact. He felt that, considering the uncertainty surrounding the outcome of the war, this had been the right, indeed almost the duty, of Mohammed V. Moreover, the Sultan's attitude toward the French had always been studiously correct in every respect, while those who surrounded him, including Marshal Pétain himself, had cringed before the Germans.

Thus, during the last spring of the war, Mohammed V found himself invited to France. He was received with deference and in style and cheered at the Opéra, an event that was new and moved him deeply after the discourtesies of the previous months. A great military display was put on for him, and this also made a lasting impression. His host then took him to the Massif Central. The two men toured the countryside, traveling from village to village without ceremony. In this way, the Sultan was able to meet the ordinary people of France and was struck by their kindness. This again was something new to him. Mohammed V, who had before known France only through official ceremonies, realized there was no fundamental human difference between the two peoples. Sharing the personal acclaim of his host, whose popularity he came to appreciate, he felt that he could rely on De Gaulle. Subsequently, the Sultan left for the headquarters of the First Army, where General Jean de Lattre de Tassigny, in his usual sumptuous and somewhat theatrical style, gave a magnificent reception in his honor. There he found many Moroccan soldiers, whose morale was as high as ever. The Sultan, won over by the brotherhood of arms, was delighted at being made a *Compagnon de la Libération*. This was no small tribute. Roosevelt had not received the honor and Churchill was only to do so long afterwards in 1958.

After all this, substantive discussions began. "Your country is just beginning," the General said. "Ours is going to begin all over again." He added that he understood the Sultan's desire to create a modern state and assured him that he alone could carry out that task and not the Istiqlal—a prediction which, as it turned out, was not quite correct. He warned Mohammed V against undue haste, stressing that, apart from the administrative system borrowed from France, Morocco was still unorganized; hence the need to proceed slowly and to plan ahead. The trip had brought the Sultan into the limelight in France, Morocco, and the outside world. In the General's opinion, this was to be the starting point, the first stage in an evolutionary process. It was agreed that there should be other visits to France, almost every year. The independent states of Morocco and Tunisia could be linked to France, each in an appropriate fashion, by federal ties. As far as Morocco was concerned, the stages and dates could be determined in the eventual treaty. De Gaulle thought that ten years would be needed to complete the process, and he laid particular stress on the problem of training cadres without which, he emphasized, nothing solid could be built.[21]

The Sultan was to visit France again in 1946. The General hoped that by that time there would be a constitution, and admitted that it was beyond his power to do anything definitive, legal, and lasting until that condition had been fulfilled. This relieved Mohammed V and allayed his misgivings. He signified his agreement, and nothing that happened subsequently would appear to give grounds for doubting the good faith of the two negotiators. On July 2, the Sultan returned to Morocco after an absence of sixteen days. He did not return empty-handed, having apparently convinced the government of the necessity of reducing the tension between the Residency and the Palace by recalling the Resident-General. Events were moving rapidly in Paris, however, where De Gaulle was preparing to leave the political scene before he had had time to launch his Moroccan policy.[22]

In October 1945, an incident once again enabled the Istiqlal to stress one of its basic grounds of opposition. A September 15 decree of the Provisional Government had called upon Frenchmen in Morocco to participate in the French October elections and in the constitutional referendum of May 1946.[23] Although the nationalists protested vigorously against the election, which they considered contrary to Moroccan sovereignty, three representatives for Morocco, Pierre Parent (Anti-Fascist League), Louis Dumat (France First),[24] and Jean Léonetti (S.F.I.O.) were elected by the settlers on September 21.

Nevertheless, the thaw in Franco-Moroccan relations continued. Some university faculty members and certain leaders of the Istiqlal had been considering for some time the conditions under which the dialogue could be resumed. Frenchmen in Morocco protested to the Quai d'Orsay about the immobility of the

21. Henceforth, Moroccans were admitted to St.-Cyr, the Polytechnique, and the École d'administration.

22. On March 2, 1946, nearly nine months later, the Gouin government finally appointed Labonne as Puaux' successor.

23. *Journal officiel de la république française* (*J.O.*), *Ordonnances et décrets*, Sept. 16, 1945, p. 5813.

24. Title of a party slate headed by Louis Dumat, representative to the Third Electoral College of the Government Council.

Resident-General. On February 13, 1946, fourteen leading Frenchmen submitted a political memorandum to the Department for
Africa and the Levant. They maintained that the protectorate
system no longer satisfied the Moroccan people and asked the
government to reconsider its attitude, proceed with the reforms,
reestablish political liberties, and restore confidence, so that a
modern state of Morocco could be brought into being.[25]

Parliament had not waited until 1946 to express its desire for
reform.[26] During a debate on Moroccan and Tunisian affairs on
August 1, 1945, following the submission of a report by a Parliamentary Commission of Enquiry, some M.R.P. and Communist
deputies came out strongly in favor of the introduction of far-
reaching reforms in Morocco.[27] The debate ended with the Provisional Consultative Assembly's urging the government to put
into effect a bold program of reforms.

The liberal views held both by the head of the Provisional
Government and by the Consultative Assembly seemed to open
the way for far-reaching developments. This consensus, however,
did not survive the blow to the decision-making powers of the
government caused by De Gaulle's departure. The Fourth Republic was to be rendered impotent by the enormous problems
raised by the revolt of its colonies as well as by internal schisms,
and was to wear itself out and finally destroy itself in a vain
effort to thwart the aspirations of subject peoples.[28] It had settled

25. Julien, p. 354.
26. The Provisional and Constituent Assemblies from 1943–46 were not completely
indifferent to Moroccan problems.
27. J.O., Débats parlementaires, Assemblée consultative provisoire, Aug. 2, 1945, pp.
1705 ff., 1719 ff.
28. One may ask whether this view is tantamount to linking the subsequent evolution
of the conflict to a simple historical accident attributable to the intransigence of one
man. Nobody would deny the role of accidents in history. But, in this case, the accident
is only apparent, in the sense that it is the inevitable product of sociological and French
political factors that so forcefully helped to shape later events.
Far from being an accident, the split between the regime and the man who had reestablished democratic and political freedom would appear to be the fatal consequence
of two incompatible concepts of political life. Democracy is not hostile to authority, but,
by its very nature, it recognizes only that governing force deriving from the voluntary
consent of the governed. De Gaulle was not opposed to democracy, but he believed that,
in a society divided to the point of impotence, representative government could only
reflect at the summit the tensions affecting the base. Hence the idea of compensating
for the congenital weakness of the French political organism by resorting to expedients
of quasi-plebiscital nature. The regime, in refusing to be saved by a man incarnating a

down into the rut of the Third Republic. However, the desire for a new era that had been apparent in Paris during the past months remained sufficiently strong to enable a change of course at Rabat. It was this that made it possible to replace Puaux by Eirik Labonne, a liberal of quite different stature. Labonne was dependent entirely on his own resources and could only demonstrate, at his own expense, that it was impossible to resolve revolutionary tensions developing in a colony without the backing of a government willing and able to make decisions, which France, now reduced to mere reflex actions, could no longer provide.

It remains for us to draw up a balance sheet of these events. In Morocco, the conflict between resurgent nationalism and the colonial system had, by the end of the war, assumed most of its characteristic features. The alliance between the Sultan and the Istiqlal had been sealed in blood and in the public humiliation of the sovereign. The partnership between the Sultan and the Resident-General had not yet, of course, been entirely dissolved. Many mistakes were to be made before a complete divorce occurred. Trapped between the Istiqlal and the Residency, the Sultan still hesitated, temporizing, changing from one extreme to another with a mixture of audacity and uneasiness. Nevertheless, the die was cast. There were already indications of the approaching union between the Sultan and that section of the Moroccan people most susceptible to nationalist pronouncements. Mohammed V was no longer merely the religious leader and the physical personification of a theoretically sovereign state. He was gradually, but very consciously, becoming the champion of his people's independence. Of course this embryonic nationalism still affected only a nucleus of the urban population. However, the

---

political philosophy not akin to its own, reacted as would have been expected, but in so doing it could no longer cope with the very problems that brought about its stagnation. De Gaulle, in refusing to abide by the rules of the game, was consciously safeguarding the prestige and support which history had bestowed upon him, but in so doing he placed himself outside the only political machinery practicable at the time. It was impossible to reconcile De Gaulle with the external forms of democracy just after the war, but this came about quite naturally twelve years later, once the regime had reached the final point of disintegration and had delivered itself into his hands. At that moment, France accepted him more or less willingly as the only alternative to social revolution or to a military coup d'etat.

popular base of the movement had been extended. From Fez, the cradle of the movement, it had spread in the direction of other northern and also western towns. It had reached Rabat-Salé, the political heart of the country. The Istiqlal had reconstituted its cadres, reaped the benefits of the National Reform Party's pre-war activities among Moroccan youth, and wiped out the effects of the 1937 crisis; it had successfully resumed its underground work of organizing the masses. It was at last at the starting point.

The cogwheels—the dialectics of repression and the growth of the repressed movement—had been set in motion. It was to this that young Moroccan nationalism essentially owed its early successes. The Istiqlal had set the repressive machinery in motion, but it was France which had made it work to the benefit of her opponent. For the more one arrests, harasses, and humiliates, the more those formerly indifferent will rally, however reluctantly, to a resistance movement, either from wounded national pride, fear, or because, since all retreat for the suspect has been cut off, there is no other way out. The time was soon to come when the nationalists had only to act; repressive measures automatically multiplied the nationalists' power of attracting the masses. It is at this point that historical causality shifts to determinism and that the sociological determinants transform historical contingency into necessity. The relative strength of the antagonists works to the disadvantage of the colonial power. Whatever the Istiqlal did worked in its own favor. Whatever France did to contain the Istiqlal worked, in the long run, to the latter's advantage by driving the Moroccans into the Istiqlal camp. It is not surprising, therefore, that France ultimately found itself isolated in a Morocco rallying entirely to nationalism, for the intrinsic strength of the colonial regime operated for ten years to benefit its opponent.[29]

The majority of the French in Morocco had not yet entered

29. Obviously, France at any given moment, at least theoretically, could have resolved the conflict by exerting unlimited coercion upon the Moroccan people. The repression in question concerns individuals who have broken the laws of a given group, as opposed to the kind of repression, completely different in principle, that seeks to destroy or terrorize that group, in order to suppress the political problem it poses. This basic distinction is not elaborated here, since it is covered more fully in volume 2.

upon the scene. They felt themselves sufficiently protected by the armed force of the regime and the conservatism of their leaders. However, they had at least become aware of the threat and were beginning to grow apprehensive, although as yet this concern was manifested only by the fact that they were gathering behind their natural protectors. From the beginning, even before this concern came into the open, their leaders had adopted what was to be their characteristic attitude throughout the crisis. The pattern had been set. The Residency had given way to the temptation of cloaking repressive measures in sham reforms, and was to depart from these tactics only in exceptional cases. The major administrative departments had become states within a state, and the Resident-General was forced to confess that he no longer controlled the police. The army, the police, and certain high officials had formed an alliance from the outset. They threw all their weight behind the policy of force and put on the brakes whenever the Residency sought to make overtures.

Most important of all, the efforts at provocation by a certain sector of the police had found a worthy protagonist from the start in the person of Boniface. Another constant factor in the conflict was that whenever it looked as though agreement might be reached between France and the nationalists, those opposing any such agreement provided the necessary impetus at Rabat to have the whole question reopened. Except for a few well-informed persons, hardly anyone believed this at the time, but it was to be a common aspect of North African colonial crises.

In France, while the battle lines were being drawn in Morocco and the two adversaries had taken up their positions, and even before the curtain rose, De Gaulle's departure had destroyed any possibility of arbitration by the Métropole. The nation was now abandoned to the conservative impulses that were to aid the supporters of the status quo until the final capitulation.

However, in this first period, which was in many respects so typical, all the wheels had not yet been set in motion. Only the black keys of Moroccan nationalism, of which each heading in the organigramme could be said to represent one note, had so far been played on the sociological and political keyboard of the crisis. The white keys for the most part had remained silent. At every phase of the future, each Resident-General would have to play his own particular variations upon this keyboard, according to particular circumstances.[30]

On the Moroccan side, there was as yet no conflict between the Government Council and the Residency. The First and Second Electoral Colleges of the Council went about their business in the comfortable atmosphere of a game which seemed to have been taken up where it was left off. The easy relationship between the Government Council and the Residency did not prevent a marked tension from appearing within the Council itself, between the first two Electoral Colleges, which were solidly behind the administration, and the Third College, which represented diverse interests and which exhibited a strong leftist tendency in this immediate postwar period.[31] Although the July 1945 session of the Council had been rather dull, the Communists in the Third College had demanded the nationalization of the state bank and of the water, electricity, and transport services. The dispute which had been latent broke out at the next session, in January–February 1946. On behalf of the Third College, a delegate demanded a decent standard of living for the ordinary white man. The same speaker demanded trade-union rights for Moroccans, the extension to them of social legislation hitherto restricted to French workers, and tremendous expansion of the educational system. Outright accusations were made and there were violent scenes which set the delegates at loggerheads with the administration. The most frequent target for these attacks was Georges Girard, head of the Department of Public Works.

It would be wrong, however, to attach too much importance to

30. This, despite the deliberate sociological character of the method, is what justifies dividing history into separate periods. While the role of basic sociological and political factors is primary in considering the internal determinism of a political phenomenon, the action of individuals comes to the fore in an historical study such as the present one. These two perspectives are not incompatible. For if it be understood that the actions of individuals constitute the basic stuff of which history is made, this is not to deny that the individuals who play key roles in history are only actors in a play of which they are not the directors—a play, in fact, that has no director. In other words, sociological, like economic, phenomena themselves determine their development, albeit by other means.

31. The rapport between the important settlers and the administration did not prevent certain high-ranking officials at the Residential level (such as Léon Marchal, defender of the peasant land-reform program) from doing everything in their power to salvage as much as possible of the Residency's reform program.

these incidents. The Council was not ready to perform its proper role until the first two Colleges took up the fight against the liberal Residents-General and until the Third College, which had become less left-wing, entered the fray and protested purely as a matter of form, when it protested at all.

The French press in Morocco purred contentedly. It gave the impression that nothing was happening in the country. The first rumblings of nationalism were ignored as being too dangerous to comment on and, moreover, of no importance in the eyes of the great economic interests, whose sole concern was to whitewash themselves and adjust to the new political context born out of the Resistance. The Mas press trust (the French newspapers in Morocco belonging to Pierre Mas) had just been dissolved for having collaborated with the enemy. However, apparently neither the press nor the authorities wanted to recognize the existence of Moroccan nationalism. As long as the Residency had matters under control, all was for the best in the best of all possible worlds. For example, in January 1944, absolutely no mention was made of the Istiqlal manifesto, or of the reasons for Massigli's arrival. On February 1–3, there was nothing about the riots at Fez. Again, nothing or almost nothing on the Puaux reforms. There was, in fact, a systematic news blackout. The Communist-inspired weekly, *Libération,* was almost alone in criticizing the inertia and lack of creative spirit displayed by the departments of the Residency. There was a similar silence or near-silence on the part of French political parties and trade unions, except for the S.F.I.O. whose leaders were at the time liberally inclined.

Everyone went about his own business as if nothing were happening, but this did not prevent either side from voting, amid general indifference, upon motions or resolutions in accordance with its traditional ideology. The trade unions followed the advice of the Resident-General and closed their eyes to membership of individual Muslims in their branches. The settlers, usually so touchy, allowed Puaux to set up his new agricultural reform program without objection. The same program was to elicit furious opposition during Labonne's Residency, but calm prevailed for the time being, as it did in other groups in the French colony. Apart from the police, the upper echelons of the administration swam with the current. All the regional commanding officers except General Suffren had been appointed at the Resident-General's request, as had the directors of the chief technical departments: Georges Girard, Roger Pasquier, René Thabault.

In France, where everything had to be rebuilt, Morocco was a minor concern. Parties and trade unions had barely reorganized and were otherwise preoccupied. Press references to Morocco were few, in view of the shortage of newsprint and the plethora of news, and were as detached as though they referred to minutiae. The Quai d'Orsay allowed the Resident-General to do as he pleased; he had full powers, and, furthermore, he belonged to the inner circle. Only De Gaulle and certain members of the Provisional Consultative Assembly had given any thought to the problem. The former, however, was leaving the stage, and Parliament, once the Fourth Republic was installed, was shortly to lose all interest in Morocco and was not to make its views known until too late.

Chapter 3

THE LABONNE PERIOD
AND THE REFORMS
THAT WERE SABOTAGED
(MARCH 2, 1946–MAY 14, 1947)

In recalling Gabriel Puaux, the Gouin government was only confirming a decision that had been virtually a foregone conclusion since 1945. It had not been acted on earlier because, under the De Gaulle regime, members of the government had not been able to agree on a successor. The ministers all recognized that Puaux could not remain much longer at Rabat without inviting disaster. The potential candidates were General Alphonse Juin, General Jacques Philippe Leclerc, and Ambassador Eirik Labonne. De Gaulle himself had looked favorably on Leclerc for the post, but after Puaux's failure it had seemed to him unwise to appoint another man of military temperament. Labonne finally won when the problem came up again after De Gaulle's departure. Neither Juin nor Leclerc was pleased. Actually, of the three, Labonne was the only possible candidate at that auspicious moment after the war when the future still seemed bright.

In France, the liberal impetus De Gaulle had given to colonial policy on the very eve of his resignation was in fact developing in a vacuum, with no one really in control. The détente that was becoming evident in North Africa, and especially in Morocco, following the abortive attempt to apply it in Indochina, was not unlike a badly supported attack that all the courage of the attackers cannot save from failure. In Paris, a succession of provisional governments continued to guide the affairs of a nation whose main concern was to provide itself with a constitution. The first governments of the Fourth Republic were shortly to slam the door that had been momentarily ajar. Very soon

41

were to come the rupture with Ho Chi Minh, Labonne's recall, and the abandonment of North Africa to conservative forces.

The new Resident-General took up his duties in a situation which had not yet wholly crystallized, but for which the chances of a liberal solution, momentarily discernible, were rapidly vanishing. Labonne was no stranger to Morocco; fifteen years earlier he had been Secretary-General of the protectorate. He was bold, visionary, unorthodox; he was not altogether a man of his time, yet in some respects he possessed an astonishing understanding of it. He was more economist than politician, perhaps even more technocrat than economist. In other respects he was imbued with an almost punctilious sense of his mission. He landed in Morocco with a well defined program and a determination to yield nothing of the patrimony he had been sent to restore and to allow no one, from the most gold-braided generals to the most powerful leading citizens, to stand in his way. He intended to re-establish contact with the nationalists in prison or in exile; to feed, clothe, and house the Moroccans; to develop the country's natural resources; and, above all, if not first of all, to regain control of the top officials and liberalize the administration without modifying its basic structure.

One week after the new Resident-General arrived, Mohammed Lyazidi, who had been leader of the Istiqlal since the exile of Ahmed Balafredj, sent him a memorandum listing the party's chief grievances against the administration.[1] The memorandum laid particular stress on the absence of civil liberties and on the treatment of the nationalist leaders who had been exiled or imprisoned in 1937 and in 1944. The appeal could not be allowed to go unheard. The Resident-General's first gesture was to release Allal el-Fassi. He sent his personal airplane for him and scandalized the Europeans by inviting him to dinner on the very day of his return. The sentence of banishment imposed on Mohammed el-Ouazzani in 1937 was rescinded. Ahmed Balafredj, in forced residence in Corsica since 1944, also received amnesty. The nationalists at once sat up and took notice. The Istiqlal, with its original leadership restored, was to enjoy a tolerance throughout

1. Istiqlal Party, "La Crise marocaine," *Documents 1944–46,* pp. 27–36.

Labonne's administration that the party used to great advantage in developing its activities.

Labonne's second gesture was to put the administrative part of his program into effect. On June 25, 1946, a Residential order abolished the Department of Political Affairs and replaced it by two new organs which took over respectively the political and administrative powers of the former body: the Political Secretariat and the Department of the Interior.[2] The Department of Political Affairs, which had long been, as it were, a state within a state, seemed to have been dismantled. In reality, this reorganization was unsuccessful. The senior officials' relative independence of the Residency was due to the influence they had managed to establish for themselves rather than to the division of powers among the departments—a mere reallocation of functions did not solve the problem.

Labonne then made two unhappy decisions, which in a few months were to bring about the failure of his policy and his own recall to Paris. Instead of appointing a trustworthy man as head of the new Department of the Interior and neutralizing Philippe Boniface's power with an honorary post, he merely transferred him to Casablanca as Regional Commissioner. Then, ignoring the advice of General de Lattre de Tassigny, he put the Department of the Interior under Colonel Jean Lecomte, no doubt hoping by this concession to win the approval of General Leclerc, who had strongly backed that officer's candidacy.

He could hardly have made more unfortunate decisions. These two men, the civilian and the soldier, so effectively combined their opposition to the Residency's policy that it is hardly an exaggeration to say that Labonne, in thus assigning them to two key posts, sealed the fate of his administration. Both were hostile to anything resembling a liberalization of the protectorate. Both were given to intrigue. One was to lead those settlers who were in the process of repudiating their allegiance to France and the other was to be the mouthpiece and incarnation, in the administration and then the general staff, of the deep-rooted hostility of certain military leaders to the political claims of subject peoples.

2. Protectorat de la république française (empire chérifien), *Bulletin officiel* (*B.O.*), June 28, 1946, p. 551.

Boniface left Rabat for Casablanca fully determined to reorganize the instruments of personal policy he had been forced
to relinquish to the new director of the Department of the
Interior. He resented a transfer he considered a demotion. Convinced that the protectorate would never survive the Resident-
General's proposals, he therefore took immediate steps to block
them. As head of the contrôle civil and past master in the use of
secret police, Boniface had hitherto been merely a senior official
who had become all-powerful in his own department. His transfer to Casablanca, the business and financial capital, threw him
into the arms of the settlers. Within a few months, the growing
anxiety of the leading citizens resulted in his becoming the chief
backstage power in the protectorate. As de facto Resident-
General of a European colony which was soon to clamor for and
obtain the head of its nominal chief, he joined the ultras and
formed what was to be an unbreakable alliance with the army.
In furtherance of his ambitions, he assumed the leading role in
the conspiracy that was to bring about Labonne's downfall.

Colonel Lecomte, who succeeded Boniface in the Department
of the Interior, was equally formidable. With a quick mind,
unquestionably superior to his predecessor, the new director declared himself against all reform, worked methodically to destroy
the Resident-General's standing in governmental circles in Paris,
and kept in constant touch from Rabat with all those in France
who might at the slightest opportunity tip the scales in favor of a
policy of force. In the end, he served the settlers' cause well. Here
again, the appointment to a key post of a personality committed by
temperament as well as by conviction to using force and trusting
to luck marked the beginning of a career of unparalleled influence, far exceeding that inherent in the post.[3]

Thus barely three months after his arrival in Rabat and solely

---

3. Colonel Lecomte was transferred again in 1948 after the Berber pamphlets affair,
and served as Chief Staff Officer for General Juin and then General Guillaume when
they were Inspectors-General of North African troops. He was subsequently a member
of Marshal Juin's special staff, military expert to the French delegation in the Franco-
Tunisian negotiations, then Chief Special Staff Officer to General Koenig, Minister for
National Defense in the Faure Cabinet. He accompanied Koenig to Aix-les-Bains and,
following his superior's resignation, submitted his own in September 1953. This did
not prevent his remaining to the end the éminence grise of the great military leaders
of the regime.

because of these two appointments, Labonne lost the game before it really began. It would be unfair for an historian today to reproach Labonne for not anticipating all the fatal consequences that reorganization of the protectorate administration was to have for his policy, but the rashness of much of his course seems obvious. In such circumstances, it is of little avail to hold the principal controls if one does not hold them all. One must be master or give up. Controlling the Residency and then generously abandoning a key departmental post and the command of the most important region to men known to be hostile to his policy, Labonne allowed his opponent to queen two pawns at the very start of the game. The Resident-General, however, did have some grounds for believing that the reorganization had strengthened his authority: at the Residential level he had Léon Marchal in the Délégation, Jacques Lucius in the Secretariat, and Jacques Vimont in Sharifian Affairs—a first-class team whose loyalty he considered above suspicion. He henceforth devoted all his efforts to drafting reforms he intended to make public in July 1946, when he opened the summer session of the Government Council.

Even earlier, on May 4, he had set up itinerant schools "under unpaid teachers, mostly the wives of settlers or civil servants, living in areas where the difficulty of recruiting teachers [threatened] to make the establishment of regular schools impossible for a long time to come." [4] His purpose was to set up a parallel, makeshift system of education at little cost which could, as a beginning, fill some of the most glaring gaps in the official educational system. The attempt, which was received with an initial burst of enthusiasm, foundered amid general hostility.

Although in the interval Labonne had been careful to give the public frequent glimpses of his reform policy, his opening speech before the French section of the Government Council on July 22, 1946, amounted to a bombshell.[5] His inimitable style, unorthodox ideas, and obvious determination to put them into effect at once despite opposition quickly plunged the representatives in

4. Rézette, *Les Partis politiques marocains*, p. 168 n.
5. *La Documentation française, Notes documentaires et études, Textes et documents*, no. 357 (July 22, 1946), pp. 1–10. See also Résidence-générale de la république française au Maroc, *Bulletin d'information du Maroc*, no. 7 (Aug. 1946), pp. 11–41.

the first two electoral colleges into mute consternation that soon
flared into open hostility.

The Labonne plan centered upon three complementary and
closely connected objectives. In production, far-reaching economic reforms were to make possible the accelerated development of Moroccan natural resources. This was to be accomplished by establishing joint companies in which the Sharifian
state would be associated with both European and Moroccan
private capital, by progressive industrialization of the country,
and by complete modernization of traditional agriculture
through extension of up-to-date farming methods. The program
was to have been launched with public funds. Subsequently, resources obtained from initial achievements would, according to
its promoters, make it possible to extend the system throughout
the country. On this triple base was to rise a whole system of
social reforms financed by taxation, borrowing, subsidies from
France, and, as progress was achieved, by the increase in the
national income generated by the application of the plan itself.
The objective was to westernize the way of life of the Moroccan
peasant, modernize the judicial system, educate the masses, organize the neo-proletariat of the large towns into trade unions,
and throw open the civil service at every level to Moroccans.
Lastly, and less important than the first two reform measures,
the government itself was to become more democratic through
the establishment of rural, municipal, and provincial councils,
with strictly equal representation for the French and Muslim
communities, and it was to be headed by a new joint Central
Advisory Council, elected by universal suffrage, which would
shortly replace the old Government Council.

Labonne's accompanying commentary—even more than the
expression of his intentions—left no doubt that this time the
Residency was deeply committed to a policy of reform. He called
unequivocally upon the Sharifian state to take charge of Moroccan economic development wherever private enterprise was
lacking, inadequate, impotent, or harmful. "Through its intervention in certain activities," he said "from participation on the
most modest scale to complete control if necessary, the state must
carry out the mandate it holds from the people, that of promot-

ing expansion and development, while at the same time properly safeguarding the rights of the people and the nation." [6]

In the field of social reforms, gargantuan efforts were needed to educate the whole population and to effect modern judicial regulations replacing the "present system, which is manifestly out of date, and whose flagrant abuses must cease." [7] Trade-union rights would have to be granted to wage earners, with the exception of agricultural workers, deemed to be insufficiently prepared as yet. All careers, particularly in the administration, would have to be thrown open to Moroccans. Finally, the new political structures at the local, provincial, and central levels were gradually to be substituted for direct administration; the protectorate would, of course, be maintained but would be renovated and made completely egalitarian in character.

The top civil servants and notables who heard the Resident-General realized that he was in earnest and determined to put his program into effect, point by point. Following hard upon the heels of the release of the nationalist leaders, the Labonne plan once more threatened the established order: the Sharifian state was asked to defend the public interest from private interest groups. The settlers were invited to sacrifice their near monopoly of the budget to the fellah and to Moroccan illiterates; direct administration and the penal powers of the pashas and cadis—the very foundation of the existing regime—were to be replaced by a modern system of administration and justice. The sacrosanct Government Council was to be replaced by a single assembly with equal membership and elected by universal suffrage.

"In our day . . . nothing is accomplished in politics without the consent of the people," Labonne had said at the end of his opening speech. "Nor can anything great be done without love, outside that communion of souls and hearts which His Majesty the Sultan enjoys with his people, and without that love which I make so bold as to say that I have for this country." [8] One can imagine the suppressed smiles with which these generous views were greeted by those who believed, not without reason, that in

6. Ibid., p. 25.
7. Ibid., p. 40.
8. Ibid., p. 41.

matters of colonization, in the short run, the consent of the notables counted for more than that of the people. The notables were preparing a striking demonstration of that political truth.

The First and Second Electoral Colleges, their backs to the wall, withdrew from the assembly hall as a sign of protest, except for the delegates of the Chamber of Commerce and Industry of Rabat, which remained in session. The debate continued in the presence of the delegates of the Third Electoral College and the members of the Moroccan section of the Government Council, although both advanced lively criticism against those aspects of the protectorate's policy with which they did not agree.

In his closing address to the Government Council on July 25, 1946, Labonne assured those remaining that his political plans had been deemed "prudent and sound" in France.[9] He regretted that the First and Second Electoral Colleges had withdrawn, even temporarily, and expressed the hope that all the members of the French section would speedily resume their collaboration with the government. Labonne's firmness won him the second round. The councillors soon changed their minds when they observed that the Resident-General, far from being intimidated by blackmail, refused to yield. They abandoned their boycott, and the situation apparently returned to normal. Labonne had foreseen this move, since the leading citizens could not afford to avoid dealing with the representative of the central power in all matters relating to the daily affairs so important to them. This sound appraisal brought him temporary victory but did not change the strategic weakness of his position. In spite of the about-face of the absentees, the conspirators among the army, the settlers, the upper levels of the administration, and the Moroccan Radical Socialists (all-powerful in Morocco since the Residency of Théodore Steeg, 1925–29) had been waiting for a chance to close in for the kill. The Sultan's speech at Tangier a few months later provided the opportunity.[10]

The press was divided, each paper following the pattern dictated by its general political views. Departing from the usual

9. Ibid., pp. 49–52.
10. See p. 57.

conformism of the Mas press, *Le Petit Marocain,* then in its liberal period, commented extensively on the events. In its editorial of July 21, the paper criticized the Council as an institution. Two days later it stressed the significance of the Resident-General's statement. "All his listeners are dimly aware that Morocco is at a crossroads and that the words pronounced will reecho throughout the country." Noting that the Resident-General in bypassing the first two Electoral Colleges had shown them up "in their true proportions," the article dwelt sarcastically and with some pleasure upon the offstage maneuvering of the delegates who "having missed their exit . . . were terrified lest they miss their next entrance." The Mas press minimized the incident, while at the same time avoiding an open break with the Resident-General for the present. *L'Echo du Maroc* printed his speech without comment on the abstentions, and urged that the dust be allowed to settle before passing judgment.[11] The newspaper did not care whether it displeased either or both parties; it was trying to patch matters up and give the Resident-General a pledge of its goodwill.

Labonne's troubles were by no means over. While the leading French settlers were preparing to defeat his policy, the nationalists were making ready to take the offensive for opposite reasons. As long as he had had to deal with the settlers alone, Labonne had only to overcome expected obstacles. The situation was drastically altered by the nationalists' entry into the fray. Their opposition to the Resident-General's plans correspondingly reduced his freedom of maneuver and, what was worse, succeeded in involving the Sultan. From then on, Labonne was almost completely isolated and had to fight on three fronts.

On July 24, the Istiqlal publicly declared itself opposed to the reforms. In a letter to the Sultan, Ahmed Balafredj charged that the Labonne plan "consolidated the bases of a colonialist policy which the experience of thirty-four years has shown to be a complete failure."[12] He expanded his grievances, complaining that the plan made no reference to civil liberties, violated the international status of Morocco by giving French capital a monopoly

11. *Echo du Maroc,* July 24, 1946.
12. Rézette, p. 159.

over the country's wealth, weakened the Maghzen by expanding
the competence of the tribal assemblies, and impeded the development of modern Arab education by reforms which concentrated almost exclusively on extending French education. Once
again, Balafredj demanded the constitution of an authentic Moroccan government that could enter into negotiations, under the
Sultan's leadership, for the conclusion of a new treaty with
France.[13] The recently founded P.D.I. took up the cry. Finally,
the Sultan himself told the Resident-General that he regarded
the proposed reforms as mere palliatives, and left unsigned the
six *dahirs* that were to have put them into effect.

It must be conceded that the Resident-General's plans had
placed the nationalists in an awkward tactical position. They had
decided in 1944 that they would not consider any reform as long
as their country had not achieved independence. They could
hardly accept the control of Morocco's natural resources by
French capital when the idea of the mobilization of the country's
wealth—launched by President Roosevelt at Anfa—had become
one of nationalism's cardinal principles. It is difficult, for instance, to imagine Balafredj disguising the deal by accepting the
vice-presidency of the Djerada Coal Company, as the Resident-
General had proposed.

Basically, the Istiqlal agreed—apart from the financial question—with the essential points of the Resident-General's economic and social program, but the nationalists did not believe he
was in a position to make his views prevail. They felt that his
policy had no future. Knowing him to be the butt of the hostility
of the French and of his immediate associates, they were particularly afraid of disarming their forces by rallying publicly to a
plan that was destined to go down with the Resident-General or
be sabotaged by the administration after his fall. Some were
equally afraid he might succeed, which they felt would consolidate the protectorate for an indeterminate period. Hence their
public opposition, which was purposefully designed to keep the
masses on the alert. It did not prevent the nationalist leaders
from explaining to their comrades in private that the party's veto
was directed less against the reforms than against the political

13. Ibid.

context in which the Resident-General was forced to defend them.

Despite its tenacity, this opposition in principle was less absolute than one might have believed. It did not prevent the Sultan and the leaders of the Istiqlal from maintaining excellent relations with the Resident-General, once the initial tension had passed. The nationalists refused to approve the Labonne plan, but were not averse to encouraging the liberalism of a man for whom they had the greatest esteem. They hesitated at the doorstep, but they had not closed the door. There was mutual sympathy between Labonne and the Sultan, who obviously wavered between collaboration and obstruction. The pending *dahirs* might have to be signed one day, and it would be difficult then for the Istiqlal to go on alone. On many occasions, Mohammed V admitted to French ministers or to foreign visitors that real progress was being made.

It appears that the Istiqlal made an appreciable error of judgment. While the party was undoubtedly correct in fearing the final fall of the Resident-General, it is questionable that that was sufficient reason for refusing to back him. As long as the experiment lasted, the Istiqlal was sure to be able to devote itself peacefully to its own reorganization and to the organization of the masses. Assuming that, as might well have happened, the ultras would finally overcome the united front of the Residency and the nationalists, the question would arise whether the party was in any worse position to resume the fight. One might say, on the contrary, that the real danger was that Labonne might succeed and give the protectorate a new lease on life. Here the nationalist leaders seriously misread the situation. The regime would not have long survived the entry of Moroccans into the higher administrative categories, cessation of fiscal and budgetary privileges for the settlers, creation of Moroccan trade unions, elimination of direct administration, and the establishment of a pyramid of joint elected assemblies, however restricted and advisory in character they might initially have been.

Although the Resident-General had said on his arrival in Morocco that he would do anything except abolish the protectorate, the settlers realized better than he that his program

implied the ultimate liquidation of the regime he sought to re-
generate. Some representatives of the French community, despite
the automatic nature of their defensive reaction, were nevertheless
acutely aware of the fundamental danger to them inherent in the
situation. The Resident-General had the settlers against the wall.
All they could do was fight back. Paralyzed by fear of making a
false move, the nationalists were the only ones who did not see
the implications of the Resident-General's program if it were
successful.

Another sign of the times was that, on August 7, the Moroccan
branch of the S.F.I.O. (S.F.I.O/Morocco) had criticized the reforms in progress, especially the failure of the itinerant schools
and the agricultural reform program. By so doing it was in fact
merely defending the French teachers whose privileges were
threatened by Labonne's bold nonconformism. The French colony, feeling itself abused, was beginning to regroup its forces.
Actually, Labonne could go no further; blocked on both sides,
he was forced to compromise. In a speech at Casablanca on September 21, 1946, he admitted frankly that the reforms would
have to proceed by long and devious routes,[14] and he let it be
understod that the Government Council would not be reorganized for the next elections. He added that it had been necessary
to reestablish censorship because of the regrettable incidents that
had marked Moroccan political life. In conclusion he stated unequivocally that things were going badly and a thorough overhaul was needed.[15]

It was becoming urgent to put the administrative machinery
into operation again. The opportunity soon arose. For a long
time, the Sultan had wanted to visit the international territory of
Tangier. The projected trip raised thorny problems of international policy and at first Labonne felt unable to approve it.
The Sultan, under pressure to sign the reform *dahirs,* brought the
matter up again at the beginning of November 1946 during a
private interview with the Resident-General. He argued that in

14. *Bulletin d'information du Maroc,* no. 9 (Oct. 15, 1946), pp. 17–22.
15. He repeated this warning on October 26 in a speech following a dinner given
by the committee director of the Association au Maroc des anciens combattants et
victimes de la guerre. Also *Bulletin d'information du Maroc,* no. 10 (Oct. 31, 1946), pp.
10–17.

view of the importance of the *dahirs,* he wished to be able to affirm his authority throughout his empire before consenting to a plan of reforms that would affect the future of all Morocco.

The hazards were considerable, but Labonne saw an opportunity of breaking the deadlock. He said he agreed in principle; nevertheless, he warned Mohammed V of the dangers he would run if he said anything politically unacceptable to France. Labonne also made it clear that if the *dahirs* were not signed on the Sultan's return, he himself would carry out the remaining reforms by Residential decree. It was, in fact, a bargain: the Resident-General authorized the journey, and, while the Sultan did not formally undertake to sign all the *dahirs,* he did bind himself morally to sign at least one of them.

Most of the more thoughtful leaders of the Istiqlal had finally endorsed the major points of the Labonne plan after innumerable interviews, dinners, and conversations. This modification of the nationalists' attitude was due to the Resident-General's persuasive charm in his contacts with the Istiqlal leaders. The party had at last realized that sabotaging his activities was not in its own interest; but this unofficial, reserved, and tentative acquiescence was far from giving Labonne the political advantages that would have accrued from the nationalists' public approval of his policy. He disregarded advice from the Quai d'Orsay to proceed cautiously, and knowingly wagered his whole reform plan and his mission at Rabat upon a single throw of the dice. Matters had reached such a point that this calculated risk might well have appeared the only policy open to him.

At the beginning of 1947, the Government Council met again for its winter session. The debates in the French section were this time uneventful. Labonne, who thought that the *dahirs* were about to be signed, had no reason to rush the councillors. He contented himself in his opening address with the traditional analysis of the economic and financial situation,[16] though not without emphasizing the progress achieved in agricultural reform, education, and the establishment of joint companies. Fourteen agricultural reform centers had been set up during the year and 6,000 more hectares put under cultivation. A whole series of

16. Ibid., supp. to no. 2 (Jan. 31, 1947), pp. 1–22.

new companies and enterprises had been created according to plan. On the educational side, it had been possible to organize 500 to 600 itinerant French schools, affecting between 30 and 40 thousand children. Thanks to the Sultan's solicitude, a parallel network of Muslim schools had also been developed. Lastly, he announced significant reforms in the administration, where wartime disorder had brought about certain abuses that the Resident-General intended to correct.

The budget was sharply criticized by Gustave Aucouturier, President of the French Chamber of Agriculture of Meknes. He said his mind reeled at the contemplated expenditure of 15 billion francs—the settlers tended to fall prey to such apprehensions whenever the proportion of public expenditure allocated to the Moroccans threatened to rise.

The birth of the Fourth Republic, the announcement of the Sultan's forthcoming visit to Tangier, the anniversary of the events of 1944, the very recent reception in Washington of the future president of Tunisia, Habib Bourguiba, by Secretary of State Dean Acheson all gave the nationalists, at the end of January 1947, an almost irresistible opportunity for publicly restating their grievances. In a memorandum to the Sultan,[17] Ahmed Balafredj again demanded a freely contracted alliance as a substitute for the Protectorate Treaty, and on January 30 Mohammed Lyazidi protested vigorously to the Sultan about the Resident's economic policy. Labonne's cherished scheme for the creation of joint companies was for the first time publicly denounced as the most dangerous policy ever followed by France in order to extend and consolidate her position in North Africa. The Istiqlal also demanded that the Sharifian government hold a majority of at least 51 percent in the large joint companies established to exploit the country's natural resources. This was a new development in the official nationalist platform. With relentless tenacity, the Sultan had argued privately for months with the Resident-General along just such lines.

As was his custom, Labonne affected officially to be unaware

---

17. Istiqlal Party, "Protestation," pp. 39–40. Translation of the protest presented to the Sultan on July 24, 1946, by a delegation from the Istiqlal, following Labonne's speech of July 22 to the French section of the Government Council.

of this development.[18] At the beginning of March, a special congress of the S.F.I.O./Morocco was held at Fez, attended by Georges Gorse, former Under-Secretary of State for Muslim Affairs; Robert Verdier, Assistant Director of *Le Populaire;* and Jean Léonetti, Councillor of the Republic for the French in Morocco. The delegates unanimously recognized the need for far-reaching reforms to facilitate the integration of the two civilizations. Thus it can be seen that the position of the S.F.I.O./Morocco was not altogether consistent.

Because of the international status of Tangier, negotiations had been taking place among Britain, France, Spain, and the United States during the early part of 1947 concerning the Sultan's contemplated visit. The Quai d'Orsay, which had initially opposed the plan, finally agreed. Once the Powers had consented, it looked as if the trip would be a success both for the Resident-General and for the Sultan. No Moroccan sovereign had set foot in the city since 1899. A tradition was to be resumed, and only the desire of France to embarrass Spain by emphasizing the Sultan's popularity throughout the Sharifian Empire had made this change in French policy possible.

Then, only three days before Mohammed V's departure, disaster occurred in Casablanca. On April 7, 1947, after an apparently commonplace brawl between a number of Moroccans and some Senegalese infantrymen, the latter returned to their barracks, broke into the armory, equipped themselves with am-

18. Labonne did not take such communications too seriously, and always refused to acknowledge them, even when they were forwarded by the Sultan. The nationalists' demands, while not necessarily unreasonable or subversive, did in his opinion constitute an attack upon French sovereignty, which it was his duty to defend in Morocco. If the Residency and Paris had replied to these messages as if they had come from a great power, this, in a sense, would have implied recognition of the nationalist movement. Such recognition might have made the Sultan more intransigent lest he be outdone by the nationalists, thus depriving France of the benefits of his role as moderator. Also, Labonne considered it necessary to set absolute limits to the activities of the nationalists. However, while he may have appeared officially unaware of their messages, Labonne had no intention of clashing with the young Turks of the Istiqlal. He tempered his official refusal to acknowledge them by numerous unofficial contacts, to avoid alienating men whose hold over the young Moroccans appeared evident. Such was Labonne's policy vis-à-vis the Istiqlal. It should be emphasized that his ideas regarding reforms excluded any infringement of the Treaty of Fez. Labonne was in Morocco to apply it to the letter, including those clauses favorable to the Moroccans. He did not intend to let it be breached.

munition, and fired on the crowd that had gathered, killing dozens of Moroccans at random and wounding many more. It was learned later that the officers in command had not appeared, and that the French police had stayed out of the way during the rioting, only appearing on the battlefield at the end of the afternoon.

The Mas press reported the affair as a routine incident, although it claimed that because of the Sultan's nationalist sympathies, disorder was sure to follow. *Le Petit Marocain* was less willing than its competitors to turn a blind eye and demanded an investigation. It drew attention to the singular absence of the police and stressed the fact that according to the testimony of witnesses, the crowd of Moroccans on whom the troops fired had been absolutely unarmed. On April 10, the same newspaper announced that the Council of Ministers had been asked to impose severe penalties on those responsible for the massacre. "The people of France," added the article, "have learned with stupefaction of the assassination of these Moroccans in circumstances with which we are all familiar."

Thus, on the eve of a step that had all the appearances of being decisive in the evolution of the protectorate and just when nationalist opposition was tending to lessen, a new outbreak of violence—occurring as in 1944 at the psychological moment and under Boniface's direction—shattered the calm that had almost been achieved and ruined all the Resident-General's efforts of the past year to persuade the Sultan to compromise. This was the second in the series of serious incidents arranged or exploited in Morocco by those who were unwilling to see matters settled and who had at their disposal more influence and more accomplices than necessary to ensure success for their calamitous policy.[19]

On April 9, the Sultan left Rabat for Tangier in an atmosphere completely spoiled by the events preceding his departure. Nevertheless, his trip through the Spanish zone was a triumph. It enabled the Sultan to form an idea of his popularity among

19. That the authorities were responsible seems almost certain. Two Residents-General and a Secretary General of Morocco formally confirmed, during interviews, the provocative role of the French police. Similar testimony was obtained from the ultras.

his subjects in the northern zone and to assure himself of the loyalty of his local representative, the Caliph of Tetuán.

The Sultan was to speak at Tangier the next day before an audience of notables from every part of his empire, the diplomatic corps, and a delegation of French civil servants led by Jacques Vimont. His text contained a eulogy of the Arab League, offset by a warm tribute to French achievements in Morocco. Mohammed V had been angered by the bloodshed at Casablanca and stirred by the reception the citizens of Tangier gave to his eulogy of pan-Arabism and the Arab League. Afraid, perhaps, as he said later, that his listeners might under the circumstances boo the tribute to France with which he was to close, he omitted it. To the consternation of his French audience, his speech thus took on the aspect of a rebuff to the protecting power.[20]

Whatever the importance of the Casablanca shooting and the dramatic moment at Tangier, these two events only precipitated a foregone conclusion. No doubt they had freed the Sultan from his moral commitments to the Resident-General. It is no less likely that even if the two incidents had not taken place, the Sultan's conversion to Moroccan and pan-Arab nationalism would have come about in the end by other means. The whole situation was leading Mohammed V in that direction: the evolution of Moroccan public opinion, the progress of Arab nationalism in the world at large, and even support from abroad. Labonne was not unaware that in Tangier itself the Spanish minister had monopolized the Sultan from the moment of his arrival and had openly incited him to a break, while the United States representative had given him to understand that his government would favor and facilitate modification of the protectorate.

The Resident-General's hopes were shattered by these events, and the calculated risk he had taken in authorizing the Tangier visit appeared, in retrospect, to have been a political error. The trend begun years before ended with a decisive stand by the

---

20. Julien, *L'Afrique du Nord en marche*, pp. 363–64, analyzes the speech and variation. For the complete text, see *Bulletin d'information du Maroc*, no. 6 (April 15, 1947), pp. 18 ff.

Sultan in regard to Moroccan nationalism. Mohammed V had burned his bridges. All things considered, the recall of the Resident-General and the reversal of French policy in Morocco had become inevitable. In the train back to Rabat, Labonne made it quite clear to the Sultan that he was certain to be recalled. The Sultan had every reason to fear that the Resident-General's departure would be followed by the arrival of General Juin at Rabat and that France's return to the policy of force would sooner or later mean his own deposition: the fate of the Bey of Tunis left him in very little doubt of that. A victim of nervous reaction after the tension of the past few days, Mohammed V gave himself up for lost.

The repercussions were considerable in France and throughout the world. The metropolitan press was not yet sufficiently involved in Moroccan affairs to let itself be drawn into violent polemics, but it reported the affair in detail, which was in itself something new.[21] The jolt to French political circles was decisive: those who in Paris as in Rabat had been waiting the past six months for a chance to demand the head of the Resident-General had their revenge. They had only to pluck the fruits of victory. This was made easier by the fact that the ground had long since been prepared by the Moroccan Radical Socialists and by the military, led by Colonel Lecomte. Georges Bidault, Minister for Foreign Affairs since January 1947, had hitherto supported the Resident-General. After Tangier, he was swept along by the current and allowed himself to be convinced by Labonne's adversaries that events had only too well justified their somber prognostications.

The Council of Ministers took up the matter on May 13, and unanimously opposed the Resident-General. The political situation was unequivocal. The eviction of the Communists had made the Prime Minister, Paul Ramadier, entirely dependent upon the M.R.P., which controlled the political balance. The Minister of the Armed Forces, Pierre-Henri Teitgen, M.R.P., was an en-

---

21. The text was first published as the Sultan was to have given it and was distributed to the press by the Residency's *Service général d'information*. Not until April 12 was the oversight noted and the omission revealed. See *Combat* and *Le Monde*, April 12, 1947; also *Bulletin d'information du Maroc*, no. 7 (April 30, 1947), pp. 31 ff.

thusiastic supporter of General Juin. He was strongly opposed to
Labonne and had recently attacked him vociferously. Teitgen's
opposition was bolstered by his M.R.P. friends. In the Council,
Ramadier, his eyes on his Minister of the Armed Forces, watched
for the approbation or disapproval of the "arbiter" who held the
fate of the government in his hands. For Ramadier it was more a
matter of the rules of the political game and the balance of forces
than of personal conviction, and he bowed to the inevitable.[22]
These are the events that led a Socialist head of government, on
May 14, to announce Juin's appointment as Labonne's successor.

It is important to take stock again, especially since this marks a
vital turning point. An epoch had just ended. Another was about
to begin, although this would not prevent metropolitan France,
absorbed in other problems, from remaining for a long time
unaware of the conflict. In Morocco, the battle lines were drawn
at last. The two communities were face to face. The die was cast.
The tensions that had plagued the country since the liberation
had this time started a rift. Of course, both sides were not
equally aware of this. Although the French community was
almost completely united (according to the Resident-General, the
French in Morocco celebrated his recall by hanging out flags),
the Moroccans themselves were only beginning the evolution
that would gradually convert them in nine dramatic years to
the nationalist cause, as embodied in the alliance between the Sultan and the Istiqlal.

So far, the conflict existed only between the settlers and an
active Muslim minority that had the Sultan as its figurehead and
that wished to snatch the Moroccan people from the grip of the
notables and launch them on the road to independence. Yet it
was already a conflict between two adversaries who rejected all
attempts at mediation and were to devote themselves with increasing fury to mutual destruction. As long as the Residency
and the Palace nostalgically hoped for agreement, tension did
not go beyond the initial stage. Once these two were completely
at odds, the mechanism would be assembled and begin to function.

22. This scene was described during interviews by persons present at the meeting of
the Council of Ministers.

This time there were no longer any silent keys on the French part of the Moroccan keyboard. The Mas press of course was still cautious; caught between the interests it defended and a liberal Resident-General who was not to be overawed, it maneuvered and criticized sotto voce. It contented itself with discreet rejoicing over Labonne's recall. The ultra press was to unleash its fury against the nationalists only during the next period, when it was certain of the Residency's support. With this exception, once it had become evident that Labonne was not playing the settlers' game, all the opponents were face to face. The Government Council had become refractory. The rebels in the administration had beaten the Resident-General as the result of the Casablanca shooting. The army had openly supported the rebel officials. The Radical Socialists had entered the fray and occupied most of the key posts. They were led by Émile Roche, who was himself linked to Boniface and the Pasha of Marrakesh.

Apart from the Communists, the other branches of the metropolitan political parties were divided and would hide behind a facade of liberalism until the end. Among the leading citizens, Gustave Aucouturier and Émile Eyraud, editor of *La Vigie marocaine,* had assumed their roles as protagonists and, according to the Resident-General himself, formed the nucleus around which the great mass of the French in Morocco were already grouped. It was to become increasingly cohesive despite its composite character.

Attitudes were to become increasingly violent. The conservative reflex had already come into play. The European colony was achieving its internal unity and—vitally important—it was doing so around a new type of leader. This was a crucial development. The settlers were shocked and alarmed by the Resident-General's liberalism and felt themselves betrayed. They repudiated their nominal leaders and acquired new ones whom they deemed more capable than their rightful chiefs of assuring the defense of what they considered their vital interests. Henceforward, the Residency would be obeyed only to the extent that it acted in accordance with these de facto leaders. With the end of the Labonne experiment, the Residency completely lost its ability to mediate and was to be drawn directly into the conflict. Although

nationalism was virtually confined to the towns, it gained daily
in numbers and cohesiveness. The Sultan was drawn to the Istiqlal
and became the symbol of their aspiration by a development
analogous to that which propelled the Residency into the arms of
the settlers. The Imam, in whose name prayers were said
throughout Morocco, publicly and openly declared himself in
favor of independence. The Istiqlal, which despite the formation
of the P.D.I. remained and was to remain practically without a
rival until 1953, had taken advantage of the liberalism of the outgoing Resident-General to reseat itself in the saddle. It had deliberately worked to expand its relations with the rank and file
and was changing from a simple political movement to a mass
party. In all the centers where any tension existed between
Moroccan notables and the populace, Istiqlal support was virtually ready-made. Wherever the party had a trained and capable
local representative, potential support became active adherence.
Paid membership increased. The movement overflowed from the
large towns to the small. A whole segment of the country's
youth, molded by nationalist teachers, was won over almost
spontaneously. Thus, for the time being, the Istiqlal exerted its
major efforts on training cadres, for it knew that wherever
trained militants could be installed, the townspeople would rally
to it. Nevertheless, with a few exceptions, the movement was
limited to the centers of population. The conquest of the masses
was only beginning. The neo-proletariat of the western towns
was to enter the fray in the years ahead, and the *bled* itself
would not begin to stir until after the Sultan's deposition.

Another permanent feature of the conflict was the importance
assumed by the problem of reform from the time of the Labonne
period.[23] From a technical point of view, the Labonne reforms
were a great achievement, but politically they failed completely.
The Sultan had not signed any of the *dahirs* presented to him.[24]

23. Actually, "the battle for or against reforms" and "colonial conflict" are almost
synonymous concepts inasmuch as "reform" is defined as "all positive or negative
change in the organizational status quo induced by existing forces."

24. The Sultan's veto undoubtedly stimulated the opposition of both nationalists and
settlers to the reform *dahirs,* but this was a mere accident of procedure. After
Mohammed V's deposition, the *dahirs* drafted by the Residency and signed by his
successor also came to nothing, thanks to the muffled opposition of the Moroccan
people to the proposed institutions. The same held true for the settlers; never, until the

Substantial results, of course, had been obtained in fields in which the Residency could act without having to legislate with the Palace's consent: expansion of the agricultural program, development of itinerant schools, creation of joint companies, reorganization of political affairs. However, these temporary achievements did not survive Labonne, whose work for the most part was to be systematically undone bit by bit by the settlers and the administration. The agricultural-reform program, purged of its revolutionary spirit, would soon be only propaganda for the glorification of the protectorate. The itinerant schools would close. The Department of the Interior, reconstituted with all its old powers, would, in the next regime, become the bastion of directorial omnipotence. Only the joint companies set up under the Bureau for Mineral Prospecting and Investment were to escape annihilation.

The failure of Labonne's reforms is self-explanatory. When the authority in power does not enjoy the support of any of the groups it governs, it cannot mediate in any dispute between them. When its executive staff refuses to carry out orders and instead sabotages them, the authority can hardly amount to anything. When authority is impotent, it cannot resist the temptation to regain its power by abandoning its position as mediator in order to ally itself with those social groups to which it feels closest. Even if the nationalists had encouraged the Sultan to sign the *dahirs,* the result would have been the same: put into effect over the Sultan's seal, they would have been whittled away by the settlers and the administration. Given the social structure of the regime, the French in Morocco were powerful enough by themselves to neutralize any reform they disliked. When it came to refusing to participate further, thus nullifying some "reformed" political institution established by the French, the Moroccans equaled the settlers in their capacity to be obstructive. Support from one of the groups involved was essential for each reform measure. Failing that, the reform was blocked or emasculated from the start.[25]

very end, did the Residency succeed in winning them over to a policy with which they did not agree.

25. It has been alleged that it is hard to reconcile this passage with censure of the Istiqlal for not supporting Labonne's reforms. Such criticism does not seem to take into account the fact that when an historian subsequently judges events, he reasons

France itself was to stay on the sidelines of the conflict for a long time. The only real participants were those organs of state constitutionally connected with implementing policy relating to Morocco. Nevertheless, some features were beginning to emerge which were later to characterize France's attitude toward the conflict. The future was already indicated. A Socialist government had recalled a liberal Resident-General and had replaced him with a military man who was a staunch supporter of a policy of force and of prestige. The Socialists had thus demonstrated that in their eyes colonial questions and matters of principle were less important than political prescriptions and the struggle for power that hinged upon considerations of internal policy. Paris colonialist circles, prodded by Rabat, had perceived for the first time that no opposition parties (apart from the Communists, who were out of the running) would use the liberalization of a colonial administration as a basis on which a government—and still less a whole regime—might stand or fall. The way was clear before them. They would go from success to success until the Right itself was forced to give up the struggle, the issue having been decided by its own propensity to resist all change.

---

within a frame of reference different from the one he had when, projecting himself into the role of the protagonists, he criticizes their tactics at the time the events occurred. In the latter case, we said previously that they erred in not seeing that realization of the Labonne plan would have precipitated the downfall of the entire regime instead of (as they feared) consolidating it. We say now, with the hindsight that the nationalists obviously did not have, that even if the Istiqlal had supported Labonne's reforms, the French administration was sufficiently powerful to have prevented their being carried out. This means the Istiqlal's error was unimportant in the last analysis; it does not mean that no error was committed within the nationalists' frame of reference, inevitably more limited at the time.

Chapter 4

THE JUIN PERIOD AND THE 1951 CRISIS
(MAY 14, 1947–AUGUST 28, 1951)[1]

General Alphonse Juin was what is often called an "Old Moroccan." He was first a member of Marshal Lyautey's staff, senior military aide of Resident-General Lucien Saint, Commanding Officer of troops in Morocco under General Auguste Noguès, and Commander-in-Chief of French North African Forces in 1942. He was given command of the French forces in Tunisia; in that capacity he proceeded in 1943, on orders, to depose the Bey for collaborating with the Axis.[2]

This was only the beginning of a military career that was to assume national importance after the Italian campaign, in which French and Moroccan forces had covered themselves with glory under his command. After being Chief of General Staff, French Armed Forces, Juin was attached in 1945, to the French delegation to the Conference on International Organization at San Francisco. In January 1947, just before his departure for Morocco, he served as French representative at the London Conference of Deputy Foreign Ministers.

1. While developments basic to the Franco-Moroccan conflict were manifest during Juin's proconsulate, the crisis of 1947–51 constitutes, in many eyes, simply a general rehearsal of the more serious and decisive one of 1952–53 under Guillaume. In both cases, the same forces were at work and the same protagonists in the limelight. Since a detailed study of these two crises would have burdened the story without appreciably advancing our knowledge of its mechanism, we have merely summarized the Juin period as background to a study in greater depth of the subsequent Guillaume residency. In an historical analysis, in which the interest lies in the chronology of specific events, it seems preferable to magnify situations in accordance with their varying importance rather than to magnify across the board and thus run the risk of losing the woods for the trees when the situation becomes complex.

2. Juin was hardly partisan to the Bey's deposition. He wrote, "I have often regretted, as I think over the circumstances that determined those events, that the pseudo-government in Algiers in its haste (and let us say also in the ignorance of the exact facts of the Tunisian political situation) should have required me to commit an impolitic act, to the detriment of a sovereign who was really above reproach and always loyal." Alphonse Juin, *Mémoires, 1* (Paris, 1959), 188.

64

In the Council of Ministers, Georges Bidault had strongly advocated the candidacy of the new Resident-General, who had become one of the settlers' heroes. Ramadier finally agreed in the hope that it would be possible, by appointing to Morocco a man of prestige with a detailed knowledge of the country, to bring the Sultan back into line by means of a judicious mixture of firmness and reform.

With this end in view, Juin had been given strict instructions authorizing him even to threaten the Sultan with deposition should such extreme measures become necessary and if he still refused to sign the *dahirs*. These instructions, which had been debated in the Council of Ministers, did not, however, authorize the Resident-General to do more than bring pressure to bear on the Sultan. But the Quai d'Orsay had gone further than the government. In fact, Juin bore a letter from Bidault authorizing him to proceed from threats to action if intimidation proved insufficient. These supplementary instructions were later withdrawn by Robert Schuman, whose views on the matter were much less clear-cut than those of Bidault.

Basically, the instructions may be reduced to two points: to force the Sultan to make his regime more democratic or else to risk abdication, and to carry on with the implementation of the economic reforms started by Labonne. By this means, the Quai d'Orsay hoped to end what it called the Sultan's theocracy and to rally the young Moroccan nationalists to the protectorate regime by associating them with the operation of democratic organs of government.

Juin's first act was to reassure the settlers and the Moroccan notables. As soon as he arrived in Casablanca he told the settlers that Morocco was not a Near Eastern country and that until she was ready for self-government the Residency would maintain order and carry out Morocco's responsibilities. He told the notables they could count on the Residency's support when they demonstrated their ability to keep control. The Pasha of Casablanca spoke of "the wave of joy that swept over the country." [3] "France," cried the President of the French Chamber of Com-

3. Juin's response to speeches by the settlers and the Pasha of Casablanca, *La Vigie marocaine* (May 27, 1947).

merce and Industry of Casablanca, expressing the general feeling, "has found in Juin Africanus the great leader she was seeking." [4] Boniface greeted the arrival of the new Resident-General as a personal victory, and publicly rejoiced that the clock had been put back twenty years. Despite this harmony of views, however, friction soon developed between the two men. Boniface opposed a return to the Labonne reforms at any price. He hoped that a trial of strength with the Palace would bring about the fall of the Sultan and made no secret of the fact. Five years were to pass before he had his way.

In the midst of the general euphoria, the Arab press and *Le Petit Marocain* sounded a less enthusiastic note. As early as May 13, 1947, the latter had expressed surprise that Ramadier had accepted Juin's appointment when a Socialist Party Congress had just condemned the Labonne reforms as inadequate. On May 12 the same paper said in an editorial that certain Socialist deputies had declared themselves in favor of the government's collective resignation, and that one of them had even gone so far as to say that if the Socialist ministers had really supported the general's candidacy, they would have to explain their actions to the party congress. These few objections were inconsequential. Embroiled in internal politics, the S.F.I.O. finally gave in with good grace, and harmony reigned.

The Arab press of North Africa had no illusions. In Cairo and Tunis, Arab newspapers denounced the policy of force and recalled the deposition of Moncef Bey. The concerned Moroccans in the Paris area nervously affirmed their loyalty to the Sultan. Fear that he might be deposed began to be expressed openly in Cairo as a result of stories emanating from London. Juin then turned to the Palace and contented himself at first with exchanging the amenities demanded by protocol. This did not deceive the Sultan. Beneath the detached friendliness of these first official contacts, he felt the Resident-General's determination to impose the reforms he had in mind. Still affected by the violence of French reactions after the Tangier affair, Mohammed V prepared for the worst and disguised his apprehensions behind an amiable smile. The Resident-General, having reassured the no-

4. Ibid.

tables and having convinced the Sultan that he was in earnest, could devote himself wholeheartedly and with the full consent of the French settlers to carrying out the first stages of his reform program.

At this juncture, a complete misunderstanding masked the change in direction of French policy in Morocco. Paris was still thinking in terms of democratizing a theocratic regime without, apparently, any clear realization as yet of the effect that such a process might have on a political system under which the French were, legally speaking, aliens. The Residency, however, backed to the hilt by the settlers, proposed to use the carte blanche given by Paris to force the Sultan to accept—under the pretext of democratization—the dismantling of the Treaty of Fez and its replacement by a regime of cosovereignty in which the French would have full citizenship.

The Sultan's difficulty in parrying this maneuver was increased by the fact that under the circumstances it was impossible for him to defend the Protectorate Treaty against the encroachments of Residential authority without laying himself open to the capital charge—given the content of the Quai d'Orsay's instructions—of opposing the modernization and democratization of Morocco.

The initiation of demands for reform by the settlers themselves was a new development that was to have a powerful effect on future Franco-Moroccan relations. There was nothing abnormal in this phenomenon. Legally and politically, the French in Morocco were in a paradoxical position which in some respects resembled that of the European proletariat before universal suffrage. With no political status, since they had de facto but no legal power, they sought to determine the future by modifying the form of the regime to their own advantage. Taking everything into account, this sociological reflex was as normal as the reverse reflex which impelled the nationalists to demand independence. The settlers, who heard of nothing but independence in a rapidly changing world, could scarcely have done other than pit their own demands against those of the nationalists who indisputably threatened what they considered their acquired rights. Obsessed with the fear that the Residency's authority would one day disappear in favor of the Moroccans in a modernized and independent country, the settlers could only maneuver to ensure that their future elected representatives would ultimately hold the real power. The basic fictions of the regime greatly facilitated this operation, since France had pledged herself in the treaty to the progressive modernization of Morocco. The two adversaries thus found themselves striving to outbid each other on the issues of democratization and modernization in a political climate made oppressive by the growing opposition of nationalism and the French settlement.

The settlers' pressure on the regime for reform did not stem only, as Robert Montagne realized, from their numerical increase and the weight of their influence on the Residential authority;[5] it was also due as much if not more to the alliance—indeed, the indissoluble solidarity—that had been gradually established among the "potentates" of the administration, the army leaders, and the most important settlers. The French colony did not actually outnumber the administration; it would be more exact to say that the administration identified itself with the colony. The most influential notables were all playing the same game, whether they were civil servants, businessmen, or wealthy settlers. The others followed willingly, for they recognized themselves in the aspirations of their leaders.

At the end of June 1947, the first series of reforms was imposed on the Palace. Delegates of the Grand Vizier were attached to the chief French technical departments. A new organ, the Council of Viziers and Directors, was set up within the Maghzen. In October, the procedure for appointing the Moroccan Consultative Chambers of Agriculture and of Commerce and Industry was expanded. Two months later, the Moroccan section of the Government Council, which was based on the Chambers, was also reorganized.

The creation of vizierial delegates was only a pseudo-reform intended to hide the real purpose of reorganization at the Residential level. At first there were five,[6] later ten, delegates of the Grand Vizier to the French departments. In principle, their role was to act as personal and permanent liaison between the Magh-

5. Montagne, *Revolution au Maroc*, pp. 205 ff.
6. Finance, Agriculture, Commerce, Public Works, Health.

zen and the neo-Sharifian government departments, but they were carefully kept out of circulation by the French department heads. The delegates rarely saw even the routine mail. Replies to important communications continued as in the past to be drafted by the departments with no thought of consulting the delegates.

The Council of Viziers and Directors was established to reinforce the personal liaison—provided by the delegates—with a functional liaison, through a joint body which reunited the "Rump" Maghzen of 1912 with the very active French administration.[7] The original *dahir* of June 21, 1947, had initially been drafted in fairly liberal form.[8] It empowered the new Council to engage in the "joint consideration of questions of general interest" at its monthly meetings. Owing to the opposition of the administration, which feared that reform would lead to the reconstitution of a Maghzen ministerial system, a vizierial order of September 15, 1947, "rectified" the institution by specifying that the Council would deal only with questions of general interest submitted to it by the Residency "for advice."[9] The Council was thus deprived of the only vestige of competence that might have justified its establishment. Neutralized by this change, from then on it simply became inactive. In principle, its meetings were to have been held monthly; in fact, it met about fifteen times in five years and bogged down in formalistic discussions that were but little enlivened at the end of the year by the ritual presentation of the budget.

This theoretical liberalization of the regime was apparently reinforced in October 1947 by the reform of the Moroccan Consultative Chambers of Agriculture and of Commerce and Industry,[10] and of the Moroccan section of the Government Council in December.[11] The former Moroccan sections of the French Consultative Chambers were transformed into autonomous Mo-

7. The Grand Vizier presided over the Council of Viziers and Directors, which was composed of members of the Maghzen and of French directors led by the Secretary General. The latter in effect assumed the presidency of the Council.

8. Protectorat de la république française (empire chérifien), *Bulletin officiel* (*B.O.*), July 4, 1947, p. 631.

9. Ibid., Sept. 19, 1947, p. 914.

10. Ibid., Nov. 14, 1947, *dahir* of Oct. 13, 1947 (27 kaada 1366), concerning the Moroccan Consultative Chambers, p. 1155; and Vizierial Orders of Oct. 14, 1947, pp. 1155–56.

11. Ibid., Dec. 26, 1947, p. 1334, Residential decision of Dec. 20, 1947.

roccan Consultative Chambers, elected by restricted suffrage.
According to Robert Rézette,

> The electors had to be Moroccan subjects, male, of age,
> to have resided in the district of the Chamber for at least
> one year, and to have engaged for at least three years in
> agriculture, industry, commerce, or a skilled trade; all
> electors were also eligible for election to the Consultative
> Chambers, provided they were not civil servants.
>   The corporative character of the Chambers was em-
> phasized by the division of the electorate into five cate-
> gories, each electing its delegates separately, and by the
> restricted nature of the right to vote which was only ac-
> corded to the Moroccan *évolués,* or those regarded as
> such.[12]

The members of the Moroccan section of the Government
Council previously appointed by the Grand Vizier were to be
recruited by various procedures. This section included, in addition to the presidents, vice-presidents, and delegates of the Moroccan Consultative Chambers elected by their peers, six delegates elected by the Municipal Commissions from their membership, six delegates chosen by the Resident-General, and six
elected by the committees of the Jewish communities.[13] Despite
the small size of the new electorate, (3,000 Moroccan electors for
the Chambers of Agriculture, 8,000 for the Chambers of Commerce and Industry for 1947) and the continuing consultative
character of the trade chambers, the reform did nevertheless
open the Government Council to the Istiqlal. Although it did
not give the future members any actual power of decision, it did
in fact confer on them a right of remonstrance which they were
promptly to utilize by extensive criticism of the regime.[14]

In some respects, the Residential plan was not without sub-
tlety. Its very gradualness was its trump card. By granting the
right of suffrage to the bourgeois merchants who were the
Istiqlal's chief support and by opening the door of the Govern-

---

12. Rézette, *Les Partis politiques marocains,* p. 41.
13. Ibid., p. 44.
14. Ibid., pp. 41 ff.

ment Council to them, the Residency also hoped to pave the way for representatives of the French colony in the contemplated municipal assemblies. The Residency was merely yielding the first round to its opponents in the hope of winning the second, which was much more important in its eyes because it would determine the whole future. Sending elected Moroccan representatives to the Government Council was only the beginning of a process intended to bring the French into the arena. As subsequent events will show, the granting of political rights to Moroccans was negated by the consultative character of the institution and was designed merely to facilitate the creation of municipal and provincial assemblies. These would also be elected, but this time vested with real powers within which the French would be in the majority once more and would enjoy effective political rights, pending the establishment of a central government and legislative assemblies along the same lines.

Although the Sultan in any case retained his right of veto, this step-by-step strategy might to some extent have foiled his opposition and the nationalists' to the cosovereignty reforms had not the Residency's policy been vitiated at the time by an internal contradiction that was shortly to neutralize any possible positive effects. Juin was caught between the hope of involving the Palace in carrying out the cosovereignty reforms and the thwarted desire to isolate Mohammed V by separating him from the Istiqlal and purging the Maghzen. He ended by laying so heavy a hand on the Palace that soon the Sultan's only course was to paralyze the regime by again refusing to sign anything.

The 1947 reforms and the apparently democratic spirit that inspired them did not prevent the Residency from continuing to govern Morocco as of old in a climate considerably worsened by the use that was soon to be made of the new institutions. Hitherto, the Maghzen had retained some semblance of autonomy because the Grand Vizier, by more or less autonomous Vizierial Order, still controlled to a certain extent the implementation of the *dahirs* submitted by the Residency for the Sultan's signature. Once the Council of Viziers and Directors was set up, the Maghzen lost even that vestige of power. Henceforward, the Residency exercised direct control over the viziers and their delegates in a joint body that deprived them of all individual initiative. The changed climate was most apparent in the matter of the Sultan's appointment of Maghzen officials. The Resident-General, not content with having forced the signature of a series of *dahirs,* at the end of pro forma negotiations with the Palace forced the Sultan to dismiss one of his viziers and certain local officials. Breaking with a long-standing practice whereby proposals for appointing members to the Maghzen were made in the form of lists that gave the Palace relative freedom of choice, the Residency thereafter pushed through its own candidates without even seeking prior agreement from the Palace. Four caids who had incurred displeasure were replaced without even a bow to formalities.

The political reforms, initiated under duress, were finally buried (as was to be expected) by the issue of municipalities. In the process of implementing the December 1947 Residential instructions on political control of municipalities, new difficulties arose in connection with the appointment of district caliphs who were to be associated with the pashas in the principal towns. The Palace, which had been consulted neither on the principle of this reform nor on the choice of candidates, protested once more. A year and a half later, the *dahir* of April 4, 1949 [15] was to settle the question of the appointment of these caliphs after a fashion, but it was to be Juin's last victory. The reform machinery was finally to come to a standstill when the Residency returned to the charge with a plan for establishing elected, deliberative municipal assemblies, which would have given every French voter twenty to thirty times as much voting power as his Moroccan counterpart. The Sultan stood his ground and the reform was held up until the advent of Mulay Mohammed ben Arafa in 1953.

Nothing more had been said of the economic reforms drafted by Labonne and for which Juin had assumed explicit responsibility on his arrival in Morocco. The itinerant schools disappeared, the agricultural-reform program disintegrated (the settlers had no difficulty in effectively vitiating it in the Government Council), and all appeared serene.

15. *B.O.,* May 13, 1949, p. 586.

As matters stood, Residential pressure on the Maghzen for reform left Mohammed V no alternative but to appeal to the French government in order to ward off, if possible, the clearly imminent trial of strength in Morocco and the accompanying veiled threat of deposition. He protested in vain to the Residency against its abuses of power and lack of courtesy. Then he turned to the authorities in France and began with them that long exchange of notes which was to continue until the coup d'etat in August 1953, the origin of which should be explained at this point.

The Palace had no lack of grievances against the Residency. The absence of any real reform, the Residency's increasing interference in the appointment and dismissal of Maghzen officials, the problem of municipalities (a perennial sore spot for the regime), the question of the caliphs, the inadequacies of the educational system, and the absolute opposition of French authorities to anything resembling the establishment of an autonomous Moroccan trade-union movement—all these factors formed the basis for a dispute that was constantly influenced by a whole series of irritations, justifiable or otherwise. The Sultan was especially concerned about the position of Prince Mulay Hassan, whose title of Crown Prince the Residency disputed. The same was true of hostility shown by the French authorities toward Muslim schools, whose inaugural ceremonies were frequently banned because they generally served as a pretext for nationalist demonstrations. Finally, the Palace was becoming increasingly impatient about the Residency's overt support of the activities of religious brotherhoods to which the Sultan was unalterably opposed. All these points of friction haunted the regime like a nightmare. On December 3, 1947, Mohammed V unburdened himself in a letter to the President of the Republic. In closing, he was careful to reaffirm his determination to modernize and democratize Morocco.[16]

As if to demonstrate publicly the omnipotence of the political departments at the very moment when the Sultan was appealing to the President, in December 1947 Juin abolished the Political

16. This diplomatic controversy continued until the deposition of Mohammed V in August 1953.

Secretariat set up earlier by Labonne. Its functions were transferred to the Department of the Interior, whose original privileges were ipso facto restored, to Colonel Lecomte's advantage.

The Sultan's Tangier speech had damaged the prestige he had hitherto enjoyed in French government circles, a fact which seriously impeded effective resumption of the dialogue with France. By an astounding reversal of fortune, the disclosure in January 1948 of the "affair of the Berber pamphlets" was to enable the Sultan to reestablish his moral position at the expense of his adversaries. Some scurrilous pamphlets, sent through the mail and openly directed against Mohammed V personally, had been circulated throughout Morocco. It was soon discovered that they had been printed on a press belonging to the Department of the Interior. The Sultan arrested a young Muslim interpreter from the Department whose handwriting was known to the Palace. He was convicted of having worked for the instigators of the affair but was released shortly afterwards at the request of the Residency, which then handed him over to French judicial authorities despite the Maghzen's protests. Lecomte, compromised by this scandal implicating one of his subordinates, was at first backed by the Resident-General, who firmly refused the Sultan's request that Lecomte, as director of the Department, be discharged. Mohammed V then obtained the intervention of a number of leading liberals in Paris, who explained the situation to Bidault and finally won their point. Even so, it was March 1948 before Lecomte was replaced by Marcel Vallat. This time the Residency had lost face. The moral consequences of the Tangier affair were wiped out. Mohammed V again found himself with the prestige necessary for resuming talks with France. These were not resumed, however, until two years later, in December 1950.

At the beginning of 1948, the change which the reforms of October 1947 had made in the enabling statute of the Moroccan Consultative Chambers and that of the Moroccan section of the Government Council obviously placed the Istiqlal in a dilemma: whether to boycott the forthcoming elections on the grounds that the above institutions were illegal, or to participate and send nationalist leaders to represent it on the Council.

Despite the disadvantages, the second course was tempting to the Istiqlal, whose means of influencing public opinion were limited. Such action would provide the party with a pulpit in the very temple of the settlers, afford its leaders practical experience in debate, show French public opinion it did not disdain the conventions of democracy, and, above all, enmesh the Residency in the web of demands supported by a lawful opposition. After much deliberation the party finally chose the more discreet course. The elections to the Moroccan Chambers of Commerce and Industry took place in February 1948. Rézette wrote in this connection:

> The limited nature of the right of suffrage accorded to the Moroccans by the 1947 reform, far from hindering the representation of the Istiqlal Party in the Government Council, was the essential condition for it. The Party's real strength lay less in mass support, the extent of which the leaders themselves were unable to gauge, than in that of an industrial and trade aristocracy anxious to control the economic system, something they could not do under the protectorate. It was the representatives of this westernized and ambitious class which the elections of 1948 sent to the Chambers of Commerce and Industry and to the Second College of the Moroccan section of the Government Council: eleven members and four supporters of the Istiqlal Party, most of them rich merchants or industrialists; that is, fifteen delegates to the Second College out of a total of twenty-one.[17]

On the other hand, the First and Third Electoral Colleges of the Moroccan section remained unchanged. Rézette added:

> The precautions taken in regulating the right to vote and the more conformist mentality of the rural population kept representatives of the political parties out of the First College of the Government Council (thirty-eight members); the Third College (eighteen mem-

17. Rézette, p. 45.

bers), consisting of delegates appointed by the Resident
or elected by the municipal commissioners (who were
themselves appointed), and Jewish representatives,
eluded all the attempts of the Moroccan political parties
to gain a foothold. Nevertheless, the fact that 19 percent
of the seats in the Moroccan section were held by Istiqlal
Party members had a profound effect on its behavior.[18]

Despite these restrictions, the Istiqlal had established a solid
footing in the Government Council. The physical contact between the nationalists and the delegates of the French colony
could only end in disaster. However, it was not in the party's interest that matters should come to a head too quickly. Apart
from the fact that the Istiqlal meant to reap the greatest possible
advantage from the political forum to which it had just gained
access, there was no reason to risk the expulsion of its delegates
as long as a complete breakdown in relations between the Residency and the Palace did not justify a resumption of revolutionary opposition. The crisis was not to erupt for two years, on
the occasion of an abortive journey to Paris by Mohammed V.

In the meantime, and apart from the twice-yearly sessions of
the Government Council, 1948 and 1949 were characterized
chiefly by economic difficulties and by the slow deterioration of
relations between Juin and the Quai d'Orsay. From March to
October 1948, the economic and social situation of the protectorate remained the Residency's chief concern. Strikes had
broken out in various sectors, and were denounced by the General Confederation of Employers on April 3, 1948, as politically
inspired. The Confederation refused to put into effect wage
increases ordered by the authorities. A lock-out followed, the
trade unions joined in, and it was not until the end of October
that a 10 percent wage increase could be carried out in both the
public and private sectors.

Then, too, Paris was growing tired of the paucity of reports
from its representative in Rabat. Ministerial and departmental
displeasure facilitated the efforts being made in Paris at that time
by the liberal protagonists in the conflict to promote the opening

18. Ibid., p. 47.

of negotiations between the Sultan and the government. The Resident-General, who was as generous with words as he was sparing of information in his reports, had allowed himself on several occasions (inter alia on August 20, 1947, at Port Lyautey and on January 25, 1948, in Paris during a press conference) to refer somewhat unwisely to the day when Morocco would regain independence. Of course, these were only fine words meant as sugar-coated pills for the nationalists, but they had been variously interpreted and had made the Quai d'Orsay more impatient than ever.

Much more serious was the address Juin delivered on November 18, 1949, before the Academy of Colonial Sciences favoring the thesis of Franco-Moroccan cosovereignty. The Moroccan delegates in the Government Council, led by Mohammed Lyazidi, recalled the unitary nature of the country's sovereignty. The Resident-General retracted his statement and declared before the Council on December 24 that there was only one sovereign in Morocco: the Sultan. The Grand Vizier ended the controversy by declaring that the Moroccans were satisfied with the Resident-General's explanation. The incident had served a purpose: at least it had shown Juin that the time was not ripe for a policy of cosovereignty, in either Paris or Rabat.

In January 1950, Paris again called Rabat to order. The Minister upbraided the Resident-General for not sending him his recent speeches or informing him of his disputes with the Sultan, which had only come to the Minister's attention by a devious route. Schuman was vexed at receiving no reports, and apparently finally sent an emissary to Rabat. Normal political channels were clearly not functioning any better between Paris and Rabat than they were between the Residency and the Palace.

The crisis that had been building up inside the Government Council became evident only in July 1950, when the Second Electoral College of the Moroccan section of the Council decided to walk out. The absentees declared that after three years of the proconsulate they wished to make a public demonstration of their determination to have their legitimate claims regarding judicial, trade-union, and social matters satisfied. The Resident denounced what he called the bad faith of the delegates and their systematic refusal to recognize France's efforts. Matters remained at that point temporarily, but the problem of reform was brought squarely before the public just when France was preparing to reopen political talks with the Sultan.

The French government was concerned over the deteriorating situation in Morocco and invited Mohammed V to come to Paris at the beginning of October 1950. The Sultan had taken the precaution of drafting a memorandum which he gave to the President of the Republic on October 11, the day after his arrival in Paris. The Sultan recapitulated the vagaries to which the protectorate had been prey and emphasized his personal neutrality toward the nationalist parties. He stated that the time for superficial reforms was past: the Moroccan people now demanded a substantial improvement in their status.

Mohammed V was courteously received but went away empty-handed. On October 31, the French cabinet held a special meeting to study the Moroccan requests, while the Director for Africa and the Levant studied the memorandum. The same day, the government gave the Sultan an evasive reply that sidestepped the problem of Sharifian sovereignty—the crucial issue—and merely hinted at a possible lifting of censorship, more flexibility in the trade-union system, and the return of the Residency to a stricter procedure in its relations with the Palace.

The Sultan was disappointed and renewed his attack on November 2 in a note, considerably less diplomatic than the first, the burden of which was that only the abolition of the Protectorate Treaty could solve the dispute between France and Morocco. This second appeal was no more successful. The government merely promised that joint committees would be organized at Rabat to try to solve the outstanding problems, but this was never done. The last resort—appeal to France—had failed. The Palace and the Residency were to find themselves face to face in a situation from which this time there was no way out.

The French in Morocco were furious at the concessions made in the government's first reply, even though they were purely formal, and did not wait to hear about the failure of negotiations before protesting angrily to Paris against the very principle of holding them. Messages and telegrams flooded in to the Quai d'Orsay. Ministers heard from every side that any alteration in the status quo would halt investment altogether and ruin the French colony. This restraining influence was enough to immobilize a coalition government condemned to inaction by its composition, the apathy of public opinion, and the absence of any opposition determined to force an "agonizing reappraisal" of the country's colonial policy.

After his return to Morocco, the Sultan on November 18 gave an address during the Festival of the Throne in which he informed his subjects of the results of his trip.[19] In reply to the campaign waged by the French press in Morocco against what it called his "medieval sovereign's megalomania," he emphasized strongly that Morocco had no intention of having anything but a democratic regime. This was, he added, quite consistent with the principles of Islam. In Casablanca and Rabat, the Festival was used every year as the occasion for a great demonstration sponsored and organized by the Istiqlal to show the solidarity of the Sultan and the townspeople. It proved beyond any doubt that on this subject they were solidly behind the Sultan.

Since Mohammed V's trip to France had been fruitless, there was obviously nothing left for the Sultan and the Istiqlal to do but resume the fight, and it was with the Palace's full agreement that the party's rapporteurs to the Government Council prepared the speeches which were to trigger the explosion.

On December 6, as soon as the winter session of the Moroccan section of the Council opened, the storm clouds gathered. Mohammed Lyazidi, President of the Federation of Moroccan Chambers of Commerce, Industry, and Handicrafts, delivered a detailed criticism before the Resident of the protectorate's budgetary and financial policy.[20] He devoted himself to showing, figures in hand, that the Moroccans had only the crumbs of the cake. Juin replied sharply and charged that the speaker had based his report on a complete distortion of the facts and ordered him to cease at once.

On December 12, Mohammed Laghzaoui, rapporteur on the

19. *Bulletin d'information du Maroc*, no. 8 (Dec. 5, 1950), pp. 143–44.
20. For the intervention of Lyazidi, rapporteur-general for the proposed budget, see ibid., no. 9 (1950), p. 157.

Public Works budget, was preparing to deliver his report when the Resident interrupted and directed him to leave the Council. Laghzaoui's criticisms had been reported at length in the nationalist press a few hours earlier and this calculated indiscretion was the last straw. The nationalist delegates left with Laghzaoui, while their pro-Residential colleagues hastened to deplore this behavior and affirmed their own devotion to the regime.

The expulsion of the Moroccan delegates from the Government Council was followed several days later by a new incident between the Resident-General and the French government. Juin, urged by Paris to take a command with the North Atlantic Treaty Organization, refused to leave his post because of developments in the Moroccan crisis, and threatened to resign altogether if he were moved before the middle of 1951. The government, which was becoming accustomed to not being obeyed but which saw itself this time openly defied, was furious but yielded nevertheless.

Juin has been reproached for taking these nationalist outbursts too seriously in December 1950. Partisans of the Resident-General have expressed the opinion in interviews that it would have been preferable at the time not to force the Sultan and the Istiqlal to a break by expelling from the regime the nationalist leaders who had only recently been given access to the Government Council by the Residency. From the viewpoint of Residential policy, these reservations seem highly questionable. The nationalists, once installed in the Council, in effect possessed the means to make life intolerable for the Residency and to force it to choose between two courses, both with disadvantages: to lose face by tolerating constant charges against the protectorate, or to confront the troublemakers and expel them. It would seem that the Residency's mistake was not so much in expelling the nationalists from the Council as in admitting them in the first place when it was not ready to work with them. Experience shows that a colonial regime which gets into difficulties owing to pressure from a subject people has nothing to gain by allowing them the right to complain if it does not, at the same time and to the same extent, grant them the right to manage their own affairs. The entry of an opposition into consultative organs in which it has no practical outlet can only poison the atmosphere. There are only two coherent policies, in the short run, for a contested colonial regime: to go in frankly for reform, knowing that the process will not stop until the opponent has carried out his program and won independence, or to stick firmly to the status quo, which ultimately settles nothing, but which for the time being deprives the opposition of indisputable tactical advantages.

The old hands in the administration sensed this as they had four years earlier under Labonne, and this was one of the reasons why they so obstinately defended the status quo. The problem had not changed; it was the solution—at least in their eyes—that had to change. The reaction of Moroccan notables backed by the regime had been no less significant than that of the Residency: the more privileged among them, threatened by the revolutionary alliance between the Sultan and the Istiqlal, had not hesitated to express their discontent. The considerable advances made in the past four years by the major nationalist party amply justified their apprehensions.[21] The organization of cadres and recruitment of members had been intensified in the towns and villages. The nationalist press, censored but not banned, increasingly attacked the regime, and unceasingly pointed out local abuses by the administration and the notables. Pressure had been brought to bear on the rural areas, sometimes successfully, through nationalist representatives in the Moroccan Chambers of Agriculture.

While nationalist activities were beginning to spread to the *bled,* the Istiqlal had embarked on a vigorous policy of trade unionization that in the end was to give it complete control of the neo-proletariat of the western towns and particularly of Casablanca.[22] The political movement of the first postwar years had become a mass party.

The intensified conquest of the townspeople at the base had been accompanied at the summit by systematic infiltration of the central political machinery. The nationalists' entry into the Gov-

21. Juin considered the Istiqlal as negligible and did not persecute it; the party had profited from this period of relative tolerance by widely expanding its propaganda and recruitment.

22. The P.D.I. at the time was a minor movement, with no appreciable influence until later, and then not much. See Rézette, pp. 178–79.

ernment Council had been only one aspect of a policy designed to ensure party representation at the highest level. It had found expression through the entry of Istiqlal militants into the Sultan's Private Council. In September 1950, two months before the crisis just described, an Imperial Moroccan Cabinet had in fact been set up at the Palace. Under Mohammed V's direct authority, it was designed to secure a vital liaison between the Maghzen and the sovereign so as to offset somewhat the partial absorption of the Maghzen into the Council of Viziers and Directors created in 1947. The nationalists were soon heavily represented in the new body, and the Sultan's refusal to sign decrees, which had been going on for three years, thus appeared in its true light as the concerted policy of the Sultan and the Istiqlal.[23] Thus the separation of the Sultan and the party—the Resident-General's chief objective—became impossible to achieve by normal means of intimidation. There was nothing left for the Resident-General but to use the threat of deposition that his instructions so unwisely authorized as a last resort.

The trial of strength between the Residency and the Palace was imminent. All the protagonists had helped to bring it to a head: the nationalists and the Sultan by sabotaging Labonne, Juin by driving the nationalists and the Sultan into a corner and forcing them to surrender or fight; the Sultan and the nationalists by attacking the Residency's prestige in the Government Council or allowing it to be attacked; the Sultan's refusal to sign the *dahirs* and the consequent paralysis of the regime.

The emotions aroused among the great notables by the attack upon the regime in the Government Council and by the entry of the Istiqlal into the Private Council soon crystallized. On December 21, 1950, during an historic interview, the Sultan broke with el-Glaoui, who had come to inform him of the notables' discontent. Mohammed V replied that he was above all parties, which infuriated the old Berber chieftain, who knew very well how things stood. They exchanged bitter words. Shortly after-

---

23. The Istiqlal was so preoccupied with matters of internal organization that it gave scant attention during the crisis to its international position, which did not take precedence until the following period. For the Moroccan nationalists' international activities at the time, see ibid., pp. 183 ff.

ward the Sultan informed the Pasha, through the Grand Vizier, that he was not to appear again at the Palace until further notice. Outraged, el-Glaoui returned to Marrakesh with his sons and his caids.

The Sultan's quarrel with el-Glaoui was soon seized upon by the French press in Morocco and by the ultras. It provided a unique opportunity to saddle the caids with an attempt to depose the Sultan by presenting the ill humor of a few notables as the revolt of a democratic Morocco against the despotism of a sovereign allied with atheistic communism. Robert Montagne wrote:

> It was then that there took shape within the mind of the powerful el-Glaoui the plan for a new version of the 1907 maneuver, whereby his elder brother el-Madani had brought about the fall of Sultan Abd el-Aziz at Marrakesh, to the advantage of his brother Mulay Hafid. The Pasha of Marrakesh, backed by the strength of the Glaoua, made contacts with the great chiefs of the Zaïans of the Moyen Atlas, the Imhazen [who] like the Glaoua . . . did not owe the origin of their power to the reigning sovereign. There followed a mobilization of the Berber tribes which found, it must be admitted, lively sympathy among those of our responsible officials who were convinced by that time of the impossibility of our ever being able to reestablish wholehearted cooperation with the Sultan.[24]

What followed has been described too often, and resembles too much what was to happen in August 1953 to merit detail. At the end of January 1951, just before leaving for the United States with René Pleven, the Resident-General handed the Sultan an ultimatum enjoining him to cease withholding his signature from the *dahirs,* and either to break with the Istiqlal or to abdicate. He gave Mohammed V until his return to Morocco to make up his mind. Juin returned to Europe without having been able to convince the United States government of the soundness of his policy, and without the free hand he had hoped to obtain

24. Montagne, p. 221.

in Washington.[25] On February 5, two days before his return to Rabat, the Resident-General had a decisive interview with Schuman in Paris. The Minister told him that although the government approved his determination to obtain a public repudiation of the Istiqlal's methods, it firmly opposed deposition, both out of concern for French interests and for reasons of strategic security. Schuman urged Juin in so many words to avoid anything that might lend substance to the belief that France was seeking to depose the Sultan and install another ruler in his place. The United States Embassy in Paris had just intervened in that connection to warn the French government of the effect the Sultan's deposition might have upon law and order in Morocco.[26] Schuman told the Resident-General of this and insisted that the joint committees envisaged at the time of the Sultan's visit to Paris should begin at once to study reforms.[27]

When Juin returned to Rabat, the conspiracy promoted by Boniface and el-Glaoui had ripened. The contrôle civil, or at least its most active members, organized petitions against the Sultan and the Istiqlal. The Palace and the party replied by producing counter-petitions and retractions. Juin brought increased pressure to bear to obtain at least the desired repudiation. Mohammed V

25. Juin was quite specific in his *Mémoires:* "I personally had the opportunity, in Washington several years ago, to tell our American friends how regrettable it was that they were taking the same line vis-à-vis North Africa as Moscow, namely, that France had better withdraw. But while the American position was taken in the hope of removing a source of friction, the Russian position was based on the not erroneous assumption that once the French departed, there would be such chaos in North Africa that communism could easily make headway.

"Unfortunately, I do not think I was understood. Moreover, this took place in the State Department, at a time when the United States was already preoccupied with its future Afro-Asian policy, a policy which is becoming increasingly evident." *Mémoires, 2* (Paris, 1960), 157–58.

26. The United States made a similar demand of the French government after the arrest of the Chenik government at the height of the Tunisian crisis. See Jacques Fauvet, *La IVᵉ République* (Paris, 1959), p. 214 n.

27. Juin protested against "this legend that it was the French government, in the person of Robert Schuman, Minister for Foreign Affairs, which opposed the Sultan's deposition in extremis. Robert Schuman did not intervene officially. I knew only that he wanted, as I did, to avoid such a denouement to the crisis." Juin, *Le Maghreb en jeu* (Paris, 1957), p. 82. If it is true that Juin's circumspection prevented a final outburst between Paris and Rabat, it seems to us nevertheless that the February 5 discussion bore all the marks of official intervention by Schuman.

fought every inch of the way in constant liaison with the Istiqlal, whose emissaries were introduced secretly into the Palace and did not emerge again until the end of the crisis. Apparently, it was at this stage that Crown Prince Mulay Hassan began to exercise over his father the influence that was soon to make him one of the chief protagonists in the conflict.

Since most of the caids had been drawn into the plot in spite of themselves by combined pressure from the Residency and the notables, the Sultan asked Juin for help, invoking the Treaty of Fez, under which France was bound to protect the person of the ruler. Juin riposted by requesting him first to repudiate the Istiqlal. The Sultan, his back to the wall, vacillated: he would repudiate the party, he would not, he would do so through the Grand Vizier. Juin rejected the first draft of a repudiation as inadequate. The Sultan then refused categorically to sign anything whatsoever. Juin broke off all relations, while Mohammed V telegraphed an appeal to the President of the Republic who referred it, according to the Constitution, to the Council of Ministers.

For the first time since the conflict began, the French government was forced to arbitrate. As has been seen, Paris was not ready to back the conspiracy. Public opinion in France was not ripe for a deposition. The Sultan had just been received in the capital. The French press was still far from being really interested in the debate. Against this fairly negative background, the move by the United States Department of State, concerned about American bases in Morocco, gave the ministers who opposed deposition the necessary weight to turn the decision finally in their favor. This conjunction of circumstances propitious to the Sultan was reinforced at the eleventh hour by a last attack by those ministers most opposed to deposition—namely Robert Schuman and Jules Moch, supported by the personal intervention of the President of the Republic. The Council finally got out of a difficult situation by means of a compromise.

The government replied indecisively to the Sultan in order to emphasize its desire that he repudiate the Istiqlal, but the agitation of the notables was secretly curbed so as to give the Palace a

way out. The Residency had to tell el-Glaoui that Paris was
unwilling to give full support to the conspirators. Thus it could
only maneuver to secure the repudiation of the Istiqlal and the
dismissals which constituted its minimum program.

Juin's position in regard to the ultras of the Residency and the
bled had not been wholly unambiguous. He was undoubtedly
behind the operation, but only halfheartedly. It certainly suited
his policy to let the great overlords and the religious brotherhoods plot against the Palace with barely concealed administration support. It was reasonable to hope that, threatened by his
own subjects, the Sultan would seek the protection of the Residency, which would have been, for Rabat and for Paris, the
perfect solution to the political difficulties Juin had been sent to
deal with at Rabat. Nevertheless, in his own way, the Resident-
General was too cautious and disliked trouble too much to become deeply involved without cover. His circumspection undoubtedly facilitated the compromise the government wanted.

Juin, hindered by the government's hesitation, settled the crisis
in the spirit of its latest instructions. On February 22–23, the
tribal horsemen levied by the administration and el-Glaoui
moved in to besiege Fez and Rabat. On the 23d, French troops
surrounded the Palace as if to fight off the "Berber revolt." An
airplane had been ostensibly made ready in case the Sultan refused to comply with the Residency's demands, which were presented to him at six o'clock that evening in a written ultimatum.
After two hours' reflection, the Sultan signed, but announced
that he did so only under compulsion.

Curiously, certain Residency protagonists tried during interviews to argue that the administration had been completely passive toward the 1951 Berber revolt, although they freely admitted
that the Residency had planned and organized the 1953 coup from
beginning to end. In making this distinction, they were perhaps
anxious to present the notables' revolt as a spontaneous phenomenon that was not utilized by the Residency until after it happened. The facts are otherwise. The former contrôleurs civils
interviewed in Morocco in the course of this study formally
stated that in 1951, as in 1953, the Berber horsemen had been
called up by the Residency on the most varied pretexts, and that

the majority were quite unaware of the reason for their mobilization.[28]

The administration's tenacious attempts to overcome the resistance of caids loyal to the Sultan were not always successful, as witness the firsthand testimony of the former Caid of Oulmes, Madjoubi Aherdan, given in May 1955 to the National Conference for the Solution of the Franco-Moroccan Problem. This statement has been singled out as a striking example of the tactics that were used in 1951 and were to be systematically resumed two years later. Aherdan described the early stages of the affair and noted that General Juin, Secretary of State Max Lejeune, and el-Glaoui were present at the hearing to which he had been summoned by the contrôle civil. He continued:

> We were taken to the District Officer's room. He had the petition in front of him. M. Pujol spoke to Caid Allal:
>
> "Whose signature is this?"
>
> "That is the signature of Caid Hadj Messaoud."
>
> "And this?"
>
> "That is mine, the fifth time I have signed." He had had to sign often to encourage others.
>
> "And Aherdan?"
>
> "Our friend did not wish to sign."
>
> M. Pujol did not mention the letter to me. He said, "Are you going to sign?"
>
> "No, I will not."
>
> "You know what will happen, the risk you are taking, if you don't sign?"
>
> "If you don't understand my feelings, obviously I know the risk I'm taking. Anyway, I shall be fired." (I had been made Caid for a two-year probationary period during which time my work was to be evaluated by the Contrôleur Civil.) "If I do sign, the Sultan will never give me my *dahir;* if I do not sign, you won't keep me

---

28. One *contrôleur* was directed to send his cavalry to a prearranged assembly point, namely Fez. Since his cavalry could not ride horseback, he was forced to ship them by truck. He and his men were unaware of the reasons for the assignment.

as Caid. I choose the more honorable course: I shall not sign."

He replied: "You've got to sign."

"I am an officer in the French army. It is there that I learned a sense of honor, and I have not come here to dishonor myself for a cause that is not mine."

We beat about the bush all morning and finally in desperation I said, "I am an officer in the French army and the regulations prohibit me from engaging in political activities." (I was at that moment on leave of absence) "I shall not sign."

The Contrôleur Civil had a determined air; he looked at my companion Allal (God rest his soul! He is dead now), who said; "We have another comrad, Caid Kebir, who is an officer like Aherdan, and he agreed." M. Pujol brightened and added, "You are going to sign." For two and a half or three hours the conversation went on like this.

Finally, tired out, he stood up and said, "Go think it over."

I got up. My wife was waiting for me in the car. I came back again to M. Pujol's office.

"Are you signing or not?"

I went out again. [He called after me,] "Come back this afternoon, then we shall see."

At noon, not wanting to wait the whole day, I forced my way into his office and said, "I have come to tell you I won't sign."

He tried to explain to me. "But do you understand what this is all about?"

"Yes, I understand, you are trying to bring the caids out against the Sultan."

"No, it is against the Istiqlal."

I replied, "Istiqlal in Arabic means Independence. I could never sign against my independence."

"The members of the Istiqlal insulted General Juin in the Government Council."

"General Juin is big enough to defend himself. He
does not need my signature for that."

At last he gave up and said, "They are telephoning
me about you. Are you going to sign?" (He had just
been speaking to someone on the telephone.) I turned
thumbs down. He stood up angrily: "From now on, I
shall regard you as an enemy of France."

I left. I regret that I must say his words hurt me
deeply. They still hurt. I wonder who are the real enemies of France.[29]

An officer in the French army, married to a Frenchwoman,
Caid Aherdan was to play a leading part in 1955 in organizing
the Moroccan Army of Liberation. In this exchange, we have a
vivid picture of the way a colonial regime can create out of
whole cloth, almost gratuitously, that individual opposition
whose weight will finally crush it.

Despite the Palace's retreat, the operation had misfired. Mohammed V had been forced—as in the Puaux period—to break
officially with the Istiqlal. Nevertheless, he had not signed the
dahirs. The Sultan's "strike" continued. The gulf between the
Residency and the Sultan remained as wide as ever, and the situation had been irretrievably damaged by the flagrant breach of
the Treaty of Fez that the Residency had committed in forcing
the Moroccan sovereign to yield under pressure of a local revolt
organized by the Residency itself.

This political failure bore within it the seeds of a reversal of
fortune. The notables felt the Paris government was only a paper
tiger; they knew at last that Rabat was the real locus of power.
They were sure the Residency would give them free rein on the
next occasion and vowed not to give in a second time.

In accordance with the conditions he had himself imposed on
the government, Juin did not leave Morocco until September 20,
1951. Shortly before the change of regime, in April, as though in
response to the abortive crisis, the four chief nationalist parties in

29. Comité national pour la solution du problème franco-marocain, *Compte rendu de
la conférence nationale pour la solution du problème franco-marocain* (Paris, 1955), pp.
12–13.

the two zones—the Istiqlal, the P.D.I., the National Reform
Party, and the Moroccan Unity Party—joined together to form a
National Front. All the leaders who signed, with the exception
of el-Ouazzani who came from Fez, resided in Tangier. The
agreement, however, merely summarized the program of each of
the member parties. The initiative they took subsequently enabled them to achieve a certain unity of action in the field of
international propaganda, but it had no other effect. The constitution of this "Front," which might have been a sign of the
times, was in fact little more than an empty gesture.[30]

On March 20, 1951, a *dahir* inspired by the Residency increased the Second Electoral College of the Moroccan Consultative Chambers (Commerce and Industry) to more than 100,000
electors by incorporating in it all persons holding business li-
censes.[31] These new electors were for the most part inhabitants
of the small centers—a fact not unfavorable to the Istiqlal's propaganda in rural areas—while the previous College had been
largely merchants from the big cities. A more comprehensive
definition of modern agricultural methods likewise increased the
size of the Third Electoral College from 3,000 to about 11,000
electors.

In June, the Sultan approved the draft of a Moroccan penal
code, which did not commit him to very much.[32] On July 6, he
signed another *dahir,* approving the principle of setting up rural
djemaas throughout Morocco,[33] but he formally refused to sign
the *dahir* instituting Franco-Muslim elected assemblies in the
municipalities. The whole problem of cosovereignty and of the
reforms as then conceived by the Resident was thus left in
suspense.

When this third period is considered in retrospect, there is a
striking contrast between the rising tide of passion in Morocco
and the indifference in France. The lag in metropolitan interest
reached its nadir at this time. In Morocco, the urban masses were

30. Rézette, pp. 190–92.
31. B.O., April 20, 1951, p. 609.
32. Julien, L'Afrique du Nord en marche, p. 386.
33. B.O., July 20, 1951, pp. 1150–51.

enthusiastically rallying to the Istiqlal banner. The Moroccan section of the Government Council was disrupted by nationalist pressure. At that very moment the notables were becoming active protagonists in the conflict, and the press was deeply involved in the caids' conspiracy. But in France, public opinion, the press, and Parliament remained on the sidelines.

The change in the position of the pro-Residential press began to be obvious after December 1950. The note of opposition sounded in the Council by the Third French Electoral College during the previous legislature had disappeared, since the elections of December 7, 1947, had shifted representatives of the various interests toward the right of the political spectrum. The French section, reassured by the new Resident-General's attitude, went about its business in newfound security. The opposition voice of *Le Petit Marocain* was growing weaker. In this atmosphere of renewed calm, the Mas press contented itself with praising Juin while drawing a modest veil over the traditional squabbles between the administration and private interests. Little was said of the difficulties with the Sultan and the nationalists. From 1947 to 1950, then, the watchword of silence had remained the rule.

Everything changed in December 1950 with the break between the Sultan and el-Glaoui. However, it was not until January 3, 1951 that *La Vigie marocaine* reported the incident, under the headline "Alarm Bell," and apologized for being unable to mention it earlier because of the censorship. From then on, the press joined fully in the game between the Residency and the notables. The major themes of the official ideology were brought out one by one in crescendo: the Berber myth; el-Glaoui, France's only friend; Franco-Moroccan solidarity in arms; the incompetence of a Métropole which no longer understood Morocco; the playing down of the international aspects of the crisis; the Istiqlal's atheism; its collusion with the Communists; the political soundness and loyalty of the Moroccan people who refused to follow a handful of agitators who represented no one—everything was there. Nevertheless, this was only a beginning: from 1951 to 1953, this work of inflaming public opinion and dressing up the facts was to continue, and was finally to be transformed into a genuine campaign to drive the public into a state of panic.

In France, on the other hand, the press did not become really interested in Moroccan affairs until 1953, two years after the French press in Morocco. This time lag did not prevent the great newspapers from playing their part in Moroccan events after December 1950. The 1951 crisis was followed carefully by moderate newspapers such as *Le Monde* and by the Leftist press. At that time, there was only factual reporting; the real press campaign did not occur until 1953. For most Frenchmen, there was still no conflict in Morocco.

The National Assembly was only intermittently concerned with Morocco during the four years of Juin's proconsulate. A whole series of parliamentary questions were asked during this period, most frequently by deputies of the extreme Left, but in general were not discussed. The technical problem of parliamentary representation of the French in Morocco was the only one really debated. Since there were no Moroccan deputies in the Assembly and since the government regarded Moroccan problems—except in the case of acute crisis—as being exclusively a matter for the Executive, no further action was taken. Only the Assembly's Committee on Foreign Affairs—that eye which a somnolent parliament kept half open on external affairs—showed any interest in the crisis developing at Rabat. Schuman was sharply cross-examined on this point on February 26, 1951, but managed to evade the issue without too much difficulty, and closed the discussion with the assurance that the campaign against the Sultan would cease.

The government itself showed little more interest in Moroccan affairs. Between January 1947 and August 1951, the first legislature of the Fourth Republic saw seven governments come and go. On the other hand, there were only two Foreign Ministers during those four years: Robert Schuman and Georges Bidault. The chronic instability of Prime Ministers had therefore no very pronounced effect on the conduct of Moroccan affairs at that level, since it remained exclusively within the competence of the

Quai d'Orsay. The Council of Ministers only intervened, as we have seen, at the end of the February 1951 crisis.

At Rabat, the Residency emerged all-powerful from a crisis which the Council of Ministers had solved by abandoning its stakes in the game in the nick of time instead of settling it by some positive act of authority. In Paris, the government remained determined not to refer the Moroccan crisis to Parliament until the pressure of circumstances made it impossible to consider the matter as theoretically within the sole competence of the Executive. Thus Morocco was left in the hands of a Quai d'Orsay, which was quite incapable of dealing with anything but day-to-day affairs.

No concatenation of circumstances could have been more favorable to the final success of the conspiracy just formed in Morocco between the ultras and the notables, whose temporary setback had only stimulated their hopes.

Chapter 5

THE GUILLAUME PERIOD AND
THE 1953 COUP
(AUGUST 28, 1951–AUGUST 28, 1953)

The Early Days of General Guillaume

General Guillaume, like his predecessor, was an old Moroccan hand. He had played an active part in the pacification of Morocco, had been Director of Political Affairs under General Noguès from 1940 to 1943, and knew the country as well as it could be known by a military man who did not find it easy to grasp problems outside his own profession.

According to one witness, shortly before his departure Juin had beseeched the French delegates to the Government Council to help him obtain Guillaume's appointment by approaching the appropriate political persons in Paris.[1] Bowing to the wishes of the future marshal, the Council of Ministers on August 28, 1951, appointed Guillaume as Resident-General to Rabat. Juin, who hoped through his successor to retain control over Moroccan affairs, was delighted. He was soon disenchanted, however, when he realized that, contrary to his expectations, Guillaume intended to keep the reins in his own hands.

Promptly following his appointment and while still in Paris, Guillaume assured the Grand Vizier of his liberal intentions. The Sultan therefore received him cordially. He did not disguise from the general his hope that the policy of the Residency and the government would soon become less intransigent. The Resident-General, not yet caught in the web of the conflict and not lacking in goodwill, asked the Sultan to be patient and wait until he had finished his coming routine tour of the chief

1. Interviews.

94

Moroccan towns. He added that he did not think the French government would take any new steps until after the sixth session of the United Nations General Assembly, which was opening in November.

The courtship, however, was brief, for the Resident-General soon fell under the spell of the French colony. He was little qualified to take the helm in such a complicated political situation and, like most old colonials, he thought that force, provided it was just, was all the natives understood. This is one of those truths of yesterday that are turned by colonial conflicts into the errors of tomorrow.

The situation quickly reverted to the point where Juin had left it. Once difficulties arose, Guillaume treated the nationalists with clumsy arrogance and even went so far as to threaten to make them eat humble pie. "Fighting is my business . . . I know how to avenge an insult," [2] he declared on October 12, shortly after his arrival. On the 28th, there was a further diatribe, this time against Allal el-Fassi, calling him a traitor "to his country, his master, and his religion. He has deemed it prudent to withdraw to Cairo, quite a distance. From there, like a serpent, he spreads his venom over the world." [3] This was enough for the nationalists to form an unflattering opinion of their new opponent, who was in other respects well intentioned.

The policy of intimidation exercised against the Palace was resumed and intensified. The fact that those responsible for the 1951 crisis were kept in office, the attack on the Maghzen by constant interference of the French authorities in the appointment of the Sultan's local representatives and in the composition of his cabinet, the ever increasing number of arbitrary arrests, which now included even the *ulama*—all these events soon convinced the Sultan that the Residency's policy had not changed.

At the beginning of November 1951, a new upsurge of nationalist feeling arose in connection with the increase in membership of the Government Council.[4] A vizierial order of October 17, 1951, had cut short the time for consulting the elector-

2. *La Vigie marocaine* (Oct. 12, 1951).
3. Ibid. (Oct. 21, 1951).
4. For the complete episode, see Rézette, *Les Partis politiques marocains*, pp. 44 ff., 195 ff. Our text closely follows Rézette's.

ate by setting November 1 as the day for elections to the Moroccan Consultative Chambers. All seats were to be filled.[5] Because of successive amendments in the provisions governing the formation of these Chambers, the Moroccan electorate had rapidly been expanded from 8,000 to 220,000 voters, 125,000 of whom were of rural stock.[6] This vast expansion of the electorate not only made consultation with the people essential to the Istiqlal, but also raised a delicate tactical problem because of the large number of rural voters who were to be called upon to vote for the first time, namely whether they would or would not rally to the nationalists. The Istiqlal had so far done little work in rural areas. By rushing the elections and the preparation of electoral lists, which had to be in by October 26 at the latest, the administration sought to deprive the Istiqlal of any opportunity for effective propaganda. This would have allowed the administration to claim, in the event of nationalist defeat at the polls, that the party had lost the support of the masses and that the *bled* would not follow its lead. The nationalists retaliated by boycotting the elections.

On October 27, the weekly *Al Istiqlal* published simultaneously a communiqué from the Board of the Federation of Moroccan Chambers of Commerce, Industry, and Trades; an interview with Mohammed Lyazidi; and a statement from the National Front announcing that the Federation and the National Front refused to take part in the elections and calling upon their members not to participate. The opposition pointed out, inter alia, that the administration had established the procedure all by itself; that the voters had been deprived of all guarantees; that no provision had been made for publicizing the electoral lists; that, contrary to custom, elections were not to be held on a holiday; and, above all, that the Moroccan candidates had not been given any of the opportunities enjoyed by the French candidates to campaign and to make contact with their voters. The percentage of abstentions was extremely high: 95.9 at Casablanca, 97.2 at Safi, 95.2 at Agadir, 93 at Port Lyautey, 98.2 at Salé, 93.2 at

5. Protectorat de la république française (empire chérifien), *Bulletin officiel (B.O.)*, Oct. 26, 1951, pp. 1651–52.
6. These figures are from Rézette, p. 47.

Petitjean, and 82.7 at Khemisset for the Chambers of Commerce alone, which involved only about 20,000 voters.[7] Robert Rézette wrote:

> On election day, violent rioting broke out in Casablanca, where the demonstrators, supplied from trucks loaded with stones brought for that purpose, attacked a polling station and stoned the voters, passers-by, and the police. Five persons were killed and forty wounded. The violence resulted in numerous arrests, as a result of which *Al Istiqlal* on November 3, 1951, appeared with the huge headline, "The Moroccan People have said No."[8]

The election boycott and ensuing disturbances took place only a few days before the opening of the sixth session of the United Nations General Assembly, at which the Moroccan problem was to be brought up. This concatenation of circumstances undoubtedly figured in the party's decision to harden its position in the hope of attracting world attention to Morocco. The Istiqlal had completely lost its representation in the Government Council. Henceforth, the two sections were to consist only of ultras and conformist notables, thus stripping subsequent sessions of all political significance. "Once again," concluded Rézette, "the Istiqlal sacrificed its domestic effectiveness to a spectacular demonstration, in order to create propaganda for international purposes."[9] This is an arguable point. By rushing the elections, the administration had in its turn confronted the Istiqlal with the dilemma: whether to lose face or to boycott. In choosing the latter course, it had probably adopted the tactic most suitable at the time. The disturbances had not really lost the party its political representation, since that in any event had already been compromised by Juin's expulsion of the nationalist delegates from the Council. In abandoning only what it no longer possessed, the Istiqlal had nothing to lose in the long run by engaging in a trial of strength, regardless of the violence of the repressive measures that might be directed against it in the near future.

7. Ibid., pp. 48–49.
8. Ibid.
9. Ibid.

For various political and sociological reasons, the party once more found itself at a turning-point. It was practically cut off from the regime; it could now count only on the rank and file, of which it was complete master, and on international support. The steady influx of lower-echelon adherents had gradually reversed the relationship of internal forces to the advantage of the middle-echelon leaders and the militants at the base. The latter were more and more eager for action and less and less disposed to be satisfied with political negotiations in which they had no part and the utility of which they did not understand. The national leaders, however, were unwilling to achieve independence by direct action, which they considered unprofitable and unsuited to their predilection for political maneuvering. They believed they could solve the problem by concentrating on international propaganda.[10] The results of this dual movement—the displacement of the party's internal center of gravity toward the base and the leaders' preoccupation with external policy—were soon apparent. While the leaders were absorbed in their international activities, the middle-echelon militants gradually assumed internal control of the party. Overwhelmed in the large towns, especially in Casablanca, by supporters ready for action, the Istiqlal's Executive Committee gave in and allowed the militants of the rank and file to reply to the Residency's policy of force by mass demonstrations and increasingly serious incidents. The regional authorities were soon to use these as a pretext for launching a merciless campaign of repression.

The Sultan, always anxious to maintain contact with the masses, took advantage of the disturbances which had accompanied the November 1951 elections to put the regime's record once more before the public. On November 18, the day of the Festival of the Throne,[11] he referred in his traditional address to

10. For a detailed account of the Istiqlal leaders' international activities in 1952, see ibid., pp. 196 ff. Briefly, this consisted of an extended trip by Allal el-Fassi through Europe and Latin America, and the establishment, in the major interested capitals, of offices of information and propaganda, which worked indefatigably to influence public opinion. In New York, the influence of the Moroccan Office of Information and Documentation under Dr. Mehdi ben Abou, through its publications, its activities vis-à-vis the press and influential circles, played a significant role in the 1952 change in the attitude of the United States toward Morocco and its position at the United Nations.

11. *Bulletin d'information du Maroc*, no. 6 (Nov. 20, 1951), pp. 112 ff.

the memoranda [12] he had sent the previous year to the French government on the occasion of his visit to Paris with the idea of obtaining the signature of a treaty guaranteeing full sovereignty to Morocco and providing a new basis for relations with France.

Guillaume, replying three days later to questions from Moroccan journalists concerning their country's future, said that although French achievements in Morocco would benefit all those living on Moroccan soil, Morocco could count only upon French capital for its continued development. He saw no solution to the crisis except by an understanding between Moroccan nationalism and French nationalism, and concluded that the problem of Moroccan independence would be resolved without difficulty once the Moroccans became capable of self-government—unless, of course, nationalist obstinacy brought about a general collapse.

The Residency and the Palace were clearly as far as ever from a basic understanding. Whether the political situation in France was not auspicious, or whether the disturbances which had rocked Casablanca were considered still too recent, the French government did not take up the Sultan's reference to his memoranda of the previous year. Not only did it make no proposal, but it took no steps to set up the famous joint committees [13] that had been promised to Mohammed V the year before.

Three months later, in mid-February 1952, new mass disturbances broke out upon the arrival in Morocco of fifteen Latin American representatives to the United Nations. In Rabat, demonstrators surrounded the Resident-General's car. Police reinforcements were called in and used their weapons. In Casablanca, 5,000 demonstrators defied the police, who also opened fire and dispersed the rioters. This second wave of incidents soon resulted in the resumption of discussions between the Palace and the Residency. Guillaume in a private audience made it plain to the Sultan that certain sectors of Moroccan public opinion were reproaching him for not adopting a policy of force toward the Palace. The Sultan replied with equal frankness that the problems troubling Guillaume were in essence due to the state of

12. See p. 78.
13. Loc. cit.

political inferiority in which the Moroccan people were kept. In substance, he told Guillaume that the country possessed neither a Moroccan government with real powers, nor an organized system of justice, nor any democratic institutions to guarantee the rights of individuals and local communities. Under such conditions, how could things fail to go from bad to worse?

All in all, nothing had changed since the first nationalist demonstrations had challenged the regime eight years earlier. The grievances the Sultan was again preparing to express to the French government had become sharply aggravated during the past few months. In fact, the Franco-Moroccan dispute had intensified throughout the Juin period, both in regard to internal and external policy, and social and economic policy.

Apart from the situation of the Maghzen, the arbitrary actions of the administration, the outworn judicial system, and the inadequacies of the educational system, the Palace laid bitter stress upon the low rate of social investment, inequities in the distribution of profits between Moroccans and French, the abysmally low wage scale, and the enormities of a mining policy which sacrificed the interests of the Sharifian state to the holders of mining concessions.

The Sultan felt that the diplomatic and domestic prerogatives of Moroccan sovereignty had been disregarded. The Maghzen was kept in complete ignorance and was informed neither of diplomatic acts affecting the Empire nor of international decisions which influenced its future. The Palace had not even been consulted when the United States, in agreement with France, set up air bases on Moroccan territory in 1953. That was only one example. The Sultan felt that, in the circumstances, Moroccan opinion had reached the point where it envisioned no remedy for these evils but modification of the regime. The Palace had therefore been compelled to open negotiations with the French authorities. This was the purpose of the memoranda which the Sultan had sent to the government on the occasion of his trip to Paris in 1950.

The failure of these negotiations had opened a new chapter in the history of Franco-Moroccan diplomatic relations. The Residency had at once taken advantage of the stalemate in France to begin plotting. Certain *dahirs* contrary to the Treaty of 1912 had had to be signed under duress. Despite the gravity of measures taken, the Sultan had not lost hope that the day would come when the French government would finally solve the Moroccan problem on the basis of the Palace's proposals. Mohammed V concluded that, since Guillaume's arrival, tension had steadily mounted as a consequence of the aftermath of the 1951 crisis and the increasing restraint exercised by the Residency on the Maghzen. He was convinced that the policy of force would only widen the gulf between the two communities. In his opinion, only the introduction of civil liberties—including trade-union rights—and the establishment of a provisional Moroccan government empowered to negotiate a change of status on the basis of his earlier memoranda could prevent the worst from happening.

Such was the Sultan's state of mind in March 1952 regarding the whole Franco-Moroccan dispute. He conveyed his views to the President of the Republic on March 20 in a new memorandum, which again gave the complete history of the problem of the protectorate regime and restated the grievances the Palace had expressed to Guillaume on many occasions since his arrival.[14]

As if to support this resumption of discussion while at the same time demonstrating the moderation of Moroccan views, the Istiqlal published an important declaration. "Moroccans recognize that France has certain legitimate rights and interests," declared a party spokesman. "These rights can be safeguarded and guaranteed in a new treaty. There is no question of breaking with France. On the contrary, it is a question of ensuring the continuity of Franco-Moroccan relations, but within a framework which will satisfy the aspirations of the Moroccan people."[15]

While Rabat awaited the Paris government's reply to the Sultan's March 20 memorandum, *La Vigie marocaine* also made a statement on April 29 in an article entitled, "What Has Happened to the Reforms?" Summarizing the reforms since February 1951, the writer first noted that there had been no real

14. *Echo du Maroc*, March 29, 1952, and *Al Istiqlal*, March 29, 1962, cited in Julien, *L'Afrique du Nord en marche*, p. 390.

15. *Al Istiqlal*, March 29, 1952, cited in Julien, pp. 390–91.

Sultan's "strike of the *dahirs*." "The legislative machine has not come to a standstill," he wrote, not without optimism. "It is merely working at low speed." He compared the reforms put through with those still pending and pointed out that under the *dahir* of July 6, 1951, the administrative *djemaas* had been reconstituted on a new basis that gave them a broader elective status than before. Thirty-one of these new *djemaas* had been set up by vizierial order on November 7 of that year. As a result of this initial reform, changes had been prescribed on March 8, 1952, in the system of rural redistricting in the Wadi Faresh.[16]

The article noted that in judicial matters the Sultan had rejected the Residential proposal for establishing regional tribunals staffed by Moroccan magistrates and for transforming the Sharifian High Court into the supreme court of the new system.[17] On the other hand, the Moroccan penal code had been signed and promulgated but could not be put into force until the regulations governing the competence of the Maghzen courts had been altered. The code of criminal procedure remained one of the stumbling blocks to reform.[18] It had been rejected by the Palace in December 1951, and a revised draft had to be submitted. The draft *dahir* providing penalties for extortion by Moroccan judges had not been accepted either, although the caids had been granted civil servant status on January 1, 1952. Administrative reform was no further advanced. The Sultan had rejected the plan for municipal reform under which mixed municipal committees with deliberative powers would have been elected. For those centers not designated as municipalities, the reform envisaged the establishment of joint committees for local affairs which would have been responsible for assisting the pashas and caids in the conduct of administrative matters. However, *La Vigie marocaine* continued, the Sultan ruled out any French participation in these organs on the grounds that it would conflict

16. *B.O.*, Nov. 23, 1951, pp. 1826–28, and March 28, 1952, pp. 471–72.

17. The effect would have been to deprive the Sultan of his remaining judicial power in exchange for a partial reform that would have settled no basic issues. Moreover, it would have remained a dead letter because of lack of credit and cadres, as long as the regime maintained the status quo.

18. Its entry into force would have implied granting to those under Moroccan justice guarantees that the Residency could not recognize without dismantling the arbitrary judicial framework that was inseparable from the regime.

with the rules of international private law, and at the same time would violate Moroccan sovereignty. As for trade-union reform, it too had come to a dead stop. The plan prepared by the Residency made mandatory the presence of French trade unionists in the offices of the trade unions and federations and restricted the exercise of trade-union rights to permanently employed workers. It had not been approved by the Sultan, who demanded greater freedom and opportunity for union members to choose their own leaders. The newspaper ended by recalling that all the projects left pending were part of the plan of reforms which had been prepared as early as 1947 when Juin had reorganized the Maghzen.[19]

The French government did not reply to the Sultan's memorandum of March 20 until September 17.[20] The reply was disappointing. After the usual glorification of French achievements, the government declared it would abide by the reform plan that had been blocked by the Sultan's withholding of his signature. It rejected any proposal for a piecemeal approach. It declared itself ready to make a solemn proclamation of the principle of Franco-Moroccan interdependence once the reforms had been put into effect, although there could be no reopening of the question of political objectives and the attribution of powers defined in the Treaty of Fez.[21] The tone was not threatening, but the Palace recognized it as a complete dismissal of its case.

Mohammed V could do little except reiterate the causes of the conflict, reaffirm the rights acquired by the French community, and note the fact that France sought to adhere to the protectorate regime in an effort to obtain at least a return to the letter and the spirit of the Treaty of Fez after twenty years of distortion. The Palace's legal position was as strong as its political position was

19. General Juin was appointed Marshal of France on May 7, 1952. General Guillaume handed him his Marshal's baton the following Bastille Day, in Morocco.

20. Indicative of the influence of the great Moroccan notables was the fact that they were repeatedly received in Paris by the highest French authorities. In September 1951, the Pasha of Marrakesh was received by the President and by Ministers Pleven, Queuille, and Schuman, and again on July 21, 1952, by Antoine Pinay, Minister of Foreign Affairs. Sharif Abdelhaï el-Kittani, mortal enemy of the Sultan, had talked with Auriol and Queuille on March 17.

21. On August 27, the International Court of Justice had reaffirmed the sovereignty of Morocco in a decision settling a dispute between France and the United States as to rights of United States nationals in the Sharifian Empire.

weak. Either France must accept revision of the Treaty of Fez, wrote the Sultan, in which case he would take into consideration all its suggestions for reform, or it must adhere to the Treaty of 1912. In the latter case, all reforms not compatible with it would have to be ruled out a priori and he would have to request the Residency to return to a strict observance of the basic agreements. This would imply elimination of the arbitrary practices which had been grafted on to the treaty and which in fact constituted the essence of the existing regime. Not only had the Residency persisted in implementing reforms incompatible with the existing regime, the Sultan continued, but it had considerably weakened his position by compelling him to accept them en bloc, thus depriving him of any freedom to negotiate. The municipal reforms would divide Moroccan sovereignty because they conferred voting rights on aliens. Franco-Moroccan government bodies such as the Council of Viziers and Directors were also contrary to the treaty since they made the administration of the country a joint affair. Implementation of any reform not explicitly envisaged in the treaty violated it by the very fact that enumeration of possible political arrangements was in itself a limitation. France wanted Morocco to be more democratic, and so did the Sultan. But the protectorate treaty did not institute a democratic regime, and only a change of regime would enable Morocco to become more democratic through the establishment of representative assemblies with powers of deliberation and decision. He said that he gave in wherever possible without abandoning what was essential. He signed the *dahir* establishing *djemaas* in rural areas. The question was settled because *djemaas* had been set up in various regions. If there had not been greater progress it was because the Residency had not yet seen fit to submit to the Grand Vizier the draft vizierial order which defined the procedure and the requisite electoral guarantees. He gave in when he could, but the Residency remained inflexible. The Sultan asked it to end this state of siege. His request was rejected. The Residency knew that since General Guillaume's arrival in Rabat the Palace had done all in its power to avoid aggravation of the dispute in the hope that Robert Schuman would keep his promise to the United

Nations that negotiations would be opened with Morocco with a view to solving the Moroccan problem. So far, this had not happened. The Sultan was reproached for doing nothing; actually, he said, it was the French who did nothing. He went on to say that he was only against whatever might make the existing situation worse, which was precisely the Residency's objective. Whether the Treaty of Fez was revised or not, one had to know what policy had been chosen. If the Residency was unwilling to modify the treaty, he asked only one thing: that it be respected. But he refused then and there to be responsible for what would happen in Morocco if the French failed to understand that the days of colonialism were numbered.

Mohammed V forwarded these views on October 3, 1952 to the President of the Republic in a note replying to the French memorandum of September 17. Anxious this time to publicize the debate, the Palace issued a statement on October 8 summarizing everything that had taken place in Franco-Moroccan diplomacy in the last two years.[22]

Meanwhile, as France's position in the General Assembly deteriorated, Schuman was obliged, on November 10, to redefine the policy France intended to take toward its North African protectorates, especially Morocco. The Minister declared that although the evolution of Franco-Moroccan relations could not be identical with that of Franco-Tunisian relations, the aims were the same in both cases: consolidation of Morocco's character as a sovereign state, development of its political and social institutions along democratic lines, safeguarding of all its interests, and the exploitation of all its resources and of all assistance within the framework of a gradually expanded autonomy. France, Schuman added, was ready at any time to come to an understanding with the Sultan on the bases for and methods of implementing such a program. However, independence was a relative concept and existed in varying degrees. The same was true of the concept of sovereignty, which had lost its absolute character. The welfare of a people was no longer identified with unbounded and unreserved independence. The perilous mirage of premature inde-

22. Julien, pp. 393–94.

pendence would endanger legitimate interests and the subsequent development of the territories in question.[23]

Once again November 18, the Festival of the Throne, arrived. Mohammed V, who had lost all hope of seeing France embark upon liberalization of the regime, was particularly uncompromising in his speech. He likened the Treaty of Fez to a garment that had been outgrown, rejoiced in the bond between his people and himself, thanked them for their support, drew up a balance sheet of negotiations since his Tangier address, and hoped that Morocco would soon join the fellowship of independent nations. The political views of the Moroccan ruler, his interpretation of the ties that bound him to the people, and his firmly expressed determination to see Morocco set free were this time openly and forcefully affirmed in an open-air meeting between the Sultan and the Moroccan people.[24]

Léon Marchal was impressed. Of course, neither the Minister nor his adviser was ready to follow Mohammed V. Marchal had no doubts regarding the guiding principles for development of the Franco-Moroccan association. His avowed aim was not to grant Morocco its independence but to "democratize" it under the auspices of France and of those Frenchmen established in Morocco. In his view, this objective had to be achieved by agreements freely arrived at in an atmosphere of calm, with due regard to the aspirations and interests of all sectors of the Moroccan community. Since the Sultan had stated his position, it became imperative for the government to spell out for the Resident-General, without delay, the policy it intended to follow at Rabat and, for the first time, the procedure for putting it into effect. Since the Sultan's withholding of his signature was paralyzing the legislative machinery and impeding the democratization of the protectorate as envisaged by Paris, the Quai d'Orsay felt that the only course open was to apply the pending reforms by means of the special powers the Resident-General enjoyed under the Treaty of Fez.

It was thought that the Sultan's intransigence could be over-

23. United Nations General Assembly, *Official Records,* 7th Sess., 392d Plenary Mtg. (Nov. 10, 1952), paras. 76–158.

24. Montagne, *Révolution au Maroc,* pp. 228–31.

come by enlarging the competence of the existing consultative bodies through support of local groups, or by setting up regional consultative councils consisting of delegates from different parts of the local organization established by the regime such as consultative chambers, municipal committees, various corporate bodies, councils of the agricultural-reform sectors, and *djemaas*. Naturally, these new organs would not enjoy any legal power of decision because they could only be vested with requisite authority by a *dahir*. However, by asking existing bodies (or those to be set up) to express opinions upon an increasingly wide range of administrative subjects, and by following their advice wherever possible, Marchal hoped the Residency would succeed in interesting the population and the nationalists in these new means of political expression. Once these new elites were drawn in, the Residency—so Paris thought—would merely have to use the emergencies it had itself created to induce the Sultan, through these subtle tactics, ultimately to grant what he had so far refused.

This curious doctrine sought to involve the nationalists in spite of themselves in a policy which would substitute for the demand for independence a program of progressive democratization that would gradually deprive the Residency of the discretionary powers it enjoyed, without, however, settling the problem of the protectorate system. It is not surprising that the Rabat administration thought the scheme unrealistic and preferred the status quo. It is a moot point whether Marchal really believed in the policy he defended officially, or whether he was already inclining toward the idea of complete independence, of which no one in the government yet dared to speak.

Having thus adapted his policy to the Sultan's, Marchal submitted it to Schuman. Whatever the Minister's opinion on the substance of the matter, he agreed to the procedure his adviser suggested. He instructed the Residency to use its special powers to prepare, as of the end of November 1952, for the inauguration of the regional and local consultative assemblies recommended by the Director for Africa and the Levant. The method was not new; Labonne had already threatened to resort to it before the Tangier speech. By adopting the idea as its own, the Quai d'Or-

say had merely returned instinctively—for better or worse—to
the only alternative means of legislation left to France once the
Sultan withheld his signature.

The 1952 Festival of the Throne was the last important event
before the December riots. All the Moroccan townspeople had
been mobilized by the Istiqlal, which proved remarkably successful in organizing this great demonstration of unanimity among
the Sultan, the party, and the politically conscious sector of the
nation. In the poor and working-class quarters of the big towns,
along the main roads, in the small centers, the accord of the rejoicing mob and local agitators made it a real political country
carnival.[25] The eagerness with which the people, especially the
young people, responded to the slogans indicated that this time
the pressure was coming from below and that those party militants who claimed to be swept away by their supporters were telling the truth. In political crises, when action at the top and reaction at the base are frequently out of step, the pressure exerted by
the rank and file may force the leaders to act when they least
want to do so. Such a reversal of pressure invariably indicates
that latent tensions are ready to explode almost spontaneously
into violence. The Istiqlal had become a mass party, seething
with ardent followers eager to prove their mettle. It recognized
that its control over the masses might be jeopardized by the
slightest incident.

Tragedy in Casablanca

The dramatic events which took place at Casablanca between
December 7–13, 1952, mark a vital turning point in the Franco-
Moroccan conflict.[26] On December 6 the news of the murder of
the Tunisian trade-union leader, Ferhat Hached, ran like the fire

25. Ibid., pp. 228 ff.

26. These events are so complex and their interpretation so difficult that a new
analysis would have required a special study. Fortunately, a résumé of the essential
aspects was prepared by *Cahiers du témoignage chrétien* as their 35th publication: *Le
drame marocain devant la conscience chrétienne: les événements de Casablanca à travers
la presse française du Maroc* (Paris, 1953). In making this the basis of our account,
we have diverged from a policy of using liberal publications only as an exception; but
this particular publication is less a polemical exposé than an objective study of the
official version. This study is even more valuable in that it is based upon a thorough
study of the press at that time. The summary we have drawn from this book has been
rounded out here and there by materials obtained from interviews and documents.

of a lighted fuse through Moroccan nationalist circles, already at fever pitch after the constantly growing political tension of the past few weeks. The crime was immediately laid at the door of French counter-terrorists from Tunisia. There is some reason to believe that the accusation was not wholly unfounded, since Robert Montagne, in his study of this period, considers it likely.[27] Emotion ran particularly high in Casablanca trade-union circles, which the U.G.S.C.M. continued to keep on the alert. Constant contact had gradually harmonized the ideas and demands of the neo-proletariat of the *bidonvilles* (literally, "tin-can towns") surrounding the city with those of the natives of the ancient *medinas* who had hitherto provided the nationalist movement's major support.

This climate made rioting inevitable. It had not come about overnight, nor without assistance from the French police, whose preventive or repressive activities had become almost routine. Since the Festival of the Throne, arrests, searches, and imprisonment by the administration had increased throughout Morocco. French newspapers in Casablanca were full of announcements of repressive measures and arrests in the Arab quarter. *Al Istiqlal,* aroused by the extent of these activities, took the offensive. In a significant article of November 27, 1952, entitled "Repression Continues Everywhere—What Is Its Purpose?", it listed the wave of arrests that had followed the Festival of the Throne and came to the conclusion that in many areas the police seemed to be trying to manufacture incidents. The newspaper was neither banned nor censored. While such passivity does not necessarily prove that the French authorities admitted the accusation, it does suggest that the police thought it opportune at the time to allow the nationalist press to step up its propaganda.

On the Moroccan side, matters had not stood still. After the election boycott of 1951, the ensuing disturbances, and the mass excitement that accompanied the Festival of the Throne, the Casablanca proletariat joined the movement.

Since August 1952, more and more meetings of an increasingly stormy character at the Maison des syndicats, the Maison du peuple, and the meeting hall of the *bidonville* of Les Carrières-

27. Montagne, p. 231.

Centrales outside Casablanca had kept at fever pitch this army of supporters who longed to demonstrate their unity and political ardor.

That the topics of these meetings had gradually become deliberately political was at once symptomatic and revealing of the close interpenetration that had progressively taken place between Moroccan trade unionism and the Istiqlal. The success of these meetings showed that the awakening of the Moroccan proletariat was frankly centered upon the demand for independence, which was the heart of the nationalist movement's position.[28] Against this background of intense political activity, a few sporadic outbreaks had increased tension since the beginning of December.[29] Despite this excitement, the Executive Committee of the Istiqlal had succeeded in restraining the rank and file and the middle-echelon leadership. It told them repeatedly that serious disturbances would give the Residency the excuse it wanted, would be fatal to the party, and would mean that the Sultan, once isolated, would risk being either promptly neutralized or deposed.

Confronted with the emotion generated by Ferhat Hached's assassination, the Executive Committee resigned itself to allowing a tremendous protest demonstration, in the belief that this would provide a safety valve for the militants' ardor. By the evening of December 6, strike orders were beginning to circulate in the *medina* of Casablanca. On the morning of the seventh, the U.G.S.C.M. General Assembly met in the Maison des syndicats on the Rue Lassalle. At the same time, the U.G.S.C.M.'s strike call "to the workers and people of Morocco" appeared in *Al*

28. While the demand for trade-union rights was not forgotten, the topics most discussed at these political meetings included: support of the Moroccan position at the United Nations, independence for Libya, the need to organize demonstrations in the event of failure at the U.N. or of a negative response by the French government to the Sultan's memorandum, union with the Istiqlal, and the role of violence in the attainment of liberty.

29. There were apparently only five such incidents: April 5, attempted arson in Casablanca against the home of an enemy of the Istiqlal; April 8–9, a similar incident; June 23, a bomb placed in the home of an Istiqlal opponent; November 14, a similar bomb in the offices of the pro-Residential newspaper *Liberté;* December 7, a similar attempt in the office of the newspaper *El Azima.* These were not the beginning of urban terrorism but of individual attacks, obviously amateurish and spontaneous. These demonstrations claimed no victims and had no legal repercussions. The French press did not even report them all.

Alam It called upon the workers to participate in a twenty-four-hour general strike on Monday, December 8, "to protest the assassination of Ferhat Hached and to ask the United Nations to intervene in the continuing dispute between France and the two North African countries."[30] At the end of the meeting, which had been quite calm, the workers left the Maison and returned through the European quarters to the *bidonvilles* without incident, vituperations, or attacks on any Europeans.[31] The afternoon was equally peaceful. Toward evening, a dispatch from *Agence France-Presse* reported that although workers' general assemblies in several Moroccan towns had approved the strike order, there was no news of any incident anywhere in the protectorate.

The atmosphere began to deteriorate during the night of the seventh in Les Carrières-Centrales. Late that night, 5,000 Moroccans, including women and children, held a violent demonstration outside the Carrières-Centrales police headquarters. According to *La Vigie marocaine* of December 14, the outbreak had been provoked by the appearance of criers sent by the pasha to order striking shopkeepers to stay open. Attacked by the crowd, the criers had taken refuge in the police station, which was soon surrounded and threatened by rioters. The police and the Maghzen militia fired to keep them at bay until 300 Goumiers arrived to disperse the crowd. An alert was sounded throughout Casablanca. Reprisals in the district continued far into the night. One by one, tenements were searched by police, and sporadic firing lasted until morning.

Monday the eighth was dedicated to the strike, which was effective throughout Morocco. At Casablanca, the picket lines were in place at dawn. Everywhere patrols of cyclists rode from barrier to barrier to see that orders were obeyed. All was quiet in the city, where, despite the events of the preceding night, the organization of the strike was obviously still the trade-union

---

30. *Al Alam,* Dec. 7, 1952, cited in *Cahiers: Le drame marocain,* p. 11.

31. The following details are confirmed in *Echo du Maroc* (Dec. 8, 1952); *La Vigie marocaine* (Dec. 8, 14); *Le Petit Marocain* (Dec. 8, 9); *Maroc-Presse* (Dec. 9); *Cahiers: Le drame marocain,* pp. 17, 19, 29–36; and Robert Barrat, *Justice pour le Maroc* (Paris, 1953), pp. 233–48.

leaders' chief concern. Even *La Vigie marocaine* on December 8
reported that by the end of the morning no serious incident had
as yet occurred.

The night's events had impelled the authorities to take important security measures. Arrests continued throughout the morning. The police intensified their searches in union circles and
rounded up about a hundred U.G.S.C.M. militants, including
three chief organizers of the movement. A protest meeting was
at once called for that afternoon in the Maison des syndicats in
the center of the European district. Also, at the end of the meeting a delegation was to go to the Regional Commissioner to protest the arrests.

The bodies of Moroccans killed during the night had been
taken to the mosque of Les Carrières-Centrales, and the Regional Commissioner had arrived about noon for the official
count and identification. The victims were hastily buried "in an
atmosphere of dangerous excitement" in a besieged quarter that
was crowded with troops and surrounded by machine guns set
up to guard roads leading into the area.

This was the state of affairs when a Moroccan mob surrounded a European automobile driving through the quarter.
Finding his way blocked, the driver shot his way out, but without killing anyone. The mob retreated, then re-formed in front
of the troops who, believing themselves threatened, opened fire.
"This moment saw the birth, in circumstances which demand
investigation, of those rumors which were to make the eighth of
December a day of tragic folly." [31a] The rumor spread that bodies
of mutilated and disfigured Europeans had been discovered at Les
Carrières-Centrales. It was soon an established belief that two
European women had been raped and slaughtered by a howling
mob. The French population of Casablanca was seized by a
frenzied thirst for vengeance. This understandable emotion was
raised to the point of paroxysm by dramatic reports of the
rumors by the French press in Morocco. *La Vigie marocaine,*
having reported on December 8 on page three that nothing had
happened, announced the next day in large type on page one:

31a. A.F.P. release, Dec. 8, 1952, *Le drame marocain devant la conscience chrétienne,*
p. 19.

"Two European Women Raped and Murdered," and "European Torn to Pieces." *Agence France-Presse,* which had reported on the morning of the eighth that two unidentified Frenchmen had been killed, by evening spoke only of one European killed that morning, but added that three on the French side had been killed the night before. Apart from the report on the victim of the eighth, none of the reports that added fuel to the flames of the French district was correct.

This mass excitement made inevitable the clash that occurred in the afternoon. After burial services for the Moroccans killed during the night, many groups of workers had gone to Les Carrières-Centrales to join the procession that was to precede the meeting to be held at 2:30 in the European district to protest the morning's arrests. The demonstrators who left Les Carrières-Centrales never got to the meeting. At the Place des Quinconces, they found their way blocked by police and troops who opened heavy fire. The crowd was fired upon again a few minutes later, on the Mediouna road at the railway bridge. The unarmed demonstrators encountered tanks and military formations which opened fire and drove them back without difficulty.

The international press reported hundreds of casualties. *Corriere delle Sera* of December 10 said that the number of deaths could not be estimated. The correspondent of the Belgian Socialist daily *Le Peuple* on December 12 reported that there were at least 300 Moroccans dead, and that witnesses had seen more than 50 bodies piled in the road outside the Carrières-Centrales police station. The same paper a day later reported more than 200 dead and wrote: "The whites of Casablanca do not feel safe, for they know that the casualties caused by the recent shootings have aroused a hatred among the Moroccans that will be difficult to appease." In *The New York Times* of December 14, Robert C. Doty also said the number of victims could not be accurately estimated, but he placed it at several hundred. *Agence France-Presse* remarked on December 11 that the number of Moroccan casualties would remain uncertain, since the rioters had carried the bodies off and buried them without ceremony.

On the French side, three civilians had been killed early in the afternoon by the crowd which the police had just fired upon and which was retreating to Les Carrières-Centrales. A Spaniard whose body had been found there the evening before beside his burned-out automobile brought the total of European victims to four.

This did not prevent the French press on December 9 from reporting seven, then eight, then nine European victims, not counting the women supposedly raped and murdered. All the newspapers on that day were forced to deny that any European women had been raped. Carrying the retraction a stage further, *Maroc-Presse* of December 11 correctly reported only four European victims, all of whom had been identified. This figure was confirmed by Regional Commissioner Boniface in a subsequent interview with Raymond Cartier published on February 7, 1953, in *Paris-Match:* "I lost two men, three French civilians were killed (one of the four European victims was a Spaniard), and we found the bodies of twenty-eight natives," said Boniface. "Others were taken into the *medina* and buried secretly. In all, probably about forty were killed."

Despite these belated corrections, the initial false reports so lavishly spread by the press produced their effect. The French population, incensed by all the rumors and newspaper reports, was beside itself with rage and clamoring for blood. Within the day, the press and the police provided the French mob with the sacrificial victims who alone could appease them. The regional authorities did this quite simply by transforming a Moroccan protest meeting called for that afternoon into a police trap. About two o'clock, when the meeting hall in the Rue Lassalle was full, Goumiers and police surrounded the district. They arrested most of the Moroccans present and took them away in buses and vehicles commandeered for the purpose; the rest were handed over to the mob and lynched. Whatever the police and the French authorities in Morocco may have said subsequently, the meeting had not been banned. It was a trap, as Montagne confirmed in his analysis of these events.

It is necessary to quote here in some detail the French newspapers of the day. They give a vivid picture of the way in which a group can be influenced in such circumstances by what are politely called the news services.

Le Petit Marocain of December 9, 1952, in an article headed "Police Trap at the Maison des syndicats" reported:

> One after the other, searched and rendered incapable of doing damage, the Moroccans were piled into buses and vehicles. . . . Previous events—the brutal assassination of Europeans and the discovery of weapons on these men—were not calculated to make the police patient. The potential criminals were vigorously hustled out of doors. . . . The police were busy all afternoon. . . . Some Moroccans were led with their hands over their heads to the end of the square, where they were seized by the waiting crowd. . . . Meanwhile, more news arrived and it was learned that in other areas Europeans had been killed or wounded. The weapons collected were thrown into an armored car, while the Moroccans were marched four by four down an energetic whipping line.

Maroc-Presse reported on December 9:

> The inhabitants of houses overlooking the little square, into which the Rue Lassalle and the Rue Blaise Pascal emerged, watched from their balconies as though at the theater, and saw the spectacular arrest of several hundred Moroccan trade unionists who, having come to attend the banned meeting, were caught like rats in a trap. . . . Suddenly, shots rang out. From the balcony above, a young girl leaned out farther to see what was happening.

Commented *La Vigie marocaine* on the same date:

> Those demonstrators not found to be carrying arms and who could not therefore be imprisoned as the search went on were allowed to escape from the trap. They did not get far. In the Rue de l'Aviation Française, the European residents of the district, both men and women, who stood in the road, fell upon them, manhandled a good many, and shouted over and over, "Murderers!"

If the local police are to be believed, the purpose of the operation was to seize the weapons the Moroccans were suspected of
carrying. Later, the French press had to confirm indirectly that
this had been only a pretext. On December 9, *Agence France-
Presse* reported that only 50 of the 3,000 Moroccans arrested were
carrying knives other than pocket knives. Neither the French
press nor those police reports which could be consulted report
the firing of a single shot by a Moroccan during all that time.

Despite the violent blow to Casablancan trade unionism, the
regional authorities seemed to hope that a final spasm of the
city's proletariat would give them an excuse for the coup de
grace. On the eleventh, more than 10,000 armed men again
invaded the *medina*. Once again, the way in which the press
reported and commented on the event leaves very little doubt as
to what was expected. "There were so many troops in the
Moroccan sections and even on the outskirts of the *medinas*,"
wrote *La Vigie marocaine* on December 12, "that the European
population was alarmed. . . . This enormous army literally
blanketed the *medinas*."

The *Giornale d'Italia* of December 12 reported the presence of
many Senegalese troops and navy commandos, at the same time
emphasizing—as the *Cahiers du témoignage chrétien* indicated
—that this display of force "[could not but] stir people up instead
of calming them down."

"However, *contrary to all expectations*," admitted *Le Petit
Marocain* on December 13, at the end of an article devoted to
these same events, "the people left the mosques in complete
calm." [32]

In accordance with a previously prepared plan, the Residency
had launched, on the evening of December 10, what *Agence
France-Presse* was to call "the biggest political roundup in Morocco since January 1944." [33] Four hundred members of the

32. Emphasis added.
33. "It was learned late in the evening of December 10 that the leaders of the
nationalist and Moroccan Communist parties were the object of extensive arrests
throughout the country. The Residential authorities and the Sécurité have so far refused
to give any official confirmation of this report. But it is confirmed by families of members of nationalist and Communist party-affiliated organizations in the large towns and
is now considered true. It is also known that the pashas have been ordered to remain
in their cities and that all police leaves have been canceled. The main center for those

Istiqlal, the U.G.S.C.M., and the Communist Party were arrested. Of those arrested, 383 were held. The 112 forming the
leadership core of the Istiqlal were put under house arrest in the
south. The Istiqlal, the U.G.S.C.M., and the Communist Party
were put out of action as unified political organizations and were
banned throughout Morocco. The chief organs of the nationalist
press were silenced. A new group of pashas and caids suspected
of pro-nationalist sympathies was dismissed. The victims of these
dismissals were replaced by Residency candidates without consultation with the Sultan. This was in no sense repressive action
based on real or supposed participation by nationalist leaders in
the recent disturbances. It was a political operation intended to
destroy the leadership of a group of organizations regarded as
morally responsible for the riots and which were—as far as the
Moroccans were concerned—accused en bloc of collusion with
the Communists and of plotting against the security of the state.

It was not easy for the Moroccans to defend themselves against
this charge of collusion, because the establishment of indigenous
trade unions was forbidden and the Communist General Confederation of Labor had been the only trade-union organization
in Morocco after the war to open its doors to the nationalist
militants. The charge was nevertheless without foundation. It
was in fact so gratuitous that the military tribunal which had to
decide the issue in 1954 dismissed the case for lack of evidence
and released the accused.[34]

Once again, this sweeping operation had taken place without
the Quai d'Orsay's knowing any more than its officials had been
able to glean from the newspapers. At the end of January 1953,
the Department for Africa and the Levant was to complain, with
justification, that it had not received the official casualty figures
until a month after the event. Despite repeated requests for
information, it received no reports regarding the brutal treatment
of the demonstrators who had been arrested. It particularly
deplored the fact that the responsibility of the Istiqlal leaders and

detained is Meknes, where airplanes are being made ready to deport them." (Free translation, dispatch of *Agence France-Presse*, Dec. 11, 1952, cited in *Cahiers: Le drame
marocain*, p. 33.)

34. See p. 222.

their collusion with the Communists had been neither proved nor disproved, although the Residency had not hesitated to advance those two allegations publicly as justification for its repressive action.[35]

Robert Schuman was no better satisfied. He had sensed the threat to Franco-Moroccan relations implicit in retaining a senior official as controversial as Boniface and had sent a cable demanding his retirement just before the incidents at Casablanca. The demand was indicative of the Minister's frame of mind and of his lack of confidence in the official who in the absence of the Resident-General was to organize the repression.[36]

The Boniface affair is characteristic of the insubordination shown by the Residency toward the Quai d'Orsay at the time.[37] In November 1952, Boniface was five years over normal retirement age. He owed his continuation in his post only to the series of prolongations annually extorted by the Residency from the Quai d'Orsay. In November 1951, the Minister had agreed somewhat reluctantly to a final extension of one year, on the urging of the Resident-General, who told the Quai d'Orsay that the Regional Commissioner for Casablanca was an avowed opponent of the Sultan. This argument was meant to overcome all opposition. On November 29, 1952, a week before the disturbances, the Residency, which had had more than a year to find a replacement, told Schuman that it could find no solution to the problem but to keep Boniface in his post, as a *chargé de mission,* although he had definitely been placed on the retired list. Confronted with this fait accompli, Schuman protested and remonstrated with Rabat during the early part of December, but to no avail. The former Director of the Department of the Interior did not leave the administration until 1954. Émile Roche then took him under his wing and found him a position with a business concern. This change of status did not prevent Boniface from

35. For example, Guillaume's speech at the American Club. See *Le Monde* (Jan. 30, 1953); also, for the Residency's mimeographed press release after these events, see *Cahiers: Le drame marocain,* pp. 63 ff.

36. Guillaume was away from Morocco during the disturbances.

37. For a more complete picture, see Robert Schuman, "Nécessité d'une politique," *Maroc et Tunisie: le problème du protectorat, La Nef,* n.s. *10* (1953), 7–9.

continuing to play a leading part in the intrigues of the final period.

In trying to formulate a judgment of this turning point in the Franco-Moroccan crisis, one must consider a thesis and a hypothesis, between which two extremes the truth presumably lies. According to the Residency's thesis, the police had confined themselves to quelling riots, directed initially against the police headquarters of Les Carrières-Centrales and then against the French city of Casablanca. These riots, they said, formed part of a vast subversive enterprise planned by the Istiqlal and the Communist Party. In order to protect the beleaguered French city, a few dozen Moroccans, at most, were killed.

The hypothesis is that of French liberals of the time, and particularly the *Cahiers du témoignage chrétien*. It is merely a hypothesis because *Témoignage chrétien* affirms nothing but merely points up the extravagances and inconsistencies of the pro-Residential press reports and official statements. According to that hypothesis, the regional authorities had "smoked out" the nationalists in order to finish them off once and for all, had misrepresented a general protest strike as a riot directed against European lives, and had killed several hundred unarmed Moroccans.

In view of these facts, it is difficult to avoid the conclusion that although the murder of Ferhat Hached gave the Moroccan nationalists the opportunity to organize a major demonstration, the Residential authorities found in that political demonstration the pretext they had long been seeking to crush the Istiqlal and at the same time to wipe out the Communist-labeled political trade-union organizations that Moroccan trade unionists had entered because they were unable to form their own unions.

Neither the repression of 1944 nor that of 1946 had created such a storm in France and abroad as that which engrossed public opinion outside Morocco after December 1952. Great waves are not caused by tossing little pebbles into the water, and although some doubt may remain regarding the exact number of deaths in the absence of any accurate casualty count, it seems highly probable that a large-scale massacre took place. On the other hand, there was obvious provocation. Nothing could be more natural than this massive recourse to repressive measures. As for the defenders of the status quo who, under one title or another, exercised the Residential authority, the only courses open at that time were either to demonstrate their superior strength or to give in without striking a blow. The Sultan and the Istiqlal had signed their political death warrants. One had paralyzed the Residential regime rather than agree to a tacit revision of the Treaty of Fez through a system of cosovereignty. The other had proved that it was rapidly expanding among the urban proletariat instead of being confined, as had hitherto been believed, to the relatively harmless traditional lower class. How could key officials, therefore, who had never even considered the possibility of relinquishing their actual power in Morocco in order to reestablish French presence on another basis, have sought anything but a decisive trial of strength?

Could not the supporters of the status quo argue with some apparent justification that "a rather rough police operation" was not too high a price to keep a prize won after ten years of bloody warfare? Were they not warranted in believing that the three hundred dead in Casablanca—if indeed there were so many— counted for little beside the human lives that would have had to be sacrificed on both sides if the movement had been allowed to grow into open revolt? Force has its logic just as generosity has. An operation based upon conquest and the belief that might is right—which does not prevent it from being in its own way a civilizing force—must inevitably choose police action, only to bow to the inevitable late in the day when its failure is too obvious to ignore.

The event, in the words used during an interview by a former Resident-General not known for his liberalism, was "the beginning of everything." After December 1952, metropolitan public opinion was awakened, a Moroccan lobby was organized in France, press campaigns and investigations on Morocco proliferated, and the first works by Frenchmen on Moroccan problems were published in Paris. The first ultra associations were on the verge of appearing in Morocco, under pressure from settlers who felt themselves betrayed by the response in France to the campaign of the liberal protagonists; meanwhile, in France itself, conservative circles were organizing to counter this adverse propaganda on all fronts.

It was also after December 1952 that the nationalist rank and file, shorn of leadership by the repression, became part of a sociological and political process that was shortly to cause them to sever their ties with the few original leaders who remained. Their new leaders were to be of a different type; they had risen from the ranks and were resolved as much by temperament as by necessity to use violence to gain their ends. This crucial development, however, did not gain its full momentum until the Sultan's deposition had forced the Moroccan people to advance from the stage of making demands to that of revolutionary action.

The emotion aroused in France by the events of the winter of 1952, although significant, did not carry sufficient political weight to force Parliament to take an active interest in the Moroccan conflict. On November 22, 1951, Schuman had reported to the National Assembly on the debates at the United Nations on the Moroccan question.[38] With this passing reference to events in the outside world, Parliament lost interest in the protectorate until the Casablanca massacres a year later again forcibly directed its attention to North Africa. On December 9, 1952, deputies François Quilici (Radical Socialist) and Roger Linet (Communist) put two questions to the Minister on events in Tunisia and Morocco.[39] Ferhat Hached's assassination aroused a violent but short-lived storm in the Assembly. On December 16, the Minister for Foreign Affairs asked that the questions be considered at some later date, a proposal tantamount to burying them. He repeated the official version of the Casablanca drama, which the Residency attributed to collusion between an extremist minority and the Communists, and promised that conversations between the Residency and the Sultan would be resumed. In conclusion, he said that, pending the outcome of these new negotiations, the government thought it inadvisable to debate the Moroccan question. However, the tragedy was still too recent for

38. *Journal Officiel (J.O.)*, *Débats parlementaires, Assemblée nationale* (Nov. 23, 1951), pp. 8323–24.
39. Ibid (Dec. 10, 1952), p. 6079.

the Assembly to be able to give full support to the Minister on that point. By a vote of 310 to 303, it rejected indefinite postponement, and, by a further vote of 376 to 226, scheduled the debate for December 23.[40]

In the meantime, the fall of the Pinay government precluded any debate. There was no further discussion on Morocco until the crisis of August 1953. Residential activists and el-Glaoui were thereafter free to maneuver against Mohammed V, who was already little more than a ruler living on borrowed time. The emasculation of the Istiqlal made it easier for them to strike at the Sultan, since he was left without political support—if not without friends—in the face of a conspiracy of notables and senior officials who expected shortly to have the upper hand over the Moroccan people once the bad shepherds had been isolated or cut off from their flock.

The 1953 Crisis and the Sultan's Deposition

The coalition of high officials, Moroccan notables, and leaders of the religious brotherhoods, which had narrowly failed to bring about the Sultan's deposition in 1951, was reconstituted at the beginning of January 1953 with the firm intention this time of forcing the issue. The way was clear. The removal of the Istiqlal leaders and the suppression of the party's organs of domestic propaganda and information marked the triumph of a policy of force and gave the Sultan's opponents virtual assurance that the disorganized Moroccan masses would be unable to react effectively in defense of their sovereign. The achievement might well appear considerable, and it was for this purpose that anti-nationalist activities had assumed their familiar guise.

The conspirators were masters of Morocco, and also had the upper hand in Paris. The retention of Boniface against the express wishes of the Minister for Foreign Affairs would have sufficed to show them that the Quai d'Orsay could no longer impose its will upon Rabat. Schuman, confirming in advance the inevitable outcome of this administrative battle, was soon to admit publicly in a lead article in *La Nef* that the Quai d'Orsay was no longer obeyed at Rabat and could not oppose the faits

40. Ibid. (Dec. 17, 1952), pp. 6465 ff., 6484, 6488.

accomplis that were "the great and constant temptation" of the Residency and its various departments. He concluded by saying that nothing could be done in Morocco until the French administration had been brought under control.[41] Rabat could scarcely have asked for more. Thus armed with official acknowledgment of their insubordination from the Minister who had for six years been responsible for Moroccan affairs, the conspirators could march boldly forward.

The first signs of renewed activity coincided more or less with the replacement of Robert Schuman by Georges Bidault, who on January 7, 1953, again became Minister for Foreign Affairs, in the Mayer government. Although Schuman was hardly authoritarian in temperament, he had nevertheless cautioned Juin after the February 1951 crisis. What had happened two years before could happen in 1953, hence the advantage which his departure from the Quai d'Orsay represented to the Sultan's opponents.

Bidault was laconic and deliberately abrupt whenever his personal authority was questioned, and was more inclined toward a policy of force and more imbued with colonial conservatism than his predecessor. He had supported Juin's appointment in the Council of Ministers in 1947. He was to defend with increasing intransigence France's imperial position against the partisans of evolutionary change. Only his most determined well-wishers could ignore his hostility to Mohammed V.[42] Those in power at Rabat could not fail to regard this change at the Ministry as one more trump card in their hand. Thus, just as the ultras for the first time felt themselves masters of the field at Rabat, the political situation in Paris, on which the success of their operation depended to some extent, was also developing in accordance with their hopes.

THE PROTAGONISTS

Since history is made by men acting under specific conditions, the study of these conditions—the ultimate aim of political

41. Schuman, "Nécessité d'une politique," p. 7.
42. This alternation between Schuman and Bidault dominated the entire conflict and embodied, in the very heart of the M.R.P., the opposition between moderate Catholic progressivism and imperial conservatism which hardened from crisis to crisis until the end of the Fourth Republic in May 1958.

science—makes sense only if one bears in mind that the web of events is woven by individuals. Our first task, therefore, is to place the individual protagonists in the 1953 crisis as correctly as possible in their respective roles.

On the French side, the conspiracy had largely retained its 1951 characteristics, but this time it was more keenly aware of the weakness of the obstacles to be overcome. Director Marcel Vallat of the Department of the Interior, and Colonel Jean Lecomte on Guillaume's staff (in his capacity as Inspector-General of French North African Forces) were the center of a conspiratorial network which rested, at the administrative level immediately below, on the regional commissioners led by Boniface. In fact, without their cooperation nothing would have been possible, since they controlled the *contrôle civil* and the notables. Apart from Boniface, who was practically a second Resident-General, General Hubert d'Hauteville was firmly ensconced in the key regional post as Chief of the Military Region of Marrakesh, and maintained permanent contact with el-Glaoui.[43] Gradually, level by level, the entire French administration in Morocco, with few exceptions, was drawn into the struggle.

Only one high-ranking official, Secretary-General Georges Hutin, was frankly opposed to the deposition of Mohammed V. He was a clear-sighted man and said openly that, although the mass of the people was still passive, attacking the Sultan would unite them against France. This isolated voice in Rabat was echoed here and there in the *bled* by the protests or opposition of a few contrôleurs civils who, by temperament or greater insight, realized that sooner or later the move would redound to France's disadvantage. These few dissidents represented the dying voice of individual reason in the storm of passionate conformism that swept the country.

The ramifications of this center of intrigue extended as far as the frontiers. Two equally important groups took turns supporting the conspiracy. The first included leading French citizens who had cooperated with the administration since the

---

43. The exception at this level was General Marie-Antoine Laparra, head of the Region of Fez. He remained on the fringe of the movement; as a result, most of the caids under his jurisdiction took no active part.

Labonne era: Aucouturier, Eyraud, Pierre Mas with his newspapers, and many more who, with Boniface as their spokesman, were continually to incite el-Glaoui and the Moroccan traditionalists against the Sultan. The other consisted of notables of the *bled* and the leaders of the religious brotherhoods: el-Glaoui, the Zaïans, and a few lesser barons represented the feudal lords; the Sharif el-Kittani and his group represented the religious side. They were especially eager for the kill because, having compromised themselves in 1951, they had no choice but to win or to resign themselves to a situation that would relegate them increasingly to the past. They were fully aware that most of the lesser caids would ultimately support the winning side and were confident they could win the *bled* officials over to their cause if France would only indicate unequivocally that she supported them.

This activist network consisted of disparate components that were nevertheless united in a smoothly working relationship based as much upon enthusiasm as upon experience. It was impelled by two social forces. One was the uneasy conservatism of the French colony, which was staking its all against nationalism in conditions that were steadily deteriorating as a result of what the settlers called their betrayal by Paris. The other was the misgivings of the traditional feudal and religious forces of Morocco, which were playing the same game in the certainty that they would be the first to go if nationalism won, and which were left by the Sultan's unequivocal stand with no source of political support but the French colony.

In this system the senior officials of the Residency provided the regulatory mechanism. The French group was the driving force, and the nobles and the chiefs of the religious brotherhoods set the machinery in motion again whenever it came to a halt. Like the rear echelons of an army in the field, the settlers pushed the front line of notables before them, while the political and administrative staff of the regime provided guidance, information, and cover. The whole movement was so strong in comparison with that of the nationalists, which had been put out of action by the December roundup, that it looked as if it might ultimately be possible to draw the still neutral and relatively malleable mass of caids and tribal horsemen into the conspiracy. All that would remain then would be to launch the *bon bled* into an attack on the Palace, representing the operation as a spontaneous revolt by the democratic forces of the real Morocco against the Sultan's despotism.

The goal was almost within reach, but to achieve it the enterprise had to be guarded in the van and on the flanks by men playing an ad hoc role. It was chiefly in that particular respect that the situation had improved since 1951. In the van was General Guillaume, who lent cover to the whole operation, although it was never quite clear whether he knew where his subordinates were leading him: he was not of sufficient political stature either to oppose the movement or to control it. His permissiveness, whether due to resignation or to his secretly favoring a move to which he could see no alternative, meant that the obstacle created by the relative caution displayed by Juin in the same position two years earlier was removed.

Freed from all political responsibility, Juin openly supported el-Glaoui and threw into the balance the not inconsiderable moral weight that attached to his prestige and his newly won dignity as Marshal of France. The notables could hardly have doubted they were on the winning side when the only living Marshal of France was holding, in the very heart of the Berber country, military reviews that were obviously intended to bring together in one place and in one common cause all the forces that the army, the contrôle civil, and the traditional officials mobilized as actual or potential support. They had no reason to hesitate, since throughout the critical period of the conflict, Juin was to lend his support to el-Glaoui in Paris in a fighting spirit that left no doubt as to the political purpose of this demonstration.[44]

There remained the question of relations with Paris. These rested in the competent hands of the Deputy Minister to the Residency, Jacques de Blesson, who, because of Guillaume's frequent absences, gradually became the man with whom the Minister for Foreign Affairs had to deal. De Blesson was the diplomatic brain of the conspiracy, and nothing would have been possible without his support. He was to work tirelessly to conceal

44. Montagne, p. 237.

the operation from the Quai d'Orsay and finally to make the Minister's personal envoy accept the fait accompli.

No operation of this kind can take place without propaganda, and the Mas press was soon deeply involved. *Le Petit Marocain's* return to the fold and the elimination of the nationalist newspapers had removed all opposition voices. With the Residency's encouragement, the Mas press devoted itself to making the administration's game look like an authentic revolutionary uprising of the Moroccan people. *Le Petit Marocain,* then under Rouault's guidance, was to take the lead. The Rouault-Mazoyer-Grimault trio was to the press what the Blesson-Boniface-Juin team was to the political and military front. While Rouault campaigned against the Sultan, wrote innumerable articles preparing the public for the deposition, and held the pen for el-Glaoui (apparently he wrote the August 1953 interviews himself), Mazoyer and Grimault took care of everything else.[45]

In France, facing this coalition of forces made overpowering by distance, events, and force of habit, Bidault held the reins at the Quai d'Orsay. He was assisted by a high-ranking official passionately opposed to the conspiracy, the Director of the Department for Africa and the Levant, Léon Marchal, whose arrival at the Quai d'Orsay was the result of one of the innumerable vicissitudes of the crisis. As Deputy Minister under Labonne and at the beginning of Juin's proconsulate, Marchal had been regarded after Juin's arrival as an inconvenient witness by those high officials who were preparing to launch their campaign against the Sultan after Labonne's recall. Marchal was then transferred and appointed ambassador to Pakistan in December 1947. He returned a few years later and was made, by an ironic twist of fate, Director of the Department for Africa and the Levant just when the 1951 conspirators were about to go into action. This ill-matched pair remained in harness together until the end of the crisis, the adviser striving tirelessly to open the Minister's eyes, the Minister playing his solitary game of bogeyman to Rabat. It was an open secret at the Quai d'Orsay that

45. Henri Mazoyer, former Director for Information under Juin, was then head of the Moroccan Bureau in Paris. Louis Grimault was a Mas factotum. Mas discharged Rouault a year later, reportedly after vehement reproaches from Edouard Herriot for his newspaper's role in the deposition.

Bidault read Marchal's reports with impatience when he read
them at all, and that their contacts were few and far between.
Bidault had not much faith in the departmental system—with
some justification in the case of so skeletal an organization—and
he tended to underestimate the Moroccan question. It is rumored
that he even flattered himself that, given the spare time, he could
solve it in a few days. His headstrong impulses, his low regard
for the Sultan, his deep-rooted conservatism, which made him
particularly sensitive to any threat to France's position as a
colonial power—all these factors were more favorable to the
conspiracy than was Schuman's timid but obstinate opposition in
the same post in 1951.

Surrounding this incongruous team in France were the pressure groups and lobbies that had appeared just after the Casablanca massacres. They were expanding rapidly under the mounting tension that was soon to bring them to grips. On the liberal
side, the Comité France-Maghreb was gradually mobilizing, in
Parliament, in the press, in intellectual circles, and even in the
army, all the opponents of a policy of force. Between January
and August 1953 it did everything possible to prevent the Sultan's deposition. After its failure it never recovered its position as
an organized group.

In the conservative camp and in the same milieux, all those
who felt they had interests to defend in Morocco banded together to uphold the status quo. On this side there was as yet no
real organized pressure group but, rather, an almost spontaneous
coalition of powerful individuals. These influential citizens were
part of the regime and were working from the inside to keep on
the right track those high officials who, at least at that stage, saw
matters essentially as they did themselves. With rare exceptions
their opponents were fighting on the fringes. They were attacking in order to ward off an objectionable decision.

These two groups were both closely and for various reasons
linked to the Moroccan centers of power, of which they were in
a sense only the metropolitan extensions. The settlers on the one
hand and the French liberals in Morocco who supported the
Sultan on the other had relatively little influence in France.

Nevertheless, it is essential to study them to understand the subsequent developments in the conflict.

While the Residency was dependent on the two social forces with which it was linked—the French colony and the great notables—the Quai d'Orsay, with a hesitant government and an indifferent Parliament behind it, was operating in a vacuum. Its policy in 1953 was determined neither by the liberals in France —the denouement makes that quite clear—nor by their opponents. The only external factor the Minister had to contend with was the opposition of the real masters of Morocco in Rabat. As for the Residency, the only unpredictable human factor in Paris was the personality of Georges Bidault. This time, the ultimate decision rested with a rampant conservative who would not be long deterred by any inclinations toward a liberal course that might be engendered in him by his authoritarian outspokenness or by French treaty obligations vis-à-vis the Sultan.

This was the equation of forces involved. It must be kept in mind if the final outcome is to be understood. To sum up, whether because chance had favored the scheme or because its leaders had played their cards well, everything pointed toward success. From the Resident-General to the Minister, down through Boniface, Vallat, de Blesson, and Mas, the high-ranking army officers and the Moroccan notables, all posts were filled by men who openly or secretly supported one idea: if a conflict broke out between France's Moroccan friends and its enemies, it was inconceivable that France would one day turn against those local leaders who had been for nearly thirty years the docile instruments of French North African policy. Equally important, there was sufficient time to widen the movement's popular foundation, to rouse the French colony to white-heat, encourage the resentment of the great notables, play up the susceptibilities of the religious brotherhoods, and postpone the final explosion until tension had reached breaking-point. Lastly, the removal of the nationalist leaders and the isolation of the Sultan safeguarded the Residency, at least in the immediate future, from any flare-up of popular feeling. The leaders no longer doubted that they could achieve their goals, because they firmly believed that the still neutral mass of the Moroccan people, freed from nationalist blandishments, would once more accept domination by the pashas and caids who would be vested with new prestige by the very success of the operation. They reduced everything to the simple notion that they were dealing with the enemies of France and that those enemies understood only force. Once the Sultan was out of the way the Moroccan people would yield to the strong side. Therefore, the only appropriate policy was to eliminate those elements in the Maghzen that had gone over to nationalism and to replace them by friends they could trust.

At first, this policy—which erred only because it had been successful too long—seemed to be justified in a series of dramatic incidents. Their origins merit examination.[46]

END OF THE FRANCO-MOROCCAN EXCHANGE OF NOTES
(JANUARY–JULY 1953)

The extensive repression of Moroccan nationalism after the Casablanca incidents made resumption of negotiations on reform difficult but essential. The speech at the 1952 Festival of the Throne had been the last public expression on this, and since the violent French reaction had put the Palace again on the defensive, only France was really in a position to reopen negotiations. Had it waited any longer, Moroccan and international public opinion might have concluded that the French authorities had been so energetic merely to avoid the trouble of further talks.

The French government realized this. On January 6, 1953, shortly after the tragedy at Casablanca and just when the notables' conspiracy was quietly being revived, René Mayer, in his investiture speech before the National Assembly, made a statement concerning the protectorates in North Africa. He said it was the duty of France to guide the peoples of Tunisia and Morocco toward self-government but emphasized that cooperation must be assured between Frenchmen and Muslims within the existing framework of governmental institutions in both countries. As part of this requisite process and within the frame-

46. Since events in Morocco during the first half of 1953 were too complex to be traced chronologically, it seemed preferable to discuss separately the diplomatic and political events of this period. See the two following sections.

work of the treaties, the Prime Minister continued, the French government would seek the accord of the Tunisian and Moroccan sovereigns. "Negotiations must be resumed in Tunis as well as Rabat," Mayer concluded. "They presuppose the maintenance of law and order." [47]

The Sultan was waiting for an opening and seized upon the occasion at once. Six days later, on January 12, he notified the President of the Republic of his desire to reopen negotiations on the basis of Mayer's statement.[48]

The basic issues were the same. But as a result of Schuman's departure and Bidault's return to the Quai d'Orsay, certain aspects of the political situation most directly concerned with the problem of the regime had altered in the past two months.

The Residency was delighted with its victory over the Istiqlal and kept the Quai d'Orsay even less informed than before. Since the end of November 1952, when Paris had ordered Guillaume to use his powers as Resident-General to circumvent the Sultan's refusal to sign anything, despite many requests the Residency had not sent the Minister any plan of action or any information regarding the primary problem of reform. The Quai d'Orsay would have continued in complete ignorance of Rabat's intentions had not an article by Henri Duquaire in Le Figaro of January 24–25 reported the imminent establishment of regional and local assemblies. This was far from true, but nevertheless the author was regarded in Paris as the customary spokesman for the administration at Rabat, and the Minister was annoyed. Coming after two months of silence, this sudden and very indirect declaration of intent hurt a number of feelings. The Minister regarded it as one more reason for demanding that henceforth he receive information from sources other than newspapers.

The Sultan had been displeased with comments made by the French press in Morocco concerning his last message to the President of the Republic. Having learned of the Sultan's action through the usual unofficial channels, the press in Morocco and L'Aurore in France had launched their customary criticism of

47. Speech of Jan. 6, 1953, J.O., Debats parlementaires, Assemblée nationale (Jan. 7, 1953), p. 4.
48. L'Année politique 1953 (Paris), p. 197.

Mohammed V. They reproached him mainly for the moral responsibility they said he had assumed for the Casablanca disturbances and for his implacable opposition to the Residency's proposed reforms. Fortunately for the Palace, the campaign started by the French Catholics after Casablanca had to some extent offset, in the Sultan's eyes, the deliberate distortions of the pro-Residential press. He considered a public protest against these attacks, but changed his mind a few days later when the Adviser for Sharifian Affairs assured him that he greatly deplored these indiscretions. The Sultan admitted that the campaign in the liberal press compensated for the slurs on his honor and prestige by hostile publications. An incident was thus averted.

With a third party working in his defense, the Sultan could afford to wait and to demonstrate a certain degree of flexibility without having his opponents interpret his silence or concessions as resulting from the daily attacks upon him since Casablanca. While he did not go so far as to consent to the suspension of various Moroccan officials, neither did he refuse to fill vacant posts or to deal with current affairs. Although he made no basic concessions, he answered the remonstrances of his French entourage by pointing out that he was fulfilling his duties as sovereign by respecting the Treaty of Fez and by not refusing to enter into any discussion. The Residency reported these facts to Paris only to counteract all conceivable consequences. It held that naturally the Sultan's policy had not changed; he was merely giving a few pledges of goodwill in the hope that the French government would be grateful and would in turn make some advance.

This was the situation in Rabat when Bidault presented the government with the draft of the reply he wanted it to make to the Sultan's letter to the President of the Republic of January 12. This reply was handed to the Sultan on February 7. It clearly reflected Bidault's desire that the forthcoming negotiations remain as outlined in the French reply of September 17. The government merely referred to this, and emphasized that conversations could only proceed satisfactorily in a calm atmosphere, which had already been promoted by outlawing the extremist parties. It again demanded that the pending *dahirs* be signed.

The only concession to the Palace was purely formal; it was understood that once the scope of negotiations had been fixed, there would be direct talks between the Sultan and the Residency to try to smooth out their mutual difficulties.[49]

Having thus nipped in the bud any hopes the Mayer statement might have aroused in Mohammed V, Bidault made a point of laying down for Guillaume the program of reforms which the government intended to effect in Rabat. He reminded the Residency of its duty to submit reports and urged it in future to present its demands for reform to the Palace more tactfully.

The following analysis reflects as accurately as possible the political theory of the Quai d'Orsay. Bidault and his advisers thought that no headway would be made in Rabat until the Residency agreed to return to a stricter observance of the Sultan's prerogatives. They ruled out any policy of violence or intimidation and trusted that the recent measures against the nationalists would be regarded as exceptional. They felt that to represent these as the first step in implementing a policy based on force would ruin everything. Fundamentally, of course, French policy and that of the Sultan remained completely opposed. France's first objective was to lead Morocco toward self-government within the framework of the Treaty of Fez. A new instrument of association could not be negotiated until that goal had been attained. But the Sultan demanded immediate independence. Therefore, the Minister believed, a drastic change was necessary in Mohammed V's attitude toward the Residency and the government. In the opinion of the Quai d'Orsay, the deadlock could be broken, as in the past, only by carrying out the proposed reforms by using the special powers vested in the Resident-General by treaty and usage whenever these reforms did not require a *dahir*. When the reforms proposed by France could not be instituted except by *dahir,* however, the procedure suggested by Marchal had no practical utility. Five years after the beginning of the difficulties that had resulted in the almost total paralysis of the regime, Paris still had neither the complete list of

49. In a press release dated February 13, the French government summarized the Sultan's letter of January 12 to the President, as well as the government's reply a month later.

the major unsigned *dahirs* nor a clear account of the fundamental issues separating the two parties. One of the Quai d'Orsay's aims was to obtain these from the Residency. (It never did.) Meanwhile, the Minister believed the only way to diminish the Sultan's objections to municipal reform was to assure him that the establishment of elected assemblies would not prejudice Morocco's future status as far as the French government was concerned. This was the spark of an idea that might have permitted a start toward a solution of the problem of municipalities by limiting its scope; but the growth of the notables' revolt in the following weeks precluded any relaxation of tension.

Measures depending on Residential action alone were easier to prescribe than to have carried out by Rabat. In this category, Bidault kept strictly to his predecessor's proposals concerning the *djemaas*, regional assemblies, the Government Council, judicial reform, social action, opening of the civil service to Moroccans, and the relaxation of direct administration. Here there was complete continuity of action. Superimposed, however, were some new touches that indicated either a tendency to define in greater detail the normally highly simplified instructions to the Residency, or a desire to impose certain new limitations on reforms regarded as liberally inspired. Thus, although the Minister wanted the 1951 *dahir* on the *djemaas* put into effect, he thought that the requisite funds should be obtained without new taxes. He also thought the regional assemblies could be created as effectively by simple Residential instructions as by Residential decree, and looked forward to the day when these intermediate assemblies would be replaced by up-to-date bodies. Ultimately, he wanted the two sections of the Government Council united into one assembly; he thought he could reduce the Residency's hostility to this idea by recommending that as a first step the two sections of the Committee on the Budget sit together. It seemed to him that Residential instructions giving effect to the new safeguards contained in the draft penal code and the code of criminal procedure would be the best means of getting judicial reform under way. This would not, for the time being, touch on the problem of confusion as to locus of power. In view of Rabat's obvious inability at the time to settle the problem of Moroccan trade unionism, Bidault believed this gap could be filled by recommending the establishment of workers' *djemaas* empowered to present the members' demands to employers. He hoped internal disputes might be settled by social welfare inspectors serving as arbitrators and attached to the districts of urban deputies. The other projects were concerned chiefly with administrative and social organization of the urban neo-proletariat, promotion of rural programs by comprehensive development of agricultural modernization sectors, and expansion of the role of the sector councils, closer association of the youth of the two communities, easier access for Moroccans to the civil service, and relaxation of direct administration. There as elsewhere, and indeed more than elsewhere, the Quai d'Orsay did not imagine it could go beyond a declaration of intent. Its job was to outline the program and set the sights. The Residency's was to work out details and put them into effect.

About the middle of February, following this reappraisal, Bidault had gleaned enough from this survey for a new set of instructions. The Residency was already deeply involved in fostering the notables' revolt and had other worries than provincial councils or the lessening of direct administration. However, it would have been somewhat impolitic to leave unacknowledged the instructions from Paris. Rabat decided to concentrate on municipal reform as envisaged by Paris—especially since on this matter, apart from a few minor points, the Quai d'Orsay's instructions coincided with its own desires. An exchange of notes, less acid than usual, followed on the subject of municipal reform. This was to continue, not without some semblance of success, until the Quai d'Orsay realized that it had been distracted for three months by a minor issue and that the crux of the problem lay elsewhere. Nevertheless, it is worth analyzing this political and administrative interlude.

The Sultan, once informed by Guillaume of the Quai d'Orsay's new policy, reiterated his belief that municipal reform posed the most serious problem that had arisen in Morocco since the signing of the Treaty of Fez. He enumerated all the obstacles of international law which to his way of thinking would be raised by the eventual participation of Frenchmen in the election of municipal assemblies. He pointed out that Spain might well follow suit. In addition, he emphasized that participation of French political parties in future elections would ultimately take the Moroccan conflict into the political sphere. Finally, he announced his intention of convening a political council consisting of persons most qualified to give him an opinion on a subject that affected the future of the empire.

In answer to the Sultan's reaction, Bidault ruled out the idea of referring the problem to a sort of Council of Empire which might be interposed between the Residency and the Palace. The Quai d'Orsay considered the plan contrary to the Treaty of Fez, and told Rabat that if the Sultan wished to protect himself by seeking the advice of a committee, he could recruit one from the Maghzen—all of which, considering how the Maghzen was recruited, ruined the Sultan's hopes on this score.

Having thus from a constitutional standpoint returned the problem to the comfortable rut of a tête-à-tête between Maghzen and Residency, the Minister turned a more sympathetic ear to the fears of the Palace. He gave precedents for participation of aliens in the elections of a sovereign state, inter alia, Iceland. He added that extending municipal reform to Spanish Morocco would be meaningless, since Spain was fully sovereign there. He promised (this was a new argument) that the right of aliens to vote would be restricted to Frenchmen; this would limit proportionately the international character of the proposal. Lastly, he conceded that future municipal committees would be prohibited from discussing anything outside their terms of reference and from making political recommendations. He explained that it was merely a question of letting the French participate in the political life of Morocco within the narrow framework of representing their own interests. As he saw it, the reform only answered a present need for representation and defense of legitimate interests. The Moroccans themselves would benefit, for they would receive training in the practice of modern assemblies side by side with the French.

In late February and early March, Guillaume tried to convince the Sultan that the new views conveyed to him by the French government opened the way to a compromise solution of the problem of municipalities. The Sultan agreed. He told Guillaume he would no longer oppose the plan if it could be presented to him in a form that would leave Moroccan sovereignty unimpaired.

Mohammed V then changed his tactics and confided to Guillaume his apprehensions about the intervention of the Moroccan French press in the debate. In fact, the press had increasingly presented municipal reform as the starting-point for a complete overhaul of the existing system. The resolutions adopted on the subject by most of the Moroccan branches of the French political parties had convinced the Sultan that the reform had been forced through by the French colony and was not the outcome of government decisions. He feared above all that the French colony would one day inherit the powers which France declared itself ready to abandon once the evolutionary process ended; this would be tantamount to substituting a protectorate of the French in Morocco for that of the Republic. In fact, that was the idea at the back of Guillaume's mind, and although the Quai d'Orsay did not perhaps see things in exactly the same way, its instructions might well have led to the same result in a colony where the local authority enjoyed all the freedom of action it needed to interpret the Métropole's instructions in accordance with its own aspirations.

Paris was struck by the extent to which these apprehensions were justified. Marchal rightly considered it essential at that stage to convince the Sultan of the sincerity of the government's intentions. He thought it particularly regrettable that the periodic reports of the Department of the Interior should be drafted in such a way as to undermine Mohammed V's prestige. Whenever the Sultan gave way on some point, there was open rejoicing over what was bluntly called a capitulation. Whenever he stood firm, it was called obstruction. "Sidi Mohammed is already trying to use the delaying tactics introduced by the Bey of Tunis in the same circumstances," stated the Department of the Interior's *Bulletin de renseignements*. "In this way, he is trying by gaining time to recreate the deadlock of last year, especially if the Arab League, as certain signs seem to show, succeeds in alerting international opinion once again. In the meantime, the real match is once more between the Palace and the Residency under the country's watchful gaze." [50] Coming just when the Residency was entering into the caids' conspiracy, this commentary by the official organ of the Department was hardly likely to induce concessions by the Sultan.

The editors of the *Bulletin* would have been closer to the truth had they written that the Sultan was in fact trying to influence Paris against the Residency by relaxing his own position regarding the problem of municipalities rather than accused him of obstruction just when he was becoming less intransigent. Mohammed V was isolated by the liquidation of the Istiqlal and by growing Residential pressure on his entourage and his officials. He was publicly challenged by every official and unofficial spokesman for the settlers. Yet he must have been aware, in March 1953, when the 1951 conspiracy was again taking shape before his eyes, that he was being drawn toward a major crisis that might well cost him his throne. The Palace had only one defense against this overt threat. It could give in on municipal reform after limiting its dangerous effects through negotiation, while at the same time informing Paris that the promise given would be fulfilled only when the Residency had in turn met its obligations by bringing the notables into line and by punishing the daily attacks that were damaging the prestige of the Throne.

It was a skillful parry and almost impossible to counter. If at that time the Paris government had had any vestige of authority over Rabat, the Sultan's tactics would probably have been deemed effective. Unfortunately for him, things had gone so far that it had become impossible for the Palace to exert pressure on the Residency by maneuvering through Paris. The normal channels of authority had been closed to Morocco. The Sultan could still hope to justify his position to the Quai d'Orsay. But he could no longer hope (although he was still probably unaware of this) to persuade the Quai d'Orsay to alleviate the Residential pressure on him in Rabat.

Whether the evidence in retrospect is correct or not, the Sultan's counterattack was carried out in two clearly defined stages. At the end of March, he informed the Residency of the

50. *Bulletin de renseignements de la Direction de l'Intérieur de la Résidence générale (section politique)*, no. 2 (Rabat, 1953).

conditions upon which he was willing to sign the *dahir* on municipalities. He began by recalling that the Treaty of Fez, in view of the restrictive nature of the reforms it authorized, precluded any unilateral modification of the political system set forth therein. He repeated that municipal reform ceased to be administrative and became political in character once the question arose of giving the French colony an electoral voice in municipal government. While the Sultan did not deny that it might be equitable to give the settlers an opportunity to protect their interests, he did point out that these were already strongly defended by the protective attitude adopted by the Residential authority toward the French, and by the various bodies it had set up for them in exercise of its own powers. Having again emphasized the gravity of the problem, the Sultan said he was ready to compromise on two conditions. First, the right to vote should be limited to the area of municipalities, which would enable the Palace to regard that right as merely a technical means of recruiting committees and as having no political character. Second, the administrative supervision of municipalities should be restored by the Department of the Interior to the Grand Vizier in his capacity as Minister of the Interior of the Empire. The Sultan stated categorically that while he had no objection to the democratic nature of the reform, he had some political misgivings, because it called Moroccan sovereignty into question. He did not oppose democratization of that sovereignty, provided its intangibility was recognized by both sides.

These were important concessions. On the Moroccan side, the door was now wide open for negotiation. Realizing the interest the Sultan's proposals would evoke in Paris, the Deputy Minister to the Residency, Jacques de Blesson (acting in Guillaume's absence), seized the opportunity to report simultaneously to the Quai d'Orsay on the petition drawn up against the Sultan by the pashas and caids. He also let it be understood that this demonstration of hostility was not worth taking seriously and that the French authorities had had no hand in it.[51] The Residency thus portrayed itself in the best possible light. It made sure the two reports coincided. It simultaneously produced the Sultan's con-

51. See p. 169.

cessions on municipal reform, and credited its success on this score to its flexibility in negotiating with him. Thus it could to a certain extent hope to convince the Quai d'Orsay of its innocence in the affair of the caids.

These affirmations deceived neither the Sultan nor the Quai d'Orsay. The Sultan knew very well where he stood and was only awaiting the agreement of Paris to impose his conditions on the Residency. The Quai d'Orsay was too well briefed by its unofficial informants to believe seriously that the caids were organizing all by themselves. The Residency knew that the Sultan and the Quai d'Orsay knew, but was anxious to preserve appearances in this early stage of the renascent crisis and believed itself strong enough to defeat the Sultan in any case.

Whatever the hidden intentions of the principal actors in this incipient drama, the Sultan's concessions did have their effects in Paris. The Minister noted with satisfaction that the Sultan did not object to the democratic nature of the reform. Without going so far as to accept the idea that administrative supervision should be entrusted to the Grand Vizier, he signified his willingness to transfer it from the Department of the Interior to a neo-Sharifian Department, and even to put the Division of Municipal Affairs under a Moroccan, with a Frenchman as second in command. Turning to the Sultan's apprehensions, he told the Residency quite plainly that municipal reform was in no case to be regarded as the first stage in a tacit revision of the treaty. He was anxious to bring matters to conclusion this time before new complications arose and gave strict instructions that the negotiations with the Palace should remain secret. This was to prevent any indiscretions by the press that might ruin everything. The Minister, alerted by the petition, added that the government was absolutely opposed to any policy of force and to any solution involving abdication or deposition at the behest of a deliberately engineered public opinion. On the other hand, it was agreed that the Residency should continue to give the Sultan to understand that if he returned to his original obstinacy, France would proceed to democratize the regime by means of the special powers of its representative in Morocco.

Early in April 1953, a solution to the question of municipal reform was close at hand. Paris and the Residency had agreed that competence of the municipal assemblies should be strictly limited to the administration of local affairs. It was understood that the electoral procedure would be merely a technical method of recruitment. There was even a question of inserting a provision into the *dahir* on the municipalities recalling that administrative supervision rightfully belonged to the Grand Vizier. The Quai d'Orsay had risen to the bait. The Residency realized, perhaps, that negotiations had been outdistanced by the mounting political crisis. Or perhaps it felt that a breakthrough, however limited, in the troublesome question of municipalities would one day make it possible to force through the greater part of the settlers' demands. At any rate, it discreetly negotiated with one hand and stirred up the notables against the Sultan with the other.

Mohammed V had only to proceed to the second stage of his counterattack; he revealed the political conditions he intended to impose on the agreement that had virtually been reached on the substance of the problem. He confided these to Guillaume at the beginning of April during a private audience. He noted with satisfaction that agreement seemed closer than ever and announced to the Resident-General that he was going to set up a committee of the Maghzen to reexamine the plan as a whole and work out a definite solution. As for the political situation, he told Guillaume frankly that as long as the atmosphere was disturbed by activities of the sort the Palace had denounced for months as incompatible with the normal functioning of the regime, it would be impossible for him to sanction the reforms. He now agreed with them in principle, but in his view they could only be put into effect when the Residency had returned to a satisfactory observance of the spirit of the Treaty of Fez.

As in the past, there were numerous sore spots in the ever deteriorating political situation. These included the suspension and appointment of pashas and caids by the Residency without consulting the Palace; the French authorities' encouragement of the political and religious activities of the Zaouïa and the religious brotherhoods committed to practices contrary to Islam and to acts which only the Sultan as Imam could consider; the rapidly developing revolt of the caids, which would have been impossible, as the Sultan rightly pointed out, without Residential support; and the campaign directed against him by the Moroccan French newspapers and the pro-Residential Arab press. The Sultan pressed his attack and asked what the Residency hoped to achieve by its direct attack on his person and prestige. He told Guillaume it would be impossible to make progress until the atmosphere had improved. He stressed the evidence of his goodwill and said it was time for the Residency to do likewise. This was asking of Guillaume more than he could promise. Mohammed V realized that all he received were fine words, and decided to appeal again to the President of the Republic. Since the French government had suggested in its reply of February 7, 1953, that the difficulties reported by the Palace should in future be settled by means of direct conversations between the Palace and the Residency, Mohammed V informed Vincent Auriol on April 14 that, far from having been smoothed over, these difficulties had been deliberately aggravated by the Residency, and urged that the matters in dispute be dealt with and settled directly by Paris.

The government was not prepared to go so far. While it did not object to acting as arbitrator as long as there was no risk of open conflict with its local representative, it did not intend to let itself be forced into a serious governmental crisis by assuming direct responsibility for a problem it had originally placed in the hands of the Residency. It therefore decided to turn a deaf ear. It ignored the Palace's objections by merely replying that it noted with satisfaction that full agreement had been reached on municipal reform, and by declaring its determination to see that law and order and the prerogatives of the sovereign were respected. The Government also urged that the disputed *dahirs* be signed without delay, and asked the Sultan to see that the attacks in Morocco against France should cease. Once again, there was a deadlock. It was now the latter half of April. The progress of the notables' revolt was soon to smother the problem of actual reform beneath the weight of dramatic events. Matters would probably have remained at that point had not the very aggravation of the crisis led Mohammed V to make a last appeal two months later to Moroccan public opinion and to the highest French authorities.

A banal accident that had forced him to cancel the festival of Aïd-Seghir provided the opportunity. Wishing to thank his people for their tokens of esteem, he took advantage of the situation to call upon his subjects publicly to bear witness to his goodwill. In a statement containing the text of the address he had intended to give at the celebration, the Sultan gave a lengthy account of his efforts to reach agreement with France. He recalled that a number of reforms had already been put into effect with his consent. He asserted that the scope, significance, and nature of the municipal reform plan was being clarified, but repeated that full agreement could not be reached in the present atmosphere of passion exacerbated by intrigue that existed in Morocco. He expressed the hope that France without delay would draw up a complete plan for the modernization of Morocco, based upon widespread social improvements and development of the Moroccan economy. He also demanded measures to provide the country with hospitals, schools, housing, and law courts, while emphasizing that judicial reform would involve the separation of judicial and administrative powers and organization of a modern system of legal officials. As for the economic situation, he fully recognized the need to draw widely upon foreign capital, and that it would be necessary to offer investors not only social harmony, but the solid safeguards resulting from peaceful cooperation between capital and labor, and from granting trade-union rights to Moroccans. Thus, the trade-union problem was linked by a skillful and unexpected move to the problem of protecting foreign investment. The Moroccan attitude during the war and the Palace's previous statements proved Morocco's friendship for France, the Sultan continued, and it was because of that friendship that he had always drawn the French government's attention to anything that might endanger Franco-Moroccan relations.

The Sultan was not content with this latest expression of his views to the Moroccan and French public, for he considered the situation too serious to let it rest there. At the end of June 1953, only two months before his deposition, he reaffirmed his views in a final appeal to the President of the Republic.[52] He had no lack of grounds for complaint. The revolt of the notables and the religious brotherhoods was clearly based upon a series of maneuvers executed according to a previously prepared plan. The Sultan declared them to be contrary to the Treaty of 1912, to the wishes of the French government, and to the desire for change he had himself shown concerning the delicate questions of judicial and municipal reform. He pointed out that if matters had rested with him, the most necessary reforms would already have been put into effect. It was impossible to ignore the fact, he said, that local difficulties, instead of being smoothed over by the Residency, had been deliberately aggravated. In the circumstances, he saw only one way of breaking the deadlock; he requested the French government to put an end to the crisis by a solemn declaration restoring the established order. He also requested that an overall plan be put into effect according to a prearranged schedule; this should reconcile once and for all the sovereignty of Morocco with the requirements of interdependence. Thus might all the problems be resolved that had poisoned the atmosphere for years.

The points made by the Sultan in his message of June 17 and in the subsequent appeal were, of course, embarrassing for the Quai d'Orsay. Although the Sultan knew he had all the urban population of Morocco behind him, he continued, as Léon Marchal indicated to the Minister, to demonstrate an attachment to France that gave every appearance of being genuine. His analysis of the causes of the conflict struck Marchal as irrefutable. The Residency had obviously not carried out the Quai d'Orsay's instructions regarding the assuaging of local difficulties. The Moroccan press had deliberately added fuel to the fire. The Residency was involved in the conspiracy of the notables. Every day the practices of the regime violated the spirit and the letter of the Treaty of Fez. How, therefore, could Mohammed V be sent back to negotiate directly with the Residency? How could the Quai d'Orsay cling to the comfortable myth, disproved by the

52. On July 3, the Sultan received Guillaume and handed him his letter to the President dated June 23. Guillaume arrived in Paris with the letter the next day.

facts, of the Residency's neutrality in a spontaneous quarrel between a feudal chief and notables? So convinced was Marchal that he was inclined to recommend that the Minister make the solemn declaration the Sultan requested, although he realized it would remain a dead letter if the Residency did not command the obedience of its subordinates. He had no objection to negotiating an overall plan, but he feared it might founder in the abyss that separated the government's position and the nationalist demand for immediate independence. He believed that if such a plan were to be seriously formulated, it would be necessary to go beyond the stage of partial reform and give unreserved consideration to a series of innovations consonant with the government's Moroccan policy. At all events, he deemed it necessary to study without delay the possibility of establishing a Moroccan legislature and executive based upon a system that would adequately safeguard individual rights.

It was the middle of July. Having presented these views to Bidault, Marchal urged particularly that the proposed plan be prepared by a special unit within the Department for Africa and the Levant. He thought that one competent official could carry out the task, provided he was empowered to call the Residency's experts to Paris for consultation. He made it quite clear to the Minister that if the studies were conducted in Rabat, they would be ipso facto doomed to failure.

The Quai d'Orsay was finishing where it should have begun, but the hour was too late to begin again. At Rabat, the machinery had got out of hand. From then until the end of August, the history of reform was to be tied to that of the conspiracy. The Sultan received no reply to his latest proposals. Overwhelmed by the crisis, the new government abandoned its efforts until, in an effort to avoid catastrophe, it authorized Guillaume to get the Sultan by hook or by crook to hand over his remaining legislative and regulatory powers in favor of joint Government Councils—thus destroying the Treaty of Fez with a stroke of the pen. Even this tremendous concession to a triumphant conspiracy did not save the Moroccan ruler. To explain this denouement it is necessary to examine the development of the notables' conspiracy while the insoluble problem of reform was being bandied back and forth interminably between Paris and Rabat.

THE 1953 CRISIS AND THE OFFICIAL VERSION (JANUARY–AUGUST 1953)

Cited below, to bring out the basic difference, so easily detectable today, between the official version of the 1953 crisis and the actual events, is the report submitted by the Quai d'Orsay to the National Assembly's Committee on Foreign Affairs as justification of Mohammed V's deposition.[53] The complete text is lengthy but of prime importance and gives a firsthand picture of the way events were reported to Parliament.

> Although the movement opposing the Sultan undoubtedly had its origin in more distant events, the starting-point can be taken as December 1950, the date on which the Nationalist Party delegates provoked the skirmish at the meeting of the Moroccan section of the Government Council. The Pasha of Marrakesh told Sidi Mohammed ben Youssef flatly that he no longer considered him the Sultan of Morocco, but "Sultan of the Istiqlal." This precipitated the public break.
>
> During the crisis of February 1951, when the Sultan refused to repudiate the Istiqlal, Berber horsemen camped before Rabat and under the walls of Fez, and demanded his deposition. This time they were appeased and order was restored.
>
> Nevertheless, el-Glaoui and his supporters had not given up. Meanwhile, the Sultan became more intransigent than ever in his demands to the French government, and the Istiqlal, encouraged by the United Nations debate on the Moroccan problem [autumn 1952], was increasing its agitation.

53. Ministère des affaires étrangères (Direction Afrique-Levant), Note du 4 Septembre 1953 (Paris 1953). While this is technically a state document, it has fallen into so many hands that it may be considered in the public domain. Incidentally, the tenor of this document was transmitted by the Minister for Foreign Affairs to all French diplomats overseas in a circular dated Sept. 13, 1953.

A few days after the twenty-fifth anniversary of Sidi Mohammed's accession to the throne, in an atmosphere of great excitement, the extremist Nationalist Party, with the help of the Communists, touched off the bloody incidents that took place in Casablanca on December 8–9, 1952. The repression which followed dealt a heavy blow to the Istiqlal and to its capacity to act.

For their part, the Moroccan circles which proclaimed their loyalty to France used the violent measures of the Istiqlal as an argument for demanding that Morocco and the Sultan extricate themselves from its grip. At the same time, the religious brotherhoods began to play a part in the campaign.

On February 5, 1953, a sharif belonging to an important brotherhood of the Derkaoua presided over a meeting at Meknes which was attended by many caids. On the twenty-third, at Marrakesh, some Zaouïa chiefs came to renew their fealty to el-Glaoui, while the Sharif Abedelhaï el-Kittani went to Algeria to make preparations for a congress of religious brotherhoods to be held at Fez in the spring.

This public opinion movement, hostile to the views and even the person of the Sultan, was echoed in certain French circles in Morocco by ever stronger complaints against Sidi Mohammed. The Ministry for Foreign Affairs therefore sent a message to General Guillaume on February 18, 1953, instructing him to be on guard.

Nevertheless, demonstrations by the Moroccan chiefs and leaders of the religious brotherhoods grew increasingly frequent.

On March 9 in Marrakesh, a public demonstration was held to protest the conduct of el-Ayadi, Caid of the Rehamna and longtime enemy of el-Glaoui.

On March 20, again in Marrakesh, following a meeting of some twenty caids with el-Glaoui, a petition was signed demanding the Sultan's removal. This document stated:

"(1) That Sultan Sidi Mohammed ben Youssef had

broken the commitments and covenants by which he was bound in regard to the Muslim religion and under which he bore obligations to the Moroccan people;

(2) That by attaching himself to illegal extremist parties and applying their principles in Morocco, he was leading the country to its doom;

(3) That in so doing, he had placed himself in opposition to all men of goodwill in the country and had embarked on a path contrary to the tenets of religion."

The signatories therefore asked the Resident-General of France and the French government to "remove" and "depose" the Sultan and to "give power to one worthy of it." This petition at once began to circulate among the Moroccan chiefs.

From April 4–6, the Congress of Religious Brotherhoods of North Africa was held at Fez, presided over by Sharif Abedelhaï el-Kittani, Grand Master of the Kittanines, in the presence of el-Glaoui and some twenty caids. The assembly was attended by about a thousand Moroccan delegates representing fifteen brotherhoods, 200 Zaouïas, 300 French Muslims from Algeria, and a few Tunisians. After listening to speeches against the Sultan, it adopted resolutions in favor of expanding the movement of the brotherhoods and of strengthening their ties in order to combat the "disturbers of Islam and of Muslim society."

On April 23, Sharif Kittani took part in a political meeting at Meknes organized by the Moroccan People's Party.

Finally, on the occasion of a military review for Marshal Juin on May 11 in the Moyen Atlas, 100,000 Berbers assembled, and in the eyes of the Moroccans this gathering took on the aspect of a demonstration against the Sultan.

In the face of all this agitation, the Sultan himself protested orally to the Resident-General of France on April 10, and on April 14 he wrote to the President of the Republic.

In this communication, Sidi Mohammed ben Youssef denied that the Congress of Fez had any competence whatsoever in religious matters. He also demanded that the representatives of the Residency display absolute neutrality, and he accused the contrôle authorities of being involved in the caids' petition.

A few days earlier, on April 1, the Minister for Foreign Affairs had confirmed his February 18 instructions to General Guillaume regarding the attitude of the French authorities toward the Sultan in the following terms:

"I am aware that certain persons already envisage the possibility that the Sultan may refuse to approve the reforms submitted to him and, indeed, are hoping he will do so. To deal with this eventuality they are advocating recourse to such extreme measures as the deposition of the Sultan or his forced abdication under pressure of carefully molded public opinion. . . . It must be made quite clear to everyone concerned that the French government would not condone recourse to such a policy."

On May 15, the Residency informed the Ministry that "the initiative [of the pashas and caids] seems to have attracted a much wider following than was at first expected." The next day, the Ministry, referring to this communication, reminded the Residency of its obligations under the protectorate treaty: the Resident's directives to the contrôle civil authorities on the attitude to be adopted toward the caids' petition were to conform with those obligations.

The petition was officially delivered to the Resident-General by the Pasha of Marrakesh on May 21. It bore the signatures of 250 pashas and caids, six religious leaders, and thirty-one notables. In his interview with General Guillaume on this occasion, el-Glaoui stressed the widespread nature of the movement of which he had assumed leadership, the firm resolve of those who had joined it, and the patriotic and religious character of the motives which guided them. He made a point of stating that the movement had arisen independently of the French authorities and that, far from being an instance of Berber anarchy, it was a sign of the awakening of the Moroccan people who opposed a Sultan "whose policy," he said, "is dangerous to the country's higher interests and whose conduct is contrary to the precepts of the Koran." He added that according to Muslim law, the *Oumna* (community of the faithful) was itself entitled to express its views on the capacity of the Imam without having to use the ulamas, who were only its agents, as spokesmen.

On May 29, *Agence France-Presse* published a report confirming that the Minister for Foreign Affairs had been informed by General Guillaume of the delivery of the petition. This report, while noting that "the importance of the sectors of Moroccan opinion from which this document emanates must not be underestimated," said that France had no "intention of taking political action, in the present circumstances, in reply to this initiative." The report concluded, "This action can only strengthen the government's determination to give democratic expression to the trends that are beginning to appear in Moroccan public opinion."

That same day, the Pasha of Marrakesh, who was passing through Paris, announced to the press that "the voice of the people has been heard through the mouths of its qualified representatives from the four corners of Morocco. For them and for me, the Sultan has already fallen. We await the approval of the French government with confidence."

On May 31, the Resident-General was given an audience at the Palace in Rabat. The Sultan protested strongly against the Moroccan chiefs' petition and against el-Glaoui's statements. General Guillaume stressed the spontaneity of the Moroccan chiefs' action and said that no doubt they were anxious to see Morocco freed from political crises caused by extremist agitation which boasted, without contradiction, of the Sultan's support, and they were worried because the reforms proposed by France had been rejected or postponed.

The Imperial Palace's reaction was embodied, on June 1, in a statement denying that the pashas and caids "vested by *dahir* of the Sultan with the power to represent him in the towns and in the country, had any right to rebel against the central authority without gravely contravening the most elementary rules of orderly government." It also refused to recognize "any capacity to express themselves concerning the general policy of His Majesty's Government, still less upon religious matters which have never been within their competence." In conclusion, the statement declared that they had no basis for "claiming to speak for those under them who had no part whatsoever at any stage in their appointment."

After referring to the "maneuvering and pressure" that had accompanied the collection of signatures to the petition, Sidi Mohammed ben Youssef called upon the French government to put an end to "this organized disaffection which is in danger of seriously compromising Franco-Moroccan relations and the tranquillity of the Sharifian Empire."

Throughout June, the dispute intensified between the supporters of the caids' movement and those loyal to the Sultan. Hundreds of cables were sent to the President of the Republic, the Minister for Foreign Affairs, and the Parisian newspapers, some affirming the signatories' unswerving support for the Sultan and others demanding an end to his tyranny and that of the Istiqlal.

The Pasha of Marrakesh went to London and attended the coronation festivities as the personal guest of Sir Winston Churchill. He then visited Paris where he was received by municipal officials and invited by Marshal Juin to the French Academy. From there he went to Vichy to take the waters.

The Sultan made a further protest in a letter of June

29 to the President of the Republic against "the machinations of the Pasha of Marrakesh," "the open rebellion of administrative officials against the central authority," and the actions of "a leader—and a disputed one at that—of a religious brotherhood," all of which constituted, according to him, "subversive activities contrary to the Treaty of 1912, and of Article 3 in particular."

In Morocco, new petitions against the Sultan were being circulated. All the opponents united in a text dated June 26 but not made public until August 1 when el-Glaoui delivered it to the Residency. It bore the signatures of 350 Moroccan chiefs and the five leaders of the principal brotherhoods. This document emphasized the "danger of disturbance" created by "the continuing delay in acting on" the March 20 petition and affirmed the petitioners' confidence in the Pasha of Marrakesh, "whom they recognized as their leader and whom they authorized to speak in their name."

The text was accompanied by a statement, dated July 2, giving "full powers" in regard to policy "to the eminent leader of the opposition movement, the Pasha el-Glaoui," and in matters connected with the Muslim religion to the Sharif el-Kittani. It recalled the opposition of the signatories to the Istiqlal Party extremists and to "anyone who assists them, even the holder of supreme power in Morocco," and requested "the French Nation to deliver our people from these Istiqlal Party extremists and anyone who helps them."

With the return of the Pasha of Marrakesh to Morocco, events followed one another in swift succession. Si Thami el-Glaoui left Paris on July 28 and on July 30 arrived in Casablanca where he was met by 150 pashas and caids, the leaders of several religious brotherhoods, and about 2,000 notables. He said to the press, "All believers should dissociate themselves from the Sultan. France must do what is right."

He then began a lengthy tour which was to take on

the aspect of a popular election campaign. On August 4, he was at Agadir, on August 5 at Marrakesh, on the sixth at Khourigba, the seventh at Marchand, the eighth at Adjir, the ninth at Sefrou, the tenth at Oudja and Taza, the eleventh at Teroual.

On the afternoon of the eleventh, the journey that had become a sort of triumphal progress came to a halt at the holy city of Mulay Idriss, where el-Glaoui met the Sharif el-Kittani. There, after a ritual sacrifice, the Pasha arranged a meeting with his supporters for five P.M. on August 13 at Marrakesh.

However, on August 11 the Moroccan crisis took a sudden turn for the worse. In a cable sent by special messenger—which was reported to the Minister for Foreign Affairs immediately upon his return from Germany—the Deputy Minister to the Residency reported a conversation he had had on August 7 with the Pasha of Marrakesh: with the backing of the Moroccan authorities and the leaders of the religious brotherhoods, the Pasha had openly declared that his aim was to proclaim the deposition of Sidi Mohammed and the enthronement of a new Sultan. De Blesson had remonstrated that such serious measures could not be contemplated without the consent of the protecting power and that the latter, owing to the obligations it had assumed both toward Morocco and to the international community, could only give its support to a solution that would take into account all the factors and interests involved, including of course the legitimate claims of the movement of the pashas and caids. El-Glaoui had promised De Blesson not to take any action before he had seen him again at the end of his tour, that is, toward the middle of the following week.

While the Minister for Foreign Affairs was being informed of this message, De Blesson telephoned Paris to say that because of the triumphal character of his tour, el-Glaoui was now having some difficulty in restraining his followers. The Deputy Minister asked for instructions on what to say to el-Glaoui in the course of the conversation planned for the next day, August 12.

In the Foreign Minister's opinion, the sudden aggravation of the crisis did not constitute sufficient justification for the French government to renounce its obligation to act as mediator. In keeping with that role, it had prepared a plan of reforms for submission to the Sultan at the beginning of August that was even then under examination by the Residency. The latter was supposed to make its views known within two or three weeks. Obviously, el-Glaoui's movement was gathering momentum and quicker action was called for.

Accordingly, the following instructions were sent to De Blesson at the end of the morning of August 12:

"The French government could not agree to being presented with a fait accompli by anyone, nor could it agree to the possibilities of arbitration being compromised by action taken without its consent. The Deputy Minister should therefore transmit as soon as possible the anticipated comments on the reforms proposed as the basis for a settlement and also should instruct el-Glaoui to call a halt for the time being in order to allow France to intervene and settle the dispute."

The task of communicating this message and of reaching a settlement fell to General Guillaume. As a result of transport and communication difficulties caused by the strikes, the Resident-General could only be reached in the course of the day of August 12. He reached Paris in the evening, was received by the Minister for Foreign Affairs and then by the Prime Minister, and left for Rabat that same night.

In the meantime, De Blesson had persuaded el-Glaoui to agree to suspend all action until he could talk to the Resident-General.

General Guillaume was the bearer of a full-fledged plan for a settlement: he was to ask the Sultan to sign a certain number of reforms enabling the French government to disarm its opponents and restore calm. These reforms had a dual aspect. They were designed to transfer a large part of the Sultan's temporal powers, which his subjects accused him of abusing and which had enabled him to frustrate the French desire for reform. His regulatory powers were to be delegated by him to the Grand Vizier sitting in a Limited Council of six members, Moroccan and French. His legislative powers, in matters not religious or constitutional, were to be delegated to the Grand Vizier sitting in the Council of Viziers and Directors (established in 1947). These practical reforms were accompanied by others of a specifically liberal character. They constituted a complete plan of judicial reform through the establishment of courts staffed by professional magistrates, the separation of executive and judicial powers, the promulgation of a penal code, and a code of criminal procedure . . . In addition, they established a system of elected municipalities and regional assemblies also to be elected . . . If the Sultan accepted the proposed plan, a joint declaration by Sidi Mohammed and the Resident-General would announce the agreement to the Moroccan people, and this would constitute both an agreement on the future of Franco-Moroccan relations and a charter between the Sultan and his subjects. The text of the declaration stipulated, inter alia, that "the problems posed by the evolution of the Sharifian Empire are the exclusive concern of France and Morocco. Any external interference could only delay or compromise the solution."

August 12, which Paris had spent in drafting these texts and giving General Guillaume his instructions, was calm throughout Morocco. The Sultan issued an appeal to the President of the Republic, the French government, and the French public to put an end to the situation in Morocco. This document recapitulated all the Sultan had said and done on behalf of Franco-Moroccan cooperation. In that connection, it is significant that he was unable to quote any of his words subsequent to

1939–40. El-Glaoui, to whom De Blesson had been authorized to convey the broad outlines of the reforms drawn up in Paris—with a view to securing his interest and thus gaining time—expressed his satisfaction with them, but nevertheless did not agree to halt his action against the person of Sidi Mohammed.

In these circumstances, General Guillaume undertook his difficult task of mediation between August 13 and 15.

The Resident-General went first to the Sultan's Palace, where he was received on August 13 at 4:30 P.M. Sidi Mohammed so clearly realized the desperateness of his situation that he agreed without discussion to the draft settlement submitted to him. By 6:30, the Resident-General had received his agreement on all points in the joint declaration and on all reforms corollary to it.

General Guillaume then turned his attention to the Sultan's opponents, who were holding a meeting at Marrakesh at which they hoped to place the seal of success on their undertaking. More than 300 pashas and caids (nine pashas out of 23 and 309 caids out of 325) were gathered about el-Glaoui and the Sharif Kittani, each accompanied by ten notables from their tribes or towns, prepared to proclaim the fall of the Sultan and announce his successor. They were excited by the atmosphere of their meeting, bound to each other by a religious vow not to return to their tribes until they had achieved their aim, and fearing that if they should fail they would lose the respect of their subjects and incur the vengeance of a Sultan still enthroned. They constituted a compact bloc which was difficult to approach and more difficult still to convince. As soon as Guillaume had obtained the Sultan's agreement, he sent Vallat, Director of the Interior, to Marrakesh that same evening and he, together with the Chief of the Marrakesh Region, General d'Hauteville, tried to persuade el-Glaoui and his associates to abandon their goal.

In the meantime, the threat of decisive action loomed

greater. On the night of the thirteenth, French and foreign press services reported that a new Sultan would be proclaimed at nine o'clock the next morning. The Minister for Foreign Affairs ordered General Guillaume by telephone and by cable to call el-Glaoui to Casablanca for a face-to-face interview, while his emissaries at Marrakesh tried to disperse the meeting. No partisan uprising was to be tolerated. But, the general excitement was such that while Guillaume carried out his instructions at once, the Moroccans did not.

On the morning of the fourteenth, General Guillaume sent further emissaries to Marrakesh. Before intervening himself, he was awaiting the arrival of Bidault's personal representative, Vimont, Assistant Director of the Minister's personal staff, whom Bidault had decided to send on condition that he was not faced on arrival with a fait accompli.

He succeeded in persuading the Moroccan leaders to agree to a further delay until August 15 at 10 A.M.

The discussions between General Guillaume, Vimont, and the Moroccan leaders began on August 15 at 9 A.M. and lasted five hours. Bidault had written to the Pasha of Marrakesh listing the concessions obtained from the Sultan and asking him to declare himself satisfied and to leave to France the responsibility for their implementation.

El-Glaoui did not give Guillaume and Vimont the impression of being absolutely opposed to compromise. However, he was swept forward by the ardor of the troops he had assembled, as was evident when a delegation of about fifteen pashas and caids was called to take part in the conversations. Not only did they refuse, for the reasons outlined above, to return home without having achieved their purpose, but their response to the account of the reforms obtained from the Sultan was that Sidi Mohammed's word was not to be trusted and that to leave him on his throne after the threat of losing it would mean that sooner or later not only would the

Moroccan leaders be exposed to his vengeance but also
the French in Morocco. They urged Guillaume and
Vimont "not to betray those who had never betrayed
them, for the benefit of a man who was their enemy
only because he was first and foremost an enemy of
France." Guillaume brought to bear all his prestige, not
only as Resident-General but also as military leader during the time of the pacification of Morocco and in the
Italian campaign. Many of the caids present were the
sons or brothers of those who had yielded to France
(and not to the Sultan). Many had fought under him in
1943. Using memories and arguments out of this common past, he succeeded after several hours in shaking
their determination to some extent. Finally, they agreed
to disperse without proclaiming either the deposition or
the replacement of the Sultan, and to leave it to France
to "settle the problem of the Moroccan throne." For
themselves, they were more than ever decided not to
recognize Sidi Mohammed as their temporal or spiritual
ruler any longer. In particular, they would no longer
agree to have the Friday prayer said in areas under their
jurisdiction in the name of a man they had repudiated
before God. Guillaume could obviously neither give nor
withhold the right to choose a new Imam for the prayer
ceremony. They were all agreed that this was a matter
of individual religious choice; no name was mentioned
for the new Imam, but many of those present thought it
preferable for the prayer to be said in the name of the
Muslim community rather than in that of a specific
person, particularly since no authorization had been
given for the enthronement of a new Imam.

The appointment of Sidi Mohammed ben Arafa as
Imam, which was carried out in el-Glaoui's gardens two
hours after General Guillaume's departure, had therefore no canonical value. When Guillaume heard about
it, he gave Rabat orders for the immediate cancellation
of other ceremonies organized by el-Glaoui that would
have given the appointment of the Imam a more official

character—enthronement in the great mosque at Kou-
toubia and installation in the Imperial Palace at Marrakesh. El-Glaoui did not demur. At the time it still
seemed as if it might be possible to settle the question of
the throne peacefully by minimizing the scope of preparations for proclaiming a new Imam and by bringing
to bear all the influence of the contrôle authorities on
the caids once they had returned to their tribes.

However, the publicity given by the Moroccan newspapers on August 16 to the ceremony at Marrakesh
(responsibility for which has been falsely attributed in
some quarters to General Guillaume) brought these
hopes to nothing.

In addition, the Sultan urged the whole Muslim community to bear witness to the insult inflicted upon him
by his "schismatic" subjects. Last, although the pashas
and caids did return to their homes, they left behind
them at Marrakesh a new Imam whom they intended to
treat as their religious leader on all occasions beginning
with the festival of Aïd el-Kebir, which was to take
place on August 21. Again, the Residency and the government were faced with an extremely short time in
which to make a major decision.

Obviously, such uncertainty could not continue much
longer; even before the Sultan's appeal became known,
there had been incidents in Rabat on the morning of
August 16, provoked by troublemakers coming especially from Casablanca. On the preceding evening, in
Marrakesh, an Istiqlal demonstration had resulted in
eight deaths. After the Sultan's proclamation, sporadic
disturbances broke out in Meknes, Casablanca, and
Oudja in particular, where they continued into the
night and caused about twenty deaths. The Grand
Vizier, undisputed and revered leader of the Sharifian
Maghzen, did not come out unequivocally on the side of
the reigning sovereign but confined himself to advising
the Residency to announce its choice without delay. The
Sultan, for his part, instructed Vimont, who had come

to pay him a visit, to ask the French government to
recognize him publicly as the sole spiritual and temporal
ruler of Morocco, failing which he would refuse to sign
the decrees implementing the joint declaration.

Faced with this state of affairs, the government had to
weigh the conflicting elements involved in order to
arbitrate in accordance with its treaty obligations as regards the future of the throne and the domestic peace of
Morocco. This it did on August 18–19.

It seemed to the government at first that it could not
abandon its task of mediation while any possibility of
reconciliation remained.

On the evening of August 19, therefore, General Guillaume left with instructions to call el-Glaoui to Casablanca to determine whether and on what conditions
the activities of his supporters could be halted and Sidi
Mohammed kept on the throne, and whether the Pasha
would regard as sufficient a formal condemnation of the
Istiqlal Party by the Sultan. If so, Guillaume was to go
at once to Rabat and obtain the Sultan's consent. In the
meantime, everything possible should be done on the
eve of Aïd el-Kebir to prevent the tribes from gathering
and marching either to Marrakesh to acclaim a new
Sultan or to Rabat to dethrone the present one by force.

General Guillaume in fact saw the Pasha of Marrakesh at Casablanca on August 20 at 6 A.M. By 7, he informed Paris that el-Glaoui maintained his implacable
opposition to Sidi Mohammed ben Youssef.

The Council of Ministers, when it met that morning,
had therefore two choices. To keep Sidi Mohammed on
the throne, it would in all probability have been obliged
to use military force against the chiefs and the many
people who were still loyal to the French presence and
mission in Morocco. In any event, this solution would
have produced lasting disillusionment, out of which
would have come either their union with the enemies
of France, or else disaffection, concealed or overt, that

would have resulted in growing insecurity throughout the country.

Exiling the Sultan would doubtless have produced certain protests, notably from the Arab states, and perhaps a reaction from supporters of the Istiqlal and elements under its influence.

However, by exiling the disputed Sultan, France would have strengthened the ties that bound the faithful majority of Moroccans to her; by keeping him on his throne, she could have expected no more than the persistent ingratitude which he had so long displayed toward her.

General Guillaume was therefore instructed to go to the Sultan and to make quite plain to him the demands of the situation. The tribes were rising on every side. The Grand Vizier had declared himself ready to support and sanction whatever solution was chosen. The Sultan could therefore no longer count on either his people or on the Maghzen. France, anxious at least to save his person and his family and to safeguard the dynasty, advised him to abdicate. Sidi Mohammed refused to abdicate but said he was ready to leave Morocco with his two sons. He departed at 4 P.M. in a military aircraft bound for Corsica.

One question remained: that of Sidi Mohammed's successor. There was general agreement that Sidi Mohammed ben Arafa was the best fitted of the Alaouit family to rule; moreover, he had for years been the choice of those concerned with the question of a successor to the throne in the event of Sidi Mohammed's death. Furthermore, the claimant had been born and brought up in Fez and would have no particular ties with Marrakesh. This was evidenced by his behavior in the first few days, especially in his initial choice of associates and representatives. On the afternoon of August 20, it was essential to reach a prompt solution if trouble was to be avoided because of the sovereign's absence on Aïd el-Kebir. The Grand Vizier beseeched the Resident-General to authorize him to proclaim, as was his traditional duty, a new sultan in the person of Sidi Mohammed ben Arafa. He claimed the latter already had the support of the rural areas; the Grand Vizier and the Maghzen would bring him support from the towns. Thus, the unity of Morocco could be immediately reestablished if France consented.

However, France could consent only after due deliberation. It was with full awareness of all the factors involved that the government decided, at the last meeting of the Council of Ministers late in the afternoon, to allow traditional procedure in the appointment of Sidi Mohammed ben Arafa. At 8 P.M., the Grand Vizier declared the throne vacant, proclaimed the new Sultan, and sent a letter to each of the pashas of the cities of Morocco requesting the allegiance of the ulama, the chorfas (nobles), and the notables to the person of the new sovereign. By the next day, testimonies of support were pouring in. The first to respond was Fez, where all the ulama of Karaouyne save one, all the members of the Alaouit family, and all the religious and intellectual leaders gave the requested oath of allegiance.

At the same time, absolute calm reigned in all the cities of Morocco. Even in those towns where four days earlier the Istiqlal had risen to the Sultan's call, there was quiet after his departure. Nor was this attributable merely to security measures, for there were only 72 precautionary arrests, and not more than a thousand arrests of persons actually committing offenses, which were made for the most part during the incidents of August 16.

On August 22, the new Sultan, Sidi Mohammed ben Arafa, took possession of the Palace at Rabat, and with this, the Sharifian Maghzen and the pashas and caids, who had grown progressively further apart since 1950, were reconciled without further difficulty.

ANALYSIS OF THE OFFICIAL VERSION

Such was the governmental version of the 1953 crisis. Although the liberals were not incorrect in their interpretation of events at the time, the government's efforts to clear itself of responsibility were not entirely wasted. In fact, it was so successful that some distinguished people in France still believe a version of the affair that is not perceptibly different from that of the government.[54] While it is understandable that a politician involved in a serious governmental crisis (in this case, Bidault) should take certain liberties with historical truth, history is not politics and it is important to reconstitute the facts as far as possible. The Residency's planning of the fait accompli, its deliberate concealment, the overt and active intervention of the contrôle civil, were all prefigured by the precedent of February 1951 and by Schuman's disenchanted confidences to La Nef.[55] But this is not all; the plot is proved beyond a shadow of a doubt by the information collected in the course of this investigation.

It is therefore essential to analyze the official version, approaching it from different angles in order to correct the errors in the government's account and to fill in the usual gaps which such a simplified analysis of the crisis inevitably involves.

THE ROLE OF THE RESIDENTIAL AUTHORITIES AND THE CONTRÔLE CIVIL

Contrary to the Quai d'Orsay's insinuations, the first shots in the campaign were fired not in February 1953 by the leaders of the religious brotherhoods but in January by el-Glaoui and the

54. A former liberal Prime Minister summarized his conception of the crisis, during an interview as follows: "The government allowed itself to be confronted with a fait accompli. Everyone deceived everyone else. The Prime Minister trusted Bidault; Bidault thought Guillaume was behind him; Guillaume, that De Blesson obeyed him; De Blesson that he influenced Boniface; and Boniface that he had a firm grip on el-Glaoui. In short, it was el-Glaoui who played his hand openly in the belief that Boniface, De Blesson, Guillaume, and Joseph Laniel secretly approved of him. Each, similarly, thought the others would agree in the end. Each moved as in a complicated machine, where each gear has greater play than the preceding." We hope to demonstrate below that this view is obviously alien to the facts. Each actor was deceived by the other but each one (at least in Rabat) knew it. This does not mean, however, that the denouement can be explained in depth by such trivia.

55. Schuman, "Nécessité d'une politique."

top French officials, with clandestine support from the Moroccan Radical Socialists.

On January 1, Émile Eyraud had conveyed to Boniface the pleas of elected officials. The latter had replied that Paris had given assurance that France would not let the French in Morocco decline from the rank of protector to protected nor be ousted from the administration of a country they had remade.[56] On January 2, in a sensational interview accorded the special correspondent of the Madrid monarchist newspaper A.B.C., el-Glaoui violently attacked the Sultan, whom he accused of encouraging a seditious movement which the Moroccan people, still incapable of governing themselves, were far from approving.[57] On January 10, the Moroccan Radical Socialists congratulated René Mayer on the formation of his government and reminded him that they counted on his understanding of North African affairs to defend the French presence in Morocco.[58] Three days later, Boniface received a delegation from the religious brotherhoods of eastern Morocco en route to Marrakesh and solemnly wished them "a good journey and every success." [59] This was the first public reappearance of the brotherhoods; the role they were soon to play is already known.

On February 7, after conducting an inquiry in Residential circles, Raymond Cartier published an article in *Paris-Match* headed, "Either the Sultan Must Change or We Must Change the Sultan." In this famous article, the whole plan that was to be put into effect from that very day was expounded in detail in striking summation: a month before the notables' petition for the Sultan's abdication was drawn up, the French public learned that 325 caids and pashas no longer wanted the Sultan—which was, to say the least, an astonishing piece of foresight. Of course, there had been a constant counting of heads among the conspirators for two years.

At first, collusion between the Residential authorities and the notables was merely passive. The administration, which had shown its hand once before in 1951, thought it preferable to

56. *La Vigie marocaine* (Jan. 1, 1953).
57. *Maroc-Presse* (Jan. 3, 1953).
58. *La Vigie marocaine* (Jan. 10, 1953).
59. *Maroc-Presse* (Jan. 13, 1953).

begin by demonstrating a policy of laissez-faire toward the notables, who were, in fact, carefully instructed by the administrative representatives most deeply involved. The complete freedom of movement and speech enjoyed by the caids and the leaders of the brotherhoods in Morocco, once action was resumed, implied open Residential approval. The system was such that the caids never took any political initiative without consulting their respective contrôleurs. No senior Moroccan official could move about the country without the approval of a contrôleur civil or of an indigenous affairs officer. The Sultan's own officials could no longer go to the Palace without authorization. Freedom of speech and assembly depended entirely upon the Residency's goodwill. The caids' plot could not have developed without the support of the French authorities, and no one at Paris could have been unaware of this.

In addition, the contrôleurs civils were openly and increasingly encouraged by the Department of the Interior's *Bulletin de renseignement,* which brought them a monthy report on the situation in Morocco and portrayed the movement in terms that left no doubt about the Department's feelings in the matter. Thus, the question of responsibility may be considered as predetermined, for an authoritarian regime that does not forbid, approves.

The relative caution displayed in the first few weeks did not prevent the leaders of the plot from shortly burning their bridges. By the end of May, Boniface (who rightly considered himself powerful enough to brave the thunder of the Quai d'Orsay) granted an interview to the journalist Alexander Werth of the *New Statesman and Nation* of London. This provided material for a series of articles on Morocco.[60] Casting caution to the winds, the Regional Commissioner for Casablanca described the Sultan with barely concealed scorn as a sort of führer seeking only to increase his influence by so-called reforms. The writer received similar statements from other high French officials. They made no attempt to disguise their intention to set the Berbers against the Arabs, encourage the religious brotherhoods

60. *The New Statesman and Nation* (May 30, 1953), p. 633; (June 6, 1953), p. 666; (June 13, 1953), pp. 695–96.

of the south and the great overlords to unite against the Sultan
and ultimately to depose him—or, at the very worst, to isolate
him once and for all. The Quai d'Orsay was furious and demanded an explanation. Boniface denied everything, and there
the matter rested.

Juin's patronage of el-Glaoui was also a striking example of
the way the highest French authorities intervened in the conspiracy.[61] At Queen Elizabeth II's coronation on June 2, el-
Glaoui stated that in the eyes of the pashas and caids the Sultan
had already fallen.[62] This announcement was more important in
context than in content, since it indicated that the Residency
would no longer be hampered by diplomatic interventions of the
kind that had cut short the 1951 attempt. The conspirators
profited, most opportunely, from accusations of collusion with
communism and hostility to the North Atlantic Treaty Organization made against the Istiqlal and the Sultan shortly after the
Casablanca incidents.

Toward the end of the month, el-Glaoui left London for Paris,
where Juin promptly took him in tow. On June 25, the Pasha
attended the ceremony under the Institute dome at which Juin
was made a member of the French Academy. In his speech of
appreciation, the Marshal made a sharp attack, in his guest's
presence, on François Mauriac. A sharp exchange ensued, which
was only one more episode in the war of words and ideas unleashed by the Moroccan lobby in Paris after the Casablanca
incident.

Throughout August, el-Glaoui and Sharif el-Kittani were increasingly threatening toward France. On the eighth, in an
interview with *Le Petit Marocain,* el-Glaoui and the Sharif requested that they be left free to choose another Sultan. They said
the movement was based solely on the will of the people and
demanded that the French authorities not hinder it; otherwise, el-
Kittani declared, "We shall accuse the French government of
being in league with the M.R.P. and communism against our

61. Bidault, who was not on the best of terms with Juin, alluded to this in his note
to the Assembly's Committee on Foreign Affairs, but did not indicate the complexity
and significance of the situation.

62. Barrat, p. 104; see also Montagne, pp. 237–38.

national religion." On August 18, in another interview in *Le Petit Marocain,* the Pasha of Marrakesh returned to the charge and went so far as to declare that the Moroccan people were awaiting a decision. He added that unless the government acted immediately and firmly there would no longer be any place for France in Morocco. He announced that he, el-Glaoui, would save Morocco come what might, even if it cost him the friendship of France he valued so much. The personal intervention of the highest ranking officer of the French army tended in any case to prove to the activists of the Residency that there was no longer any great risk and that the time had come for them to leave the wings and make their entry upon the stage. To succeed in the operation that had failed two years before, they had only to mobilize the Berber horsemen: this was promptly done by the contrôle civil, and on August 19 they besieged Fez.

Almost nobody now in Morocco denies the administration's intervention. Only one or two of those directly responsible for the movement professed, during interviews, to uphold the threadbare argument of a local uprising that the authorities had allowed to develop "because it was tempting to see a pro-French movement come to grips with France's Enemy Number One." [63] This is mere fiction. On the second occasion as on the first, the horsemen were called out and assembled by orders of the contrôle civil, which was itself set in motion by the regional authorities.

A former government adviser, a well-known settler, explained matters with great detachment:

> The year 1951 was an unsuccessful dress rehearsal for the 1953 affair. It is indisputable that there was even then a coalition involving nearly all the senior French civil servants, the army, and the loyal Moroccans. General Juin did not push the operation very far. He thought it needed more time and feared that by supporting it he might compromise the extra two stars he was still hoping for. It was then that he thought of General Guillaume for the future. . . . The same operation was

63. From an interview with a high Residency official.

launched in 1953. As under Juin, the regional officials
urged us on. The conspiracy profited from circumstance
—the August strikes and so on. Even the Resident's absence was useful to us, since it made the revolt look
more spontaneous. Only one official opposed it: Hutin.
. . . Once again, in 1953, there was unanimous opposition to the Sultan, at least among the French.

One of the few contrôleurs civils who frankly opposed the
pressure of the regional authorities provided the following account of a tragi-comic scene in which he was a most unwilling
actor.

In August 1953, as in February 1951, I was almost the
only senior official on duty in the territory who refused
to participate. General d'Hauteville telephoned me to
send my men. I refused and told him they wanted peace
and had no use for el-Glaoui. I only agreed to send ten
of them to the assembly point, but warned the general
they would refuse to join the movement. That was what
happened. A little later, General d'Hauteville told me
over the telephone: "The Sultan has gone. We now
have another, a nice old chap who won't bother us."
The general asked me to send him a list of names to be
purged. I refused. He warned me I should be called
again. Vallat called me. Finally, I hung up.

When, a few months later, a parliamentary committee of inquiry arrived in Morocco, Eyraud made no effort to conceal the
fact (according to certain respondents) that the French authorities had fostered the operation from the start. Although their
leading role in the August 1953 affair is undeniable, it must be
recognized that the coup could not have succeeded if many
Moroccan notables had not considered themselves threatened by
the policy of the Sultan and the Istiqlal: the Residency would
have been helpless had it not been able to base its activities on the
genuine hostility of a group of notables toward the Palace. The
majority were trapped between the Residency, the great caids,

and the fear of having the Sultan emerge victorious from the struggle. They temporized, signed the petition, then retracted, and abandoned the Sultan again, with the Grand Vizier at their head, when it became obvious that the Residency was winning. To this body of notables, handpicked by the French and so often purged in the past, it was essential not to be caught on the losing side. The most loyal followed the movement reluctantly once there was no other choice. The rest were influenced by a mixture of conservatism, opportunism, and fear.[64]

INTERVENTION OF THE DEPUTY MINISTER AND THE CAMOUFLAGE
OF THE PLOT

The way Bidault was deceived by his representative at Rabat reveals, even better than the events recounted in the last section, the Residency's double game. Although the notables' petition was signed on March 20 and the Residency learned of it the same day, De Blesson did not inform the Quai d'Orsay until two weeks later—and then he did not attach the text to his report. The petition was not officially delivered to the Resident-General until May 21, but it was not until the end of May—two and a half months after signature—that Guillaume gave Bidault the original text, in Paris.

De Blesson's first report to the Quai d'Orsay at the end of March was a masterpiece of its kind. He viewed the petition as a simple demonstration of Moroccan conservative opposition. As the delayed expression of a crisis already over, he said, it presaged no new events and was unimportant. El-Glaoui himself had had nothing to do with it. The text had appeared spontaneously and had had random circulation. The French authorities had not been involved at all.

After such a soothing preamble, Bidault's sharp reaction to De Blesson's May 15 dispatch, which for the first time intimated to Paris the real gravity of the situation, is understandable: hence the Minister's cable of the 16th, enjoining the Residency to remind the contrôle authorities that their attitude toward the movement must conform with France's obligations under the

64. See pp. 496 ff. and 566 ff.

protectorate Treaty. Either these instructions were meaningless or they meant that the Residency should take el-Glaoui into custody, send the caids back to their districts, and take all the necessary steps to preclude further talk of the petition.

De Blesson, despite this sounding of the alarm, continued to lull the Ministry by minimizing the importance of events and by either delaying information or by meting it out in small doses. In June, the Residency went so far as to inform the Quai d'Orsay that it was the administration's duty to allow Moroccan public opinion to express itself freely against the Sultan, adding that the caids should not be compared to civil servants but to feudal chiefs in conflict with their suzerain, which was precisely el-Glaoui's argument.

This shift in the Residency's thinking came just at the moment when heavy pressure was being exerted on the Grand Vizier, Hadj Mohammed el-Mokri, to force him to withdraw a protest issued by the Sultan against the petition. On June 1, in the very midst of the crisis, a significant incident occurred in Rabat that set the Grand Vizier and De Blesson at loggerheads. The latter, although he regarded the caids' petition as a legitimate demonstration of Moroccan public opinion, balked when the Grand Vizier released to the press the protest the Sultan had just made against the notables' manifesto. De Blesson at once urged the Grand Vizier, without success, either to withdraw or to amend the Palace's communiqué.[65]

In July, when a new series of petitions began to circulate in the protectorate, De Blesson pretended to know nothing about them, and continued to report to Paris as if nothing of importance was brewing in Morocco. El-Glaoui, returning from Paris at the end of the month, landed in Casablanca, where Boniface gave him a ceremonial reception. This was just before the tour the old Berber chieftain was preparing to make of Morocco, starting from Agadir, in order to rouse his supporters. De Blesson,

65. El-Glaoui, who participated as a third party in all important aspects of Moroccan policy, attempted a strange move the next day that was presumably intended to alienate the Sultan and the Grand Vizier. Calling upon De Blesson as witness, he maintained that the Grand Vizier had released the communiqué without having had the chance to read it.

reporting to the Minister on the Pasha's departure for Agadir, merely remarked with his usual apathy that el-Glaoui was making the journey in response to private invitations received on his return from France.

Bidault was vexed at receiving no news from Rabat which, to use the words of one of those interviewed, "he could not have got out of the papers," and demanded a complete report on the aims of the movement's leaders. He emphasized again that the government would not recognize any fait accompli that might compromise its position as mediator. De Blesson replied that nothing seemed to herald such an eventuality, that it would suffice for the Residency to instruct the regional commissioners to keep careful watch, and that he himself would ask el-Glaoui to be prudent.

El-Glaoui's great tour through Morocco from August 4 to 7 was reduced in De Blesson's reports to a kind of folk festival with no political overtones. According to him, there was nothing but banquets, games, and dancing. Thus, according to the Deputy Minister, on August 7, the very eve of the denouement, nothing at all was happening in Morocco. Even if anything were, the Residency would have been ill advised to pay attention. This feeling was so prevalent at Rabat that Guillaume, then at Vichy, was planning to continue his holiday in the Alps.

The climax came August 7. Until then, all was quiet in Morocco. The next day, it was too late. On the eighth, Paris learned from De Blesson over the telephone that el-Glaoui, surprised by the success of the movement, was no longer in control of his forces. The die was cast. There was nothing to do but "fire upon the friends of France" or recognize the fait accompli.

Léon Marchal then learned through the Pasha of Sefrou, Si Bekkaï ben M'Barek, that the proclamation of a new sultan was imminent and would be followed shortly by a politico-religious demonstration to be held at Mulay Idriss, near Fez. On August 11, therefore, the day Bidault returned from Germany, Marchal persuaded him to call Guillaume to Paris, and to hand him that evening instructions which could now be considered final.

FAILURE OF THE VIMONT MISSION AND THE ATTITUDE OF THE FRENCH
GOVERNMENT

Since the formation of the Laniel government at the end of
June 1953, no cabinet had received any communication from the
Quai d'Orsay regarding Morocco. Edgar Faure, Minister for
Finance and Economic Affairs in the Laniel Cabinet, had received a visit from Guillaume in July. The latter had not concealed the fact that certain circles in Rabat were working actively
for the Sultan's deposition. He had even told Faure that pressure
had been put on him to bring this about during the governmental crisis prior to Laniel's entry into office, but that he had
refused. Guillaume's manifest determination to act as the faithful
executor of the government's instructions and the fact that he
had not felt obliged to forgo his vacation had led Faure to
conclude that the rumors he had heard were exaggerations, or at
least premature.

It was not until about August 10, when news of De Blesson's
pessimistic cable began to circulate, that certain ministers realized something out of the ordinary was brewing at Rabat.
Once again alerted, Faure went to Laniel on August 13 to
inform him of his fears. The Prime Minister told him he had
just seen Guillaume, who was returning to Rabat with a settlement plan drawn up by the Minister for Foreign Affairs and
approved by the Prime Minister. This plan, to which the Quai
d'Orsay's report repeatedly refers and the preamble of which has
been discussed in the course of this study, is of first importance
not only because it reveals that the Prime Minister knew exactly
what was happening in Morocco at that moment, but also because it assumed in advance responsibility for all the cosovereignty
reforms the Residency was to put into effect in Morocco immediately after Sultan ben Arafa's accession to the throne.

The preamble to the Ministry's instructions noted first that the
strategem being elaborated was contrary to the country's traditional policy and that realization of the conspirators' aims would
mean the end of France in Morocco. It was also affirmed, with
some justification, that the attitude adopted hitherto by the
Deputy Ministry toward Paris was unacceptable. The instructions

entrusted the Resident-General, and him alone, with the task of persuading the Sultan to agree at once to the transfer of his regulatory and legislative powers to the Grand Vizier, sitting either in the Limited Council or in the Council of Viziers and Directors; and to sign en bloc all the administrative and judicial reforms previously submitted to him. Paris considered the establishment of elected local and regional assemblies especially urgent. It was formally stipulated that once the Sultan had agreed, the notables would have to comply.

As soon as Guillaume arrived in Rabat, he set about carrying out the first point in his program. On the fateful day, August 13, 1953, French forces surrounded the Palace. While the Crown Prince was kept under surveillance, the Resident-General was received by the Sultan at four P.M. After a fifteen-minute audience, the Resident-General handed the ruler the text of a protocol stripping him of all his essential powers and demanded its immediate signature. After confirmation in writing that the document did in fact emanate from the government, the Sultan signed at 6:55 P.M.; he had been told that if he refused to give in, a telephone call from Paris would order his deposition.[66]

The second part of the settlement brought back by Guillaume from Paris was put into force with much less determination than the first. Once the protocol had been signed, the next step was to get the notables to abandon their project. The Resident-General might have been expected to assume personal responsibility for this delicate task, the success of which depended primarily on the prestige and determination of the person undertaking it. This was not the case. Either through resignation to the inevitable or through collusion with his subordinates, on the evening of August 13, Guillaume delegated the task of persuading el-Glaoui to be reasonable to Vallat, Director of the Department of the Interior, and d'Hauteville, Regional Commissioner for Marrakesh. El-Glaoui and his supporters were duly reprimanded by those who had been inciting them to extreme measures for the past six months, and remained unmoved.

On August 14, Bidault congratulated Guillaume on the success of his interview with the Sultan the evening before and then

66. Barrat, p. 198.

drove him into a corner. He told him in substance that the government did not approve of the financial and reactionary aims of the conspiracy and that any personal policy would be punished, even if successful. He added that in view of the difficult times the country was going through, (referring to the transport strikes that had begun August 9), he would not tolerate, at Rabat, any policy but the government's. The supporters of that policy, Bidault continued, must be brought into line, particularly now that the Sultan had yielded and no further concessions could be requested. Considering the report of the imminent proclamation of a new Sultan as a defiance of French authority—in view of the agreement reached with Mohammed V and the promises made by the conspirators—the Minister formally instructed his representative to send the caids back to their districts and to forbid them to leave, to forbid any gathering of partisans, and to meet el-Glaoui personally and in private at Casablanca in order to bring him into line.[67]

There was nothing for Guillaume to do but to speak up. With his back apparently against the wall, he managed to extricate himself again and said he was awaiting the arrival of the Minister's personal representative, Vimont, before he intervened personally. In the meantime, as if to exert the strongest possible pressure on the Pasha of Marrakesh during this lull he had created, he again dispatched Vallat, accompanied this time by De Blesson and Boniface so that the conspirators could no longer claim to have misunderstood the Residency's orders.

The official entry onto the scene of the conspiracy's general staff on the morning of August 14 met with the success one would expect.

> Toward noon we were astounded to learn that De Blesson, Vallat, and Boniface had been despatched to Marrakesh. This was sending the arsonists to put out the fire. . . . The evening papers printed a fantastic statement by Boniface and Vallat, who addressed the pashas and caids in Arabic.
>
> "Wait twenty-four hours. Paris is wrongly informed

---

67. For these instructions, see the official version, pp. 155.

of your intentions and of the situation in Morocco. Sit tight.[68] Stay at Marrakesh until tomorrow, but do not take any decision. Give us a little time. In France, they do not realize the importance of your movement. They have not understood the reasons for your complaints against the Sultan. We are asking the government to analyze the situation more carefully, to go over the information, and to take action. We need twenty-four hours. Wait until tomorrow."

El-Glaoui spoke next. "Good-for-nothings like Si Bekkaï have been in France stirring up trouble and spreading lies about our movement. Wait at Marrakesh, all of you. We have agreed to postpone any decision for twenty-four hours. But tomorrow, whether the government agrees or not, we shall act. Meet me here tomorrow at nine." [69]

Now the Minister's personal envoy could come to Morocco. The ringleaders succeeded in neutralizing the Vimont mission in circumstances bordering on farce, since they had themselves been thrown into the assault against el-Glaoui by Guillaume. Vimont had hardly reached Marrakesh when he was taken in charge by De Blesson, Vallat, Boniface, and d'Hauteville, who told him with greatest solemnity that it was too late to do anything. They insisted that a real conspiracy was in being, that by opposing it France would irrevocably forfeit the notables' cooperation, and that if the notables persisted there would be no alternative but to bar their route to Rabat by shooting. Indeed, matters had reached a point where the argument had taken on some semblance of truth. Vimont was so convinced that, from then on, he thought only of gaining enough time to obtain the Sultan's abdication according to protocol, with the agreement of Paris and without seeming to have been forced into it by the notables. In any event, this was how he reported the situation to Paris. Obviously, Vimont and the government did not give up the struggle. They intended to fight every foot of the way, and that was how they

68. The Residency, it will be recalled, had just received official orders to send them home.

69. Barrat, p. 199.

spent the next few days. However, it was tacitly understood from the beginning that if the notables persisted, Paris would not, in any event, go so far as to make them lose face by publicly repudiating their action. The authorities would try to make them listen to reason. There was no longer any question, however, of forcing them to do anything. The conspirators were assured in advance of having the last word.

While Guillaume was talking with el-Glaoui at the Residency of Regional Commissioner d'Hauteville, Vimont had just left the conspirators and had had an interview with Maurice Fauré, S.F.I.O. delegate to the Third Electoral College of the Government Council for Marrakesh. He confirmed in all respects what had just been said by the Resident-General's four envoys.[70] Thus Vimont was able to verify the truth—that the French colony in Morocco wholeheartedly supported the Residency and el-Glaoui in opposing the Sultan.

Vimont had been duly indoctrinated. On August 17, at the end of his mission, he could only conclude on behalf of Bidault that France had to choose between its friends and its enemies, that it was too late to resume control over the pashas and caids, and that the government would have to make the decision after listening once more to the Resident-General. Under pressure from those members of his government who were exhorting him to be firm, Laniel was, at this point, considering sending to Rabat a member of his staff, Pierre July, then Secretary of State in the Office of the Prime Minister, with instructions to see that the government's orders were fully carried out and to take such decisions as the situation called for in the light of the facts. Thus, just as Vimont was reporting from Rabat that he considered the cause lost, July was preparing to leave Paris. He would in all probability have left for Morocco had not Bidault, on the same day, formally opposed his trip.

When the Cabinet met on August 19 to discuss the Moroccan crisis, the government was to all intents and purposes confronted with a fait accompli. All the ministers agreed with Bidault that it would be impossible to use force to compel the notables to

70. The era of liberal resolutions by the S.F.I.O. was past, but was to return.

acquiesce. They also realized that only the complicity of the Residency had made the conspiracy possible. Once again, Faure reverted to the idea of sending a government delegation to Rabat to settle the crisis of authority. In an effort to assuage Bidault's sensibilities, he proposed that the Minister for Foreign Affairs or, failing him, the Secretary of State should undertake this delicate mission. The suggestion was ultimately rejected, which was not surprising: France would hardly have fought to prevent the fall of the Sultan when it had stripped him a week earlier of all the political powers that had been at stake in the crisis. There was nothing to do but to ask Guillaume to make a last attempt to bring about a reconciliation at Rabat, and this was what was finally decided.

Since the fatal step had been taken in the meantime, the meeting of the Council of Ministers on the morning of August 20 could hardly have been more than an endorsement of faits accomplis or an expression of reservations. Edgar Faure and François Mitterrand intervened at regular intervals throughout the meeting to record their objections and to ask for clarification, which no one seemed able to supply. When Faure left the meeting for a moment, the liberal ministers, Corniglion-Molinier, Coste-Floret, July, and Houdet, followed to consult him. They considered the problem less one of government than of governmental authority, since Laniel and Bidault had apparently been confronted with a fait accompli they were forced to endorse. Faure told his friends that, considering the situation, he did not see how they could break with the government. He preferred to express his reservations in a personal letter to the President and to have it attached to the record of the cabinet meeting.[71] The other ministers agreed to this solution. Bearing

71. Faure's letter of August 26, 1953, to the President systematically set forth his formal reservations on the way the government had been induced to conceal the notables' conspiracy. He also developed substantive arguments, contending especially that it was not in keeping either with France's interests or international position to have violated on its own initiative the principle of legitimacy embodied in the fallen Sultan. In some respects, Faure continued, he would normally have resigned. But he could hardly relinquish his position as Minister for Finance and Economic Affairs in a period of strikes and great crisis, since to do so would have appeared tantamount to disavowal of a Prime Minister whom he certainly did not mean to incriminate.

Faure's decision in mind, Mitterrand took the same course, but at the same time asked for certain future guarantees (which he did not, incidentally, receive).

A final meeting was held the same afternoon. Only then did the ministers learn that the Sultan had been deposed and was en route to Corsica. Confirmation of the decisions made appeared in the following communiqué:

> The Council of Ministers met again at six-thirty P.M. to consider the latest developments in the political situation in Morocco.
>
> It noted that, in accordance with the government's instructions and in view of the impossibility of maintaining the Sultan without grave risk of civil war breaking out in the protectorate, the traditional procedure had been invoked in order to assure the succession to the throne.
>
> The government trusts that the new investiture will open an era of far-reaching political, economic, and social reforms, since this inauguration will be accompanied by administrative changes permitting close and essential cooperation between France and the protectorate.[72]

The declaration of intent which ended the communiqué and which concealed the acceptance of the fait accompli was a mere formality. By forcing the Sultan, through its instructions of August 12, to divest himself of all his essential temporal powers in favor of governmental councils controlled by the Residency and designed to serve as the apex of a pyramid of mixed assemblies, the Quai d'Orsay had endorsed a priori and with the agreement of the Prime Minister the series of cosovereignty reforms that were to strip the protectorate treaty of all substance in the first few days of the new Sultan's reign. To Paris, democratization could no longer mean anything but cosovereignty. This time, France completely endorsed the political demands of the French colony and its local representatives.

72. *Le Monde* (Aug. 22, 1953).

OTHER ASPECTS OF THE CRISIS

This reconstruction of the facts would be incomplete without emphasis on certain aspects of the crisis that were skimmed over in the official version. These must be brought out if this phase of the conflict is to be understood. These supplementary details concern the attitude of those loyal to Mohammed V, his final negotiations with the French government, the position of the Istiqlal, and the way in which French newspapers in France and Morocco reported events in August 1953.

As the climax approached, the Sultan's margin for maneuver was drastically reduced. Spurred on by the personal attacks on the sovereign which proliferated in the higher ranks of the administration, the French press in Morocco, and the groups of notables, the Palace counterattacked by seeking to give the weight of a national plebiscite to the loyalty demonstrations emanating from the most varied sectors of the Moroccan population. Entering into the spirit, the loyal caids, the intellectuals, and the trade unionists—backed by all that remained of the organized forces of the Istiqlal and by gatherings of petitioners and schoolchildren—multiplied their declarations of loyalty until the end of August.

By the first half of June, there were far more protests by the loyal caids and other dignitaries than the official version implies. On June 3, the Pashas of Fez, Salé, and Meknes, backed by Si Bekkaï, rose up in protest against what they called "the demented statements of el-Glaoui." [73] On June 5, 318 ulamas favorable to the Sultan launched an appeal at Tangier to the Moroccan people and to the Arab and Muslim world, to Christendom, and to world conscience. The appeal branded the signatories of the petition as "tools in the hands of an individual who assumes the gravest responsibility for this affair," who was himself a "puppet worked by other hands." [74] Toward the end, the Sultan was able to show Deputy Pierre Clostermann 343 letters of retraction from signatories of the petition protesting their loyalty and stating that they had signed under duress. [75]

73. *L'Année politique 1953*, pp. 250–51; *Le Monde* (June 5, 1953).
74. *Combat* (June 6–7, 1953).
75. Pierre Corval, *Le Maroc en révolution* (Paris, 1956), p. 70.

Pressure on the loyal caids increased constantly. Fifteen caids, pashas, and caliphs dismissed from their posts in 1951 or 1953 for refusing to yield to the injunctions of the contrôle civil wrote a letter on June 30, 1953, to the Minister for Foreign Affairs protesting the petition in their capacity as illegally suspended officials. They drew the Minister's attention to the measures taken to suspend or dismiss them, and ended by saying that the Moroccan people were gradually losing confidence in their pashas and caids. This, they asserted, endangered Franco-Moroccan amity.[76] As has been implied, these retractions should not be taken entirely at face value. Apart from a few loyal supporters such as Si Bekkaï, the former Caid Aherdan, Dr. Mohammed el-Khatib, and several others, the notables were chiefly concerned with protecting themselves. That at least appears to have been the Sultan's feeling, since as soon as he returned to Morocco nearly all the pashas and caids were replaced so that the signatures to the retractions of August 1953 seem to have counted for very little.

By the end of July, the pressure on the Maghzen hierarchy from every side had isolated the Sultan completely. He was cut off from the Istiqlal and increasingly abandoned by his local representatives. Even the Grand Vizier was about to turn against him. Mohammed V was forced to throw men of a new type into the fray. Hence, the Bekkaï and Khatib missions, and the dispatch on August 11 of Si Bekkaï, Pasha of Sefrou, to Léon Marchal to inform him of el-Glaoui's most recent machinations.

The political promotion of Si Bekkaï was in some respects the result of an inquiry Le Figaro had conducted in Morocco a few months earlier.[77] When its reporters arrived in Morocco, they had written an article on Si Bekkaï, who was the perfect embodiment of a moderate nationalist free from all political ties. As President of the Moroccan Association of Ex-Servicemen and War Victims, linked to none of the nationalist parties and a great friend of France, Si Bekkaï was appalled by the attacks of el-Glaoui and by the campaign being resumed against the

76. This letter was made public on July 2. See Le Monde (July 4, 1953).
77. Le Figaro announced the investigation on January 9, 1953. It was conducted from Paris by François Mauriac and lasted from January 12 through March 20.

Sultan. Having been brought into the limelight by *Le Figaro's* investigation, this attractive figure who symbolized the loyalty of Moroccan ex-soldiers to France and of the pashas to the Sultan came to the fore because the national leaders of the Istiqlal had been put out of action, and his house became a place of pilgrimage for loyal Moroccans and French liberals. In July 1953, while the last leaders of the Istiqlal still at liberty kept aloof from the Palace, and the dignitaries and erstwhile friends of the Sultan were fleeing one by one to the winning side, Si Bekkaï, Caid Aherdan, and Dr. Khatib remained almost the last of the faithful. The Sultan rightly regarded them as his only possible intermediaries. Accordingly, he made use of them in various capacities, sending Si Bekkaï and then Dr. Khatib to Paris with final messages to the French authorities. He entrusted Deputy Pierre Clostermann with a final appeal to the President of the Republic. Dr. Khatib returned to Morocco on August 23 after carrying out his mission. He was soon to distinguish himself in the resistance movement at the side of the former Caid Aherdan. These nonpolitical figures were deeply involved in the struggle and an increasingly large number of the population was soon to follow their example. Their entry into the fray was in fact the prelude to the tremendous upheaval which was to culminate in the months ahead in the mass replacement of the major protagonists of the crisis, both in France and Morocco.

At the same time, the evolution which had begun among the lower and middle-level leadership of the Istiqlal in 1952 took final shape. Under the authority of a provisional executive committee, the party militants embarked decisively upon the path which was to separate them from their former leaders and to lead them to combine with the terrorist organizations and the future Army of Liberation, together with volunteers from every political quarter in Morocco. At first, for some four or five months the new leaders were completely cut off from their imprisoned leaders and from those who, like Allal el-Fassi and Ahmed Balafredj, were continuing their fight from abroad. But then little by little they succeeded in reestablishing contact with the former through their lawyers, Bachir Ben Abbès and Ahmed Boucetta. Having hesitated between violence and resignation to the inevitable, the members of the new executive committee rightly decided in favor of prudence, knowing full well that as long as the Sultan was on the throne, any rash act might precipitate his deposition or force him to repudiate the party. Nevertheless, pressure at the base continued to grow, and this new period of enforced waiting merely fostered the spirit of resistance which was soon to take the upper hand.

The disturbances which ultimately broke out at Rabat, Meknes, and Casablanca were of the usual type and posed no great problem, except that it is rather difficult today to trace their exact origin.

On the other hand, the events at Oudja, where a furious attack by the Beni Snassene tribe caused eighteen deaths, had a very different meaning. They were part of the already lengthy series of shocks which had agitated certain sensitive areas of the *bled*, particularly since 1951. The official version was completely silent on this aspect of affairs, which was beginning more and more to belie the theory of the *bon bled* so dear to the Residency and on which its entire policy was based. Nevertheless, the warning was not lost on those who, innocently or for ulterior motives, stubbornly clung to the idea that nationalism was a surface phenomenon strictly confined to the towns.[78]

The French press in Morocco played a vital part in the conflict. The publicity given by the Mas press on August 16 to the fait accompli with which the conspirators had confronted the Residency by appointing a new Imam, despite the agreement reached and in defiance of orders, constitutes a typical example of political maneuvering linked to a concerted press campaign. It reported the appointment of the new Imam under enormous headlines and falsely attributed his enthronement to the intervention of the Resident as mediator. It ignored the joint declaration of August 13 confirming Mohammed V as the lawful Sultan, and laid heavy stress on the fact that the declaration stripped all essential temporal powers from a sovereign who had just been deprived of his spiritual powers. Thus, the press deliberately destroyed the few small achievements obtained by the Vimont

78. The critical problem of the political shift in the *bled* is discussed later in relation to the events of Oued Zem. See p. 286.

mission and the Resident-General's more or less sincere attempts to avoid the inevitable.

Guillaume was overwhelmed by the press and cut off by the Sultan, who considered in the circumstances that the declaration of August 13 had gone by the board. The Resident-General could do nothing but yield. This he did, after belatedly denying the report which announced as a matter of course that the new Imam would be enthroned that same day and then installed in the Palace.

The triumphal chorus with which the Mas press greeted the appointment of the new Imam climaxed an impassioned campaign that had lasted eight months. There had been no question of censorship, although it was obvious that only by curbing the Mas press could the Residency have enforced a solution, assuming it had been so inclined. In point of fact, it was hardly to be expected that the notables should take seriously the official efforts of the Resident-General and the Minister's personal envoy, when at the same time the French newspapers were without restraint advocating a policy opposed to that of the government and its representative in Morocco.[79] The press would hardly have abandoned its position at the last minute; it had entered upon the scene only in full accord with the highest authorities in Morocco. The most blatant disagreements between the local newspapers and official Residential policy were not even reprimanded.[80]

The metropolitan newspapers opposed to the policy of force were kept informed by the Moroccan lobby in Paris, and missed nothing of any importance. As early as August 14, Jean Rous revealed in *Franc-Tireur* that el-Glaoui was preparing to name a new Sultan and that Guillaume had deliberately disobeyed instructions from Paris. The same day, *Le Figaro* recalled that the Treaty of Fez obligated France to support the Sultan wholeheartedly, while *L'Aurore* came out against any governmental intervention in the dispute.

On August 18, *Franc-Tireur* reported bluntly that Bidault had

79. Censorship was only imposed in extremis after Vimont's return to France when the game was already over.

80. It would be gratuitous to engage in a detailed study of this campaign, which was developed with so little discretion that it is enough to leaf through a set of *Le Petit Marocain* or any other Mas publication.

gone over to the Sultan's enemies. *Le Figaro,* in turn, revealed that el-Glaoui had received official support; *L'Aurore,* on the other hand, took a completely opposite stand and declared that France could no longer disregard the wishes of the Moroccan people. The attack was intensified on the nineteenth: "This crisis exemplifies the decadence of the state," declared *Combat.* It was supported by *Le Monde* which demanded a list of those responsible for the conspiracy, and by *Le Figaro* which urged the government to make its decisions respected. This did not prevent *L'Aurore* from stating that it was not difficult to choose between the Sultan and el-Glaoui.[81]

On August 24, in an editorial in *Le Figaro,* François Mauriac openly denounced the men responsible for the crisis and violently attacked Bidault and those he called the "ringleaders." De Blesson had not been spared. On August 20, in an analysis of the latest events attacking the Deputy Minister personally, *Le Figaro* had asked:

> Is this what the producers of the drama wanted? For the producers certainly exist. It was not without support, discreet authorization, indeed open encouragement, that el-Glaoui was able to organize his petition against the Sultan, his trip to England . . . Although the French government and the President of the Republic himself hoped to find grounds for agreement, after the Sultan's conciliatory declaration on July 14, preparations for the coup de force continued behind the scenes in General Guillaume's absence. How can a diplomat representing the Quai d'Orsay in Morocco, the guarantor of the application of the treaties, cover up actions by senior local officials that contravene the very principles laid down by the government?

At the moment when the highest French authorities were asserting that the Moroccan people were in full agreement with

81. On August 21, each great metropolitan daily derived its own moral from the events. "France has torn up the Protectorate Treaty" (*L'Humanité*); "Reparations and Suffering Necessary because of Marrakech Conspirators" (Mauriac in *Combat*); "Government Prisoner of Intrigues in Marrakech and Rabat; Tries to Throw People off the Scent; Mitterrand Apparently Not Deceived" (*Combat*); "Situation Clarified" (*L'Aurore*).

what had just happened, the Residency was so afraid of a popular reaction that the entry of the new Sultan into his capital looked like the arrival of a conqueror into a defeated city. Tank regiments supported by regiments of infantry flanked by armed police escorted the victors, while the civil police forced open and ransacked the closed shops of those Moroccan shopkeepers faithful to the deposed Sultan.[82]

On August 25, *Le Monde* published an article on the events by Charles Faverel that bluntly contradicted the official version of Mulay ben Arafa's entry into Rabat: "The procession formed successfully and turned toward the Imperial Palace in a somewhat embarrassing silence; there was no crowd of spectators along the way, for police barriers prevented the people from emerging from the *medina*." Mulay ben Arafa was acclaimed in Rabat, not by the populace but by tribal horsemen from outside the city. There is no need to say more.

The Ben Arafa Reforms [83]

In the eyes of the Residency, the deposition of the Sultan was to the reform of the regime what the opening of a floodgate is to waters that have been too long held back. In less time than it takes to tell, all the backlog of reforms accumulated during the six years of the so-called Sultan's strike flooded into the gap. The vestiges of sovereignty hitherto retained by the Moroccan ruler and his Maghzen were taken over by the Residency with a stroke of the pen. The French in Morocco, no longer considered aliens, took their place as co-citizens with the Moroccans of the Sharifian state. The Treaty of Fez was to all intents and purposes abolished.

After this it was plain that the war of the *dahirs* which the Residency had so long waged against Mohammed V had been designed purely to replace the protectorate by a system of co-sovereignty for the benefit of the French community and its leaders. The stubborn opposition which the fallen ruler had

---

82. For detailed confirmation, see *France-Soir* (Aug. 21, 1953).

83. While the ben Arafa reforms belong technically to the subsequent period (since they were effected after Mohammed V's deposition), it seems preferable to introduce them here in order to maintain the unity of an account to which they are the obvious conclusion.

maintained toward this policy, at a time when the attempt was still made to disguise it with trappings of democracy and progress, was justified.

The 1953 reforms were the work of two men. One was De Blesson, who had been as active in determining the objectives of the 1953 coup as in carrying it out. The other was the Contrôleur Civil, Maurice Guiramand, then Adviser to the Council of the Sharifian Government. Since De Blesson did not consider himself an expert on Arab problems, he had thought to find in Guiramand the specialist he perhaps regretted not being himself. Thus armed with the trust and support of the Deputy Minister, Guiramand had set up a sort of brain trust within the Department of Sharifian Affairs which had very soon become the final arbiter on matters of reform, although it played very little part in actual policy-making. It would be an exaggeration to say that the idea of cosovereignty originated with this group. That idea expressed the general feeling of the French in Morocco too well to have needed an inventor. It had taken shape there, however, and been given a sort of doctrinal polish.

The original idea of the Residency reformers had been to embody the future regime in a sovereign with limited prerogatives, flanked by a Council of Empire consisting of the former viziers, representatives of the religious brotherhoods, great caids, pashas, dignitaries of Karaouyne University, and Jews. The Residency would have governed Morocco at its ease behind this stage-setting, with the place of honor reserved for the victorious notables. When the success of the August 1953 plot made it possible to pass from theory to practice, the idea of the Council of Empire suddenly seemed dangerous and was abruptly discarded.

Disagreement then centered on the much more concrete problem of powers to be reserved to the new Sultan. Was he to be deprived of power entirely and given a purely ornamental role? Alternatively, should he be left a residue of legislative power which would make it possible to retain the myth of Moroccan sovereignty, while at the same time giving the Residency all real authority? De Blesson and the "hard core" at the Residency favored complete liquidation of the Maghzen's traditional powers. Other Residential officials, at heart opposed to such plans, pointed out that this radical departure would be ill-advised. They advocated a policy more subtle in form if not in substance, and in the end they won. For form's sake, promulgation of laws and a right of suspensive veto at first reading were left to the Palace. Apart from these, the Sultan lost all legislative, executive, and judicial powers which the Treaty of Fez had recognized as his. The customs of prostration before the Throne, tribute, and the *heydia* (giving of presents) were abolished, ostensibly with a view to modernization but in fact to please the notables. However, this tremendous upheaval only altered the style of the setting. Behind the scene, the Residency continued to exercise alone, with growing difficulty, all real power.

To understand the scope of the operation it is necessary to go into a few details. Although the 1951 reforms had merely sanctioned the apparent reentry of the traditional Maghzen into a system whose basic juridical structure remained unchanged, the 1953 reforms sanctioned—or very nearly—the unilateral suppression of the protectorate treaty and its replacement by an embryonic Franco-Moroccan state.

At the end of this second wave of reforms, the Sultan's legislative and executive powers were in fact handed over to two Franco-Moroccan governmental assemblies: the Council of Viziers and Directors (reorganized) and the Limited Council. The former became the legislative organ of the Sharifian Empire. The Sultan retained only the right to request a second reading of draft *dahirs* he disapproved of, although if the council insisted on the original text by a two-thirds majority, he was forced to sign it. The council consisted of an equal number of Frenchmen and Moroccans. The former exercised the actual power, based on a procedure which guaranteed them a majority in all circumstances.[84] The Limited Council inherited the regulatory powers hitherto enjoyed by the Grand Vizier. It consisted of the Grand Vizier, who presided, his two Assistant Viziers, the Secretary-General of the protectorate, the Councillor of the Sharifian Government, and the Director of the Department of the Interior. Hence it possessed, in theory at least, all the characteristics of a council of ministers.[85]

---

84. *B.O.* (Sept. 11, 1953), p. 1268 (*dahir* of Sept. 9).
85. Ibid. (Sept. 4, 1953), pp. 1240–41 (*dahirs* of Aug. 13 and 31, 1953).

Municipal reform, held up so long by the Sultan's "strike," came into force almost at the same time. The old municipal commissions were replaced by joint elected deliberative assemblies that were given authority over municipal affairs. One of the principal demands of the French colony was thus satisfied; the door was open to them for gaining citizenship rights.[86] Also in September, a *dahir* decreed that the Government Council should lose its status as a Residential organ and become part of the Sharifian government. Its two sections were henceforward invited to sit together, but this did not prevent the council from continuing to operate, as in the past, in a state of complete indifference.[87]

By the end of October, the first *djemaas* set up in 1951 were to begin to function. "The success of this long-term project," wrote Robert Montagne, "would have . . . required considerable financial assistance, which a centralized administration was reluctant to assume. Once again, the administrative and technical organization that we had set up and that had for so long, out of inertia, depended upon the Sultan's despotic system of government, paralyzed any true reform." [88] Aside from the decrepitude of the Maghzen, a condition in itself only an effect of the political stagnation the Residential authorities had imposed on Morocco, this criticism was well put: even if the *djemaas'* plan had offered a starting point for effective renovation of Moroccan local government (which is debatable) it would have failed in any event for lack of financial support from the Residency.

Reform of the Moroccan judicial system followed in November. The Sultan abandoned his reserve judicial powers to the Sharifian High Court. In theory, the separation of powers was now complete. The status of the Moroccan magistracy was modified, at least on paper. Work began on new codes.

Everything had been achieved, or so it seemed. At the summit of the hierarchy, the Sultan had divested himself of his traditional powers in favor of joint committees consisting of officials without responsibility. At the base, the French of Morocco had

86. Ibid. (Sept. 25, 1953), pp. 1339–43 (*dahir* of Sept. 18, 1953).
87. Ibid. (Oct. 16, 1953), p. 1431 (*dahir* of Sept. 16, 1953).
88. Montagne, p. 228.

made a breakthrough on the municipal front. They were preparing, through their elected representatives, to gain access to all levels of authority in the future Franco-Moroccan state. The fact of colonization was finding legal sanction in a series of measures designed to place real power in the hands of the French colony or of its representatives. The Residency did not doubt that it had succeeded. All the observers interviewed agreed on the extraordinary self-confidence exhibited at that moment by the victors. Vallat declared to all who would listen that Morocco was assured of twenty years of peace. De Blesson and his cohorts sincerely believed their problem was solved. They were profoundly convinced that the campaign which they had pressed to a victorious conclusion gratified the wishes of the majority of the Moroccan people. At the Residency, the skeptics could be counted on the fingers of one hand. The enthusiasts made common cause and gave the skeptics to understand it was high time they returned to the fold.

In spite of this euphoria, the reforms remained a dead letter. Most important to the Residency, the Istiqlal and the Sultan had been eliminated and the regime so reorganized as to give the Residency full control. For the present, it cared little whether or not the organs created by virtue of this reinforcement of the status quo worked. Perhaps it thought, not without justification, that, until the situation returned to normal, to set up the Franco-Moroccan state of which it dreamed was premature. It is instructive, nevertheless, to point out that none of the cosovereignty reforms designed to set up a new organ achieved its purpose. The Council of Viziers and the Limited Council were little more than chambers for rubber-stamping the Residency's wishes. The municipal reforms were outstripped by events and remained meaningless. Apart from a few superficial improvements, Moroccan justice remained to the end the product of a complete confusion of powers. The *djemaas* never really participated in the political life of the country, even in the few regions where the French authorities did not thwart their development. As for the Government Council, it foundered amid general indifference.

It is possible for a time to base a regime upon force when its subjects no longer want any part of it. It is impossible to force those same subjects to breathe life into representative institutions which a large part of the community regards with suspicion. Any institution that does not respond to a social need is condemned in advance to stagnation. The Residency had believed for ten years that only the Sultan's obstruction was holding up the legislative plan so dear to its heart. Once Mohammed V was exiled, it realized that the real obstacle was not the Palace but the Moroccan people themselves, of whom the Palace had been only an advance outpost.

In Morocco in 1953, there were only two political realities: a Residential absolutism in the process of being rapidly transformed into military occupation, and the remnants of a nationalist political leadership that was soon to be forced by circumstances to transform itself into a terrorist general staff. Everything which fitted these two realities succeeded automatically. The Residency had no difficulty acquiring all the power in a Morocco which had been systematically purged of any political life of its own. In the same way, the nationalists were to see their dismantled networks reconstituted almost spontaneously. On the other hand, everything counter to this process remained in the limbo of stillborn reforms. The municipal elections had to be postponed from one legislature to the next. The Residency hoped for support from the new governmental organs but did not get it. At every level of the structure, the Moroccan people held aloof from the executive or administrative organs when only their participation could have given the system life by linking the summit to the base. The mountain of reform had brought forth a mouse.

The part played by Paris in this organizational upheaval—which in fact merely adapted the public law in force in the protectorate to the fact of the Residency's omnipotence—remains to be considered. There are still some today who believe that the 1953 reforms were imposed on the Quai d'Orsay by the Residency after its triumph of August 20. It has been shown that this was not at all the case. Actually, the instructions Guillaume took back from Paris on August 12 contained the complete plan of cosovereignty reforms that was put into effect by the Residency between September and December 1953.[89] However, Paris had merely returned to Rabat as orders the suggestions received previously from the Residency. Matters could hardly have been otherwise. Once Paris had rejected the idea of independence, while at the same time feigning to assert officially that the system of direct administration was outmoded, only one solution remained: to make the French in Morocco full citizens in an equal democracy in which the French voters would constitute the most powerful section politically, by virtue of constitutional arrangements since they could not do so through force of numbers. The only disagreement between Paris and Rabat had been on procedure. Paris wanted flexible negotiations that would gradually have drawn Mohammed V into the path of democratization in a Morocco having joint sovereignty. Rabat, on the contrary, wanted to use the Sultan's opposition to policy to get rid of him altogether. Essentially, both sides were in agreement.

It is hard to know today on what ideas about the future Léon Marchal (the man behind it all at the Quai d'Orsay) based his policy. It must have been one of two things: either he really hoped to stabilize Morocco under a regime of cosovereignty in which the real power was reserved to the elected representatives of the French colony; in that case it must be concluded that his policy was no more realistic than that of the Residency, for such a crude solution would not have had much more effect on the crisis than maintenance of the status quo; or else he believed, without daring to say so officially, that cosovereignty was a stage on the way to independence, and in that case his policy appears in retrospect the only possible one in a situation in which the Quai d'Orsay's hope was to liberalize the regime by concealing its final objectives from the French colony in Morocco, which was opposed to any policy of overt decolonization.

The tension between Paris and Rabat was soon to be revived, but this time on a quite different basis.

89. Nevertheless, the Residency refused to the end to set up the regional assemblies that would have allowed the settlers to participate in the political administration of the regions.

END OF THE GUILLAUME PERIOD; THE LACOSTE PERIOD; TERRORISM AND PASSIVITY (AUGUST 28, 1953–JUNE 20, 1955)

After Mohammed V's deposition, nationalist opposition and the problem of reforms continued to dominate the conflict. These two related problems were merely intensified by the deposition of the man who embodied both the religious beliefs of his subjects, and the Empire. Nationalist activity took the form of urban terrorism and guerrilla warfare, although the desire for political action remained. The perennial problem of reform was absorbed into the problem of the Throne. In Morocco, the conflict reached its climax. Once this had happened in France, the denouement was inevitable.

End of the Guillaume Period
(September 1, 1953–May 20, 1954)

The first manifestations of urban terrorism coincided with the beginning of the new regime.[1] Between August 20 and October 2, 1953, the authorities recorded 45 incidents, including eight murders, nine fires, and about a dozen acts of sabotage. Although these outbreaks were still few in number and limited for the most part to the urban center of Casablanca, their significance was clear. They were a matter of immediate concern to the Residency, on its own admission. On September 11, only three weeks after Mohammed V's arrival in Corsica, Sultan ben Arafa narrowly escaped assassination on his way from Rabat to the Mulay Idriss mosque for the Friday prayer ceremony. This

---

1. The first terrorist acts thus began in August 1953. No time was lost between the Sultan's deposition and the unleashing of actual terrorism.

violence marked the rift between the new sovereign and his people immediately after his coronation, and was the starting point of real terrorism. From then on, there was a constant succession of attacks on prominent Frenchmen or Moroccans, intensified from time to time by some spectacular act of sabotage. On November 3 a bomb exploded in the *medina* of Fez, and thereafter the attacks were increasingly frequent. On November 7, saboteurs derailed the Casablanca-Algiers Express and seven passengers were killed. On December 24, a bomb thrown by a terrorist acting under orders claimed 60 victims, including 18 dead, among the French and Moroccan Christmas shoppers at the Central Market in Casablanca. "The French chose the great Muslim festival on August 20, 1953, to exile Mohammed V," said the Tangier *Bureau du Maghreb arabe* in a statement published by the Egyptian newspaper *Al Gomhourya* under the heading, "Vengeance at Christmas-time." [2] "Our commandos avenged themselves by setting off several bombs in Casablanca. Thus France's Resident-General spent Christmas Day accompanying the funeral processions of the French victims." This brutal attack, directed indiscriminately against both communities, plunged Morocco into a state of civil war. There was no respite. On February 13, 1954, Commandant Si Fathmi, a friend of Mulay ben Arafa and an officer in the Black Guard, was murdered. On the 20th, el-Glaoui escaped death by a hair's-breadth.[3] On March 5, the terrorists of Marrakesh again attacked Mulay ben Arafa, although without success. On May 25, the day of General Guillaume's farewell at Marrakesh, a grenade thrown among the security forces killed one soldier and wounded dozens of people.

These spectacular incidents were merely the high points in a series of daily attacks directed primarily against Moroccan informers employed by the police in Muslim milieux. Terrorism mounted and rapidly developed a characteristic pattern. Victims

2. *Bulletin d'information du Maroc,* no. 38 (Jan. 1954), p. 17.

3. If Mulay Arafa and el-Glaoui had been assassinated early in 1954, the final period of the conflict would have been completely different, and so would the denouement. Accidents play their role in history, but if history is the result of an accumulation of accidents, few particular events are capable of determining it. For every battle of Poitiers that changed the face of the world, how many Waterloos did nothing but fulfill destinies that might as well have been fulfilled by other means?

were predominantly Muslim. Repressive measures were useless in a community that protected the outlaws. Security measures were inadequate because the police were overworked and three-quarters blind. There were also police brutality and counter-terrorist activity against Moroccans and French nationals whom the European public, maddened and exasperated by the terrible impending threat, rightly or wrongly considered responsible.

The first organized retaliation attributable to counter-terrorist activity was the so-called kidnapping affair, which occurred in November 1954. Five members of the Istiqlal party disappeared from their homes between the sixth and eighteenth. The press let it be understood that most of them had been abducted by French civilians posing as policemen. Moroccans and French liberals at once accused the French police. The Residency denied the charge. When, two months later, a parliamentary commission of investigation[4] made an on-the-spot inquiry, Jean Dutheil, head of the D.S.T., formally denied that the administration had had any hand in the kidnappings. In the meantime, however, the Sultan's advisor, Maître Georges Izard, had learned the whereabouts of the five from a colleague. The letter assigning their place of detention was discovered, and it made clear beyond doubt where the responsibility lay. In fact, the whole affair had been organized by a senior Residency official, who had succeeded in convincing Guillaume that counter-terrorism was the only possible reply to Moroccan terrorism. What was needed, in his view, was to throw the nationalists off balance by systematically interning those directly or indirectly responsible for the attacks. (According to a high-ranking official whose backing was essential if the operation was to succeed, it was finally decided to go ahead. The Resident-General agreed, and the five were kidnapped and kept under guard in a supposedly secret spot.) Two of the leaders were from Fez, and for ten days there were no further incidents there. Those responsible subsequently maintained that, had they been able to continue this policy, terrorism would have been eradicated. Unfortunately for them, Paris reacted. The Resident-General, disturbed by cabled accusations, again denied the charge, but the five internees had to be released.

4. See p. 198.

It must be admitted that the counterattack had been mild. Despite its clandestine nature, it had been inspired by feelings that were in the circumstances understandable. The idea was far from novel; one might hope that terrorism could be temporarily discouraged by taking hostages, but this method of repression never has been particularly successful. Even if the Residency had subsequently shot the nationalist leaders, all those with any moral responsibility for the terrorism would have gone underground, and the nature of the problem would have remained unchanged.

While terrorism and counter-terrorism were being organized, a far-reaching reorganization was going on among the protagonists in the conflict which was to put the key positions in both countries into new hands. On September 3, 1953, François Mitterrand (U.D.S.R.) had resigned from his post as Deputy Minister to the Council of Europe, although he remained one of the most confirmed parliamentary opponents of the ultras. His departure was less a sequel to the previous month's coup de force than a gesture of protest against the government's inertia in regard to Tunisia.

On the Franco-Moroccan side, Boniface, who retired in September, was the first to leave, although he continued to play a part in the games in which he had excelled. In November, De Blesson also retired. In June and July 1954, he was followed by the Director of the Department of the Interior, Marcel Vallat; the Director of the D.S.T., Dutheil; and by the Adviser to the Sharifian Government, Louis de la Tour du Pin. Since the protagonists' attitude in crises of this kind is normally merely the product of the political situation, the departure of the Regional Commissioner for Casablanca and of the Director of the Interior and the Deputy Minister did not prevent growing disaffection of the French in Morocco. Indeed, when Grandval arrived early in July 1955, he found himself faced with a staff of Residential officials who were as intransigent as ever.

Among the Moroccans, a resistance movement was secretly being organized while the Istiqlal leaders moldered in prison. Once the nationalist leaders arrested in December 1952 were released in 1954, two types were to vie for the leading roles: the

"civilians" of the political period and the résistants of the terrorist period. The classic conflict between these two was to be one
of the characteristic features of the conflict until the end, despite
the fact that many résistants were former Istiqlal recruits who
had been driven to direct action by the force of events and by the
forced absence of the party's original leaders.

In France, changes were to be even more marked. The two
Ministers for Foreign Affairs prior to August 1953, Robert
Schuman and Georges Bidault, were to throw in their hands.
Two newcomers to the office of Prime Minister, Pierre Mendès-
France and Edgar Faure, were to settle the Tunisian and Moroccan crises, and a right-wing Minister for Foreign Affairs,
Antoine Pinay, was to hold the infant Morocco at the baptismal
font. This is not so paradoxical as it might seem: in a political
phase in which the Right is arbiter, a political problem of this
type can only be solved with the tacit or explicit consent of its
representatives.

The emergence of terrorism and the first manifestations of the
major reshuffle of the protagonists were not the only developments in the last months of 1953. Two lesser but nevertheless
significant new events—the switch of *Maroc-Presse* to the opposition and the resistance of leading citizens to the Residency's
reforms—were to help to make the change even more apparent.

At first, Jean Walter of *Maroc-Presse* had adopted a wait-and
see attitude, and the paper's transformation was not accomplished in a day. The change began gradually with the editorial
writer, Henri Sartout, who took more than three months to
consolidate his new position. On September 4, 1953, Sartout was
still stoutly denying the liberal version of the August events. It
was not until November 21, with the publication of his famous
article, "Day of the Dupes," that the paper's new political line
was confirmed after weeks of vacillation. For the first time, the
crisis of the summer of 1953 was presented as a political comedy
by a French newspaper in Morocco. The conversion of *Maroc-
Presse* was not completed until March 1954, when it published a
series of articles on the Moustier mission headed, "Lessons of an
Investigation." [5]

5. See p. 199.

While the Residency was reforming the regime to suit itself, terrorism was being reorganized. *Maroc-Presse* was slipping slowly into the opposition camp and the conspirators of the 1953 coup were retiring from the field. At the same time, the influential citizens of Morocco, disappointed at having been excluded from the discussions of the ben Arafa reforms, began their own revolt. The hostility of this group to the Residency's omnipotence had been discernible for some time. On September 12, 1953, the editorial writer of *La Vigie marocaine* had maintained the necessity of the Residency's holding consultations before implementing the reforms. On the 17th, he expressed hope that the Residency would not confront the French in Morocco with a fait accompli. These misgivings were echoed at the Radical-Socialist congress held at Aix-les-Bains from September 17–22. Émile Eyraud was managing editor of *La Vigie marocaine* and president of the Moroccan branch of the Radical and Radical-Socialist Party. Léon Martinaud-Déplat, administrative head of the party and at that time Minister of the Interior, had just rendered him "a special tribute for his courageous and clear-sighted action, which had provided the basis for the present reforms." The Moroccan Radical-Socialists, Martinaud-Déplat continued, had always fought valiantly for the accomplishment of France's mission in loyal collaboration with the Moroccans.[6] In retrospect, the resolution adopted by the Aix-les-Bains congress on September 19 has its humorous aspects. It noted the relaxation of tension in Morocco following the events of August, events which it regarded as an earnest of a "future full of promise" in the political, social, and economic fields. This new situation, the resolution continued, "marks the dawn of the era of democratic reforms so long urged by the Radical and Radical-Socialist branch of Morocco. It guarantees frank and friendly cooperation between the two communities and is a pledge of a lasting French presence in Morocco."[7] The congress thanked those who had so accurately estimated the political situation in Morocco in the last few years,

6. For the account of this congress, see *La Vigie marocaine* (Sept. 18, 1953). This admixture of Moroccan Radical-Socialist leaders and ultras did not prevent the former from having their liberals. One of these, *bâtonnier* Yves Bayssières of Rabat, was an active protagonist in the liberalization of the protectorate.

7. *Le Monde* (Sept. 20–21, 1953).

in particular the Radical and Radical-Socialist branch of Morocco, the Radical ministers, and especially Henri Queuille, René Mayer, and Martinaud-Déplat. It congratulated the chairman, Émile Roche, on his active role in the satisfactory outcome of the Moroccan crisis, and urged that "those who had been the first to study the reforms to be applied in Morocco should be called upon to discuss them freely with the authorities responsible for carrying them out."

Maroc-Presse, although still uncertain of its line, had no hesitation in writing on September 19 that the Radical-Socialist delegates from Morocco had taken advantage of the congress to start campaigning against the reforms, particularly the municipal ones, which they regarded as too democratic. This comment was directed against Eyraud, who, as everyone knew in Rabat, wanted to be mayor of Casablanca, an event which might well become impossible if the new municipalities were created. By attacking the municipal reforms, he hoped to kill two birds with one stone, since the opposition of the Radicals and Socialists might well result either in associating the notables more closely with discussion of the municipal reforms if they were put into effect, or in shelving the project, which would have suited the personal ambitions of the managing editor of *La Vigie marocaine.*

The rise of terrorism and the kidnapping affair had disturbed Parliament so much that the National Assembly's Committee on Foreign Affairs decided at the end of 1953 to send a commission of investigation to Rabat. The commission, headed by Roland de Moustier (Independent Republican) and consisting of Raymond Laurent (M.R.P.), Robert Verdier (S.F.I.O.), and Jacques Genton (Radical-Socialist), arrived in Morocco on January 2, 1954. The investigators began work at once, impressing the public with their obvious determination to make contact with every sector of opinion. The industrialist Jacques Lemaigre-Dubreuil, who had accompanied De Moustier and his colleagues, paved the way for them among the French liberals and the Moroccan underground. Guillaume, assured by the investigators that they had obtained similar authorization from De Hautecloque in Tunisia in 1953, agreed to let them see the imprisoned nationalists. Thus, the investigating team was able to interview such men as Omar Abd el-Djellil and the trade-union leader, Mahjoub ben Seddik. They succeeded in seeing Abdelkrim Bendjelloul, one of the underground leaders of the Istiqlal. This came to the attention of the administration, which never forgave them.[8]

De Moustier, whom the Socialists had chosen as rapporteur because he was a moderate, appeared before the Committee on Foreign Affairs on March 3 to outline the findings of the commission of investigation. Verdier submitted a written report at the same time to the S.F.I.O. group in Parliament. This report, whose basic conclusions are summarized in the next few pages, gives a valid picture of the attitudes of the various sectors of Moroccan public opinion immediately following the coup de force of August 1953.

After emphasizing that moderates in both camps were effectively silenced by the climate of fear and hypocrisy which reigned throughout the country, the author of the report made it quite clear that the August 1953 coup had merely aggravated the conflict and provided no solution. He noted that it was difficult to ascertain the feelings of the Moroccan populace with any accuracy, and expressed the view that although a considerable number of Moroccans were still linked to France by ties of self-interest, the Sultan's deposition had nonetheless created, even in the opinion of such a man as Aucouturier, a general coldness toward the French. The Moroccan notables approached had confined themselves to praising France's achievements. They avoided expressing any opinion on the state of mind of their compatriots, made neither criticisms nor suggestions, and merely urged more effective repressive measures. In contrast to the notables' conformism, the mass of the urban population seemed hostile. The report observed that censorship, suppression of opposition newspapers, and outlawing parties and trade-union organizations open to Moroccans had not prevented Moroccan public opinion from taking shape. The formation of that opinion had received a powerful impetus from the existence of a network of

8. According to one member of the commission, the Residency was informed by an S.F.I.O. member of the Government Council.

120,000 radios, the organization of listening parties, and the rapid transmission of news by word of mouth. Apparently 90 percent of the Moroccan population in the towns was opposed to the deposition. Even the townsmen who had been somewhat reserved in their attitude toward nationalism had been affected by that event. The nationalist intransigents unanimously regarded the Sultan as their symbol, even when their ultimate hopes were secretly republican. Among the masses, devotion to the Sultan was becoming almost mystical. Nobody believed that the August 1953 conspiracy had been spontaneous. "We had been planning the operation for four years," Eyraud told the investigators. The Moroccans for their part incessantly underlined its negative character. There was general hostility to the "old turban-wearers" whose privileges had been confirmed by the administration. Thus, the opposition between youth and age became one of the main-springs of nationalist action, an inevitable phenomenon in a country in which the majority of the population was under twenty years of age. According to the Resident-General himself, the Istiqlal had the support of the educated young people, many of the merchants, and the urban proletariat organized by the trade unions.

The predominant nationalist trend, which supported the Istiqlal, did not appear to be entirely homogeneous. Mahjoub ben Seddik, who claimed to be a member of the Istiqlal, had told inquirers that he needed the party's support because infant trade unionism could not rely upon communism, employers, or the administration; nevertheless, he had admitted he felt closer to the French proletariat than to certain bourgeois elements in his own party. As was to be expected, the P.D.I. was regarded as much less important than the Istiqlal.

The report stressed the fact that the nationalists to whom the commission had talked were not demanding the departure of the French or the weakening of French influence. "How can we be intransigent?" one of them had said. "We have everything to ask and nothing to give." The real issue, in their view, was to know where French policy was leading them. They had lost faith in partial reforms and were awaiting a declaration of intent from France announcing a gradual evolution and a new definition of

Franco-Moroccan relations. They all denounced police brutality, arbitrary actions by the administration, and the exploitation to which Moroccan workers were subjected, both by French employers and by certain Moroccan employers.

De Moustier saw the French community as divided between a liberal minority and the monolithic ultras who were supported by most of the European group. Only a few senior officials and a very few leading citizens seemed to have understood the urgency of the political and social problems confronting the regime. This enlightened minority realized that to solve existing problems of health, housing, and education—fields in which major efforts had already been made—a tremendous financial outlay would be necessary, in addition to political and social reforms impossible under the present fiscal regime. The report recognized that the attitude of the French colony and of its representatives precluded any reform. It attributed this negative state of mind, rather narrowly, to two factors which were really effects rather than causes: the near monopoly exercised by the Mas trust over the French press in Morocco, and the method of appointing the three French Electoral Colleges of the Government Council. In this connection, the report stressed that the French in Morocco had little interest in the Government Council; as a result, many abstained from voting and thus artificially inflated the importance of those elected. The report described these representatives as interested only in the application of police measures: they rationalized the brutality, wanted Mohammed V removed still farther from Morocco, and claimed that the entire country had approved of his dethronement. They justified the 1953 coup by stating that the deposed Sultan had been blocking the reforms, but recommended that these be implemented slowly and prudently. Although hostile to any change in the regime, they adamantly demanded revision of those articles of the Treaty of Fez which incommoded them. A number of the French Chamber of Agriculture of Fez had begun by criticizing the agricultural reform plan, only to end by declaring that modern farming methods should be reserved to the French and that it had been a great mistake to teach the Moroccans to use machines. The report noted that this obstructionist attitude impeded even the administration's faint desire for reform: having recently decided to reduce the exemption from the *tertib* (agricultural tax) enjoyed by modern farmers from 45 to 25 percent, it had been forced to raise it again to 30 percent under pressure from the settlers. By and large, the French in Morocco were described as being drawn more and more toward an aggressive separatism. They incessantly berated France and the metropolitan government, and openly regretted that the Residents-General did not enjoy greater freedom of action in relation to Paris.

Trapped between the two communities, the administration was felt to be generally hostile to any form of nationalist opposition. The investigators had found this strikingly confirmed by the fact that the Moroccan People's Party—a wholly artificial creation which had been vigorously encouraged in its activities by the administration in order to check the Istiqlal—had just been forbidden all activity because it had taken a stand against the Sultan's deposition.

De Moustier concluded that in such conditions there was little chance of any successful reform, since both the French and the Moroccans were against it for opposite reasons. The fact that in August 1953 support had been derived from all that was most reactionary in traditional Morocco and among the French made the deadlock even more complete. In fact, in twenty years, he stated, only one reform had been put into effect: abolition of the letter of the Treaty of Fez and the institution of a system of cosovereignty under cover of a reorganization of the central administration.

The argument the liberals had used against the ultras since the beginning of the Moroccan controversy was largely confirmed. Of course, the commission's majority report was more moderate in form and less positive in substance than the Verdier report. As the investigators noted when they presented their conclusions to the Assembly's Committee on Foreign Affairs, all had made certain individual concessions to avoid the necessity of a majority and a minority report. Nevertheless, the two versions were in essential agreement.

After reporting its conclusions, the De Moustier commission

expressed the hope that a bold and effective social policy could be put into effect in the protectorate.

While the commission proceeded with its investigations in Morocco, French and Spanish relations, never good, had reached their nadir. The Spanish authorities were piqued at having been ignored by the French during the 1953 crisis, and allowed the Moroccan notables in their zone to demonstrate openly against the spiritual rule of Mulay ben Arafa. The Tetuán petition affair, summarized elsewhere, aroused considerable feeling both in France and in Morocco. On the northern frontier of the protectorate, Spain opened a political second front which was soon to become a base for military operations by the Moroccan Army of Liberation. As early as January 1954, at the close of the Tetuán affair, Goum units were stationed on the frontier between the two zones. On January 24, Mulay ben Arafa appealed to Moroccans in all provinces of the empire to reaffirm its unity. On the 25th, as if in reply to the threats from across the frontier, Mohammed V was removed farther from Morocco and transferred from Corsica to Antsirabé, on the island of Madagascar. An epoch was drawing to its close.

On March 4, 1954, as the military situation in Indochina grew steadily worse, the Comité France-Maghreb passed a resolution denouncing the inadequacy of the Laniel government's policy in Tunisia. It declared that the time had come for France to define her North African policy and called for a change in the senior administrative officials in Morocco and for an end to police terror.[9] The return of France-Maghreb to the political scene was in itself a sign of the times. For the first time since the August crisis, Moroccan affairs had again become a pressing issue in France. From then on, France-Maghreb was to work actively for a change of Residents-General. Throughout March, the French press in Morocco devoted long articles to the recrudescence of terrorism which coincided with a rapid deterioration of the military situation in Indochina.

9. *France-Maghreb,* no. 1 (1954), with an editorial by Mauriac. There were several issues of this bulletin.

In April 1954, a final series of ministerial instructions gave proof that though Paris would make no decisions, it still intended to exercise its remaining power to give advice on reforms. All that could possibly be said in this connection was paraded, from the need to end terrorism to the necessity of rallying the Moroccan people around the new Sultan, admission of young Moroccans to administrative posts in the public and private sectors, reduction of the rebate on the *tertib,* action in rural areas, development of farm cooperatives, action in regard to workers, and the development of workers' councils. Particular emphasis was placed on the importance of speeding up the work of a joint committee on reforms set up by a Residential order of January 30,[10] of having the two sections of the Government Council sit as one, and of loosening the vise-like grip of direct administration.

Despite the August 1953 coup and the resigned acquiescence of Paris to the will of the Residency and of the leading citizens of both communities, the dialogue between Rabat and the Quai d'Orsay continued. Until the deposition of Mohammed V, Paris and Rabat had agreed in principle on the goal of creating a Franco-Moroccan state by means of reforms establishing a system of cosovereignty. Since August 1953, Paris and Rabat had agreed as to aims; but a new, tacit, but nonetheless perceptible conflict had arisen over procedure.

Whereas for Paris the August 1953 crisis ought to have constituted the point of departure for a policy of democratization intended to vest in the French colony in Morocco the powers formerly exercised by the Residency, for Rabat those same events constituted an end in themselves, a perfect solution, a masterly return to the purity of the colonial covenant which any further action might have ruined irreparably. Of course, the Residency still regarded the creation of a democracy in which the French and Moroccans would be on an equal footing as the ultimate objective, but it was convinced that it would be utter folly to try to effect such a system while the terrorist crisis continued. As long as the trial of strength in progress had not been settled in

10. Protectorat de la république française (empire chérifien), *Bulletin Officiel (B.O.),* Feb. 5, 1954, p. 172.

favor of the regime, the diminution of direct administration, modification of the judicial system, and establishment of elected bodies vested with powers of deliberation were bound, in the eyes of Rabat, to represent only drawbacks similar to those which the Sultan's deposition had been designed to avoid.

The Residency was so determined to adhere to the status quo that it found itself outdistanced both by Paris and by the ultras. While the Quai d'Orsay struggled in vain to make Rabat return to a policy of movement, the ultras took offense at the authoritarian complex which was causing the administration to concentrate all powers in its own hands. Matters were becoming ever more complicated in Morocco, where new problems seemed to arise in waves under pressure of political difficulties of every kind stemming from the abortive denouement of August 1953.

In such circumstances, the appointment of a new Resident-General seemed essential to all who were in any way involved in the conflict. On May 20, 1954, the Laniel government took advantage of the psychological shock caused by the fall of Dienbienphu on the 7th to appoint Francis Lacoste as Resident-General to Rabat. Paris liberals, aided by the return of France-Maghreb to the offensive, had played a considerable part in a decision they had been insistently demanding ever since terrorism first raised its head in Morocco. On May 21, the former Pasha Si Bekkaï held a press conference in Paris at which he urged the recognition of Moroccan sovereignty and the constitution of a Supreme Council. That same day, Jacques Lemaigre-Dubreuil in *Maroc-Presse* demanded the restoration of Moroccan sovereignty. On June 1, Guillaume left Rabat to the sound of gunfire. Slowly but surely, the end was approaching.

The Lacoste Period and the Mendès-France Government
(May 20, 1954–February 23, 1955)

Moroccan affairs had reached such a state by the spring of 1954 that the only possible impetus had to come from Paris. Thus it is necessary to study the metropolitan political situation in order to understand what was to happen at Rabat during the Mendès-France regime.

The government of Joseph Laniel had been shaken by North African events and worn out by the crisis over the European Defense Community (which had divided the majority parties as well as the Socialist opposition), and by the stunning disaster of Dienbienphu. On May 13, one week after Dienbienphu, the government had won its final extension by a mere two votes. Its fate had been virtually sealed since June 9, when the Prime Minister's proposed agenda had been refused priority after a meeting dominated by fiery attacks from Mendès-France; its final defeat came on June 12 by a vote of 306 to 293, with 12 abstentions.[11] The political offensive waged by Mendès-France against Laniel was designed less to put an end to the war in Indochina—the outcome of which was more or less a foregone conclusion once the Geneva Conference (April 26–July 17) had opened—than to take advantage of the breach in the metropolitan political front caused by the defeats in the Far East so as to bring about a complete overhaul of French policy. The new Prime Minister's main objectives appear to have been to put the government back in control, grant domestic self-government to the rebellious colonies, and settle the E.D.C. problem in order, by this sacrifice, to permit constructive negotiations with the Soviet Union, where the process of de-Stalinization was then in full swing.

On June 18, after a brief crisis, the Radical-Socialist leader was elected Prime Minister by 419 votes to 47, with 143 abstentions.[12] The political composition of the Mendès-France government did not differ essentially from that of its predecessor. This was not so strange: individuals had begun to count for more than opinions, since the right-wing and center parties had split under the stresses created in the French body politic by the vast problems confronting it, particularly the E.D.C. On the other hand, the parliamentary positions of the two governments differed considerably. The Laniel government had been right-of-center. The Mendès-France government was left-of-center; this did not prevent it from gleaning a good deal of support from a right wing

11. *Journal officiel (J.O.), Débats parlementaires, Assemblée nationale* (June 13, 1954), p. 2988.
12. Ibid. (June 18, 1954), p. 3037. The M.R.P. resented Mendès-France's policy on E.D.C. and overwhelmingly abstained.

which the defeats in Indochina had forced, willing or unwilling, into a policy of action.[13]

No sooner had he been invested by the Assembly than Mendès-France applied himself to the task of liquidating the war in Indochina. This was not a matter of choice, but a decision that could not be postponed in view of the stage developments had reached at the Geneva Conference. On June 17, 1954, in his inaugural speech, the Radical-Socialist leader had made the famous "Geneva wager" from the rostrum of the Assembly: "The government I am setting up will give itself—and our opponents —a time-limit of four weeks in which to . . . achieve [a cease-fire]. Today is June 17. I will come before you on July 20, and I will report to you. If no satisfactory settlement has been achieved by that date . . . my government will hand in its resignation to the President of the Republic." [14]

On July 22, the Prime Minister returned to Paris from Geneva bearing the international agreements which ended the war. The military settlement consisted of regrouping the two armies on either side of a provisional demarcation line drawn across the seventeenth parallel. France undertook to evacuate the Tonkin redoubt, but the Vietminh lost the vast dissident areas they controlled in the south and center of Indochina. On the political level, general elections designed to reunite Vietnam were to be held in July 1956. The international character of the peace settlement was only partially achieved. The President of the United States declared that his country would not consider itself bound by any agreement involving Communist China. At the same time, he indicated that the United States would regard any reopening of hostilities as "a matter of extreme gravity." [15] A defense committee had been set up consisting of Marshal Juin; General Pierre Koenig, Minister of War; General Paul Ely,

13. Since the Socialists refused to participate, Mendès-France had to move his government more to the right than he liked. The S.F.I.O., moreover, continued to support him. So did the Communists, who did not join the opposition until October 1954, thus accentuating even more the trend to the right of the group in power. It should be noted, however, that in calculating his majority in the Assembly, Mendès-France discounted the Communist votes as a matter of practice.

14. *J.O., Débats parl., Ass. nat.* (June 18, 1954), p. 2993.

15. François Mitterrand, *Présence française et abandon* (Paris, 1957), p. 60.

High Commissioner in Indochina; and General Guillaume, Chief of Army General Staff. On July 28, it was forced to affirm on behalf of the government that the delta and the battle of Tonkin had been lost. Any plan to continue the war in Annam and Cochin China in an attempt to recover lost territory, according to the committee, would require calling out the reserves.[16] On July 23, the National Assembly ratified the Geneva agreements by 462 votes to 13, with 134 abstentions, 70 of them from the M.R.P. For a time, Mendès-France had a free hand.[17]

The settlement of the Indochinese conflict in fact undermined the basic premises of French colonial policy. A seemingly endless colonial war had just terminated in resounding military defeat. The country's lassitude had made it necessary to seek a negotiated settlement long before the beginning of the last campaign. Except for a last little band of diehards, the Right had been forced to liquidate an operation it had supported for ten years and which, despite its domination of French policy since the Liberation, it had been unable to carry out. Parliament and the country, still stunned by the fall of Dienbienphu, greeted the compromise ending the crisis with almost unanimous relief. Not a single voice was raised on the Right, either in Parliament or the press, to demand reconquest of the lost Asian territories. The expeditionary force had been bottled up in the Far East for months. At any time, increased terrorism in North Africa might demand a military effort from France equal to or greater than that which had been necessary in Asia. The reverses in the Far East had shown that, in a crisis of this kind, internationalization apart, no stable solution can be found short of abandonment of the struggle or general mobilization. And so, for the first time, the colonial problem was laid squarely before the public. Colonialist groups in Parliament and in the country at large were thus faced with the choice of either a negotiated settlement or of general mobilization should the situation deteriorate in North Africa. Those in favor of the status quo at any price, who had dictated French colonial policy for the past decade, found themselves suddenly incapable of opposing a decolonization program

16. Ibid., pp. 22–23.
17. J.O., Débats parl., Ass. nat. (July 24, 1954), p. 3619.

for North Africa, as long as it was carried out vigorously and they were spared the embarrassment of having to direct it themselves.

Mendès-France was wise enough to realize the unique opportunity of settling with a flourish that North African conflict which had almost ended.[18] Since there could be no question of the course to take, he had addressed himself to the Tunisian problem as soon as he took office. In his inaugural speech, he had expressed himself categorically on the Tunisian and Moroccan questions:

> The accomplishment of the tasks I have just cited must go hand in hand with the reestablishment of peace and security in those two North African countries which at this very moment are beset by terror and fanaticism. Morocco and Tunisia, for whom France has opened the way to progress . . . must not become foci of agitation and insecurity on the borders of our Algerian departments. This is unthinkable.
>
> At the same time, I must state unequivocally that I will not tolerate any hesitation or reservations in carrying out the promises which we have made to peoples who have placed their trust in us.
>
> We promised we would train them to manage their own affairs. We shall keep that promise, and to this end we are ready to resume the negotiations which have, unfortunately, been interrupted.
>
> I am convinced that it is possible to reconcile the existence of common organs within the French Union with the steady evolution of governmental institutions within each of these two countries.[19]

18. He had to choose between settling the Tunisian problem or the Moroccan one. The choice was obvious. The former involved only the promise of internal autonomy made long before, and beyond dispute. This was the most that could be expected, considering the continuous opposition of political and social forces to fulfillment of this promise. By riding blindly into the Moroccan thicket, on the other hand, he would most certainly have come a cropper over the thorny problem of the Throne. This might have left the government without support in the face of a counterattack by partisans of the status quo.

19. *J.O., Débats parl., Ass. nat.* (June 18, 1954), p. 2994.

On July 17, 1954, even before the die was cast at Geneva, Mendès-France had brought Habib Bourguiba, previously interned on the island of Groix, to Paris. He sent the Socialist deputy Alain Savary to negotiate an unofficial agreement with the Neo-Destour leader. At Geneva, direct conversations were held between the Prime Minister and the Tunisian nationalists through Mohammed Masmoudi, representative of the Neo-Destour in France; while Christian Fouchet, first incumbent of the new Ministry of Moroccan and Tunisian Affairs, sounded out representatives of the Tunisian traditionalist or independent circles.[20]

Mendès-France's Tunisian campaign was waged on two fronts in masterly fashion. On July 30, the Prime Minister persuaded the Council of Ministers to approve granting immediate internal autonomy to Tunisia. France reserved to herself control over foreign relations and national defence. In addition, the rights of French nationals who had settled in Tunisia were to be protected by conventions to be negotiated between the two states. The real difficulty lay in obtaining a free hand from the Council of Ministers to carry out the decision, but this was obtained the same day, the Prime Minister having skillfully commandeered the good offices of Marshal Juin. This in itself was a revelation of a new sense of authority, and the Marshal was the first to recognize it. The next day, Mendès-France landed at Tunis with Juin and Fouchet. He then delivered an historic address at Carthage in the presence of the Bey which marked the end of the crisis: "The French government unreservedly recognizes and proclaims the internal autonomy of the Tunisian state. . . . The degree of development attained by the Tunisian people . . . the remarkable qualities of their leaders, justify their being called upon to govern their own affairs"[21] The Tunisian question had been

20. "There was much conjecture in political circles. M. Voizard and General Boyer de la Tour, commanding officer of troops in Tunisia, arrived in Paris. M. Colonna came to inform the Prime Minister of his fears. A Franco-Tunisian group established itself in the Palais Bourbon under the leadership of M. Médecin. The Independents and the A.R.S. opposed all negotiation with the enemies of France. The Gaullists were equally uneasy and René Mayer, followed by a significant part of the Radical Party, was positively menacing. It was necessary to act quickly to keep the opposition from reforming." Félix Garas, *Bourguiba et la naissance d'une nation* (Paris, 1956), pp. 253–54.

21. *La Documentation française, Articles et documents, Textes du jour,* 088 (Aug. 3, 1954); *Le Monde* (Aug. 1–2, 1954).

settled in principle; it still had to be settled in practice. A negotiating government was set up on August 7, 1954, consisting of nine ministers (four from the Neo-Destour party), with Tahar ben Ammar as Prime Minister. The opponents of the Carthage settlement, led by the Radical-Socialist Martinaud-Déplat, made a parliamentary counterattack on August 10 which failed. Questions on Tunisia and Morocco were postponed to August 27, by 397 votes to 114.[22] Despite their preference for a liberal colonial policy, most of the M.R.P. deputies had refused to vote for Mendès-France because of their hostility to his European policy: only 16 of them had supported the government.

The Franco-Tunisian negotiations, which had opened in Tunis on September 4, were resumed in Paris on the 13th. It may be useful to summarize their course up to the fall of the government. Although Bourguiba was still under house arrest at La Ferté, he had become the undisputed inspiration of the Tunisian delegation. In the beginning, the French attempted to limit participation by the Neo-Destour (the new Tunisian Prime Minister was not a Neo-Destour supporter). But they finally recognized the importance of the movement—a change of attitude that immediately increased the chances for success. Although the Tunisian ultras had not laid down their weapons, the government was wise enough to keep their representatives, Senator Antoine Colonna and Gabriel Puaux, away from the conference table. Their opposition, supported by their allies in Parliament and the press, was nevertheless a source of anxiety because of the continued activity of the *fellaghas* (terrorists). The new Resident-General, General Pierre Boyer de Latour, had proposed a truce to the outlaws, but they were unwilling to lay down their arms as long as negotiations continued. In the circumstances, it was difficult for the French government not to insist on the prior reestablishment of order. It is to Boyer de Latour's credit that he shouldered the full responsibility which this delicate political situation placed upon him. After difficult bargaining, he and Tahar ben Ammar resolved the issue on November 22 in a joint declaration calling upon the fellahin and the French in Tunisia to lay down their arms, and assuring the Tunisian freedom

22. *J.O., Débats parl., Ass. nat.* (Aug. 11, 1954), pp. 4047 ff., 4069.

fighters that they would not be molested. Boyer de Latour took vigorous steps to put the declaration into effect. By mid-December, the majority of the fellahin had laid down their arms.

The moment seemed ripe for concluding negotiations. The Mendès-France government, weakened by unprecedented political activity, ran out of time. Anxious to ward off the Opposition's increasing attacks, the Prime Minister had not dared to release Bourguiba or to negotiate directly with the Neo-Destour leaders. He was absorbed by the parliamentary battle over the Paris agreements and left Fouchet to his own devices. Negotiations bogged down, as much because of the inability of the head of the government to give them his personal attention as because of the intransigence he had been forced to show in order to stay in office. The Mendès-France government finally fell on February 5, 1955, leaving the Faure government to bring the Tunisian affair to conclusion.

This brief digression has been necessary for an understanding of the passivity displayed throughout by Mendès-France regarding Morocco. To have taken on Morocco when he was unable to solve the Tunisian question (which was already three-quarters settled) would have been the last straw for a policy which had been made generally vulnerable by seeking to settle all the problems at once. Nevertheless, at the beginning of August 1954, barely six weeks after taking office, Mendès-France had liquidated the problem of Indochina and had succeeded, for the first time since the war, in imposing the will of the executive upon those who had worked unceasingly and indefatigably to maintain the status quo in Tunisia.

What had been happening in Morocco? By sending Lacoste to replace Guillaume, the Laniel government, which knew it was doomed, had merely replaced a Resident-General worn to a shadow by one who was relatively fresh, but who was quite as attached to the status quo as his predecessor. Bidault had cut the ground from under the feet of Mendès-France, who was thus prevented for the time being at least from appointing a man of action to Rabat who would be energetic enough to assume on the spot, and if necessary at his own risk, the responsibilities which the head of the government might perhaps be unable to assume from Paris. As usual in the appointment of Residents-General, Guillaume's successor was no newcomer to the seraglio. A career diplomat, Deputy Minister, and then Secretary-General of the protectorate under Juin, he had won a narrow victory in the last days of the Laniel government over two other distinguished contestants whose names were to become household words: Koenig and Grandval.

Francis Lacoste took over the Residency on June 14, 1954, two days after the fall of the Laniel government and four days before the investiture of the Mendès-France government, at the very moment when, in Paris, a new man was bending all his energies to breathe life into a body politic paralyzed by internal dissension.

The two men were virtually destined to misunderstand each other. One envisaged the problems before him solely in terms of action. The other was obsessed by the idea that no reform was possible in Morocco until order had been reestablished. In France, the dizzy round of problems was beginning. At Rabat, passivity was to reign for the next twelve months.

The need for immediate restoration of order was the dominant theme in Lacoste's program, which he announced on the day he arrived in Rabat.[23] Evolution would only be possible, he said, if law and order were respected. Outside influences were the prime cause of terrorism (this was one of his idées fixes) and he would not allow himself to be drawn into the vicious circle of terror and collective repression, or into the error of confusing the genuine supporters of nationalism with the enemies of France. Unwilling by his silence to encourage the violence he feared, he closed with a pious warning to those troublemakers in the security forces who might be tempted by the situation to resort to cruelty. This mixture of platitudes—the cycle of terror and repression could hardly be broken if the primary objective was restoration of order—and dislike of violence was characteristic of the man. Despite this somewhat academic approach, Lacoste's advent was greeted with some hope by the nationalists and the French liberals, who little realized what disappointment Guillaume's successor had in store for them.

23. *Bulletin d'information du Maroc*, no. 43 (June 1954), pp. 154–55.

This apparent break in the clouds did not prevent terrorism from increasing, or even from using the French authorities as a target. On June 20, General d'Hauteville, head of the Military Region of Marrakesh, was wounded during an attempt on his life. On July 23, Claude Thivend, civic affairs deputy at Marrakesh, was assassinated. On July 30, Émile Eyraud was also killed in Casablanca. His murder aroused intense feeling among the French colony. They had deluded themselves into believing that the August 1953 coup would be accepted by the Moroccan populace, and were beginning to realize that civil war was at their gates. The authorities were increasingly alarmed. The closing of small Moroccan shops was clear indication of the growing domination of the nationalist agitators over the ordinary people. There were daily attacks on the state tobacconist's monopoly. The boycott spread to rural areas. Traditionalist officials, impressed by urban terrorism and by events in Tunisia and Indochina, grew more and more uneasy. The French police on numerous occasions had stressed the effect of the defeats in Indochina on Moroccan morale. The new flare-up of terrorism in the towns was certainly due in large part to Dienbienphu.

This new outbreak of violence was merely the outward sign of a political situation that was deteriorating at frightening speed. The townspeople and pro-nationalist notables had been profoundly stirred by events in Indochina and Tunisia, and were preparing to return to the fray after eleven months of submission. On July 24, 128 leading Moroccans addressed a letter to the Resident-General in which, after deploring the violence, they urged that steps be taken to relax tension and to settle the problems raised by the Sultan's exile, while duly recognizing the need to respect legitimate French interests.

As early as the end of July, petitions in favor of Mohammed V's return were pouring into the Residency. The movement had started among the ulama of Fez, and the small merchants in the towns immediately made common cause with them. In the towns, where emotions had reached fever pitch, the exiled Sultan's prestige was higher than ever. In the meantime, the internal autonomy of Tunisia had been proclaimed, and all Morocco was to be on tenterhooks. On August 1, a rumor that the Sultan was returning began to circulate in Fez. Soon thousands of Moroccan demonstrators were gathered. Women and children were trampled upon by the crowds or injured by the police. From then until about August 20, the town was in a constant uproar. On August 2, five Moroccans were killed and twenty-five injured, while shops were ransacked and the crowd acclaimed Mendès-France. Troops surrounded the *medina,* but the demonstrations increased. On the fifteenth, a sweeping roundup by the French forced the ulama to take refuge in the mosques. Finally, on the eighteenth, the ulama who had taken refuge in the *Horm* (sanctuary) of Mulay Idriss were arrested by the Sultan's Black Guard and taken to Rabat. Fez had been merely the epicenter of a political earthquake which had spread to all the principal towns of Morocco. While the people of Fez were defying the French authorities, Petitjean, Casablanca, and Port Lyautey had been the scene of incessant disturbances. At Petitjean alone, eleven people were killed and twenty wounded on August 3. Two days later, reinforcements had to be flown in, while at Khemisset the French settlers threatened to march on the Residency. Because of a harbor strike at Casablanca, it was necessary to concentrate sizable military forces there.

The P.D.I. took advantage of these circumstances to return to the political scene and to take its stand in favor of Mohammed V's return and the establishment of a Moroccan government. On the other side, el-Glaoui and the notables who had taken part in the Sultan's deposition made every effort in Paris and Rabat to see that the government did not waver in its support of Mulay ben Arafa. In an August 22 broadcast, Lacoste could point to something of a lull, but he was forced to admit that 32 Europeans and 129 Moroccans had been killed.[24] He recalled his declaration of June 14 and concluded by saying that neither letters nor petitions would lead him to make any changes in the program he had proclaimed upon his arrival. He was not the only one who refused to yield. On August 9, the Executive Committee of the S.F.I.O./Morocco had demanded the repres-

24. Ibid., no. 46 (Sept. 1954), p. 249.

sion of terrorism and had said that the problem of the Throne was irrelevant.[25] In less than a month, the Moroccan crisis had crystallized around the problem of the Throne.

Despite its small margin for maneuver in the Moroccan crisis, the French government had not remained wholly inactive. Mendès-France's statements in his investiture speech were not the first in which he had taken a stand on Morocco.[26] On June 9, nine days before he came to power, he had said in Parliament:

> Certainly, you have dethroned the former Sultan, or rather you have allowed him to be dethroned. But the change of sovereign has solved nothing—quite the contrary. And then you consent to mitigate the deficiencies in your policy . . . by recourse to the most oppressive police violence in complete opposition to France's fine liberal tradition.
>
> However, the force which was designed to prevent or to delay events has in fact accelerated them. It is, among the most advanced, transforming demands into open revolt, and, among the hitherto indifferent masses, it is creating the . . . concept of a national conflict and driving them to take arms against us.[27]

On June 19, one day after the vote of investiture, the Ministry of Moroccan and Tunisian Affairs had been set up in Paris. One month later, the Department of Sharifian Affairs was reorganized in Rabat. Liaison with the viziers was entrusted to the head of the department, while liaison between the Resident-General and the Sultan continued to be carried on by an adviser. At the same time, a whole series of appointments was announced. Maurice Papon became Secretary-General of the protectorate, Maurice Guiramand became Director of the Department of Sharifian Affairs, Colonel Georges Hubert took over the Department of the Interior, and Raymond Chevrier the D.S.T. There was nothing revolutionary in these changes and the problem of

25. Ibid., no. 45 (Aug. 1954), pp. 226–27.
26. For his investiture speech, see *J.O., Débats parl., Ass. nat.* (June 18, 1954), pp. 2992 ff.
27. Ibid. (June 10, 1954), p. 2853.

direct administration was left untouched. Since the reins were in the hands of the Prime Minister and Lacoste, such small-scale bureaucratic manipulations could not fundamentally improve the political context in which the two men had to operate.

The incidents at Fez had forced the Prime Minister to make two statements on Morocco in August 1954. Between July 20 and August 9, nine questions had been submitted to the officers of the Assembly. The debate to determine the date for discussing these items, most of which concerned Tunisia, was held on August 10. Mendès-France and Fouchet used the occasion to outline the policy they intended to adopt in Morocco. Christian Pineau (S.F.I.O.), Jacques Fonlupt-Esperaber (M.R.P.), and Pierre Clostermann (Social Republican) supported the Prime Minister. Deputy Jacques Bardoux (Independent), General Adolphe Aumeran (Independent), and Deputies François Quilici (Radical-Socialist), Jacques Vassor (A.R.S.), and Joseph Halleguen (Social Republican), supported by Léon Martinaud-Déplat (Radical-Socialist), vigorously attacked the government's Tunisian policy, emphasizing the potential repercussions in Morocco for the position of the ex-Sultan. Martinaud-Déplat exclaimed:

> If . . . wherever French blood flows . . . France negotiates with the assassins, new crimes will follow the old, and France, . . . one day bled white, will find herself reduced to her metropolitan territory, too small in this modern world to allow her to play the role of a Great Power.
>
> Now, Mr Prime Minister, you can understand my despair. I beg you to listen to me while there is still time.[28]

After explaining his Tunisian policy, Fouchet defined his Moroccan policy in these terms:

> As soon as the period of crisis has ended, it will be possible to undertake constructive political action in Morocco. The government will then embark on a large-scale program of activity. Those best qualified to repre-

28. *J.O., Débats parl., Ass. nat.* (Aug. 11, 1954), pp. 4049–50.

sent the Moroccan people will participate in its preparation, and it will give the Moroccans, the young people in
particular, increasing responsibility in the management
of their own affairs. . . . Such an overall program, ignoring none of the problems that have now plunged
Morocco into anarchy, and opening the way for a definitive solution, requires a minimum of calm and serenity
for its introduction and implementation. It is to this end
that the government intends to devote its immediate
efforts.[29]

The Prime Minister then rose to say that France could not
remain indifferent to the events which were rending Morocco
asunder. He added that an effort would be made, in agreement
with Sultan ben Arafa, to reduce tension and reestablish peace.
He repeated that though he would not yield to blackmail, it was
nonetheless necessary to have the courage not to use disorder as
an excuse for postponing essential political reforms.[30]

The great debate on the questions took place on the 26th. The
time allotted to each group had been strictly limited, and individual speakers had only a few minutes in which to explain their
views.[31] Certain truths hitherto misconstrued began to emerge.
Pineau read a letter he had received from a French officer serving
in Morocco which stated that the Berber tribesmen retained
warm feelings toward the deposed Sultan and that the Berber
troop concentrations at Fez should not be taken too seriously.
The former Minister said that he was personally in favor of a
third solution to the problem of the Throne, which did not, he
added, necessarily imply the intervention of a third person.[32]
Pierre Clostermann, also speaking in an individual capacity,
explained how the coup of August 20, 1953, had been organized
by the contrôle civil and in turn denounced the artificiality of
the conflict between the people in the towns and those in the
mountains. He asserted that the policy of restoring order as a

29. Ibid., p. 4046.
30. Ibid., p. 4052.
31. Although this was routine procedure, it is nonetheless remarkable that such
serious questions were treated with such concern for brevity.
32. J.O., Débats parl., Ass. nat. (Aug. 27, 1954), pp. 4256 ff.; ibid. (Aug. 28, 1954),
pp. 4313 ff.

precondition created a vicious circle, and concluded that the fact that Mohammed V had been deposed because of his so-called obstruction of the reforms had not prevented his successor from taking refuge in passivity.

The Muslim deputy Caid Abd el-Kader (U.D.S.R.) protested the Sultan's deposition, agreed that the Arab-Berber distinction was meaningless, told Fouchet the apparent restoration of calm in Morocco was deceptive, and berated Mendès-France for his weakness and inactivity concerning the Moroccan question. Speaking at the end of the debate, Mendès-France admitted that the government had not been able to devote sufficient time to Moroccan affairs. He declared his readiness "to take steps to improve the personal situation" of Sidi Mohammed ben Youssef, but said that he "could not, however, contemplate his return to the throne." [33] He added that, in agreement with Sultan ben Arafa, the government intended to organize local and regional assemblies vested with real powers. Representative assemblies could be installed side by side with the central authority at a later stage. He announced the establishment of a council to study reforms in which all shades of opinion would be represented, and concluded with a promise to raise agricultural wages, recognize trade-union rights, and apply labor legislation. The agenda item "approving the action of the government" was adopted by 419 votes, including the Communists, to 112, comprising Independents and most of the M.R.P. delegates.[34]

For the first time since the start of the North African crises, the Assembly was showing a direct interest in Morocco. The government's Moroccan policy had now been defined. It was almost indistinguishable from Bidault's. Its two guiding principles were opposition to the restoration of the deposed Sultan and recognition of the necessity for moving slowly in carrying out the reforms.

In Morocco, the notables expressed their satisfaction. But nationalist pamphlets distributed in Casablanca branded as traitors all those who responded to the French advances as long as the deposed Sultan could not make his voice heard, the imprisoned leaders had not been released, and Morocco had no promise of

33. Ibid., p. 4335.
34. Ibid., p. 4370.

complete independence. The Prime Minister's policy was so akin
to total immobility that even the French press in Morocco
commented on his August statements without hostility. It noted
with satisfaction the irrevocability of Mohammed V's deposition
and even contemplated his possible installation in France with
equanimity. The deadlock was worse than ever.

The Prime Minister had been forced to make the best of a bad
job. He was reduced to hoping that measures of clemency
together with a close association of the nationalists in the discussion of pending problems (the question of the Throne excluded)
might make it possible to await in relative calm the liquidation
of the Tunisian question and the opening of final negotiations on
Morocco. On September 8, 1954, Mendès-France, who had just
had a lengthy interview with the Resident-General in Paris, laid
down for him in a personal letter the political program whose
broad outlines he had sketched before Parliament. The Prime
Minister's plan was arranged under five headings: (1) relaxation
of tension through the release of deported nationalist leaders and
amnesty or conditional release for all persons sentenced for
political crimes; (2) creation of a council to study reforms, to
which the nationalists would be admitted after being warned
that the question of the Throne would not be raised; (3) return
to the policy of control within the framework of administrative
action designed to permit wider access by young Moroccans to
the civil service; (4) adoption of social and economic measures
aimed at raising wages of agricultural workers and granting
trade-union rights; (5) reorganization of the regime through
establishment of a Moroccan government consisting of Moroccan
ministers and French heads of departments, creation of a council
of notables and a representative central assembly, and decentralization of the executive.

Obviously, this compromise formula could lead nowhere. If
the question of the Throne was eliminated, what was there to
discuss, and, above all, with whom? Reforms of the usual kind
had failed because of the hostility of the Moroccan people; they
no longer interested the nationalists, who had heard more than
enough of them for ten years. As long as Mulay ben Arafa was

on the throne, no genuine spokesman would assume responsibility for an agreement on any important point. Even democratization of the country was blocked by the people's attitude toward the *djemaas* and the municipal elections. One may wonder how regional assemblies, still less central assemblies, were to be set up when the principle of election had been rejected at the local level, or how the political problem posed by general elections was to be solved when no one on the Moroccan side had any confidence in the Residency. If the elections were fair, the French candidates would be beaten. If they were not, there would be no genuine candidates. These are not reflections formulated in the light of hindsight, but commonsense comments found in the writings of most of the unofficial observers of the time.

Coming in the wake of Mendès-France's speech at Carthage, this program, though moderate, failed to please Lacoste. Apart from the provisions for releasing prisoners and initiating social reforms, Mendès-France's Moroccan plans seemed to him in flat contradiction to the policy of first restoring order with which he wanted his name associated. This policy was undoubtedly also the government's, officially at least. To the government, it was merely a face-saving device; to Lacoste, it had all the force of dogma.

Therefore, his speech on September 20, which informed Moroccans of the plan of action on which the Residency had embarked in compliance with the government's recommendations, did not go nearly as far as the Prime Minister had intended. Lacoste explained that the points he was to make were merely an outline for the Moroccans' consideration. He then took a stand in favor of the establishment of municipal, regional, and central assemblies in which the Moroccans would serve apprenticeship in democratic institutions. He also advocated reforms of the executive and judicial branches, and of decentralization of the administration. He went on to explain that the program would not be put into effect until after the establishment of a council to study reforms, which would in turn be preceded by amnesty arrangements and unofficial consultations with spokesmen of the various sectors of Moroccan public opinion. A few economic and social improvements were also promised for the immediate future, pending initiation of a constructive program of social action.[35]

Since the Resident-General had not disputed the need for steps to bring about a détente, these were duly taken. On September 29, the Military Tribunal of Casablanca dismissed the charges in the "1952 Communist plot" case and discharged the fifty-one Istiqlal and General Federation of Labor leaders held for the past two years.[36] On October 5, forty political detainees were also released. This was a major attempt to turn over a new leaf, all the more surprising in view of France's refusal at the same time to enter into discussions with the nationalists who had thus returned to circulation. This achievement was due in part to the efforts which the young Moroccan underground in Paris had been making since the autumn of 1953 in liaison with the nationalist leaders who had taken refuge abroad. They received effective support from the Comité France-Maghreb and Maître Georges Izard, and had used every possible procedural tactic to ensure that the trial of their interned political friends should open when the political climate was most auspicious. The decisions to be made depended primarily on Ahmed Balafredj and Allal el-Fassi, who conducted the defense with an anxiety which is understandable when it is borne in mind that their slightest miscalculation might have cost the lives of their friends. By the end of the trial, the group of nationalist protagonists had been reinforced by such Moroccan defense lawyers as Ahmed Boucetta.

The recently liberated nationalist leaders could choose between two lines of conduct. Some stayed in Morocco to resume control over the movement and review contact with the French authorities. Others, such as Omar Abd el-Djellil, Abderrahim Bouabid, and Ahmed Boucetta, settled in Paris, both to assume responsibility for public relations in connection with unofficial negotiations

35. *Bulletin d'information du Maroc,* no. 46 (Sept. 1954), pp. 241–44.

36. While the decision of the Military Tribunal had been in some respects circumstantial, it was certainly not a question of clemency, but of dismissal for lack of evidence. Had the Tribunal considered the indictments well founded, it would have pronounced sentence as a matter of course and would have left to the Resident-General responsibility for measures of clemency.

Lacoste was preparing to conduct with their friends in Rabat over the problem of the Throne, and to reorganize the defense of the nationalist cause in France itself, as the center of gravity of the conflict gradually moved from Rabat toward Paris.

With the release of the Istiqlal and U.G.S.C.M. leaders, Moroccan nationalism entered a new political phase. The failure of Mulay ben Arafa's policy and the prestige of the exiled monarch in Madagascar were gradually to place the nationalist leaders in a position from which they could really negotiate with France as equals. Increasingly, the Istiqlal leaders acquired the status of recognized political negotiators, although they never ceased to combat the protectorate. Nevertheless, the Istiqlal had lost the unparalleled position it had occupied in the nationalist camp up to December 1952. It was to remain to the end the most important Moroccan party, but was to be forced, irrespective of its wishes, to operate in a political context in which the resistance movement represented by the terrorist groups and the Moroccan Army of Liberation was to play an increasing part. It was the growing politicization of the conflict that was to enable the P.D.I., at the very end, to play a significant diplomatic role. It was never to become a mass party, but its pro-Residential sympathies became so diluted by the force of events that, when peace was restored, it was able to constitute itself an opposition to the monopolistic power of the reconstituted Istiqlal.

The unofficial consultations which the Resident-General had announced in his speech of September 20 took place immediately after the release of the nationalist leaders.[37] The council to study reforms which the conversations were intended to set up was the part of the governmental program that caused the Resident-General the greatest anxiety, since it implied opening de facto negotiations with the nationalist leaders.

Lacoste did not have long to worry. On September 29, on the eve of the liberation of the nationalist leaders, the Executive Committee of the P.D.I. announced from Lausanne that it did not intend to negotiate with the Residency.[38] The P.D.I. had

---

37. *Bulletin d'information du Maroc*, no. 46 (Sept. 1954), pp. 241–44.

38. This declaration could not be found in the press but was ascertained from unofficial Residential documents.

abstained from all political activity since August 1953; its reentry onto the scene was characteristic of the times. Lacoste, not wishing to let the Istiqlal monopolize any future negotiations, had thought to avoid such difficulty by encouraging the P.D.I. to resume its political activities. Lecomte was no stranger to this action, which brought a republican nationalist party back into political circulation just when Mohammed V and the Istiqlal were, willingly or unwillingly, becoming the real negotiators with the French government. Unfortunately for the Resident-General, the time for such subtle tactics was past. The P.D.I. leaders had been forced into intransigence in order to outbid the nationalist leaders who had taken refuge abroad: they were irrevocably bound by the Arab radio broadcasts of their slogans. They had not even awaited the opening of consultations announced by the Residency to make known their hostility: hence their statement of the twenty-ninth.

Obviously, in such an atmosphere, discussions between the Resident-General and those nationalist leaders still in Rabat were doomed. The Istiqlal leaders flatly opposed any participation by their representatives in the council to study reforms as long as the exiled Sultan had not been released. Those who talked to Lacoste on behalf of the P.D.I. were more flexible in private than their friends at Lausanne. They did not hide their personal opposition to Mohammed V's return to the throne; but this unofficial support for the Residency's argument was of no political use in view of the stand taken by the party leaders in Switzerland.

In the circumstances, Lacoste had no choice but to inform the government of the negative results of his consultations. This he did in October, the tenor of his report being that the demands of what he called the Istiqlal and P.D.I. "extremists" were unacceptable to France and that, consequently, France could maintain herself in Morocco only at the cost of a prolonged struggle with them. Lacoste hoped the measures of clemency just granted would allow the mass of the population to be reconciled with France, provided she did not compromise herself by clumsy attempts to enter into impossible alliances with the extremists. While recognizing that the idea of installing Mohammed V in France after he had abdicated still had merit, he emphasized that the problem of the throne could not be tackled officially until it had been unofficially clarified by preliminary contacts he had made with what he termed "the moderate elements in the P.D.I. and the Istiqlal." Lacoste's conclusion was that although there was some hope that most of the traditionalist elements and the moderate nationalists would adhere to the government's program (assuming an early compromise on the question of the throne), it was still necessary to negotiate with prudence; contact with the Istiqlal and the P.D.I. had been reestablished thanks to the unofficial negotiations begun by the Residency.

Since the moderate elements in the Istiqlal and the P.D.I. to which Lacoste referred were by definition unrepresentative, the problem of the Throne remained as pressing as ever. Once again, Rabat had lost the game before it had really started. This time, however, the Residency could fairly plead extenuating circumstances. The French government's plan had no chance of acceptance by the nationalists. Although the Resident-General had defended it with a manifest lack of enthusiasm, if must be recognized in his defense that he had no reason to fight for a policy in which he did not believe, while the government itself admitted it could not take public responsibility for the policy it ostensibly supported.

Not only was the government's plan blocked; the political house-cleaning which had accompanied its announcement had aroused new ferment among the French in Morocco. As a result of the activities in Paris by nationalist spokesmen whose movements had been the subject of extensive comment in the press, it had been bruited in Rabat that the government's program was merely a maneuver to pave the way for a decisive political campaign that would include, inter alia, a settlement of the problem of the throne in the nationalists' favor. On all sides there was open talk of the departure of Sultan ben Arafa, the return of Mohammed V to France, and the appointment of a Council of Regency. The excitement spread to the nationalist leaders still in Morocco, who talked only of going to Paris to negotiate with the French government.

The Resident-General went to Paris at the end of October. He surveyed the political scene there, complained bitterly of the activities of the Moroccan lobby, and declared himself in favor of replacing ben Arafa by a third man—an apparently innocuous solution that was more astute than it looked, as will be seen subsequently. Lacoste returned to Rabat on October 27, declaring that the next move was up to the government, which, having been counting on the Resident-General to act in its stead, was thus back where it had started.

So widespread was the feeling that Mendès-France would be forced to take a stand that the Federal Executive Committee of the S.F.I.O./Morocco adopted a resolution on October 30 stating that "at a time when the French government is preparing to define its Moroccan policy, the S.F.I.O./Morocco hopes that no decision affecting the future of the Franco-Moroccan community will be taken without first considering the desires of the various sectors of the Moroccan population." [39] In deference to this resolution and similar appeals, Fouchet announced on November 8 that the government would make no decision on Morocco without the agreement of all parties, which was one way of yielding to the inevitable. [40]

On the night of October 31, the Algerian insurrection broke out in Aurès, marking the beginning of a military crisis of the first order in North Africa. Although initially the incident had no appreciable effect on French policy in neighboring territories, it was to prove decisive for the future of Franco-Moroccan relations. The Algerian revolt did more than hamper the military effort France was to make in Morocco the following year; it also brought much closer the time when the Métropole would have to choose more or less deliberately between reconquering all three territories or concentrating its military might on Algeria alone. [41]

The deterioration of the situation in Morocco and the outbreak of the Algerian insurrection, which coincided with Boyer de Latour's appeal to the Tunisian fellahin on November 22, 1954,

39. *Bulletin d'information du Maroc,* no. 48 (Nov. 1954), p. 303.
40. *Le Monde* (Nov. 10, 1954).
41. The effect of the Algerian rebellion on the Moroccan conflict might have been even greater had the Moroccan insurrectionists been able to launch their campaign simultaneously. This was impossible, due to circumstances beyond their control, and the Algerians went into action alone, followed the next year, on October 31, 1955, by the Moroccan Army of Liberation.

made a new debate on North Africa essential.[42] It took place between December 9–11.[43] Sharply attacked on every facet of their North African policy, the Prime Minister, the Minister of the Interior, and the Minister for Moroccan and Tunisian Affairs reaffirmed the line they intended to follow in the three territories.

One interpellator, Jean Grousseaud (moderate), said that never had a government done so much harm to the country. René Mayer (Radical-Socialist) vehemently criticized the conduct of the Franco-Tunisian negotiations and expressed the fear that the policy adopted in Tunisia would have disastrous repercussions in Algeria. Bidault, who had asked a question regarding the "government's rumored intention of bringing the former Sultan of Morocco from Madagascar to France and the guarantees . . . given to His Majesty Sidi Mohammed Mulay ben Arafa in regard to the continuity of French policy in Morocco,"[44] told the Assembly of his anxiety over reports which had appeared in the press in that connection, but declared himself satisfied when Fouchet replied that, as far as the French government was concerned, there was only one ruler of Morocco.

The government's Algerian policy, as set forth by Mitterrand, Fouchet, and Mendès-France, was based on three points: repudiation of any solution through surrender, defense of the unity and integrity of French territory, and the need to proceed with widespread reforms without awaiting restoration of order. As Mendès-France said in regard to Tunisia: "M. René Mayer used a phrase echoed by M. Fouchet which seems to me admirable in its clarity and simplicity. He said: 'Self-government, yes; independence, no.' On behalf of the government, I reply: 'Agreed.' "[45] On the other hand, the Prime Minister made no promises regarding Morocco. "Few speakers . . . have referred to Morocco," was all he said. There, too, the "situation has improved considerably in the countryside and nearly all the towns." One had only to bear in mind "the acute crisis" of August to "realize what a considerable advance the situation of today represents, al-

42. While most of the interpellations concerned Tunisia, a few applied to Morocco.
43. *J.O., Débats parl., Ass. nat.* (Dec. 10, 1954), pp. 6017–32; ibid. (Dec. 11, 1954), pp. 6047–59, 6083–6108.
44. Ibid. (Dec. 10, 1954), p. 6017.
45. Ibid. (Dec. 11, 1954), p. 6093.

though . . . of course, we cannot claim to have settled all the problems." [46] While it is true that the hopes aroused by the change of government had probably made it possible to avoid the worst in Morocco, Mendès-France was nevertheless forced to take the wish for the deed. Deputy Robert Verdier (S.F.I.O.) was not deceived. He adjured the government to settle the Moroccan problem as quickly as possible, and to start by solving the problem of the Throne.

The debate concluded with the adoption of a resolution approving the government's declaration, by 294 votes to 265. The opposition included the Communists, the M.R.P., and various right-wing members. The hostility of a Radical-Socialist like Mayer was a clear sign of the slow but certain deterioration of the parliamentary position. The government had never had so small a majority.[47]

Anxious to be done with the problem of the Throne at all costs, Mendès-France made his decision. On October 23, he resorted to one of the unorthodox moves which were his trademark and sent Mohammed V's personal physician, Dr. Henri Dubois-Roquebert, to Madagascar to explain unofficially to the exiled monarch that although the French government still opposed his restoration, it was willing to install him in France, provided he would first agree to the designation of a new sultan.[48]

As might have been expected, Mohammed V refused. There was, he said, no justification for an abdication, no matter what it was called, either in any error of his own or in the will of the Moroccan people. He pointed out that the designation of a third ruler would simply aggravate the crisis and would solve none of the existing problems. He declared his readiness to join the government in studying any solution that might restore calm in Morocco, provided he was first brought to France. He explained that he could not play any political role while in Madagascar. Morocco would have no confidence in decisions taken by a captive sovereign. In any event, it was essential that he be able to

46. Ibid., p. 6092.
47. Ibid., p. 6116.
48. George Izard, "Le 'Secret' d'Antsirabé," *Études méditerranéennes*, no. 4 (1958), pp. 62–63.

consult freely with representatives of Moroccan public opinion before he made up his mind.

Despite this refusal, developments since August 1953 in the various circles concerned with the problem of the throne did not appear to be absolutely incompatible with the working out of a political modus vivendi. Even the most convinced nationalists realized that no French government could restore Sidi Moham- med ben Youssef without risking immediate overthrow; this awareness led them spontaneously toward the idea of a third solution. The Moroccan traditionalists ruled out any return of the ex-Sultan to the throne, but they were ready to envisage any other formula. As for the French in Morocco, they had realized for some time that Mulay ben Arafa threatened to become more of a nuisance than an asset, and they too were forced to admit that the constitutional status quo could not go on forever. When each party had made its reservations, there was still sufficient room for maneuver to begin unofficial negotiations, with some chance of success.

To understand subsequent events, it is necessary to examine in turn the attitude of each interested party that had officially or unofficially taken up the question of the Throne during the pre- ceding months. There were four such parties and they came upon the scene in approximately the following order: liberal circles in Paris; Mohammed V himself, negotiating from Mada- gascar with the nationalists through his adviser and confidant Maître Izard; the Residency; and the French government.

The idea of a Council of the Throne was first publicly formu- lated at the end of the Guillaume period. It seems to have been the idea of a liberally inclined metropolitan study group: the Centre d'études et de documentation, run by Jean Védrine, Assistant Director of the Carven Perfume Company. The inter- vention of this unofficial body in the Moroccan question is a typical example of the part unauthorized persons can play in the genesis of a political idea, and an unmistakable sign that the Moroccan problem had come to a head in France. The aim of the Centre, whose principal figures seem to have had no political ambitions, was to study the Moroccan problems objectively, to try to find some solution, and to have that solution adopted by

the French government. It appears to have been motivated by
Védrine's intense pleasure in the roles of *éminence grise* and
organizer of brain-trusts. At first, the Centre favored complete
and unconditional independence for Morocco, but after the deposition of Mohammed V it moved toward the idea of setting
up a Council of Regency. On May 15, 1954, immediately before
Guillaume's departure, a mimeographed note put out by the
Centre had taken a stand, apparently for the first time in France,
in favor of the elimination of Sultan ben Arafa and the constitution of a Council of Regency.[49] Thus began the idea of the
Council of the Throne. On October 10, the Centre reiterated its
suggestion in a new bulletin which emphasized its timeliness and
reformulated it, after once again denouncing the myths of el-
Glaoui and the Arab-Berber opposition.[50]

In the meantime, in September, Maître Izard flew to Antsirabé,
the Sultan's Madagascar home-in-exile, in answer to a call from
Mohammed V, who wished to review the political situation with
him. Whether Izard knew of the Védrine document or whether
he had come to the same conclusion—it was after all a fairly
common suggestion in times of monarchical crisis—he had left
Paris convinced also that the establishment of a Council of the
Throne was the only possible means of breaking the Moroccan
deadlock without forcing any of the parties to lose face. He
thought even then that the future council should consist of at

49. Centre d'études et de documentation, *Un Processus d'évolution du Maroc,* Maroc
A6 (Paris, 1954).
50. Centre d'études et de documentation, *Urgence d'une politique française au Maroc,*
Maroc A8 (Paris, 1954). The political activities of the Védrine group began to take shape
in the summer of 1953. At that time, Védrine met Si Bekkaï and soon aroused him to
action. Si Bekkaï at first considered the idea of the Council of the Throne unsound but
finally allowed himself to be persuaded. The group then turned its attention to French
public officials and tried to convert them by sending them mimeographed documents.
Védrine later estimated that of the 200 members of Parliament approached, some 20
were interested. Appeals to officials, trade unions, journalists, and government advisers
were equally futile. Of the speaking tours arranged, only Si Bekkaï's were well attended. This intellectual pressure group, according to one of its leaders, was interested
less in defending interests than in launching key ideas, and was the first to elaborate
the real Moroccan policy of France and to impose it, first on the Moroccans, then the
Sultan, and, finally, on the French government. This group was unquestionably instrumental concerning the Council of the Throne, but such claims seem to be based upon
an exaggerated evaluation of the role of these ideas. At that time, theory was less
important than practice, and that, in the end, was to depend upon the concerted action
of all the interested protagonists.

least three persons: a representative of Mohammed V (possibly Si Bekkaï), a representative of Mulay ben Arafa, and a representative of the traditionalists.

At first Mohammed V was cold to the idea. He could not see why any representative of Mulay ben Arafa should serve on such a council. Later he realized that this was of no importance, since Si Bekkaï would be his own representative on the council and nothing could be decided without his consent. Finally, therefore, Mohammed V gave his consent on condition that the Istiqlal, with which he authorized Maître Izard to enter into negotiations, also approved. At this stage, it was no longer simply a question of setting up a Council of the Throne, but of negotiating a durable political solution pending the formation by the council of a provisional Moroccan government empowered to settle with France all the outstanding questions.

On his return, the Sultan's negotiator got in touch with the newly released leaders of the Istiqlal. Throughout the autumn of 1954 there were active negotiations between the Istiqlal and Antsirabé, through the intermediary of Maître Izard, who reported regularly to Mohammed V and each time brought back the requisite instructions. In the course of these negotiations, every aspect of the problem received detailed study, especially those relating to the actual constitution of the future council, its competence, its procedures, its relations with the two Sultans, the powers of the provisional government, and the form of relations to be established between the two sides. The principle of the establishment of a constitutional monarchy was also adopted. The Istiqlal laid particular stress on the problem of sovereignty raised by the 1953 coup. Opposed to the abdication of Mohammed V and hostile to the opening of any negotiations before the departure of Mulay ben Arafa, the party finally signified its assent to a gradual course whereby Sidi Mohammed ben Youssef would be installed in France and a Council of Regency would be set up, consisting of a representative of the Sultan; representatives of the P.D.I., the Istiqlal, and the ulama; and a Moroccan traditionalist appointed by the Residency (el-Glaoui and the Sharif el-Kittani being ruled out). It was understood that a provisional government consisting of Istiqlal leaders, P.D.I. representatives, and Moroccan independents would be set up at the same time.

The contacts made by the Sultan's envoy were not restricted to the Istiqlal. Agreement of the P.D.I. was also obtained, and opinion in French political circles was sounded out by various intermediaries, including the editor of *L'Express,* Jean-Jacques Servan-Schreiber, who apparently had been taken into confidence.

At Rabat, meanwhile, the Resident-General was pursuing a very different political course. Lacoste was entirely opposed to the idea of a Council of the Throne and had unveiled his own plan in conversations with the nationalist leaders. The Lacoste plan advocated installation upon the Sharifian throne of a third man, who would succeed the reigning Sultan after Mohammed V's abdication. The change of ruler would have been accompanied by the introduction of reforms already announced by the Resident-General and also, at some unspecified date, by some kind of internal self-government à la Bourguiba. The Resident-General's idea was to offer the throne to the Caliph of Tetuán, which was rather clever. By crowning the Caliph, the Residency would have killed two birds with one stone: It would have brought Spain and France together again, and it would have deprived the nationalists of the support of the northern zone. In this way, the Residency hoped to rally international opinion to its side and so eliminate any danger of the return to the throne of the man who had become the embodiment of Moroccan nationalism. This politically astute plan, so full of potential danger for the nationalists, was the work of Colonel Aymé Pommerie, Director of Industrial Production and Mining and principal political adviser to Lacoste. The Istiqlal immediately concentrated on blocking this solution. Abderrahim Bouabid and Omar Abd el-Djellil made a special trip to Paris for this purpose and, spurred on by the knowledge that the third-man scheme appealed to the Prime Minister, did their utmost to torpedo it.

Lastly, there were the ideas of Mendès-France himself, which were not far removed from those of the Resident-General. Mendès-France was not sympathetically disposed toward the exile in Madagascar. He knew little of the Sultan and believed him to be both discouraged and not very eager to regain the throne. He had told Maître Izard he intended to make Sidi Mohammed ben Youssef choose between abdication and exile on a distant island, and Dubois-Roquebert had finally been instructed to advocate the third-man formula at Antsirabé.

The failure of the Dubois-Roquebert mission seemed to have brought the Franco-Moroccan problem once again to a complete deadlock. The government demanded Mohammed V's abdication and his agreement to the investiture of a new Sultan. Mohammed V refused to make any decision before being brought to France. The nationalists refused point-blank to negotiate with France until that condition had been fulfilled.

Nevertheless, Maître Izard believed that this conflict of views did not necessarily destroy all chance of success for his transitional formula, since the failure of Mendès-France's envoy in effect forced the Prime Minister to reopen negotiations at once. As Izard saw it, the position after the failure of the Dubois-Roquebert mission was as follows: the French government had just made two unsuccessful attempts to ensure that the question of the Throne would not remain a stumbling block. It had released the 1952 detainees in order to facilitate the establishment of a council to study reforms, in the hope that this body would serve as an acceptable spokesman. That procedure had been stillborn because of the nationalists' refusal to serve on the council until the problem of the Throne had been settled. Paris had then tried to approach Mohammed V through Dubois-Roquebert, thus bringing about the definitive rejection of the third-man solution. Therefore, the Council of the Throne became the only possible solution. It would be to the French government's advantage because the Sultan would not be restored and France would not be obligated to restore him, and the nationalists who had sponsored the plan would become acceptable spokesmen in the negotiations. Thus tension in Morocco would be relieved. Mohammed V himself would obtain satisfaction on two essential points: the spectacular liquidation of the 1953 coup would point up for all concerned the inconsistency of the present occupant of the throne, and the public, in France and abroad, would realize once and for all that nothing could be done without the lawful sovereign's consent.

This time the problem was clearly stated. Because the Residency and the notables were beginning to suspect the plot between Paris and Antsirabé, it became more necessary than ever to act quickly. It was now mid-December 1954. There remained only the question of where to record the Sultan's official consent to the formula suggested and prepared by his negotiator. The French government wanted Madagascar, fearing that the Sultan, once settled in France, would increase his demands. The Sultan, who was afraid that anything decided in Madagascar would be suspect in the eyes of the nationalists, was unwilling to commit himself until he had set foot on French soil. Again, Maître Izard found a way to compromise: he proposed that the final plan be negotiated in Madagascar, but that its signature and publication should not take place until after Mohammed V's arrival in France.

The exiled ruler made a final statement of his position in a letter to Izard from Madagascar on December 26. This letter marked the turning point in the crisis.[51] The formula for the Council of the Throne and for the provisional negotiating government, previously agreed upon with the nationalist leaders, was this time accepted by Mohammed V as a basis for unofficial negotiations with the French government. Sidi Mohammed ben Youssef specified that the role of the provisional government would be to negotiate an agreement affirming the integrity of Moroccan sovereignty, to organize relations between France and Morocco on a basis of interdependence, and to put into effect reforms that would transform Morocco into a modern country governed by a constitutional monarchy. It was stipulated that the economic and cultural rights and interests of the French colony would be defined and guaranteed. Lastly, the Sultan demanded that once calm was restored, the Moroccan people should freely choose their own sovereign. Izard at once informed Fouchet of this basis for discussion. The Minister took note of it, at the same time raising certain objections to the role envisaged for the future provisional government and the use of the term "interdepen-

51. For the text, see Izard, "Le 'Secret' d'Antsirabé," pp. 61 ff.; see also *L'Année politique 1955* (Paris, 1956), pp. 663–65; also *Le Monde* (Sept. 14, 1955).

dence." The Sultan explained a few days later that he had used the term advisedly because it implied the whole range of possible forms of association between France and Morocco.

The initial Izard mission, crucially important, had ended. For the first time since the crisis began, the French government had before it a compromise formula for a settlement that had the approval of the nationalists and the Sultan. All that remained was to persuade France to agree to discuss it officially. A second Izard mission, under the Faure government, was to devote itself to this end, with the same nationalist interpellators. It was to begin in February 1955 and to end with Lacoste's recall and his replacement by Gilbert Grandval in June 1955.

In the meantime, the government's Algerian policy had grown still more complicated. On January 5, Mitterrand submitted to the Council of Ministers the plan of administrative reform [52] he had outlined in Algiers the previous September. The aim was still to give effect to the 1947 statute by various electoral and administrative measures favorable to the Moslems. Anxious to crush the opposition he anticipated in Algeria, Mendès-France replaced Roger Léonard at Algiers with Jacques Soustelle, who at the time enjoyed a solid reputation as a liberal. This appointment, coinciding with publication of the Mitterrand plan, elicited sharp reactions in Algeria and in Parliament. The Algerian Assembly objected that it had not been consulted when the government was drawing up a program which in fact came under its jurisdiction. [53]

In Paris, the Mendès-France government was nearing its end. Fenced in by growing opposition after nine months of frenzied activity, the Prime Minister had his back to the wall and was fighting adversaries who were only awaiting the moment for the final blow. The Residency in Rabat, realizing the end was coming, gambled on the fall of the government and confined itself to dealing with day-to-day matters. The last debate opened

52. This plan had already been brought up in the National Assembly during the December debate on North Africa. See *J.O., Débats parl., Ass. nat.* (Dec. 11, 1954), p. 6080.

53. For this period of the Algerian conflict, see in particular "Le problème algérien," *Chronique de politique étrangère, 8* (1955), 677–740.

on February 2 with a series of interpellations on North Africa and more particularly on the government's Algerian policy.[54] New "explanations" were quite uncalled for, since the Assembly had discussed the same problems at length six weeks earlier. In reality, the opposition was seeking a parliamentary fight that would enable it to finish off Mendès-France on ground where he had become particularly vulnerable.

Fifteen Independent, Social Republican, A.R.S., and Communist interpellators were listed. The Communist spokesman, Raymond Guyot, demanded an end to ben Youssef's exile and said that ben Arafa "should be chased off the throne." [55] He did not go so far as to propose restoration of the ex-Sultan, which shows how sensitive the French Parliament still was to any thought of restoration in Morocco. The decisive attack was led by René Mayer, Radical-Socialist deputy from Constantine. He told the Prime Minister at the end of his speech that if another vote of confidence were demanded, "I shall regretfully not be able to give it to you, for one simple reason . . . related to policy as a whole and also to international affairs. . . . I have no idea where you are going. I cannot believe that a policy of action can find no middle course between passivity and wild experiment." [56] It could hardly be more clearly implied that the debate on North Africa was mere pretext, but in reproaching the Prime Minister for basing his foreign policy on ulterior motives to which Parliament was not privy, the Radical-Socialist deputy was perhaps not wholly wrong. However, whatever those secret designs relating chiefly to foreign policy might be, the Communists did not seem to take them very seriously, for once again they were preparing to vote against the government.

Mendès-France vigorously defended his position on North Africa:

> Only two policies are possible there; the policy of agreement and reform. . . . Or the policy of force and repression, with all its horrible consequences. I have urged

54. *J.O., Débats parl., Ass. nat.* (Feb. 3, 1955), pp. 603 ff.; (Feb. 4, 1955), pp. 662 ff.; (Feb. 5, 1955), pp. 737 ff.

55. Ibid. (Feb. 3, 1955), p. 629.

56. Ibid. (Feb. 4, 1955), p. 666.

you again and again, with all my strength and with all my conviction, to choose the first—and so far, despite all difficulties, the National Assembly has followed the government in this course. I cannot allow the policy which I believe to be sound and necessary to be condemned today. I shall defend it to the end, in defiance of all political trickery.[57]

The results of the voting on the government's resolution were announced on February 5 after the Prime Minister had denounced the motley coalition formed against him and had stressed the danger of open political crisis in the present state of French affairs. The government lost by 273 votes to 319, including 20 Radical-Socialists.[58] Contrary to established practice, Mendès-France mounted the rostrum again after the announcement to make a final statement that was the target of lively protest from the Communist benches, the Right, and the M.R.P. The divorce between the regime and the man who had tried to breathe new life into it was now complete.

Once again, the Assembly's vote was directed against the man and his personal idea of French policy far more than against his North African policy. Parliament had no fundamental disagreement with his Tunisian policy, which it was to continue to support under the next government, his Moroccan policy (far from bold in any case), or his Algerian policy, which bore no trace of any spirit of compromise.

The failure of the Mendès-France experiment put an end to a policy of decolonization that had barely begun. Actually, the Prime Minister had regarded Tunisia as a kind of pilot project. Morocco, the African colonies south of the Sahara, and Algeria were to have followed. Each community was to have been granted a certain measure of self-government over a period of time. Mendès-France said in the course of an interview that in one more year he would have reached his objective. His view was confirmed by the fact that various North African nationalist leaders admitted in private that it would not be in their interest

57. Ibid., p. 691.
58. Ibid. (Feb. 5, 1955), p. 782.

to attain independence too soon. Believing himself incapable of settling the fate of both protectorates at once after the Geneva armistice, Mendès-France had chosen to begin with Tunisia, where the line of resistance was weaker. The Right, confronted more or less with a fait accompli, had gone along with him, but his enemies had recovered and given him to understand that he would not take them in a second time.

Another expert on Morocco implied during an interview that Mendès-France ought to have gone from Tunis to Rabat to do in August 1954 what Edgar Faure was to try to do in August 1955.

> He would have got them to agree to anything, for he had the wind in his sails. But he had got himself involved in European affairs, the Brussels Conference, the rejection of E.D.C., the establishment of the Western European Union, not to mention the Saar agreements with Adenauer. On November 1, the revolt broke out in Algeria. On the 13th he left for Canada. The situation could have been saved if he had had time. In Morocco he would not have had Marshal Juin's support as he did at Tunis. He would probably have said to Sidi Mohammed ben Youssef: There are islands even further off than Madagascar.

Of these two explanations—progressive whittling away of his freedom of parliamentary maneuver or failure to exploit the political situation properly through trying to do too many things at once—the Prime Minister's seems on reflection to have been the sounder, although overwork and accumulation of responsibilities undoubtedly played their part. Had there been any solution to the Moroccan problem in August 1954, it would not have entirely disappeared by February 1955; and Mendès-France's successor, who was watching Morocco closely, would have been able to take the initiative as soon as he came to power. Yet Faure was also to be reduced to admitting that nothing could be done in Morocco while the Tunisian problem remained. He was to have to put up with Lacoste. Not until five months after his investiture, in July 1955, was he able to take a step forward by replacing Lacoste with Grandval.

To conclude, in spite of these facts, that the Moroccan question could have been settled out of hand in August 1954 would be to substitute groundless assumptions for the normal process of retrospective speculation.

End of the Lacoste Period: From the Investiture of the Faure Government to the Appointment of Gilbert Grandval (February 23–June 20, 1955)

The Faure government was installed on February 23, 1955, by 369 votes to 210, with 28 abstentions. As in the time of Joseph Laniel, it was right-of-center. The Communists, Progressives, and Socialists voted against it as a bloc, but the Right and Center gave the government massive support. The new team included five Radical-Socialists, four M.R.P. members, and three from the R.G.R.; three Independents and Independent-Peasants, one Peasant, one U.D.S.R. man, four Social Republicans, and one member of the A.R.S. This time the Ministry of Moroccan and Tunisian affairs went to Pierre July (A.R.S.). Antoine Pinay was given the Quai d'Orsay, where he was to play a decisive role in the next period. In the Ministry of National Defense, General Koenig brought a watchful and censorious eye to bear on the government's Moroccan policy until his resignation in October 1955.

It is symptomatic that the Prime Minister who was to lance the Moroccan abscess felt Parliament to be so sensitive on anything relating to the protectorate that he omitted reference to Morocco in his inauguration speech. Until Lacoste was replaced by Grandval, furthermore, the government paid much more attention to Tunisian and Algerian affairs than it did to Morocco. As for Tunisia, Faure declared on the day his government took office that he intended to continue his predecessor's work and to conclude negotiation of the conventions begun on the latter's initiative.[59] There was no objection from Parliament, a clear indication that the Right had no intention of questioning the change in approach and concept which the outcome of the war in Indochina had imposed upon its colonial policy.

Unreservedly supported by Pierre July, whose political beliefs

59. Ibid. (Feb. 24, 1955), p. 868.

did not prevent him from professing and applying very liberal ideas in regard to decolonization,[60] Faure set to work. As Assembly susceptibilities were impeding the drafting of the remaining articles of the Franco-Tunisian conventions, the Prime Minister took the bull by the horns. He released Bourguiba, who he knew was willing to compromise to end matters, summoned him to Matignon, and in consultation with him settled all remaining problems. It was now April 22, 1955.

The protocol completed by the two men included a general convention embodying the principle of Franco-Tunisian cooperation and internal autonomy of the former protectorate, while safeguarding (subject to Tunisian agreement) the diplomatic and military prerogatives of France. Provision was made for recourse to a council of arbitration if difficulties arose. The Bizerte-Ferryville zone was accorded special status, with the French retaining exclusive control over military establishments there. The general convention was accompanied by a second convention setting forth the special rights of French nationals in Tunisia, and various agreements relating to judicial, administrative, technical, and cultural matters. These agreements were the outcome of a compromise; the internal self-government of the Tunisian State was limited by the privileges granted to French residents there, and the exclusive competence France had tried to retain in matters of foreign relations had been replaced by a simple treaty of cooperation between the two countries.[61] The conventions were initialed on May 29 and signed on June 3. On May 31, Bourguiba had embarked for Tunis after stating that independence was still the supreme objective but that it would have to be attained in a manner consistent with the conventions and free association with France.[62] The National Assembly approved the Franco-Tunisian conventions on July 8 by 538 votes to 44, with 89 abstentions.[63] They were ratified by the Council of the Republic on August 3 by 253 votes to 26, with 36 abstentions.[64]

60. July was excluded from the A.R.S. on October 7, 1955, for his attitude on Morocco, but he remained part of the independent center and connected with the R.G.R.
61. See "Evolution de la question tunisienne," *Chronique de politique étrangère*, 9 (July 1956), 516, 528.
62. See *Le Monde* (June 1, 1955); *La Documentation française, Notes et études documentaires*, no. 2026 (May 31, 1955), p. 10.
63. *J.O., Débats parl., Ass. nat.* (July 9, 1955), p. 3780.
64. *J.O., Débats parl., Conseil de la république* (Aug. 4, 1955), p. 2200.

Not all the difficulties had been smoothed out, but the Tunisian crisis was nevertheless resolved on the basis of a statute that seemed to define in advance the task of the negotiators who would one day have to untangle the Moroccan conflict. No one could have foreseen that in a few months the deterioration of France's position in Morocco would have brought about, by a relentless chain reaction, the total demolition of the conventions so happily drafted by Faure and Bourguiba.

While passions were dying down in Tunisia, the situation in Algeria grew steadily worse. Here again, the Prime Minister had committed himself in his inaugural speech to continuation of his predecessor's policy.[65] The retention of Jacques Soustelle as Governor-General exemplified the continuity of French policy in Algeria. Separatism was politically inconceivable and the government had little room to maneuver. On March 31, 1955, the National Assembly passed the act declaring a state of emergency by 361 votes to 227.[66] The measure at that time was limited to Aurès and a part of Kabylia. It was very poorly received by the Muslims, who thought it discriminatory, and by the parliamentary Left, which thought that it was undemocratic and created a dangerous precedent.

The effect on Algerian nationalism of the entry into force of the state of emergency, whether coincidence or reaction, was the reverse of what had been anticipated. The revolt in Aurès continued on a larger scale throughout April. Although the French military machine had been reinforced by the arrival of Moroccan Goumiers and the formation of Tabor units, this time the military and judicial repressive action was ineffective. The outlaws had learned a lesson from the initial French reaction, and the 18,000 men who were trying to control Aurès wore themselves out in unsuccessful pursuit of an elusive adversary whose surprise attacks were increasingly savage.

Soustelle managed to resist the creation of vigilante groups by the French settlers, but had to sanction the organization of local auxiliary forces to operate under control of the authorities. The Governor-General's idea had been to reestablish order through

---

65. *J.O., Débats parl., Ass. nat.* (Feb. 24, 1955), pp. 866–68.
66. Ibid. (April 1, 1955), pp. 2158–75, 2190–2219, 2289. For text of the law of April 3, 1955, see *J.O., Lois et décrets* (April 7, 1955), p. 3479.

ideological reconquest of the population, by moving up indigenous troops commanded by Muslim Affairs officers, by opening
work camps, and by finding work for the unemployed. As early
as May, General Gaston Parlange was given this mission as his
objective and was instructed, under Soustelle's authority, to coordinate civil and military operations in the emergency zone.
This appointment was no better received by the outlaws than the
proclamation of the state of emergency itself had been.

In May, disturbances increased in Kabylia and spread out from
the Constantine area. French circles in Algeria took advantage of
this to create difficulties for the Governor-General, whom they
criticized both for adopting a negative attitude toward the vigilante groups and for having ordered wage increases for Algerian
workers. The Chambers of Agriculture of Algiers, Constantine,
and Oran suspended operations in protest. On May 20, the
Governor-General summarized recent happenings in a broadcast
address.[67] He agreed that the military situation was disquieting,
reaffirmed his determination to treat the outlaws with utmost
severity, but chiefly emphasized the need to remedy those economic and social defects which were in his view the real cause of
the disturbances.

Meanwhile, Soustelle had vigorously urged the government to
reinforce his military strength. The state of emergency was soon
extended to all of Constantine. French forces were increased
from 70,000 to 100,000 men. The auxiliary units included groups
from Tunisia and Morocco, as well as metropolitan reinforcements designed to replace the Algerian rifle regiments that had
gone over to the rebels. One of these divisions had been taken
from Lorraine and had been under NATO command.[68]

The repercussions of events in Tunisia and Algeria on the
Moroccan crisis were now at their height. On one hand, granting
Tunisians internal self-government that practically amounted to

67. *Le Monde* (May 22–23, 1955).
68. There was no advance notice of this transfer of troops, which annoyed the
NATO Council. In addition, the United States refused the French authorization to
use in Algeria American helicopters lent for the campaign in Indochina; Paris complained somewhat bitterly of this attitude. When Pinay arrived in San Francisco
in June 1955, one of his objectives was to try to explain the positive aspects of French
North African policy. This period is discussed in "Le Problème algérien," *Chronique
de politique étrangère, 8* (1955), 715–27.

independence greatly helped to strengthen the Moroccan nationalists' belief that the goal they had pursued since 1944 was perfectly realistic; at the same time it made increasingly untenable the position of the French in Morocco and in France who persisted in clinging to the Treaty of Fez. On the other hand, reinforcement of the French army in Algeria was beginning to weaken Moroccan security; this was soon to shift the balance toward those who believed the requisite effort in Algeria would be impossible without compromise in Morocco.

Under these manifold pressures, the hour of decision for Morocco was fast approaching. The few months remaining before Grandval's dispatch to Rabat were the last in the phase of total passivity that had started two years earlier with Mohammed V's deposition. A study of the end of this period should begin with an examination of the Moroccan crisis on the day the Faure government took office.

Initially, neither Faure nor his Minister for Moroccan and Tunisian Affairs had pronounced views on the policy to be adopted in the protectorate. Both tended to regard Mulay ben Arafa as the only possible spokesman in any negotiations, and dismissed any idea of Sidi Mohammed ben Youssef's return to the throne. At most, they envisaged the constitution of a Moroccan reform government. The only apparent difference of opinion between the two men was that July thought that the Moroccan problem would soon become acute while his Prime Minister, more sensitive to the Parliamentary situation, wanted to resolve the Tunisian problem before taking any decisive move in the Moroccan crisis. Hence, the maintenance of Francis Lacoste in his post. Hence, again, July's fruitless attempts to make the Resident-General assume the responsibilities incumbent upon him without delay. One week after the government took office, July summoned Lacoste to Paris and told him it was going to be necessary to introduce dramatic reforms to prevent a political hiatus at the very time the Tunisian crisis was drawing to a close. The Resident-General was noncommittal. His chilly demeanor turned to dismay when the Minister, revealing his plans, asked Lacoste to submit the names of several prominent Moroccans, whom July intended to substitute for two French heads of departments. Lacoste replied that the two men to be sacrificed were excellent civil servants. The Minister said that he was sure of it, but insisted that it was essential to take some such step in order to produce a psychological effect perceptibly improving the situation. He therefore requested Lacoste, despite his objections, to take the necessary steps within two weeks. When the two met again a little later, nothing had been done, and the Resident-General was forced to tell his chief that what he asked was impossible. July insisted, but got nowhere. There the matter rested, since the situation had changed in the meantime and necessitated a change of Resident-General.

While the government was formulating its plans and the Resident-General was countering his Minister's proddings with imperturbable inertia, the positions previously adopted by the various sectors of Moroccan opinion had apparently crystallized. El-Glaoui seized every opportunity to declare the question of the Throne a closed issue. Si Bekkaï replied that nothing would be done until the problem was settled. The French in Morocco displayed their usual gamut of reactions, ranging from support of el-Glaoui's argument to liberal declarations by the progressive protagonists. All these conflicting views were bound up with the period of expectancy that had as usual followed a change of government. They were displayed throughout March 1955 and a good part of April without the addition of much that was new.[69] During this period, terrorism ebbed and flowed, with no real period of calm.

Tired of the Resident-General's negativism, July went to Morocco on April 1 to form his own opinion on the spot. In accordance with a well-established tradition, the Residency had arranged the Minister's visit to ensure that he met no nonconformists. The Minister saw el-Glaoui, who reproached France violently for having made use of him in August 1953 and afterward "letting him drop." The Pasha concluded that if the

69. On March 6, the S.F.I.O./Morocco took a new tack and announced that the hopes engendered by Mendès-France's policy had been destroyed by the colonialists and the Communists—which was true. It declared itself in favor of setting up a temporary Council of the Throne to create constituent organs, abolish privileges, and arrange for the unrestricted consultation with the public concerning the creation of an authority to negotiate a new Franco-Moroccan statute.

government went on making concessions, he would make some too—an indication that he was already prepared for his about-face of the following autumn. His chief aim (he made this very clear) was less to keep Mulay ben Arafa on the throne than to prevent his rival from returning to it. He declared himself ready to make any concessions to achieve this end. Equally important was the fact that even the most conservative French residents in Rabat did not hesitate to tell the Minister that henceforward they regarded the Arafa formula as impracticable and outworn.

Thus something new had occurred. Although the French and the Moroccan notables were still unalterably opposed to Mohammed V, they were nevertheless disposed, in private, to consider any solution which did not imply the return of Sultan ben Youssef. It was undoubtedly too soon to solve the problem of the Throne, but the time was approaching when it was going to be possible to raise it officially. The whole Grandval experiment two months later was to be based on this political theme. Mulay ben Arafa, sensing the changing wind, wrote to the President of the Republic on April 8, 1955, asking to be consulted on any plans the French might make in connection with reforming the regime.

A decision was imminent. In France, this became so obvious that private circles concerned with Morocco decided to convene a National Conference for the Settlement of the Franco-Moroccan Problem, which was held May 7–8. This time it was no longer a question of discussion among liberal protagonists, but of a wider debate in which Moroccan nationalists and French liberals could pit their ideas against those of the other faction. The attendance of the former Director of Finances of the Protectorate, Emmanuel Lamy, was symptomatic in this respect. Among the sympathizers who were not present but who had agreed to have their names printed in the records were such widely differing men as Michel Debré and Claude Bourdet, François Mitterrand, and Marcel-Edmond Naegelen. The principal statements were made by Paul Buttin, former leader of the French Bar at Meknes and one of the leading French liberals in Morocco; Jean Védrine, of the Centre d'études et de documentation; and André de Peretti (M.R.P.), former adviser to Union française. The most significant speeches were those by Caid Aherdan, Robert Verdier, Pasha Si Bekkaï, François Mauriac, and Jean Rous, a journalist for *Franc-Tireur*. The chairman was Léon Marchal. The general conclusions of the debate were summarized by the secretariat in a document read to the meeting. A second document, relating more particularly to the problem of the Throne, was supported by some of the participants.[70] It is impossible to measure accurately the meeting's influence on the development of the Moroccan crisis. It was closely linked to the activities of the Centre d'études et de documentation, and was also a sign of the times.

Lacoste was forced to realize that his silence was not in keeping with the general climate of opinion. He suddenly decided to reveal his plan of action, and arrived in Paris on May 15 determined to defend it. He pointed out quite correctly that the political context of the Moroccan conflict had been radically altered by the development of the Franco-Tunisian negotiations and by the spreading disturbances in Algeria, which threatened to draw Morocco into a general movement linked to this revolt. He again advocated the third-man solution, while at the same time enumerating with grim pleasure the disadvantages this course would entail. Not the least of these, in his eyes, involved sacrificing Mulay ben Arafa, who he said was progressively strengthening his position. He emphasized that the Algerian troubles and consequent need for manpower necessitated considerable caution in France in framing its Moroccan policy. He concluded his preamble by repeating that, in view of the situation, the disadvantages of the status quo were still less than those of a deliberate change of policy.

This argument had been handed down from one Resident-General to the next, and it retained its ambiguous force. Any change of policy at Rabat, when there was no official consent either to the return of Mohammed V or to independence for the protectorate, was in fact completely impossible. Grandval was to realize this shortly, at his own expense.

This being the situation, what was to be done? The operative

70. Comité national pour la solution du problème franco-marocain, *Compte rendu de la conférence nationale pour la solution du problème franco-marocain* (Paris, 1955).

part of Lacoste's plan rested on four main points: appointment of a new Grand Vizier to replace the centenarian el-Hadjoui, reorganization of the Maghzen, abolition of the Council of Viziers and Directors (now considered a nuisance because of its equal membership and because of the implied confusion between legislative and executive branches), and institution of a Moroccan government responsible for preparing for the protectorate's independence. Lacoste proposed that the future government consist of a Moroccan majority flanked by civil servants appointed by the Resident-General, and by representatives of the French in Morocco. The Residency would retain its power of preliminary reading and promulgation. The government's competence was to be discreetly limited, moreover, to the study of draft *dahirs* at present submitted to the Council of Viziers and Directors, and to the consideration of whatever problems of general policy the Grand Vizier or the Resident-General might submit to it. Lastly, it was made clear that the Residency was to be free to accept or reject suggestions made by this curious body that was obviously no more than the illegitimate offspring of the Council of Viziers and Directors and the Council of Government. The Lacoste plan concluded with a few ritual remarks regarding the judicial system, trade unionism, and admission of Moroccans to the civil service.[71]

Lacoste left Paris without governmental authorization to put his plan into effect. Apart from the fact that the Council of Ministers continued to hesitate concerning various possible solutions to the problem of the Throne, Faure could not afford to associate any action he might take with a Resident-General who personified a policy of passivity and a reform program that amounted to bandaging a wooden leg. The Prime Minister, having judged Lacoste by his program, was now determined to replace him at the first opportunity.[72]

In Morocco, tension had reached the breaking-point. Terrorist

71. The idea of replacing the Grand Vizier with a younger man lent itself to humorous but perceptive remarks. Forty years after the Treaty of Fez, said Lacoste, that treaty by which France undertook to reform and modernize the country, the Maghzen was still directed by the same Grand Vizier, by then a centenarian. *Conscience française* could not have put it better.

72. For Faure's speech to the National Assembly, see *J.O., Débats parl., Ass. nat.* (June 22, 1955), pp. 3179 ff.

activities and the political conflict had been further complicated by a strike of Moroccan shopkeepers which the merchants of Casablanca had set off on May 20 and which had gradually spread to the other towns. Jewish merchants, threatened by terrorists, had joined the movement. A large number of European shops had closed on June 27, in compliance with a strike order of the Anti-Terrorist Defense Organization in protest against an investigation into counter-terrorism being conducted in Morocco. Some French business circles feared a general strike and complete breakdown of commercial operations.[73]

Suddenly, on June 11, 1955, the assassination of Jacques Lemaigre-Dubreuil by French counter-terrorists made Faure decide that the time had come to act. The murdered man, who had just declared war on the ultras in the columns of *Maroc-Presse,* was well known to the ministers. His relations with the French government were closely linked with the history of Moroccan counter-terrorism. Toward the end of 1954, the first specific information on counter-terrorist activities had been brought to Paris by a journalist who had received it from a young police official, Albert Forestier. Apparently his was a dangerous trade, for on January 3, 1955, Forestier was the victim of an automobile accident, the cause of which was never fully explained, while the man in whom he had confided barely escaped with his life from two successive attacks. It emerged from the inquiry undertaken by Forestier that most French counter-terrorists in Morocco were well known and had willing accomplices among the local French police and even among the French magistrates. Mendès-France ordered a thorough investigation, which confirmed Forestier's findings.[74] The government then instructed Lacoste to take the requisite steps. The results were disappointing, so much so that on the fall of Mendès-France, Fouchet could do no more than pass on the information to his successor.

As soon as the Faure government was set up, Lemaigre-

73. See the article on Jacques Lemaigre-Dubreuil, *L'Express* (June 18, 1955).

74. On August 14, 1954, Mendès-France authorized Fouchet to set up a committee to investigate detention. It consisted of Mouguilan, then Presiding Judge of the Division of the Paris Court of Appeal, and Commandant Vincent Monteil. They inspected the Moroccan prisons between September 20 and 30 and submitted their report on October 20, 1954.

Dubreuil, who had serious grounds for believing his life in danger, requested an interview with Pierre July. He told him he was in a position to buy *Maroc-Presse* from the son of Jean Walter, but would decide definitely to do so only if the government were willing to inaugurate a liberal policy in Morocco. In support of his case, Lemaigre-Dubreuil emphasized that unless liberal circles replied publicly to the slanders of the Mas press, it would be impossible to create a climate in Morocco conducive to opening negotiations. At his request, July gave him a letter to prove, if necessary, that he had official support.

Lemaigre-Dubreuil returned to Rabat, where he plunged into a campaign against the ultras. Meanwhile, Faure instructed the head of the D.S.T., Roger Wybot, to examine the reports of counter-terrorism received from the previous government. Wybot had no difficulty in establishing complicity between the counter-terrorist organizations and the Moroccan police, and concluded that a complete overhaul of the protectorate's police system was necessary. When the government showed no signs of taking action, Lemaigre-Dubreuil requested a meeting with the Prime Minister, who received him on June 10. He returned the same day to Casablanca, wrote a final letter to the Prime Minister again stressing the deterioration of the Moroccan economic situation and the imminence of a general strike, and that night he was murdered.[75] This violent death of a man who had just left the Prime Minister's office after predicting his own imminent assassination made a deep impression on the head of the government. As one of his ministers said in an interview: "It was now proved that there was a clique, backed by the shadowy figures of certain military leaders and of Boniface—who remained very active despite his retirement—which was determined to oppose by every available means any favorable development in the Moroccan crisis, no matter what government took the initiative."

From all sides, events impelled Faure toward a decision to which his own inclination would have led him before long. On the whole, the parliamentary situation was still good. Twice

---

75. Most of this information came from *L'Express* (June 18, 1955), except as modified by interviews.

during this period, on May 12 and 26, July had been asked to report to the National Assembly's Committee on Foreign Affairs on the result of his trips to Morocco; no particular tension had ensued between the government and Parliament. The government was so aware of the growing interrelationship of North African problems that at the beginning of June 1955 it had set up an interdepartmental Committee for Coordination of North African Affairs, consisting (apart from Marshal Juin and General Koenig, Minister of War) of Gaston Palewski, Deputy Minister to the Office of the Prime Minister; Maurice Bourgès-Manoury, Minister of the Interior; Pierre Pflimlin, Minister of Finance; and Gilbert Jules, Secretary of State for Finance.

While the Assembly retained its confidence in the government, the second mission of Maître Izard, undertaken at Mohammed V's request at the time of the fall of the Mendès-France government, was drawing to a close. There was a decisive interview on June 14 between the Sultan's envoy and Faure, who told the former of his decision to recall Lacoste. He said he was personally in favor of the political formula accepted by Mohammed V in December 1954, insofar as political circumstances would allow it to be put into effect. The two men met again on June 20. The plan drawn up at Antsirabé was this time unofficially handed over to the Prime Minister by Izard with the Istiqlal's consent.[76] In deference to Mohammed V's wishes, Izard presented it as the fruit of his own initiative, which was very close to the truth. Always with an eye on the political situation, Faure replied that he hoped the new Resident-General, once he had judged the situation in Morocco for himself, would be able to propose a plan to the government that would be very similar to the one now before him. Grandval was to fulfill this hope shortly.

Faure was determined now to press forward, and appeared before the National Assembly on June 21 to expound the policy he proposed to apply in Morocco.[77] He explained that the government's concern with the problem had predated the most recent events. He said he had been unable to accept all the con-

76. Izard, "Le 'Secret' d'Antsirabé," pp. 61 ff.
77. J.O., Débats parl., Ass. nat. (June 22, 1955), pp. 3179 ff.

clusions of the plan submitted by Lacoste on May 15, and that consequently he had decided only the day before to replace him at Rabat by Grandval. The Prime Minister, not wishing to reveal the full extent of his plans to an Assembly he did not wish to offend, confined himself to implying that the new Resident-General would put into effect a program, within the framework of the Treaty of Fez, that would be drawn up point by point with his assistance and would be based upon the following principles: permanence of the French presence in Morocco, abolition of the system of direct administration, creation of modern governmental institutions, and organization of genuine interdependence between the two countries. The concept of interdependence that had languished in the political correspondence of Sidi Mohammed ben Youssef had at last made its official entry into the political vocabulary of the French government. Henceforward, it was to dominate the evolution of Franco-Moroccan negotiations. The Prime Minister concluded with humor:

> This coexistence is indispensable to both the material and moral interests of the people of both countries. It forces us to avoid the fatal dilemma, which would be either departure and abandonment or an intransigence so conservative that one could attach any virtue to it except the virtue of conserving anything at all.[78]

These commonsense proposals were received without enthusiasm by the Right.[79] But for the first time since 1944, the die had been cast. Though the gambler was cautious and unwilling to take unnecessary risks, this time the will to act coincided, in Paris, with the first indisputable expansion of the government's freedom to maneuver.

78. Ibid., p. 3180.
79. See *Le Monde* (June 23, 1955).

Chapter 7

THE GRANDVAL PERIOD;
THE HARSH BLOW
(JUNE 20–AUGUST 29, 1955)

On June 14, 1955, the Prime Minister recalled Gilbert Grandval to Paris from Saarbrücken; six days later he appointed him Resident-General to Rabat. It had been the Prime Minister's personal decision to replace Francis Lacoste with a man who had been in turn France's Military Governor, then High Commissioner, and finally Ambassador of France in the Saar. He had offered the post first to Marcel-Edmond Naegelen, then to André Dubois (at that time the Paris Prefect of Police),[1] and finally to Grandval, who accepted. Faure had good grounds for considering Grandval the right man for the job. His firmness in the Saar, both toward the Germans and his own government, had favorably impressed the Prime Minister. Moreover, it was well known that Grandval had the ear of General de Gaulle. At one time, he had even been Georges Bidault's candidate, when the latter had been asked to find a new occupant for the Residency in Rabat. This was sufficient reason for some right-wing politicians to consider him—though very wrongly—a "strong man" after their own hearts. Initially, everyone in Paris and Rabat expressed satisfaction at the choice.

"Such was the misunderstanding which made my name acceptable in the most surprising quarters," noted Grandval, after reporting how Colonel Lecomte had been the first to be misled. "I was more uneasy than flattered, for I knew perfectly well that my first moves would be enough to destroy this unanimity. In fact, Colonel Lecomte was to oppose—a little late—my appointment."[2]

1. Neither was enthusiastic: the former did not feel he could accept unless the S.F.I.O. met his demands; the latter preferred to keep his job in Paris.
2. Gilbert Grandval, *Ma mission au Maroc* (Paris, 1956), pp. 16–17.

From June 20 to July 7, 1955, the date of his departure for Rabat, Grandval spent his time in consultations, recruiting his staff, and preparing his governmental instructions. Faure had authorized him to work on this document with Pierre July and his advisers, chief of whom was Jean Basdevant, then head of the Department for Moroccan and Tunisian Affairs; there was nothing unusual in such procedure. Although the salient points in those forty-five pages have been made public by Grandval himself,[3] the contents are summarized below. The explanatory statement centered upon the simple but long ignored idea that the inertia of the Moroccans could only be transformed into active cooperation by granting them power to govern and to administer their own country. It was made clear that under the Treaty of Fez, Sharifian sovereignty could not be shared or shifted; any formula of cosovereignty must definitely be ruled out as contrary to the letter and spirit of the treaty. It was explicitly stated that the desired objectives could be achieved neither by the maintenance of direct administration nor by the relinquishment, through a series of concessions, of the status of protecting power which France had enjoyed since 1912.

The immediate measures designed to bring about relaxation of tension were broadly and generously defined. They involved reestablishing control over the French police, releasing nationalists sentenced for their opinions rather than for terrorist activities, liquidating direct administration by replacing French officials whose transfer to France appeared necessary, and appointing young Moroccans to senior administrative posts.

The problem of the Throne was analyzed in detail. The arguments the Resident-General would have to use with various groups received individual attention. All possible solutions to the problem of the Throne were examined: the retention of Mulay ben Arafa, the Caliph, a third man, a Council of the Throne, a Council of Regency. The idea of a third man (possibly the Grand Vizier) particularly appealed to the government since it would have had the virtue of leaving an occupant on the throne: The present Sultan would merely delegate his authority temporarily to a representative, and so would remain nominally in

3. Ibid., pp. 26, 27, 86, 121.

possession of it. However, it was explicitly recognized that such a procedure would serve no purpose without support from the nationalists and the traditionalists. The instructions did not therefore direct the Resident-General to adopt this course, but gave him full freedom to recommend to the government whatever solution he thought best, with the proviso that the possibility of Mohammed V's return to the throne was ruled out.[4] Having made that point clear, the French government did not exclude the idea of bringing Mohammed V to France once the question of the Throne had been settled and the future government of Morocco established.

Although the method of implementation was left to the Resident-General's discretion, the instructions were quite specific as to the establishment of a Moroccan government. They stipulated that the abolition of the Council of Viziers and Directors and of the Limited Council should coincide with the appointment of a new Grand Vizier, who would assume the title of Prime Minister. The future government was to be composed chiefly of Moroccans, Frenchmen being represented only in the transition period. The government was to enjoy the prerogatives normally pertaining to the exercise of executive power; and the holder of the Seal—whether a third man or a Council of Regency—would exercise legislative powers. These would be enlarged by the repeal of Article 3 of the *dahir* of September 9, 1953, which required acquiescence by the Sultan if the Council of Viziers and Directors adopted a draft *dahir* in second reading by a two-thirds majority.[5] The instructions as they stood laid down clearly the successive stages of the new Resident-General's task: first, exploration of the situation and measures to bring about a détente; next, preparation of a plan of action, including settle-

4. When he received Dubois and then Grandval at Matignon, Faure did not conceal the fact that no progress would be possible in Morocco until the question of the Throne had been settled. The main point, he said in essence, was not to know who should be Sultan but to negotiate an agreement with the intellectual elite of Morocco and thus with the nationalist parties. But it was his feeling that no agreement could be concluded until the question of the Throne had been settled. Faure tried expressly to avoid imposing this personal opinion on Dubois and Grandval. "You must make up your own minds," he said. It was this concept of their mission that was reflected in Grandval's instructions.

5. See p. 187.

ment of the problem of the Throne and establishment of a Moroccan government; last, implementation of this plan after its approval and possible revision by the French government.

Although the government's instructions gave Grandval an opportunity to solve the Moroccan problem in accordance with his liberal views, they did not provide him with the essential key. This was none other than Mohammed V's letter to Maître Georges Izard on December 26, 1954, which had confirmed, for the benefit of the French government, the agreement of Sidi Mohammed ben Youssef and the Moroccan nationalists on a formula for a settlement. It involved the creation of the three-member Council of Guardians of the Throne, a Moroccan government to carry out reforms and negotiations, the return of Mohammed V to France, and a Sultan definitively chosen by the Moroccan people. It will also be recalled that without going so far as to commit himself to the formula, Faure had told Maître Izard quite openly that he was in favor of it and he hoped that political circumstances would permit its being put into effect.[6]

Grandval subsequently interpreted this silence on the unofficial negotiations of the spring of 1955 as a trick deliberately designed to involve him unwittingly in a course that would ultimately lead to the restoration of Mohammed V. In other words, he felt the Prime Minister had concealed the Sultan's letter because he knew the Resident-General opposed any backstairs restoration of Sidi Mohammed ben Youssef, and because the unofficial formula for a settlement set forth in the letter was obviously a first step in that direction. However, any idea of deliberate chicanery by the Prime Minister should be ruled out for the simple reason that the 1954 stratagem was no longer secret to anyone by the time Grandval was preparing to leave for Rabat.[7] All the nationalist

6. See above; also Izard, "Le 'Secret' d'Antsirabé," p. 70.

7. The Prime Minister had not, moreover, been completely silent on this point. He had said to Grandval during their first talk on June 15, "You are having dinner at Bérard's with Izard. Listen to him." Grandval, p. 3 (Bérard was Faure's diplomatic adviser). The Sultan's confidant was no more loquacious than Faure. According to one of the protagonists interviewed, Izard "scarcely mentioned the substance of the matter with the future Resident-General," although he hid nothing from him. Coming from one who more than any other had been "in the thick of it all," the formula is not without piquancy. "There I was in the temple of opposition to the Sultan Mulay Arafa," Grandval reported in his book when describing his talk with Izard at Bérard's: "The whole evening was spent discussing the blunder of August 20, 1953, and

leaders had been involved in one way or another with the Izard-
Mohammed V transactions, and those with whom Grandval was
to negotiate were well aware of them. Even if Grandval had not
initially known about Mohammed V's letter, there was always the
chance that he might have found out about it, unless one imagines
that those acquainted with it were all linked in a single conspiracy
of silence toward the Resident-General. Such a supposition is
manifestly absurd. What apparently happened was much simpler.
"The Prime Minister," Izard noted on June 20, 1955 when he
handed Mohammed V's letter to Faure, "was anxious to have
the new Resident-General lay before the government a plan
similar to ours after judging the situation at first hand." [8] If
this important comment in fact reflects the thought of the two
men, the Prime Minister's behavior ceases to present a problem.
Since Grandval asked for no explanation regarding unofficial
negotiations of which he would normally have been aware,
Faure might well have believed that the Resident-General would
make his own appraisal of the situation at Rabat with a more
open mind if that thorny issue were temporarily bypassed. It is
conceivable that, knowing his man, Faure was afraid to ask him
to assume explicit responsibility for a settlement that would
make Mohammed V the arbiter of France's Moroccan policy, lest
his last candidate refuse to go to Rabat because of his instinctive
hostility to a solution which he regarded, rightly or wrongly, as
dangerous.[9]

Having succeeded in making a liberal Resident-General appear
to the ultras as one of their own men—in itself no mean feat—
Faure was to eclipse his first achievement by playing so skillfully
on Grandval's character as to lead him, almost despite himself, to
reinvent a settlement plan that had already been thought out, if
not negotiated, by the principal parties concerned. In any event,
everything transpired as Faure had hoped in June. On August 1,
1955, after several days of negotiations with the Moroccan nationalist leaders, Grandval sent the government a plan which

---

methods for undoing the damage. It was an exciting conversation. Izard did most of
the talking, fulfilling brilliantly and faithfully his function of counsel to Sidi Mohammed.
But I had been forewarned, and only listened." Ibid., p. 6.

  8. See p. 251.
  9. Grandval, p. 9.

coincided almost exactly with the proposal previously accepted by Mohammed V: a Council of the Throne, a negotiating government, and return to France of Mohammed V. There was also to be a declaration by the Sultan endorsing the transaction and explicit recognition of his rights in regard to the Throne.

While Grandval helped in preparing the instructions, there were two important reactions in France to the government's alleged plans. De Gaulle emerged from retirement and used a press conference on June 30 to make a significant statement on Morocco. "Association, for certain states such as Tunisia and Morocco, signifies a tie of a federal nature with France. I recall that Sultan Sidi Mohammed ben Youssef is a Companion of the Liberation." [10] This open support for a "Tunisian" solution to the Moroccan crisis was too close to what Faure and Grandval themselves wanted not to constitute solid encouragement for the government, especially since the General's reference to Mohammed V was tantamount to a public stand in favor of the exiled Sultan's restoration.

As if to offset the benefit Faure reaped from this event, Marshal Juin resigned on July 2 from the Committee for Coordination of North African Affairs. His action followed a letter of June 21 to the Prime Minister in which Juin said he could only give public support to the new committee if the government based its Moroccan policy on strengthening the powers of the Maghzen and of Sultan Mulay ben Arafa.[11] When Faure refused to make such a commitment, the Marshal resigned in protest to a policy which in his view could only end in Mohammed V's prompt return to the throne.[12] Juin was the standard-bearer of those French circles which defended the Moroccan status quo. Coming at this time, his resignation could only be interpreted as a declaration of war against the Prime Minister by the ultras, whose strategic position had never been so strong. In France, the Right and the Extreme Right—the Independent and Social Republican ministers—controlled the government. In Morocco, the ultras had an equally solid hold on Mulay ben Arafa

10. *Bulletin marocain d'information et de documentation* (*B.M.I.*), 5th year, no. 101 (1955), p. 2.

11. Juin, *Le Maghreb en jeu*, pp. 190–91.

12. Ibid., pp. 93, 96, 97.

through el-Glaoui and the "mayor of the Palace," the famous Hadjoui.

Cornered, Faure could hope to win only by rallying the Independent Ministers to his Moroccan policy, thus isolating the Social Republicans, and making use of the support of Pinay and Roger Duchet, Secretary-General of the National Center of Independents and Peasants, to force Mulay ben Arafa's protectors in Morocco and France ultimately to accept his departure. This masterly maneuver was to be carried out step by step, although too late to be completely successful.[13]

Grandval arrived in Morocco on July 7. After a fairly warm welcome from the French residents of Casablanca, thanks to Émile Roche, the Resident-General at once set out to apply the corrective measures in his instructions.[14] Between July 12–15, 1955, seven French department directors and two other high officials were relieved of their posts with a stroke of the pen. "The Departments involved," wrote Grandval, "were Sharifian Affairs, Industrial Production and Mining, Commerce and the Merchant Marine, Education, Agriculture and Forests (the assistant chief was removed also), Public Works, and Labor. An Inspector-General of Administrative Services was relieved at the same time." [15] The Resident-General's civil, military, and diplomatic staffs and the general services of the Department of the Interior were regrouped under Grandval's principal assistant, Pierre Laurent.

Aware of "the extraordinary overlapping of the various Residential staffs . . . and the Departments of the Interior and of Security," [16] Grandval sought to complete his attempts at improvement by creating a General Department of the Interior, to which he attached the two traditional Departments of Interior

13. See pp. 323–24.
14. Émile Roche had intervened and had requested Bernard Le Coroller, Vice President of Présence française, to publish (or else be ostracized from the Radical Socialist Party) a communiqué asking the people to welcome the new Resident-General. See Grandval, p. 36. But Roche had also informed Grandval that he would consider any measure against the former director, Boniface (perennially active behind the scenes) as a declaration of war.
15. Ibid., p. 54.
16. Ibid., p. 56.

and of Security. This new body was instructed to "centralize intelligence and information services, make arrangements for the proper use and interpretation of intelligence received, and, lastly, regroup under a single authority all the forces and services used in maintaining order—it being understood that the director of the new Department was to be closely associated with the Residential team." [17] There was something to be said for the idea, although it is always dangerous to upset an administrative structure when one is wholly dependent upon its smooth operation. Moreover, if this reform was to justify any reasonable expectations, the critical listening-post and action center would have had to be entrusted to someone dependable.

Grandval, however, repeated the fatal mistake of his predecessor Labonne nine years earlier. He appointed General Georges Leblanc as director of his new General Department of the Interior on the recommendation of General Koenig, whose personal chief of staff was Colonel Lecomte.[18] "The mistake," Grandval was to write later, drawing his lesson from the episode, "lay not in the reform, which was necessary, but in the choice of the man." [19] He added, "Even more serious was the fact that General Leblanc was to prove incapable of effectively organizing that 'intelligence center' from which I expected so much. Thus it was all the easier for him to isolate my authority because I had—with good faith so naive that I almost blush for it— stripped myself of all the means of information my predecessors had been forced to create within their own staffs in order to escape the isolation in which the Residential services deliberately kept them." [20]

Once again, the military men most strongly opposed to a liberal solution to the conflict had succeeded in gaining control

17. Ibid., p. 57.
18. Oddly enough, Lecomte, when called in for consultation by Grandval before the latter left for Rabat, had spontaneously suggested getting rid of the diehards in the Residency as soon as he arrived. Lecomte's list gave star billing to men like Girard and Mazoyer. He may have thought Grandval would not survive this housecleaning, but this is merely speculation. Carried to such an extreme, a spirit of intrigue is ultimately self-destructive.
19. Grandval, p. 58.
20. Ibid.

of the central command post of the Residential establishment. Even worse, Koenig's ministerial status gave the extreme Right of the government a direct hold on the Residency.[21]

The key point is that, in the circumstances, the perennial opposition of the French administration and of the settlers to the government's policy had ceased for a time to be decisive. The center of gravity of the conflict had shifted from Rabat to Paris. Even if the administration and the leading settlers could have been brought into line, a veto by the Right in France or a word whispered to the Sultan by el-Glaoui would still have sufficed to maintain the status quo. Grandval did not know Morocco, and so he was not altogether aware of these developments. As he saw it at the start of his mission, Rabat was still the center of gravity of the crisis; the chief obstacle was the omnipotence of the heads of departments. Hence his idea of beginning, as instructed, with reforms in the higher echelons of the administration—which could not solve any problems—while behind the scenes his adversaries in Morocco and in France prepared to nullify his activities by manipulating Mulay ben Arafa with invisible strings.

All his reforms failed. The question of the Throne had become so central that any other reform was ipso facto doomed. By disrupting the administration *before* the question of the Throne had been settled, Grandval merely sanctioned the ultras' determination to do their utmost to prevent Mulay ben Arafa's departure. This substantially aggravated the internal contradiction that ultimately defeated his policy.

Despite this premature coup, the entry of the new Resident-General onto the scene was not wholly unsuccessful. The nationalist leaders, attracted by his liberalism and by his character, had done their utmost to ensure him the warmest possible welcome from the Moroccan people. They did not, obviously, control the terrorist organizations, but the hope of change

21. Grandval's error was particularly surprising in that Koenig had initially persuaded him to add Lecomte to his team—a significant commentary on Koenig's reservations concerning Faure's Moroccan policy. On June 20, Grandval had dined with Labonne, who had informed him of Lecomte's role in the affair of the Berber tracts. (Ibid., pp. 13–15.) All things considered, it is difficult to understand how Grandval could have appointed to such an important post a military man he did not know and whose backing must have seemed dubious to him.

seemed to have permeated throughout. Apparently held in check by Émile Roche, Présence française merely bided its time. As for the higher administrative echelons, the sudden transfers had at least administered a shock that made it possible to expect some relief.

This promising start was utterly ruined by a new and serious incident. On July 14 at Casablanca, a bomb exploded at the Mers-Sultan intersection, in front of a cafe in the middle of a crowd. Six Europeans were killed and a number of people wounded.[22] Slumbering passions were again aroused. European crowds immediately demonstrated spontaneously in front of the regional headquarters of the contrôle civil. Inflammatory pamphlets were distributed that night and groups of demonstrators organized by Présence française commandos again overran the town, looting and burning shops, and lynching Moroccans. The next day, Grandval had a stormy interview with Dr. Fernand Causse, president of the organization, who told him his supporters would never agree to the application of a Tunisian policy in Morocco. Afterward, *Le Petit Marocain* published a statement issued by Présence française without Grandval's agreement and alleging that he intended, with government support, to apply a policy in Morocco that was contrary to the interests of his compatriots. "Nothing," wrote Grandval, "could be more calculated to inflame the masses and provoke new disturbances." [23] More rioting broke out in the next few days under the conniving eye of the police. There were answering demonstrations on July 16 in the *medina* of Casablanca that were immediately dispersed by police gunfire. On the same day, funeral ceremonies for the victims of the fourteenth gave rise to indescribable scenes; after the religious ceremony, the European crowd harried and insulted Grandval right in front of the police, who were entirely on the side of the rioters.

Following this flagrant collusion between the police and Présence française, Grandval decided to expel Causse, together

22. The Istiqlal leaders played no part in this attack; they had no control over any of the various terrorist groups in the Casablanca region. The initiative could have come from a rank-and-file cell acting without orders. The hypothesis of counter-terrorist provocation is unlikely.

23. Grandval, p. 76.

with several others responsible for the riots. He was aware of the kind of help he could expect from the police, and he replaced them on the eighteenth with mobile gendarmerie in the *medina* of Casablanca, while the Casablanca region of the contrôle civil was made into a military region under the command of General André Franchi. The Resident-General had not let himself be intimidated, but the damage was done: in forty-eight hours, the gulf between the two communities had reappeared, now deeper than ever.[24]

Although relations had been severed between the Residency and the French in Morocco, the favorable impression Grandval had made on the nationalist leaders largely remained. Si Bekkaï was summoned to Rabat. On July 20 he had a fruitful interview with Grandval. That same day, in Egypt, Allal el-Fassi made a moderate statement to a correspondent for *France-Soir*. While continuing to advocate total independence, he declared that for the moment he favored a return to the letter of the Treaty of Fez, and added that he saw no objection to members of the Istiqlal entering, on an individual basis, a Moroccan government formed by the Residency.[25]

On July 12, Grandval had also seen el-Glaoui, who had not demurred at the idea of a spontaneous departure by Mulay ben Arafa but would not consider any replacement not from the Alaouit family. The two men met again on the twenty-third, when the Resident-General came to Marrakesh. Again Grandval urged the necessity of the reigning Sultan's speedy withdrawal. Again he emphasized that there was no question of restoring Mohammed V to the throne, or of giving it to one of his sons. The Pasha made no comment. He sent his eldest son, Si Brahim, to Paris to consult with his friends, apparently to secure further information before deciding on a course of action. They—and we know how powerful they were—were to have the last word. They quickly showed their hand.[26] The Social Republican members of Parliament, as though echoing el-Glaoui's misgivings,

24. The three days of rioting resulted in "66 dead (55 Moroccans and 11 Europeans, 6 of whom were at Mers-Sultan) and 306 wounded (218 Moroccans and 88 Europeans, 30 of them in the explosion)." See ibid., p. 80.

25. Ibid., pp. 134–35.

26. Ibid., pp. 61, 90 ff.

adopted a resolution on July 23 which ruled out the return of Sidi Mohammed Ben Youssef, or any of his descendants, to the throne.[27]

Grandval did not wait for the resumption of intrigues between Paris and Rabat before taking action. He was anxious to force the reigning Sultan to a decision as soon as possible, and requested an audience with the ruler, whom he had first seen on July 10; at that time, he had been unable to entice the Sultan onto the dangerous ground of discussing the problem of the Throne.[28] The situation had hardly improved in the interval. In fact, the Pasha of Marrakesh had taken the precaution of visiting the Palace the previous evening to make sure Mulay ben Arafa did not change his mind. Afterward, el-Glaoui told *Le Petit Marocain* and *La Vigie marocaine* that the Sultan had reiterated his intention of remaining on the throne—this was going a good deal further than the evasive reply that Mohammed V's rival had given Grandval on July 10, 1955.[29] "These concurrent and unexpected developments," wrote Grandval, "gave the impression of a carefully concerted plot. Who was pulling the strings in Morocco or Paris and trying to frustrate my efforts at conciliation?" [30] Duly reprimanded, the Sultan, who cared less about his throne than did those who were pressing him so hard to cling to it, evaded the issue and confined himself to presenting the Resident-General with a list of 85 names of possible Moroccan candidates for office, which turned out upon examination to be absolutely useless.

The intrigue was directed from Paris by Marcel Boussac, who worked closely with el-Glaoui, his son Si Brahim, Juin, and Émile Roche. Boussac's opposition to Faure's Moroccan policy had developed slowly. The two men had known each other a long time. They had not clashed on Indochina or on the European Defense Community, but Boussac's attitude had changed when Morocco came to the fore. He had large-scale interests there and close ties with el-Glaoui, who, it is said, exerted an absolute fascination over him. As early as August 1953, Boussac

27. Ibid., p. 96.
28. Ibid., p. 44.
29. Ibid., p. 99.
30. Ibid., pp. 99–100.

had approached Faure to try to persuade him to show some
flexibility in the Cabinet. When Faure became Prime Minister
and decided to take action on Morocco, he tried vainly to rally
Boussac to his views in the hope of averting an opposition, the
force of which he was fully conscious of. He put Boussac in
touch with Lacoste and then Lecomte, whom he did not know
very well. Unfortunately for Faure, these subtle tactics worked to
his detriment. Boussac, not content with gathering information
from these sources, went over to their side and soon became the
chief inspiration of Grandval's opponents. The polite obstruc-
tionism with which Mulay ben Arafa had just greeted the
Resident-General was the first sign of these underground activities, and this was only the beginning. The curtain had barely
risen on the Arafa comedy, and it was not to descend until three
months later, in November 1955, after countless dramatic events.

Since Grandval's plan had miscarried, thanks to el-Glaoui's
Paris advisers, his only course was to proceed to the second phase
of his mission and to open the consultations he hoped would
enable him to formulate the plan of action requested by the
Prime Minister.

The Grandval plan was drawn up between July 24–30, 1955,
in the course of incessant conferences with the leaders of the
various political factions of Morocco. Just as these talks were beginning, Si Brahim returned from Paris with news that was to
give fresh impetus to the conspiracy the ultras were organizing
in France and Morocco against the Grandval policy. Si Brahim
reported that the government was preparing to have the throne
vacated; to set up a Moroccan government approved by Mohammed V and consisting of nationalists, moderates, and supporters
of el-Glaoui; and to bring the ex-Sultan to France. The main
point was that Si Brahim had been told that "the reactions of the
Rightist parties still provided a good opportunity for a counter-
offensive, which the Pasha [ought] to undertake for the sake of
his friends and the prestige of France." [31]

For the ultras, the new development was neither the plan
approved by Mohammed V nor the fact that Faure had not expressly rejected it when Maître Izard presented it to him in June.

31. Ibid., p. 118.

It was that the government—no doubt in conjunction with the Resident-General—now seemed to look upon the plan with favor. These intrigues in Paris, though full of danger for the immediate future, did not prevent Grandval's talks from proceeding according to the Prime Minister's wishes.

The caids were apparently resigned to Sultan Mulay ben Arafa's departure, provided they received assurance that Mohammed V and his descendants would be kept off the throne. The Istiqlal wisely abided by the Izard formula: departure of Arafa, and a Council of the Throne consisting of the Grand Vizier, a representative of Mohammed V (Si Bekkaï, in fact), and an Arafist representative—probably one of el-Glaoui's sons.[32] "As for the Prime Minister," noted Grandval, "although there again I could hardly lay my cards on the table, it seemed to me that without being very enthusiastic they would not be unalterably [opposed] to the appointment of Si Fatmi ben Slimane," the former Pasha of Fez.[33] The P.D.I.'s position was "almost indistinguishable from that of the Istiqlal on problems of dynasty, the government, and the agreements to be concluded." [34]

There remained the problem of Mohammed V's future status, on which Grandval's nationalist spokesmen divided into two camps: the faithful, who, like Si Bekkaï, felt the crisis could only be solved by the return of Mohammed V to the throne at the call of the appropriate Moroccan bodies; and the politicians, who saw in Mohammed V's popularity a means rather than an end, and who demanded his return to France without caring very much what happened afterward.[35]

The Grandval plan was sent off on July 31 in a long cable that has been analyzed in detail in Granval's book [36] and need only be summarized here. Its forceful preamble stated that no one in Morocco still disputed the necessity of solving the problem of the Throne by an act of governmental authority; parties of the most divergent views agreed on this without exception, although they remained fundamentally divided on the means of implementing

32. Ibid., p. 135.
33. Ibid.
34. Ibid., pp. 137–38.
35. Ibid., p. 130.
36. Ibid., pp. 150 ff.

such a formula. It stressed even more forcefully the need to put
the proposed plan into effect before August 20, the anniversary of
Mohammed V's deposition. Grandval considered this time limit
extremely important; his nationalist interlocutors had convinced
him, quite rightly, that he would lose all credit with the Moroccans if he let that fateful day pass without taking action.

Once those two points had been made clear, Grandval advocated persuading Sultan Mulay ben Arafa to abdicate voluntarily
without designating a successor, so that a vacancy of the throne
would be created, making it possible to set up a temporary
regime consisting of a Council of Regency and a negotiating
government, publicly and freely backed by Mohammed V. The
exiled Sultan's installation in France was expressly recommended, since the Resident-General regarded Mohammed V's
approval as the key to success. Grandval planned to ask the
Grand Vizier to preside over the Council of Regency, which
would neutralize the opposition forces by including a representative of the Sultan and one of the notables. The Seal—that is, the
legislative power—would be delegated by the Council to the
Grand Vizier. Finally, the Council would appoint the negotiating
government, the actual formation of which Grandval recommended entrusting to Si Fatmi ben Slimane, who would be free
to choose his ministers.

One difficulty remained—the fact that the formation of a
Moroccan government with full executive powers would have
implied prior abrogation of the Treaty of Fez, the demise of
which was precisely what the negotiating government was to
negotiate. Grandval proposed to get around this procedural difficulty by limiting the powers of the provisional government to the
conduct of these negotiations, and by leaving responsibility for
current affairs with the traditional Franco-Moroccan bodies on
the understanding that a definitive Moroccan government would
be set up once arrangements had been completed for the replacement of the protectorate by a new regime.

Grandval summarized his entire plan as follows:

> The people should be informed simultaneously, in a
> statement by the Resident-General, of the voluntary

departure of Mulay Arafa, the composition of the Council of Regency, and of the negotiating government, the return of Mohammed V to France, and his message to them. The statement should also outline in very general terms the aim of the forthcoming negotiations.[37]

It was July 31. Only three weeks remained in which to settle the problem. Grandval knew the French government would make no decision before August 5, the beginning of the parliamentary recess. He therefore asked Faure to let him know his decision by the sixth at the latest, which would leave just enough time to obtain Mohammed V's agreement and to prepare the statement the Residency planned to make public on the eighteenth. Grandval concluded:

> If, owing to failure to receive instructions from the government within the time limit I have indicated, the large-scale political operation I propose were not immediately put into effect, the present relative calm would be followed by a dramatic new outburst of terrorism, and we should find ourselves embarked irretrievably upon a course wholly different from the one I propose, and upon a policy quite the opposite from that which I imagined I was called upon to pursue in Morocco.[38]

Faure had succeeded. The Grandval plan not only conformed strictly with the government's instructions but also duplicated the formula proposed in previous months by Si Bekkaï, Maître Izard, and the nationalists. Although originally hostile to a formula he feared would one day result in the restoration of Mohammed V, Grandval had ended by being convinced that this was the only solution. Despite the differences of character and political temperament dividing the two men, they had both finally arrived, by separate courses, at the same conclusion. It would be hard to find a more striking example of the constraint which the nature of a political problem can exert on the freewill of those who seek to solve it.

Although the Grandval plan was the same as the Izard plan, it

37. Ibid., p. 154.
38. Ibid., p. 155.

was the Izard plan with a time limit and a head of government added. Grandval demanded nothing from the French government that did not conform with his instructions, or that was not made imperative by the force of circumstances. Nevertheless, this decision which had to be made "within the next six days" must obviously have had the ring, in the more sensitive ears of the Right, of an ultimatum regarding a date, August 20, and a name, that of the future head of the negotiating government.

Faure had succeeded in one sense; he had transformed Grandval and the negotiators at Rabat into a testing-ground for the solutions he personally thought the most reasonable. But it was still only a partial victory, for a division of opinion in the government on these ideas was developing just when they were becoming politically feasible, thanks to Grandval's firm action in Morocco. Once again, hopes for a solution were to recede. Actually, complications had arisen in Paris during the last days of July. The Resident-General's negotiations had created such a backwash in the French capital that Faure, as early as the twenty-ninth, and even before being informed of the plan nearing completion at Rabat, had been obliged to write Grandval to ask him to make arrangements for a "short pause, so we can take the necessary precautions." [39] Grandval, dismayed by what he regarded as a complete failure to understand the importance of the time factor, replied the next day that the date of August 20 was vital. He assured the Prime Minister that once that date was past, he would have lost the Moroccans' confidence. He urged the government to determine its policy by August 5 at the latest.[40] The impending departure of the deputies for the recess inevitably increased the uneasiness of the Right, particularly the Independents. Alerted by Grandval's initial steps at Rabat, "heated by the controversy that had raged during the debate on Algeria," [41] fearing above all to see the government take advantage of the parliamentary recess to confront them with a fait accompli, the moderate members of Parliament became intractable. On July 30, Pierre July was put through a long inquisition by the Com-

39. Ibid., p. 141.
40. Ibid., pp. 144–45.
41. Ibid., pp. 145–46.

mittee on Foreign Affairs. To the consternation of the Moroccan nationalists, he had to deny officially that there was any possibility of the Sultan's restoration.[42] The moderate deputies, not content with this fundamental concession, insisted that Mohammed V should not be installed in France without Parliament's formal consent.[43] Pinay and Duchet had to go so far as to promise "if necessary, to convene the Executive Committee of the moderate groups and to expect their resignation from the government if they disagreed with the solutions adopted."[44] The Prime Minister was apprehensive of the effect the revelation of the Grandval plan might have in such an explosive political atmosphere, and instructed July to telephone Grandval and to persuade him not to send his proposals to Paris. But Grandval was unwilling to assume a responsibility that properly belonged to the government, and he cabled his plan to Faure that same day.

The ultras did not wait for the government's reaction to the Grandval cable before attacking. On August 2, *Paris-Presse* published verbatim, on its front page under an enormous headline, the text of a letter from el-Glaoui to Faure. In this letter—which *Paris-Presse* made public even before Si Brahim had placed the original in the hands of the Prime Minister—el-Glaoui attributed to Grandval entirely different political plans from those the latter had conveyed to him a few days earlier. He declared that he and his friends found these plans unacceptable, and emphasized that Mulay ben Arafa would never renounce his throne unless forced to do so by improper pressure from outside. This new maneuver[45] finally convinced Grandval that the political correspondence of the Sultan and the Pasha of Marrakesh was drafted in Paris, and that the two men were only tools in the hands of those who pulled the strings there. "Once again," he commented, "I had the feeling that matters were passing out of my control and

---

42. Ibid., p. 147. Furthermore, Faure refused to commit himself on this point, figuring rightly that it would have been illogical to mortgage the future when his entire policy depended upon Mohammed V's agreement to a temporary solution to the Moroccan crisis.

43. Ibid., p. 146.

44. Ibid., p. 147.

45. Ibid., pp. 160–61.

that the battle would be won or lost at Paris rather than Rabat." [46]

By way of counterattack, Grandval attempted anew to persuade the Sultan to abdicate, after trying in vain to free him from the domination of Si Abderrahim el-Hadjoui. This direct attack might perhaps have been decisive had not *Paris-Presse's* publication of el-Glaoui's letter parried it in advance. Once again, Mulay ben Arafa evaded the issue. For the second time, the attempt was a failure.[47]

The Resident-General laid his plan before the commissioners of the regions on August 5. "While I spoke," wrote Grandval, "I watched the faces of my listeners around the vast table. What attention—but what hostility! One grew pale, another crimson, a third had the condescending air of one listening patiently to a lunatic, another's lips were fixed in a sickly grin." [48] In the face of such opposition, the Resident-General, who had hoped for approval of a plan for the return to their districts of nationalist leaders who had been sent away as an administrative precaution, dared not proceed and abandoned the idea.

Things were no better in France. El-Glaoui's letter had not quite nipped in the bud any chance of success for the Grandval plan. However, by implying publicly that the Resident-General was preparing to depose the reigning Sultan against his will, the Pasha of Marrakesh had given his Parisian friends the pretext they needed to attack the Grandval plan. This new about-face by Mulay ben Arafa was, like the first, the result of the delaying action Boussac had been maneuvering so successfully from Paris ever since the idea of the reigning Sultan's abdication had arisen. Realizing that the government was working along those lines, Boussac had in fact sent Maître André Lénard to the Sultan to try to persuade him to assert publicly his intention of remaining on the throne. The Lénard mission, with the other pressure groups surrounding the Sultan, succeeded. Mulay ben Arafa was defenseless against his entourage and had finally decided to adopt the attitude demanded of him by his friends in Paris—hence el-Glaoui's letter. Boussac had only to explain to those who

46. Ibid., p. 161.
47. Ibid., pp. 162–63.
48. Ibid., p. 167.

still vacillated that the Prime Minister had been abusing the good faith of his ministers when he told them Mulay ben Arafa was ready to abdicate. The Sultan himself was soon to give decisive weight to this maneuver by officially informing the President of the Republic of his determination to remain on the throne.

On August 5, the day before the parliamentary recess, Faure made a statement on Morocco to the National Assembly that was along the lines of his statement of June 21. He confirmed that the government intended to press forward simultaneously with the restoration of law and order in a seriously disturbed situation and with the search for a political solution. He explained that the Resident-General's proposals would be examined by the Committee for Coordination of North African Affairs and by the government as a whole, and he assured the deputies that Parliament would in no event be confronted with a fait accompli.[49]

The next day, July had to inform Grandval by telephone that the Council of Ministers, which had debated his plan for nine hours, had decided it contained an implied threat. Its opponents had argued that France could not accept an ultimatum.[50] At least, that was the only explanation Grandval received.

In fact, something momentous had just occurred that placed an unforeseen and temporarily insurmountable obstacle in the Prime Minister's path. Shortly before the council meeting, Faure had been informed of an official letter from Mulay ben Arafa to the President of the Republic, dated July 28.[51] In this letter, impeccably written and based upon an incontrovertible legal argument, Mulay ben Arafa announced that under no circumstances would he consider withdrawing, that the dynastic problem could not be raised, and that no one could release him from his oath. This new document was even more important than the

49. *Journal officiel, Débats parlementaires, Assemblée nationale* (Aug. 6, 1955), pp. 4660–61. Since Parliament was to reconvene on the first Tuesday of October, the government had two months in which to act.

50. Grandval, p. 178.

51. This letter was slightly delayed, partly because of Mulay Arafa's vacillation and partly because communications of such importance were drafted and sent from Paris before submission to the Sultan for signature. Be that as it may, Mulay Arafa's letter was not sent back to Faure from the President's office until August 5, at the insistence of Charles Merveilleux du Vignaux, who had sent it directly to Jacques Duhamel.

letter el-Glaoui had just released to the press.[52] It was in outright contradiction to the principles of the Grandval plan which envisaged—and indeed assumed—a voluntary withdrawal by Mulay ben Arafa in favor of the Council of the Throne.

Faure had had too much experience to wage a parliamentary battle that was doomed to fail. For the moment it was impossible to counter the Sultan's latest maneuver; there was nothing to do but wait for an opening.[53] The Council of Ministers therefore confined itself to a general exchange of views, and Faure concluded by calling a meeting of the Committee for Coordination of North African Affairs for August 11.[54] It was agreed that the meeting should be open to any minister who wished to attend, which meant it would be a meeting of almost the entire council. Faure and July thus had five days to deal with the new situation. They also planned to use them to try to appease Grandval's understandable impatience.

A meeting was organized for this purpose on August 7-8 at Sanary, near Toulon, between July, Jacques Duhamel, Director of the Office of the Prime Minister, Koenig, and Grandval. The Resident-General arrived at Toulon on the morning of the seventh and was joined secretly later in the day by July and Duhamel.[55] July told him that it would be impossible to persuade the government to accept his plan within the time prescribed. "Some don't want Arafa to go, others are furious at the idea of ben Youssef's returning to France, and nearly the entire Council of Ministers thinks it highly improper for France to let herself be forced into accepting a deadline as early as August 20." [56]

Everything was in a state of suspense. Duhamel, who had no

---

52. See p. 269; for the text of this letter, see *Le Monde* (Aug. 5, 1955).

53. Before the meeting, he had talked with the President, who agreed with him. Coty, a man with somewhat liberal views, personally favored the Grandval plan. They were not prepared to accept Mulay Arafa's letter as a temporary stumbling block. Coty at one time had thought of neutralizing the right-wing opposition by suggesting to Faure either that he himself get the Socialists to join forces with the majority, or get someone else to do it. The latest event had made this procedure impracticable. It is possible that the letter had been sent with the idea of leaving Faure with no room to maneuver in the Council meeting, which immediately preceded Coty's vacation.

54. *Le Monde* (Aug. 9, 1955).

55. Officially, Grandval returned to France for personal reasons.

56. Grandval, p. 180.

illusions regarding the political situation, told Grandval privately that in his opinion the climate in Parliament was such that there could be no solution of the Moroccan problem before the next session. This forecast was to prove correct. July made no secret of the fact that Faure was much troubled by the attitude of Pinay, who had been opposed to Grandval ever since the two had clashed over the Saar. He added that this attitude was one reason the Prime Minister had decided that further consideration by the government was necessary.[57] To his great regret, Grandval was unable to see Pinay, but he did meet Koenig on August 8. The latter reproached him for having allowed himself to be won over by the Moroccan masses and for not taking the advice of Colonel Lecomte, who wanted Mulay ben Arafa to be given a chance. The Minister of War also said that the government could not agree to the August 20 deadline, and that the requisite decisions could be made just as well and better after that date. "Lecomte had made up his Minister's mind," Grandval concluded in his account of this interview, "and I knew I could not get him to change it."[58]

The Resident-General returned to Rabat empty-handed. The game was not yet lost, since the government's decision had been put off to August 11, but the political climate was becoming patently worse. Just when it had seemed to the Resident-General that a shift in attitude was opening up prospects for a political solution in Morocco, the obstinacy of the most energetic segment of the Right in France, based on a strong and official protest by Mulay ben Arafa, threw open the whole matter once again. The nationalist leaders' obvious dismay, when Grandval revealed to them that August 20 might well pass without any political settlement, clearly revealed the crucial nature of that fast-approaching date.

But Grandval had not lost all hope. For the first time since the crisis began, the French in Morocco and their local leaders showed signs of a willingness to compromise. They were still far from ready to accept the political consequences of the possible

57. On August 7, no one had as yet informed Grandval of Mulay Arafa's letter to Coty. It was not possible to uncover the reason for this strange reticence.
58. Grandval, p. 182.

withdrawal of Mulay ben Arafa, but their growing recognition
of the necessity of such an event was bound to lead them ultimately to accept its implications, unpalatable though they might
be. This major and still incipient trend resulted from the constitutional deadlock arising out of the August 1953 coup and from
the growth of terrorism. In an acute conflict, a time arrives when
the recourse of the parties to force compels one or the other to
envisage the possibility of a political solution which it had initially regarded as unacceptable. Once the French in Morocco
began to consider the mere possibility of the abdication of their
chosen Sultan, they virtually admitted defeat, since Mulay ben
Arafa embodied their only conceivable solution to the conflict.

Grandval realized that the question was no longer whether the
nationalists would win, but in what way and how quickly they
would achieve their objective—whether France could resolve the
conflict along lines conducive to a compromise formula such as
internal self-government, or whether the government's paralysis
would entail such political and military atrophy that France
would have no choice but to surrender the unconditional independence of Morocco to the nationalist leaders who had been
overwhelmed by their own supporters.

Everything depended on the tone of the discussions in the
Committee for Coordination of North African Affairs called for
August 11. Grandval, an ex officio member of the Committee, left
Rabat for Paris on the tenth, after devoting two days to a thorough examination of the political and military situation. In Paris,
he was immediately received by De Gaulle and then by Faure.
The former approved of the plan but warned against the government's vacillation and advised Grandval to resign at once if he
felt anyone was trying to make him a scapegoat.[59] Faure reaffirmed his confidence in Grandval and outlined his approach.
Grandval wrote:

> I was . . . to trust him to keep calm and poised, and to
> let him do the maneuvering. It was most important for
> him to convince Pinay. The moderates would follow him
> and once their support was gained, Koenig would have

59. Ibid., p. 185.

to give in—or resign. In any event, he assumed full responsibility for the plan I had submitted to the government. Nothing in it had to be changed, except perhaps a slight alteration in the timetable, but that, after all, was of no importance.[60]

In fact, the two men agreed on the substance of the problem. But whereas Grandval believed that everything must be settled by August 20, Faure, being more sensitive to the parliamentary implications of the problem, refused to be bound by a deadline which Mulay ben Arafa's letter had made it impossible for them to meet.

Grandval has described with great clarity the course of the August 11–12 negotiations in the Committee for Coordination of North African Affairs.[61] The theme of this political bout was simple. The Council of Ministers agreed unanimously that it was essential to break the deadlock as soon as possible by negotiating large-scale reforms with a representative Moroccan government. However, the same council threatened to split as soon as there was any attempt to make it accept a solution to the problem of the Throne that implied Mulay ben Arafa's departure. Because the Grandval plan made this departure the necessary preliminary to any reform program, it endangered the government's existence. Rather than recognize that the Moroccan problem could not be solved while Mulay ben Arafa was on the throne, the Arafist ministers preferred to believe, or pretended to believe, that there was no need to settle the question of the throne first, that the abdication of Mulay ben Arafa was not essential, that nationalism was just a bogey given importance only by the Resident-General's reports, and that consequently there was no reason why the reforms—which all agreed to be necessary—should not be carried out within the framework of the existing system.

60. Ibid., p. 186.

61. Grandval was still bound to secrecy when he wrote his book, and based his description of the tenor of these discussions solely upon secondhand sources: accounts in the French press and political statements by the major political participants. See ibid., pp. 189 ff. This was, obviously, only a device. Grandval was present at the discussions and if he chose to describe them as an outsider, he did so by discretion rather than ignorance.

The government found itself in such extreme danger that only a brilliant maneuver by the Prime Minister could ward off disaster. Faure suddenly changed his tactics and decided on August 11 to adopt his opponents' argument in order to force them to prove to themselves the futility of the political solutions they advocated. Substituting a plan of his own for the Grandval plan, he proposed to his astounded ministers a compromise formula which Grandval reports in these terms:

> I was to suggest to Mulay Arafa the immediate constitution of a widely representative Moroccan government whose members would be chosen from a list agreed upon by a "Committee of Five" consisting of the Prime Minister, Schuman, Pinay, July, and Koenig. If the Sultan could constitute such a government, its members were to be invited to go to France by August 18 and be received by a government delegation. If he failed to do so, it would rest with me to choose from the list a certain number of Moroccans who would be received on the same day by the same delegation. After this exchange of views, the government would determine, if possible before August 25, the necessary steps to resolve the Moroccan crisis, which in any event should be "out of the critical stage" by September 12 at the latest.[62]

A few days later, Faure explained his intentions to Grandval in terms that left no doubt as to what he was trying to accomplish. "You are to return to Paris on August 18. Since Arafa will have been unable to constitute his government by that date, we shall reach the second phase, the consultation between the Moroccans and the French government's delegation. This will enable us to get past August 20 without trouble." [63]

The Faure plan was adopted by the Committee for Coordination of North African Affairs on August 12 and then by the Cabinet.[64] On the thirteenth, the Prime Minister went to Vizille to bring the President up to date. With Coty's approval, he made a statement the same day to a correspondent of *Agence France-*

62. Ibid., p. 193.
63. Ibid., p. 200.
64. *Le Monde* (Aug. 14–15, 1955).

Presse which, while it did not reveal the tenor of the government's plan, informed the public that the government had agreed upon a plan and that the Prime Minister intended to press forward quickly and terminate the critical phase of the crisis within a month.[65]

The government now had a plan, a method, and a timetable. If the Prime Minister had really believed it possible to solve the Moroccan problem within the framework of the Arafa regime, his plan would have been only the most commonplace political scheme. Actually, it was a masterpiece; Faure was fully aware of having put on a show, and he intended to make the Independents and the Social Republicans pay the cost. By forcing the Right to admit that it accepted the principle of large-scale reforms, by luring it on with the notion of negotiating these reforms with a "widely representative" Arafist government, by asking Mulay ben Arafa to set up such a government within a short space of time, and by reserving the right—if he failed—to make the Right fall back on direct negotiations with the Moroccan nationalists, Faure had set in motion a policy that could not thereafter be halted either by the clandestine maneuvers of the ultras or by the obstinacy of the diehards in his own government.

The new point of departure in Faure's maneuver was the natural outcome of the government's need to respond to Mulay ben Arafa's letter. The Sultan's theme had been, in substance, that France should proceed with the awaited reforms on the basis of the treaty—the initiative rested not with him, but with France. The obvious rejoinder was to ask him to form a government. However, the reply was aimed less at the Sultan than at the ultras. Faure, July, and Grandval had no doubt that Mulay ben Arafa wanted to escape from his advisers' grip. In asking him to form a government, they were lending him a helping hand, while at the same time setting a trap for the ultras. Faure, in a masterstroke, hid nothing from his opponents. When he proposed his plan to the committee, he did not try to lure his colleagues blindfolded into an adventure of unforeseeable consequences. He made no secret of the fact that he considered the

65. Ibid.

Sultan incapable of persuading the nationalists to enter a government, no matter how much time he was given to do it. None of the ministers had disagreed with him on that point. The blow could not be parried, not even by an opponent who realized the risks he was running. The Right had wanted Mulay ben Arafa to be given a chance; it had been given. The Right, then, could hardly refuse to enter the trap Faure had set.

Faure knew Mulay ben Arafa would achieve nothing. He foresaw that once Pinay was involved in direct conversations with the nationalists, he would be forced to recognize that the only solution lay in Mulay ben Arafa's abdication, the establishment of a Council of the Throne, and the eventual return of Mohammed V to France and then Morocco. Once the power of the Independents had been offset, the resignation of Koenig and his cronies in A.R.S. would be unimportant. They would be allowed to leave, and the government would have survived the crisis intact. It was not even a question of abandoning the Grandval plan, but merely of providing a political digression between August 12–25 to force the Right to confess its impotence and to do, despite itself, what it did not wish to do. The Prime Minister's methods had not changed. Having led the Resident-General to reinvent the Izard plan, he was trying to persuade the Independent leaders to reinvent the main clauses of the Grandval plan. It was almost like the application of judo tactics to politics, with the fighter taking advantage of the strength exerted by his opponent to reverse their positions by feigning first to yield to his adversary's attack or defense.

Although by devious means it approximated the Izard-Grandval plan, the Faure plan presented certain disadvantages that made it unacceptable to the Resident-General. The Grandval plan had advocated settling the Moroccan crisis before August 20 by securing the agreement of all parties concerned, thus allowing Morocco and France to work out the details in a more pacific atmosphere. The Faure plan, on the contrary, amounted to letting the Right begin political negotiations with the Moroccans in a completely disorganized fashion, thus forcing it to pull chestnuts out of the fire once the situation had deteriorated so far that France had no alternative but to accept her adversaries' conditions. By obliging Grandval to give public proof of Mulay ben Arafa's political inadequacy, the Faure formula ipso facto strengthened the political position of the nationalists. By accepting the risk of unleashing full-scale political horse-trading in France itself, in the midst of the crisis, it guaranteed in advance the success of the bargain that was to emanate this time from the Moroccan camp. In abandoning the fateful date of August 20, it condemned all future Franco-Moroccan negotiations to the pressure of flaring passions instead of avoiding the risk of an explosion by concluding an agreement in principle with the other side, at the proper time, as Grandval would have liked.

This disintegration of the political situation was the inevitable result of Mulay ben Arafa's letter to the President of the Republic. Faure's response had offset its most dangerous effects, but it could neither recapture time lost nor, consequently, enable the government to solve the crisis before August 20. Purely from the point of view of the deadline, the ultras had won the round. One week had been sufficient for the French government to be seized of the Moroccan problem and, because of the Right and Extreme Right, at the same time to ruin whatever chance of a peaceful settlement the situation still held out. From then on, the outcome was settled. Since Paris had not taken a stand, the forces involved were to operate exclusively to the nationalists' benefit until the conflict was totally resolved.

Grandval's only alternatives were to go back to Morocco to implement a plan that was no longer his, or to resign. Because he had just been told that Faure had deliberately failed to submit the main part of his instructions to the Council of Ministers when the Resident-General left for Rabat early in July, he was more inclined to take the second course. Grandval could not understand why the government should be divided in August on a plan that remained so consistently within the limits of the July instructions; he concluded that Faure had tricked him and had sent him to Rabat to carry out a policy which, assurances to the contrary, had not been approved by the government.[66]

---

66. See Grandval, pp. 28, 196–97. This stemmed from a misunderstanding which derived from the fact that the text of the instructions read on July 6 in the Council of Ministers was not distributed to the Committee of Five until August 11. Grandval

Grandval had reached this stage in his thinking when July filled his cup of bitterness by giving him to understand at the last minute that the timetable in the government's plan would probably not be respected.[67] The Resident-General had had enough of such procrastination and told Faure on August 13 at the end of the day that he would not return to Morocco. Henri Yrissou and Pierre July, however, persuaded him that the disturbances expected on August 20 might be attributed to his resignation; Grandval finally accepted their argument and left for Rabat, where he arrived the next day.

Events were soon to prove Grandval's fears well-founded. The revelation of the government's plan at once led the parties involved to harden their positions. The commandants of the regions, once informed, made no secret of their gloomy expectations for August 20. Si Fatmi ben Slimane refused to enter the ben Arafa government. The Istiqlal and the P.D.I. announced that the French plan did not conform to the nationalists' aspirations and that they would not participate in the conversations to be held in France. Moroccans who had so far held aloof from the conflict began publicly to side with Mohammed V.[68] Sensing that the Resident-General's prestige had been diminished by the government's decision, the French in Morocco became uncompromising. Grandval commented,

did not deny either that his instructions had been submitted to the Council on July 6 (information obtained from interviews) or that the text submitted on August 11 to the Committee of Five actually included the paragraph providing for the eventual return of the Sultan to France. (Ibid., p. 197.) The only dubious factor is that, according to Grandval, the instructions were not read in full to the Council of Ministers because of their length—45 pages. This leaves the theoretical possibility of a breach of confidence, which does not withstand examination. It is difficult to imagine that the ministers, some of whom were old hands, could have approved on July 6 instructions, whose extreme political importance they must have known, without taking care to verify the content. Instructions to Residents-General were, in effect, official documents carefully preserved and elaborated with the assistance of competent officials. They were read in the Council of Ministers but not distributed; the original document could be consulted on request. It would be even more extraordinary, if one accepts the fact that there had been a breach of confidence, for the Committee of Five not to have realized this in August when it had the chance to read the text just sent them. If, on August 11, the Social Republicans had possesed such a strong political weapon, they could have used it to cause the government's downfall.

67. Grandval, p. 201.
68. Ibid., p. 208.

Exactly as I feared, the announcement of the forthcoming effort not only did not reduce tension but, by emphasizing that the game was not yet over, it encouraged all sides to redouble their efforts on behalf of their own cause, and to defend it more stubbornly than ever. The ambiguity in which we tried to seek refuge merely exacerbated the conflict.[69]

Moulay ben Arafa, well advised by his prompters in Paris and Rabat, replied in friendly fashion to Faure's letter, delivered by Grandval. He averred that the time allotted for constituting his government was too short, but promised to do his best. He also noted, not without humor, that if certain factions of Moroccan opinion refused to participate in such a government, they would be able to form an organized opposition. On August 17, he sent Grandval a plan for a "homogeneous traditionalist" government consisting of 20 names, more than half of which had not figured on the list Grandval brought back from Paris. The Sultan pretended to join in the government's game and rounded off with slapstick the political comedy the Prime Minister had made him play. In the circumstances, it was no longer possible to proceed to the second stage of the Faure plan and to have Mulay ben Arafa's candidates (or, failing them, those of Grandval) received by the government delegation on August 18. Not only had Mulay ben Arafa failed to appoint any ministers, but his list was so impossible that Grandval would have achieved nothing by sending a group of the Sultan's nominees to meet with the delegation in Paris. August 20 was to dawn under an ominous political cloud.

Meanwhile, Si Abbès Tazi, Pasha of Rabat, told Grandval secretly that the Sultan was willing to leave the throne in the next few days and to withdraw to his palace at Tangier. Fearing the reactions of his entourage, the Pasha asked the Resident-General to keep this absolutely quiet. But this unexpected turn seemed to reopen the whole question once again; Grandval had no course but to cable the details, and Pinay unfortunately felt

69. Ibid., p. 210.

duty-bound to reveal them on August 21 during a conversation with el-Hadjoui at Aix-les-Bains. Mulay ben Arafa's advisers immediately descended on him again, and for the second time he reneged. Thus an unforeseen chance had been lost of announcing his abdication before it was too late.[70]

While the signs of impending storm multiplied in Morocco as far as the frontier of the Spanish zone, a new meeting of the Council of Ministers took place in Paris on August 18. Faure managed to persuade it to confirm the necessity of proceeding without delay to the formation of a representative Moroccan government. Pressed by General Koenig and Raymond Triboulet, Minister for Ex-servicemen, he survived the storm only by giving way and again affirming his willingness to compromise.[71]

A final meeting of the Committee of Five had been set for the nineteenth. As the Resident-General was again thinking of resigning, Faure invited him to Paris once more to try to dissuade him by involving him in the work of the committee. Unmoved by the news of serious disturbances that had broken out the same day at Khenifra, the "Five" decided that the Franco-Moroccan conversations planned since August 12 should open at Aix-les-Bains on the twenty-second. The principle of sending a French delegation to Madagascar—an essential element in the Grandval plan—was again approved, but no date was set. Faure considered appointing Pinay to head this delegation, then decided to postpone the decision for discussion at Aix-les-Bains,[72] since he believed that no contact with Mohammed V was possible until the roundtable discussions had thrown some light on the political situation. "So," wrote Grandval, "that day's balance sheet added up to precisely nothing! We were approaching August 20 in the worst possible condition. Heartbroken at having wasted my time in Paris, as I expected, there was nothing for me to do but return

70. Ibid., pp. 215–16.
71. Ibid., p. 221.
72. Ibid., pp. 225–26. According to Grandval, as early as August 19, Pinay had appeared disposed to go to Madagascar vested with full power to settle the problem of the throne in a tête-à-tête with Mohammed V. Only the fact that the Tunisian and Moroccan problems no longer fell within the competence of the Ministry for Foreign Affairs seems to have kept him from taking this initiative earlier. The idea of ending the Moroccan crisis by direct negotiation with Mohammed V seems thus to have been envisaged by the Independent leader as early as the middle of August 1955.

to Rabat—where my plane landed at two o'clock in the morning." [73]

Morocco was on the brink of "unprecedented crisis." [74] The large towns did escape, thanks to the cooperative attitude of the nationalist leaders and (since the worst was expected) to the concentration of troops there. But the *bled* and the small towns, left to themselves, were about to erupt. At Khenifra, Khourigba, and above all at Oued Zem, the alliance between the townsfolk and the tribal horsemen was to be disastrous.

The disturbances expected for August 20 broke out before Grandval returned. At Khenifra, on the nineteenth, town dwellers mingling with Zaïan hillsmen had attacked a police station and set fire to buildings after marching in a procession brandishing flags and portraits of Mohammed V. The disturbances were initially quelled by the Foreign Legion, but broke out again in the afternoon during funeral ceremonies for the morning's victims. The rioters, bottled up in the *medina* by the military within sight of the Zaïan horsemen who patrolled the neighboring hills, laid down their arms on August 21. The affair had cost 40 lives and 60 people had been wounded. [75]

On August 20, at 8:30 A.M., the contrôle civil at Oued Zem learned from a caid of the Smaala tribe that a large body of the tribe's horsemen were marching on the town. Oued Zem, which had sent off part of its gendarmerie to a neighboring locality where acts of violence had been reported, was delivered up almost defenseless to looting and rioting. The regional reserves did not arrive until too late, and it was 5 P.M. before the French forces regained control. By evening, half the town was in ruins. Forty-nine French residents had been savagely massacred, including eight women and five children. That same day, thirty kilometers away, the French personnel of the Aït Amar mines were besieged by "a thousand Moroccans, mineworkers, and horsemen from the neighboring tribes. Barricaded in their offices with their wives and children, [the] engineers and foremen

73. Ibid., p. 226.
74. Ibid., p. 239.
75. Ibid., p. 227.

[fought] desperately for several hours. Toward 1 A.M. on the twenty-first, the army finally intervened." [76] In addition to the deaths at Oued Zem, 19 Frenchmen had lost their lives. On the morning of the twenty-first, at Khourigba, another riot caused over one billion francs of damage to the premises of the Sharifian Phosphates Office. There were many French deaths there also. Grandval, who had left for Algiers that morning on his way to Aix-les-Bains, returned to Rabat as soon as he heard of the new disturbances. [77]

Khenifra, Oued Zem, and Khourigba had been hit hardest by the wave of violence that engulfed Morocco, but French and Moroccan blood had been shed almost everywhere: at Khemisset, Rabat, Casablanca, and Mazagan. The Oued Zem incident seems to have been the crowning event in the political reconversion of the Moroccan notables who, caught between Mohammed V and Mulay ben Arafa, were trying desperately to restore themselves to their former sovereign's good graces. Four important Zaïan caids who had been compromised in the crisis of August 1953 had taken the bull by the horns and sent a cable to the French government on August 11 requesting it to put an end to the myth of el-Glaoui, whom they now denounced as an "agitator" and an "obstacle in the path of Franco-Moroccan friendship." [78] There is every reason to believe that when the two caids of the Smaala tribe learned that their colleagues at Khenifra and Khourigba had sent off cables hostile to el-Glaoui, they were filled with anxiety and allowed their followers to get in touch with the Istiqlal-dominated townsfolk of Oued Zem, without informing the contrôle civil. The Smaala horsemen knew that Muslims had been lynched at Casablanca a month earlier, after the Mers-Sultan incident, and this knowledge must have added to their fury. [79]

76. Ibid., p. 231.

77. The reason for his trip to Algiers was to persuade Si Mammeri, one of Mohammed V's faithful followers-in-exile, to participate in the Antsirabé mission. Si Mammeri had already come secretly to Rabat on August 6 to discuss the question of the Throne with Grandval and had assured him of Mohammed V's full support, provided France did not force him to abdicate.

78. B.M.I., 5th year, no. 101 (1955), p. 4.

79. The violence of public reaction to this tragedy of uncertain origin gave rise to the most contradictory interpretations. Grandval's opponents did not hesitate to accuse

At the height of the disturbances in Morocco, the Algerian insurrection flared up again. There was nothing fortuitous in this timing. The insurgents of both countries had got together, weapons in hand, to commemorate the second anniversary of Mohammed V's deposition. "With almost foolhardy audacity [the Algerian outlaws] chose as the terrain for their attacks a region the authorities had placed on the alert only the day before; it was a vast quadrilateral in the north of Constantine Department, with Collo, Philippeville, Constantine, and Guelma as its four corners." [80] This time there were real military operations carried out by men in uniform. French military casualties numbered 123 dead and 223 wounded. The insurgents left 1,273 dead on the field and lost 1,024 prisoners.[81] In this situation, it was becoming increasingly impossible to make any decisions about Morocco without being influenced by events in Algeria.

The trial of strength of August 20 showed up not only the weakness of the protectorate's defense forces, lack of intelligence,

---

him of laxity in connection with Oued Zem as subsequent justification of his forebodings. See Grandval, p. 231. Conversely, a high official of the erstwhile protectorate stated in an interview that the Commanding Officer of Troops, General Duval, had sanctioned the incident in the hope of torpedoing Grandval and his liberal policy. Accusations of this nature certainly do not constitute either definite proof or even hypotheses, but they do reveal the prevailing state of mind in Morocco toward the end of the conflict. In this embittered climate of the summer of 1955, everyone from the highest rank to the lowest ended by believing his neighbor capable of anything.

Duval's attitude was nevertheless exceptionally odd throughout this residency. Grandval writes that, just before Oued Zem, Duval refused a metropolitan reinforcement division previously promised to Grandval by the government. See ibid., pp. 16, 31, 99, 206. Furthermore, according to information obtained from interviews, Duval did not hesitate to get in touch with Koenig in Morocco in order to destroy the Residency's liberal policy. Matters went to such extremes that, in July, Pierre July was forced to write to Schuman (then acting President of the Council of Ministers) suggesting that he remind the Minister for National Defense that military authorities in Morocco were of necessity subject to the Residency. In particular, he drew Schuman's attention to the intervention of Grousseaud (moderate deputy), who wanted Grandval replaced by Duval and Cause's expulsion annulled.

Moreover, Duval was universally known to be a partisan of force. Governmental circles were not unaware that he would have liked to bring matters to a head, even at the expense of killing 10,000 Moroccans. These are the views of a tactician, and can be defended as such; Duval had first applied them ten years earlier, in Algeria. In fact, Duval had directed the repression of the Sétif riots in 1945, in which thousands of indigenous Algerians were killed. While it has not been definitely proved that Duval was one of the generals who openly tried in Paris to thwart Grandval's policies, his lack of sympathy for Grandval's so-called "liberal" policy is certain. See particularly Berger-Levrault, *Le Général Raymond Duval* (Paris, 1957).

80. "Le problème algérien," *Chronique de politique étrangère, 8* (1955), 735.
81. Ibid., p. 735.

inexplicable ineffectiveness of communications, and growing isolation of the upper administrative and political circles from Moroccan life, but also the emptiness of the Berber myth and the theory of the *bon bled*. An alliance between the tribesmen and the town-dwellers had now been formed against a regime whose control was gradually breaking down.

Yet there had been ample warning. As early as 1949, long before the first disturbances, a visit by the Sultan to the Berber country had turned into a triumphal procession. To the great surprise of the authorities, the tribes had given their ruler an enthusiastic mass welcome. Some contrôleurs civils had the impression that one day the hillsmen might demonstrate more tenacious nationalist fervor and greater loyalty to the Sultan than the more passive and stolid peasants of the plain. Apart from such precedents, the first signs of serious tribal disaffection went back to Whitsuntide 1951 and the so-called incident of Ahansali, the El Tadla killer. At that time, El Tadla was being stirred up by a particularly active and bellicose section of the Istiqlal. Ahansali was known to be in touch with a Moroccan auxiliary and was approached by an Istiqlal militant who was looking for weapons and knew the *mokhazzenis* (native gendarmes) had some. The Istiqlal man explained "that he needed a rifle because there was going to be a war." Ahansali seized the weapon, killed the *mokhazzeni,* and took to the maquis, shooting six French nationals at random and wounding three others in his solitary ambushes. An entire division under General Boyer de Latour carried out energetic reprisals against the Aït Saïd tribe, which lost dozens of men. The instigator was unquestionably an Istiqlal cell, more militant than the movement at that time, but the point is that the *bled* sheltered the assassin, thus demonstrating its discontent, its local sensitivity to nationalist propaganda, and the tribe's solidarity with the extremists claiming to act on its behalf.[82]

Throughout 1952 disturbances followed by repressive action had broken out here and there in the mountains, especially at M'rirt, where there were ten deaths and several deportations; at

82. The trial of Tadla's murderer and his alleged accomplices, which took place in Casablanca in February 1951, aroused considerable interest.

Khenifra; at Tedders in the Zemmour; and at Beni Mellal, where there were seven dead and many wounded in December at the time of the Casablanca incidents. In August 1953, riots at Oudja in connection with a revolt by the Beni Snassene were followed by reprisals and police round-ups, as a result of which hundreds fled to the Spanish zone.

Of course, it was difficult for the authorities to determine whether events of this kind were merely the exception that proved the rule of the *bled's* loyalty or whether they marked the beginning of a drift toward the nationalist camp.[83] The military leaders and contrôleurs civils were accustomed to the loyal demonstrations—often solicited—of the hillsmen, who were influenced by the undeniable brotherhood of arms that had developed between the Moroccan and French soldiers. There was therefore some excuse for their assertions that nationalism had not affected the mountain regions. The trend existed, but it was to a large extent masked by the extraordinary ambiguity that generally characterizes the attitudes of colonial peoples toward the men who embody the contradictory forces competing for their support. The difficulty of diagnosis was increased by the reverse pull that set the notables in opposition to the Palace, in this as well as other areas. Seeing the masses only through a screen of notables more or less hostile to Mohammed V, often unaware of the tensions between the notables themselves and the people under them, the contrôle civil remained wrapped in the comfortable illusions bred by the theory of the *bon bled*. However, although diagnosis was difficult, it was not impossible. A number of contrôleurs civils and French liberals had long since done just that. In most of the areas of the *bled* affected before Oued Zem, the same two factors were found in conjunction: extortion and arbitrary actions by the cadi, often complicated by rivalry among notables, and inflammatory activities by local propaganda agents for the Istiqlal, for example, merchants traveling on the great inland routes, bus drivers, and even local party cells. The corrupt caid created discontent. The nationalist agitators stirred people up and in the most serious cases succeeded in kindling a brush

83. For more details on the precursors of Berber dissidence, see Centre d'études et de documentation, *Urgence d'une politique française au Maroc*, Maroc A8 (1954).

fire. For a long time the conflagrations were limited. The periodic purging of nationalist notables and the natural docility of a rural population, with a solid social organization less affected by colonization than was often thought to be the case, enabled the French to control the *bled* easily until the deposition crisis, extension of repression, and damage done to the prestige of the French forces by urban terrorism completely altered the particulars of the problem and gave rise to the massacres of August 20, 1955.

While the regime tottered upon its foundations, suddenly deprived, by the attacks, of its traditionalist supports and the political doctrine that had hitherto made its subsistence possible, Grandval calmly analyzed the situation. He had been stripped of all authority by the violence of August 20, and was to be circumvented by the roundtable conference at Aix-les-Bains. He was fully determined not to become the tool of a policy of which he did not approve—even though it was almost identical with the one he had recommended. On August 22, he asked the government to replace him. The last days of his mission were no less disturbed than the preceding ones. On the same day, General Duval was killed in an airplane accident. The funeral, cleverly transformed by Présence française into a mass demonstration against the Resident-General personally and against the government,[84] took place two days later amid the jeers of a mob infuriated by Grandval's public appearance.

Having put his affairs in order, Grandval left for Paris on the twenty-sixth at the request of the Prime Minister, who hoped again to persuade him to change his mind. Faure rightly thought the recent events in Morocco should not influence the government's action, and so the roundtable conference opened on the appointed day. For the first time, a ministerial team representing all shades of French colonial policy was to find itself in physical contact with representatives of the various factions of Moroccan opinion, and in particular with those nationalist leaders whom the right-wing leaders had known hitherto only by reputation. For six days, August 22–27, the Moroccan dele-

84. Grandval, p. 247.

gations laid their political views in turn before the Prime Minister and Ministers Schuman, July, Pinay, and Pierre Koenig.[85] This time, the Independents and the Social Republicans were fully involved.

The Aix-les-Bains meeting was obviously not conducive to the conclusion of an agreement between the French ministers and the nationalist leaders, who by the end of the conference had become the only ones who counted on the Moroccan side. The real work was done, as is usual in such circumstances, behind the scenes. The procedure for deposing Mulay ben Arafa was discussed in detail on August 27 by the Grand Vizier on the one side, and on the other by Pierre July, Jacques Duhamel, and Henri Yrissou (directors on Pinay's staff), and Olivier Manet (a member of July's staff). The same day, July, Duhamel, Yrissou, Jean Basdevant (Director of Moroccan and Tunisian Affairs), and Manet continued their political talks until the conclusion of an unofficial agreement with the Istiqlal delegates (Omar Abd el-Djellil, Mehdi ben Barka, Abderrahim Bouabid) and the P.D.I. (Maître Abdelkader Bendjelloun, el Hadj Abdelhadi Boutaleb, Mohammed Cherkaoui, and Ahmed ben Souda). The Grand Vizier, when invited to give his opinion on the course to be followed in removing Mulay ben Arafa, proposed to his interlocutors that if the Sultan refused, the Maghzen should meet in plenary session and depose him, proclaiming him unfit to reign for reasons of health. He added that Mulay ben Arafa would only withdraw voluntarily if el-Hadjoui did not object, and that in any event it was necessary to the success of the operation for the regional leaders to stop backing el-Glaoui and to support the Maghzen. Furthermore, he explained, it would be desirable for the Sultan to withdraw to Tangier, preparations for his departure had been made, and the operation could be carried out by the following Monday if Boyer de Latour replaced Grandval in the interim.

In substance the Izard plan, which Mohammed V had just approved again, was unofficially adopted by the second group as the basis for a settlement. Since the delegates were unable to agree on the idea of Mohammed ben Youssef's immediate return

85. *Le Monde* (Aug. 23–28, 29, 1955).

to France, it was understood that while the Istiqlal would not participate in the government to be set up until after his return, neither would it boycott it. There was heated discussion concerning the composition of the Council of the Throne (it was decided to maintain its three-man membership), the Moroccan government, and the respective capacities of the two bodies. The Istiqlal leaders insisted that the French government's declarations should make perfectly clear the principle of the unity and integrity of Moroccan sovereignty and the parties' determination to enter into negotiations to define a new framework for the two countries' relations. The future declaration of La Celle-Saint-Cloud was contained in embryo in these terms.[86]

However, this was merely an agreement in principle which July was to lay before the government the next day, the twenty-eighth. Actually, the Prime Minister's political position remained too uncertain for the next Cabinet meeting to be expected to give outright endorsement to the talks at Aix-les-Bains. On August 23, in Paris, the five moderate groups (Peasants, Independent-Peasants, Independent Republicans, Social Republicans, and the A.R.S.) had threatened to withdraw their support from the government if concessions were made to "those directly or indirectly responsible for the massacres designed to evict France from Morocco." [87] On August 27, the Palace at Rabat had released its own statement, through el-Hadjoui, in which His Sharifian Majesty expressly reiterated his official determination to retain and to exercise the divine mission imparted to him and to remain at Rabat in the midst of his subjects.[88] While the Sultan was hastily having his Palace at Tangier put in order, the Imperial Chief of Protocol was not wasting his time packing his sovereign's bags.

The day this statement appeared, Faure told the press as he was leaving Aix-les-Bains that he was now convinced the crisis could be solved, that the second stage envisaged in the government timetable would be concluded in another twenty-four hours, that it was possible that the Cabinet, which was to hear

86. See p. 335.
87. *B.M.I.*, 5th year, no. 102 (1955), p. 3.
88. Ibid.

July the next day, would not be able to work out all the details of its policy immediately, but that the policy would be fully worked out by September 12 as previously planned.[89] The Cabinet, for its part, issued a statement the following day; after taking cognizance of July's report, it confirmed its previous decisions and remained in favor of forming a Moroccan government with full responsibilities.[90]

The government had not been able to bring itself to ratify explicitly all the decisions of principle made at Aix-les-Bains, but this reluctance did not alter the state of affairs. As Faure had expected, Aix-les-Bains forced the leader of the Independent-Peasants to negotiate with the nationalists. Henceforward, a tacit agreement existed between them and the French Right concerning the Izard plan. The striking contrast between the westernized nationalist leaders and the traditionalist delegates who seemed to have stepped straight out of the Middle Ages had helped considerably to persuade Pinay that the only persons with whom France could negotiate in Morocco were those who for two years had been calling so insistently for Mohammed V's return to the throne. Koenig and his friends of the A.R.S. could resign if they liked, then and there; affairs could be conducted without them.

Oued Zem had not only precipitated the evolution of Franco-Moroccan negotiations; the events of August 20 had made France realize that unless it gave in completely on Morocco, reserves would have to be called out. Faure had had to announce to the press on August 24 the recall to active duty of fifty to sixty thousand men.[91] The conjunction of the Algerian and Moroccan disturbances had suddenly created a crisis exceeding the capabilities of the regular army. To keep Algeria, France obviously had to negotiate with Morocco as quickly as possible. From day to day the pressure exerted by the Algerian crisis on the Moroccan status quo increased.

In the meantime, relations between the resigning Resident-General and his Prime Minister had grown steadily worse. Even

89. *Le Monde* (Aug. 28–29, 1955).
90. Ibid. (Aug. 30, 1955).
91. Ibid. (Aug. 25, 1955).

before his departure for Paris, Grandval had issued a statement at Rabat specifying that he had "had no part in the conversations at Aix-les-Bains." [92] The two men met again on the twenty-seventh at the Chateau of La Celle-Saint-Cloud. Despite the Prime Minister's urgings, Grandval insisted that his resignation was final. It had looked as if the matter would end amicably when new grounds for friction were created by a conversation between Grandval and Maître André Lénard, a friend of Boussac and el-Glaoui. Grandval was told by Maître Lénard that in circles closely connected with *L'Aurore*'s editorial policy, the Prime Minister and the Resident-General were regarded as conscious agents of Mohammed V's restoration. Added to the suspicions which the Resident-General had nourished for some time concerning Faure's real intentions, this information came to him like a sudden ray of light. He was furious, and certain he had been duped. He immediately decided to write to the President of the Republic and disassociate himself from the government.[93] On August 29, *L'Aurore* published extracts from Grandval's letter of August 27 to the President even before it could be forwarded to the members of the government.

To the end, the relationship between Faure and Grandval was full of grounds for recrimination. Having interpreted the silence surrounding Mohammed V's letter [94] as a maneuver by the Prime Minister, the Resident-General thought he had discovered that his instructions had not been submitted to the Cabinet in their entirety. He had hardly recovered from his annoyance at this when he finally departed on bad terms with Faure, whom he now accused of having sent him to Rabat as the unwitting tool of a plot to restore Mohammed V contrary to the government's official policy and the feelings of its representative in Rabat.

As for this last grievance, the Prime Minister had put the Resident-General on guard. "Your policy," Grandval had said to him on August 13, "is going to put ben Youssef back on the

92. Grandval, p. 253.
93. Ibid., p. 255; also *L'Année politique 1955* (Paris, 1956), pp. 667 ff.
94. See p. 255.

throne." "Did you not guess?" Faure replied.[95] Not until two weeks later, after Maître Lénard's revelations, did Grandval perceive the pejorative interpretation that might be placed on the Prime Minister's reply. Despite its possible implication, the quip did not necessarily mean what has been supposed. It could mean, of course, "I assume you have realized we are both working to restore Mohammed." But Faure could just as well have meant, "How can you not realize that the force of events will bring the ex-Sultan back to Rabat, whether we like it or not?"

The second interpretation is more consistent with the facts than the first. As soon as one thinks in terms of the plan originally prepared by Izard, rediscovered by Grandval, and finally applied by Faure in circumstances which from the beginning nullified its positive aspects, Mohammed V's restoration becomes the only possible solution. Since the failure of the August 1953 coup, Mohammed V in Madagascar had become the idol of his subjects. No recognized Moroccan negotiator would have been able to disassociate himself from him. Neither the Izard plan nor the Grandval plan had made his return to France conditional upon his abdication. Both plans admitted implicitly or explicitly that the new Morocco would be democratic and would therefore be free to choose its sovereign. When these facts are added up, the answer is almost automatically "restoration." The only way to prevent Mohammed V's return to the throne would have been to force him to abdicate from Madagascar, an impossibility because he refused, and because his cooperation was needed to solve the problem of the Throne. However, Grandval was categorical on this point: his own plan did not imply any renunciation by Mohammed V of his sovereign rights, but merely his public acquiescence in working out a transitional constitutional formula.

During a conversation at the end of June 1955, De Gaulle had told Grandval that he could see no way out of the crisis but the "reinstallation of Sidi Mohammed ben Youssef on the Sharifian throne. However, it would be necessary," the General had added, "for the French government itself to take the initiative, and this

95. Grandval, p. 201.

it is quite incapable of doing." [96] It is surprising that Grandval should not have realized from the start that there was no other answer to the problem he was about to tackle. It is true that he had just come from the Saar and could have had, in June 1955, only the most meager knowledge of the Moroccan question.[97] As his book indicates, Grandval's ideas were to evolve considerably in the course of his mission. He left for Morocco strongly opposed to the solution endorsed by Mohammed V, which obviously ran the risk of being "only a phase that must inevitably end in restoration." [98] In three weeks he rediscovered the Izard plan, adopted it after introducing a deadline, and at once became—subject to that reservation—the plan's warmest supporter. "Perhaps," he concluded in the epilogue,

> [the restoration of the Sultan] might have been inevitable in any event and perhaps even desirable. . . . All the same, his return in such circumstances was a blow to French authority and was fraught with consequences. In Morocco, instead of appearing as the result of our voluntary consent, and of being, as it conceivably could have been, a symbol of authentic reconciliation, it took place amid a general outbreak of emotion.[99]

Grandval had initially opposed Mohammed V's restoration, but, as the facts of the Moroccan problem became gradually more familiar to him, he recognized its inevitability. Thereafter, he fought only against a restoration that was premature and agreed to in the midst of disorder. That, in the end, was the real reason for his resignation. Having previously reproached Faure for permitting Mohammed V's restoration, he ultimately reproached him only for letting it happen too soon. His epilogue admits the injustice even of this grievance:

> If the Prime Minister decided, in the light of the particular political situation as viewed from his essentially

96. Ibid., p. 8.

97. Grandval himself toyed momentarily with the possibility of restoring Mohammed V, with France taking the initiative in the hope of avoiding an ultimate restoration in circumstances France could no longer control. The idea, which he mentioned to Faure, was finally rejected as impracticable. Faure's "Did you not guess?" is thus self-explanatory.

98. Grandval, p. 9.

99. Ibid., p. 263.

parliamentary viewpoint, that he could not, at the time, go any faster or any further and that I was asking the government to do too much in too short a time, am I qualified to hold an opposing view, a conviction? On the contrary, is it not probable that from his viewpoint, he was better placed to appreciate the situation and was therefore most likely to make the right decision? [100]

Faure, in his turn, was to write the following passage in a letter of November 17, 1956, to the weekly newspaper *Jours de France* which had espoused his cause:

During this period, the supporters of this calamitous policy increased their machinations and their attacks. Although this time they did not succeed in defeating the nation's lawful authorities, I must admit that they did to some extent succeed in delaying the most urgent action and in diminishing the effectiveness of its results. . . . Would the departure of ben Arafa and the establishment of the Council of the Throne have made it possible to avoid or postpone the return of Mohammed V? Grandval believes this could have been done, if his plan could have been put into effect before August 20. He may be right. We cannot rewrite history. But if this is what you believe, and since you are opposed to this return, you must not rail at Pierre July or Pinay or myself but at those men who, by making Si Mulay ben Arafa change his mind so often, first delayed and then defeated Grandval's action (by risking Oued Zem), and then delayed by two weeks the activities of Boyer de Latour (by risking Imouzer).[101]

Ultimately, each side did justice to the other. The political balance that governed governmental decisions clearly admitted of only one solution. Since the question of the Throne could not be settled without the sanction of Mohammed V, who refused to abdicate, and since the Faure government could not remain in

100. Ibid., p. 272.
   101. Cited in François Mitterrand, *Présence française et abandon* (Paris, 1957), pp. 156–57. For the reference to Imouzzer des Marmoucha, see. p. 319.

power unless it officially pronounced its opposition to his restoration, the Prime Minister could only let events run their course to the point where the restoration would be brought about not by the decision of any one man but by the forces of circumstance. These, once again, were to prove stronger than human will.

Chapter 8

THE BOYER DE LATOUR PERIOD;
THE ULTRAS' LAST COUNTERATTACK
(AUGUST 29–NOVEMBER 16, 1955)

On the surface, the replacement of Gilbert Grandval by General Pierre Boyer de Latour—who had accepted the position of Resident-General on August 29, 1955—made no change in Edgar Faure's Moroccan policy: the dispatch of a mission to Antsirabé, the abdication of Si Mulay ben Arafa, the constitution of the Council of the Throne, and the formation of a Moroccan Government of Negotiation were now more important than ever. The new Resident-General was to arrive in Morocco on August 31. The instructions he received in Paris reflected this surface continuity perfectly. The preamble explained that the instructions given to Grandval at the beginning of July remained in force, but that recent developments in the political situation had led the government to expand them on certain points. As the Resident-General wrote, these supplementary instructions centered on three points: (1) to persuade the Sultan ben Arafa to withdraw voluntarily; (2) to set up the Council of the Throne, under the chairmanship of the Grand Vizier, with Si Bekkaï and another prominent Moroccan, sympathetic to el-Glaoui, as members; and (3) to form a Moroccan government representing every shade of Moroccan opinion, but in which the undisputed friends of France would constitute the majority. The French councillors would retain control of certain technical branches of the administration under the authority of the Prime Minister. All of this was to be accomplished by September 12.[1]

It was further specified that Mulay ben Arafa should merely announce his retirement into private life (any formal abdication

1. Pierre Boyer de Latour, *Vérités sur l'Afrique du Nord* (Paris, 1956), p. 149.

might complicate the situation even more by leaving the throne vacant), and that the Moroccan government would be empowered to manage the country's internal affairs and to negotiate a new contractual basis for Franco-Moroccan relations.

Despite the absence of overt change in French policy, the choice of the individual entrusted with its execution signified a complete reversal of the attitude that had heretofore prevailed. Boyer de Latour was no longer the man who had so ably seconded the action of Mendès-France in Tunisia as long as he believed the operation had the approval of Juin and the Right. Once he felt the latter was regaining control, his only thought was to keep on friendly terms with the faction working under cover to keep Mulay ben Arafa on the throne.[2]

This brief sketch of the Resident-General's psychology appears to be fundamentally sound, but it leaves unsolved a few problems of interpretation. Some people believe Grandval's successor was merely seeking to gain time in order to be in a position to carry out the government's instructions under favorable conditions. Others consider that he deliberately allowed the situation to deteriorate, hoping along with Juin, Koenig, and Lecomte that the government would fall when Parliament reconvened in October, and that it would then be possible to set things right. The Resident-General's character and the nature of his activity point rather to the supposition that while he was not absolutely opposed to the government's plan—at least in the early days—he had no intention of putting it into effect except on his own conditions and with the agreement of the French in Morocco, who were themselves supported by the right-wing of the now very battered ministerial team on whose behalf the instructions had been issued.

It must be conceded that these instructions provided advance justification for any recanting. To prescribe Mulay ben Arafa's "voluntary" abdication, when everyone knew he was merely a tool in the hands of el-Hadjoui and el-Glaoui,[3] was tantamount

2. It was easy for Boyer de Latour to subscribe to the Residential hostility toward the Quai d'Orsay and Parliament because from February to September 1951 he had served as Secretary-General for Political and Military Affairs under Juin. Ibid., pp. 1 and 17.
3. Boyer de Latour himself realized this. Ibid., p. 148.

to making the future of Morocco dependent on the whim of the notables. It was not much better to speak of a government with a traditionalist majority in a political situation that required Mohammed V's consent for any action. Such reservations were conceivable in Grandval's time. They ceased to have any validity after the failure of his policy of controlled evolution.

His successor's entourage was, to say the least, bizarre. We have seen liberal Residents-General betrayed by their immediate staffs. We have seen Residents in uniform maneuvered more or less successfully into extremes by associates even more diehard than themselves. This time we are to see a Resident-General paralyzed by his fear of the extreme Right, pushed forward by two members of his entourage who were themselves spurred on by ministers determined this time to bring matters to a conclusion. The first of the Resident-General's "keepers" was Jan de Lipkowski, Assistant Director of the Residential staff. He was a career diplomat who had become a U.D.S.R. deputy in 1956 and had followed Boyer de Latour to Morocco after working with him in Tunis. This recent association did not prevent the Prime Minister and his Staff Director, Jacques Duhamel, from expecting great things from De Lipkowski's spirit of determination if the Resident-General should not prove up to his task. The second keeper was François de Panafieu, also a diplomat, whom Rabat had just got Faure to appoint as Deputy Minister.

In short, although there was nothing really premeditated about it, the Residential team was hardly more homogeneous than the government. While the latter slowly approached a split, the Residency in Rabat was falling apart under tensions similar to those developing in Paris. The direct contact soon established between De Lipkowski and De Panafieu on the one hand and the Prime Minister's entourage on the other merely offset the equally direct relationship that was to develop simultaneously between the Resident-General and the diehards in the government. On both sides, this stemmed less from Machiavellianism than from the restrictions of a political situation in the last stages of disintegration.

On September 5, 1955, Boyer de Latour requested an audience with Sultan ben Arafa in order to sound out his intentions. After many recriminations, Mulay ben Arafa changed his mind for the third time and announced his readiness to leave the throne and withdraw to Tangier. A settlement seemed almost in sight. Unfortunately, news of the Sultan's imminent departure rapidly leaked through the usual channels to those circles that had pinned their political fortunes to the presence of Mohammed V's successor on the throne. They immediately prepared to bring Mulay ben Arafa back into line. In France, the ultras, who perhaps did not realize as yet that Boyer de Latour's scruples were to constitute their trump card, took advantage of the situation to prepare a last-ditch delaying action.

While intrigue, more vigorous than ever, was being rekindled from its ashes at Rabat, the government dispatched to Madagascar the mission that Grandval had been so anxious to see arrive a fortnight earlier. Further procrastination had become impossible. Faure had at first considered entrusting the mission to the nationalist leaders themselves but had changed his mind lest they force the Sultan's hand. Since they were becoming impatient he had to outsmart them by a quick decision. The decision was made in the Committee of Five in early September. The idea of sending Pinay to confer with Mohammed V had been abandoned, and so it was agreed that one of the French envoys should be Henri Yrissou, director of the Staff of the Minister for Foreign Affairs. Someone still had to head the mission. To everyone's surprise, Koenig suggested General Georges Catroux, despite his established reputation as a leading liberal. Political prejudice for once gave way before the moral sway which the great Chancellor of the Legion of Honor had always exercised over the Minister of War. The government's two ambassadors were joined in Madagascar by a third emissary, Colonel Alfred Touya, who had been at Antsirabé since August on behalf of the government. He was closely connected with the Catroux mission's negotiations and was to remain at Antsirabé until the Sultan's return to France.

The government's instructions to Catroux clearly reflected the Prime Minister's uncertainty as to Mohammed V's intentions: they recalled that according to certain reports the Sultan had previously signified his agreement to the establishment of a

Council of the Throne—this was a reference to the Dubois-Rocquebert and Izard missions and to the statements of Si Bekkaï—but that his position had probably changed and hardened since. They also specified that Mohammed V would be authorized to establish himself in France, south of the Loire, after October 15, provided he agreed to a compromise in the spirit of previous negotiations. Lastly, he was asked to state, in a message to the Moroccan people, his approval of the agreements to be entered into, and in particular to reaffirm that he would henceforth abstain from all political activity. Because of its ambiguity, this last requirement did not exactly conform with the formula previously negotiated by Maître Izard, which had merely implied that the Sultan would voluntarily abstain from all political activity until the Moroccan people were in a position to choose their sovereign freely, which undeniably left open the possibility of his subsequent return to the throne. In the Catroux instructions, on the contrary, the clause excluding all future political activity could also be interpreted as a veiled demand for abdication. The need to secure agreement from all sides had again forced the government to adopt an ambiguous political tone.

The Antsirabé negotiations were concluded September 8–9 by an exchange of notes in which Catroux and Mohammed V confirmed the result of their conversations.[4] In his letter of September 8 to the Sultan, Catroux noted that he and Mohammed V had reached an agreement designed to "make Morocco into a free, modern, and sovereign state, bound to France by permanent ties of freely accepted interdependence, *with the reservation*,"[5] added the General, "that in view of the indissoluble nature of the ties that bound the two countries, France's major rights and interests in strategic, political, diplomatic, economic, and cultural matters should be guaranteed, and French nationals established in the empire should be accorded a status in keeping with the important contribution they had made."[6] The letter also specified that Mohammed V had accepted the pro-

4. *Le Monde* (Nov. 8, 1955).
5. Emphasis added.
6. *Le Monde* (Nov. 8, 1955).

cedure for setting up a Council of the Throne and a Moroccan government for administration and negotiation, and that he had undertaken to commend this procedure to the Moroccan public. Finally, it stated that the Sultan's reply would be made public and that Mohammed V would address his people as soon as he arrived on French soil, and would call upon his subjects to have confidence in France's policy.

In his reply of September 9, Mohammed V confirmed without qualifications the intentions that Catroux had attributed to him except—and this necessarily affected the nature of the contractual engagements undertaken—that the principle of freely accepted interdependence was no longer subject to any reservation. Whereas Catroux had explicitly referred the previous day to freely accepted interdependence *subject* to prior guarantee by Morocco of France's major rights and interests, Mohammed V spoke the next day only of "freely accepted interdependence in *areas* strategic, diplomatic, political, economic, and cultural." [7]

As far as the French negotiators were concerned, Morocco was to obtain freedom within interdependence only to the extent that certain fundamental privileges were granted a priori to France. For Mohammed V, on the other hand, Morocco was to receive freedom in exchange for freely accepted interdependence, of which the strategic, diplomatic, political, and other aspects constituted the substance and not the condition.

Nevertheless, the Prime Minister had achieved his aim in bringing together his negotiators and Mohammed V. The unofficial agreements of Aix-les-Bains had been approved by the man the Moroccans regarded as their rightful sultan. The compromise formula accepted by the nationalists, subsequently "rediscovered" by Grandval, and suggested again to Catroux in the Prime Minister's instructions, had been minutely scrutinized by every side and had at last become the official charter of France's Moroccan policy. The unofficial agreements of Aix-les-Bains were ipso facto confirmed by the device of a simple exchange of letters between the exiled Sultan and a French general. They resulted from action taken by the committee of five on its own authority; the Cabinet had not been forced at any time to depart

7. Ibid.

from the wait-and-see attitude adopted after Aix-les-Bains under pressure from the Social Republicans.

While in some respects Antsirabé only consolidated the agreements of Aix-les-Bains, the trend begun there was nevertheless accelerated in Madagascar. At Aix, the French government had done no more than give de facto recognition to the Moroccan nationalists as genuine spokesmen at a time when no decision had been achieved. At Antsirabé, however, the orientation of French policy toward Mohammed V's restoration and Moroccan independence became irreversible, since Mohammed V was officially requested by France to endorse her Moroccan policy and since the Mohammed V-Catroux "agreements" were tantamount—de facto if not de jure—to a declaration of quasi independence: to talk of a "free, modern, and sovereign state" and of "freely accepted interdependence" was tantamount to promising action without as yet calling it by its name. Ironically, this new trend was not the government's doing. The Catroux instructions contained no reference to freedom, sovereignty, or interdependence, but only to the elimination of ben Arafa, to the creation of the Council of the Throne, and to the liquidation of direct administration. Actually, the French negotiators had been able to exceed so easily the letter, if not the spirit, of their instructions only because the instructions represented a backward step from the Izard-Grandval-Faure plan. Yet this plan still contained the only possible solution to the conflict, since France could not eschew the Sultan's endorsement, and the Sultan remained in a position to withhold it as long as the French government affected to ignore the unofficial conversations the Prime Minister had held with the Sultan's envoy.[8]

Apart from their immediate political significance, the Antsirabé conversations were to have almost equally important indirect results. It will be remembered that as early as August, Pinay had begun to entertain the notion of resolving the Mo-

8. It is difficult to know exactly what happened at Antsirabé. By some accounts, the Sultan initially accepted the idea of internal autonomy, and the concept of interdependence was advanced later by one of the French signatories. By others, Yrissou went beyond the original Catroux proposals. A third version is that it was Catroux who "let everything go." It does not really matter, since the Catroux concessions went no further than the solution previously approved by Mohammed V, which, in any case, constituted the only possible basis for negotiation.

roccan question once and for all by a man-to-man talk with
Mohammed V. This was only the first step. When Yrissou left
for Madagascar, Pinay was still far from having made up his
mind about his policy of decolonization. Yrissou himself had not
left France any better disposed toward Mohammed V, but he
returned from Madagascar a changed man and thereafter remained the Sultan's most determined advocate with the Foreign
Minister. Pinay, pressed by his own staff and the Prime Minister
in the same direction, shortly made new and substantial progress
along the liberal path. Like all neophytes, he was prepared to
jump from one extreme to the other, and was now ready for the
revelation of the "spirit of Bandung" that was to strike him a
few weeks later in the middle of the United Nations General
Assembly. After this, the time was ripe for a decisive interview
between the Independent leader and Mohammed V.

It will be recalled that, according to the government's instructions to the new Resident-General, the third member of the
Council of the Throne was to be an el-Glaoui traditionalist.
However, on September 8, Boyer de Latour received a cable from
Antsirabé saying that the Sultan had entrusted the choice of the
third member to France provided he was not a militant supporter of el-Glaoui. In fact, Mohammed V had only partially
resigned himself to the idea that the Council of the Throne
should include an active protagonist of the August 1953 coup. He
recognized the need for a balanced political composition, but felt
that the traditionalist appointee should not also be an activist.
Thus ended the Resident-General's hope of controlling the future
Council of the Throne by introducing a third member aggressive
and subtle enough to neutralize the Sultan's representative by his
mere presence. He regarded this henceforth inevitable disruption
of the balance of power as particularly disastrous, for he saw in
it—not unreasonably—an earnest of Mohammed V's ultimate
return to the throne.[9] Boyer de Latour, like all convinced opponents of this solution, did not understand that this had become
inevitable in the long run, and that all he could do was to take
advantage of Mohammed V's apparent lack of impatience to
return to Morocco to settle as many outstanding problems as

9. Boyer de Latour, pp. 149–50.

possible before the Sultan's supporters with one accord recalled him to the throne. The alternative notion of compensating for Mulay ben Arafa's departure by neutralizing the Council of the Throne was, and could be, only an illusion. Any attempt to embody the sovereignty of a passionately Youssefist state in a constitutional organ in which the political forces would offset each other was tantamount to assuming that the problem of the ruler had been solved—a problem that had arisen only because, in the eyes of the Moroccan people, the equilibrium between the Youssefists and the traditionalists had been disrupted completely. If Boyer de Latour had succeeded in effectively neutralizing the Council of the Throne by the inclusion of an Arafist member who could have offset Si Bekkaï, the policy the Resident-General wanted would still not have become any more feasible, for nothing could have prevented Si Bekkaï from breaking up the Council of the Throne altogether by resigning from it, all of which would have put the Moroccan question back where it was after Oued Zem.

In the Morocco of autumn 1955, there might still have been some point in going through the motions of playing off Mulay ben Arafa against Mohammed V. But it was supremely inconsistent to recognize the necessity of Mulay ben Arafa's departure, to have the policy of the Council of the Throne backed publicly by Mohammed V, and still to hope that he and his nationalist allies would accept the transformation of temporary constitutional bodies, subject to their consent, into docile instruments of a Resident-General who did not understand that the era of the notables had ended.

Boyer de Latour was not so farsighted, and he was inclined to feel that Paris had betrayed him. What was his obligation to a government which was following a policy that could only end in restoration? If that was to be the result, was it still his duty to persuade Mulay ben Arafa to depart? Since governmental solidarity had become only a fiction, would it not have been better to follow the dictates of his conscience and the views of the Arafist ministers in Paris?[10] Whether he had been looking for

10. There would have been grounds for such scruples if the equivocal nature of the government's policy and the consequent unquestionable risk of premature restoration

an excuse, or whether the cable from Antsirabé had really shaken his loyalty, Boyer de Latour soon ceased to react at all, and let himself slip into the rut of Residential obstruction. Thus he informed Paris that he was keeping to the government's plan, but that he could no longer put it into effect by the appointed date since it was his intention to settle the problem of the throne simultaneously with that of the formation of the Moroccan government, "in such a way that [the friends of France] are not excluded from the Cabinet." [11] The government's timetable was again upset, but on this occasion by a Resident-General who was more than sufficiently covered by the ambiguity of instructions, which the requirements of governmental solidarity had prevented from being drafted in more explicit terms.

All in all, despite their apparently innocuous character, the Antsirabé conversations had three political consequences of fundamental importance. The Sultan had officially become, by almost universal consent, the arbiter of France's Moroccan policy. Pinay was closer than ever to regarding Moroccan independence as the only valid solution. As for Boyer de Latour, he had emerged from his first difficulties completely demoralized and almost at loggerheads with the government he represented. The ultras in Morocco and in France could launch their counterattack. They were sure in advance of the Residency's sympathy.

While the government's plan was blocked by Boyer de Latour's scruples at Rabat, the political situation in Paris had grown even more complicated. On September 7–9, even before the results of the Madagascar negotiations had been made public, the Independent Republicans, the Social Republicans, and the Independents and Peasants had publicly taken a stand against Mohammed V's possible return to the throne. The government therefore addressed itself to the task of assessing the Antsirabé conversations in a climate darkened by the hostility of its Right and by the uncertainty surrounding the reigning Sultan's intentions.

---

had not been due to the procrastination of the extreme Right, which had paralyzed the Executive for two months. Only a policy that maintained firm control over the time schedule could have allowed France to play her few remaining trumps to any advantage.

11. Boyer de Latour, p. 150.

On September 11, 1955, the Committee of Five met to hear Catroux and Yrissou, who had just returned from Madagascar.[12] At the end of this meeting, July read a communique announcing that Sidi Mohammed ben Youssef had accepted the plan drawn up by the government after the conference at Aix-les-Bains, and that implementation of the plan would follow shortly.[13]

On the twelfth, the Council of Ministers heard a draft governmental declaration on Morocco and discussed the problem raised by Mulay ben Arafa's attitude. The latter, in a letter to Boyer de Latour, had just confirmed his readiness to withdraw, provided the President of the Republic assured him that his friends would not be molested after his departure from Morocco and that Mohammed V would never return to the throne.[14]

July drafted a reply reflecting the view of the majority of ministers and in which France accepted Mulay ben Arafa's conditions. Catroux, when consulted, objected on the ground that since the government was sufficiently safeguarded by the Antsirabé agreements, it would be imprudent to make any commitments over and above the stipulations contained therein. He maintained that it would be particularly unwise to take an advance stand against the eventual restoration of Mohammed V, since it might be necessary to ask the former Sultan to intervene again at any time if there was difficulty in the formation or operation of the Council of the Throne. He emphasized the lack of any guarantee that the Moroccan people would not one day pronounce themselves in favor of restoring a monarch who had explicitly reserved his right to the throne. Faure and most of his ministers—including Schuman and Pinay—agreed. Catroux accepted responsibility, with Faure's approval, for trying to win over Koenig and his friends. The meeting broke up without agreement on a text for the governmental declaration on which Faure had his heart set.[15]

12. *Le Monde* (Sept. 13, 1955).
13. Ibid.
14. Boyer de Latour, p. 152; *Le Monde* (Sept. 14, 1955).
15. President Coty's first reply to ben Arafa has been the source of much controversy. According to some of the major protagonists, Coty had received July's draft response in the meantime and had assumed responsibility for modifying it. The text was then sent to De Panafieu, who was to give it to Mulay Arafa. When certain ministers threatened to resign, Faure decided to reconsider the whole problem,

At the end of the meeting, Faure said in a broadcast that the next few days would be decisive, and that the settlement adopted by the government would constitute an important step in the evolution of Franco-Moroccan relations. He admitted that a difficulty had arisen in implementing the plan, but added that he believed a solution was almost in sight.[16]

The Committee of Five met again on the thirteenth. It had been enlarged by the addition of Ministers Palewski and Teitgen, who were instructed to revise the governmental declaration on Morocco. The committee was so far from a solution that on the same day Koenig announced his disagreement with the plan envisaged by the Council of Ministers the previous day, and the moderates, echoing him, requested that Parliament be convened before any final decision was taken on Morocco. The government was virtually split in two.

In Rabat, the Residential team was in little better shape. It had vacillated, sought advice, said the Sultan was impossible, then retracted when the ultras objected. Boyer de Latour had gradually reached the point of deliberately frustrating the government's intentions. Despite increasingly frantic telephone calls from Paris, he was soon saying that the installation of Mulay ben Arafa at Tangier would be impracticable until he had formally abdicated. He took refuge behind the alleged conditions placed by ben Arafa upon his departure. Since the Resident-General himself recognized the Sultan's objections as directly inspired by Hadjoui or el-Glaoui, it became obvious that at that rate nothing would ever get done. Boyer de Latour climaxed the confusion by agreeing to discuss the settlement of the problem of the Throne with Présence française.

The net result was acute strain between Boyer de Latour and De Lipkowski, who was soon backed by De Panafieu. Convinced, rightly or wrongly, that their chief had turned traitor, they placed themselves at the government's disposal to try to compensate by their own initiative for the Resident-General's inaction.

Both teams—the government and the Residency—had reached

and countermanded Coty's orders to De Panafieu. Although this version was corroborated by several individuals interviewed, Faure himself has formally denied it.
16. *Agence France-Presse* (Sept. 12, 1955). See *Le Monde* (Sept. 14, 1955).

the same stage of disintegration and had gradually ceased to communicate, except among groups with the same views. While on one wire the office of the Prime Minister tried to advance its cause by negotiating directly with De Lipkowski and De Panafieu,[17] Koenig and his friends on another line daily urged the Resident-General to stand firm. These functional substitutes for a normal state of political communications had been organized only because the hierarchical channels were blocked by the insurmountable differences of opinion that separated the principal protagonists in the political drama. Instead of negotiating Mulay ben Arafa's departure with the party most directly concerned, the Resident-General held interminable conversations with Présence française and the activists of the Arafa clique. Instead of trying to settle difficulties with the Prime Minister, Boyer de Latour multiplied them by going for his political guidance to ministers who had practically left the government, and by refusing to answer the telephone when the Prime Minister called. It was inevitable, therefore, that the government should be reduced to conspiring with its representative's entourage at Rabat in the hope of finally achieving indirect implementation of its own directives.

Such a blatant decline of authority could produce only decayed fruit. Astounded at being again treated like responsible spokesmen after the sharp lesson administered to them by Grandval, the leaders of Présence française (or what was left of it) resumed their former arrogance. Day by day the movement regained its influence, thanks only to the respect accorded it by the Residency. As De Lipkowski correctly wrote,

> General de Latour's incessant efforts to win over the extremists had exactly the opposite effect from that intended. By endlessly prolonging discussions and consultations with this group, he gave it more importance than it deserved. Certain now that it would not be overruled, the group had no reason to be conciliatory. Thus, precious weeks were lost in futile conversations.[18]

17. From Paris, Duhamel systematically cabled the government's moves as soon as he was informed of them.

18. Jean de Lipkowski, "Comment le 30 septembre 1955 le sultan ben Arafa renonça au trône chérifien," *La Nef* (March 1957), p. 37.

On September 15, 1955, at Rabat, Présence française staged a demonstration for the first time in a month against the departure of General Roger Miquel, Commandant of the Region of Meknes.

On the sixteenth, the Sultan informed Boyer de Latour that he had changed his mind again and was now convinced that his departure would be contrary to the interests of France. The Arafist comedy was becoming a farce. The plot had become so complicated that on the same day the Prime Minister summoned Boyer de Latour to Paris in the hope of finding a compromise solution to the question of the Throne by bringing him face to face with the nationalists.

As soon as he arrived in Paris, Boyer de Latour went to the Ministry of Moroccan and Tunisian Affairs, to which July had summoned Si Bekkaï and Si Fatmi ben Slimane. They were joined during the afternoon by delegates from the Istiqlal and the P.D.I. The conference came to grief over the choice of the third member of the Council of the Throne because the nationalists maintained their opposition to the appointment of a traditionalist. In fact, July had reached a behind-the-scenes agreement with the Istiqlal on a name acceptable to them, that of the *fqih* ben Kadra. This did not improve the Resident-General's temper.[19] Faure thought he had solved the difficulty at one point by offering the disputed post to a Moroccan officer serving in the French army, General Kettani ben Hamon, but he arrived in Paris the eighteenth and refused the office the next day. The situation had reached a deadlock.

The Council of Ministers met in the late afternoon of the seventeenth, with Boyer de Latour in attendance. The liberal ministers, especially Schuman, were anxious to settle the problem before a new outbreak of violence again bathed Morocco in blood. Boyer de Latour, however, insisted that France could not give up the guarantee afforded by Sultan ben Arafa's departure until the creation of a Council of the Throne and a Moroccan government that accorded with French interests. The meeting ended without any decision.

Since the opposition of Koenig and his friends had been

19. Boyer de Latour, p. 156.

temporarily weakened, a final meeting of the Council of Ministers was held on September 20. An agreement was reached at
last. New instructions for the Resident-General were approved
which called upon him to invite the Sultan to delegate his
powers immediately to the Grand Vizier. They instructed Boyer
de Latour to go directly to the Grand Vizier to ask him to set up
a Council of the Throne with Si Bekkaï and a third person to be
chosen from a list of six names. Finally, it was understood that
the proclamation of the Council of the Throne would be followed almost at once by a declaration by the French government, and that the *dahir* setting up the Moroccan government
would be published without delay.

Boyer de Latour at once threatened to resign. However, the
Prime Minister smoothed matters over at the eleventh hour
during a dinner that evening at the Hotel Matignon, attended by
Émile Roche (President of the Economic Council, but also a
charter member of Présence française), July, Duchet, and
Yrissou. It was agreed that if the Resident-General judged it
impossible to set up the Council of the Throne, he could confine
himself to persuading the Sultan to delegate his Seal to the
Grand Vizier before leaving for Tangier. Boyer de Latour signified his approval of this compromise formula, which he
thought was likely to promote a resumption of negotiations with
the nationalists. He returned to Rabat the next day.[20]

In the meantime, those who favored retaining the reigning
Sultan had not been idle. On September 17, the day Boyer de
Latour departed for Paris, the Chairman of the National Committee for Defense, Deputy Pierre Montel, had arrived in Morocco with orders empowering him to inspect the French military forces. When presented to the Sultan by De Panafieu, he
had urged him strongly to remain on the throne, and had used
his inspection tours to preach the same doctrine to French groups
and Moroccan notables. When Boyer de Latour returned to
Rabat on the twenty-first, he refused to receive Montel and had
his orders rescinded.[21] Montel's activities had nevertheless been

20. Ibid., pp. 159–60.
21. This unusual action was apparently due less to basic disagreement than to
personal enmity. Montel had vehemently attacked Boyer de Latour during the Franco-

effective; Mulay ben Arafa promptly reaffirmed his intention of remaining on the throne.[22]

July had reached the limits of his patience. He told Boyer de Latour two days later "that the French government was determined to set up the Council of the Throne even if the Sultan would not withdraw." [23] The Resident-General replied that although he agreed essentially with his instructions, he could only "make the Sultan go voluntarily after certain conditions had been fulfilled." [24]

The government had to choose between looking ridiculous or taking extreme measures. Duhamel thought the necessary steps could only be taken by or under the aegis of a colleague of the Prime Minister acting on his own responsibility. An opportunity soon arrived. De Lipkowski, returning to Rabat after a brief visit to Paris, told him, as he boarded the plane, that the Resident-General would never force the Sultan's departure on his own initiative. He offered to arrange it himself, despite Boyer de Latour. Hesitant at first, weighing the gravity of the risk involved, Duhamel finally agreed to be responsible.

Boyer de Latour himself facilitated the operation: worn out by the insistence of his associates, on September 25 he authorized De Panafieu to try to ascertain the Sultan's plans through one of his close associates who would be brought from Tangier. This was all the Resident-General's two assistants needed to go into action. First, they wrote a circumspect letter to Boyer de Latour on the twenty-sixth, refusing to be responsible for the outcome of his policy and explaining why they disagreed with it. Their main argument was that although the General's desire not to relinquish the "Arafa guarantee" prematurely was theoretically understandable, it failed to take account of the time factor which, as had been the case just before Oued Zem, was again working against France and made it essential to liquidate the crisis. This was only too true. Although the first two weeks of September had been more quiet than usual, terrorism was again on the rise.

Tunisian negotiations, even accusing him of following Mendès-France to Tunis in the hope of obtaining a fourth star before he retired.

22. Boyer de Latour, p. 161.
23. Ibid., p. 162.
24. Ibid.

The nationalists were convinced once more that the French government had lost control of the situation. Morocco had grown weary of waiting for the departure of the reigning Sultan and the return to France of Mohammed V, which had been promised nearly two weeks earlier. A fresh wave of violence was in the offing. In these circumstances, it was inexcusable to risk a revolt in order to preserve the illusion of using the notables to neutralize the Council of the Throne and the Moroccan government.

The letter brought on a series of heated discussions starting on September 23, in the course of which the two men had tried to persuade the Resident-General to listen to reason. They finally gave up in the belief that he was systematically using the government's lack of cohesion to take refuge in a wait-and-see attitude, banking on its probable fall.

Two days later, Robert Gillet, adviser to the Sharifian government, had a long interview with the Resident-General, at the end of which he said he had stayed in Morocco only to put the government's plan into effect, and that since he was no longer agreed with Boyer de Latour's policy, he was returning to France.

The rest is like a cloak-and-dagger story. Since the Sultan was a prisoner of his entourage, De Lipkowski and De Panafieu had no hope of reaching him except through emissaries trusted by both sides and sufficiently neutral to avoid making the Palace jailers uneasy. De Panafieu had been Deputy Minister of France to Tangier for a long time. He sent for the majordomo of the Sultan's sister who lived in Tangier, and also a French Muslim from Algeria, Maître Mohammed Madjid Chérif, a member of the Tangier bar on whom they were counting to broach the substance of the matter after the first emissary had paved the way. At first, everything seemed to go well. The Sultan fell in with the plot without hesitation. He approved the declaration of voluntary withdrawal and the declarations delegating the Seal submitted for his signature. He soon informed De Panafieu—it was now September 28—that he would receive him at five o'clock that same day; De Panafieu was to bring the originals of the documents submitted to him, the purport of which he fully approved. De Panafieu at once informed Paris that he had high hopes of finishing the job in the next few hours. The last act would probably have gone off as smoothly as the first had not De Panafieu committed the error of revealing to Boyer de Latour that he had succeeded in obtaining an audience at the Palace. Since the General was anxious to remain in the good graces of the Arafist clique, he at once warned the Imperial Chief of Protocol, el-Hadjoui. When De Lipkowski and De Panafieu arrived for their audience with the Sultan, they found Hadjoui at his master's elbow. Hadjoui interrupted the conversation to say the Sultan had told him all about the negotiations of that day and the day before, and that although he was in agreement with the text of the declarations submitted to the ruler, the person to whom the Seal would be delegated still had to be named. De Lipkowski said the Sultan had told him previously he intended to delegate his Seal to one of his nephews, Prince Mulay Hassan (the namesake of Mohammed V's eldest son), who had agreed to accept it.

Hadjoui had only to persuade Mulay Hassan to revoke his decision, and this he promptly did. Pressing his advantage, Hadjoui got in touch with De Panafieu at the end of the evening and said that, after thinking it over, he could not approve the text of the two declarations submitted to the Sultan and that the latter's departure was now subject to further conditions. De Panafieu retorted that any further obstruction would be useless because the government was determined to set up the Council of the Throne, come what may. Driven into a corner, Hadjoui ended by consenting with ill grace to see De Panafieu again at eleven-thirty, after making the Sultan sign the declaration.

Although the situation looked hopeless at that point, De Panafieu and De Lipkowski still had two allies at the Palace. One was Captain Oufkir, Boyer de Latour's Moroccan interpreter, who had been present at De Panafieu's audience and whom Mulay Arafa, sensing the impending storm, had asked to dinner. The other was Hadjoui's own assistant, the Moroccan Ben Omar Bennasser. At three in the morning, De Panafieu learned from him that, instead of keeping his promise, Hadjoui had brought Maître Bernard le Coroller, acting president of

Présence française, to the Palace and had just telephoned to Marrakesh to alert el-Glaoui. Shortly afterwards, Captain Oufkir telephoned to confirm that Hadjoui was at the Palace with a group of Europeans. It turned out that a demonstration by Présence française was being organized in Rabat and that the demonstrators were planning to seize the premises of Radio-Moroc and the Central Post Office.[25]

After dealing with the most immediate danger by prohibiting all vehicles on the road to Casablanca and from Casablanca to Marrakesh, De Panafieu had a last bout with Hadjoui, who eluded him and lost no time in persuading the Sultan to sign a declaration of his own drafting that reopened the whole matter.

Apart from the fact that it was no longer a question of voluntary departure but of a withdrawal ordered by the French government, the Sultan's pledge was accompanied by a series of conditions intended to provoke a breach between France and the nationalists. De Panafieu lost all patience at this point and telephoned Paris to ask the office of the Prime Minister to summon Hadjoui to France. Hadjoui was invited by Pierre Petitjean, Director of Security Services, to accompany him to the airfield at Rabat-Salé on the morning of the thirtieth. Hadjoui was not officially under arrest, however, and refused to comply. De Panafieu had him watched at home, but he escaped the same day with the connivance of the six French police detailed to guard him and under the sardonic eye of the group of Présence française militants who had gathered in front of his doorway. Early on the morning of the thirtieth Ben Omar Bennasser at last brought De Panafieu the original declarations, which Mulay Arafa had hastened to sign as soon as his Chief of Protocol had taken flight. The Seal was delegated to a cousin of the Sultan, Mulay Abdallah ben Mulay Abd el-Hafid. De Panafieu promptly reported to Boyer de Latour, who took cognizance of the two documents and instructed De Lipkowski to arrange with the Sultan the details of his departure, which was to take place by mutual agreement at seven A.M. on Saturday, October 1.

Just when it looked as if a settlement would be achieved without a battle between the Resident-General and his assistants,

25. Confirmed by interviews with the leaders of Présence française.

a telephone call from Boyer de Latour interrupted De Lipkowski's audience and ordered him back to the Residency. The
Resident-General received him in the presence of the Chief
Commandant of Troops, General Leblanc, and a number of
other officers. This reception committee had before it the text of
a telephone conversation intercepted during the night, on the
strength of which the Resident-General and the officers present
alleged that the two assistants had exerted pressure on the Sultan,
contrary to the government's express instructions. There was a
grand finale in which everyone threatened to resign. Nevertheless, the Sultan left for Tangier the next morning after giving
General Leblanc confirmation of his decision, while the Resident-
General obtained, via Émile Roche, Faure's telephoned consent to
the delegation of the Seal to Mulay Abdallah.[26]

Boyer de Latour, in his eagerness not to offend the French in
Morocco, had made a final compromise the night before with
the president of Présence française, Maître Le Coroller, on the
problem of the Throne. They had agreed that the Sultan should
not leave until he had appointed an heir to the throne, to whom
the Seal would be delegated, thus precluding any possibility of
forming a Council of the Throne. The next day, the Resident-
General had to retract that pledge, but this did not prevent him
from telling Duhamel by telephone the same day that the procedure accepted by Mulay Arafa made the future establishment
of the Council of the Throne impossible.[27]

This hybrid formula was the outcome of the final concession
made by the weary Prime Minister to Boyer de Latour after
dinner on September 20. Theoretically, it reopened the whole
question; actually, it was unimportant. The crucial point to Faure
was that he had persuaded the Sultan to leave. Obviously, once
that had been done, it would be much easier subsequently to
obtain the withdrawal of the conditions attached to his departure, since Sidi Mulay ben Arafa was now a free agent at
Tangier.[28]

26. Boyer de Latour, p. 166.
27. Ibid.
28. This belated denouement seems to have resulted from last-minute arrangements
between Faure and Boyer de Latour. In our opinion, it would be wrong to conclude
therefrom that the two men had suddenly decided to join forces. The tenor of the

The Resident-General's final acquiescence to the quasi solution of October 1 had been decisively influenced by an occurrence on September 27 of an entirely different kind which had dealt the final blow to his determination to resist. A cable from July had reported that Pinay—then in New York, where he was leading the French delegation to the United Nations—had just informed the Prime Minister that the government's plan must be put into effect at once if France was to avoid being placed in a very delicate position over the Moroccan affair.[29]

In his speech to the United Nations General Assembly on September 29, 1955, Pinay pronounced for the first time the magic word "independence."

> But, in a world today, there is no *true independence* without freely accepted interdependence. . . . Last year, the Minister for Foreign Affairs of my country referred in this very hall to the negotiations then in progress between the governments of France and Tunisia: he expressed the hope that they would speedily produce results . . . The promise has been kept. . . . France intends to make of Morocco a modern, democratic and sovereign state, united with France by the ties of freely accepted interdependence. . . . Decisions have been taken. These decisions will be translated into reality. A Moroccan government will be set up. I can say definitely, and with assurance, from this rostrum, that the reforms will be carried out.[30] [Emphasis added]

The commitments made on behalf of France at Antsirabé by Catroux were thus reaffirmed before the whole world by the leader of the French Right.

Pinay had been deeply impressed by the revelation of the anticolonialist spirit that had developed in the third world after

---

Resident-General's book leaves no doubt on the subject. He believed so strongly that Faure was betraying French interests that during a dinner he even went so far as to tell him the whole affair would end up in the High Court. See ibid., p. 159. Actually, despite the spirit of his instructions, the Resident-General did his utmost to safeguard the notables' policy. He gave in because he could not do otherwise.

29. Ibid., p. 164.

30. United Nations General Assembly, *Official Records,* 10th Sess., 1955, 528th Plenary Mtg. (Sept. 29, 1955), paras. 51–54.

the Bandung Conference,[31] and even more particularly by the very explosive demonstrations of the African and Asian delegates when the result of the voting on the inclusion of the Algerian item was announced. He had joined once and for all the ranks of the partisans of Moroccan independence. Roger Duchet was carrying on at the Ministry for Foreign Affairs in the minister's absence. He, too, changed his stand, and from then on railed ceaselessly against the Resident-General's inertia. Boyer de Latour found Pinay's attitude particularly disconcerting, for until then the latter had strongly supported his desire to set up only a Council of the Throne that would be neutralized by the introduction of a trustworthy traditionalist element. Now, to conclude matters quickly, he brusquely abandoned the idea of a "balanced Council of the Throne."[32] This retreat made the Resident-General incapable of further resisting the pressure from Paris. However, he did not resign himself to the inevitable until he had tried to offset the government's plan by delegation of the Seal to the heir apparent. Whether disheartened, as he himself says, by so much maneuvering "from which [he] was excluded"[33] or whether wishing to vindicate himself to Présence française, or for some quite different reason, on September 30 Boyer de Latour cabled his resignation to the government. The latter did not feel in a position to accept it and was thus forced to keep at Rabat a Resident-General on whom it could no longer count.

Mulay Arafa's departure for Tangier came too late to prevent the explosion that inevitably resulted from the Moroccans' growing exasperation after so many wasted weeks. On the night of October 1, 1955, three Moroccan commando groups, formed and trained in the Spanish zone with the tacit compliance of the authorities, attacked two frontier posts in the Rif: Tizi Ouzli and Boured. The next night the observatory at Bou Zineb, an enclave in the Spanish zone, was also attacked. At the same time, another group of Moroccan guerrillas—also setting out, apparently, from the northern zone, having infiltrated south of Taza

31. April 18–24, 1955.
32. Boyer de Latour, p. 164.
33. Ibid., p. 166.

on the Fez-Oudja route—attacked the outpost of Imouzzer des Marmoucha in the Moyen Atlas. Tizi Ouzli resisted, but first Boured and then Bou Zineb were taken. The situation was even worse at Imouzzer des Marmoucha, where the garrison of 180 men from the Twenty-second Moroccan Goum had had their weapons removed as a precaution. The attackers broke into the armory while the police unit, the only one capable of self-defense, continued to fight. Air intervention and the ultimate arrival of a relief column prevented the worst. But on Boyer de Latour's admission, the attackers seized 300 rifles, one 60 mm. mortar, 10 automatic rifles, and 48 submachine guns.[34] Many of these weapons were subsequently recovered, but those from the captured posts enabled the rebels to equip supporters who were only waiting for a rifle to take the field. While a section of the Moroccan Gznaian tribe rebelled and fled to the other side of the frontier, other Moroccan commandos made several unsuccessful but symptomatic attacks in the eastern section, near Oudja. The troops put into the field by the Moroccan Army of Liberation were few in number, but the connivance of the population, the difficulty of the terrain, the nature of guerrilla warfare, and the lack of a seasoned army (it consisted in part of conscripts only recently arrived in Morocco) created a threat on the Spanish zone border that could only have been offset by the concentration in the north of a large part of the troops available to the Chief Commandant.

While Boyer de Latour was forced to strip the other regions of Morocco dangerously bare to reinforce the troops on his northern frontier,[35] the Arab and Spanish press of Tetuán gave great publicity to the first communiqués of the rebel leaders. On October 3, 1955, *Al Oummah,* a Tetuán daily newspaper, published a proclamation by the Army of Liberation of the Arab Maghreb announcing a national insurrection against the French, encirclement of the military posts in the Rif and the Moyen Atlas, and continuation of the fight until Morocco and Algeria achieved full independence.[36] The announcement of national

34. Ibid., p. 169.
35. Ibid., p. 171.
36. Ibid., p. 173.

insurrection was premature, to say the least, but the reference to encircled posts was no exaggeration. The post at Imouzzer could not be freed until a relief column arrived; the frontier post at Tizi Ouzli was not liberated until October 7, and then by the Foreign Legion.

On October 4, Allal el-Fassi issued a declaration of war on France from Cairo and announced that henceforward the Moroccan and Algerian rebellions would be under joint command. This proclamation, as much an instance of psychological warfare as a genuine communiqué, had a tremendous effect in Paris, where the virtual impossibility of staving off such a threat made responsible circles most uneasy. The army reinforced the beleaguered posts and partially recovered control of communications, which were constantly harassed by the enemy commandos who never laid down their weapons. Finally, the French forces were able to organize themselves on the high ground bordering the Spanish frontier.[37] At the end of October, the situation was stabilized for the time being. Boyer de Latour wrote, "On the twenty-third, I went to the danger points of Morocco: Imouzzer and the northern front. Calm had been restored in the Moyen Atlas, thanks to the measures taken. The Moroccan front opposite the Spanish frontier was also quieting down, despite the presence of guerrilla bands installed on the other side of the frontier."[38]

Nevertheless, the warning salvo of the Moroccan commandos had achieved its purpose. Although only a few dozen were armed at the outset, several hundred men on the frontier had succeeded in bottling up the bulk of French troops in Morocco. The rest of the protectorate lay open to any further disturbances, and thousands of French settlers scattered throughout the *bled* were seized with apprehension.[39] A material though indirect

37. Ibid., p. 171.
38. Ibid., p. 185.
39. The French government, well schooled in Algeria and Tunisia, recognized the gravity of the situation and decided to call up the contingents of 1951 and 1952, and send them to Morocco. *Bulletin marocain d'information et de documentation (B.M.I.)* 5th year, no. 104 (1955), p. 3. The conscripts of 1953 had been mobilized several weeks earlier. The embarkation of those bound for the Rif caused some disturbances in France, too, but never of a nature sufficiently serious or widespread to trouble the authorities.

result of the situation created by the attacks on the French posts was that the Moroccan auxiliary troops began to show serious signs of demoralization. This was only the beginning; in the months to come, their rout was to contribute decisively to the downfall of the protectorate. The Moroccan commandos vanished into the mountain country of the Rif, and were thereafter in a position to resume their activities whenever it became politically expedient to remind the French negotiators they must choose between mobilizing half a million men or accepting the enemy's conditions.

Spain's attitude added the last dark touches to the picture. There could be no doubt of the complicity of the Spanish zone. The second Rif war was beginning under the ominous shadow of French-Spanish rivalry, whereas, during the first, France and Spain had marched shoulder to shoulder. The effect of Spanish support was not only to increase the Moroccan rebels' confidence in their cause, but also to plunge the French high command into great disorder. Had they repeated so often that North Africa was not Indochina only to find themselves, here too, held back every day by a frontier that seemed to open every night to let out the revolutionary commandos?

Despite the revolt in the Rif, the political problems burned as brightly as ever. Mulay Arafa's withdrawal, while it had clarified the situation, did not enable Faure to proceed immediately with the formation of the Council of the Throne and the Moroccan government. The declaration on Morocco, which the government had been preparing for months, lay dormant in the files. The delegation of the Seal raised a procedural problem that had to be settled at once. The attitude of the Social-Republican ministers continued to impede governmental action. Parliament's return, traditionally scheduled for the first Wednesday in October, posed a threat to France's entire colonial policy that had to be removed as soon as possible.

Thanks to the tenacity of the Prime Minister and his direct associates, these three obstacles were in turn overcome in the first two weeks of October. First, it was necessary to regain the public's confidence. Mulay Arafa's voluntary retirement had been officially reported on October 1, by proclamation of the outgoing Sultan and a letter from the President of the Republic;[40] on the same day the French government was able to publish its long-projected declaration on Moroccan policy.

The governmental declaration of October 1 was in some respects a retreat from what had been agreed upon earlier. It reaffirmed the intention to establish a permanent union between the two states, and a community of the two peoples. Respect for Moroccan sovereignty, settlement of the problem of the Throne, the establishment of a negotiating government, and the organization of ties of freely accepted interdependence were all given prominence in the text.

All this was in line with France's commitments at Antsirabé, afterwards so solemnly confirmed from the rostrum of the United Nations General Assembly. If the government had not felt obliged to add that its Moroccan policy would continue to be based on "respect for the treaties relating to Morocco,"[41] the declaration would have raised no problem. Saddled with this restriction, which implicitly reaffirmed the intangibility of the Treaty of Fez, it was merely a compromise—perhaps skillful in form, but clumsy in substance—among three different political concepts: independence, internal self-government, and maintenance of the Treaty of 1912. When the emissaries of the French government were negotiating at Madagascar with Mohammed V, they had carefully eschewed any mention of the Treaty of Fez. When the government made statements intended for internal consumption, however, it became a useful reference. This was perhaps less inconsistent than is first apparent. The treaty was so loosely drafted that it could be used either as an alibi for a policy of direct administration or as the charter of a system of internal self-government. In trying to pass, under cover of the treaty, from direct administration to independence in interdependence, the government's declaration was not necessarily a denial of what had been promised. Nevertheless, it left the impression

40. President Coty recalled in this letter that Mohammed V, on behalf of himself and his descendants, had renounced all political activity in France. He made no reference, however, to the fact that Mohammed V had reserved his future rights to the throne, which seriously disturbed the nationalists. *Le Monde* (Oct. 2–3, 1955).
     41. Ibid.

that the differences of opinion that split the government were too serious to be wholly overcome.

Still with an eye on the impending parliamentary debate on Morocco, Faure made a speech at Amiens on October 2 which dwelt at length on the reasons for the priority recently given to Moroccan affairs.[42]

Then came the question of the Seal. This was settled so quickly it hardly seemed to have arisen. On October 5, the Prime Minister sent De Panafieu to Tangier with instructions to obtain the ex-Sultan's assurance that his delegation of the Seal was not incompatible with the establishment of a Council of the Throne. Mulay Arafa was now his own master. Freed from the over-powering solicitude of his entourage, he willingly consented to the request. The way was now clear.

With the same celerity, Faure drove the dissident ministers into a corner. They found themselves isolated by the change of heart of the Independent-Peasants who had been duly repri-manded by Pinay and Duchet. On Thursday, October 6, the day debate opened in the National Assembly, the Prime Minister summoned the five Social Republican ministers to the Hôtel Matignon and invited them to leave the government if they felt they disagreed with him. He was determined to obtain their departure, for he had every reason to fear they would resign during the debate and thus make matters difficult for him. When the ministers replied that they had no intention of resigning, Faure asked them to agree unconditionally to support his policy. They replied that they would make no such radical commit-ment, but that, as matters stood, they would not disagree formally. Faure then decided to interview each one privately. He began with Palewski, who was anxious to resign and had indeed drafted a letter to that effect. He did not oppose the Prime Min-ister's policy but based his decision upon the overall considera-tions set forth in his letter. He had, in fact, been one of the few ministers in the group who had supported the Grandval plan from the outset.

Strengthened by this first encounter, Faure then interviewed, in turn, Triboulet; Maurice Bayrou, Secretary of State for Over-

42. *Le Monde* (Oct. 4, 1955).

seas France; and General Koenig. He informed each of them of Palewski's decision and suggested that it would be better if they followed suit. He made an exception only in the case of General Edouard Corniglion-Molinier, whose position had been slightly different and whom he urged to stay in the government.

The office of the Prime Minister then issued a statement to the effect that the ministers had been invited to leave the government.[43] Shortly afterwards, they submitted their resignations, in such a manner as to indicate that they were doing so of their own accord although this, of course, was only partly true. Koenig was promptly replaced at the Ministry of National Defense by General Pierre Billotte, a member of the A.R.S. who had recently taken a stand in favor of Faure's policy (he assumed his duties that same afternoon). The day before, the Social Republicans had still been demanding the "immediate constitution of a Government of Public Safety," [44] but the Right was too divided by then to be dangerous, and this was their last offensive.

Once again, Faure had triumphed. He had associated Pinay so closely with his policy that, supported by developments, the Independent-Peasants had found in their leader's reversal of position the pretext they needed to do likewise. Most of the moderates threatened opposition in the debate, but Pinay took a stand against the recalcitrants and managed to rally them without too much difficulty. Thus, the time had come when the diehards, reduced to their own resources, automatically ceased to be dangerous. Their resignation reestablished unity in the government; one month earlier it would have been most upsetting.

Only the problem of Parliament remained. Debate on Morocco began on October 6, 1955,[45] with the numerous interpellations submitted since the government's declaration of June 21. It ended three days later, after six consecutive meetings, in the adoption of a resolution favorable to the government.[46] For the first time since the opening of the legislature, the Moroccan

43. Ibid. (Oct. 7, 1955).
44. Ibid.
45. *Journal officiel* (J.O.), *Débats parlementaires, Assemblée nationale,* Oct. 7, 1955, pp. 4805 ff.; Oct. 8, 1955, pp. 4871 ff.; Oct. 9, 1955, pp. 4912 ff.
46. Ibid., p. 4985.

question received the exclusive attention of an Assembly which had hitherto concerned itself with Morocco only as a side issue in the debates on Algeria and Tunisia.

The Prime Minister opened the debate with an introductory statement. This was not standard procedure, since in debate on interpellations he ordinarily speaks last. Faure did not conceal the gravity of the threat which North African terrorism and the international support of it posed to the French mission in North Africa. He justified calling up the reserves, explaining a little later that he had done so only to create a screen of troops behind which the government could continue its policy of negotiation and pacification.

Faure pinpointed the locus of responsibility by emphasizing that the present situation resulted from the weakness of the executive branch. He justified in detail his reasons for concluding that the government's policy was the only one possible. Each aspect of the plan was examined seriatim in terms of the relevant political context: the spirit of Bandung; the problem of the traditionalist cadres; Spain's assistance to the Rif Commandos; the history of the question of the Sultans; the need to base governmental policy on the nationalists while at the same time paying due regard to the traditional officials; the inevitability of ultimate independence for Morocco, but recognition by the nationalists of the need to provide for independence by stages; the necessity of reaching a settlement without delay if events were not to get out of hand; the internal divisions within the government. He omitted nothing.

As the debate continued, Faure relaxed his taut nerves by apostrophizing the deputies in a style to which they were hardly accustomed:

> I realize today, more vividly than ever before, that we are on the verge of a kind of disintegration that, as the examples given indicate, is not new, but that now, perhaps for tactical reasons, has been brought to light.
>
> It is time for all of this to end. No more of these resignations offered and retracted! No more resignations by civil servants! Obedience! . . . This evening I have

grasped what before I only glimpsed. . . . I will not
come back here to discuss with the various groups . . .
the choice and appointment of Residents and civil servants.

It is the government that governs.[47]

The illusion did not last, but nevertheless, despite itself, the
cowed and divided Right did allow the executive a fairly good
imitation of what under another regime would doubtless have
passed for authority.

The speeches that followed the Prime Minister's statement on
October 6 and 8 were characteristic of a debate which this time
went to the heart of the matter. Alain Savary (S.F.I.O.) was
indignant that those responsible for the August 1953 coup had
never been brought to book. Roland de Moustier (Independent)
regretted that Marshal Juin had received no punishment. The
right-wing deputies violently attacked the Istiqlal, Mohammed
V, Anglo-Saxon interference, and the Arab League. They proph-
esied that Mohammed V would return to the throne despite the
will of Parliament, but they refrained (understandably) from
any attempt to define a substitute policy. Carried away by their
own logic, the diehards ended by turning against the Faure
government the criticism the liberals had formerly leveled at the
instigators of the 1953 coup: its refusal to defend the reigning
Sultan; its disregard of the Treaty of Fez under which France
was bound to accord him protection; the utilization of the
parliamentary recess by the government, which was accused of
having taken advantage of the deputies' absence to confront the
majority with a fait accompli. To the extreme Right, October
1955 was in the final analysis only August 1953 in reverse. It is a
splendid illustration of the vicissitudes of history: two years
earlier, the ultras, with suppressed glee, had reaped their harvest.
Now they reaped the whirlwind.

Faure, replying on October 8 to a question from André
Mutter regarding Mohammed V's future intentions, took the
opportunity to dispel any ambiguity by explaining that the
Sultan's Antsirabé agreement (not to leave French territory and

47. Ibid., p. 4956.

not to engage in political activities) in no way constituted a renunciation of his right to the throne.

In the end, five resolutions were proposed. On a series of votes, the Assembly gave priority to the third, proposed by Edouard Depreux and supported by the Socialists.[48] It demanded the establishment of a Council of the Throne and the formation of a Sharifian government consisting of all representative elements of the Moroccan people; it expressed regret, however, that the government had compromised its own policy by hesitation. This proviso enabled the sponsors to back the government's plan without thereby approving the way those in power had carried out their policy. The Depreux resolution was voted on paragraph by paragraph,[49] and the text as a whole was adopted by 462 votes to 136.[50] Deserted by a large part of its Parliamentary support on the Right, the government survived thanks to the majority provided by the Left and the extreme Left. While the bulk of support came from the Left, the right-wing backing essential to any decolonization policy had come from those Independents who followed Pinay.

In the middle of the October 7 debate, July had been expelled from the A.R.S. by 14 votes to 5 with 2 abstentions, while Billotte was asked to resign by 16 votes to 5.[51] He did nothing of the kind, but left the same day for Morocco to investigate the mili-

48. Ibid., pp. 4956, 4970, 4979.

49. Ibid., pp. 4970 ff. The paragraph providing for a Council of the Throne was passed by a vote of 320 to 287; that concerning the creation of a Moroccan government was adopted by a show of hands; the one approving the Aix-les-Bains agreements received 468 votes in favor, 139 against. Ibid., pp. 4980, 4982.

50. Ibid., p. 4985. The breakdown of this important vote was: extreme Left, Left, and Center; the Communist, Progressive, Socialist, Radical, U.D.S.R., Overseas Independent, and M.R.P. representatives had overwhelmingly supported the motion. Only five Radicals (as against 68 in favor) and three from the M.R.P. (as opposed to 84 in favor) were opposed. The Right and extreme Right had split: 39 Independents, four Independent-Peasants, seven Peasants, four Social Republicans, five A.R.S., and 13 without party affiliations voted in favor. Thirteen Independents, 22 Independent-Peasants, 13 Peasants, 55 Social Republicans, and 25 A.R.S. were opposed. This significant tally would not have been achieved except for the wording, which distinguished between the objectives of the government's policy and the conduct thereof. The opponents considered as Left by the government (the Socialists and Communists were opposed from the beginning) had had no difficulty in joining its supporters in a vote into which they could read whatever they chose. Moreover, it could equally be considered as condemnation of the Prime Minister's actions or as approbation of his goals in Morocco.

51. *Le Monde* (Oct. 8, 1955).

tary situation. He was accompanied by De Panafieu who received a most unfriendly welcome from the Resident-General[52]
and from Présence française.[53]

The Moroccan debate was followed on October 12 by a full-
dress discussion of Algeria, which ended six days later with the
adoption of a vote of confidence of 308 to 254. This was important because it implied a reaffirmation of approval of the government's Moroccan policy.[54] France's need to make a massive
military effort in her Algerian departments once again explained
the relative ease with which the Right was resigning itself to
relinquishing Morocco. Because the adoption of the resolutions
of October 9 and 18 and the resignation of the Social Republican
ministers had restored the government's mandate, there was no
further obstacle to setting up a Council of the Throne and a
Moroccan government.

In Morocco, there were unmistakable signs that French opinion was beginning to change. Présence française fired its last
volley when it organized a protest meeting at Rabat on October
10 against the Assembly's vote. However, the branches of the
M.R.P., S.F.I.O., and Jeune République, which had previously
united in a vigilante committee, "joined the local liberal groups
and set up a French Committee of Cooperation among liberal
groups and parties in Morocco, designed to watch over the implementation of the Aix-les-Bains agreements."[55]

On October 15, a proclamation by the Grand Vizier and a
communiqué from the Office of the Prime Minister jointly
announced the formation of the Council of the Throne.[56] It
consisted of the Grand Vizier, Hadj Mohammed el-Mokri; Si
Bekkaï, representing the Youseffists; a former officer labeled as
"moderate nationalist" by the Department of the Interior, Caid
Si Tahar ou Assou; and the Pasha of Salé, Si Hadj Mohammed
Sbihi. The third man was indeed a Residency appointee as Boyer
de Latour had wished. But at the last minute, the Istiqlal had

52. Boyer de Latour, p. 178.
53. *B.M.I.*, 5th year, no. 104 (1955), p. 3.
54. *J.O., Débats parl., Ass. nat.* (Oct. 19, 1955), p. 5161.
55. *B.M.I.*, 5th year, no. 104 (1955), p. 3.
56. *Le Monde* (Oct. 18, 1955).

succeeded in persuading the government to offset his appointment by recruiting a fourth member, a nationalist sympathizer,
Hadj Mohammed Sbihi. Those traditionalists most deeply compromised by the August 1953 coup were finally kept out of the
council by a foreseeable turn of events. El-Glaoui had lost face.
As for the Grand Vizier, that centenarian embodiment of "the
old turban-wearers," he did not preside over the council but sat
as an equal with his three colleagues.

Mohammed V was anxious to bring matters to a close. Reserving judgment on the Council of the Throne until he had seen it
in action, on October 12 he cabled to Si Bekkaï that he approved
its composition and asked the two nationalist parties to accept it
as constituted.

The P.D.I. at once utilized this approval to set itself off from
the Istiqlal. On October 20 at Casablanca the Acting Secretary-
General of the P.D.I., Abdelkader Bendjelloun, published a
party statement accepting the council in its present form, despite
its imperfections, because that was the Sultan's wish and because
it would hasten the establishment of institutions that would
make it possible to satisfy the legitimate aspirations of the Moroccan people.[57]

The next day, the Executive Committee of the Istiqlal met at
Rabat and announced that the party rejected the council as
constituted and thus would not participate in the formation of
the Moroccan government. The Istiqlal justified its decision by
arguing that the Council of the Throne did not accord with
what had been envisaged at Aix-les-Bains and approved by
Mohammed V at Antsirabé in the course of his conversations
with the nationalist delegates. "The substantial modifications
subsequently introduced," the communiqué added, "together
with vacillation, hesitation, and maneuvering, have not failed to
arouse the universal indignation of the Moroccan people."[58]
Basically, the party could agree neither to Mohammed V's having been persuaded to approve the Council of the Throne, as
revised, before returning to France, nor to the assumption in the

57. *B.M.I.,* 5th year, no. 105 (1955), p. 2.
58. *Le Monde* (Oct. 23–24), 1955.

October 1 French declaration of the sacrosanctity of the Treaty of Fez.[59]

On October 22, 1955, Si Bekkaï took a stand in his capacity as a member of the council.[60] He recalled the terms of the Aix-les-Bains compromise, confirmed that the creation of a four-member Council of the Throne had been approved by Mohammed V, and announced that the so-called delegation of the Seal by Sultan ben Arafa to Mulay Abdallah ben Mulay Abd el-Hafid should be considered null and void because of the latter's voluntary retirement. He especially regretted that Mohammed V had not yet been brought to France, and declared that the reference to the Treaty of Fez contained in the French declaration of October 1 was binding only upon its authors. It emerged clearly from statements prior to the constitution of the Council of the Throne, Si Bekkaï pointed out in this connection, that the Moroccan government's specific task would be to work out with the French government a new definition of the relations between the two states. The negative effects on Moroccan public opinion of the communiqué published two days earlier by the Istiqlal were thus largely offset by this statement of the Sultan's personal representative on the council.

These three successive declarations sharply highlighted the characteristic features of the political trends arising out of the Franco-Moroccan conflict. While the rivalry between the Istiqlal and the P.D.I. was taking shape, the legitimist and moderate trend embodied by Si Bekkaï was coming to the fore in the transitional institutions being created in Morocco. All that was missing was a declaration from the terrorist organizations (especially the Army of Liberation), which from their redoubts in the Rif and the *medinas* of the great cities, were exerting a decisive pressure without which the recent successes of the nationalist negotiators would have been inconceivable.

In the meantime, on October 20, the decision to abolish the Ministry for Moroccan and Tunisian Affairs in Paris was announced. July became Deputy Minister to the Office of the Prime Minister and Pinay resumed direct control of Moroccan policy.

59. See pp. 103–05 and 322.
60. *Le Monde* (Oct. 25, 1955).

This reorganization was essential, and enabled the Minister for Foreign Affairs to make the necessary arrangements personally with Mohammed V two weeks later at La Celle-Saint-Cloud. General Leblanc, who had remained as head of the Department of the Interior despite his skirmishes with Grandval, became Chief Commandant of Troops at Rabat on October 18.

The formation of the Moroccan government followed as a matter of course. Only two months had elapsed since Grandval recommended to the Prime Minister the appointment of Si Fatmi ben Slimane. The Moroccan crisis had evolved more during that time than in the ten preceding years. As expected, on October 22 the Council of the Throne instructed Grandval's candidate to form the first Moroccan cabinet. Two days later, Si Fatmi ben Slimane began his consultations in a leisurely fashion. After two months of procrastination, the Council of the Throne and its government were beginning to take shape, at the very moment when they were being invalidated by all that had happened since summer.

The plan for the Council of the Throne had lost all significance for the French government since the nationalists who ought to have supported it were currently refusing to endorse its creation. The same was true of the Istiqlal, which had agreed to support transitional governmental institutions in the belief that the French government intended to make a clean break with the past. Once the Istiqlal realized that the Residency was merely trying to check the growth of the nationalists by returning to the policy of the notables, it reverted to its former intransigence. There was nothing to do but restore Mohammed V, preserving the transitional arrangements, if possible.

El-Glaoui was the first to realize the game was lost. He left Marrakesh for Rabat without telling anyone. It was October 25. After talking to the members of the Council of the Throne and Si Fatmi ben Slimane, he made a statement to the press that fell upon his supporters in Morocco and France like a thunderbolt. Inter alia, he said:

> My visit to the Council of Guardians of the Throne is not to be construed as recognition of this council, whose

legitimacy I have continued and will continue to dispute.

I share the joy of the whole Moroccan people at the announcement of the return to France of His Majesty Sidi Mohammed ben Youssef.

I share the hope of the Moroccan nation for the prompt restoration of Sidi Mohammed ben Youssef and his return to the throne which is alone capable of uniting our hearts and minds in peace.[61]

The Pasha returned to Marrakesh. He opened the palace gates, did a dance step beating on a tambourine, served tea, said there would be enough for everyone, and thereafter affected to ignore the crisis as though it had never existed. From the town, which was at first struck dumb, arose a tremendous outcry. Some misguided witnesses thought there was a riot. The population, worn out by months of unprecedented mental and physical tension, contented itself with shouting for joy at its liberation. The idol who for two years had been the hope and inspiration of so many French in Morocco had suddenly crumbled, leaving only a tired old man very close to death.

The simplicity, spontaneity, and extent of the movement that flung the whole of traditional Morocco at Mohammed V's feet by the end of October 1955 proved that el-Glaoui's about-face was not an old man's sudden whim, but an act of political realism instinctively understood by all who shared his position. The atavistic reflex had come into play. In traditional Morocco, it was not good form to follow the vanquished into defeat. This is understandable in a country where the best that political losers could generally hope for was to have their heads chopped off. The 1953 conspirators had only two choices: to be the strongest, or to join the strongest. Seeing the Residency swept away by the storm they themselves had unleashed, they simply collaborated.

Bidault's fears, expressed as early as August 1953, were at last realized.[62] The leader of traditional Morocco was trapped between the mounting tide of nationalism and a French administration which was losing ground because it had for too long been

61. Ibid. (Oct. 27, 1955).
62. See p. 160.

based on a social group that was in turn only using it as a support. And so the Pasha abandoned the Residency, and went over bag and baggage to the Sultan's camp.

On October 26, the Istiqlal announced that the Aix-les-Bains agreements were obsolete and demanded the Sultan's immediate return to the throne.[63] The enthusiastic welcome given to Mohammed V by every sector of French and Moroccan public opinion immediately assumed the weight of an impromptu plebiscite. On October 28, the Sharif el-Kittani made his *amende honorable.* The next day, Mulay Arafa wrote to President Coty renouncing all his rights and urging his subjects to rally to the person of Sidi Mohammed ben Youssef.[64] During October 27–31, countless demonstrations for Mohammed V's return were organized in Moroccan towns. In Paris, an avalanche of messages, cables, and telephone calls—most of them from French nationals—urged the government to restore Mohammed V immediately. Such encouragement was no longer necessary. Once the opposition of the traditionalist chiefs to Mohammed V's return had crumbled, deferment of his restoration became impossible, even if the government had considered it.

In Morocco the Mas press and Présence française climbed onto the bandwagon. As soon as el-Glaoui's message was published, Boyer de Latour, then in Paris, had told Pinay that the only solution was to restore Mohammed V, after first making him proclaim the "sacrosanctity of the Treaty of Fez." [65] Decidedly, the Resident-General's illusions were longlived.

Mohammed V landed at Nice on October 31, 1955. The last item in the Grandval plan thus became fact. The Sultan's arrival in France was in no way the result of recent events in Morocco. He had reached French soil at the appointed time in accordance with decisions made long before el-Glaoui's about-face. The French government had had nothing to do with the fact that this critical event coincided with the decisive change of climate produced by the Pasha's conversion. This masterstroke had been the work of the ultras and the Residency who, having procras-

63. *Le Monde* (Oct. 28, 1955).
64. Ibid. (Nov. 1, 1955).
65. Boyer de Latour, p. 185.

tinated too long, saw themselves being hoist with their own petard.

The idea of the Sultan's immediate return to Morocco had been so far from the thoughts of the French authorities that they had arranged for a house for him at Beauvallon, on the Côte d'Azur, for at least six months. Mohammed V was delighted to savor the end of his exile. He had agreed to abstain from all political activity while in France and had no reason to be impatient. It looked, therefore, as though there would be time to settle things in an orderly fashion. But the press of events, reinforced by the impatience of Pinay, who thought himself better fitted than anyone else to settle the crisis, determined otherwise.

The Sultan had barely set foot on French soil when Pinay resolved to get in touch with him. Arrangements had been made to prevent the nationalists (the Guardians of the Throne had arrived in Paris the same day) from seeing the Sultan before he had talked with the Minister for Foreign Affairs. However, owing to the negligence of a police inspector, the Moroccan leaders succeeded in foiling arrangements. Pinay was most annoyed, and decided to proceed at once. Yrissou escorted Mohammed V from Nice to Paris that same night. The sovereign was immediately installed at Saint-Germain-en-Laye, where, on November 1, he had a preliminary interview with the Minister for Foreign Affairs. "The Sultan and I embraced," Pinay was to declare shortly afterwards to a member of the Prime Minister's entourage, "and that is worth more than anything."

After this encounter, Mohammed V issued a public statement in which he said particularly that he had noted "the unanimous desire of the Moroccan people to adhere to the full exercise of their democratic rights within the framework of national sovereignty and a freely negotiated Franco-Moroccan interdependence based on justice, friendship, and the preservation of economic interests." [66]

Events then proceeded rapidly. The Council of the Throne resigned on November 2. From November 2–5, at Saint-Germain-en-Laye, the Sultan held endless consultations with the nationalist leaders and a growing number of important French-

66. *B.M.I.*, 5th year, no. 105 (1955), p. 2.

men. On the third, Balafredj called for the abrogation of the Treaty of Fez and the possible convocation of an international conference. On the fifth, while the Antsirabé agreements were being made public, the French Council of Ministers approved the reestablishment of Sidi Mohammed ben Youssef on the throne and confirmed the commitment made by France at Antsirabé.[67]

On November 6, Mohammed V and Pinay had an historic talk at the Château of La Celle-Saint-Cloud, after which they published a joint declaration. It ran as follows:

His Majesty the Sultan of Morocco, Sidi Mohammed ben Youssef, and President Antoine Pinay, Minister for Foreign Affairs, met on November 6, 1955, at the Château of La Celle-Saint-Cloud.

President Pinay stated the general principles of the French government's policy as laid down in the Council of Ministers' communiqué of November 5, 1955.

His Majesty the Sultan of Morocco has confirmed his agreement with these principles. Pending his return to Rabat, he has, in accord with the French government, instructed the Council of the Throne, which was set up on October 17, 1955, and resigned from its functions on November 3, 1955, to continue to direct the empire's current affairs.

His Majesty the Sultan of Morocco has confirmed his desire to constitute a Moroccan Government for Administration and Negotiation representing all shades of Moroccan opinion. This government will be charged particularly with drafting institutional reforms that will make Morocco a democratic state under a constitutional monarchy, while conducting negotiations with France for the purpose of giving Morocco the status of an independent state united to France by permanent ties of freely accepted, clearly defined interdependence.

His Majesty the Sultan of Morocco and President Pinay are agreed in confirming that France and Morocco must build their common future together, without

67. *Le Monde* (Nov. 8, 1955).

outside interference, in affirmation of their sovereignty
through the mutual guarantee of their rights and the
rights of their nationals, and in respect for the situation
created by treaties with foreign powers.[68]

Taking into account the government's aims, and despite the
reference to the general principles of French policy, the promise
of independence contained in the declaration seems very rash,
particularly as it was no longer tempered by any explicit reference to the Treaty of Fez. Of course, the only aim of the La
Celle-Saint-Cloud declaration was to settle the dynastic problem.
It remained implicitly within the political framework of previous
commitments by both sides. Nevertheless, by introducing for the
first time the concept of independence into a bilateral declaration, Pinay had gone further than the government and its leader
expected. The Foreign Minister had made no concessions. But
the reference to guarantees claimed by France and granted by
Morocco was made in such terms that the least one can say is
that, on the French side, they betrayed a total lack of conviction
regarding any remaining chance of organizing interdependence
on a solid basis before relinquishing to Morocco the limited
sovereignty that had been promised.

The possible reproach to the French government at this stage
might be that it had not from the beginning recognized that the
explicit objective of the Franco-Moroccan negotiations was internal autonomy. Since this was what the government wanted,
one may wonder why it did not use this undeniably franker term
rather than the somewhat ambiguous "independence in interdependence." The objections of the extremists in both camps had
made this impossible. The nationalist intransigents had so often
proclaimed from Cairo that the internal autonomy accorded
Tunisia was inadequate; and the French in Morocco had so often
repeated, for diametrically opposed reasons, that they would not
tolerate the Tunisian formula in Rabat that the government had
been forced to use another term in the hope of making the facts
more palatable.

Otherwise, the status accorded Morocco by France with the

68. Ibid.

backing of the Right was in no way different from what Mendès-France had given Tunisia the year before, except that in 1954 he had outdistanced events by a bold coup that had enabled him to settle the crisis on his own terms, whereas in 1955, the Faure government, restrained by the extreme Right, had allowed events to outdistance it.

Faure thought little of such questions of terminology. He was too good a judge of men and events to believe in the importance of words in a crisis which no one, either French or Moroccan, could control. Apart from military reconquest, which nobody envisaged, France's only alternative was to negotiate with Moroccan spokesmen over whom it no longer had any hold.

On November 9, while Bouabid, on behalf of the Istiqlal, was demanding immediate revision of the Treaty of Fez,[69] the Council of Ministers replaced Boyer de Latour (who had never withdrawn his resignation) by André Dubois, the Paris Prefect of Police. On the eighth at Saint-Germain-en-Laye, el-Glaoui was pardoned after prostrating himself at the feet of Mohammed V. Dubois left for Rabat on the thirteenth. On the sixteenth, Mohammed V left France for Morocco. The same day, Balafredj set off for Spain to join Allal el-Fassi.

All the actors were on stage for the last act, except in Paris, where Faure was shortly to relinquish his role to Guy Mollet.

69. *B.M.I.*, 5th year, no. 105 (1955), p. 3.

Chapter 9

THE DUBOIS PERIOD; LIQUIDATION OF THE PROTECTORATE (NOVEMBER 16, 1955–JUNE 13, 1956)

Increasing tension between the rapidly changing Moroccan situation and the legal framework within which France sought to confine it had dominated the period between the talks at Aix-les-Bains and the restoration of Sultan Mohammed V. This dichotomy between law and reality reached its culmination in mid-November 1955, while France's last Resident-General was getting settled in Rabat. Thus the last period of the conflict was characterized by an accelerated adaptation of law to reality. Since the elements of the Moroccan problem had been irrevocably changed, the declarations and conventions so laboriously prepared by the Faure government had to be brought into harmony with a political reality that had conclusively outdistanced them. In the six months that followed, France was never able to stabilize her position at some intermediate level along the road to decolonization. She slipped downward, step by step, until the proclamation of independence for the Sharifian state put a definitive end to the conflict.

From this viewpoint, the denouement is virtually self-explanatory. It is possible to manipulate an ambiguous political situation: the Residency had tried to do so for the past ten years. But it is not possible, by normal means of repression, to combat the dissidence of an entire people. This abridged version, however, cannot by itself serve as conclusion to the historical study of the conflict. In the last analysis, the rapid liquidation of the protectorate is explained by the irreparable loss of strength by the regime once the Moroccans rallied en masse behind the Sultan, and by the success of the guerrilla movement in a political

338

context that prevented France from mounting an Algerian-type military effort in Morocco.

The complexity of the diplomatic, psychological, and military interaction that must be analyzed to justify this conception of the denouement has made it difficult to pursue a strictly chronological narrative. Accordingly, it seemed preferable to analyze this last period in three sections devoted respectively to the French-Moroccan negotiations, the evolutions of political attitudes in Muslim circles, and the ultimate failure of pacification. These three sections, therefore, deliberately emphasize the succession of contemporaneous events.

Dissolution of Franco-Moroccan Ties

"We are trustees in bankruptcy," André Dubois had announced to his colleagues when he arrived in Rabat. He was absolutely right, and sensed perhaps better than anyone the degree to which the concessions of substance that France had obtained at La Celle-Saint-Cloud had been rendered obsolete by events. Despite the deliberate ambiguity of certain clauses, the gist of the legal commitments entered into by the two states in the autumn of 1955 was clear. Indeed, by signing the Declaration of La Celle-Saint-Cloud, the Sultan had implicitly subscribed to all the conditions France had previously attached to the evolution of Franco-Moroccan relations, including those contained in the governmental declaration of October 1, 1955, which called for respect for the Treaty of Fez and unimpaired exercise by the protecting power of its responsibility for internal security, defense, and foreign affairs.

At the same time, by agreeing to promote in Morocco the establishment of a Government for Administration and Negotiation, France had pledged herself to hand over to the Moroccan authorities, as a first step, all administrative powers not explicitly reserved to the protecting power under the 1912 Treaty, pending subsequent negotiations by the Moroccan government on the establishment, in the interests of Morocco, of a regime of independence within interdependence. According to the French government, this was to constitute the final and permanent stage in the evolution of political relations between the two countries.

Since the about-face of the notables and the Sultan's recall by
the unanimous will of the people, previous Moroccan commitments had become so outdated that, by the second half of
November, the Sultan and the nationalist leaders were forced to
utter public statements amounting to unilateral denunciation.

In his Speech from the Throne in Rabat on November 18,
1955, two days after his triumphant return to Morocco, Mohammed V was very specific in regard to abrogation of the Treaty of
Fez: "During our stay in France, we held conversations with the
French government on the subject of Morocco that were both
cordial and understanding. These conversations culminated in an
agreement on basic principles. . . . We are happy to announce
the end of the protectorate and the system of guardianship, and
the advent of an era of freedom and independence."[1] The
previous day, Ahmed Balafredj had been even more explicit in
an interview for the newspaper *Combat*. When asked whether he
was still opposed to having the Treaty of Fez remain "the
sacrosanct basis of Franco-Moroccan relations," he answered in
the affirmative. He added that while he was not formally opposed to the declaration of La Celle-Saint-Cloud, he rejected the
October 1 declaration, and concluded that he did not believe the
Sultan, with whom he had discussed the matter, felt the Treaty
of Fez "could constitute the juridical framework for Morocco's
future status."[2] On December 2, at the Istiqlal congress,
Abderrahim Bouabid was still more forthright. His expression of
misgivings about the declaration of La Celle-Saint-Cloud indicated that, in Moroccan eyes, this political document clearly
implied the subordination of the new Franco-Moroccan relations
to the Treaty of Fez. He recalled that the Sultan had announced
in his Speech from the Throne the end of the protectorate era,
and explicitly capitalized on the fact that at the time the French
government had not objected to this important statement.[3]

The idea of independence within interdependence was similarly vitiated by several other pronouncements. This inevitable
trend was facilitated by the inherent ambiguity of the concept.

1. *Le Monde* (Nov. 19, 1955).
2. *Combat* (Nov. 17, 1955).
3. *Le Monde* (Dec. 4–5, 1955).

Strictly construed, it meant Morocco had voluntarily renounced part of her sovereignty to unite with France within a framework closely akin to internal self-government. Loosely construed, it merely meant that once Morocco's independence had been recognized, the country would negotiate freely with France political agreements that would imply no loss of sovereignty. The Sultan and the nationalist leaders immediately adopted the second interpretation. "For us," Mohammed V declared in an interview with two representatives of the French press immediately after his return, interdependence "is a reinforcement of independence and not a limitation on our independence. The more independent Morocco becomes, the closer she will be to France. We shall put in common all that is common and we shall keep apart all that should be apart." [4] Balafredj was of the same opinion:

> The basic question is Moroccan independence. This independence must of course be limited, if not in principle at least in its outward aspects, by respect for the legitimate interests of France and of French citizens in Morocco. . . . There has been talk of interdependence: the word has no precise legal meaning. . . . The very notion of interdependence is valid only insofar as it expresses an inherent equality, for peoples can only be interdependent if they are first independent. [5]

These statements abrogating political agreements on which the ink was barely dry were, significantly, noted by the French without protest and even without comment. One wonders whether those responsible for French policy understood that it would have been morally and politically impossible for the leaders of the new Morocco to return to their country announcing that the protectorate system was still in force. Perhaps they were momentarily preoccupied with domestic policy, or perhaps they felt proposals made during the excitement aroused by the return of the Moroccan leaders could have no adverse effect upon the agreements of La Celle-Saint-Cloud. Whatever the reason, there was no reaction. Even the major newspapers continued to

4. Ibid. (Nov. 18, 1955).
5. *Combat* (Dec. 3–4, 1955).

act as if everything was for the best. Thus, on November 19, *Le Monde* printed Mohammed V's Speech from the Throne with no mention of the fact that it flatly contradicted the official principles of French-Moroccan policy.[6]

In less than a fortnight, merely as a consequence of a series of unilateral declarations by the Moroccans, the principle of Morocco's interdependence was again called into question without protest by the French. As if to complicate still further an already delicate situation, an acute ministerial crisis had arisen in France. For two months, she was to be left without a government in the face of a Moroccan crisis that was developing at lightning speed. On November 29, with Mohammed V barely reinstalled at Rabat, the Faure government was overthrown by an absolute majority of 318 votes to 218.[7] Dissolution of Parliament thus became constitutionally possible, since Mendès-France had been similarly defeated the preceding February. The Popular Republicans and the moderates demanded it. The Cabinet did not resign, and on November 30, despite opposition from the Radical-Socialists, especially five of their ministers, the government decided to dissolve Parliament.[8] This decision ruined the political hopes of Mendès-France, who was then engaged in a bitter struggle for control and reorganization of the Radical-Socialist party. The success of this effort demanded both time and the adoption of an electoral system more favorable than the existing

6. According to certain sources, on November 24, 1955, five days before the fall of the Faure government, Antoine Pinay (then Minister for Foreign Affairs) gave a complete account of the Moroccan question before the Assembly's Committee on Foreign Affairs. He explained that Mulay Arafa's abdication and Mohammed V's subsequent recall had made settlement of the problem of the throne possible and desirable. He referred to Mohammed V's speech from the throne of November 18, qualifying it as most satisfactory insofar as it affirmed Franco-Moroccan friendship and solidarity. At the conclusion of his statement, deputies representing every shade of political opinion are said to have pressed Pinay hard to define his policy. But he did not commit himself and stated only that the declaration of La Celle-Saint-Cloud and the restoration of Mohammed V in no way changed the legal situation, which derived from prior agreements. That the committee took no further action, only a few days after Mohammed V's public repudiation of the Treaty of Fez, shows to what extent the fighting spirit of the extreme Right had been attenuated.

7. *Journal officiel* (*J.O.*), *Débats parlementaires, Assemblée nationale* (Nov. 30, 1955), p. 6067.

8. *Le Monde* (Dec. 1–2), 1955.

one to the Radical-Socialist leader's political programs.[9] By holding elections before Mendès-France could present his case to the
people, Faure dealt his predecessor a hard blow, which promptly
boomeranged. On December 1, Faure was expelled from the
Radical-Socialist party. Despite Mendès-France's procedural vic-
tories within his own party, there was now an almost complete
split between his supporters and the diehard wing of the party,
led by Léon Martinaud-Déplat.

The fall of the Faure government coincided almost exactly
with the formation at Rabat of the long-contemplated Government for Administration and Negotiation. On November 22, six
days after his return, Mohammed V accepted the resignations
which the Guardians of the Throne had submitted on November
2. On the twenty-third, Si Bekkaï came out in favor of a "government of national union." The Istiqlal promptly stated the
political conditions attached to its future participation: national
independence and unity of the country, adoption of a democratic
regime based upon a constitutional monarchy, and formation of
a responsible government.[10] On December 7, only five days after
the dissolution of the French National Assembly, Si Bekkaï presented to the Sultan the first government of independent Morocco.[11] It consisted, apart from the Prime Minister, of twenty
ministers, nine of whom were leaders of the Istiqlal, six from the
P.D.I., and five Independents. Si Mohammed Mammeri (also
Independent) assumed the title of Minister of the Imperial
Household. Four ministers, Abderrahim Bouabid (Istiqlal), Mohammed Cherkaoui (P.D.I.), Maître Driss M'Hammedi
(Istiqlal), and Ahmed Rida Guedira (Independent) were made
responsible for the conduct of negotiations with France in their
capacity as ministers of state. The Ministry of the Interior went
to the Berber caid Lahcen Lyoussi.

The honor bestowed by the Sultan on the mountain regions in
entrusting the Department of the Interior to a Berber proved his
awareness of the need to incorporate the rural population into

9. Throughout November 1955 the Assembly had been absorbed by the problems of
setting the election date and of reforming the method of balloting.

10. *Le Monde* (Nov. 27–28), 1955.

11. Ibid. (Dec. 8, 1955).

the new regime. It also resulted in giving to a Palace loyalist the post upon which the internal reorganization of Morocco was to depend. Significantly, the new minister took up his quarters in the *mechouar* (palace courtyard), thus making the Sultan the effective head of the country's administrative reorganization. The formation of the Moroccan Cabinet was followed on December 17 by the designation of thirteen *oumals,* or provincial governors. Meanwhile, the new pashas and caids gradually began to take up their posts in tribe and village. At all levels, a new Moroccan administration was set up paralleling the French administration. The protectorate had not yet been abrogated, since theoretically the French retained the powers reserved to them under the Treaty of 1912. Nevertheless, in a manner of speaking, the question of succession came up while the deceased was still alive. The heir, not content with claiming the routine administrative powers he had been promised, was already demanding full internal sovereignty as a prelude to the rest of his inheritance.

In a speech on December 13, 1955, Si Bekkaï, now Moroccan Prime Minister, finally recalled the need for French assistance in technical, economic, and defense matters. "We will be the allies of the French people," he said, "for they are fundamentally a democratic and anticolonialist people, and we are assured of loyal, fruitful, and close Franco-Moroccan cooperation." [12]

Negotiations on the division of administrative powers opened in Rabat on December 8, 1955, during the French political interregnum. They were designed to elaborate the means of implementing the Treaty of 1912 during the transitional period, which had opened with the formation of the Moroccan government and would end when the last conventions on independence were concluded. While these events were taking place in Rabat, the French cabinet set January 2, 1956, as the date for elections. [13] The campaign was dominated by the political activity of the Republican Front, which consisted—except for the U.D.S.R. and some Social Republicans—of the S.F.I.O and the Radical-Socialist party. The legislative elections in January brought the interregnum to a dramatic end. The Communists were returned in

12. Ibid. (Dec. 15, 1955).
13. Ibid. (Dec. 4–5, 1955).

strength, with 144 seats as against 93. The R.P.F. disappeared. The Poujadists were enormously successful, gaining more than 2,600,000 votes and 52 seats. All the political prospects of those behind the elections were dimmed. The government was more than ever hemmed in between an extreme Left and an extreme Right, which fought each other unceasingly.[14] On January 31, the government of Guy Mollet appeared before the Assembly. The Republican Front had succeeded in obtaining power, but the presence at the head of the ministerial team of two such disparate personalities as Mendès-France and the Secretary-General of the S.F.I.O. boded ill.

In his investiture speech, the new Prime Minister said,

> The government will have to embark immediately upon negotiations with the government of His Majesty the Sultan of Morocco. This will result in a new definition, based on a recognition of the independence of the Sharifian state, of the ties that bind the two countries together. . . . In the negotiations which will open shortly in Paris, France will, of course, see that international commitments concerning Morocco are respected. She expects other countries to recognize, as she has, that the evolution of the Sharifian Empire cannot be shackled by the antiquated provisions of certain treaties.[15]

Mollet ended that part of his speech devoted to the three North African countries by emphasizing that the principles guiding France's Tunisian policy were the same as those being applied in Morocco. The government received a vote of confidence on January 31 by 420 votes to 71, with 83 abstentions.[16] From the extreme Left to the Center-Right, all deputies present had voted for the government, with the exception of one R.G.R. deputy and nine M.R.P. members, who abstained. The core of the opposition consisted only of the 49 Poujadist deputies present, together with a fifth of the Independents and Peasants. Once again, control of France's foreign policy had passed into new

14. Ibid. (Jan. 25, 1956).
15. J.O., Débats parl., Ass. nat. (Feb. 1, 1956), p. 136.
16. Ibid., p. 163.

hands. Foreign Affairs went to Christian Pineau (S.F.I.O.—the M.R.P. had objected to Mendès-France's holding that portfolio); and another Radical-Socialist, Alain Savary, became Secretary of State for Moroccan and Tunisian Affairs.

Although the dissolution of Parliament and the election had disturbed French domestic policy, the change in the legislature did not entail any revision of colonial policy. Faure had not fallen because of his North African policy any more than had Mendès-France, although this served as the pretext. The new Assembly, like the old one, did not intend to reopen issues already settled by the pressure of events. The new Parliament would not try to act either in regard to Morocco or Tunisia.

On February 11, 1956, the day Mollet returned to Paris,[17] Andrè Dubois and Si Bekkaï signed, at Rabat, a provisional protocol which ended the negotiations begun on December 8 and which regulated the division of administrative power between the Residency and the Moroccan government.[18] The Sultan retained legislative power, but the right to propose laws was divided between the Moroccan government and the Resident-General, who kept the rights he enjoyed under the Treaty of Fez concerning promulgation of laws and political control over pending legislation. Until further notice, the Resident-General retained the powers reserved to him under the same treaty— foreign affairs, security, territorial defense, finance, and administration of the affairs of the French and foreign communities. The former French heads of departments in the neo-Sharifian administration took the title of Secretaries-General of the new Moroccan ministries, and were made responsible for coordinating activities under authority of the ministers in charge. The Secretary-General of the protectorate lost certain of his traditional privileges, including his right of inspection. On the surface, France had won the day on maintenance of the protectorate treaty. Actually, this turn for the better in the curve of negotia-

17. Guy Mollet's first political act was his trip to Algiers, where he was welcomed, on February 6, 1956, by the tomatoes of the *petits blancs*. Mollet gave up the battle. A Committee for Public Safety was created in Algiers. General Catroux, Resident Minister for one day, resigned, to be replaced three days later by Robert Lacoste. The fate of the Fourth Republic was sealed.

18. *Le Monde* (Feb. 12–13), 1956.

tions was more apparent than real, since both sides understood that the protocol would become obsolete once the negotiators, who were to start work the following week, had succeeded in drawing up a new agreement.

Since disagreement between Moroccans and French was confined to the reserved powers, Moroccan ministers took over the neo-Sharifian departments without much difficulty once the government began to function. In general, French civil servants at the top level adapted well to their roles as technical advisers. The Moroccan ministers could do nothing in such areas without French administrative and financial cooperation, and the Residency had decided to consider all technical problems in the light of the interests of the new Morocco. And so, on the whole, continuity of political action was safeguarded, despite the inevitable difficulties caused by disorders and the need for the psychological reorientation of French officials.

However, there was complete disagreement on the means of implementing the reserved powers, especially those relating to internal security. The new Moroccan minister enjoyed authority over the pashas and caids he had appointed, but the material means of command—premises, communications, vehicles, technicians, and security forces—remained in French hands. Conversely, the French Director of Security had lost his power to command the Sharifian officials, but the technical means of authority were still under his control. The French chief urged his Moroccan minister to assume responsibility and, above all, to restore order. He declared his readiness to assist him and to use his reserved powers whenever the new regime took steps to that end. The Moroccan minister refused to govern until the means of maintaining order had been handed over to him and France had relinquished her reserved powers. The same problem existed at every level of the hierarchy in central, provincial, and local administration. In these circumstances, discussions on division of security powers could only drag on interminably, yet neither party wished to break them off. The Moroccans were satisfied with having shown that the Treaty of Fez no longer existed and that new authorities ruled the political roost. France was content to retain theoretical control over the reserved powers so that

France's loss of face would not be too obvious when the forth-coming Franco-Moroccan negotiations began. This explains the provisional protocol of February 11, 1956, which confirmed on paper the agreements of La Celle-Saint-Cloud two days before the Sultan's arrival in Paris and the opening of the talks that were to end in recognition of Morocco's independence.[19]

The time had come for France to capitulate on basic issues. The Moroccan delegation, led by Mohammed V, arrived in Paris on February 13. Despite the constructive and friendly nature of speeches by President René Coty and the Sultan at the opening session, it soon became clear that the two sides were diametrically opposed.[20] The Moroccans, faithful to their concept of inter-dependence, wanted confirmation of complete independence of their country prior to discussions. In their view, the sole objective of talks should be the negotiation of political arrangements for so-called interdependence between two sovereign states. The French, on the other hand, insisted that Moroccan independence was to be but the consequence of the entry into force of conven-tions for interdependence that had first been negotiated with a Morocco still bound during the discussions by the provisions of the Treaty of Fez. This reservation was not insignificant. If the Moroccan delegation had accepted it, the French delegation would ipso facto have been in a position to put the future con-ventions on interdependence within the compass of an agreement limiting the sovereignty of the new Morocco. Actually, this basic disagreement on principles was of little significance, since France no longer had the opportunity or the will to refuse what the Moroccans demanded as rightfully theirs. The Moroccans, there-fore, won the day. The first stage of negotiations concluded on March 2 with the publication of a joint declaration establishing Moroccan independence without reservation:

> The government of the French Republic and His Majesty Mohammed V, Sultan of Morocco, hereby affirm their determination to give full effect to the dec-

19. El-Glaoui died on Jan. 23, 1956.
20. *Le Monde* (Feb. 16, 1956).

laration of La Celle-Saint-Cloud of December 6 [sic], 1955.[21]

They note that in view of progress made by Morocco, the Treaty of Fez of March 30, 1912, no longer corresponds to the requirements of modern life and can therefore no longer govern Franco-Moroccan relations.

In consequence, the government of the French Republic solemnly confirms its recognition of the independence of Morocco, which is understood to include the Foreign Service and Armed Forces, and its determination to respect and to secure respect for the integrity of Moroccan territory as guaranteed by international treaties.

The government of the French Republic and His Majesty Mohammed V, Sultan of Morocco, declare that the negotiations recently opened in Paris between Morocco and France, as sovereign and equal states, have as their purpose the conclusion of new agreements which will define the interdependence of the two countries in those fields in which they have joint interests. . . . [They] agree that, pending the entry into force of these agreements, the new relations between France and Morocco will be based upon the provisions of the protocol annexed to the present declaration.[22]

This protocol was important, since it immediately recognized the full legislative powers of the Sultan. However, in return, the French representative, who acquired the title of High Commissioner, obtained the right to be informed of draft *dahirs* and decrees and to formulate observations when such legislation concerned the interests of France, French citizens, or aliens, but only during the transition period. France also undertook to assist Morocco in setting up its armed forces.[23]

An exchange of letters between Pineau and Si Bekkaï regulated a whole series of related matters.[24] The most important

21. The date was November 6, 1955.
22. *Le Monde* (March 4–5, 1956).
23. Ibid.
24. Ibid.

provisions of this correspondence concerned: foreign relations, the conduct of which was to remain in French hands during the transition period; and, especially significant, the transfer to Moroccan authorities of those internal administrative powers still reserved to the Residency. It was understood that the transfer would be made at Rabat without further delay.

The only concession obtained by the French negotiators was purely formal. At the close of the talks and with the approval of the Moroccan delegation, the French government issued a unilateral declaration to the effect that the agreements of March 2 and subsequent arrangements for interdependence would in due course be submitted to Parliament for ratification "in accordance with French constitutional provisions." [25] This was an admission that the Treaty of Fez, although nullified in advance, could not be abrogated without parliamentary approval. Above all, it was a reminder that abrogation would not take place until after the conclusion of arrangements for interdependence. Thus, Moroccan independence and entry into interdependence were placed on an equal footing, in theory if not in fact.[26]

In three decisive weeks, all the nationalists' demands had become the basis of new Franco-Moroccan relations. The Treaty of Fez had not only ceased to govern relations between the two states but had been replaced by independence, instead of by more-or-less limited internal autonomy.

Tunisia and Spanish Morocco were too closely linked with the French zone not to be immediately affected by the outcome of the Paris negotiations. Up to the last minute, Spain had pressed for the unconditional independence of Morocco.[27] The Franco regime was soon faced with the consequences of its Moroccan policy. On April 7, in Madrid, a joint declaration drafted in the Sultan's presence recognized the Sharifian Empire's full sovereignty over the Spanish zone. Thus the complete independence

25. Ibid.
26. In a press conference on February 23, 1956, Pineau said, "We cannot ask Parliament to abrogate the Treaty of Fez without, at the same time, submitting a text defining the new relations between France and Morocco." (*Le Monde,* Feb. 25, 1956.) This was the reason for the French government's unilateral declaration at the conclusion of the negotiations. Again, on March 8, Pineau stated before the Committee on Foreign Affairs that the treaty had not been abrogated.
27. Ibid. (March 8, 1956).

and reunification of Morocco took place simultaneously.[28] Only Tangier remained to be brought back into the empire.

As Tunisia was still bound to France under a regime of internal autonomy, it was becoming equally necessary to recognize its claim to independence. On February 29, negotiations to that end were opened on Bourguiba's initiative. On March 20, Pineau and Tahar ben Ammar signed a protocol of agreement recognizing the independence of the former regency.[29]

All that the Paris diehards could do was to put their doctrine to the supreme test in Algeria. The size of the French colony there, the special status of the territory, and the absence of any distinct Algerian national character were to enable the colonialists to fight a last-ditch battle against the spirit of the times on terrain as favorable to their position as possible.

In Morocco itself, not everything was settled, since the two countries still had to negotiate the means of implementing the March 2 agreements. Even more serious, although the exchange of letters accompanying those agreements had determined the immediate transfer to Moroccan authorities of the administrative powers formerly reserved to France, a last offensive by Paris revived the controversy. The Secretary of State for Foreign Affairs insisted that the appointment and transfer of French public security officials continue to be subject, despite the March agreements, to prior approval of the High Commissioner, and that territorial security should remain a French department directly under his aegis. This was tantamount to reopening the quarrel over technicalities of implementation after yielding on the substance. In theory, France should have reserved her authority and made any transfer of security powers contingent upon the surrender of the insurgents as was done in Tunisia. As we shall see, this was out of the question.

The dispute on security was resumed at Rabat more bitterly than before. Mohammed Laghzaoui, appointed Director for Public Safety since the relinquishment to the Moroccans of reserved powers, refused (as had the Moroccan minister before him) to

28. Ibid. (April 8–9, 1956).
29. *La Documentation française, Articles et documents, Textes du jour,* no. 0335 (March 22, 1956), p. 1.

assume his duties until his authority had been fully recognized. This confusion as to the locus of power resulted in complete chaos. French troops began arresting members of the Moroccan Army of Liberation, which, in reprisal, arrested French officers. The Moroccans liberated political prisoners and the French promptly threw them back into prison whenever they could. This extraordinary situation lasted until the end of April, at which time the means for implementing the March agreements were finally settled.

On April 25, a convention concerning an agreement calling for the formation of a Moroccan armed force of 15,000 men was signed in Paris.[30] The next day, in Rabat, France transferred the security services to the Sultan's government in implementation of the March 2 protocol, although not before the Moroccans had made a last protest, on April 19 and 23, against French procrastination.[31] A few days later, the powers of regional administration were handed over to the new governors of the Moroccan provinces. On May 6, a statement published after a meeting between Mollet and Si Bekkaï affirmed the intention of the two Prime Ministers to speed up the negotiations then in progress.[32] Only the interdependence conventions remained. The diplomatic convention was initialed at Rabat on the nineteenth and signed in Paris on the twenty-eighth.[33] Morocco attained full sovereignty over her external affairs. The two countries agreed to work together on matters of foreign policy. Under the terms of this convention, the French High Commissioner became Ambassador Extraordinary to Rabat and doyen of the diplomatic corps. In accordance with the March 1956 agreements, application of this convention remained in suspense until the French Parliament ratified Morocco's new status. The Moroccan government, however, did not wait for this parliamentary sanction and on April 26 appointed Ahmed Balafredj as Moroccan Minister for Foreign Affairs.

On June 5, the French Parliament confirmed the Mollet gov-

30. *Le Monde* (April 27, 1956).
31. Ibid. (April 21, 1956).
32. Ibid. (May 8, 1956).
33. Ibid. (May 29, 1956).

ernment's Moroccan policy.[34] The deed was done. In a little over six months, from November to June, negotiations had proceeded step by step to interdependence. It remains to see why.

Psychological Evolution in Muslim Circles and Collapse of the Protectorate's Administrative Apparatus

The ambiguity of the Franco-Moroccan agreements concluded before the Sultan's return to Rabat had undoubtedly fostered Moroccan demands. This semantic argument had been further reinforced by the long political interregnum that preceded the French elections. However, these were but contributing factors. Even if Pinay had negotiated a proper agreement on internal autonomy at La Celle-Saint-Cloud, and even if the Mollet government had succeeded the Faure government without a battle, the outcome would not have been appreciably different, for in Morocco itself the protectorate's political and administrative armature had begun to disintegrate long before the diplomats could foresee the consequences.

To understand the reasons for the decisive victory of the Moroccan negotiators in Paris in April, one must go back to November 1955. André Dubois had arrived in Rabat fully determined to press forward frankly with a policy of conciliation and transfer of powers. On November 15, in the midst of the crisis and despite the traditional opposition of the regional commissioners, he had abolished the curfew in the medinas. During November 16–18, in preparation for the Sultan's return, 1,713 Moroccan prisoners were liberated and 750 more on the twenty-third.

Dubois' immediate associates were equally determined to wipe out the past. Roger Lalouette, soon to serve as French Ambassador to Morocco, had been appointed Deputy Minister in place of De Panafieu, whose anti-Arafist activities under Boyer de Latour had brought about his downfall. The most important change occurred in the Department of the Interior, where Colonel Édouard Méric had replaced General Leblanc on September 1. In this transitional period, it was essential that the chief of security and

---

34. *J.O., Débats parl., Ass. nat.* (June 6, 1956), p. 2337.

of the contrôle civil unreservedly carry out the Resident-General's policy. This condition was fulfilled to the letter, in contrast to former practice.

No observer has disputed the mass movement which in less than forty-eight hours rallied all Morocco to the Sultan. This was not merely the effect of Istiqlal propaganda but a simultaneous reaction of the entire population, town and country dwellers alike, who instinctively united behind the only authority capable of embodying, without dividing, the nationalist fervor that had seized them. As long as the *bled* remained aloof, many people had considered Mohammed V merely the Sultan of the towns. After November 17, 1955, no one could doubt that he was the supreme political leader of Morocco.

There was another essential political fact which reinforced both the prestige of the leader of the new Morocco and the nationalists' hold, with his consent, over the population. The Sultan's return was not marked by any collective explosion of violence: contrary to many fears, there was no massacre either of the French or of the traditionalist notables. Of course, the coming months were to see some settling of accounts among Moroccans, and even between Moroccans and Frenchmen. After the fearful tension which the policy of force had imposed on the population during recent years, repercussions were inevitable, but they were less serious than might have been expected. Expiatory victims were sacrificed in haphazard fashion. At no time did the *bled* return to anarchy and endanger the fundamental relations of the two communities. There was no wave of xenophobia among the Moroccan people.

The first and most important of such clashes deserves comment because it was characteristic of the new climate in Morocco, and also because it brought into bold relief the almost insoluble problem of relations between the Palace and the traditional officials. It had been the custom for the pashas and caids to pay homage to the Sultan on the feast of Aïd Seghir.[35] The regional commissioners, when asked by the notables what the Palace expected of them, turned to Colonel Méric for instruc-

35. This celebration took place on November 19, the day following the Festival of the Throne.

tions. The latter asked the Prime Minister elect, Si Fatmi ben Slimane, who replied that the Department of the Interior could summon the caids to Rabat as usual. Whether Si Fatmi ben Slimane and Colonel Méric each thought the Palace had been informed by the other, or whether for some other reason, no steps had been taken in the *mechouar* to receive the notables who were already en route. Three notables from Fez became lost in a solid crowd of Youssefist hillsmen from the Atlas. They were soon recognized as confirmed Arafists and were attacked. One was lynched and his body burned on the spot. Another died a few days later. The third, although seriously injured, survived. The Sultan said the caids had not been invited and implied that, while he could excuse, he could not prevent the paying off of old scores. On the advice of the Resident-General, however, he expressed publicly his regret, suspended his receptions, and promised to visit the principal towns of Morocco where there had been scattered incidents of this sort.

The lynchings in the *mechouar* had repercussions in the French Parliament. Deputy Raymond Dronne was to tell the National Assembly on May 31, "It is inconceivable that the government should maintain an official in Rabat who is despised by everyone from the French he betrays to the Moroccan nationalists he serves and flatters. The case is too scandalous to be ignored. I mean the Director of the Interior, the man who personally summoned the caids to the *mechouar* in the Palace at Rabat, where they were massacred." [36] It was to be expected that the extreme Right should be irate with a director who was determined to carry out faithfully the Paris government's policy. Nevertheless, the Residency had made a technical error in not safeguarding the security of the Arafist notables it had summoned to Rabat.[37]

36. *J.O., Débats parl., Ass. nat.* (June 1, 1956), p. 2152.
37. Since each social group has its own values, liberals and ultras could not judge similar actions by the same standards. To the former, the nationalist victims of the policy of force were only rebels, but the murder of each Arafist caid cried out for vengeance. To the latter, the accounts settled during this transition period were but the regrettable, although inevitable, consequences of the atrocities previously committed by the protectorate. It would be futile to attempt to judge between such different concepts of human relationships, but the problem subsists despite the relativity of values. The army did not forget that it was unable to guarantee the security of the notables who had

The political problem confronting the new Resident-General was as easy to state as it was impossible to solve. Dubois arrived in Rabat as the meetings at La Celle-Saint-Cloud were coming to an end. Thus his policy had to be the one just officially defined by France. His objective was not abrogation of the Treaty of Fez but a strict return to the regime of 1912 by means of elimination of direct administration and the transfer of technical departments to the Moroccans. The basic hostility of the Sultan and the nationalists to this program is well known.

The hopeless character of Dubois' task resulted less from this radical difference of views than from the way events tended to drive them still further apart. By their solid support of a Sultan who demanded independence as a precondition, the Moroccan people had freed themselves from French control. The notables who had formerly spoken on behalf of the towns and tribes were politically annihilated by the disaffection of the masses and the sovereign they had deposed two years earlier. The protectorate still had some legal arguments to turn to account, but no longer had at its disposal the sociological props which had enabled these arguments to prevail.

Decisions concerning the notables had been swift. The Sultan had dismissed the members of the Maghzen shortly before he arrived in Morocco. He made it quite clear that he did not want them to participate in any ceremonies marking his return. Initially, he dismissed only 20 pashas and caids out of the 400 implicated in the August 1953 coup; the number was subsequently raised to 30. Actually, the entire body was deprived of all authority by the hostility of the people of the *bled* and of the towns. The notables who felt most threatened by public resentment disappeared quietly. The whole administrative apparatus gradually fell to pieces. A mood of insubordination developed among the tribes now left to their own devices, which partially explains the ease with which bands of the Moroccan Army of Liberation were to infiltrate and spread disaffection all around them.[38]

Thus, almost without transition, a vast political and adminis-

---

trusted it. Fear of similar situations on a large scale was a strong factor, several years later, in the get-tough policy of the military in the Algerian conflict.

38. See p. 358.

trative vacuum had been created at the local level. On one hand, the French administrative system retained only the semblance of authority: the contrôleurs civils and indigenous affairs officers, face to face with local Istiqlal and resistance leaders, retained only that small measure of control over the Moroccan people that the latter permitted. On the other hand, the Sultan, the political parties, the trade-unions, and the resistance groups were the only bodies able to control the passions of the masses, although, for lack of trained officials and technical means, they were as yet unable to govern and administer them.

In these circumstances, it would have been impossible for the regime to return to its pristine state, since its original foundations were gone. How could the government negotiate the division of administrative powers—that is, relinquish control over the technical departments—and retain under Residential control the political departments? This was especially true of the Interior, which was the central command post for internal security. The Residence lacked any effective authority; it was no longer capable of ensuring security. Only the Moroccan authorities had influence over the population. Only they could actually guarantee order—but they were denied the means to do so. Above all, how could the French government end direct administration when there were no trained Moroccan officials, when the only administrative core still functioning was staffed with French civil servants?

Dubois realized better than anyone the paradox of the situation. Although prepared to defend the reserved powers, he had decided to prevent the Residency and the Palace from clashing again in a vain dispute over positions already lost. He was deeply convinced that the Moroccans, once they had obtained what France could no longer deny them, would realize their weakness and draw closer to France. This realistic view, while it could not restore to France what had been virtually lost, was to prove fruitful once the independence agreements were signed.

Aside from the military aspect of the problem, which remains to be examined, the Paris agreements were much less attributable to the relative skills of the negotiators on both sides than to the consequence of the interplay of objective factors which made the

privileges demanded by France meaningless even before final
negotiations began. Furthermore, in the weeks immediately following Dubois' arrival in Rabat, the administrative apparatus of
the protectorate had been emasculated by the removal of the
traditional officials, the formation of the Moroccan government,
and the appearance at all levels of the nationalist ministers and
officials invested by public acclaim with full de facto authority,
and these developments were irreversible. All that remains in our
analysis is to consider the use of force by the insurgents of the
bled.

The Final Failure of Pacification

The collapse of the regime's political and administrative
foundations is an essential factor in the diplomatic victory of the
nationalist negotiators, but it is not the complete explanation.
The Moroccan spokesmen would not have succeeded in defeating their opponents so easily if the first factor—the development
of institutions—had not been strongly reinforced throughout this
last period by a second: increased military pressure from the
Moroccan outlaws in the towns and in the *bled*. It is, therefore,
necessary to analyze the second phenomenon. The starting point,
again, is November 1955.

The appearance on the Rif frontier of the Moroccan Army of
Liberation's commandos in October 1955 had been a mere cur-
tain-raiser. Once the Sultan landed in France, on the eve of La
Celle-Saint-Cloud, the attacks were resumed more vigorously
than ever in the Boured and Tizi Ouzli sectors. Insurrection
flared up again on the night of November 9–10. Although aircraft promptly intervened to relieve the besieged units, the French
troops were hard pressed.[39] Between the Sultan's return and the
formation of the Moroccan government (November 16–December 7), there were increasing ambushes, raids on patrols, and
attacks on outposts. From then on, the army lived in constant
fear that the revolt would spread to the entire northern front. At
the beginning of December, raids had become a daily occurrence
in the eastern section, and the environs of Oudja were classified

39. Casualties totaled 10 dead, 24 wounded, and 16 missing, a considerable number
for an operation of this kind.

as a continuing trouble spot. The initial skirmishes developed
into small-scale battles that sorely tried the morale of the French
troops, who had seventeen killed and ten wounded in an ambush
between Tizi Ouzli and Boured on November 25 alone. On
December 2, the army estimated its total losses in the Rif since
October 1 at 101 men killed and 173 wounded. The two months
between the formation of the Moroccan government and the
signing of the provisional protocol on division of administrative
powers were marked by a new and appreciable increase in the
pressure exerted on the French forces by the Moroccan Army of
Liberation commandos and by terrorist groups. Guerrilla bands,
now installed in the French zone along the Spanish frontier,
began to operate to the south. The military authorities estimated
that during December at least one hundred men equipped with
automatic rifles had engaged in attacks on roads and trails
behind the front. Not satisfied with stirring up the people north
of Taza and in the east, they extended their raids as far as the
hills around Meknes, in the Moyen Atlas.

The effects of the ever widening circles of commando raids
and tribal defections were soon compounded by lowered morale
among the Moroccan auxiliaries that within a few weeks was to
spell the complete collapse of the mobile Maghzen and Goum
units which had hitherto been the formations best adapted to the
struggle against terrorism. Actually, the Sultan's return had
placed the Goum and Maghzen units in an untenable moral
position. He could not openly support them, since they were
fighting against his own subjects; nor could he urge them to
insurrection and desertion, since the hour of reconciliation was
fast approaching. His silence ultimately drove the Moroccan
auxiliaries to despair. They were trapped between their French
officers whom they could not and would not turn against, and
the rebels whom they refused to fight once the *bled* began to stir.
Subjected day after day to nationalist propaganda, they reached a
degree of disaffection which needed only the proper moment to
manifest itself. On December 13, after one of them had been
murdered, the *mokhazzenis* of Fez gathered in a house in the
native quarter and declared that they would ignore all orders
until the Sultan told them where their duty lay. On the eight-

eenth, a *mokhazzeni* post was captured in the Fez region. Desertions, collective refusals to obey orders, and thefts of arms thereafter became a daily occurrence. The Maghzen units had ceased to be trustworthy. When attacked, the auxiliaries gave up their weapons without resisting or else deserted to join the dissidents. A few days later, while the northern front was bursting into flame and terrorist attacks were multiplying throughout Morocco, the same symptoms of disintegration appeared among the Goums.

On December 24, rebel commandos attacked the Casablanca-Oudja railway. Since the *mokhazzenis* assigned to guard it were now suspect, the army advised halting night traffic; but the Resident-General opposed such action, and in the end the trains ran without hindrance. On December 30, the rebels pressed their advantage, infiltrated in the direction of Beni Oulid and Tahar Souk, and succeeded at several points in cutting the supply route for the northern French posts. Although the ultimate effect at the front was greater on morale than it was on supplies, the rebels had scored a major success in making the army believe its communications were threatened. One by one, French troops had to relieve the posts held by *mokhazzenis* and Goums, while the commanding officer regrouped in the rear those formations withdrawn from action. Within a month, purely political and moral factors had deprived the French forces—already less than 100,000 men—of all Moroccan formations: one-quarter of their front-line troops had gone over to the enemy.

On January 7, 1956, the Sultan added the crowning blow to demoralization of the auxiliaries by refusing to receive their leaders and give them the encouragement he had once seemed ready to bestow. It was becoming evident that Mohammed V could do nothing to restore order as long as the fighting lasted, and that it would continue until Morocco was independent. Attacks on outposts, desertions, and terrorist incidents were routine throughout January.

When the provisional protocol on administrative powers was signed on February 11, the military problem was virtually settled to the rebels' advantage. French forces were outnumbered on every side and were by then fighting only in self-defense. The rapid collapse of the Maghzen and Goum units not only deprived the French units of the indispensable assistance of local inhabitants; it also solved in advance all the manpower and munitions problems of the Moroccan Army of Liberation. Morocco was full of weapons and of deserters trained to use them. Inevitably, whatever the protectorate attempted in its own defense turned to its opponents' advantage, and every threat meant still more men and weapons for the other side.

The crest of the wave was not to come until after the Sultan's departure for Paris, when the leaders of the Moroccan resistance decided to reinforce the incipient negotiations by threatening France with general insurrection if Moroccan independence was not recognized. On February 15, two days after Mohammed V's arrival in Paris, pamphlets put out by the terrorist organization, the Black Crescent, announced the beginning of an attack on French forces. To back up the argument, in the next few days grenades were thrown at army vehicles in all the chief Moroccan towns. Isolated soldiers were attacked, and the troops in the rear had to be confined to barracks, which did not improve matters. On the eighteenth, pamphlets put out by the Moroccan Army of Liberation in turn declared total war if the negotiations were unsuccessful.[40] They disclosed the "establishment, on February 15, of the combat zone of the eastern Grand Atlas, following upon the opening of fronts in the Rif, the eastern zone, and, most recently, the Moyen Atlas." The influence of these proclamations upon the Paris negotiations was far from negligible. Everywhere, as far as Marrakesh, French outposts were under fire. In the northern zone and the Moyen Atlas, tribal dissidence increased steadily. "In the territory of the Beni Snassen," ran a headline in Le Figaro of February 24, "the machine gun is law." Except in the north, where most of the available forces had been concentrated, Morocco was dangerously short of troops. A massacre of settlers would have posed a problem which the General Staff could have solved only by evacuating the *bled* and by having the settlers fall back upon the Atlantic ports. Both sides

40. Le Monde (Feb. 21, 1956).

knew this, and so the mere threat gave the attackers a greater political advantage than they would probably have reaped from its execution.

The signing of the Franco-Moroccan protocol on March 2 did not end the rebel activities. A movement of this kind does not halt on command. Nevertheless, recognition of Moroccan independence deprived nationalist military activities of their raison d'être. After several days of complete confusion, marked here and there by increasingly large thefts of arms, a détente began. On March 18, Allal el-Fassi gave public support from Tangier to the appeals of Mohammed V for calm, although he also declared that the combatants would remain on the alert.[41] That same day, Bouabid announced that the question of the Rif had been settled.[42] Calm had been restored all along the northern front. On the twenty-eighth, the Moroccan Army of Liberation acknowledged its responsibilities in a pamphlet saying:

> In deference to the wishes of His Majesty the King regarding the observance of calm pending the announcement of France's intentions . . . the High Command of the "Army of Liberation," in agreement with the Resistance Movement, has decided to halt temporarily all military operations, although the Army of Liberation will maintain its positions until Moroccan sovereignty has been completely unfettered, without conditions or reservations.[43]

On the same day, Allal el-Fassi proclaimed Morocco's right to the Sahara.[44] On March 30, Mohammed V received the leaders of the insurrection, over whom he assumed nominal control in the following diplomatic phrases:

> We address to you our wholehearted thanks, and in receiving you today we receive faithful and loyal subjects. Now that independence has been achieved . . . and all Moroccans aspire to order and stability . . . it has pleased your Sovereign to receive you . . . on this

41. Ibid. (March 20, 1956).
42. Ibid.
43. *Le Monde* (March 30, 1956).
44. Ibid.

blessed day on which you have come, in answer to the call of your King, to listen to his words and to heed his counsel.[45]

It was very obvious that although the new regime did not yet control the resistance movement, it counted on its loyalty and royalist zeal not to create trouble. The time had not yet come to demobilize this quasi-political, quasi-military formation, whose activities had done so much to show the French authorities they were losing control of the country. After taking advantage of recent events to recruit men and improve its military strength, the Moroccan Army of Liberation retired on April 5 to positions from which, without embarrassing the Rabat government, it could still influence political events. At the same time, it continued to threaten the French with resumption of guerrilla warfare if the Paris agreements were not carried out. There was a gradual change in the atmosphere of unrest and insecurity. Settling old scores among Moroccans, and between Moroccans and Frenchmen, took precedence over the so-called terrorist activities, until calm was ultimately restored.[46]

The French forces had not been conquered by their elusive adversaries—a manifest impossibility. They had merely lost control over disorders which enveloped them from all sides and which they were powerless to master. The material defeat of the army—as far as its repressive activities were concerned—was nonetheless overwhelming. Its three main objectives had been to prevent dissidence by its mere presence, to defeat the armed bands whose formation it had been unable to prevent, and to contain those it was unable to defeat. In the end, none of these objectives had been attained. The army, concentrated on the northern frontier since October 1955 with orders to keep it closed

---

45. *Le Monde* (March 31, 1956); ibid. (April 1–2, 1956).

46. On June 1, 1956, Alain Savary could inform Parliament that, "Attacks against the French, which numbered 73 in July 1955 and 66 in October, diminished to 32 in February, 17 in March, and 8 in April. In the second half of 1955, 108 French civilians were killed and 186 wounded; from January through April 1956, the figure fell to 8 killed and 26 wounded. Attacks against property during the same period fell from 716 in August 1955 to 96 in April 1956. There has been no burning of crops since the beginning of 1956, as opposed to 120 in the single month of May 1955. The boycott of French products has completely ceased since the beginning of the year." *J.O., Débats parl., Ass. nat.* (June 2, 1956), p. 2217.

and to cut off the Rif zone to the south, had been gradually obliged to assign its best troops for the protection of its own security and communication lines. Since it could neither pin down nor destroy the armed bands, it had had to be content with air bombardment of villages in the Rif. This had merely accelerated the flight of the population from the French forces. The army was supposed to destroy the traffic in arms from outside, but in a few weeks it had furnished the rebels through its own disintegration with more arms and more men trained to use them than foreign sources could have supplied in a year. A few hundred armed guerrillas had finally imposed their will on 100,000 metropolitan troops trained in the art of modern warfare.

The outcome of the Franco-Moroccan negotiations is more comprehensible when viewed against the background of the daily military and administrative situation prevailing in Morocco, while the representatives of both sides sat around the green baize table and professed to regard the problem solely from the legal point of view.

It remained for the French Parliament to approve the government's action and to draw a lesson from what had transpired. Thanks to the efforts of several speakers, this self-appraisal assumed the unexpected aspect of a political demonstration, and point by point confirms the dual analysis just attempted.

The debate on the Mollet government's general North African policy opened May 31, 1956.[47] The diehards had no difficulty in proving that the Moroccan policy, which the Assembly was being asked to approve, was no longer the one it had ratified in principle in October 1955. They sought particularly to show that the emancipation of Morocco and Tunisia would necessarily compromise the defense of Algeria. This did not inhibit the same speakers from giving explicit approval to the government's Algerian policy and the massive military effort behind it.[48]

47. Ibid. (June 1, 1956), pp. 2150 ff. It was not really a debate on ratification of the new Franco-Moroccan and Franco-Tunisian conventions but a discussion based on interpellations that soon assumed the character of a second vote of confidence. The vote of closure was tantamount to ratification of the conventions already concluded. Ibid. (June 6, 1956), p. 2337.

48. See especially Raymond Dronne's interpellation, ibid. (June 1, 1956), pp. 2151 ff.

The government replied to these attacks with a defense of its policy that left nothing to the imagination. The Minister, while acknowledging the part played in the final period of the conflict by the magic concept of independence.[49] and the long political interregnum of the winter of 1955–56, concentrated on demonstrating the irreversible nature of the situation. Alain Savary declared that:

> When the present government took office, it found, both in Morocco and Tunisia, a dichotomy between the legal position and reality.[50]
>
> The Sharifian authorities took office in a state of de facto independence. . . . The French administration, badly shaken by these developments, had lost some of its cohesiveness and organization. Even private individuals began to have doubts about the future. The only restraining influence was the authority of H. M. Mohammed V, although he had no material means of enforcement.
>
> Ultimately, the disorder and growing anarchy were expressed in bloodshed in the war which broke out in the Rif on October 2 and which continued, expanded, and threatened to spread elsewhere, confronting the French armed forces with a difficult problem they could not completely resolve by themselves, given their numbers and the morale of the native Moroccans serving in their ranks.[51]

Savary explained how similar tension had developed in Tunisia between the juridical system defined in the conventions and the political demands provoked by the proclamation of Moroccan independence:[52]

> The Tunisian government and the more reasonable political leaders could not let the crusade for independence get out of hand without consequent impairment of their authority and prestige. . . . In both countries,

49. See Pinay's defense, ibid. (June 2, 1956), pp. 2229 ff.
50. Ibid., p. 2215.
51. Ibid.
52. A reference to the pressure exerted on the Bourguiba government by the extremists of the Salah ben Youssef faction.

therefore, no solution remained but to recognize unequivocally their independence, if we wanted to reinforce the authority of governments menaced by such
crusades or by anarchy, if we wanted to make progress
once more.[53]

The minister finally turned to the question of whether it would
have been advisable to "make recognition of independence subject to a precise definition of interdependence." He demonstrated
that such an unreasonable demand might well have compromised what was still salvageable.

> What would have actually happened? Interdepen-
> dence negotiated in this fashion would soon have been
> challenged on the pretext that it had not been freely
> accepted. Moreover, negotiations would have dragged
> on for months. Hopes and impatience would have in-
> cited increased demands and violence. External develop-
> ments would soon have outdistanced the normal course
> of negotiations, and interdependence would have come
> about without us, or despite us.[54]

He concluded:

> Is it not . . . obvious that the restoration of order in
> Tunisia and Morocco and the stabilization of sovereign
> and independent states, constituting peaceful areas on
> either side of Algeria [interruptions from some right-
> wing and center benches], in which the people look to
> the future, will help bring about peace and Franco-
> Muslim reconciliation?
> To extend the conflict would have been a tragedy.[55]

Intervening in the debate, Christian Pineau concentrated on
analyzing the military problem posed by the Moroccan rebellion.
In this connection, his exchange with Pierre Clostermann is

53. *J.O., Débats parl., Ass. nat.* (June 2, 1956), p. 2215.
54. Ibid.
55. Ibid., p. 2218.

highly germane to the theory of conflict and therefore merits citation. Pineau said:

> I believe that no speaker has yet referred to the real problem of Morocco and Tunisia. I heard it said yesterday that the weakness of our policy in Morocco and Tunisia was extremely dangerous for Algeria and that the consequences of the insecurity of Algeria's western and eastern frontiers might be serious. . . . Let me for a moment put myself in the position of those who criticize [the policy of conciliation]. I would ask them: What other policy would you put into effect? . . . How many men would you have needed if the war had gone on in the Rif, and if fighting had continued in Tunisia, and what influence might that number of men have had on the Algerian affair?
>
> Let me remind you, esteemed colleagues, that in 1926 we needed 325,000 men to bring the Rif campaign to successful conclusion. At present, there are about 105,000 men there; we should need 220,000 more and probably an additional 150,000 or 200,000 in Tunisia.[56]

Clostermann then broke in, with the minister's permission:

> Abd el-Krim had at his disposal only a fraction of the Beni Snassen, about 75,000 men, of whom 20,000 were armed. We had thirty-two line divisions and forty-four squadrons, under the command of sixty generals led by Marshal Pétain.
>
> This was the French army which had just won the Great War of 1914–18, and it was well trained. It was supported by four-fifths of the population of Morocco, which had supplied some 400,000 auxiliaries[57] recruited by our friend el-Glaoui, Pasha of Marrakesh, who won his *médaille militaire* there.
>
> On the other side of the Atlas was a Spanish Army of 100,000 men, 40,000 of whom were regular soldiers.

56. Ibid., pp. 2234–35.
57. Probably a reference to the Moroccan auxiliaries called up during World War I.

. . . These are the exact figures, and they confirm your argument in every respect.[58]

Pineau continued:

> Thus, it is perfectly clear that those who favor a policy of force in Morocco and Tunisia must realize now that it would require 400,000 to 500,000 more men.
>
> Where do our colleagues propose to find these men? I have not heard anyone say from this rostrum, "I call upon the government to mobilize 400,000 or 500,000 more men for Morocco and Tunisia and I agree, of course, to pay the additional taxes this will require." . . . Moreover, this so-called policy of force would have considerably weakened our campaign in Algeria. This is only one reason which led the government to decide . . . to follow a policy of conciliation and negotiation in Tunisia and Morocco, and to reserve our major military and financial effort for Algeria.
>
> I think, therefore, that it is wholly misleading to assert that there are two governmental policies: a "strong" policy in Algeria, and a policy of compromise in Tunisia and Morocco.[59]

The alternative that had dominated the Moroccan conflict ever since the initial appearance of terrorism in the protectorate was this time brought into the harsh light of day. Of course, the government had made praiseworthy efforts to show that despite the independence agreements, Morocco and Tunisia remained bound to France by their former treaties until conventions on interdependence had been ratified. It had also attributed to the declaration of La Celle-Saint-Cloud [60] and the December 1955 political interregnum a circumstantial importance they did not actually possess. It was good strategy for the Mollet government to try to foist at least part of the responsibility for its difficulties onto its predecessor. But the facts, as they emerged from the explanations of the Minister for Foreign Affairs and of Alain

58. *J.O., Débats parl., Ass. nat.* (June 2, 1956), p. 2235.
59. Ibid.
60. See especially ibid., p. 2215, Savary's analysis of these agreements.

Savary, showed overwhelmingly that the emancipation of Morocco had become inevitable because of the activities of the terrorist groups and the commandos of the Moroccan Army of Liberation on one hand, and the spontaneous disintegration of the protectorate's political and administrative machinery on the other. Apart from reconquest, which was inconceivable, the overwhelming change of heart and the rebels' resistance had left France no course but to consent.[61]

The debate on North African policy closed on June 2, but the vote on a motion of confidence did not take place until the fifth. The motion was adopted by 271 votes to 59, with 200 abstentions.[62] The Communists abstained. Only 57 deputies from the Right and the extreme Right, one member of the M.R.P., and one Progressive voted against the government. Fifteen Social Republicans, twenty-nine Independents, and four Peasants voted in favor. The extreme Right had finally bowed to reality, but its defeat was paltry reward for victory, since events showed that it had implicitly bartered Morocco and Tunisia for assurance that no stone would be left unturned to keep Algeria. Both the attacks of the diehards and the government's reply made it quite plain that this bargain was the real and tacitly understood theme of the debate. Following the vote of confidence, the Franco-Moroccan diplomatic convention initialed at Rabat on May 19 came into force after being explicitly approved. On June 13, 1956, Dubois exchanged his title of High Commissioner for that of Ambassador Extraordinary of France in Morocco.

The parliamentary vote did not, however, conclude the transition period, which ended with the signing of the last so-called interdependence agreements.

The convention on administrative and technical cooperation was initialed at Rabat on February 6, 1957. The French officials in the Sharifian departments thereby lost their civil service status and were employed under contract, while provision was made for the gradual return to France of French civil servants released by Morocco. The cultural convention was initialed at Rabat on

61. This proposition seems self-evident on the plane of simple historical analysis, but it remains to be proved in the realm of political science. Its validity for the latter will be demonstrated in volume 2.

62. *J.O., Débats parl., Ass. nat.* (June 3, 1956), pp. 2252 ff.; (June 6, 1956), p. 2337.

May 30. It stipulated that the university and cultural mission which France was to set up in Morocco should operate six lycées, a technical school, and 1,024 primary classes. The Moroccans and the French colony received this agreement most favorably. The conventions on legal matters and mutual legal assistance were initialed at Rabat on June 11. It was understood that Morocco, in setting up her model courts, would continue to give preference to French magistrates. Certain safeguards were laid down in respect of these magistrates. A series of provisions also regulated legal relations between France and Morocco. At the end of 1957, only the enabling conventions and the consular convention remained unsigned. Talks on delimitating the frontiers were left in suspense because of Moroccan claims to the Sahara.

The end of the transition period was marked simultaneously by a progressive return to normal of Franco-Moroccan relations and by a number of political incidents which despite their gravity were not insurmountable, thanks to the radical change of climate resulting from recognition of Moroccan independence. While the French troops in Morocco were able to move freely again, the leaders of the Army of Liberation had sworn an oath of allegiance to Mohammed V on July 3, 1956, barely one month after the close of the debate on the interpellations. On the fourteenth, France brought before the United Nations Security Council the question of Moroccan membership in the organization.[63] On the Council's recommendation, the General Assembly on November 12 decided to admit Morocco to membership.[64] On October 29, the diplomatic conference at Fedala had put an end to the international administration of Tangier.[65]

The previous week, at the Imperial Palace in Rabat, Prince Mulay Hassan had officially received five leaders of the Algerian rebellion who had been brought from Nador. This precipitated a serious crisis between France and Morocco. On October 22, the

63. For the French representative's letter of July 14 to the President of the Security Council, see United Nations Security Council, *Official Records,* 11th Sess., Supplement for July, August, and September 1956 (S/3619). For the letter of July 4, 1956, from the Moroccan Minister for Foreign Affairs to the Secretary-General concerning the application of Morocco for membership in the Organization, see ibid., Doc. S/3617.

64. United Nations General Assembly Res. 1111 (XI), Nov. 12, 1956.

65. *Le Monde* (Oct. 31, 1956).

French government suspended negotiations on the conventions in protest against the intervention of Mohammed V in the Algerian crisis. That same evening, the airplane carrying Mohammed ben Bella and the other Algerian leaders from Rabat to Tunis was intercepted by French aircraft and forced down at Algiers. Moroccan reaction was initially extremely violent. On the following day, settlers were massacred in the Meknes region, and the Moroccan Ambassador to Paris was recalled. On November 3, Savary resigned in protest against the arrest of the Algerian leaders and was immediately replaced by Maurice Faure.

The de facto solidarity established between France and Morocco during thirty-five years of joint existence was too great to permit an irreparable breach at this late date. By October 30, France had sent Jean Basdevant to Rabat to try to resolve the crisis. Both sides worked to this end. The French military command took the necessary steps to safeguard the French colony in Morocco, while a Moroccan governor and military tribunal were installed at Meknes on October 27. The next day, a new Moroccan government, composed of members of the Istiqlal and moderately inclined Independents, took the situation in hand. On December 4, 112 new caids were invested under a *dahir* that was accompanied by forthright instructions concerning the protection of aliens and their interests. Several Moroccans found guilty of taking part in the October 23 massacres were sentenced to death. This strong action ended the crisis that had followed the Meknes incident in circumstances that gave the French nationals still in Morocco no grounds for doubting the Moroccan government's determination to protect foreign nationals settled on its soil.

On January 20, 1957, Mohammed V and Faure had a conversation at Cannes which marked a return to more normal relations. On February 1, the Moroccans issued official instructions restricting a proposed strike of solidarity with Algeria to a symbolic cessation of work. This moderate attitude showed clearly that the government of Mohammed V had decided to place the requirements of Franco-Moroccan cooperation above those of Arab solidarity. Many Moroccans criticized the measure. However, having held the legal aspects of interdependence so cheap, Morocco obviously did not wish to break the de facto state of solidarity between France and Morocco.

These last occurrences are a striking illustration of the change of political climate which independence and the suppression of disturbances had brought about in Morocco. By subjecting the new Franco-Moroccan relations to a real test, the Meknes massacres had forced the two governments to consider their mutual relations with a realism which no future considerations of sentiment or prestige would alter. Since nothing more could be gained in the field of sovereignty, the Rabat government realized more clearly than it ever could have done in the past how much Morocco's economic future depended upon maintaining on its soil the foreign colony established there under the protectorate. Having nothing more to lose in terms of colonization, the French government and the French public realized ever more clearly the importance of the human, material, and moral interests which France retained in the Sharifian Empire. At an earlier time such a political incident might well have permanently wrecked the relations of the two states. Instead, it demonstrated the desire of both sides to consider the ten-year crisis as definitely ended.

The almost magic properties of political independence should not obscure the fact that sovereignty is no panacea. In a colonial conflict, emancipation of colonies serves merely to put an end to the political tensions inevitably created between the colonizing country and the colonized peoples. It cannot solve the gargantuan technical, psychological, and political problems posed by the economic development of the emancipated colony, especially when a significant group of Europeans continues to live there. This study has attempted to show how the chain of historic events culminated finally in the victory of Moroccan nationalism in the conflict that had set it in opposition to French authority. It is not concerned with problems of post-independence, which fall within the realm of the theory of economic development in former colonial territories and are thus foreign to the present study.

VOLUME 2

METHODOLOGICAL INTRODUCTION

A study of the Franco-Moroccan conflict involves theories of both domestic political science and international relations. The conflict belongs in the category of political and social revolutions because it is indissolubly linked to the deterioration of the relationship uniting government and subjects. It also remains a distinctive type of revolution displaying several internal characteristics relating it to the field of international relations.[1] The people and their rulers did not belong to the same ethnic group. Until Moroccan emancipation, the rulers were the emissaries of a conquering metropolitan power. The subjects never completely abandoned their role of a conquered people, even when, for a time, they willingly accepted the fact of colonialism. Shifting completely from an internal to an external point of view, and placing the conflict in its international context, there is no doubt that the decolonization of Morocco was strongly influenced by events in the rest of the world. The emancipation of the Sharifian Empire is but one example of the Arab world's political awakening. It was encouraged by precedents, accelerated by events in Tunisia and Algeria, and supported until the end by the international sympathy that freedom-seeking colonies enjoy in the modern world.

Placing the decolonization of Morocco at the crossroads of domestic and international political science is the least of our problems. Difficulties arise only when an attempt is made to qualify the phenomenon by reference to a precise concept of the discipline. Since there is no agreed framework, the author of a study on decolonization who hopes to communicate meaning-

1. Concerning the problem of connections between domestic revolutions and international relations, see especially George Modelski, *The International War*, Research Monograph No. 11 (Princeton, Princeton University, Center of International Studies, May 24, 1961).

fully with his readers must first define his conception of the
sociological method and the political theories that provide the
backbone of his exposition.[2]

The present introduction has a dual purpose. On the one hand,
it serves as a reminder that political phenomena are essentially no
different from those normally dealt with by the sociologist, social
psychologist, or anthropologist. On the other hand, it attempts to
show that structural-functional theory, which today constitutes
the framework of general sociology, is the only conceptual system of reference that will enable political science to make progress and to take its place alongside the other social sciences.

The first objective requires no justification. In fact, the need to
combine political science and general sociology is less and less
open to question. Thus, rather than indulging in abstract specu-
lations on this theme, our purpose is to distinguish between the
political system and other social systems without thereby disrupting the coherence of the sociological analysis.

The second objective does require some clarification. The more
we attempted to apply structural-functional theory to the political system, the clearer it appeared that this theory had to be
adapted to the current capacities of sociological thought. We
certainly believe, along with Kingsley Davis and a number of
other research scholars, that structural-functional theory, far
from being only one theory among others, is actually the only
instrument of conceptual analysis now available to sociology.[3]
However, we believe that this instrument should be interpreted
and expanded if it is to be considered the framework of a unitary
sociological theory.

2. This initial obstacle is not usually encountered in other fields. Nobody expects a
physicist to preface the study of physical phenomenon by a dissertation on his scientific
aims and the method utilized. Although fated to be less fortunate, the more advanced
social sciences, such as political economy, sociology, social psychology, and ethnology
each have a certain accepted foundation. True, a standardized theory is still a remote
ideal, and intramural quarrels are still the price of scientific progress. However, and
this is what is important, practical research tends more and more to develop on the basis
of an implicit methodology applied by most research workers. This is not true in regard
to political science, whose objectives, methods, and vocabulary are less clearly agreed
upon.

3. This is what Kingsley Davis emphasized in "The Myth of Functional Analysis as
a Special Method in Sociology and Anthropology," *American Sociological Review*, 24
(1959), 757–72.

Besides its great advantages, structural-functional theory presents some real disadvantages. The advantages are obvious. The theory enables sociologists to carry out parallel investigations of the structural and functional aspects of life in societies. It also provides investigators with systems of concepts and reasoning well adapted to the study of the social structure and its functions. Hence, it provides sociologists with an explanatory framework to which the study of any social phenomenon can be validly applied; one of the fundamental requirements of scientific theory is thus satisfied on a particularly high level of effectiveness and conceptual cohesion. Unfortunately, there is a reverse side of the coin, due more to sociologists' limited application of the theory than to any defect within the theory itself. Structural-functional theory, by relating structure too narrowly to social function, by studying structure only in terms of its functions, and by analyzing social functions only in relation to the structures they sustain, mistakenly identifies functionalism with sociology, thus making it incapable of integrating without distortion another basic aspect of the study of societies, namely, social change seen as the result of the interaction of socio-cultural variables within a sociological context.[4]

Structural-functional theory cannot exclude either analysis based on relations among variables or analysis based on the study of social functions. The two approaches have the same historical and theoretical significance. To present these as alternatives is to mutilate sociological analysis. In our opinion, structural-functional theory will be fully rewarding only when analysis of the concept of social structure has been carried far enough to make it possible to understand how this structure can be studied by means of categories as different as sociological functionalism and mathematical or quasi-mathematical functionalism.[5] It will be-

4. One must be clear about the importance of this reservation. We are not claiming that sociological functionalism cannot account for social change. We are merely stating that the structural-functional theory as it is understood today cannot satisfactorily integrate analyses of social changes expressed in terms of sociological variables.

5. The concept of a functional relationship between variables is related to mathematical functionalism when it is used in accordance with the definition of logico-mathematicians. It can be considered to be related to quasi-mathematical functionalism when sociologists use it with the analogous although less precise definitions that form the basis of the non-mathematical theory of social change.

come the theory of all sociologists only when the advocates of variable-based reasoning feel as much at ease with it as the functionalists. This means that ambivalences affecting the concepts of structure and function should, for a time, become the primary concern of the theorists.

This approach to the problems raised by the elaboration of a structural-functional theory of the political system led us to subdivide the present methodological introduction into four sections covering the following subjects: (1) the concept of political system and the different modes of explaining it; (2) the biological mode and the concept of social function; (3) the logicomathematical mode and the concept of sociological law; and (4) relationships between the two modes and an attempt at their synthesis.

The Concept of Political System and the Different Modes of Explaining It

The concept of system is one of the basic concepts of modern scientific analysis. A given constellation of material elements constitutes a mechanical system. A given set of organs and body tissues forms the nervous system. The totality of factors concerned with political economy comprises the economic system. By the same token, the totality of factors concerned with political analysis comprises the political system. This comparison between the political and nervous systems is one of those rare organicist analogies that is not misleading: an individual whose nervous system does not function properly has difficulty in solving his problems; a society whose political system functions badly is in the same position. The consequences may be disastrous in both cases.

In sociology as in biology, the adoption of the concept of system involves a preliminary investigation of the factors that distinguish the system under study from other related systems. In physiology, this is a fundamental procedure, since a clear idea of the object can only be obtained by carefully distinguishing the different organic systems. Political science would be incapable of distinguishing itself from the other social sciences had it not first isolated those factors intrinsic to the political system. But it is much more difficult to isolate social systems than physiological ones; each cell of the organism tends to belong to only one physiological system, but each individual belongs to a large number of social systems.

Given these conditions, how can the political system be distinguished from the related systems that concern the other social sciences?[6] The first possibility that comes to mind is to postulate that a given individual, group, or political factor is or is not part of the political system according to whether it does or does not pose political problems for the leaders of that society. If this hypothesis is accepted, two types of social factors have to be considered: those which raise or are likely to raise political problems, and those which do not create or are not likely to create political problems. Attractive as it may appear, this hypothesis does not hold up under analysis. There are no individuals, groups, or social factors that are not likely to create political problems, that are not related, if only in one facet, to the political system. Every individual, every social factor has a political aspect, a vocation to become part of the political system. Obviously the individual exceeds in many ways the limits of the political system, since other facets of his personality, other sociological dimensions draw him into other systems—familial, economic, religious, and so forth. It would be impossible, however, for the individual to free himself from the political system and impossible for him to avoid either supporting or opposing, by his attitudes, political decisions taken by the government. In short, political phenomena are not merely one class of social phenomena among others. They are synthetic phenomena implying involvement in and, consequently, study of every aspect of social life.[7] Political science has a specific nucleus, but it has no specific field of action. Its field of action is the whole field of sociological research. Thus understood, political

6. Our intention here is not to define the political system, but to find a criterion enabling us to define its limits, in order to distinguish it from other social systems. In advanced societies, the political system can be recognized by the fact that its centers of decision are controlled by the political leaders of the entire society.

7. Talcott Parsons was fully aware of this when he mentioned in a well-known passage that political reality cannot "be treated in terms of a specifically specialized conceptual scheme . . . precisely for the reason that the political problem of the social system is a focus for the integration of *all* of its analytically distinguishable components, not of a specially differentiated *class* of these components." *The Social System*, (Glencoe, Ill., Free Press, 1951), pp. 126–27.

science can only be considered an applied science. To engage in political science means applying sociology, social psychology, ethnology, history, and so forth to the study of political aspects of social phenomena. It does not mean creating a distinct discipline, separate from the other social sciences. It means applying all the social sciences to a particular field.

It is not enough to circumscribe a system without analyzing it. Apart from the specific criterion which distinguishes them from the other social systems, political systems may be studied in terms of two fundamental modes of explanation: mathematical functionalism and sociological functionalism. Every natural system can be reduced to a set of variables or of organic functions. The very fact that the concept of system was evolved by the physico-mathematical sciences and biology leads the social sciences, somewhat wary heirs, to adopt the typical argumentation used by the more advanced sciences in their study of systems. The social sciences accept this heritage without acknowledging any liability for it. Obviously, they reserve the right to adapt the argumentation to their own needs. As far as explanatory categories are concerned, however, social sciences have invented nothing, and their use of the concept of system is clear proof of this.

Considered from the point of view of mathematical physics, and more particularly, from that of mechanics, systems are material structures whose constituent magnitudes are related to each other in such a way that if one of the variables in the system changes, the other variables tend to change in a predetermined way.[8] These interactions among variables constitute, by definition, the laws of the system. The law of universal attraction,

8. Any part of the universe considered, for the sake of research, as separable from the whole is, by definition, a material system. An air pump, the sun and its planets, and the steam engine are material systems in this sense. All material systems are not necessarily reducible to laws. The evolution of the system, formed by an experimenter and the test tube he is utilizing, is only partially determinable. To the extent that its behavior can be determined, a material system can be described as deterministic. Material systems considered *concretely* should not be confused with the more or less complex mathematical expressions which express their real behavior in the form of the requisite numerical relationships. In practice, however, physical mathematics is confined to deterministic systems, and considers them directly from the angle of the mathematical laws that govern them. What is known as the "state" of a system is determined at any given moment by the values of the variables used to describe it. The goal of the physico-mathematical theory of material systems is to foresee the subsequent state of these systems from their original state.

applicable to all Newtonian mechanical systems, is defined as a mathematical relationship concerning characteristic magnitudes such as mass, force, and distance. This manner of considering the theory of systems is currently applied in general sociology. Social systems are also composed of factors whose variations are studied through sociological analysis. The correlation of these variations reveals the laws governing the systems in question. Undoubtedly, these laws are less imperative than physical laws. Nevertheless, they govern the essential aspects of social phenomena. In political analysis, the situation is the same. Authority, force, collective attitudes, and social situations are the basic variables of the poltical system. The study of political authority as a function of other independent variables such as consent and force would reveal one law of the system.[9]

Physiological systems, for their part, appear as organic structures exercising one or more vital functions. All organic systems are in fact reducible to constituent elements with definite functions and subfunctions which may operate normally or may be affected by clearly identified characteristic abnormalities. The nervous system, with its great structural diversifications—encephalic, medullar, sympathetic, vagus, and so forth—offers an ideal physiological analogy to political analysis. This method of considering things is completely applicable to sociology and to political science. The political system fulfills a social function. It is made up of elements that support specific social subfunctions. These functions and subfunctions, in turn, can operate normally or can be affected by abnormalities that political science has to examine as it becomes aware of them.

The two modes of explaining systems introduced above are not restrictive. The concept of interaction among variables, for example, can be divided into two subordinate categories: the mathematical concept of "function" and the mathematical concept of

9. This is qualified by what is said below regarding the concept of sociological law. See p. 413. The distinction between coercive and less coercive laws approximates, at a certain point, that between strict and less rigid determinism. In mathematical usage determinism is always absolute. In this usage it is the opposite of stochastic logic. In the broader and less rigid definition of the methodologists, determinism embraces all the forms of necessity with the exception of unique causality. It is thus permissible to talk about flexible, attenuated determinism. It is, of course, to this second definition of the concept that we refer when we talk about historical and sociological determinism.

"correlation." As the concept of correlation is, in its turn, linked to the concept of probability, the theory of sociological systems ultimately relies upon four main *explicanda:* the mathematical concepts of function, correlation, and probability, and the organico-sociological concept of social function. The methodological problems raised by the development of a coherent political sociology would be easily solved if sociological language respected the definitions and usages laid down in treatises on applied mathematics and physiology. As these are generally employed loosely, usually without specifying the modifications that have been made, it is essential to review briefly the problems raised by this rough and ready use of precise concepts of mathematical logic and biology, even though our objective is less to solve these problems than to call attention to them.

THE MATHEMATICAL CONCEPT OF FUNCTION AND
QUASI-MATHEMATICAL SOCIOLOGY

Mathematical functions have been little used in classical sociology, although modern theories—especially game theory—employ them routinely. This reluctance stems from the fact that the elementary functions that sociologists of the classical period might have been tempted to use are designed to express rigorously determined phenomena that have no counterparts in social reality. It is nonetheless true that contemporary sociological speech is full of modes of reasoning and concepts borrowed from mathematics. Any social factor is a variable for the theorists of social change; any loose relationship between two social variables justifies the use of the term function. It has become commonplace in non-mathematical sociology to speak of technology as a "variable" or of social change as a "function" of technological change. In other words, with the exception of certain strictly limited fields in which it has become openly mathematical, sociological speech now appears as ordinary language "improved" by the adoption of quasi-mathematical modes of reasoning and terminology. This is not a question of premature reasoning, of empty arguments, doomed to remain void of any real meaning until the mathematical theory covering the phenomena in question has been constructed. On the contrary, it is a question of intermediate reasoning used instinctively by sociologists to avoid the pitfalls of common causality in those areas of their discipline which have not yet yielded to mathematics. When a sociologist writes that a given non-numerical factor is a "function" of another given non-numerical factor, he means that the changes affecting the first are closely enough related to those affecting the second for these changes to be described and empirically related to each other. It is in this sense that we are using the concept.[10]

However, the sociological method cannot limit itself to this basic minimum without running the risk of leaving unsubstantiated its fundamental line of reasoning. The modern theory of functions is a branch of the logico-mathematical theory of classes. It should be remembered that when two mathematical variables x and y are given, y is defined as a function of x when one or more values of y correspond to each value of x. Every function thus expresses a definite and restrictive relationship between two or more classes of numbers or objects.[11] When, in non-mathematical verbal sociology, all the possible or simply assignable sociological "states" of two non-numerical social variables are given—for example, an instrumental technique and an institution—it is generally possible to establish only a roughly

10. Robert K. Merton says that "since it was first introduced by Leibnitz, the word function has its most precise significance in mathematics. . . . This conception, in a more extended (and often more imprecise) sense, is expressed by such phrases as 'functional interdependence' and 'functional relations' so often adopted by social scientists." *Social Theory and Structure,* (rev. ed., Glencoe, Ill., Free Press, 1957), p. 21. It is the broader and less precise meaning of the mathematical concept of function, in itself quite distinct from the concept of social function, which, in our opinion, should be elucidated if one wants to have a clear idea of the nature of sociological determinism. If mathematical functions are laws by definition, then sociological arguments expressed in terms of functions are laws that are not precise. In other words, the clarification of the notion of sociological law requires clarification of the verbal approximations of the mathematical concept of function. This is a major problem to which very little attention appears to have been paid so far.

11. *Encyclopaedia Britannica,* 9 (1953), 916, defines function as "in mathematics, an expression, rule or law which makes correspond to each value taken by one variable, called the independent variable or argument of the function, one or more values of another variable, called the dependent variable. In its most general usage in mathematics the word 'function' refers to any correspondence between two classes of objects. A simple example under this general definition would be afforded by a group of people seated in a room, with the independent variable standing for any person in the room, while the corresponding value of the dependent variable is the chair in which he sits. But for most functions occurring in mathematics, the variables range over classes of numbers."

corresponding relationship between these two classes of states. Nonetheless, even in this oversimplified version, the concept of function remains synonymous with that of law, every function being a law by definition. When sociologists use the concepts of "variable" and "function" in non-mathematical sociological parlance, they are opting, not always consciously, for a deterministic approach to science. This is a quite particular determinism, the extent of which it will not be possible to ascertain until criteria have been established for distinguishing between the inevitable and the accidental in the social phenomena whose behavior is being studied. It is our feeling that this research should focus on the point at which sociological theory of ideal types and logico-mathematical theory of classes intersect. There can be no question of undertaking a project of this type in the present work, but we had to make it quite clear that when we use expressions such as "political authority is a function of consent," we are not overlooking the fact that such judgments raise problems of interpretation which are far from having been satisfactorily resolved.

THE CONCEPT OF CORRELATION

The mathematical concept of correlation, as distinct from that of function, is widely used by sociologists whenever they study a phenomenon to which statistical analysis may be applied de plano. Electoral sociology is a good example of the application of this second approach to political sociology. In this connection, it is well to remember that the mere expression of a mathematical correlation does not provide by itself an adequate explanation of a social phenomenon. The correlation must be interpreted, and in the social sciences this interpretation generally involves a return to everyday speech. It must be admitted that even in electoral sociology, progress has been slow in the interpretation of correlations that have been found between social groups and their political attitudes.

Aside from its basic meaning in statistical analysis, the concept of correlation can also be applied much more roughly. When, for want of sufficient data, it becomes impossible to enumerate exactly the classes of individuals or factors being correlated, the concept can still be of some use in ordering the correlation indices obtained using the ordinal scale analogous to that used for weighting attitudes in social psychology. It might be stated, for example, that the correlation obtained is almost perfect, very high, high, and so forth—each qualification weakening the argument somewhat without necessarily destroying its significance. This procedure will be used later to explain the correlations obtained between different classes of Moroccan society and their political attitudes.

CONCEPTS OF PROBABILITY

While the application of the concept of correlation to non-mathematical or quasi-mathematical sociology raises few problems, the same cannot be said for another closely related technical concept: the concept of probability. As we know, statistical analysis is closely linked to the calculation of probabilities. The statement that the correlation index between a given social class and a given political attitude is 90 percent means that for every individual born into that group, there are 90 chances out of 100 that this attitude will one day be his, provided that the observed correlation index remains constant. In mathematical logic, this type of probability is called an *empirical probability*. Such a judgment can only be used when the classes of individuals to which empirical reference is made are large and homogeneous enough to make the statement meaningful.

In the "improved" everyday language that is the normal working idiom of the sociologist's discipline, the concept of probability is often used in another currently accepted sense which logicians have carefully distinguished from the first. This is what Carnap and his school call *a priori probability* or *subjective probability*.[12] The statement often appears in the press or in political

12. In the first draft of the present study, we failed to distinguish between the two concepts of probability. Morido Inagaki was kind enough to draw our attention to the problem raised by the lack of specificity in the argument, and we finally eliminated all references to the concepts of probability in the first draft of the text, leaving only the passages based on the empirical notion of correlation. It seemed to us that the formulation of our conclusions in terms of probability would carry us further than was necessary to treat the subject proposed by the Carnegie Endowment for International Peace. Nevertheless, the transition from a given potential authority to actual political decisions can only be adequately judged in terms of subjective probability. For a given level of authority, a given concrete decision would be, subjectively speaking, highly probable, moderately probable, or highly improbable. The ordinary concepts of impossible, possible, or necessary decisions are finally no more than the current syntactical equivalents of the subjective probability of the decisions under study. Impossible acts of authority are only very improbable acts of authority. Similarly, necessary decisions are only highly

science studies that a given event, e.g. the final victory of the indigenous population in a given colonial conflict, is extremely probable. The Carnap school believes that judgments of this type express a probability which differs from empirical probability. To give an empirical character to this type of probability, there would have to be a sufficiently large and homogeneous class of colonial conflicts available which could be correlated with a sufficiently homogeneous class of conflicts that had ended in the victory of the indigenous populace. This, however, is not the hypothesis. When we say that a colonial nationalistic victory is extremely probable, we are really using an inductive type of reasoning that expresses the functioning of the particular political system within which the conflict is taking place. The validity of this type of prediction depends upon the validity of the inferences upon which it is based. Stating that the probability of a revolutionary faction's victory increases as the consent potential of the system's established leaders decreases does not imply that valid statistics are available for past revolutions that ended in victory for the enemies of the established order. A priori, the appraisal in question is worth no more than the inductions linking the authority of the leaders of the political system to the attitudes of the people.[13] Although the logicians are aware of the problems raised by this second type of probability estimate, we feel, once again, that much remains to be done. Interpretation of the a priori probability concept comes back to the classical problem of relations between probability and induction. This brings us to the significance of sociological laws, for if an a priori probability is based upon inductive inference, its full significance can become apparent only to the extent that the import of these inductions (laws) has been elucidated.

THE ORGANICO-SOCIOLOGICAL CONCEPT OF SOCIAL FUNCTION

In themselves, the categories and vocabulary of biological functionalism are no more applicable, without modification, to sociol-

---

probable acts of authority. See Rudolph Carnap, *Logical Foundations of Probability* (2nd ed. Chicago, University of Chicago Press, 1962).

13. This does not mean that statistics for this kind of phenomena are available, nor that the inductions in question apply specifically to the special case of decolonization.

logy—as was indicated by the organicist impasse—than the mathematical notions discussed above. However, the situation is far more satisfactory with respect to biological functionalism. The elaboration of a specifically sociological functionalism is now so far advanced that it is no longer possible to speak in terms of a lacuna. From Bronislaw Malinowski to Robert King Merton, a bevy of first-rate research scholars have distinguished themselves in this area. What is lacking is the application of this sociological functionalism to political science. In his remarkable introduction to a recent work devoted to the political structure of under-developed regions, Gabriel A. Almond states: "Nothing much has happened to the functional theory of politics since the doctrine of separation of powers and the lively discussion of it in the great era of constitution-making in the United States." [14] Disturbing as this observation may be, it is nevertheless well-founded. Wherever the responsibility may lie for this gap, sociological functionalism was applied unhesitatingly to the study of the Franco-Moroccan conflict whenever it seemed worthwhile to do so. As for the significance of the functionalist analysis in general sociology, this has been sufficiently dealt with by authors specializing in the study of these questions.

Enough has been said to make it quite clear that a study of the political system can only be made within the appropriate expanded framework if this system is considered *conjointly* as a set of variables and as a segment of the collective organization invested with a particular social function. When things are considered from this complex viewpoint, three questions of theory immediately come to mind: (1) What happens when the political system is considered as an element of a collective structure invested with a specific social function? (2) What happens when the same system is seen as a set of functional relationships among variables? (3) How and to what degree are the two functionalisms related insofar as they are based upon a common social structure?

These three questions have served as the guidelines of our analysis. We believe that they should be made explicit at the be-

14. *The Politics of the Developing Areas,* edited by Gabriel A. Almond and James Coleman (Princeton, Princeton University Press, 1960), p. 13.

ginning of a structural-functional theory of social systems if it is ever to be applied successfully to the study of political systems.

The Biological Mode and the Concept of Social Function

Let us first consider the political system from the functionalist point of view. The concept of social function is directly derived from biology. Every living organism is characterized by a specific activity (life) and by a characteristic structure, every diversification in this structure fulfilling, by definition, an organic function as long as it contributes to the maintenance of the vital activity of the whole. Sociological functionalism, after working its way into the social sciences—where it first served to classify the main functions of collective life: production, exchange, social control, and so forth [15]—soon acquired, thanks to the ethnologists, a meaning at once more general and more specific. In the broader sense, every significant element of the objective or subjective structure of a society or of its culture tends to fulfill a social function.[16] The attitudes of a nation toward its own birthrate have the function of ensuring its demographic equilibrium. The political ideology of a dominant social class justifies its position in relation to other classes and makes it seem in conformity with the "natural" order of things or with the prevailing morality. Magic humanizes the universe by providing formulae likely to attract the attention of good or evil powers, and so forth.

Having very broadly delimited sociological functionalism, it remains to define political functionalism, which is only a particular aspect of functionalism applied to the social sciences. Nobody contests the fact that the political centers of society fulfill a function, but what exactly is this function? As we have already implied, the function of political power consists, in our opinion, of resolving social problems that the people, left to their own devices, would not be able to solve, or might attempt to solve only by jeopardizing the group's cohesion.

This concept immediately raises the problem of why certain social problems are considered of political importance by the government, while the solution of other problems, apparently

15. Hence, the classical concept of the division of functions.

16. As in the physico-mathematical sciences, it is a question of studying the relationships of the parts to the whole, but according to modalities characteristic of living organisms. These are not found as such in the study of true material systems.

just as important, is left to the people. The question solves itself as soon as the attitude adopted by the people toward these problems is considered instead of their intrinsic nature. A social problem becomes a political one as soon as the actual or potential disturbances created by the situation that led to the problem induces all or part of the people to turn to the public authorities and demand a solution. In the nineteenth century, an economic crisis was hardly considered as posing political problems. Today, it does raise governmental problems, because the people, or at least some of them, demand governmental intervention in order to solve, by political decision, the social difficulties relating to this phenomenon.[17]

Engaging in political functionalism involves consideration of the most diverse social situations from the point of view of the political problems that they raise, or are likely to raise, for the government. Political "decisions" are seen as more or less necessary solutions or elements of solutions to the problems concerned. This means, still more broadly speaking, studying political centers by considering their social functions, the changes that may modify these functions, and the transformations that tend to occur in an evolving society when the nature of the problems posed for the government is also modified, thus entailing a correlative modification of the types of solution previously applied.

The usefulness of this concept for political research needs justification. The functionalist approach has, first of all, profoundly modified the relationship between the observer of political life and the phenomena observed. As long as the political scientist's reasoning is based on variables, he can view the observed phenomenon from a distance, thus putting the stress on the formal aspect of his objectivity. On the other hand, when he becomes preoccupied with the manner in which the government fulfills its social function of attempting to resolve the problems posed by the people, the research scholar tends to look at things from the same point of view as the government. The result, and

17. Thus, there are no theoretical limits to the sphere of governmental competence: the delimitation of this sphere is not a question of principle but of social attitudes. Most social problems are not political by nature. There are only political problems by agreement, it being understood that the more a social situation causes, or threatens to cause, serious disorders, the more chances there are of an agreement between some subjects and some rulers that these disorders pose a political problem.

this is another aspect of its usefulness, is that political functionalism helps to explain the "why" of phenomena whose "how" has been explained by analysis based on interaction between political variables. This partial elimination of the distance between the observer and the observed phenomenon reveals to him what might be called the human aspects of political objectivity, since one can never judge men's actions more objectively than when one puts oneself in their place.

Political functionalism is, finally, an interdisciplinary method of reasoning particularly well-adapted to the synthesizing discipline of political science. The study of a phenomenon as complex as decolonization brings into play the whole range of the social sciences—from sociology to political economy—by way of ethnology, social psychology, and the theory of underdevelopment. Under these conditions, the concept of political problem appears to be the simplest common denominator of the enormous mass of heterogeneous data that the research scholar must integrate in order to demonstrate the mechanism of a colonial crisis. It enables him to isolate, almost automatically, the political aspects of the nonpolitical elements of the phenomenon under study. This eliminates the necessity of an exhaustive study of those aspects of the phenomenon with which his research is not directly concerned.

It is with these three particular advantages in mind that the functionalist argument has been employed in the second volume of this work.

The Logico-Mathematical Mode and the Concept of Sociological Law

Let us now see how the concept of law, or, if one prefers, of functional relation between variables, has permeated the social sciences after acquiring its classic significance in the physical sciences, and by what devices the study of objective interactions uniting the major sociological variables has tended to become an orthodox method of interpretation in the social and political sciences.

In classical terms, the elaboration of physical theories and the discovery of laws which form their basic structure assumes the existence of a certain determinism as well as the use of a ready-made arsenal of general principles, of units of magnitude, and of mathematical operations indicating how the physical quantities should be dealt with. Mathematical physics would be meaningless if material phenomena did not follow a fixed pattern. It would not be an exact science if it were not based upon general principles, such as those of inertia, least action, and conservation; upon technical concepts such as mass, temperature, time; and upon mathematical operations capable of providing ad hoc connections between the numerical expressions of these concepts—functions, derivatives, differentials, integrals, and others.

The same applies, in some respects, to the social sciences. True, social phenomena display only *formal* analogies with material phenomena. Even when they are quantitative, sociological theories can thus only offer analogies with physico-mathematical theories. Nevertheless, these analogies are sufficient to establish, in both cases, the similarity of explanatory procedures. Like classical physics, sociology assumes that the phenomena belonging to its field of research involve a certain determinism. Like the exact sciences, it tends to seek basic principles, to develop a special vocabulary, and to relate these technical concepts by propositions having the form of laws. Each of these points requires separate analysis.

IN REGARD TO DETERMINISM

A full demonstration of sociological determinism would fall outside the scope of this introduction. It is enough to bear in mind that human societies could neither remain true to their own image during a period of equilibrium, nor transform themselves by shifting from one typical form to another during a period of evolution, if the behavior of the individuals belonging to these societies were not determined, to a certain extent, by their psychic make-up as social beings and by the multiple influence that collective living has upon them. Human societies would not exist if their members behaved in a completely random fashion. Moreover, social sciences postulate this determinism, since they all attempt, in one way or another, to reduce the disorder engendered by our immediate knowledge of social facts to a specific and, to a certain extent, inevitable order.

A sociology that did not postulate the determinism of its subject matter would have no raison d'être. The real question is not whether or not there is sociological determinism, but rather how sociological determinism differs from the determinism governing material phenomena. A problem of such complexity can only be resolved by degrees through the discussion of increasingly significant examples. It is from this point of view that the theoretical ideas we have developed concerning the decolonization of Morocco should be considered.

IN REGARD TO CONCEPTS

Again following the example set by the physical sciences, sociology has gradually developed a lexicon of special concepts without which it would be impossible to study its subject matter and to formulate the regularities disclosed by the study of social phenomena.

In sociology, a concept such as *attitude* plays a technical role similar to that played in physics by the concept of *mass*. Mass is a concept derived from everyday language which, under the exigencies of theory, has gradually become endowed with a precise and abstract meaning. In the physico-mathematical sense of the term, mass is no longer a thing, it is a coefficient and, more generally, a magnitude. Mass in itself is not important for classical mechanics: it is the relationship between this magnitude and the other magnitudes usually associated with it. The sociological concept of attitude is also derived from everyday speech. It grew more abstract as it became specialized and has gradually acquired a more and more precise meaning. Here again, the study of attitudes is important only to the extent that it permits expression of the sociological relationships among the components of the social structure. Like physical mass, an attitude is an abstract entity that is normally used only as the expression of a relationship.

Close as these two concepts may be from the point of view of their respective roles, they do differ on two essential points. Mass is a measurable factor, while attitudes are not, although this has not prevented sociologists from overcoming the problem by enumerating attitudes and ranking them according to intensity. Furthermore, while mass is a clearly defined concept, a definition of the concept of attitude has yet to receive unqualified acceptance by all sociologists. This further limits the technical significance of this concept.

Nevertheless, the fact remains that the special modalities of sociological reasoning would lose most of their utility if the social sciences did not have at their disposal a vocabulary capable of qualifying with sufficient precision the data upon which analysis is based. The concepts of *system, factor, action,* and *reaction* are probably the most common categories in quasi-mathematical sociological language. The concepts of *power, authority, decision,* and *force* are the principal variables of objective political science. The concepts of *situation, attitude, motivation,* and *ideology* are, mutatis mutandis, the principal variables of political psychology. As for the more general concepts of *culture, structure, productivity,* and *underdevelopment,* they are of no direct interest to political science, but must be taken into account in any attempt to place the study of a political phenomenon within the broader sociological context of which it is a part.

IN REGARD TO PRINCIPLES

The phenomena exhibited by social systems have certain general characteristics capable of expression as principles. These principles, which are at the same time points of departure and analytic guidelines, tend to play a role similar to that played in physics by its basic principles. Among the basic principles of political sociology are the concepts of *factor, action,* and *reaction.*

Factors are the constituent elements of social systems, forming the active or passive framework of interacting influences within these systems. Power, beliefs, ideologies, attitudes, behaviors, techniques, and so forth are factors in this sense.[18]

Actions are the characteristic influences that these factors exer-

18. There is no more practical difference between the sociological concepts of *factor* and *variable* than between the physical concept of *magnitude* and the mathematical concept of *variable.* The gap is of the same order when it comes to method. A physical magnitude such as mass is a fragment of a phenomenon, an element of reality turned by abstraction into an autonomous entity. The corresponding variable is only the mathematical concept, the X which expresses numerically the modifications that may affect the size of this magnitude. The same is true in sociology where *factor* is the element of reality and the *variable* only a concept of ordinary speech expressing the actual transformations undergone by the factor.

cise upon one another. The reverse action exercised by an influenced factor upon an influencing factor is called the reaction of the influenced factor upon the influencing factor. Actions and reactions within the social systems may be abstract or concrete, depending upon whether their supporting factors are abstract or concrete. It is also just as legitimate and generally acceptable to speak of the action of a need upon a technique or of a technique upon a belief as it is to speak of the action exerted by one individual upon another.

While no formulation of the general principles of sociology has ever been systematically attempted (at least, not to our knowledge), current theories tend to be based more or less explicitly on two essential principles: the principle of global interdependence of factors within the social context, and the principle of reciprocity of actions. We believe it is both possible and desirable to increase these principles to four by adding a principle of inequality of actions and a principle of subordination of the reaction to the action. Only a brief explanation of these four principles will be given here.

The principle of *the global interdependence of factors* means that at any moment every sociological factor is potentially under the influence of the totality of the other factors constituting the system to which it belongs, and, reciprocally, that the system is itself at any moment potentially under the influence of each of its constituent factors. This does not mean that the web of possible interaction which is coextensive with every sociological system is activated every time a phenomenon occurs within the system. The determination of the extent to which this plexus is activated by a given phenomenon is a purely factual question. Nevertheless, the number of social factors to be taken into consideration when accounting for a particular phenomenon is usually very large. Most of the errors of interpretation committed by sociology in the course of its development are the results of a failure to grasp this primary principle, either because one particular factor was treated as the only relevant one (monism) or because, within the framework of pluralistic interpretations, some factors were ignored that should not have been.

The principle of *the reciprocity of actions* is only a corollary of the preceding principle. It means that within social systems there is no one-way action. Every action exercised by factor A upon factor B implies a reverse action of B upon A. There is another classical mistake made by those who do not take into account this second principle, thus losing sight of the fact that the action of one social factor upon another can only be meaningfully incorporated in the theory of the phenomenon in which they are both involved to the extent that the reverse action of the influenced factor upon the influencing factor is also taken into account.

The principle of *the inequality of actions* implies that the interactions of sociological factors combining to produce a given phenomenon are not, generally speaking, of equal strength. The strength of an action can be measured by its effects. To say that factor A exercises an action of maximum strength upon factor B means that B's activity is entirely attributable to the action exercised by A over B. To say that A exercises a low-powered action upon C means that only a small part of C's activity is attributable to the action exercised by A over C. Thus there are, in social systems, strong and weak factors, strong and weak actions, and, consequently, strong and weak systems of action. This third principle is no less important than the first two. The significance of a sociological theory depends in the last analysis on the way in which it weighs the relative influences that the factors concerned exercise upon one another. Any political analysis is likely to be invalidated if the strength of the action exercised by society upon its government is underestimated, or if the government's capacity for action upon the society is overestimated.

Finally, the principle of *the subordination of the reaction to the action* means that to the extent that factor A acts upon factor B, the reaction exercised by B upon A appears as subordinate to the action from which it springs, so that events transpire as if A were acting upon itself through the intermediary of B.[19] The

19. Given two related sociological actions, the problem of deciding which should be considered as the reaction is partly an arbitrary decision. The situation is similar in the field of mathematical laws where, given two variables, the choice of the independent variable is partly determined by the nature of the experiment from which conclusions are to be drawn, and by the more or less arbitrary method devised by the experimenter to analyze the phenomena. If the influence of society upon the government is to be considered as the main action, the reverse action of the government upon society becomes

enunciation of this principle obviously becomes more complicated as the number of factors involved grows larger. If A and B
act upon C and if C reacts upon A and B, events transpire either
as if each of the factors A and B had acted upon itself through
the intermediary of C, or as if A and B had interacted, through
C, depending upon whether their actions were reflected back
upon themselves by C or, on the contrary, "crossed" in C in
order to influence the opposite factor through C.

As political science and sociology are mutually coextensive,
these four sociological principles are automatically transformed
into principles of political science, once political factors or politically oriented factors are substituted for the sociological factors
involved in the statement of the problem. For example, if we
consider society S, governed by political organs p, the separation
of S from p automatically reveals the two complex sociological
factors (S-p) and p.

The principle of the global interdependence of factors within
the whole makes it certain that all the factors constituting the
social system S have a tendency to become involved in the creation of *political* phenomena affecting the interaction of (S-p)
and p.

The principle of the reciprocity of actions ensures that there
inevitably will be an action of (S-p) upon p and an inverse
action of p upon (S-p).

The principle of the inequality of actions finds its application
in the fact that the action of (S-p) upon p and the reaction of p
upon (S-p) are not of equal strength. In fact, it is always true
that the way in which a power p imposes its norms on the
totality of social behavior characteristic of the social root-sign (S-
p) depends more upon the nature of these behaviors than these
behaviors themselves depend upon the normative activity of p. To
make this proposition intuitive one can say that each internal
sociological factor in the social root-sign (S-p) tends to depend
more upon the totality of the other factors constituting (S-p)

---

the reaction. When the actions are of an equal force, the two formulations come to the
same thing. When the two actions are not of equal force, it may be preferable to
consider the stronger action as the principal one and the action exercised by the weaker
on the stronger as the reaction, but there is no reason why the reverse assumption
cannot be made if it is adhered to.

than upon power p. The activity of power p tends, on the contrary, to depend more upon the factors inherent in $(S\text{-}p)$ than upon whatever may be sociologically unconditioned in the activity of the government. The partial independence of p in relation to $(S\text{-}p)$ naturally can limit the action exercised by $(S\text{-}p)$ over p but is incapable of taking its place. This can be shown by an example. Let us consider an internal factor of $(S\text{-}p)$ such as the political attitudes of the people toward a decision affecting their social situation made by the power p. There is little doubt that this attitude a depends, to a certain extent, upon p. But it depends far more upon other sociological factors with which it is normally associated in the root-sign $(S\text{-}p)$: political ideologies, norms contained in habitual social activities, and, especially, social situations. This basic dissymmetry is expressed by the principle of the disparity between action and reaction. Government and society are in a state of constant interaction, in which society is normally the victor. One can express the disparity between these two actions by letting A represent $(S\text{-}p)$ and b represent p, the upper case A indicating that the root-sign $(S\text{-}p)$ is the strong factor, and the lower case indicating that the political factor p is weak as compared with $(S\text{-}p)$.

This rough justification of the inequality of sociological actions between government and society is not in itself sufficient. The mere statement that the action of government upon society is not as strong as that of society upon government is not enough. It must also be shown that the nature and varying intensity of the reaction of government upon society are essentially dependent upon the stronger action of society upon government. This is where the fourth principle comes in. It implies that, to the extent that the social root-sign $(S\text{-}p)$ conditions the normative activity of the political centers p, the normative reaction exerted by p over $(S\text{-}p)$ itself depends on the main action exerted by $(S\text{-}p)$ over p. Let us now consider the mutual but disparate interaction of $(S\text{-}p)$ and of p, or, more simply, of society A and its ruling center b. To say that A acts strongly upon b is tantamount to saying that the action exerted by A upon b strongly conditions b's activity.[20] To state that b reacts weakly upon A is tantamount

20. Strongly but not entirely. A part of the activity of a politician is always free of all social conditioning.

to stating, conversely, that the activity of political centers b exercises a weaker control or a weaker conditioning effect upon the activity of the social root-sign A. The reaction of the political center b upon the social complex A is thus identified with b's activity, itself strongly influenced by A; it follows that b can only have a significant effect upon society A insofar as A provides its own political centers b with the possibility of affecting it.[21] In the final analysis, this is what the concept of social control implies. The proposition that the government of a society exercises social control means that this society controls itself through its government, and not that the government has an unconditional and unlimited control over society.

The application to political science of the principle of the subordination of reaction to action does not provide a means of determining the absolute value of the capacity for authority in a given society at a given moment. This principle merely states that it is society that determines the value of this capacity, not the government. Relatively speaking, this capacity may be very strong (Stalin) or very weak (the Fourth Republic). The fourth principle merely teaches us that it does not rest with those who are invested with a given capacity for authority to modify it arbitrarily.

The result is—and this corollary of the fourth principle is essential to the understanding of political phenomena—that *the government of a society is obviously incapable of endowing itself with the additional authority required to make decisions falling beyond its usual scope.* Under the Fourth Republic, Guy Mollet could make decisions A and B. The prevailing system did not enable him to make decision C. The head of the Fifth Republic, General de Gaulle, can make decisions A, B, and C. The present state of French society does not enable him to make decision D. General de Gaulle's capacity is superior to Guy Mollet's, since he can make decisions that Guy Mollet could not make. But, like his predecessor, he is conditioned, and incapable of endowing himself with a capacity for authority superior to the one granted him by the existing situation; his personal prestige and his grasp

21. Excluding that part of the government's activity not conditioned by A.

of problems are, of course, included in his usual decision-making capacity.

The proposition that the authority potential of the political leaders depends upon the political attitudes of the subjects would be completely meaningless if the political leaders could manipulate the attitudes of the subjects to reinforce their own authority arbitrarily, neutralizing, as it were, resistance on the part of the people. Once again, in the balance sheet of this internal interaction, society must take precedence over the government. It is the essence of political phenomena that government depends more upon the sociological factors conditioning its authority than that these factors depend upon the government itself. The way in which the government is sociologically conditioned varies according to societies and circumstances. This conditioning itself is largely immune to governmental action. It is possible to imagine a political universe where things would be different. However, a political science that escaped the constraints of the third and fourth principles would be unable to provide an adequate explanation of political phenomena as revealed by experience.

In our opinion, a recognition of the relatively limited capacity for action available to a government within a given social context is essential for a full understanding of the mechanism of social conflicts. Since these conflicts are indissolubly linked to certain failures of authority, one's view of their mechanism will depend essentially upon the question of whether these failures are considered as inevitable or accidental. In the present state of political science, inevitability cannot be proven but it can be postulated, and it can be shown that the consequences of this postulate in the actual situation are more in accordance with experience than those derived from the inverse postulate.[22]

---

22. The same is true in mechanics, where it is impossible to attempt a demonstration of the principle of inertia without postulating its validity. The formulation of the principles referred to above is to a great extent the author's own. Although it may be basically valid, the very provisional manner in which the principles are elaborated and supported raises many problems of interpretation. If we have decided to publish this essay in its present state, though unquestionably it would have benefited from further development and precision, it is because, rightly or wrongly, we found it impossible to work on any other basis. In these circumstances it seemed preferable to us to make the major elements in the argument explicit rather than to submit the results to the reader without any explanation.

Once the political system is accepted as being a complex of
variables, it is immediately apparent that it is made up of three
successive levels of factors: the first level is that of the *situation* of
the various groups among the governed; the second level is that
of the *attitudes* adopted by these groups toward the government,
the most important being *consent* and *opposition*; the third level
is that of *political authority* and its principal attribute, force.[23]

Quite apart from the fact that all the variables in the political
system exercise a reciprocal influence over each other, this system
is based upon two main relationships: that linking the political
attitudes of the people to the collective situations that condition
them, and that linking the decision-making and force-using
capacity of the system's leaders to the political attitudes (consent
and opposition) upon which this capacity depends. The capacity
for authority in a political system is thus primarily a function of
collective attitudes, and secondarily a function of the collective
situations that condition these attitudes. It is essential that these
two relationships be analyzed in some detail and that problems
of interpretation they create be defined.

The Situation-Political Attitudes Relationship

Electoral sociology of democratic regimes has familiarized
political science specialists with the idea that the political attitudes of people are largely conditioned by their social situation.
Since these attitudes are generally expressed by votes in democratic regimes and since votes are publicly counted, mathema-
ticians have been able to apply statistical analysis to the overall
correlations between each group of people and the various political attitudes that characterize their members. In addition, it has
been apparent that the distribution of political attitudes within
each social class is influenced by a very large number of factors
(i.e. standard of living, religion, regional peculiarities, historical
traditions, etc.) whose relative influence is generally impossible to
determine with any precision. We know how the different social

23. At this stage, the ideological factor will be excluded in order not to complicate
the introductory essay unduly.

classes vote in a democracy. We do not know the relative importance of the different situational factors conditioning the distribution of votes, nor the mechanism governing the transformation of these systems of political attitudes over a period of time. Above all, we do not know why this evolution seems to have as its fixed limits a state of affairs in which conservatives and progressives tend, under various names, to come into equilibrium. This phenomenon betrays the democratic elector's fundamental opposition to any political solution that will subordinate him to a permanent absolute majority, whatever it may be. The full significance of this has yet to be explained.

Similar problems exist in regimes that are not governed by democratic procedures. Among them, colonial systems undergoing decolonization are of particular interest to us. The attitudes of the various social groups in Moroccan society during the conflict were just as much conditioned by their social situation as they would have been had colonial Morocco been a democracy; however, the modalities of this conditioning are not identical with those observed in a representative system. This fact presents both advantages and disadvantages for the student of the political sociology of decolonization. The disadvantage stems from the fact that, generally speaking, in systems of this type, attitudes are not expressed through votes. Therefore, the correlation of attitudes and social groups can only be made in an approximate nonnumerical manner. The advantage is that in a decolonization crisis, the correlation of the situational factors conditioning an attitude, with the different elements of the attitude itself, can be made in a much simpler and much more satisfactory manner than in a democratic regime. While the precise correlations studied in electoral sociology of democracies generally raise problems of interpretation too complex to be completely explained, the rough correlations of political sociology within the context of decolonization reveal a simple split in society along the lines of two dominant attitudes: the anticolonialism of the indigenous population, and the conservatism of the settlers, with marginal groups in each faction having an attitude opposed to the prevailing current of opinion. We have precise knowledge of the voting patterns in a democracy, but our knowledge of why democratic citizens vote as they do is still very limited. We know even less about the exact degree of correlation between the political attitudes and the collective situations of subjects under a colonial regime, but we can analyze these correlations more meaningfully, particularly in periods of crisis, when their significance becomes obvious.

Whatever the political regime and the social environment, the attempt to relate political attitudes to collective situations raises four problems: (1) the enumeration and classification of attitudes characterizing each social group; (2) the overall correlations between social situations and the systems of attitudes based upon them; (3) the factor by factor interpretation of these correlations; and (4) the clarification of the mechanism by which these systems of attitudes evolve as a function of changes in the situations under examination. Electoral sociology of democratic systems resolves the first two problems beautifully, but it fails in regard to the third, thus making it impossible to deal with the fourth. Political sociology of decolonization evades the first, solves the second qualitatively, but perceives more or less satisfactorily the solution of the last two. These four problems will be examined in detail in the analyses that follow this introduction.

The Authority-Force-Political Attitudes Relationship

If the basis of political analysis is the relationship expressing a political system's consent and opposition potential as a function of the situation of the principal groups among the people, the complementary relationship expressing the system's authority as a function of its potential for obtaining support and using force leads straight to the heart of the problems of political science. The fact that Vilfredo Pareto gave an extremely clear description of the course to be followed in studying this second relationship makes it even more astonishing that so far the discipline has shown so little interest in doing so. In a famous passage from his *Mind and Society,* Pareto writes:

> Ignoring exceptions, which are few in number and of short duration, one finds everywhere a governing class of relatively few individuals that keeps itself in power partly by force, and partly by the consent of the subject

class, which is much more populous. The differences lie principally, as regards substance, in the relative proportions of force and consent; and as regards forms in the manner in which the force is used and the consent obtained.[24]

These few lines, in which every phrase is crucial, summarize all there is to be studied on the upper echelon of the political system.

Explicitly or implicitly, this extraordinarily pregnant text brings four well-known variables into play: authority, force, consent, and opposition.[25] Some further elaboration will be necessary if these fundamental concepts are to be succinctly defined. It is generally agreed that *political authority* consists of the ability to induce the people to do or not to do certain things, to express or not to express certain feelings, and even to think or not to think in a certain way, by means of persuasion or force, most often an appropriate combination of both. *Force* is the government's capacity to constrain, a capacity that rests upon the spontaneous or ordered obedience of the selected groups to which the government has devolved its monopoly of the material means for enforcement. Its purpose is to intimidate those who might be tempted to disobey the government, to ensure that the people fulfill their public obligations, and to prevent those who have infringed the norms sanctioned by the government from doing damage. *Consent* and *opposition* are political attitudes or, if one prefers, predispositions to obey or to disobey the orders of authority.

While it is relatively easy to formulate an adequate definition of authority or of force, the same does not apply to consent and opposition, since these two variables lie along the same continuum, and only an artificial distinction can be made between them. In fact, properly speaking, an individual or group attitude

24. Vilfredo Pareto, *Mind and Society*, Eng. trans. Andrew Bongiorno and Arthur Livingston (New York, Dover Publications, 1958), para. 2244. It should be noted that we are more concerned with the relationship between those who govern and the mass of the population than with the relationship between the upper and lower classes within society.

25. In French, *consensus* and *consentement* are practically synonymous. In English, however, "consensus" is not synonymous with "consent." In the present edition, "consent" is used in the special sense defined below.

toward a governmental decision should be described by two numbers, one giving the consensual elements of the attitude and the other its oppositional elements. The people rarely fully consent or fully oppose. Generally speaking, they do both at the same time. Thus, if the pairs of numbers expressing the consensual and oppositional factors in an individual or group attitude are recorded on a graduated axial segment, the extreme points of this segment will represent, respectively, the point of maximum consent and no opposition and the point of maximum opposition and no consent. These two extreme stages are separated by an infinite number of intermediary stages characterized by decreasing consent and increasing opposition. In our opinion, *consent* corresponds to that half of the segment symbolized by a tendency to obey which is only marginally affected by a tendency to oppose. Reciprocally, *opposition* corresponds to that half of the segment symbolized by a tendency to disobey which is only marginally affected by a residual tendency to consent.[26]

As an initial approximation, the interactions among the variables just defined can be expressed in terms of the following propositions easily deduced from a simple observation of the facts of political life:

> Political authority is a function of consent; it tends to increase when consent increases in number and intensity; it decreases as the consent changes to opposition.

> Political authority is, furthermore, a function of governmental force; it increases or decreases as this force increases or decreases.

> Governmental force, in turn, is a function of the consent of the specialized groups that apply it, and of the groups of the governed to which it is applied and from among

26. Thus authority does not depend solely upon the variable ratio between consent and opposition characteristic of the political attitudes of the ordinary people. It depends still more upon the varying tendencies toward consent and opposition displayed by the agents of the government which bring the force to bear. Furthermore, it may become increasingly dependent upon the attitude of foreign groups whose reactions have an influence on the decision-making ability of national governments. One should add that it is useless to make opposition explicit when reasoning in terms of consent, since the increase or decrease of consent automatically implies a reciprocal effect on the degree of opposition.

which government agents are recruited; it increases or decreases according to variations in the consent-opposition ratio within these two types of groups.

Governmental force is also a function of authority; in civilian as well as military affairs, it increases or decreases according to whether the government exercises its authority well or badly over the particular groups that are its agents for enforcement.

Inversely, the consent of the people and of the government agents is a function of force. Within certain limits, recourse to force can neutralize opposing elements inhibiting consent, and enhance the residual tendencies to agree that coexist with the individual's opposition, thus ensuring greater obedience.

Social consent, finally, is a function of political authority insofar as governmental force is held constant. This means that the government is not incapable of influencing the people's attitudes, even when it decides not to increase existing sanctions for ensuring obedience. News, propaganda, and the indirect rectification of social attitudes through the manipulation of the juridical norms conditioning them are the principal methods employed for this purpose.

Independently of these three pairs of relationships, political authority also depends upon the nature of the regime exercising it. Political authority is not the result of a simple numerical combination of the consensual and oppositional attitudes displayed toward it. Every regime tends to combine these attitudes according to a more or less false scale. It maximizes the consent and the opposition of certain groups, and minimizes the consent and opposition of others. This tendency to maximize and minimize consent is what can be called the regime's *authority structure*. This determines the relative importance that the political system attributes to each social group, or, if one prefers, the sensitivity of the political institution to the attitudes of the various groups of citizens.

Using quasi-mathematical language, political authority appears to be, generally speaking, a function of a constant,[27] the authority structure of the regime, and of two related variables, consent and force. This relationship, in turn, calls for some interpretation to make it possible to define the authority structure's role in political questions.

If the government's authority and resort to force were too directly dependent upon the consent it enjoyed, the government would be incapable of dealing with a drop in its reserves of consent. A decrease in consent would compel it to increase the amount of force being used and at the same time make it incapable of achieving this increase. Normally and within certain limits, political systems use two devices to maintain their authority potential at the required level when their consensual base decreases. A government can ensure a normal authority potential disproportionate to its consent so that its authority decreases less rapidly than social consent. This goal is usually achieved, as we have already implied, by minimizing the political influence of the least favored social groups or those least friendly to the regime, and by maximizing the political influence of the most favored social groups and those most favorable to the regime. The means used by a democracy to this end are: electoral qualifications, weighted voting, disproportional representation, and recruitment of state employees among certain privileged classes. Totalitarian regimes merely stretch this process to its limits when they keep entire groups of citizens beyond the political pale to make opposition less of a threat to their own authority. Secondly, governments can seek to ensure a proportionately greater capacity to use force than the increase in authority obtained by the first device, in such a way that their capacity for resorting to the use of force decreases less rapidly than the additional authority. Normally, a government achieves this second goal by exercising stronger authority over its executive agents than it does over the rest of its subjects. This is achieved by submitting them to a rigorous discipline, by modifying their spontaneous attitudes by

27. It would be more exact to say that in many political phenomena, the authority structure may be regarded as a constant. Then one would argue on the basis of a constant authority structure. In other phenomena, however, the authority structure appears as a variable.

strict training, and by recruiting them from the most loyal social classes, which, it has reason to hope, will continue to back it when all others have yielded to the temptations of the opposition. This brings us back, in a roundabout manner, to the previous method.

Despite use of these two devices, there is a point beyond which force can no longer compensate for a massive drop in consent. This phenomenon inevitably occurs either when the groups upon whose support the use of force depends join the opposition, or when virtually the whole society unites against a police force and an army still loyal to a regime that considers itself incapable of restoring order by a reign of terror. The first situation applies mainly to revolutionary opposition to a national regime. The second is particularly applicable to revolutionary opposition to an occupying power. It is therefore of direct concern to the theory of decolonization. The relative subordination of governmental force to social attitudes, the fact that force depends more upon consent than consent depends upon force, is one of the keys of political science. When a drop in the consensual capacity of a political system can no longer be compensated for by an ad hoc increase of available strength, the system has reached its breaking point. Its decision-making capacity no longer meets its needs. The relative strength of its domestic opponents has inevitably increased as its own strength has decreased; it is no longer capable of controlling them, and a revolutionary situation ensues.

Since a colonial regime borrows some of its characteristics from authoritarian regimes and others from consensual forms of government, it might be well to indicate here how the authority structures of democratic and authoritarian regimes influence their respective capacities for authority. This will make it easier to understand the part played by this essential factor when we deal with the decolonization of Morocco.

Let us consider a modern democracy functioning under ideal conditions. It is apparent that the *authority-force-consent* relationship materializes in the following manner:

The consent of virtually the entire population is the obvious and exclusive source of the regime's authority.

This consent is also the source of the force at the government's disposal, since this force has no other possible base than the consent of those applying it and of those to whom it is applied. This force plays two essential roles. The first is to bring to order the few individuals who infringe upon the estabished norms. The second is to stabilize and consolidate the consent of the vast majority of individuals who support the existing norms; the principal mark of a good citizen is fear of the police.

The regime is representative in form, which means that all social groups take part in the government both because of existing electoral procedures and because the various arms of the state (army, police, civil service) are normally recruited from every social class.

Obviously, a regime of this type can only work on the basis of general consent: any revolutionary alienation of society would result in a corresponding alienation both of the consensual basis of governmental authority and of the political organs (army, police, civil service), which incarnate the authority and are the direct sources of its capacity to use force.

Under these conditions, variations in the authority of the regime considered as a function of the factors in question can be expressed as follows:

Maximum governmental authority and force correspond to a maximum social consent implying a negligible number of revolutionary opponents.

Governmental authority and force are nonexistent when social consent is split, with half the population in revolt against the other half, while the political organs are paralyzed by a parallel division in their own ranks.

Governmental authority and force go from the maximum to the minimum between these two limits as the number of revolutionary opponents approaches 50 percent of the population.

Three complementary remarks are needed for an understanding of this phenomenon:

1. Before a loss of consent becomes disastrous for a democratic government, it has to involve a challenge to the very existence of the regime. As long as the majority and the opposing minority accept the regime, consent is by definition complete and no unusual problem arises.

2. The loss of consent is even more serious in a democracy because it is irremediable. A democratic regime presupposes universal consent. By definition, it is incapable of restoring a diminishing consent by recourse to authority, since the greater the decrease in consent and force, the less authority the regime will be able to wield over the people. This is a particular instance of the principle of the subordination of reaction to action.

3. The determinism of the phenomenon is particularly apparent in the extreme case when the collectivity is split in two by a revolutionary struggle: two social groups of the same size confront each other within the context of a power relationship; that cancels out the political capacity of the group defending itself within the framework of the regime and favors to the utmost the political capacity of the group attacking it. In the end, leaving historical accidents aside, the result is that the revolutionary group will be in a much stronger position than its opponents since the latter are dependent upon a paralyzed state while the former is based upon its *sui generis* capacity to destroy public order.

Let us now consider a typical revolutionary regime during the nascent phase of tensions. The *authority-consent-force* relationship here appears in a form which, in some respects, is very different from the preceding one. From the beginning, the society finds itself split into two violently opposed factions, one of them seeking to achieve the forcible liquidation of the traditional way of life of the other. Under these conditions:

> The revolutionary regime's authority depends only upon the consent of that fraction of society it represents. The opposing fraction is kept outside of the political system.

The numerically restricted but unswerving consent of those social groups supporting the revolution is, moreover, the only possible source of the force available to the revolutionary government. However, this does not prevent this force from having an impact upon the consent. Once again, governmental force fulfills its two essential roles, but in a fashion which is qualitatively and quantitatively different from that typifying its action in a democracy. Its first task is to impose an evolving social order no longer upon a small group of individual opponents but upon a massive opposition that includes a large section, perhaps even a majority, of the population, even if it is not the most organized. Its second role is to strengthen the consent of the revolutionary fraction by applying unlimited coercive pressure, made necessary by the exigencies of political discipline inevitable in a civil war.

The regime is not representative because of its authoritarian form and because the social groups supporting the revolution are the only ones to participate in the government, the organs of government (the army, police, etc.) generally being recruited from among supporters, although in the early states they may be reinforced by renegades from the old privileged classes.

Such a regime does not require universal consent to keep itself in power. The consent of the social classes with which it shares a common interest is enough. It is designed to destroy opposition ab initio. Opposition, therefore, cannot affect its stability, although opposing groups can display an astonishing capacity for passive resistance.

Despite variations, the fluctuations of authority which typify this second kind of political system remain similar in form to those during the cohesive phase. Authority always appears as a function of social consent and of force on the condition—and this reservation is critical—that the relationship in question involves only the regime and its partisans. This relationship may be expressed as follows:

Governmental authority and force will be at their maximum when maximum consent prevails within the revolutionary fraction of society alone; to simplify matters, the opposing faction's capacity for passive resistance has not been taken into account.

Governmental authority and force are at their minimum when the political dissociation of the revolutionary fraction and of the instruments of power emanating from it (army, police, political structures, civil service, etc.) is at its maximum.

Governmental authority and force decrease as the political dissociation of the revolutionary fraction of the society increases vis-à-vis the government.

Thus both the democratic and revolutionary regimes confirm the law of political authority, but this law operates differently in each case. Democracy is organized on the basis of a general or assumed consent and does everything to maintain it, but it ceases to function normally when consent diminishes. Regimes based on force are organized on the basis of a consent limited to one segment of society, but they endow it with de facto value of a general consent by recruiting their administrative agents exclusively from among their supporters and excluding their opponents from political participation. In certain respects, it is as if only the supporters had any political existence.[28]

28. This particular authority structure explains the mechanism of political purges. In a regime of this type, when the administrative groups upon which power is based become divided, their opposing elements are thrown into that outer darkness where subjects without any political existence are already vegetating. Thus the consent of the state's auxiliary bodies is recreated in its pristine state. But, as there has been a loss of consent, the system's equilibrium can only be maintained through an ad hoc increase in coercion. The consensual basis of the regime is thereby reduced, from purge to purge, while its coercive basis is proportionally reinforced. In the end, as during the last years of Stalin's reign, the system rests upon a consent no greater than a pinhead, and, to compensate for this weakness, upon a formidable apparatus of coercion. When a balance sheet of this kind is drawn up, one must, of course, take into account all the factors contributing to the political attitudes of the governed since their opposition to the regime is partially compensated, without any need for government intervention, by positive attitudes toward other problems. These may be relations with foreign countries, the achievement of undisputed goals of domestic progress, etc. Even during the worst period of Stalinism, the Russian people were not solely in opposition. Be that as it may, during the entire evolutionary period the sociological sum of consent and force

Political theory as we understand it is obviously threatened by a vicious circle. If the government could act only to the extent that the people agreed to obey, it would be no more than the servant of the public's whims and would lose all sociological consistency. A glance at the facts of political life indicates that this is not so. To govern is not to follow the masses. To govern is to rule. This apparent paradox is resolved when one recalls that consent does not exclude opposition, and that people always tend to obey and disobey at the same time. Two main cases deserve mention. In the first, one part of society is behind the government while the other is in revolutionary (nondemocratic) opposition (the hypothesis is the revolutionary detachment of social groups). In the second, the nation as a whole, and consequently every individual, shows a simultaneous tendency to submit and resist. This is particularly obvious in the example of tax collection. This fundamental ambivalence of popular political attitudes is essential for an understanding of the phenomena and of the theory of political authority. It means that the consent behind authority and the opposition that makes the authority necessary do not necessarily pertain to the same individuals, or in the case of a single individual to the same aspects of his personality. Authority, considered in its dual aspect of consent and coercion, is possible and necessary in the final analysis only because each member of the public is permanently afflicted by political schizophrenia. In the real sense of the term, to govern is not to follow the people, although, as we shall see later, a government whose authority is dwindling has no other choice. To govern is to rely upon the social predisposition of the people to obey in order to counteract the tendency toward opposition that the same people manifest. This is why, if the government depends upon the consent of each individual subject, the final obedience of each subject depends, in turn, upon the capacity to command and coerce invested in the government by society as a whole.[29]

We do not intend these few brief remarks about what might

remains constant, but its quality is continually reduced, this quality being at a maximum when the consent is very great and the force used very small and at a minimum when the opposite applies.

29. Political science should study two fundamentally different kinds of authority relationships: the relationship between the government and society as a whole, and the

well be described as the law of political authority to be taken to imply that this is a law in the physical or mathematical sense. Nevertheless, by definition, in everyday sociological speech "laws" are to physico-mathematical laws what "functions" are to mathematical functions. The laws of mathematical physics are imperative laws which make it possible to predict particular events or to determine their degree of empirical probability. The laws of verbal sociology are "loose" [30] laws which merely shape the general balance of the reciprocal influences between two or more non-numerical variables. Undoubtedly, these laws do permit certain broad conjectures, but their main purpose is to support the argument and to provide a frame of reference for research by revealing the different types of phenomena to be dealt with. Who would dream of studying the influence exercised by consent upon force or by the authority structure upon a system's decision-making capacity except upon the basis of quasi-mathematical argument? This does not mean that there is no further progress to be made toward quantifying these ideas. The more one can assign a numerical value to them, the more political sociology will fulfill its goal, even if this quantification is only partial, and even if improved everyday language still has to be used for some aspects of authority phenomena or for the interpretation of quantitative relationships which may have been established.

Relationships between the Two Modes and an Attempt at Their Synthesis

From a methodological point of view, modern sociology is thus simultaneously related to classical physics and to biology. From the one, it has borrowed the concept of interaction between variables, enabling it to demonstrate the manner in which the different factors involved in sociological phenomena exercise reciprocal influences upon each other.[31] From the other, it has borrowed the concept of organic function and, by transposing

---

relationship between the government and each individual subject. In the first case, society "controls" the government. In the second, the government "controls" each subject. Generally speaking, the government's authority over the individual is the greater the more closely it conforms to the needs and aspirations of society as a whole.

30. This formulation comes from Morido Inagaki, and it provides an apt commentary on the problem of sociological determinism, which is a rough, incomplete determinism.

31. In certain extreme cases and under optimum circumstances, this kind of research can lead to the formulation of a law. The mathematical concept of function is not of

this second concept into its own field, has developed a theory of social organization which overlaps the first concept and is just as valid.

The amazing thing is that sociologists rarely attempt a deliberate association between these two modes of thought to gain a deeper insight into social phenomena by playing simultaneously upon the two explanatory keyboards. Ethnology is almost entirely based on the concept of social function. Social psychology tends to reason on the basis of variables; this, however, does not prevent it from turning, when necessary, to functionalist categories. As for sociology, it is constantly oscillating between the two schools of thought. Either one is ignored completely or else they are used alternately. They are almost never combined so that a study of the *same* phenomenon can systematically profit from the particular advantages of each.[32] It would appear to be far more useful to employ them conjointly to derive all-embracing explanations.

To understand how either of these two modes of explanation can be used to study identical phenomena, it is necessary to consider the relationship existing between the concept of social *structure*[33] and the various interpretations of the concept of *function*.

---

course restricted to the laws of matter but it is especially applicable to the determinism governing those phenomena studied by classical physics.

32. Some methodologists, apparently aware of the solution of continuity that the alternating method has introduced into the growth of the social sciences, have asked themselves just how far explanations based on the concept of social function are reducible to explanations based on the concept of interaction between variables. In biology, there is no longer any need to demonstrate this since all the major organic functions can today be explained in physico-chemical terms. The studies mentioned above indicate that the same transposition is possible in sociology. Ernest Nagel in particular has shown that the *sociological* mechanism of homeostasis can be explained in terms of the physico-mathematical properties of a mechanical system and there is no doubt that this approach is subject to generalization. Methodologically, this sort of research is highly interesting, but its practical applications concern future rather than present-day sociology. In current research, there is little point to expressing sociological functionalism in physico-mathematical categories until the quantification of sociological theories has made further progress. Ernest Nagel, *Logic Without Metaphysics* (Glencoe, Ill., Free Press, 1956), pp. 247–83.

33. Here we are using the concept of structure in its mathematical sense of the relation of the part to the whole. We know that various sociologists have attempted to give more elaborate sociological definitions of this notion, but they seemed too complicated to be of use in the present case study.

The concepts of structure and function should be clearly distinguished from each other. Social systems are, first and foremost, structures. The two functionalisms (either quasi-mathematical or quasi-organic) are only modes of explanation that make it possible to undertake a scientific study of activities peculiar to these structures, or of changes affecting them.

The evolution of the biological sciences has demonstrated that the possibility of applying physico-chemical explanations to the study of the main organic functions resulted from an ambivalence inherent in the structure of living organisms. If the human body could not be simultaneously considered as an organism and as a complex of physico-chemical phenomena, biology would be unable to explain the body's activity by linking together physico-chemical magnitudes and by describing organic functions. To be precise, it is because these two aspects of the living organism are indivisible within the same structure that the association of physico-chemical and physiological reasoning is possible in biological description.

This structural ambivalence apparently stems from the fact that when a living organism is considered as a complex of organs, it has structural properties which are not apparent when this same organism is studied from the angle of physico-chemistry. In its specifically organic aspects, the structure of living beings can be defined as a relationship of the parts to the whole so that every constituent element implies the present or past existence of the entire organism. The same material structure loses these properties as soon as it is considered only as the biological location of a complex of physico-chemical factors. It is impossible to isolate the heart of a frog in a test tube unless that frog has existed in the past or still exists in some shape or form. On the other hand, no constituent atom of an organic or mineral molecule implies the past or present existence of this particular molecule. Speaking more generally, none of the physical magnitudes or chemical elements which constitute the substance of a given organism are specific to this organism.[34]

34. This distinction between physico-chemical and organic structures tends to become blurred when the lower levels of organizational life are examined. A given protein is still a macromolecular physico-chemical structure whose constituent atoms are interchangeable. But it is also a non-interchangeable element of the biochemical heritage of

Thus the living structure possesses two different and complementary aspects. Although all organic functions can be interpreted in physico-chemical terms, the physico-chemical and organic languages are still far from being equivalent in the natural sciences. It is true that the division of organic functions can be studied by using either concepts of physico-chemistry or of physiology. This does not mean that the two sets of concepts are interchangeable. The brain, the liver, the gall bladder are neither physical variables nor chemical elements. Carbohydrates, ions, and concentrates are not organs. To move from one process of reasoning to the other, the concepts of the first system must be abandoned for those of the second, and the mode of explanation must be modified.

Now one must examine the extent to which the link between the ambivalence of biological structures and the modes of biological reasoning can be rediscovered, mutatis mutandis, when one moves from biology to sociology. If sociology succeeds in combining functionalist reasoning with reasoning by variables, then it must be presumed that the social structure displays an ambivalence similar to the one displayed by organic structure. This assumption must now be justified.

The point of departure for such reasoning is identical with that in the preceding hypothesis, for as it is true that every element of an organic structure implies the existence of the entire organism, so each element of the quasi-organic structure of a society implies the existence of the whole of that society. A man-made flint produced for purposes other than entertainment cannot exist unless the society which used this tool existed or still exists. On the other hand, the social structure is also reducible to an inorganic material aspect which is disinguishable from its quasi-organic aspect by virtue of the fact that the existence of the part here no longer implies the existence of the whole. The meteorite revered as a totem by a so-called primitive culture does not imply this culture any more than a given atom implies the existence of the particular molecule of which it is accidentally a

a particular species, and it will not be found with an identical structure in other members of the same species. Although it is still a lifeless material structure, it tends to assume the value of a specific organic factor. It is not interchangeable as such, whereas a glucose is.

part. The meteorite existed before the society, and it could have existed without it; the same applies to all other material substances of which the culture is made up.[35] In this respect, there exists an unquestionable symmetry between the ambivalence of organic structures and that of the structure of societies.

Unfortunately, this first aspect of the ambivalence of the social structure is not much help to us. No doubt it is real. No doubt it conforms to the state of ambivalence which characterizes the structure of living organisms. If, despite formal analogies, it remains unusable, this is for the simple reason that sociology does not study lifeless social substances, whereas biologists normally study the physico-chemical aspects of living structures without exceeding the limits of their own discipline. Inorganic substances only concern the physical sciences. The fact that social structure is both inorganic substance and structural organization at the same time thus remains outside the scope of this analysis.

The ambivalence of social structure can only be considered from the viewpoint adopted in the present work if it remains within the order of sociological phenomena. Contrasting the quasi-organic aspect of social phenomena with their inorganic material aspect leads nowhere. If the problem is to be defined correctly, this quasi-organic aspect must be linked to a complementary structural mode which is no less social than the other.

It seems to us that current sociological analysis is based upon a structural ambivalence of this kind. Sociologists view the social structure either as a complex of quasi-organic elements which fulfill specific functions, or as a network of sociological factors in a state of constant dynamic interaction. In the first instance, social structure assumes a quasi-organic form. In the second, it appears as a quasi-physical complex. Sometimes it seems to emerge from the realm of life, and sometimes it lets itself be treated as an inert object.

35. As we have already implied, this concerns inorganic substances and not social instruments. The existence of a tool implies the existence of a society. A tool plays the role of a quasi-social organ. This is why it is possible to say that a given automobile's engine part fills a mechanical function while it would be meaningless to speak of an inorganic body's function or utility in relation to other inorganic bodies. It would be absurd to say that the moon's function is to cause tides. What does this imply if not that man-made physical structures form a part, like man himself, of the organic universe?

The ambivalence of social structure having been defined in sociological terms, it now becomes possible to reveal the connection between this structural ambivalence and the two modes of explanation which make its study possible. Social structure can be analyzed in terms of sociological functionalism because, in one respect, it appears as a quasi-organic relationship between the parts and the whole. From other points of view, this same structure appears as a complex of factors linked to each other like physical magnitudes. This is why it can also be analyzed in terms of variables and of mathematical or quasi-mathematical functions.

The relationship between the two sociological functionalisms and the two aspects of the social structure to which they are related displays two notable properties that are not found when studying the structure of living organisms. These, in our opinion, are at the root of the methodological differences between biological and sociological analysis.

The first of these properties relates to the explanatory framework. While physiological concepts as such cannot be broken down into the concepts of physico-chemical language, it would appear that the concepts of sociological functionalism can be transposed without difficulty to the domain of interactions between sociological variables. As we have already pointed out, the brain and the liver are not variables according to the meaning of the term in physico-chemical analysis. However, sociological "variables" may be viewed as structural elements having a social function. Collective attitudes and political decisions are at the same time sociological variables and elements fulfilling definite social functions.

The other property concerns the structure itself and we consider it to be basic to the understanding of the structural-functional theory of social systems. While each organ of the living being merely implies the past or present existence of the organism from which it has become separated, it is easy to see that certain pseudo-organs of the social structure are also able to signify the future as well as the past and present existence of the society to which they belong. A shattered flint usually implies a society which no longer exists. A generating plant implies today's industrial society. However, an automated factory suggests a society which does not yet exist. Organ by organ, human societies go through constant mutations, and these mutations affect their entire future.[36] It is because every structural element of society is quasi-organically linked to all the others, even in the future dimension, that the structural factors supporting the various social functions can be seen directly, and without any change in terminology, as variables. On this level of reciprocal involvement between the parts and the whole, concepts of sociological variables and of social function inevitably tend to merge. Each social quasi-organ is also a sociological variable because it can force all the others to change with it. Technology exercises a social function because it is quasi-organically linked to all the other social factors. Since it cannot change unless a readjustment of the whole of society to its material instruments also takes place, each factor of the whole is inevitably, at the same time, a function of the technological variable. It is because it exercises a *social function* within society that technology is also, in addition, a *socio-cultural variable*.[37]

36. One might be tempted to say that biological mutations are a similar type of phenomenon; this would result in putting transformism and social change on the same footing, and would be stretching the comparison too far. Mutations affecting the hereditary patrimony of a living being are extraordinary changes which affect the organic structure only through the intermediary of a gene. Social change, on the contrary, is the result of a direct modification of an element in the socio-cultural complex. The two phenomena would be comparable only if the living being mutated directly, organ by organ, and if these mutations resulted from a conscious effort of the individual or of the species to adapt to the environment. This is not the case. Considered as a specific entity, aside from any false analogies, social change thus appears as a sui generis characteristic of the social organism.

37. This essay on the integration of sociological and mathematical functionalism stems from a highly significant comment by Professor Henri Janne. After noting that the relationship between variable and function and not the causal approach was most appropriate for sociological analysis and that "in principle, *every* element should be considered successively as a variable and all the others as a function of each variable," he went on to ask in effect: what then is the nature of this mutual interdependence or of this relationship between variables? Here, Professor Janne continues, "We come across an element that has already been introduced . . . by other sociologists: the concept of function. Thus, analysis by variables and functions (the mathematical term 'function' should not be confused with the normal meaning of the word, used in a somewhat specialized way in sociology) should, in our opinion, be based on—or if one prefers used as a hypothesis—the approach designated as functional. Thus this type of analysis has a twofold claim to the title 'functional.'" Henri Janne, "Function et Finalité en Sociologie," *Cahiers Internationaux de Sociologie, 14* (1954), 51, 53. The ambivalence of functionalism is clearly illustrated in this quotation which stresses opportunely the fact that the interaction of sociological variables is *based* on the inter-

To conclude our discussion on this fairly abstract but essential aspect of our analysis, let us say that in sociology the relationship between the organic interrelationship and the interdependence of variables is the opposite of what it is in biology. In biology, organic structures emerge as a result of interaction between physico-chemical variables. In sociology, on the contrary, it is the interplay of variables which emerges from the morphological and functional correlations which bind together the various elements of a society's structure. A structural ambivalence exists in both cases, but in each case the nature and the meaning of the ambivalence are different.

Since every sociological factor thus tends[38] to appear simultaneously as a variable and as the support of a social function, every relationship between sociological variables inevitably possesses a functionalist aspect. It is just as important to study how the authority of a political regime varies as a *function* of attitudinal and situational variables which condition it, as it is to study how this regime fulfills its *social function* by using its authority to solve the social problems it faces.

Passing from one explanatory method to another is no less simple when the order is reversed and one shifts from categories of sociological functionalism to those of quasi-mathematical sociology. The function of society's political organs is to solve certain social problems by appropriate decisions. But these problems and the decisions which resolve them are also variables, since their solutions vary as a function of their specifications, and these specifications themselves vary according to the elements of the social structure which are incorporated within them.[39] The social norms are variables as well as products of the functional activity of political centers, and it is this ambivalence of the

---

dependence of social functions, the quasi-mathematical method ultimately deriving from the quasi-organic method which thus retains its primacy in the conceptual hierarchy, if not always in practice.

38. We say "tends" in order to avoid the problem of deciding whether every structural element is necessarily linked to the exercise of a social function or whether there are exceptions to the rule.

39. In this respect, the main difference between geometry and sociology is that solutions of geometrical problems are determined strictly by the problems while sociological problems only determine their solutions thematically. This leaves a considerable amount of initiative in producing variations on these themes.

categories which makes it possible to move directly, with a minimum of terminological changes, from one perspective to the other.

The association of sociological functionalism with reasoning based on variables is not only possible and useful; it is methodologically essential.[40] The dualism which has been established at the very heart of sociology since functionalism began to emerge on the fringes of the logico-mathematical approach is more than intellectually painful; it stunts the growth of the discipline by creating a competition between two modes of reasoning which should be working in unison. There is reason to believe that by combining the two methods, one is in a better position to understand phenomena which might possibly have been studied according to one method alone, but which will reveal their true complexity only when they are treated both as inanimate objects and as manifestations of human behavior. This is at least what we have in view when we plead for an enlarged structural-functional theory.

Political science, long hampered by obstacles which prevented it from developing at the same rate as the other social sciences, has never fully adopted reasoning by variables (except in limited fields, such as electoral sociology, which is eminently suited to a classical mathematical approach) nor the functionalist approach, which it ignores almost totally. It will not catch up with the other social sciences until it integrates the arguments developed by the pioneers so as to make them serve jointly the ends of political analysis. So far in the social sciences this has been done only in a fragmentary manner.

---

40. A simple reductio ad absurdum might well have taken the place of the analysis which has just been attempted. One could have merely stated that ambivalence in sociological language necessarily implies ambivalence in the social structure. The relationship between concepts expressed in words and the phenomenon to which they refer is such that any statement must necessarily have a counterpart in the reality that is being expressed, provided of course that the propositions under study are empirically valid. If a flower is described as both a rose and a peony, this means that it is really a rose and a peony; in other words, a hybrid. If sociological speech is allowed to develop on the levels of sociological functionalism and of arguments based on variables, this means that the social structure is at the same time both organic and mechanistic. This can be proved, once again, by the fact that functionalism could not be applied to a purely physical theory since material phenomena are free of the structural ambivalence that typifies biological and social phenomena.

The problems that one attempts to solve when undertaking the explanation of a social phenomenon should not only be related to a well-defined methodological conception. They must also be related to everyday experience, and on this level the abstract and concrete must meet. The theory of a political phenomenon can and should be abstract, but the phenomena it deals with must be consistent with common sense.

What does one see when one examines a colonial conflict? First, that the behavior of opposing groups does not depend upon chance: there is a definite link between each social group's way of life and its political attitudes in the conflict, and this link must be studied first of all. One then sees that there is just as definite a link between these attitudes and the margin of authority, or, if one prefers, the decision-making capacity of the colonial regime. Finally, one sees that the way in which the regime fulfills its social function, which is to find answers for certain problems on the basis of its margin of authority, is strongly conditioned by the nature of the problems which arise; some are satisfactorily resolved, others less so, and some not at all, which generally results in putting the government at a disadvantage vis-à-vis the colonial peoples in revolt. Once again, one must find out how and why.

A valid theory of a colonial conflict can be outlined only to the extent that precise and adequate answers are found to the three following questions:

1. To what extent are the political attitudes of conflicting groups a function of their social situation?

2. To what extent is the decision-making capacity of the political centers concerned a function of these attitudes?

3. To what extent does the specific nature of the problems raised by the milieu condition the ability of the colonial regime to fulfill its social function?

The overall plan for a systematic study of the conflict was based upon these three questions. The first part of the study is devoted to a functional analysis of the main problems that France and the Residency in the Moroccan protectorate had to deal with; the relationship between the nature of these problems and their solution is explained in each case. The second part seeks to qualify in terms of political variables the material derived from the history (Volume 1) and from the study of social groups and institutions on both the metropolitan and Moroccan echelons (Volume 3 of the French edition). The third part is devoted to the study of the interactions observed between the variables previously analyzed, and to the construction of a model integrating these interactions, with the international aspects of the conflict included at this stage of the demonstration. The conclusion reestablishes the overall unity of the analysis by combining the functionalist and quasi-mathematical aspects of the argument.[41]

41. The ideas developed in this introduction and their elaboration in the following chapters were presented in more summary form in an earlier study entitled "Note on the Theory of International Conflicts" (mimeo., Congress of the International Political Science Association, Rome, 1959).

PART ONE

THE FUNCTIONALIST ASPECT

The objective of utilizing the functionalist aspect in the systematic study of the decolonization of the protectorate is to reveal the degree to which the technical aspects of the problems posed by Morocco for the authority of the French determined the positive, negative, or imaginary solutions which the decision-making centers, whose social function was to resolve them, attempted to find.[1] It would be difficult to use this method of argumentation, even summarily, without first defining the concepts of "political problem" and "technical aspects of a political problem."

The concept of political problem has a flexibility which makes it unusable as long as the order of magnitude of the technical objectives of the ruling power has not been linked to a clear definition of the political ends pursued. Thus, the problem posed for the protectorate of developing the traditional sectors of the Moroccan economy remains indeterminate as long as there is no criterion which makes it possible to determine objectively the magnitude of the development the regime intended to carry out annually. As long as the ruling power was in a position to control this arbitrarily, the statement of the problem remains vague, since the objective can always be attained if it becomes sufficiently restricted, so that the task corresponds to the normal capacities for action of the regime assuming the task.

1. The functionalist analysis of political activity being equivalent to the study of the interactions between political variables, there was no reason to initiate the theory of Moroccan decolonization according to one mode of reasoning in preference to another. If problems are discussed before variables, it is because in the present state of knowledge political functionalism is a cruder method of analysis than reasoning through variables. The study of Moroccan problems clears the ground. It already establishes the main variables to be studied in subsequent chapters. It calls for a systematic analysis of their interactions by treating in general questions it does not explicitly answer. The analysis was initiated with the functionalist study of Moroccan problems to safeguard the progression of the argument which might have become unbalanced if the starting point had been the demonstrative method.

This arbitrary manipulation of technical objectives can be avoided only if the ends pursued on the economic and social level are linked to well-defined political exigencies. When the protectorate decided to modernize traditional Morocco, it was not motivated by the gratuitous desire to afford a demonstration of applied economic sociology for the benefit of ivory tower scholars. Its conscious or unconscious motivation was to avoid imperiling its colonization by the political upheaval created by its implantation in a primitive environment. The increase in agricultural production, the de-proletarization of urban masses, the promotion of social welfare facilities were not ends in themselves. They were only means used to achieve minimum political stability. It is thus in relation to this objective that the ability of the regime to develop the traditional sectors of the Moroccan economy must be evaluated.

The same example makes it possible to define the notion of the technical aspects of a political problem. Obstacles to development are technical as well as political. They are technical when the manpower, goods, and capital for a satisfactory solution to a given problem are inferior to the needs. They are political when the objective could be reached on the technical level, but the ruling power is paralyzed by the resistance of the social groups from which it derives its authority.[2] Every problem of this kind tends to have a limited technical aspect and a broad political aspect. The technical aspect concerns only the question of knowing whether there is enough time and enough resources to reach the desired objective within a given length of time. The political aspect is found by reincorporating into the problem the attitudes of the interested groups toward the technical solution sought by the ruling power. It involves only the question of knowing the full extent to which one can hope to attain objectives which are technically feasible despite political attitudes thwarting their fulfillment.[3]

2. This distinction between the technical and political aspects of a governmental problem corresponds, to some degree, to the distinction that Anglo-Saxon authors make between politics and policy. Cf. Raymond Aron, *Sociologie des sociétés industrielles: esquisse d'une théorie des régimes politiques* (Paris, 1958), pp. 1–2.

3. In spite of its normative interest, the distinction between the technical and political aspects of the problems under consideration has not been used with the same results

These categories must now be applied to the problems studied in the following chapters.

---

in the six studies discussed in the following chapters. It is clearly at the root of the analysis of the first three problems studied: creation of modern sectors within the Moroccan economy; development of its traditional sectors; and political liberalization of the regime. It concerns the problem raised by the functional degeneration of the protectorate only incidentally. It ceases to apply as such to problems raised by the military and political repression of nationalism. The outward manifestation of the political attitudes adopted by a society toward the technical solutions that the ruling power attempts to impose operates with varying clarity in each case. The more technical the problem, the easier the distinction. The more political the problem, the vaguer the distinction becomes, although it does not disappear altogether. When the totality of the Moroccan crisis is considered, the maintenance of law and order in an environment which protected outlaws remains a technical problem, despite the importance of the political attitudes that envelop it.

Chapter 1

THE PROBLEM OF CREATING MODERN
SECTORS OF THE MOROCCAN ECONOMY

The history of the protectorate between 1912 and 1956 shows striking contrasts of success and failure. The success compels our admiration: in a few decades, 300,000 Europeans attained a standard of living often higher than they would have in metropolitan France; large cities, railroads, highways, ports, and mines appeared, and crops doubled wherever the colonists settled; the industrial, commercial, and financial structures of a modern economy were established in a few years; law and order was assured; health services were constantly being improved; Moroccans served in all ranks of the French army. France extended into North Africa and assured the European safety and protection in a land as vast as France itself. All this was achieved with so little perceptible effort that it seemed to have taken place automatically, through the simple multiplication of actors playing roles learned in advance. It was as if an entire society had been sown from a first seedling and had grown without effort or struggle.

But the failure was as striking as the success: traditional agriculture languished beside the miracles of colonialism; the hideousness of the *bidonvilles* was the shame of the large European communities; schools and housing were inadequate to meet the needs of the indigenous population; improvements in public health were in large part nullified by an increasing population; a handful of militant nationalists defeated the prestige and strength of the colonizer; the urban Moslems seceded from the regime. The French army was first held in respect, then paralyzed by a few dozen guerrillas supported by an unarmed population that was finally victorious in its struggle with a great modern power. One can conceive of a metropole with diminishing population, resources, and vitality becoming incapable of imposing its will on its empire, and Rome is an example. But it is less clear at first sight how a fully developed great western power, in a situation where the only political difficulties are those affecting the supporters of decolonization, could be compelled to give way to a weaker opponent.

The success and the failure are incomprehensible only if one forgets that political regimes, and colonial regimes in particular, can resolve certain types of problems and not others. As long as a regime restricts itself to its sociological limits of operation, it can, in principle, successfully meet any political difficulties which may arise. As it loses its ability to function, or as it encounters problems beyond its scope, its resistance to political upheavals is seriously weakened. Colonialism has a clear-cut objective: to create a modern economy in an underdeveloped area. It is not designed to ensure the development of the indigenous inhabitants, or to govern them effectively once its normal capacity for enforcement can no longer keep them in check.

The gradual solution of this specific problem depends strictly on conditions of authority, supplies, finance, remuneration, and protection of the market. Whenever these have been resolved, modern producers can recreate an element of western society in proportion to their numbers. Not only does a colonial regime limit beforehand its aims regarding the exploitation of human, material, and geopolitical resources of the colony,[1] but from the beginning it equips itself with the structural and institutional features necessary to fulfill its function. It is an enlightened despotism, and its initiative is institutionally subordinate to none of its component groups. It is an expatriate regime that recruits its agents almost exclusively from the metropole, with the exception of the local elite which serves it in return for advantages received. It is a government of occupation whose authority permanently rests on a military apparatus acting as its police force. It is a regime based on economic and financial privileges and its attraction for the human and financial resources of the métropole must always

---

1. Colonialism only fixes humanitarian ends for itself insofar as they are necessary to the achievement of its ultimate objective.

remain superior to that in any competing economy. It is finally in certain respects a consensual regime, for it can function only with the consent of the indigenous population. This consent is the basis of the whole political system. It is obtained by two complementary methods: first of all, a military conquest bolstered and stabilized by a fraction of the traditional elite; and, second, respect for and maintenance of local institutions insofar as they coincide with the ultimate aims of the colonial regime.

The successful functioning of a colonial regime requires the capacity to use force, consent of both communities, concentration of power in European hands, integration of the local elite into the colonial order, and special privileges accorded to the settlers. With these prerequisites established, the regime's functional integrity is automatically assured and its ultimate objectives can be fulfilled by the private initiative of the settlers operating within the institutional framework provided. The French protectorate was able to resolve the problems posed by the creation of modern sectors of the Moroccan economy because it was created to solve them. Mutatis mutandis, the same can be said for all colonial regimes since the beginning of colonialism. In this respect, a comparison of the results obtained with the institutional and the psychological factors upon which the regime is based is sufficient proof of the ability of the political organism to achieve its ultimate objectives.

These considerations might have been sufficient if the protectorate had not continued to fulfill its economic function at a time when its capacity for enforcement and authority had been seriously impaired. How can one explain the fact that the normal activities of production, investment, and exchange went on almost as usual, in spite of the challenge to its authority by the political opposition of the indigenous population? The anomaly is obvious and must be resolved if the preceding argument is to be convincing, but it can be explained rather simply.

In the first place, the Moroccans continued to behave as disciplined workers long after they had ceased to be acquiescent subjects; thus the change from consent to opposition on their part did not bring the economy to a halt. It is easier for a person to oppose for two years a regime to which he is subject than to stop work for eight days. A strike is a luxury of the western proletariat. In a country where workers can fall back neither on union funds nor on personal savings, anything but a short-term work stoppage is out of the question. Nothing illustrates more clearly the difference between these two pressures on modern man— politics and economics—than the enduring quality of the worker's participation in the production of goods and services in a society in which that same worker has ceased to cooperate in the making of political decisions and in their implementation.

In the second place, the economy of the protectorate continued to invest and produce despite the political conflict, because private enterprise continued its contribution until the final months of the crisis, and because the protectorate continued to receive increasing amounts of financial aid from the metropolitan government until the very end of its official economic activity in Morocco. The regime lacked neither disciplined labor nor capital, and it is for this reason that the economy continued to operate while the political organs were being slowly paralyzed.

This illustrates a more fundamental phenomenon: the gradual transition of the Moroccan economy to its post-colonial phase of development. The relative economic stability of the protectorate between 1953 and 1956 was due not only to the weak influence of political events on the economy but to the preparation of this economy for post-colonial conditions of operation. The economic trend of 1953–56 had its raison d'être in both the past and the future. The vitality of the regime's productive apparatus was not the aberrant survival of a function within a moribund political organism. It is one of the aspects of this economy's adjustment from one system to another, even before the advent of independence.

Because of the attraction of the country's natural resources for metropolitan France, the modern sectors of the Moroccan economy had been constantly expanding since 1912. The transition of this economy to its post-colonial phase of development was made possible by the attraction of its modern sectors for both the indigenous population and metropolitan France. Experience has shown that when the death knell sounds for a colonial regime, the indigenous population can no longer remain aloof from the means of production and exchange created by colonization, and the mother country cannot remain indifferent to the fate of its overseas establishments. Barring a total breakdown, the deterioration in, or even the disappearance of, the normal functioning of a colonial economy tends to be offset by the institutionalization of factors of economic and sociological solidarity whose role is to link together the ex-colonial economy and that of the former colonial power through financial and technical assistance, economic agreements, and so forth. It is obvious that this institutional trend began before France actually granted Morocco its independence.

The post-colonial economy, moreover, functions under political conditions similar in many ways to the colonial economy. Security and protection must be ensured for foreigners, law and order enforced among the indigenous inhabitants, and acceptable relations maintained with donor countries. Certain post-colonial regimes smack incontestably of neo-colonialism; nonetheless they function under very different conditions from those which made it possible to create the modern sectors of the Moroccan economy. In the waning years of the protectorate, the modern sectors of the economy functioned only partially on the basis of the human and financial means which had characterized the regime since its beginning. They were also based on local attitudes and sources of metropolitan finance which were to characterize the regime after independence. It is this phenomenon, more than any other, which enabled the protectorate to continue to solve its economic problems even after its political integrity was no longer assured.

Chapter 2

THE PROBLEM OF ECONOMIC AND
SOCIAL REFORMS IN MUSLIM CIRCLES

As the protectorate solved its problems by encouraging European settlers and creating a modern sector in juxtaposition with the traditional sector of the Moroccan economy, a new set of problems arose. Like colonial peoples everywhere, the indigenous population began a dual movement of cultural separation and the creation of new social structures. The extension of health services caused a demographic upheaval. The rural exodus rid the countryside of overpopulation, while depriving it of the most dynamic elements. The urbanization of the neo-proletariat was achieved at the lowest standard of living. The needs of the colonized with regard to housing, schooling, health services, and administrative training were translated over the years into higher and higher budget estimates and more and more credits. But none of these reforms succeeded in heading off the change in political attitudes caused by this upheaval in the lives of the Moroccans.

Did the protectorate have sufficient economic, financial, and human resources to achieve a rapid and substantial improvement in the lives of the inhabitants of both cities and rural areas? Could it at least hope to combat the appeal of nationalist propaganda to the Muslim masses merely by social reforms? Such is the political statement of the problem, and it is in these terms that the willingness and capacity of the regime to meet the problem must be judged.

As an example, the urbanization of the new *medinas* in Morocco encountered three basic obstacles: lack of resources, lack of will, and lack of time. The lack of resources is of course relative, but in practice it was conclusive. The financial and human resources needed to raise substantially the level of existence and living standards of the Moroccan neo-proletariat would have been enormous. All large countries have shrunk from the sacrifices required to urbanize the slum districts on the outskirts of their large cities. In theory, such reforms are financially possible. But the essential investments are so great that to undertake them would require a motivation greater than normally exists.

This lack of incentive is at the heart of the problem. Why should France urbanize Casablanca rather than Saigon, and why Saigon rather than the area surrounding Paris? To be effective, the urbanization of the new Moroccan *medinas* would have had to keep pace with their growing importance. The necessary reforms would have had to be carried out well before 1939. But any French resident-general who proposed such a plan at that time would have been considered a dreamer. When it might have been tried, the lack of incentive made it utopian. When the incentives finally provided the goal for the government, it was too late for effective action.

In such a situation, lost time can never be made up. Once a nationalist movement is under way, it can only be stopped by a pace of reform which is inherently impossible to realize. Once a certain pace of development has been attained, time cannot be gained even by huge investments of men and money. Even if France had increased its social investments tenfold in postwar Morocco, it could not have improved the lot of the neo-proletariat in time to achieve its proposed political objectives.

This inherently slow pace of development is in dramatic contrast with the explosive momentum of the nationalist movement that it attempted to combat. The formation of the independence movement, Istiqlal, dates from December 1943. Within five years, nationalism had swept the cities. To attain its objective, the regime would have had to carry out, in less than five years, a radical reform of the living conditions of the urban neo-proletariat. Even if the will of the Residency had not encountered political opposition, the technical nature of the problem would have made it insolvable. How could the protectorate gain time on the nationalists with a remedy that acted more slowly than the disease, and that was only feasible politically after the disease had become incurable?

The situation in the rural areas was no less discouraging. Attempts to increase agricultural yields where ancient farming methods still prevailed faced similar difficulties stemming from the interdependence of the factors of production—everything had to be changed simultaneously, or defeat admitted—and the peasants fiercely resisted political constraint. Even in communist countries where industrialization has made great strides, farm production is static, if not retrograde. In underdeveloped economies under the western sphere of influence, small-scale but promising experiments with new farming methods have been achieved. But it does not yet seem possible to use them to achieve a self-sustaining evolution of ancient farming methods.

In Morocco, where all peasants were small landowners, any serious attempt at collectivization or consolidation of holdings would probably have triggered a mass uprising. Jacques Berque and Julien Couleau apparently partially overcame this obstacle by concentrating on arable collective farms and by beginning with a small number of pilot projects. By minimizing the political and psychological shock of the reform in the *bled* and by demonstrating that the effort was sufficiently profitable to become self-supporting within its chosen limits, the promoters of *paysannat* gave their name to a remarkable achievement. The question is whether this reform was still only at the experimental phase when it was challenged by the settlers and their spokesmen. Berque and Couleau were sure they had achieved a breakthrough. But in our view, lack of time, lack of incentive, and the huge financial effort required, as in the cities, would have nullified any political advantages gained from the reform. Even if the engineers of the reform had been given a free hand, the ten percent of arable land in the *bled,* which was to be cultivated by modern farming methods in eight years, would not have made much difference in the long run. At this pace, it would have been as impossible to overtake the nationalists in the rural areas as in the cities, even if one takes into account the fact that the revolt broke out first in the cities and took several years to reach the rural areas.

Thus far, the argument has assumed that a nationalist movement for independence can be kept dormant by raising the living standards of colonial peoples, and that the only insolvable problem stems from the technical obstacles to a rapid and large enough improvement in living standards. But the problem becomes more complicated if one questions this initial hypothesis and asks whether the very idea of neutralizing a nationalist movement by raising living standards has any meaning. In this broader context, the problem not only seems insolvable, but misconstrued. First, the immediate effects of economic and social growth are not necessarily beneficial. One has only to consider the industrialization of Europe to realize that in terms of well-being the costs of growth may be greater than the benefits over a long period of time. Moreover, the desire for liberty is an exclusive passion and cannot be disarmed with investments. It cannot be killed in embryo by keeping its adherents in a gilded cage, nor can it be deflected once it has crystallized.[1] Colonialism awakened civilizations asleep in their ancestral misery. It could not keep them torpid while it transformed them, still less could it send them back to sleep after awakening them. The discrimination of which colonial peoples feel themselves to be the victims only serves to intensify their desire for liberty. The elimination or attenuation of this discrimination does not, however, make them free.

To neutralize the Moroccan masses by radical social reforms and to disarm the nationalist elite by investments would have been vain. On both the technical and psychological planes, the achievements of the regime in this domain were unrealistic solutions to a problem enunciated in insolvable terms.

---

1. To convey the mechanistic aspect of animal behavior, certain specialists in the study of dogs explain that a dog which is confined does not bark "because it wants to be let out," but "because it is confined." The distinction is equally valid for sociological behavior caught in the cog of a given mechanism. Colonial governments do not develop the indigenous milieu *in order* to neutralize it politically. This is only a rationalization a posteriori of their behavior. They develop the milieu *because* they and the nationalists are embarked on the same ship, and action is necessary, even if it has nothing to do with the ultimate objective. This does not mean that there was not a certain evangelical quality in colonialism: many colonists were certainly apostles in their own way. In sociology, all contradictions exist side by side. Some were plainly there to make money; others were altruists; but in large part, the humanitarian ends of colonialism were subordinated to the pursuit of material advantage.

Chapter 3

THE PROBLEM OF POLITICAL REFORMS

The protectorate, unable to forestall or disarm the nationalist drive through extensive development of the traditional sectors of Moroccan society, attempted during the Labonne period to neutralize the demands of the Moroccan elite through political reform. The official objective was not to clear the way for ultimate independence, but to stabilize the regime through the progressive participation of the Muslims.

It is not our intention here to see whether the Residency had enough control over its officials and the other Europeans to enforce such reforms; this aspect of the question will be discussed later. Our only concern is to investigate whether reform of a colonial regime is technically feasible. This is not to say that progressive liberalization of a regime of this type is impossible; many examples prove the contrary. The objective is to investigate what kind of "progressive political reform" would be acceptable to both communities. Does it really make sense to attempt to liberalize an authoritarian regime in order to give it stability? Would not the anticipated reforms have the opposite effect of speeding up, rather than slowing down, the dynamic forces of evolution? This is the technical side of the question which interests us, and on which the liberals and ultras were sharply divided.

The liberals hoped to bring the nationalist movement under control through granting reasonable concessions. They took no formal stand on the question of independence, preferring to put it off to a later day. The ultras held that such a policy was self-defeating: it would merely accelerate the evolution in progress, spur the nationalists to intensify their demands, and weaken the ability of the protectorate to withstand the nationalists as long as

436

its institutional integrity remained.[1] Which side saw the true technical nature of the problem—the liberals who argued that liberalization of the regime would gain time and pave the way for an orderly transition of Morocco to independence, or those who held that the slightest concession would throw the edifice off balance and lead to its destruction in short order? It is clear that the burden of error lies with the liberals who sought to be reformers, for, as the ultras feared, the partial reform of the protectorate did lead to its downfall.

The introduction into Morocco of the principle of the separation of powers, which implied that the population was no longer subject to traditional Moroccan penal justice but to magistrates appointed for life and applying modern concepts of jurisprudence, would have been enough by itself to bring down the regime. How can self-government be denied to a people exempted from arbitrary justice? Accelerated education of the Moroccan people would inevitably have diminished the leadership of the small European group. Even with the best intentions in the world, the creation of mixed regional and central elected assemblies, as well as the substitution of personal security for the *bon plaisir* of the regime, would have created conditions of instability conducive to the exercise of growing pressures by the Muslims on an administration less and less able to resist them. The large-scale entry of westernized young Moroccans into the administration would have caused a disequilibrium within the regime by subjecting it to an uncontrollable demand for reform, and exposing it to permanent administrative sabotage. A colonial regime which speeds up the westernization of the indigenous population becomes weaker, not stronger. It weakens psychologically—as a people evolve and become emancipated, the weaker become the colonial arguments in defense of trusteeship. A technical imbalance occurs—any partial reform of the injustices of an authoritarian regime is a threat to the system as a whole. The so-called injustices of colonialism are but the by-products of its normal conditions of operation. As in the case of

---

1. The European colony's opposition to reform was above all an instinctive conservative attitude unencumbered by explanations. It nevertheless may be said that colonialist leaders possessed a doctrine founded upon a rational appreciation of the dangerous pressure that partial reform could bring to bear upon the regime.

the reform of the Moroccan penal system, elimination of injustice means the eradication of the technical means of action to which it is linked. It is a contradiction in terms to refuse independence to a people who demand it and to give them at the same time the technical and psychological means to claim it through the granting of partial and successive concessions.

Progressive reforms make sense only if the ultimate goal of the colonial regime is independence. So long as the colonial regime has not resigned itself to independence at some predetermined date, it cannot afford to embark on partial reforms. Without provision for ending a colonial regime, partial reforms are sterile. By the same token, the indigenous population can agree to take the path to progressive decolonization only if the date of its independence has been fixed beforehand.

In these circumstances, the only reasonable solution to the colonial problem is to emancipate a colony before it attains full development but after training local cadres to assume responsibility when independence is achieved. As the European group is in a position to oppose the peaceful transition to independence, once it grows large enough to impose its will, this rational solution can usually be achieved only provisionally and after a political struggle of varying intensity and duration. As will be seen below, the get-tough policy of the ultras was just as inadequate a solution as the liberal policy of partial reform.

Chapter 4

THE PROBLEM OF THE DEGENERATION
OF THE REGIME

The residents-general who attempted to liberalize the protectorate promptly encountered opposition from within their own ranks. This opposition was based on deep anomalies in the division of political and administrative functions. Before going further, it is important to analyze the residential, directorial, regional, and local aspects of this functional degeneration and its effect on the conflict.[1]

Deterioration in the Function of the Residency

At the war's end, various factors, some new and some old, combined to impair more and more seriously the authority of the Residency. Entrenched behind the de facto or de jure powers acquired in wartime, the major political departments sharply opposed any attempts by the Residency to bring them back into line. Unable to reassert authority over them, the residents-general attempted to get around the problem by having the most important matters handled by their own cabinets.[2] This only aggravated the situation. The continuous and excessive centralization of the technical services of the regime only served to glut the machinery of residential decision-making by overloading it with an enormous volume of business. The opportunities for sabotage and obstruction of the authority of the regime increased danger-

1. A detailed study of the problems at these different echelons would fill a volume. Thus only the conclusions of the analysis made in the course of the study are presented schematically here. The analysis reinforces in its broad lines the criticism directed at the regime by students of the problem, particularly by Gilbert Grandval.

2. Grandval, *Ma mission au Maroc,* pp. 48, 56. The deleterious effect of the confusion of lines of responsibility on the Department of Information and on the activities of the police have been analyzed elsewhere in the light of critical observations made by Gilbert Grandval. See volume 1, pp. 258 ff.

ously.[3] As the Residency was generally only a technical inter-mediary between the sultanate and the ministries in Paris, to which it was subordinated, it found itself constantly short-cir-cuited by departments which had fallen into the habit of nego-tiating directly with Paris on affairs within their competence. Moreover, these departments as well as certain residents-general were profoundly influenced by interest groups, the local press, and metropolitan political circles. Robert Montagne has rightly emphasized the extent to which ties between the Moroccan ministries and these pressure groups increased the impotence of the residents-general.[4] The temporary character of the function, the virtual absence of control by the government in Paris, as well as the assimilation of French officialdom into the European community, gave this weakness a permanent character. In such a situation, a temporarily appointed resident-general is in danger of finding himself being used as a tool by those who are perma-nent, unless each appointee attempts an impossible palace revolu-tion. Virtually left to his own devices by the Métropole, his theoretical authority is transmuted into isolation and he has no choice but to become a part of the local milieu in order to regain a semblance of authority. The few residents-general who refused to do so found their subordinates unwilling to carry out their policy.

Deterioration in the Function of the Secretary-General

In theory, the secretary-general of the protectorate had the last word on the centralization of administrative affairs and on the control of technical departments of a non-political nature. But in practice his authority was gravely infringed upon and weakened by the competing authority of other high officials. A brief ex-amination of these infringements suffices to show the extent to which the actual functioning of the regime was at variance with the letter of the regulations. For example, although the secretary-general's office was theoretically in charge of all matters having to do with municipal administration, urban development, and indigenous affairs, these matters were in fact handled by the De-

3. Grandval, pp. 48–49.
4. Montagne, *Révolution au Maroc*, pp. 337–38.

partment of the Interior. The same confusion prevailed in the realm of indigenous agriculture. The *paysannat* and the irrigated perimeters were handled by the Residency. The Department of the Interior was in charge of the cooperatives. For a whole series of reasons too involved to be analyzed here, the secretary-general, realizing the impossibility of coordinating the various departments in charge of indigenous policy, was led to create others himself. The disorder became total when the secretary-general, thus deprived of an essential part of his authority, was invested by General Guillaume with specifically political powers as a member of the restricted council.[5] Certainly the personality and the idea of the officeholder might, on occasion, compensate for the downgrading of the institution. A secretary-general who took his role seriously might succeed in imposing a better than usual degree of coordination on his departments. Another, more subject to the prevailing esprit de corps, might find himself in sufficient psychological agreement with subordinates over whom he had no control, so that a minimum of coordination might be obtained by this coincidence of independent impulses. It is true, nonetheless, that the effectiveness of the office continued to deteriorate in both cases.

Deterioration in the Function of Leadership

It should be clear by now that the real policy makers in Morocco at the central echelon were the heads of the various political and technical departments. The authority of the Residency was irremediably dissipated at this level, and taken over by the Department of the Interior, the Department of Finance, and the Department of Public Works.

The Department of the Interior controlled a substantial share of the political power in Morocco, but this invisible government was blinded by the continual need to defend its prerogatives and to maintain the status quo at all costs. The Department of Finance made policy as it saw fit, in agreement with Paris, within the sphere of autonomy granted it by the metropolitan government. This independence was further strengthened by the weak financial powers of the Residency. The Department of

5. See volume 1, pp. 186 ff.

Public Works generally determined on its own initiative all matters concerning budget appropriations for public and semi-public investment in Morocco. In contrast with this directorial absolutism, the Department of Agriculture had no apparent policy and was usually content to place its officials at the disposal of departmental services which, by fact or by law, determined indigenous agricultural policy.[6] This usurpation of residential power by these administrative bastilles, each of which had become practically autonomous, has been described and confirmed by many authors.[7]

The Problem of Direct Administration on the Regional and Local Levels

The situation was no better at the lower echelons. Gilbert Grandval writes that "the breakdown of central authority had repercussions even in the *bled*. The district officers, supervisors, and officials of Indigenous Affairs attached to the Department of the Interior, which was itself completely independent of the secretary-general, were overloaded with minor administrative matters and could not coordinate locally the activities of the various services emanating from different departments."[8] It is enough to add in this respect that regional autonomy superimposed on directorial autonomy made the administrative distance separating the *bled* from the Residency astronomical. Between the Residency and the lower echelon, the director and the district officer set practically insurmountable communication barriers if the Residency or secretary-general did not share their views.

The problem of direct administration is closely linked to that of local government. The phenomenon has been considered by a number of authors, particularly liberal authors, as one of the most flagrant vices of regional and local administration. This criticism is too sharp. In fact, the protectorate used very flexible methods in governing Morocco. Direct administration was the undisputed master at the summit of the hierarchy. The govern-

6. Barrat, *Justice pour le Maroc*, p. 149.
7. See particularly Grandval, pp. 49–50; Montagne, pp. 336–37; Pierre Boyer de Latour, *Vérités sur l'Afrique du Nord*, p. 26. On the exaggerated technocratic character of this directorial government, see Grandval, pp. 50–52.
8. Grandval, p. 49.

ment of the notables was generally maintained at a less central echelon in order to gain the support of the traditionalist elite. Generally the notable was just another name for the local French agent. It is true, nonetheless, that in some cases the great notable governed his subjects as he saw fit, with the tacit approbation of the French authorities.

In any case, it would be an exaggeration to consider direct administration as a vice peculiar to the French colonial system in North Africa. France governed Morocco according to methods and norms common to all colonial systems. One may regret that the new Muslim elites were not associated more closely with the country's administration, in order to assure a more orderly transition to independence. But one cannot take this as grounds for reproaching the protectorate for never respecting the Treaty of Fez. Direct administration is not an accidental vice of colonialism, but one of its fundamental techniques. The transition from a state of underdevelopment to one of development implies, for all regimes, undisputed political authority. Direct administration is only the application of this principle to a colonial regime.

Although the regime was in theory based on protection and supervision, it considerably worsened its own moral position by resorting to the inevitable practice of direct administration. It was thus particularly vulnerable to nationalist propaganda, but this does not mean that any other course was open to it. If the regime had from the beginning limited itself to the kind of control implied by a literal construction of the treaty, the French could certainly have continued to establish precarious enterprises in Morocco as they had done before 1912, but colonialism as such would never have developed.

Status of Colonial Administrators

The statutory privileges enjoyed by French civil servants in Morocco appear to be both the cause and symptom of the breakdown of the regime. Apart from the supervisory and technical services, the French cadres in Morocco were nominally subordinate to the metropolitan administration; but they had special privileges. Except for the secretaries of the administration, who were subject to a common set of regulations, the status of the

35,000 French officials in Morocco was determined either by particular regulations for each service, or by special regulations covering in language "comprehensible to the initiates, a number of personnel problems," [9] or by established practices capable of sanctioning the most flagrant administrative irregularities. Abuses were rife. Gilbert Grandval has stated that it was commonplace for a high-ranking civil servant, retired for reasons of age, to be assigned on a contractual basis to a post or para-administrative position while continuing to draw his retirement pay and other benefits. It was equally customary for a military officer on active duty to be assigned to a civilian post or for the head of an office, after several years of service, to have the rank and salary of director without exercising the functions of a director. An official who might be called upon to perform temporarily higher functions might not return to his old post on completion of this mission but continue to draw the higher salary while doing nothing. Sanctions were practically nonexistent, and the greatest risk to an incompetent official was that he might be reassigned to a post where his negligence would once more be given free rein.[10] According to Grandval, "this situation was not only an insurmountable obstacle to necessary integration . . . but it encouraged an egotistical, jealous, and defensive attitude among the French officials. This explains the almost total absence of Moroccans in the civil service, which was to have grave political consequences." [11] The complete integration of French civil servants into the colonial leadership resulted in a complete harmony of viewpoint. As beneficiaries of the special privileges of the colonial regime, they had to adopt a fundamentally conservative attitude. The strength and homogeneity of this reaction was not, however, without certain nuances.

Some civil servants assigned to the *bled* have been described as "conscientious, interested in, and devoted to their work" with "a thorough knowledge of indigenous administration on the local level, its operation, and its 'ins and outs'. It was this competence, this knowledge of the caids which was the supreme and magical

9. Ibid., p. 50.
10. Ibid., p. 50–51.
11. Ibid., p. 51.

virtue that the 'old Moroccans' found wanting in the laymen sent from metropolitan France." [12] Others have been denounced as displaying a "sort of insensitivity, a social and political aloofness. They have an inveterate hate of everything in Morocco which is not in accordance with the feudal tradition. They erected a political, even a social and moral system, based on force and characterized by immobility." [13] Even among the most outstanding,

> rare are they who are able to derive from their daily experience with the people and the environment of Morocco anything but a more or less enlightened paternalism. Rare are they who take the trouble to see how the people live and evolve under their very eyes. Rare are they who really know any of the Moroccans of the future. Even in the cities, most officials deal only with the chiefs or traditionalist notables. They are almost totally ignorant of popular aspirations, even of the feeling of bourgeoisie. Their only knowledge is based on police reports. They do not understand or try to understand the development of present-day Morocco and are concerned with it only negatively, in order to contain it.[14]

Once again, this description is accurate only in a very general sense. In the *bled* there were, until the last months of the conflict, many civilian officials and indigenous affairs officers who saw clearly the impending catastrophe, and did what they could at their own level to forestall the breakdown of the regime.

It is relatively easy to describe the main symptoms of the organic malady of the protectorate. But to appreciate fully the role this factor of disorganization played in the conflict is not as simple.

Steps taken by Residents-General Labonne and Grandval to reorganize the administration met with failure. If this reorgani-

12. Ibid., p. 126.
13. Ibid., p. 59.
14. Ibid., p. 127.

zation had been attempted by residents-general who favored the status quo, and who simply wished to regain control of the administration, the obvious explanation for the failure would have been the natural inertia of any cadre faced with an attempt to bring it back into line. This classic explanation unfortunately loses its validity because the efforts of Labonne and Grandval were only the first steps toward the eventual liquidation of the regime. Under these conditions, the resistance of the cadre clearly appears as a particular case of resistance to decolonization. Technically speaking, the two problems, that of regaining control of the administration and that of actual political reform, are not identical, but the fact that those concerned tended to confound them helped conceal their separate identities.

If one distinguishes by analysis the two elements that became amalgamated in reality and isolates the real role of administrative breakdown in the conflict, its minor importance becomes evident. When the residents-general and the metropolitan authorities attempted to substitute an evolutionary policy for the Moroccan status quo, they were met by overwhelming resistance. Deeply impressed by this fact, most authors have reasoned a contrario that the failure stemmed from the lack of discipline and the conflict of authority to which the regime normally was subject. This implicit reasoning is not convincing. The regime being what it was, it is natural that French officials would have defended the status quo, within the framework of their self-constructed administrative citadels, and continued to rely on the habits of *bon plaisir* and the indiscipline they had cultivated over a long period of time. On the other hand, there is no proof that the opposition to decolonization of this cadre would have been less effective if the Residency had normally had a firmer control over its services. It is indisputable that the obstructionist attitude of French officialdom was reinforced by the privileges it enjoyed. But one cannot avoid the question of whether its defense reflex is not more fundamentally related to the problem it faced when the French authorities asked it to step aside in favor of Moroccanization. The question has both a theoretical and practical importance.

The policy of the liberal residents was based on the questionable assumption that a redefinition of roles, accompanied by a few spectacular dismissals, would eliminate French officialdom's opposition to liberalizing the regime. The whole inquiry, however, would have been fruitless if, sacrificing reality for appearances, one had succumbed to the temptation of explaining the conflict on the basis of maladministration. Obviously, one has to describe the functional breakdown and to evaluate it. But this was only a secondary factor; the deeper reasons for the obstructionist attitude of the administration lay elsewhere.[15]

The problem posed for the liberals by the functional breakdown of the regime can now safely be stated. Either it is identified with the problem of the liberalization of the protectorate and becomes a part of the more general theme of the political paralysis of the regime considered in relation to the attitudes of the Europeans, or it becomes an entity in itself, in which case it is of secondary importance. In the first case, an analysis of it would encroach upon the questions discussed in the following part. In the second, it may be considered as accessory.

15. The idea of "breakdown" requires further clarification. It would be erroneous to assume that the political system instituted by the Treaty of Fez functioned normally at the outset and only broke down later. Morocco knew no golden age of colonization, if we understand this to be a state of affairs characterized by strict application of the regulations under which the regime functioned. The legal fictions of the Treaty of Fez covered, from the outset, a complete colonial regime. If Lyautey had better control over his staffs than his successors, he was no more obedient to the metropolitan authorities than they, although his attitude was very different. The seeds of the functional breakdown that became so flagrant toward the end of the conflict were sown in Morocco in 1912. What was remarkable was the steady growth and gradual institutionalization of the malady.

Chapter 5

THE PROBLEM OF POLITICAL REPRESSION
OF NATIONALISM—ANALYSIS
OF A CONJECTURE

Since the protectorate was incapable of making the Europeans accept a liberalization of the regime, it had no choice but to try to win Moroccan acceptance of the status quo. This aspect will be considered here within the confines of the problem posed for the regime by the rise of political nationalism. The conditions under which a colonial nationalism can be put down by force will be investigated afterward. The question is whether, granted the time, place, and social milieu described, a growing colonial nationalism, when pitted against an intransigent regime, can be checked in its course by methods similar to those applied by the supporters of a policy of force in Morocco in 1952 and 1953. Could the Residency hope to prevent, before time ran out, the outbreak of terrorism by regaining psychological control of the masses through police action designed to neutralize the pole of nationalist attraction? We know this policy was a complete failure. Sociological analysis will demonstrate that the failure was inevitable and inherent in the nature of the problem posed.

The point of departure is a dual assumption. By decapitating the Istiqlal and the U.G.S.C.M. in 1952–53, and by purging the Sultan's followers and deposing Mohammed V, the Residency not only thought it had dealt its adversary a rude blow but that it had settled the nationalist question for the next twenty years. In its optimism it committed the future to a course of action that only a few civil servants in official circles in Rabat sought to question.

The French liberals of both Morocco and the Métropole were no less categorical in their appraisal of the future. Two days

448

before the deposition of Mohammed V, an unofficial source at the Foreign Office set down the probable results of the operation and concluded the report with a prognosis tending to prove that, contrary to the general view, forecasting is possible in political matters if the underlying situation has been adequately taken into consideration. Virtually the whole future chain of events was predicted in a masterly fashion in this document: an increased number of disturbances ending in fatalities; the outbreak of a Tunisian-style terrorism with bomb attacks; the assassination of notables and the massacring of the isolated; the inevitable transformation of the protectorate into an occupation regime destined to a dramatic collapse; a future precluding all possibility of Franco-Moroccan cooperation; identification of the Sultan's cause with that of Moroccan patriotism; increased political and psychological separation of the Spanish and French zones of Morocco; the chaining of the regime to a local feudal elite whose predatory instincts were given free rein; the French in Morocco becoming the rulers of the country; the trusts in Casablanca formulating Moroccan policy on an ad hoc basis; French interests in the Arab world at the mercy of a caprice; international opinion convinced of the falsity of the French position. Everything was included.[1]

In what way did the implicit concepts of the problem on which the ultras and their opponents based their views of the future differ fundamentally?

Theorists of the residential camp and prophets of the liberal lobby began with similar data. Both knew that the Moroccans were torn between two opposing political poles: the Residency and the nationalists. Both were aware that the residential pole had exerted a predominant influence for the past thirty years. Neither ignored the fact that since 1944 growing segments of the

1. This faithful reproduction contained only three important errors of judgment. The effect of the colonial conflict on later possibilities for Franco-Moroccan cooperation was grossly exaggerated. In 1961, seven years after the outbreak of the Algerian conflict, chances for cooperation between France and the Maghreb countries still seemed good: it would have taken much more than the deposition of Mohammed V to affect France's position in North Africa and the Middle East. In both cases, the end is not yet in sight. The role that international organizations were to play fully for the first time in a colonial conflict in the Congo crisis was already implicit. Apart from these qualifications, the chain of events leading to the downfall of the protectorate was predicted with incredible accuracy.

population had been falling under nationalist influence and abandoning the Residency. The past ten years had witnessed a relative weakening of the power of attraction of the Residency, and a corresponding strengthening of the nationalists' hold over the population. An essential fact to bear in mind, however, is that only that fraction of the population which had the loosest ties to the regime had weakened in its allegiance; in the midst of the crisis over the monarchy in August 1953, the rural inhabitants, four-fifths of the Moroccan population, showed no flagrant signs of disaffection, with a few highly localized exceptions.

In spite of this common ground, the two analyses of the Moroccan situation branched off in different directions from the outset and were thus oriented toward opposing perspectives for the future. These analyses were posited on incompatible hypotheses which need to be made explicit.

The theorists of the regime saw the Moroccan population as politically neutral, incapable of spontaneously affecting its own destiny in any way. In their view, Morocco had been faithful as long as the Residency had been the strongest force. If allegiance was gradually changing to dissidence, it was because the regime had allowed another political pole to establish itself. The Residency did not consider the nationalist movement as a preestablished harmony of popular aspirations and propaganda themes. The force of nationalism sprang from the vestiges of sovereignty that the Treaty of Fez had imprudently left to the Sultan, and from the past tolerance of the Istiqlal: freedom granted to its oral propaganda, press, and enrollment of militant politicians and trade union leaders, and the inadequacy of police measures against nationalist outbreaks. The weakening of the authority of the Residency was merely the consequence of the freedom of action unwisely accorded to the adversary. In one sense, nothing had changed, since the French and the notables continued to support the regime. Destruction of the opposing political pole by ending the tolerance and legal fictions which had led to its formation would suffice a priori to redress the situation. Therein lay the solution to the problem, and it was to this end that the strong men of the Residency had struggled since the war. The action of December 1952 had made it possible to liquidate the

Istiqlal and to place the nationalists outside the law. That of August 1953 had made it possible to depose the Sultan, replace him with a notable who supported the Residency, restore the prestige of the great feudal lords, and, through appropriate reforms, transfer the last vestige of Moroccan sovereignty to French hands. How could success be doubted under these conditions?

Advocates of a liberal solution to the problem based their protests on an inverse view of the role of the masses in the conflict. In their eyes, the Residency's facile victory was only a paper victory since it assumed the problem solved by eliminating the most vital factor of the situation—the Moroccans themselves. Objective observers of the Moroccan situation saw the indigenous population as the driving force of the evolution. To assume that the masses will remain neutral during a revolt is to assume that there is no revolt. The assumption that the masses are not neutral inevitably implies that all counterrevolutionary action based on the inverse postulate will end in failure.

When the hypothesis of the a priori involvement of the masses is substituted for that of their political neutrality, the thesis of the ultras is turned inside out. The evolution of the force relationship between the poles of attraction fighting for the allegiance of the Moroccan masses is no longer seen as dependent upon the manner in which the two active minorities constituting these poles maneuver vis-à-vis each other against a background of popular indifference. On the contrary, it is seen as a direct result of the attitude of the masses toward these minority poles. The behavior of the masses in a revolution is not the passive result of two outside forces, foreign to its feelings and substance. On the contrary, it is the masses that make the sovereign choice between the two forces seeking their support, and the side to which they swing gains a decisive advantage.

Let us consider this phenomenon without taking up the question of whether it can be thwarted by a brutal and totalitarian use of force. Since 1912, the Residency's ascendance over the indigenous masses was based on their acceptance of the regime following a military conquest psychologically stabilized by a wise dosage of intimidation, respect for local customs, and, when the immediate interests of colonialism were not endangered, good administration. As allegiance turned to opposition, growing numbers of Moroccans began to destroy progressively what might be called the protectorate's ordinary capital store of authority. Since the Residency's power of attraction decreased as the indigenous masses turned away from it, its only alternative was to admit defeat, or to try to reassert its jeopardized authority by a crushing show of force. Seeking instinctively to avoid this, it resorted to the classic method of regaining control of the masses: the arrest and imprisonment of nationalist leaders. It is understandable that it took this course, but it is nonetheless astonishing that the Residency thought it could settle the immense problem posed by the rise of nationalism with such prosaic limited measures.

When this argument is extended to the relationship of the Moroccans to the nationalist pole, it becomes obvious that this repressive technique could not succeed. As the Moroccans weakened the regime by withdrawing their support, they fed the power of attraction of the nationalist pole, either by obeying more or less spontaneously its injunctions or interdictions, or by reconstructing from within themselves the nationalist cadres each time they were destroyed by repressive measures, as was the case after December 1952. The falseness of the thesis that the masses would remain neutral during a revolt is proven not only by the factor of collective attitudes conditioning the authority of the leadership on both sides but also by the fact that the revolutionary cadres manifest themselves not as independent and isolated from the masses but as a direct emanation of them. We have seen how, once the first nationalist leaders had been disbanded, a new, different, and more militant leadership arose in its place, ready to satisfy the mass thirst for direct action, and how terrorism was naturally born of this conjunction of popular aspiration for revolt and the creation of a group of leaders capable of organizing it.

From this particular vantage point, the complex interplay of sociological influences which throws one pole off balance with regard to the other appears as an irreversible change in attitude which turns indigenous acceptance into open revolt. Put another way, popular indifference to the first political manifestations of nationalism was transformed into characteristic revolutionary fever. It remains to be seen why this change, so far assumed to be irreversible, really is irreversible and what are the elements of this irreversibility. As will be seen in the following chapters, the only factor which might explain this irreversibility is the situational factor.

When seen in relation to all of the factors of the political system, the two theses can be reduced to a disagreement on the significance and intensity of the reciprocal influences of the factors in question: granted the two prevailing collective situations, the attitudes of the social groups in these situations, as well as the centers of political decisions exerting opposing influences on the groups having these attitudes, it remains to be seen what directions these prevailing influences will take.[2]

The residential thesis implied a *descending* conception of these influences. The attitudes of the neutral mass were considered to be basically determined by the political centers, and the relationship of the attitudes to their corresponding situations were not taken into account. In such a framework, higher factors act upon the lower ones, which is to say, once a revolution starts, its outcome depends solely on the maneuvering ability of the political centers in conflict.

The liberal thesis, on the contrary, implied an *ascending* conception of the same influences. It is the situation which is completely responsible for the change in attitude and, in turn, determines the relative strength of the two competing political poles. The lower factors determine the higher ones. Tactical errors committed by either side are negligible in the face of the overwhelming influence these collective attitudes exert on the evolution of the force relationship between the political centers.

When a political change appears as the inevitable complement of a sociological transformation which has already taken place at

2. Although the preceding considerations encroach, in certain respects, on the following chapters, the two approaches to the problem are not synonymous. For the time being, the objective is to investigate how the protectorate hoped to be able to check the spread of nationalism on the local level by *manipulating* the collective attitudes barring a solution. The investigation is thus based on functionalist principles. But the subsequent analyses bear on the objective interaction of political variables. It is the same phenomenon, but the method of approach and the reasoning remain distinct.

the situational level, a relationship is established between political and sociological dynamics. All sociologists and economists agree that changes taking place on the lower levels of society will have repercussions on the higher ones, and there is no reason why these induced changes should not be political in nature. To speak of inevitable political changes is to express a theoretical point of view similar to those that have become commonplace in the related domain of technical sociology or economic dynamics.[3]

This being so, could the Residency have forestalled the outbreak of terrorism by devoting all its available human and material resources to a more effective policy of forceful conversion of the attitudes? As has been seen, the failure of its repressive policy stemmed primarily from a ruthless manner of determining the political objective, from a false conception of the problem itself. The mistake of the French authorities was to have believed that revolutions are made by leaders, by militant minorities. In fact, in a revolution, the leadership is only an extension of the mass—certainly indispensable, but also replaceable as long as the masses can turn out other leaders. In a revolution, the real enemy is not the leadership; it is the organized masses. Thus, if repressive measures are to be effective, they must be aimed at the masses' capacity for reorganization.

To settle the nationalist problem, therefore, the Residency would have had to concentrate its efforts on the Moroccan people, to liquidate through an ad hoc policy of force not only the existing nationalist leadership but all the elites from which new leadership could be recruited. It would have been necessary to put all the rural and urban Moroccan elites into camps and to exile or disband all integrated military units capable of furnishing the soldiers of a future rebellion. The protectorate would have had to take deliberate steps to prevent the population from

3. Why is it difficult for political science to deal with the concept of inevitable political change? Apparently it is because numerous sociological changes occur without being obstructed by social control, but political changes threaten directly, and by hypothesis, a power that reacts. It is therefore not enough to show that these political transformations rest on an irreversible tendency to change. If their inevitability is to be established, it must be shown that the political bases threatened by this evolution cannot counterbalance by an ad hoc use of force the psychological transformations undermining their authority. Seen this way, the problem of change gives way to the problem of resistance to change. This will be fully examined in the following pages.

reconstructing its revolutionary cadres for years to come, and to transform the protectorate into an armed camp. Such an extreme policy would have been the only possible alternative to decolonization as it is theoretically possible to offset, at least for a time, lack of acceptance on the part of the indigenous populace by unlimited use of force. But in practical terms it would not have been feasible. One can imagine that a regime, a la rigueur, might take such steps to quell an armed revolt. But to adopt them before the outbreak of terrorism would have been unthinkable. Such arbitrary use of force would have unleashed opposition all over the world, including the Métropole itself and even in French colonial circles, where it would have sounded the death knell of economic activity. Moreover, no one at Rabat ever dreamed of such a policy at the time, and nothing demonstrates more clearly the political absurdity of such a hypothesis.

The regime, wanting neither to decolonize nor to use sufficient force to extirpate nationalism, for the time being, was forced to adopt police measures inadequate to solve the problem but more than sufficient to unleash, by reaction, terrorism and guerrilla warfare in Morocco.

Since the problem of the *prevention* of terrorism and guerrilla warfare by simple political neutralization of the nationalist pole is insoluble, it remains to be seen if, and under what conditions, the problem posed to the regime by the *outbreak* of terrorism and guerrilla warfare could have been settled by force.

Chapter 6

THE PROBLEM OF MILITARY REPRESSION
OF TERRORISM AND OF
REVOLUTIONARY GUERRILLA WARFARE

Having vainly tried to halt the surge of nationalism by a policy of development, then by liberalization of the regime, and finally by police measures designed to prevent the outbreak of terrorism and guerrilla warfare, the protectorate found itself confronted with a final problem: the forceful elimination of the outlaws of the cities and the *bled*. Since this test of strength was decisive, it is of vital importance to ascertain the extent to which a problem of this kind can be solved and why it was not in Morocco.

To understand how the nature of a problem of public order can affect the success of forceful measures, one must first review the different social functions that force fulfills within the political system. The first political function of force is to inhibit, repress, and prevent the spread of antisocial behavior of individuals in conflict with the accepted norms of society as sanctioned by the authorities. This could be called the *police* function of force. Its second political function concerns the methods of constraint used by revolutionary factions as they attempt, through direct action, to resolve the social problems which traditional authorities cannot or do not want to resolve themselves. This is the *revolutionary* function of force. The third political function of force is to inhibit, and, if necessary, repress threats to public security by that fraction of the community in revolutionary opposition to the state. This is the *counterrevolutionary* function of force. The fourth political function of force is to settle by force of arms the community's conflicts with its outside enemies— military means used either for self-defense or for aggression and conquest. This is the *military* function of force. Last, there is the sort of force used by leaders of militarized groups to reinforce the component of spontaneous loyalty and adhesion among their members. Neither police, nor gendarmerie, nor army, nor revolutionary organization could function if, in each of these authority structures, the respective leaders did not create a common bond of attitude and feeling among their followers through ad hoc coercion, i.e. disciplinary constraint. We are no longer speaking about subduing by force a dissident individual, an outdated regime, a revolutionary faction, or a rival group, but of reinforcing, through a special kind of constraint, the attitudes of individuals and groups upon which the authorities depend in their struggles against enemies, within and without. The *disciplinary* function is the last major political function of force.[1]

For the purposes of the present analysis, it is sufficient to consider only three of these: the police function, the counterrevolutionary function, and the military function of force as used by the state.

The Function of the State's Police

Although the police function of the state is only indirectly related to the theory of conflict, we must nevertheless present a brief analysis of it. Sociological factors conditioning the efficacy of resort to force are most evident at this level. The police function is generally a normal social function of the state. It is important to know why and how this is so before attempting to understand the mechanism of the considerable difficulties the state

---

1. Strictly speaking, the phenomenon is concerned solely with the internal structure of militarized groups. But in a broader sense, it concerns all of the relations between political leaders and their troops in time of acute social upheaval. Force used by a communist regime, by a colonial nationalist regime, or by a fascist regime always contains a disciplinary component aimed not at the enemy, or the adversary, but at the faithful, the soldier and the citizen. Force is not only applied against the enemy, the out-group, it is also applied against the faithful, whose loyalty is assured, and against the traitor whose treason is to be prevented or neutralized. There is an obvious connection between these two kinds of restraint. An army would not know how to range itself against the enemy if its strength was not partially based on its discipline. Revolutionary leadership could not effectively fight against the existing regime if it did not base its intrinsic strength on the working discipline and the spontaneous support of its own troops. The sole difference is that in the case of the army, the enemy is clearly distinguishable from a friend, whereas in the revolutionary hypothesis, friend and foe generally belong to the same group.

encounters when called upon to fulfill its military and counter-revolutionary functions in order to combat a colonial revolt.

It is well-known that the effectiveness of the police function is linked to the instinct of primordial defense which, in all societies, tends to set witnesses of a crime or offense against its author. The authorities, by punishing a criminal, are only taking upon themselves the necessity for enforcing law and order agreed upon to a greater or lesser extent by the quasi-totality of members of the society.

Successful state action in this realm depends on four interrelated conditions: a monopoly of organized force, legislation adapted to the difficulties to be overcome, a penal code severe enough to discourage potential lawbreakers, and public support of the repressive system. The importance of the psychological factor is obvious in the extreme case in which the norm sanctioned by the governing authorities is considered unjust by the conscience of society. If the violated norm does not have sufficient support from the group, the search for lawbreakers becomes a mere formality, the judiciary becomes lax, and the law is openly disobeyed. The necessity for the conscience of the community to adhere to a norm that is threatened or violated is not merely moral; it is also technical. The detection and punishment of lawbreakers requires the active cooperation of all classes within the community. Law enforcement becomes impossible when society itself sides with the lawbreakers. All citizens are voluntary members of the repressive system. For sociologists, the witness who helps to uncover a crime and the policeman who brings the criminal to justice are inseparable.

The existence of "milieux" that sustain organized antisocial behavior illustrates, even better than the previous example of the unjust or unpopular norm, the vital role of social conscience in law enforcement. Such "milieux" are those sectors of society that no longer feel at one with its community norms and oppose them with norms of their own production. When a crime is committed under such circumstances, the "milieu" covers for it, and repressive action rapidly drops below its acceptable level of effectiveness.[2] This review of the basic concepts well known to penologists confirms the fact that collective support of a govern-

2. No doubt the relative immunity of the "milieu" is greatly reinforced by the

ment's repressive action is the sine qua non of the normal exercise of the state's police function.

There is no reason, however, why one cannot modify the formulation of the question and ask whether the problem posed for society by the antisocial behavior of a fraction of the governed can be dealt with by reforms or repressive action directed at the *"milieu" itself.* Delinquents who are products of a certain milieu may evade control, but this milieu itself cannot escape. Is it therefore not possible to make the milieu the object of an effective policy of constraint or of an acceptable reform program? Theoretically, this phase of the problem has two extreme solutions.

The first would consist of a fundamental reform of the social situations constituting the milieu, by raising the living standards of the most impoverished elements of the population and by inaugurating appropriate remedial measures. In an urban area, these would include a fight against juvenile delinquency and against slums, work rehabilitation of the unfit, therapy for the mentally disturbed, and a program to eliminate alcoholism. A quick glance at the record of most civilized countries in this realm tells us that no modern state has ever successfully applied such reforms to its urban slum zones. Generally speaking, public officials are content to make symbolic gestures. Waves of public opinion that might make such reforms practicable fade away quickly and are seldom powerful enough to sustain to the end the half-hearted action of the government. A society can only reform itself if it has the will to do so, and apparently no modern state has ever really wanted to solve the problem of its urban slum areas.

The second solution would be to destroy the milieu, or to subject it to unlimited constraint by executing or imprisoning families of suspected lawbreakers or those refusing to testify, by segregating men and women in rehabilitation camps, by razing the urban districts depopulated by these methods, and so forth. Technically speaking, nothing could be simpler for a modern country. But the destruction or neutralization of dissident groups

---

constraint brought to bear on their own members. This is only a secondary phenomenon. In refusing to cooperate with repressive action, the individuals who feel akin to the gangster or the trafficker at large already assure his essential safety.

by terrorism would be morally impossible. Aside from Nazi Germany, this has never been done in a civilized country, nor, it would seem, even in antiquity. For both ancients and moderns, the guilty one has been the sole object of sanctions. Whatever the nature of the crime, governments have rarely resorted to the extreme solution of resolving the problems posed by one segment of society by amputating the diseased part.[3]

The study of the regular and special use of the police function demonstrates the vital role of the attitudes of these "milieux." Even in ordinary cases, the problem of repression has only two solutions: punishment of particular crimes with the consent of the milieu, or punishment by terrorism, by segregation, or by dispersion of the milieu itself when it becomes allied with the guilty individuals. This last encounters obvious sociological obstacles. We will see that the problem posed by the entry on the scene of terrorist groups and the outbreak of guerrilla warfare in a colonial revolt is of the same nature.

The Antirevolutionary and Military Role of a Colonial State During a Revolutionary War

A French military expert has defined revolutionary, guerrilla, or partisan warfare as "the armed struggle of a minority that gradually gains control over the population, providing it with incentives for action against the established authorities or against an authority it repudiates" [4]

The phenomenon can take three distinct forms. In the first case, the irregulars operate in constant or intermittent liaison with a friendly regular army: the Spanish war under Napoleon, the European Resistance after the landing in 1944, the Soviet partisans who fought with the Red Army, and so forth. In the second case, the insurgents work alone but with the support of a foreign army able to furnish them cadres, materials, and instructors. This is admirably illustrated by the activities of the

---

3. The only known exceptions are political or ideological: the deportation of minorities, the extermination of religious sects, the collective massacres of European Jews or of "antisocial" elements by the Nazis during the last world war.

4. Ximenès, "La Guerre révolutionnaire et ses données fondamentales," *Revue militaire d'information*, no. 281 (Feb.–March 1957), p. 11.

Vietminh groups in Indochina and their progressive transformation into a people's army with the human and material support of the Chinese Communist Army. In the third case, the insurgents receive neither direct nor indirect support from a regular army; their only support is the people themselves and their only source of supplies is the adversary or the international market. The colonial conflicts in North Africa are a striking illustration: the insurrection of the *fellaghas* in Tunisia, the Franco-Moroccan conflict (apart from the help of Spanish Morocco to the insurgents), the Algerian conflict (aside from the F.L.N. bases in Tunisia), and the Cypriot crisis.[5] The present analysis is concerned solely with the third form of revolutionary warfare.

Revolutionary wars can be differentiated not only by the kind of support the insurrectionists enjoy but also by the ability of each side to adapt to the struggle. Metropolitan forces and insurgents can either be highly specialized or relatively unprepared for the struggle at hand. The armed operations which toppled the protectorate in 1955–56 had two distinct characteristics: the obvious unpreparedness of the French forces, and the embryonic organization of the nationalist bands. The guerrilla war which developed in Morocco to the advantage of the nationalists was still in its first phase of development. It is the problems posed for the forces of law and order by this primitive type of insurrection that will be dealt with first.

The question can be put as follows: to what extent could a modern army, inexperienced in guerrilla tactics and operating in the geographic and social environment of Morocco, hope to defeat nationalist commando bands that had the backing of the people but were confined to their own military zone and were not in communication with an outside army capable of supplying them with food and arms? To quote Colonel Lacheroy: "Why were the strongest defeated by the weakest?"[6]

The answer is that a revolutionary war is more a revolution

5. Concerning this last point, see François Crouzet's remarkable study on the insurrectional phase of the Cypriot crisis, which will be published in this same series.

6. Charles Lacheroy, *Action Viet-Minh et communiste ou une leçon de "guerre revolutionnaire,"* S.l.n.d. (roneographed, Centre militaire d'information et de spécialization pour l'outre mer, Section de documentation militaire de l'outre mer), p. 2.

than a war. The strongest is only the strongest in appearance since its full military strength cannot be thrown against the enemy. Second, the weakest is only the weakest on a strictly military plane. Popular support gave the nationalists a clearly irreversible advantage over the French army and was a weapon against which force was unavailing.

The functionalist nature of this dual explanation is obvious. A modern army is a military tool, created for a specific use. Its function is to combat a similar army within a framework which forbids civilians to extend any direct assistance whatsoever to the contending forces. When an instrument of this type is engaged in partisan warfare, its immense destructive capacity can no longer be effectively used. Apart from tanks and helicopters, all other heavy and average size weaponry becomes unusable. The bulk of its strength is used to occupy the terrain and to defend itself. Only a fraction of its forces can be used against the guerrillas, and it is only effective if it is versed in the latest guerrilla tactics. T. E. Lawrence criticized the Turks and the Germans for believing "that rebellion was absolute like war" and for dealing with it "on the analogy of war." But "war upon rebellion was messy and slow, like eating soup with a knife." [7] This formula admirably illustrates the material ambiguity in developing a clear-cut method of stamping out the sort of insurrection that broke out in Morocco.

If we shift our point of view and place ourselves in the position of the nationalists, it is no less clear that a heavy, unwieldy military apparatus plays into the hands of the insurgents. Lengthy, complex supply lines and the necessity of being constantly on guard from all sides leaves the metropolitan forces open to successful surprise attacks by the guerrillas. Numerous attacks are not required to paralyze the adversary. Each attack has endless repercussions: a few ambushes oblige the metropolitan forces to consider the possibility of each host being besieged; a few cases of sabotage on the railroads or road junctions oblige it to guard every kilometer of the line of communications; the least evidence of a popular uprising will give it the feeling of being threatened on all sides.

7. T. E. Lawrence, *Seven Pillars of Wisdom*, (New York, Doubleday, 1938), p. 193.

Let us suppose that the actual forces of the two adversaries have been reduced to equal proportions. The metropolitan forces would retain a certain technical superiority over the insurgents, which would, however, be offset by popular support for the insurgents. This leads us back to a problem similar to that studied in regard to the state's police function. Without the active support of the population, the insurgents would not hold out a week. Once this support is acquired, they become, if not impossible to destroy, sufficiently elusive so that the elimination of guerrilla groups is impossible. If the indigenous group is not a "milieu" in the pejorative sense, it benefits nonetheless from two advantages which shield it from standard repressive techniques: the solidarity of the "milieu" and the outlaws; and the inversion of political and moral values that makes the dissident groups hostile to the attitudes of cooperation on which the functional effectiveness of the repressive apparatus is normally based.

The impossibility of maintaining law and order in a social milieu that makes common cause with a revolt is a sociological phenomenon going beyond the theory of war. This is frankly admitted by experts on revolutionary warfare even when they are convinced, as are the French theorists of the Algerian war, of the existence of pacification formulas other than the standard one of repression. A French expert writes:

> In a revolutionary war, victory cannot be won by arms alone. As long as there remains the basic "infrastructure," the organization that exercises its control over the population, the decimated guerrilla bands continue to regroup themselves and the task of the troops ordered to destroy them recalls that everlasting "clean-up operation" that we have already known in Indochina! [8]

The same writer maintains: "As long as the population is not won over psychologically, as long as the people are not organized to fight (by the forces for pacification), any peace-making effort is too fragile to be of any real significance." [9] "As for guerrilla

---

8. J. Hogard, "Guerre revolutionnaire et pacification," *Revue militaire d'information,* no. 280 (January 1957), p. 14.
9. Ibid., p. 18.

warfare," observes another writer, Ximenès, in summing up a formula that is very applicable to the Moroccan situation,

> its effect cannot be judged only by the number of casualties inflicted on the enemy, nor by the number of arms recouped. By its relentless harassment of the administrative machinery, the police, and the armed forces, this type of warfare puts the regime on the defensive; by its creation of a situation of constant insecurity, it cuts off the masses from the government.[10]

Thus the failure of the type of military repression carried out in Morocco was not accidental. It stemmed from the fact that the repressive measures were aimed at the elusive by-product of the revolt, the revolutionary commando groups, rather than at the real adversary, the indigenous population—or that segment of it which supported the insurrection. In the case before us, the classic form of repression showed itself inadequate to resolve the situation, since the functional prerequisites for the neutralization of the armed groups by metropolitan forces were not present in the milieu.[11]

The conclusion needs a strict interpretation. The French army in Morocco could not stamp out terrorism and guerrilla warfare

---

10. Ximenès, p. 12.

11. The ineffectiveness of a policy of classical repression does not take into account the ups and downs of daily action, where the rebels cease to observe the rules of partition on which their security depends, where the French forces shift without warning from legal to arbitrary repressive measures, and where the urban terrorists find themselves at a disadvantage for a certain period of time. The destruction of terrorist groups in the Algerian *medina* by paratroopers seems to explain itself through a connection of analogous circumstances. When insurgents become too militarized, too heavily equipped, they run the risk of being destroyed by the pursuing army. Once a guerrilla movement is transformed from small elusive terrorist bands into a professional army, it loses its relative immunity. Aside from the closing of the Yugoslavian frontier in 1949, it is this phenomenon which seems to be the origin of the defeat of General "Markos" during that phase of the Greek civil war. Cf. Gabriel Bonnet, *Les Guerres insurrectionnelles et révolutionnaires de l'Antiquité à nos jours* (Paris, 1958), pp. 181–82, 191. As a general rule, such occurrences favorable to repression are incapable of sufficiently modifying the relations of the forces. When terrorist bands are dismantled, they are reconstructed on the spot or elsewhere. Outclassed, partisan groups that are too highly militarized must break up into smaller groups, sacrifice their heavy weapons, and return to simpler tactics that assure their impunity. Both adversaries can make positive or negative variations on the struggle which pits them against one another. They cannot emancipate themselves.

by the methods it employed. This does not mean that, under more favorable political conditions, it could not have neutralized the threat by an extensive occupation of the country, as in Algeria. This method of reacting to the revolt was never considered in Morocco, thanks to an ad hoc metropolitan effort, because it was politically impossible. The granting of internal autonomy to Tunisia, the restoration of the Sultan, and the increased needs for men and weapons for the Algerian war deprived the protectorate of this last recourse.

Having demonstrated the impossibility of dealing with the problem of repression in classical terms, it can no longer be argued that France could have attempted to resolve the problem either through radical reforms, or by recourse to indiscriminate or selective genocide. As for the possibility of crushing the rebellion by an all-out military action aimed at the populace, this would no doubt have resolved the problem on a technical plane, but it would have run up against political and psychological obstacles that must be analyzed for a full understanding of the mechanics of the conflict.

Putting aside for a moment the psychological obstacles that recourse to indirect or direct genocide would have created on the international level,[12] it is evident that this type of extreme action would have engendered more problems than solutions from a purely technical viewpoint. It is easy to crush a people in revolt by force, but it is another matter to apply repressive tactics to all those who merely afford protection to the insurgents among their ranks. A sweeping massacre of passive citizens might have stamped out terrorism in the cities, but it would have resulted in a general retreat to the *bled* of all those able to bear arms. Indiscriminate extermination of the rural population would only cement the unity of tribes and rebels. The only practical solution would have been to destroy selectively the Moroccan elite of the cities and of the *bled* by eliminating all those among the indigenous population who had a capacity for leadership. But how could this be done if all the groups in question were capable of escaping to the hills? This solution, technically feasible before the outbreak of disturbances, would have been inapplicable at

12. See pp. 619 ff.

that phase for lack of political incentive. At the guerrilla stage, it was politically conceivable, but technically unfeasible.[13]

There is a striking similarity between the state's police function and its military and counterrevolutionary functions. In both cases, the reestablishment of order by classical repressive methods becomes impossible when the populace protects the insurgents. In both cases, reforms or destruction of the milieu are as a general rule hard to put into practice for technical, political, and psychological reasons.

The Modern Theory of Colonial Methods of Repressing a Revolutionary War: Case Studies of Indochina and Algeria [14]

Failure of classical forms of repression led military theorists on decolonization to reexamine the entire problem. This doctrinal movement dates back to the war in Indochina, particularly to the battle of Dienbienphu. The functional impotence of the regular army in its struggle against the Vietminh commandos was demonstrated daily. Witnessing the efficacy of propaganda techniques and of the training and mobilization of the opposing masses, and staggered by the results of the brain-washing techniques inflicted on French prisoners by communist experts, officers of the French expeditionary force promptly set about studying their adversary's doctrine. This effort resulted in a concept of pacification consisting of three relatively independent constructions: a theory of revolutionary warfare as practiced today by colonial peoples; a theory of methods of regaining control over the population by metropolitan forces; and application of a repressive policy that differs from the theory on essential points. It is this triple structure that needs schematization and discussion.

13. Except to the extent that repressive measures were used against the fraction of this group which could be effectively apprehended. It is one thing to place a few thousand suspects in rehabilitation camps, but quite another to arrest and imprison tens or hundreds of thousands of individuals, active collaborators or neutrals, who constitute a future source of sociological recruitment for nationalist cadres.

14. Morocco knew only the initial phases of an insurrectional phenomenon that reached full magnitude in Indochina and Algeria. It is necessary to take into consideration Indochinese and Algerian developments on the problem of repressive action if we are to determine in which manner such action could be successful once the insurrection spreads.

SCHEMA OF A REVOLUTIONARY WAR

French experts generally reduce the plan for colonial revolutionary war to the five following steps: (1) planting clandestine groups of agitators and propagandists; (2) creation of secret political organizations—so-called "parallel hierarchies"—whose task it is to enroll the local population in political revolutionary organizations, parallel to those on which the regime relies, and, in the last resort, to ensure the complete militarization of the whole indigenous population to the utmost limits; (3) training and use of terrorist groups and guerrilla bands; (4) creation of "liberated zones" under a revolutionary government, and, finally, the appearance of a regular revolutionary army working hand in hand with the irregulars; and (5) general offensive of revolutionary forces against the established regime, and the accelerated defection to the revolutionary forces of military cadres and elements of the population still controlled by the regime.[15]

This plan may, of course, be complicated or simplified according to the circumstances and may even be confined to some of the initial steps. "Parallel hierarchies" may range from a simple organization of a part of the population by the political and syndical organs of a movement, such as the Neo-Destour or the Istiqlal, to a complex network of hierarchies such as that of the Vietminh, which grouped the entire population in a dual network of local committees and a popular front, the so-called "Lien Viet," both of which were controlled by the Communist Party.[16] The fourth phase, which includes the opening of liberated and occupied zones by a regular revolutionary army, is possible only when the rebellion has at its disposal an adequate foreign base, as was the case in Indochina. It is incompatible with the situations in Tunisia, Morocco, or even Algeria. It was not the pacification activities of the French army that prevented the creation of a regular F.L.N. army in Algeria, but rather the insufficient military aid given by Tunisia and Morocco to the insurrection.[17] The fifth phase, with its final military onslaught,

15. Hogard, p. 11.
16. Ibid., p. 8.
17. If the French army was able to prevent the formation of a regular F.L.N. army, it is because the creation of such an army was against the nature of things. Tunisia

has occurred only in China when the nationalist government of Chiang Kai-shek suddenly lost its popular and military support to the communists. Such a phase would be impossible in a colonial revolt, where the repressive apparatus is made up of metropolitan forces. They can certainly be demoralized or even militarily defeated, but one cannot imagine them swinging over to the rebels as in a national revolution.

THEORY OF COUNTERACTION AND REASSUMPTION OF CONTROL
OVER THE POPULATION

The French doctrine concerning reaction to a revolutionary war is based on awareness of the fact that an insurrectionary movement of the population can only be combatted through that population. Hogard writes that "the only successful pacification policy rests . . . on the coordination of our efforts in all domains, on an extensive use of psychological warfare with a view to radically destroying the basic infrastructure that is the source of our enemy's strength." [18] He adds that

> the military leader, in close collaboration with the civil authorities, must seek by all possible means—political, administrative, economic, social, cultural, and military —not only the annihilation of enemy units, which cannot be accomplished by arms alone, but the destruction of the politico-military organization of the rebels. The leader must work for the psychological conquest of the population so that it can be organized and participate actively in the fight on our side.[19]

In other words, it is a question of borrowing the adversary's methods, transplanting them to the domain of repressive action, and using them against him. Thus, it is not by pure chance that the plan for suppression contains the five following points:

1. Setting up a *"human contact"* policy based on the analysis of social inequalities favorable to revolution and "the implemen-

_____

was too vulnerable, too reluctant, and too parsimonious of aid to be for North Africa what China was to Indochina. Moroccan support was even more measured.

18. Hogard, p. 16.

19. Ibid., p. 24.

tation of reforms designed to suppress or at least alleviate the 'internal contradictions' which form the grass roots of the rebellion."[20]

2. Parallel development of a policy of counter-propaganda and information designed to immunize the mass against the adversary's psychological warfare, to "unmask the mechanism" before their eyes, and to establish instruction for the colonized.[21]

3. Creation on this basis of "a centralized information agency" with maximum ramifications as well as the installation of a system of politico-military defense over a territory that is largely decentralized.[22]

4. "Physical and moral mobilization of the population—the real stake in the struggle—without which the regime is destined to collapse sooner or later, depending on the adversary's strength."[23] This mobilization tends to thwart the enrollment of revolutionary troops by a counterrevolutionary regimentation, and helps the wavering populace to resist the adversary's pressure by installing a system of self-defense.

5. Final reconquest of a population still controlled by the nationalists through an increased military effort, reinforced by the elimination of suspects and the internment of recalcitrants or well-known rebels into camps for reindoctrination.[24]

The difficulties involved in the implementation of this pacification program were perceived, if not fully understood, by French authors. The elements of weakness and illusion that must be guarded against if successful pacification is to be achieved have been analyzed by Hogard. The first weakness is the flexibility of the adversary's defense. The adversary who is "defeated in the third, fourth, or fifth phase of the struggle . . . can return to the preceding one, to the first phase, if necessary, and start over again." Under the circumstances, the only thing to try is to "make him go back to the initial phase, and force him to stay

20. A. Souyris, "Les Conditions de la parade et de la riposte à la guerre revolution-naire," *Revue militaire d'information,* no. 281 (February–March 1957), p. 101.
21. Ibid., pp. 102–03.
22. Ibid., pp. 104–05.
23. Ibid., p. 106.
24. Ibid., pp. 108–09.

there." [25] The second weakness is the danger of confusion about the real causes of the struggle, or differences between the aims of the party that controls the insurrection and the roots of popular discontent it exploits. The real cause of the Algerian war, writes Hogard, gathering his thoughts into a formula confusing illusion and reality, was the "determination of Cairo and the F.L.N. to drive the French from North Africa. It is therefore futile to attempt to put an end to revolutionary war only through political, economic and social reforms." Finally, there is the previously mentioned impossibility of "victory by arms alone," [26] and the fact that negotiations strengthen the adversary's position rather than force him to compromise.

According to French theorists on revolutionary warfare, pacification cannot overcome its own inherent weakness except by taking into account, and fully exploiting, those of its adversary. Hogard continues that the weaknesses of the insurrection are the attraction of the western ideal in its struggle against the perverted morality that characterizes all revolutionary undertakings, the "academic" slowness of the processes of revolutionary war, which is forced to develop under the eyes of its adversary, and which is easy to stop "in the first or the second phase and even the third or fourth"; and, last, the dependence of the opposite side's politico-military organization on the population which can be easily voided of its substance by rallying the indigenous population to the side of pacification. Peacemaking in practice was marked by efforts to organize and reconquer the masses.[27]

The inconsistency of the last three arguments is obvious. The pacifier may well judge his moral values to be superior to those of the enemy, but nothing obliges the adversary to share these sentiments. The slowness of the organizational revolutionary processes does not imply in any way that a mass movement is easier to stop in its initial manifestations than in its later developments. As for the necessary reassumption of control over the masses, it is less a case of finding a sociological condition for a solution to the problem than of assuming that it is solved by

25. Hogard, p. 13.
26. Ibid., p. 14.
27. Ibid., pp. 14–15.

gratuitously turning the oppressed masses into a sort of human clay that the colonizer can mold to suit himself.

THE USE OF COUNTERACTION

While there is no question that this concept of pacification was largely inspired by the operations of the French army in its struggle against the F.L.N., these operations diverged so widely from the theory that they took the form of a third concept which it is essential to analyze. The practice of pacification diverges from the theory in two important respects: (1) the organization and reconquest of the masses was pushed to such a point that it was transformed into an actual campaign of nerves and thus of disintegration of the colonized peoples; and (2) the need for reform and human contacts which is at the heart of the concept was translated into truncated programs and into sterile social activities.

There is no doubt about the effects of pacification on the Algerian people. Under the banner of purification, organization, and rehabilitation, the pacification policy achieved the partial destruction of the nerve centers of the population. On the pretext of reorganizing and of regaining the support of the population, people were uprooted and transferred from their lands and a serious blow thus dealt to the existing social structure. On the pretext that reprisal was necessary, counter-terrorism against the population was instigated to compensate for the F.L.N.'s hold over this same population. The policy was never pushed to the point of reestablishing a rapport between the indigenous masses and the forces of colonialism. These minor and selective forms of genocide nevertheless did help the French forces to hold out, which demonstrates the inadequacy of classical forms of repression and the impossibility of adhering strictly to the theory of pacification formulated by the army.

The theory assumed that the indigenous mass would rally to a political organization which was more effective and more equitable than that of the revolutionaries. The practice resulted in the prostration of the population by harassment, segregation and terror—the net effect of which was to strengthen the hold of the insurgents, who were already trying to convince young Muslims that the F.L.N. was the only solution to their problems. This doctrinal distortion in favor of force is the normal counterpart resulting from the postponement of social reform measures and of social justice basic to the pacification policy. It would be unfair to deny the positive results on social justice instituted in Algeria, by a pleiad of administrative officers, but, even in the best cases, the effort remained sterile because it was conceived as a means of pacifying the population and not as the first step toward their eventual political and social emancipation. Not being able to destroy colonialism, the practitioners of pacification, with one exception, satisfied themselves by destroying it in name only with the adoption of the formula of integration. The vicious circle was changed. Either integration is undertaken seriously and can only result in the election of nationalist leaders, followed, at the first signs of difficulties, by secession, the ultimate disaster which integration itself is precisely intended to avert. Or integration has no goal other than change for the sake of change, and nothing is settled. In the best of hypotheses, it is predicated on a doctrinal interpretation based on the contestable idea that the easiest way to delay emancipation of a colonized people is to quicken the pace of western development.

Such as it was, pacification in practice was in keeping with the theory, but the theory itself was mitigated by its exigencies of reform and weighted down by the many cruelties inflicted on a people that it had given up trying to convert by psychological methods.

CRITIQUE OF THE THEORY OF PACIFICATION

The doctrinal readjustment affected by the French army in North Africa hinges on an attempt to transpose to the realm of pacification a strategy and tactic of revolutionary action that is the work of communist theorists. It is nonetheless true that such a transposition would not have been possible if the officers who formulated it and put it into practice had not made themselves into self-styled sociologists, administrators, politicians, and social reformers. This diversification of military action is one of the traditions of the colonial army, but this time it was pushed to its extreme limits. The importance given to the psychological factor, the minimized role of arms, the necessity of transforming the classical functions of the army into politico-military functions were as clearly recognized as was possible by the officers, whose limited training and prejudices were the only obstacles to a full implementation of this program.

This logical, and in a sense balanced, structure was basically vitiated by a postulate which is familiar to us: the essential neutrality of the masses which are considered a priori as an inert factor that opposing organizations fight over and manipulate. It is an explicit postulate this time and is seen as a leitmotiv by French authors. According to Hogard, "parallel hierarchies" deliver "individuals to the mercy of the authorities."[28] The psychological basis of the enemy organization is from the beginning considered as "rigged."[29] There is nothing simpler than "to propose an ideal around which people can rally. If this ideal has to be defined at a very high level, it must suit them and be presented to them in an appealing manner."[30] Ximenès declared the mass to be "fundamentally inert and amorphous."[31] For him, the opposing organization is the only obstacle to the psychological mobilization of the masses. The ultimate objective is the "conquest of the human milieu."[32] Captain A. Souyris considers that only the action of the revolutionary organization is the "determining cause" of the revolution.[33] And to eliminate any doubt about this statement, he quotes Colonel Lacheroy: "If you hold a receptacle firmly in hand, you can put what you wish inside."[34] In this extreme case, it is a question of lending a concept to the adversary, but lending it only to withdraw it as the cornerstone of the pacification policy.

In Rabat and Algiers, in both civilian and military circles, by De Blesson or Colonel Lacheroy, the same mistake was made. But in Rabat under De Blesson it was instinctive and unformulated, whereas in Algiers under the reign of the army, and after

28. Ibid., p. 9.
29. Ibid., p. 23.
30. Ibid., pp. 20–21.
31. Ximenès, p. 14.
32. Ibid., p. 20.
33. Souyris, p. 97.
34. Ibid., p. 101.

years of doctrinal elaboration, it became explicit, "formulated," and even more subtle. In Rabat the two opposing poles were still composed of only a handful of French and Moroccans, whereas in Indochina and in Algeria the two poles developed so as to include the whole population in a double net wherein all individuals were, in fact, prisoners. From 1955 to 1960, the only real progress made in the doctrine was the increased importance given to the role of the masses and the realization that standard military methods would not work against a rebellion. At Algiers and Rabat, the analysis was rendered sterile by the idea that revolutions are made by leaders who manipulate the people as they see fit. It was felt that the work of the rebels could be nullified by an effective program of pacification, and a theory of action was formulated, based on the notion that the mass was an inert, amorphous factor in the struggle.

All the vices of the doctrine of pacification stem from these fundamental misjudgments: minimization of the factors which condition the attitudes of colonized people in revolt; exaggeration of the role of revolutionary and counterrevolutionary organizations, and consideration of them as the only active elements; misunderstanding the real psychological nature of the rebellion and correlative falsification of the role of pacification; underestimation of the real significance of the first nationalist outbreaks; and the fatal instability engendered by a policy of pacification that vacillates perpetually from attempts at reforms to a repression which is ineffective because it is not aimed at the true adversary—the masses.

French theorists borrowed their techniques for warfare and control of the mass from the communists, but they failed to see that these techniques were only the obvious superstructure for a revolutionary upheaval, of which the mass was the driving force. From Marx to Lenin to Mao Tse-tung, professional revolutionaries have always considered the masses the prime mover in social upheavals. Marx considered the revolutionary leader the pilot of the ship with the real force coming from below. Lenin in his famous formula said that he wished to be one step ahead of his troops, but only one step. In modern revolutionary warfare the increased importance given to disciplinary constraint and persuasion techniques might lead the uninitiated astray. The fundamental nature of the phenomenon remains the same. By ascribing everything to the hierarchy, to the pilot and the motor, to the brain which directs, and to the factor which propels, western military men have stood Mao Tse-tung's theory on its head and transformed a theory of revolution by the people into a theory of revolution by cadres.[35]

Apart from the ideological distortion which was inevitably to lead the theorists of pacification to a misconception, this doctrinal inversion has two rational causes. The first is the extreme complexity of the problem. A very subtle analysis is required to evaluate exactly the role of leadership in revolutionary sociology. More so than in other realms, the superficial factors conceal the deeper ones. It is evident that an unorganized movement is from the beginning destined to fail, that the masses make their demands heard through their leaders, and that without disciplinary constraint the spontaneous attitudes that cement the bonds between social groups would not suffice to prevent an anarchic dislocation. The mistake is to assume that organization, discipline, and leadership are enough in themselves. It is not organization that molds collective attitudes, but collective attitudes that serve as the foundation for organization. Leaders cannot majestically halt the course to be followed. They can only resolve, to a greater or lesser degree, the problems posed by the contradictory demands of the governed. Discipline does not create the morale of an army. It can only stabilize and give value to a preliminary accord between leaders and their troops that, far from seeming to be the result of action by the leaders, is instead the condition. If the doctrinal movement of the French army in North Africa had been purely rational, it would have been sufficient for these leaders to consider the sociological structure of the military phenomenon in order to immunize themselves against the difficulties of the problem. The first mistake not to be made when considering the nature of revolutionary theory is to forget that a "civil war" is nonetheless a "war," and that these two phe-

35. The two terms can, in a certain way, inverse their roles in the latter phases of a revolution, but this Stalinization of command is impossible in the initial phase of the movement. The masses must "bring" their leaders to power before the leaders can bring their power to bear on the masses.

nomena are sociologically similar. At the basis of all armies as in all revolutions, there is a consensual element not attributable to the actions of its leaders. Patriotism, in modern warfare, is that spontaneous esprit de corps of the troops, its preliminary moral component, the leader, being merely a guardian. In ancient warfare, it was the contractual adhesion of the mercenary who had sold his physical self for pay. When this foundation is given, leaders can build their hierarchy and rely on it to react on this basis through discipline. Failing this, an army cannot function. In any case, no proof of strength is possible with an adversary in moral agreement with the objectives of the struggle. There is no more neutrality among troops in war than among masses in revolt; there is no moral accord that can be formulated by the leaders unless the base contributes to its primary components, and there is no discipline without consent. The mass cannot be governed by spontaneity alone, or by organization alone. In these circumstances, the only coherent doctrine is one that rejects both extremes and sees the masses and the hierarchy as complementary. However interdependent they are, the fundamental collective data remain sociologically more vital than the organizational factor.

The second error stems from the complexity of real situations. We may, in an attempt to simplify theoretically, reason as if the totality of the colonized population supported the nationalist organization and as if the enacting terms of pacification found themselves in a milieu radically hostile to them. In reality things are not so simple. A colonized populace in revolt is made up of three distinct political factions: those who support the revolution, those who remain neutral or who "wait and see," and those who collaborate with the colonial authorities. The sociological rapport that is established between pacification and each one of these factions necessarily differs in each case. Moroccans who were favorable to the regime were the pillars of colonial order—the regime could not function without the support of at least one fraction of the traditional cadres and their popular following. The neutralists partially justify the French doctrine of pacification, since a theory that postulates the neutrality of the mass is necessarily true with regard to the fraction of this mass that is really neutral at the given moment. The fraction which voluntarily and spontaneously supports the insurrection necessarily puts the theory and practice of pacification in question. Its irreducible hostility to colonization removes from the influence of the regime the irreducible nucleus that must be pacified if their objective is to be obtained. The converse is true. The constraint exercised by the revolutionary organization on the authentic revolutionary fraction of the population is purely disciplinary. It does not create the attitudes of this social group. It is based on a preliminary coincidence of desire and sentiment between the leaders and the masses to reinforce that accord.Where it concerns the neutralists and those with a "wait and see" attitude, the constraint is neither pure discipline nor pure terror, since those intermediary groups are composed of individuals who have not yet rallied to the revolution, but who will eventually be swept up into it, or die-hards who will always escape the revolutionaries, and who could only be neutralized through coercion. To deal with the regime's collaborators the revolutionaries evidently employ purely terroristic techniques, since only physical destruction or intimidation could break them away from the opposing organization.

This introduction of necessary nuances in no way nullifies the overwhelming advantage which the insurrectionists enjoy by comparison with the forces of pacification. First, this is because the fraction of the population that supports the insurrection includes the youth and the new elites who are the most dynamic and vital elements of the present. Second, the insurrection is carried on by the modern and advanced elements of the community, whereas pacification is founded on the vestigial and archaic remains of traditional society (those who resist change or those who have not yet been eliminated by it). Moreover, the neutralists constitute in themselves only a provisional group destined to split in the near future into proportions favoring either of the two extreme groups.

Seen in this more subtle perspective, the conflict between the revolutionist forces and those of pacification no longer appears as the struggle between absolute truth and absolute falsehood, but as the failure of a truth yielding to a stronger truth. The statement should be taken literally. The advantages that accrue to the

forces of change over the conservative forces are only decisive because they are able to transpose to the political plane the irreversible evolution which gradually replaces outdated social structures
with those of a future which is in fact half realized. The irreversibility of a political transformation does not necessarily imply
its simplicity. Sociological phenomena are only simple in the
theories that simplify them. These facts must certainly be reduced to their essentials in order to be understood, but once the
explanatory schema is stopped, it is indispensable to return to the
facts in order to explain the situation and express its differences.
The first movement produces the groundwork of the explanation. The second restores to the phenomena the imprecision of
contours, the indistinctness, and the ambiguity which characterize sweeping sociological transformations. In social evolution,
the winners need not hold all the trump cards to be the victors.
It is possible to slow down an evolutionary process by using
the factors favorable for a conservative or "wait and see" policy.
So that history may continue, it is enough that those who have
the future in their favor and those for whom the future is
condemned establish a difference in positive historical potential,
however minimal it might be. Even on the most level plains,
rivers never flow back toward their source.

In political struggles of the Franco-Moroccan or Franco-Al-
gerian type, where the elimination of evolutionary solutions
leaves the Métropole no other choice but to pursue repressive
policies, we can imagine four a priori solutions to the military
problem posed for the force at grips with the insurrection: (1)
liquidation of the insurgents and stabilization of the regime by
standard military measures aimed particularly at the armed
enemy bands; (2) complete elimination of the insurgents
through mutilation of the colonized people, accomplished
through a policy of ad hoc collective violence; (3) reciprocal
confrontation between the revolutionary and repressive forces,
eventually resulting in a deadlock until the métropole abandons
the war effort; or (4) placing the metropolitan army at a
strategic disadvantage by the insurgents, leading to a forced
evacuation of the colonial territory by the metropolitan forces.

Even military experts agree that the first solution would be impracticable once the insurrection gains broad popular support. The second solution is conceivable, but rendered unworkable by the grave moral and political objections it would encounter. The fourth solution assumes that the insurgents had access to a foreign base potentially equal or superior to that of the metropolitan forces, which was not the case in North Africa. There remains the third solution which is the most consistent with North African crises. It has both a major and minor form. In its minor form (Tunisia, Morocco), the metropolitan forces abandoned the terrain after a brief show of force because they allowed themselves to be drawn into a classical war. The forces were not willing or able to make the necessary military effort to hold out, or did not make it because the insurrection had gained time on the metropolitan forces, who had neither the time nor the local support necessary for organization. In its major form (Algeria), metropolitan France launched upon a war effort that absorbed a vital part of its armed forces and relied on the partial destruction of the colonized. This mutilation was ideologically camouflaged or portrayed as meeting the normal needs of pacification.

The result is that, on the one hand, in a conflict of the North African type, the insurgents have the means to engage the metropolitan army as long as they wish. On the other hand, the metropolitan forces cannot balance the pressure of the insurgents except at the cost of an exceptional military effort, which implies the settlement of other colonial crises in which the mother country is involved and the concentration of all its available resources in a single theater of revolutionary war. The insurrection, however, is hard put to defeat the metropolitan forces. Revolutionary war can seldom hold within itself the decisive factor. Only the central argument of the constellation of material, political, and moral forces will eventually persuade the metropolitan power to abandon the struggle; but this would be inoperative if local nationalism renounced the use of force.

PART TWO

THE VARIABLES IN THE SYSTEM

Having examined the main political problems which the two communities of Morocco posed for France and her local representatives, we can now move from the functionalist aspect of the argument to its quasi-mathematical aspect.

The purpose of this second part of the analysis is to requalify, conforming to this explicative method, the historical and sociological data set forth in the other volume, thus permitting the major variables of the political system in the conflict to become apparent.

The metropolitan and Moroccan echelons of this system were reduced finally to four groups of variables: situational, attitudinal, ideological,[1] and decision variables. The phenomena which appeared on the international plane will be the subject of a sociological analysis in Part III.

1. Regarding metropolitan ideologies, see p. 513 n.

SECTION ONE: THE MOROCCAN ECHELON

Chapter 1

SITUATIONAL VARIABLES

The situation of a social group can be defined as the whole complex of relationships that bind this group together or that link it to the society of which it is a part, to its source of livelihood, and to the techniques which characterize its level of sociological development. Thus, the situation is equivalent to the social existence of the group, but it comprises neither the group's attitude toward its living conditions, nor the ideas which it derives from these attitudes, nor the decisions taken by its leaders with regard to its situation.[1] From the point of view of method, the analysis of situations is the necessary starting point for any study of conflicts, attitudes, ideologies, and decisions that form the raw material of political crises and only become meaningful when considered in relation to the collective situations from which they derive. Once the knowledge of situations is given, everything projecting from this on a higher level of attitudes, ideas, and political decisions becomes intelligible. To attempt the study of any conflict, especially a colonial one, without basing it on the study of situations facing one another would be to place the theory on an unsound basis.

1. The highlighting of certain attitudes with regard to the situation of a group is a somewhat arbitrary process. A number of attitudes remain an integral part of the situation. The discrimination practiced in everyday affairs by the Europeans in Morocco against the Muslims was, in its strongest sense, part of the situation. On the other hand, when the Europeans defended their situation against Muslim demands, this defensive attitude in part transcended the European situation, since it was partially determined by it.

The Situation of the Muslims

The situation of the Muslims has been schematically reduced to seven components expressing, respectively, the political, ethnic, socio-cultural, economic, demographic, technological, and psychological aspects of this group's social existence. Each situational component is reduced, in turn, to a certain number of constituent factors which summarize the analyses described elsewhere, and which we will schematically enumerate.

POLITICAL COMPONENTS

Transformation of the Sharifian Empire into a French protectorate as a result of a military conquest;

Subsequent breakup of Morocco into two political zones under the jurisdiction of different colonial powers;

Contractual establishment in the French zone of a protectorate regime granting nominal sovereignty to the Sharifian Sultanate;

Progressive development by a covert legal regime of a bicephalous political organization in which the Sultan, apart from his spiritual authority, retained only the right to put his seal of approval on laws promulgated by the French;

Subdivision of the traditional political-administrative framework through the addition of a French official to control the activities of Muslims in the cities and the rural areas;

Correlative transformation, through selective recruitment and administrative shakeups, of the Sultan's agents into puppets of the French regime;

Maintenance and reinforcement of privileges for eminent Moroccans by consecrating to them the sources of prestige which they enjoyed prior to French conquest and through the concession of new favors which tie them to the colonial regime;

Ignorance of the political role of the traditional urban elites and of the westernized Moroccan youth;

Relative stability of the political system in the rural areas through the control of the elite that were supported by French authorities;

Lack of political framework in the large *medinas* suffering from a chronic state of inadequate administration;

The absence of political representation, personal security, and social rights, but toleration by the French authorities of a Muslim trade-union movement.

ETHNIC COMPONENTS

Gradual establishment, alongside the indigenous community, of a European community that was at the same time a political minority and a privileged group;

Flagrant materialization, at all levels of this social structure, of economic, political, and cultural factors of superiority and inferiority that characterized these two communities;

Almost complete segregation of the two communities in urban areas, in effect, contact between the two only in public places and at work;

Attenuation of segregation in rural areas of mixed population was less feasible because farming implied a certain amount of necessary cooperation between the two groups.[2]

SOCIO-CULTURAL COMPONENTS

Disintegration, varying according to the intensity of the contact, of the existing institutions, attitudes, and values involved in the adaptation of traditional Muslim society to the needs, resources, and techniques characteristic of underdeveloped societies;

Partial replacement of traditional cultural factors by embryos of western culture (institutions, attitudes, and values).

In the Towns

Gradual westernization of the way of life of the upper classes;

Training and development of a small intellectual elite in French schools;

Slow regression of the traditional class of artisans;

Growth of a middle class in the western sense;

Increased exodus of peasants from rural areas to European centers creating a neo-proletariat, the result of urbanization of a large portion of the agricultural class, freed of the restraints of rural life but unassimilated into traditional city life;

2. For a detailed study of the situation of the European group, see pp. 486 ff.

The absolute poverty in living conditions of this social group;

Intensification of the political and social role of the cities in traditional Muslim society.

In the Rural Areas

Apparent stability of the rural areas, concealing a gradual deterioration;

Permanence of traditional modes of existence of a stationary nature: great feudal lords, middle-sized landowners, small landowners (fellahin), salaried workers (agricultural laborers and *khammès,* or sharecroppers);

Permanence of nomadism, but the relative disappearance of the phenomenon, due to the appropriation and the parceling out of the arable land by the European settlers, to the advantage of the small Moroccan landowners;

Increasing proletarianization of rural Morocco;

Massive rural exodus resulting primarily from the pull that urban centers exercised on the *bled*.

In General

The weakening role of religion in the life of westernizing Moroccan groups;

Deterioration of religious cohesion in the Muslim milieu due to opposition by a modernist trend and a traditionalist trend to Islam;

Gradual penetration of western values into Muslim culture.

ECONOMIC AND FINANCIAL COMPONENTS

Intensive development, until the last months of the protectorate, of the infrastructure in the two communities, but principally "consumed" by the Europeans;

Inadequate social improvements for the Muslims, particularly in the domain of housing, education, and health, and the late development of these reforms;

Fiscal and financial discrimination favorable to the colonizers and in general tied to the profit exigencies of the colonial economy;

Stagnation in the productivity and living standard of the traditional Moroccan farmer, in spite of the mechanization of some large feudal domains, the creation of advisory centers for the peasantry, and the implementation of marginal measures of protection of the peasants;

Four million hectares of arable land belonged to Muslims, and one million hectares to European settlers;

Stabilization of the living standard at the subsistence level for Muslim groups involved in the European economy with the exception of a privileged faction and the new rising middle-class.

DEMOGRAPHIC COMPONENTS

An extensive increase of the Moroccan population, from 4,000,-000 in 1921 to roughly 7,500,000 in 1951–1952;

Inequality of this increase in the rural and urban centers (between 1912 and 1952, the urban population increased from 500,-000 to 1,500,000; the increase in the rural areas for the same period was from 3,500,000 to 6,000,000);

Numerical predominance of the rural elements of this population in which the urban fraction represented less than a quarter of the population in 1951–1952.

The extreme youth of this population (the average age of 30 percent of the whole population was 20 to 40);

Relative decrease in the number of rural landowners with medium and small holdings (between 1932 and 1952 this group's percentage of the rural population fell from 50 percent to 30 percent); Relative increase in the number of salaried agricultural workers (between 1932 and 1952, this group's percentage of the rural population rose from 33 to 60 percent);

Gradual disappearance of nomads;

Increase of urban neo-proletariat, which in 1952 accounted for almost one-third of the Muslim city population. This exodus from the rural to the urban areas represented only 35 percent of the increase of the rural population. The remainder stayed.

TECHNOLOGICAL COMPONENTS

Stagnation of traditional techniques of agricultural production;

Integration of a part of the urban population into the attractive area of modern techniques of production and exchange;

Extension of preventive and curative medicine for the masses;

Improvement of the geographical integration of the country
and the intensification of contact between city and *bled* through
the development of a complex network of modern communications;

Extension of modern techniques of information and the advent of a tight network of radio receiving stations, putting the
inhabitants of the most isolated regions into immediate contact
with the cities and the outside world;

Partial compensation for the weakness of intercultural contacts
in the *bled* by the militarization of an extensive portion of the
rural population.[3]

PSYCHOLOGICAL COMPONENTS

The refusal of the Europeans to permit the Muslim group to
move beyond the caste barrier that separates the colonized from
the colonizers in a colonial regime;

The unusual character of this caste barrier, which led the
colonized to consider other factors of inequality inherent in their
situation as simple corollaries to this major discrimination;

Psychological and political integration of opinion through
modern techniques of information.

The Situation of the Europeans

The situation of the Europeans is characterized, like that of the
Muslims, by a certain number of components reducible to a
multiplicity of constituent factors. We have retained here only
the components and factors which characterize the particular
situation of a European group living in a colonial environment.

POLITICAL COMPONENTS

The monopoly of political influence and of governing force by
the French in a regime tending to assure, above all, the progress
and security of the Europeans;

Exclusive control of public functions by the French through
French administrators who governed, administered, or judged
directly, or through representatives;

---

3. 150,000 voluntary recruits, for the most part peasants, served in the French Army
during World War II.

A foreign statute imposed European-style by a regime that acknowledged the nominal sovereignty of the Sultan, as a result of which the settler in Morocco had neither political rights, guarantees of personal security, nor the possibility of participating in the municipal government of which he formed the majority.

SOCIOLOGICAL COMPONENTS

Minority character of this group;

Attainment by the Europeans of a western way of life that tended to give them a higher standard of living and more prestige than a group with their social status would have enjoyed in France;

Intensified internal stratification of the group (the numerical preponderance of notables, merchants, officials, employees, and skilled workers; the absence of peasantry in the European sense of the term, the settlers being the only farmers; the absence of a wage-earning class, but the development, in the slums of Casablanca in particular, of a relatively important neo-proletariat of Mediterranean origin);

Voluntary and spontaneous isolation of the Europeans living in the cities, although not always in the *bled*.

ECONOMIC AND FINANCIAL COMPONENTS

Economic activity characterized by the gradual incorporation of the natural and human resources of Morocco, the traditional peasantry excepted, into a western type of economy;

Rapid upswing of the modern sectors of the Moroccan economy, the phenomenon being linked to the economic, political, and fiscal privileges of the Europeans at the expense of the native labor force;

Budgetary and financial policy conditioned by the necessity to guarantee a greater profit to metropolitan or foreign investors than they could normally obtain from their own economies;

Financial priority for investments destined for the development of the economic activities of the Europeans and the satisfaction of their needs;

Limited financing for support and modernization of traditional sectors of the Moroccan economy, due to the priority character of the needs enumerated above;

Economic activity of the European sector based on the mobilization of the country's natural resources, on their commercialization, and on the development of activities indispensable to the growth of the group (construction, irrigation, etc.);

Very limited or nonexistent industrialization;

Appropriation of 15 percent of "arable" Moroccan land (1 million hectares) by 20,000 settlers, 8,000 of whom represented 3 percent of the rural Muslim population;

Relatively weak sociological impact of colonization on traditional rural life.

DEMOGRAPHIC COMPONENTS

The numerical weakness of this group, which, in 1951–52, represented about one twentieth (350,000 individuals) of the whole Muslim population;

The essentially urban character of the group, 80 percent of which was concentrated in the cities;

The numerical predominance of the French, representing in 1951–52 six-sevenths of the expatriate community.

PSYCHOLOGICAL COMPONENTS

The psychological isolation of the Europeans behind the caste barrier separating the two ethnic groups;

The importance of this barrier in the psychology of the Europeans, the inferiority imposed on the Muslims having a tendency to appear to the colonizer as the justification of his presence in the colony, as the reason for his settlement in the country, and as the safeguard of the privileges attached to his social condition.

Chapter 2

ATTITUDINAL VARIABLES

If political conflicts are rooted in determined social situations, they only become consistent, as we have said, at the level of attitudes which stem from these situations, and the political behavior is derived from these attitudes. Attitude, individual or collective, is essentially "anticipated behavior." [1] It is nothing more than the common denominator of a characteristic type of behavior. Thus, it is through the interpretation of collective attitudes that social behavior acquires specificity and homogeneity. Attitudes, like situations, are sociological variables. Given a situation, a certain type of attitude will necessarily derive from it. If this situation is changed in a determined manner, the corresponding attitude tends also to change in a determined manner. The attitude is defined as soon as its contents, intensity, and the sociological factor to which it refers are determined. A subject's motives for adopting a certain attitude with regard to a certain sociological factor do not help to determine the attitudinal variable. Thus motivations form a variable different from the attitudinal one. The two variables interact on each other, but one is not necessary for an explanation of the other.

It appears, on the whole, that the cohesion of the Franco-Muslim community in Morocco gradually altered after 1943 as a result of a complex system of psychological tensions which put into opposition, on the one hand, the political attitudes of the two ethnic groups and, on the other hand, the varying proportions of partisans and adversaries of the status quo within each of these groups. These different attitudinal systems are studied below from the dual vantage point of the content of the attitude and its generalization within the group in question. The reasons

1. As defined by Kimball Young, cited in Roger Girod, *Attitudes collectives et relations humaines* (Paris, 1953), p. 9.

for a change of attitude will be examined at the end of the analysis, and for the groups in toto.

Muslim Nationalism

COMPONENTS OF THE ATTITUDE

The political attitude which was to spread, within ten years, to the greater part of the Muslim population may be defined as anticolonialism in principle based on *demands* implying the following:

Gradual elimination of economic and financial discrimination tied to the protectorate regime, and the adoption of a budgetary policy resolutely based on the modernization of traditional agriculture, the promotion of social reforms in the Muslim community (e.g. health services, education, housing), and an increase in the salaries of the indigenous workers;

Correlative elimination of political, socio-cultural, economic, financial, technological, and psychological factors of inequality in the Muslim situation;

Creation of temporary legislative, executive, and administrative organs purged of all archaic and arbitrary features;

Correlative concession to the Muslims of the individual security and political rights that characterize a modern democracy;

Final crowning of these transitory preparations through the recognition of independence of the country and the establishment of a fully sovereign modern regime.

The conversion of an initial consent into political opposition for the conservative decisions of the regime, and subsequent conversion of this political opposition to insurrectional action occurred as these demands were not satisfied.

Although this nationalist program was primarily made up of the maximum demands elaborated by the most conscious elements of the Muslim population, it nonetheless expressed the source of weakness and the subject of true discontent of the greater part of the colonized group. It therefore reveals the attitude of this group.

GENERALIZATION OF THE ATTITUDE

The gradual spread among the Muslims of the characteristic attitudes of nationalism took place along such different lines and at such a different pace in the urban milieu and in the rural milieu that the two aspects of the phenomenon should be analyzed separately.[2]

In the cities, it was the westernized youth, allied with the anticolonialist fraction of the intellectual and religious traditionalist elites, that prepared the way for the political change. Moroccan nationalism derived from this combination of opposing forces a composite character, at once modernistic and traditionalist, rationalist and religious, extremist and moderate, which shows how complex this sociological structure was. The support at first given to this movement, under different names and with varying intensity by the composite elite of the cities, was echoed immediately by the artisans, the new middle class, and the neo-proletariat of the *medinas,* whose natural *encadrement* these elites constituted. The neo-proletariat of the cities of western Morocco joined the movement only as Istiqlal succeeded in assuring its political *encadrement*. The commercial bourgeoisie either remained aloof or remained attached to a relatively moderate nationalism, with few exceptions, until the end. The conversion of the majority of the urban population to nationalism was achieved in 1952; but the outbreak of terrorism soon revealed very different levels of intensity in the attitudinal system expressing opposition to the regime by the citizens. These psychological differentiations were only obliterated during the scenes of popular enthusiasm that accompanied the restoration of Mohammed V in November 1955.

The evolution of political attitudes was very different in the rural areas. Despite premature signs of tension, large-scale popular opposition to the regime did not manifest itself until August 1955, almost ten years after it had begun in the cities. Urban Moroccans had been supporting urban terrorists for a year and a

2. The attitudinal change of the groups under examination is analyzed from a purely descriptive viewpoint. The same phenomenon will again be studied in the following part in order to establish the degree to which the procedure previously described was necessary. See pp. 545 ff.

half. Rural opposition was at first limited to the northern zone, where it silently supported the operations of the Moroccan Army of Liberation throughout the Rif campaign. It spread only toward the end of the crisis, with the restoration of Mohammed V, when the fate of the protectorate was virtually sealed.[3]

It is clear that the revolt in the *bled* was brought on by the revolt in the cities and by the defeat of the French forces in the cities. In certain respects, nationalism in the *bled* was a resurgence of the dissident spirit of the first years of colonization, but the rural milieu was scarcely touched by the modernization of the country and its political evolution had been halted by the integration of traditionalist cadres into the regime. On the other hand, nationalism in the cities was the specific protest of the urban groups most affected by the sociological upheaval provoked by colonization.

The relative independence of the two branches of the phenomenon in no way destroys its underlying unity. Even when order seemingly prevailed in the rural areas, discontent nevertheless existed. If it appeared so late, it was because, apart from the sociological factors which inhibited its appearance, it had had two safety valves: the induction of tribesmen into Moroccan contingents of the French army, and the rural exodus. The militarization of the Moroccan warrior is often described as a proof of solidarity in the rallying of tribesmen to the colonial order. It also meant, for those inducted, a break with their traditional way of life. There was no emigration that was not a sign of protest. Military life can be a form of evasion and it is significant that the

3. The first evidence of the phenomenon was concealed for the most part until August 20, 1955, by the ambiguity of the attitudes that prevailed among the rural population and especially among the notables. It seems that this ambiguity is due less to a conscious desire to dissimulate than to the juxtaposition of the two incompatible attitudes (pro-French and anti-French) within the indigenous group that was slowly swinging from one side to the other. In such circumstances, the colonized tends to adopt the attitude his interlocutor expects of him, but quickly modifies his response and behavior when his interlocutor changes sides. When solicited by the French authorities to show their loyalty to the regime, they often did so with the best faith in the world. This did not prevent them from reacting in a diametrically opposite manner from one day to the next when the stimulus came from the other side. The balance of two contradictory attitudes can last only a short time. The new attitude rapidly becomes the predominant one. The ambiguity which affects the attitude in the course of the period of readaptation is nevertheless characteristic. We will see below that a similar phenomenon occurred among the Europeans. See p. 495.

tribes which furnished the highest proportion of recruits to the French army were, at times, those who had been the most strongly repressed by the colonizing authorities. The same reasoning can be applied a fortiori to the rural exodus. The influx of peasants into the cities implied a clean break with the basic conditions of peasant existence. In certain respects, it reveals an even more intense rejection of the traditional way of life than that which occurred in the urban elements of the population, since the urban Moroccan, in rising up against the colonizer, only rejects certain aspects of his condition; the peasant who emigrates to the city rejects everything. These two attitudes of rejection differ only in one way. The urban Moroccan translated his grievances directly into political protest. The peasant, who had scarcely emerged from military defeat, and who remained psychologically beaten, began by emigrating to the cities; only when he had settled there did he enter the second phase of his protest, laying the blame on the regime. The neo-proletariat of the large cities in western Morocco was made up of individuals born in the *bled* who had come to the cities of their own volition. The political activity of this particular group can then be considered as a delayed rural protest, and, if it is true that the dissidence in the *bled* was brought on by that of the cities, it is nonetheless true that the revolt in the cities was in large part the work of rural Moroccans who had been only briefly exposed to urban life.

On the whole, the adoption of nationalism in the *bled* seems to have been only the last stage of a psychological evolution that can be outlined as follows:

The formation in the *bled,* as a result of the French conquest, of a complex attitude consisting of an acceptance of colonization and a sensitivity of suppressed people;

Progressive reinforcement of this residual discontent as a result of the extension of European colonization, the vices of the caid regime, and the impasse in which the Moroccan peasant found himself as a result of his deteriorating situation;

Neutralization of the dangerous aspects of discontent through the rural exodus and the militarization of tribes;

Neutralization of latent aggressiveness in the *bled* through conformist pressure exercised by the elite on the peasants;

Psychological shock administered to the rural areas by the deposition of the Sultan;

Defeat of the French force in the cities by a nationalism backed by a neo-proletariat group which had emigrated to the cities as part of the rural exodus;

Implantation in the *bled* of contingents of the Moroccan Liberation Army combined with a great number of tribes who had been trained by the French army, and the correlative appearance of a reflex of popular solidarity favorable to these formations;

The shift by the entire *bled* to the nationalist camp as a result of the successes of the Moroccan Liberation Army and the restoration of Mohammed V.

Thus outlined, the phenomenon regains its unity. In the cities as in rural areas, the conversion of political attitudes seems to be an immediate or postponed rejection of the conditions of existence of the masses under the colonial regime. According to the Moroccans, the regime was either directly or indirectly responsible for these conditions.

Conservatism of the European Colony

COMPONENTS OF THE ATTITUDE

The attitude of the European minority in Morocco is reducible, by analysis, into these distinct components:

Intransigent and aggressive defense of the social privileges attacked by nationalist demands;

Obstinate demand for political rights denied to the foreign community by the Treaty of Fez (voting rights and participation of European representatives elected to the administration of the country in local, regional, and

central assemblies, which would have established the
political preponderance of the governing group);

Political minimization of the inequities existing
within the European group and the alliance of its different strata before the exigencies of the Muslim community;

Conversion from an initial political acceptance into
opposition to the regime at each attempt by the Residency to liberalize the protectorate.

The political rights demanded by the Europeans demonstrate
an unusual phenomenon. The temporary suppression of internal
dissensions that affect the existence and cohesion of a threatened
group is a common psychological reaction; many examples can
be found in the sociology of war. The linking of a conservative
component with a demanding component within the political
attitude of the European minority shows, strikingly, on the other
hand, that a privileged caste may be led to base the defense of its
privileges on the type of demands that characterize, in general,
the groups in the lower echelons of society.

GENERALIZATION OF THE ATTITUDE

While the Muslims swung over to nationalism only gradually
and in successive segments, the conservatism of the Europeans
crystallized at the first attempts made by the Residency to liberalize the regime in favor of the Muslims. Again, qualifications
must be introduced here, for the intensity and the modalities of
the reaction of the European minority changed appreciably in
the course of time. Until the deposition of the Sultan, antinationalist action was carried out essentially by French officials and
the privileged class. The majority of Europeans were content to
give passive approval. After Dienbienphu, the speech at Carthage, the deposition of Mohammed V, and the outbreak of
terrorism in the cities, the situation changed. The Residency lost
control of the situation just when it thought it had won the
country. The European community became worried and created
its own organs of defense. The French colony was prey to a
curious ambivalence of attitudes that combined a deep-seated

pessimism with supreme self-confidence. While the Europeans showed an instinctive fear of a nationalist victory, they nonetheless persisted in the belief that this same nationalism was the work of a handful of agitators who enjoyed no real support among the indigenous classes. From this stemmed the instability and the internal contradictions of the European reaction to nationalist pressure. The colonists and their leaders acted simultaneously or alternately as if the adversary represented only negligible numbers and as if this adversary were on the point of sweeping away the established regime.

Aside from the particulars which affected the intensity and coherence of the European reaction, it seems that the generalization of dominant attitudes took place in quite a different manner in each community. It was gradual and selective among the Muslims. It was sudden and complete among the Europeans. To be thorough, we must consider the attitudes of the marginal groups in the two camps: the traditional Muslim elite and the European liberals.

Conservatism of the Muslim Notables

The attitudes of the Muslim notables are not simple to circumscribe or to describe.

If by "notables" we mean the Muslim officials invested with power by the Sultan, with French approval, it is clear that the dominant attitude of this group was one of conservatism, but we must add that it is less a question of a natural group than an artificial group—the result of careful political selection. The conservatism of this restrained group is explained by the fact that only the notables known for their loyalty and sympathy to the regime had a chance of making a career in the Maghzen. The others were not appointed, or were regularly purged.

If by "notables" we mean the complex social strata from which the officials of the Maghzen were recruited, we can no longer maintain that conservatism was the dominant attitude of this fraction of the Muslim population. Among many, this conservatism was nullified by the varied acceptance of nationalist propaganda and, among others, by actual loyalty to the Sultan. Torn between their position as privileged members of the regime, and their status as members of the colonized group, the notables were in large part divided. There remains the fact that the protectorate would not have had at its disposal a body of Muslim officials loyal to the cause until the end, even if, on the whole, there existed a group of the Muslim notables who spontaneously favored the status quo.

We will attempt to clarify the ambiguous concept of "notables" by considering first only the group of Muslim officials, and re-establishing later the liaison between these individuals and their social milieu—which will necessitate a study of the evolution of this attitude in its social milieu and qualification of its different levels of intensity.

COMPONENTS OF THE ATTITUDE

The attitude of the Moroccan notables, considered in a limited sense of the term, may be analyzed as a conservatism based simultaneously on the support of the foreign regime that reinforces its social preponderance and on the rejection of innovations that threaten the traditional stability of Muslim society. The Maghzen officials certainly defended the caids' function against the modernism of the Sultan and Istiqlal, when it became clear that the privileges granted to them by the protectorate would cease with the triumph of the nationalist cause. This immediate defense reflex was only the most obvious component of a fundamental and instinctive protest directed by the most representative of the traditional social leaders against the modernism of the nationalists and their popular backing. Seen from this vantage point, the negative attitude adopted by the caids and pashas with respect to the nationalism of the Sultanate can be considered as a manifestation of the classic quarrel between the Ancients and the Moderns in an ambiguous state of affairs created by a colonial regime that was upsetting the social structures of the country while continuing to link its fate to that of the traditional authorities whose hold over the population was weakening as the old Morocco was disintegrating.

GENERALIZATION OF THE ATTITUDE

The attitude of the notables loses its relative homogeneity and differentiates itself, once we reestablish the complexity of the group by distinguishing between the activists of antinationalism (great chiefs and heads of religious brotherhoods), the local officials of the Maghzen, and the complex social milieu from which both sides were most often recruited.

At the level of the great caids and brotherhood chiefs who instigated the so-called plot of the notables, the conservative reaction came into play once it became evident that the Sultan was losing the support of the French. It attained its maximum intensity and coherence during the crisis which took place during the summer of 1953. Once Mohammed V had been deposed, it was only necessary for el-Glaoui and his rivals to prevent his return. This political theme dominated the scene until the collapse of December 1956.

The pashas and caids of lesser importance reacted like the great protagonists of the movement, but in a manner obviously tempered by the fear that they would eventually find themselves on the losing side. Whereas the great notables were quick to burn their bridges behind them, the lesser members of the conspiracy were content to demonstrate a conservatism strongly tainted with opportunism that makes perfectly clear the tragicomedy of the petitions and the counter-petitions of 1953. The final volte-face of el-Glaoui revealed that opportunism was not the exclusive property of the lower class.

The true nature of the attitude of the notables is only revealed when we place the officials of the Maghzen and the heads of the brotherhoods that were hostile to the Sultan in their proper social milieu. In a Morocco thrown into confusion by colonization and dominated by the nationalist ideology, it was normal that the pressure exerted by nationalism on the privileges of the traditional elite should lead to a political rupture. At this level, it is no longer the relative predominance of one type of attitude over another which is the rule, but the instability of the fundamental attitude. Torn between contradictory feelings, the notables divided: some rallied to Istiqlal, others threw in their lot with the colonial power. It is the political conservatism of this "social residue," so characteristically embodied by the caids and pashas which could not be assimilated by the nationalism. For want of data, it is impossible to know at what pace the attitudinal change of this group took place, and what this conservative balance of Muslim elites represented, but, as is the rule, it is probable that the cleavage of attitudes took place between the young and the old.

Pronationalism of the French Liberals

While a fraction of the Muslim population resisted the teachings of the nationalists, at the other pole a small number of Frenchmen in Morocco adopted attitudes at variance with those of their group and put their talents and energies to work for the nationalist cause. The attitudes of these two dissident groups, the Moroccan notables and the French liberals, seem at first sight to have played symmetrical roles in the conflict, but a close examination of this dual anomaly shows that the attitudes of the marginal groups in both camps were in reality of a very different sociological nature.

COMPONENTS OF THE ATTITUDE

The attitude of French liberals in Morocco is distinguishable from that of the notables in three fundamental ways:

1. From the beginning, it proved itself incompatible with the immediate interests of the individuals who adopted it, as these individuals were promptly excommunicated from their own group for political ideas they maintained.

2. The attitude was based on disinterested moral values and was aimed, above all, at redressing wrongs and exposing injustices.

3. It singled out individuals who considered themselves supporters of the nationalist cause, although the need to find equitable solutions for the two groups was not entirely absent from their preoccupations.

GENERALIZATION OF THE ATTITUDE

When we consider the relationship of the attitude to the group which holds it, it becomes difficult, at this particular point, to speak of the evolution of an attitude in time. The French who proclaimed themselves liberals in 1955–56 had probably been so since the outbreak of the conflict, but this tendency was intensified through the effect of the psychological shock that was created in Franco-Moroccan circles by the great repressive acts of the regime: December 1952, August 1953, counter-terrorism, and torture.

The Appearance of These Four Attitudes Over Time

The problem posed by the generalization of the four systems of attitudes which have just been studied should not be confused with that of their gradual appearance. Why the conflict was initiated at one time rather than at another is a question that will be studied in the following part.[4] For the moment, it is sufficient to observe that the question was only significant for the nationalist fraction of the Muslim population. For the other three groups, it was a chain reaction. The defense reflex of the Europeans came into play as soon as the nationalist threat became evident. The defense reflex of the notables was unleashed on the same basis as that of the colonizers after the first successes of Istiqlal. As for the political alignment of French liberals, this occurred once the repressive policy of the regime became incompatible with the political and moral values that they held to be more important than the pursuit of their immediate self-interest.

4. See pp. 559 ff.

Chapter 3

IDEOLOGICAL VARIABLES

The conflicting groups are not in opposition solely because of the political attitudes and actions involved. They are also in opposition in the development of different systems of ideas and values that are as irreconcilable as their attitudes.

Ideology, in turn, may be defined as the group's concept of its own position, used to justify attitudes linked to its way of life. It is of little importance whether this concept is true or false, objectively accurate or distorted. By definition, an ideology comes into existence once a concept of the situation emerges at a given political juncture. A group cannot survive if it takes a desperate stand to defend its position and at the same time formulates a theory about this position that might bring on the condemnation of its own political attitudes. Any ideological slackening involves the risk of neutralizing the collective personality under the weight of the contradictions engendered by the incompatibility of the spontaneous attitudes, and the concepts which should be supporting them. We will therefore consider ideologies as both conceptions (*idéations*) rising out of the situation and as rationalizations (*motivations*), the subject more or less consciously justifying his adopted attitudes by adjusting his concept of the situation to explain them.

Neither Europeans nor Muslims in Morocco were exempt from this rule: in each camp, the most skilled propagandists formulated ideologies that did nothing but provide explicit rationalizations of the attitudes that were adopted by the two communities and played such essential roles.[1]

1. It remains to be explained why the four groups described formulated but two distinct ideologies, when each of them had a different set of original attitudes. There actually is no mystery here. The ideology of the colons was a priori suited to the Moroccan notables since both groups worked toward the same ends and enjoyed, to a certain extent, the same privileges. The ideology of the nationalist Muslims suited the

Pro-Residential Ideology

The particular brand of colonial ideology that developed in Morocco during the last years of the protectorate can be outlined as follows:

Affirmation of the objectively progressive and modern nature of the protectorate, with a constant propaganda display of the social and technical achievements of colonization;

Affirmation of the subjectively progressive nature of the protectorate toward the Moroccans, who were officially credited with better living conditions than previous generations and with being on the whole satisfied with their lot;

Attribution of the political difficulties of the regime to the actions of a minority of irresponsible agitators without any real influence on the population as a whole, and to the manipulation of this minority by foreign elements seeking to sow discord;

Minimization or ignorance of all the facts not matching this optimistic view of the colonial situation;

Dissimulation or minimization of the extreme measures employed by the regime to maintain power; justification of those extreme measures that could not be concealed on grounds of legitimacy and defense of public order supported by some elements of the Muslim population;

Singling out of the civilizing and progressive character of colonialism as central to the pro-residential ideology.

Nationalist Ideology

Similarly, the nationalist ideology can be reduced to the following components:

More or less explicit denial of the objectively progressive and modernistic nature of the regime, the positive

French Liberals as, for the most part, they had formulated it. Both groups did little but refer in various ways to the basic values of democratic ideology.

achievements of colonialism being viewed as benefiting only the Europeans and emphasis also being given to the disintegration of the traditional Muslim way of life under colonial rule;

Categorical denial of the subjectively progressive nature of the regime, the protests of the Muslim masses being represented as a revolutionary attitude linked to their political, economic, and cultural discontent resulting from colonization;

Refutation of the nationalist theory adopted by the colonists; the affirmation of solidarity between the nationalist movement and the masses; the correlative affirmation of the secondary role played by foreign aid to the colonized;

Focus of attention for propaganda purposes on the socially inferior and superior status of the two communities involved in the struggle;

Affirmation of the legitimacy of the acts of violence committed by terrorist gangs and guerrilla groups;

Singling out of the needs for political emancipation and for modernization as central in the nationalist ideology.

Comparative Appraisal

The comparative study of these two ideologies reveals similarities and differences that deserve to be highlighted. It will be noted that these two systems of ideas and values are not demonstrative of anything. They constitute a collection of aphorisms which can be accepted or rejected but which cannot in either case be identified as a complete and consciously objective theory concerning the situation. The emphasis laid on modernization and development occurs in each case, but with this difference: the colonized people see self-government as a fundamental aspiration, while the effort made by the colonial power to make the colony capable of self-government is obviously nothing but an argumentative device.

The manner in which the two sides viewed their respective uses of violence might lead one to believe that they appealed to different moralities. Yet when we examine the matter more closely, it appears that the two adversaries were linked by a common scale of value: one which admitted the legitimacy of violence when committed by people struggling for freedom, yet condemned the same violence when employed by regimes or dominant factions attempting to impose their authority on people who contest it—hence the ease with which the nationalists admitted the various outbreaks of violence committed in their name, and, conversely, the constant tendency of the opposing group to conceal its own violence or the attempt to conceal its dubious nature.

Finally, it will be noted that if the two opposing ideologies played essentially auxiliary roles, the distortions of the colonial situation by the pro-residential ideology were much stronger than those by the nationalist ideology. In the case of the colonial powers, the ideological distortion of the situation was flagrant and fundamental. In the case of the colonized, the distortion was much weaker and involved nuances and omissions necessitated by propaganda requirements rather than by a fundamental urge for distortion. This ideological distortion, varying according to situations, will be justified later.[2]

We can see that the two ideologies that have just been briefly examined approach an objective theory of the colonial situation. Discussed from this point of view, there would be a great deal to say, and the pro-residential concept of the colonial situation would not necessarily lose out. Our aim does not lie in this direction; therefore only a few remarks will be made concerning this aspect of the problem.

It should first be noted that if the achievements of colonization are of immediate benefit to the colonist, the colonized is his heir presumptive; one day the roads, bridges, and dams of which the colonist is so proud will belong to the colonized. The date of coming of age can be tampered with but the heir's vocation is neither disputed nor disputable. It follows that if the colonial structure has been built up by the suffering and exploitation of past and present indigenous generations, these sufferings are, to a

2. See pp. 570 ff.

certain extent, capitalized for the profit of generations to come. Here, the colonial proletariats find themselves in a position similar to that faced by western proletariats in the nineteenth century. In each case there was exploitation of one class by another, and in each case the final result of this exploitation favored the masses.

It will also be noted that the benefits derivable from colonization do not lie exclusively in the future. They also involve the present. Colonial powers, of course, waste no time in listing them: improved public health, the elimination of internal warfare through the stabilization of government, the political centralization of the territory improved or built up from nothing, and the initiation of development in every sphere in the colonized nation. All these changes, if not subjectively satisfactory, do represent positive advantages for the subjugated masses, and it is difficult to see how they cannot be credited to the colonizing power.

An objective view of colonization should also take into account the fact that this phase is historically necessary. When the modern colonies were founded at the end of the nineteenth century and the beginning of the twentieth, there was no alternative to colonization for the colonized nations. One could say, paraphrasing Marx's eulogy of capitalism (although colonialism is, of course, only one aspect of capitalism), that it has been the best and the worst of things. It is impossible not to see colonization as an essential step in the socio-cultural evolution of humanity.

Finally, it must be admitted that overpopulation, the decline of traditional culture, and the proletarianization of the masses—evils that generally accompany colonization—would have occurred even if the development had been the work of the colonized people, and even if they had received impartial assistance from the world's most highly-developed countries. Certainly all this is true, but these arguments are only polemically useful within the framework of a distorted view of the problem. It is the objectivity of the analysis that is debatable. The question is not whether the balance of advantages and inconveniences of colonization favors the colonized nations but to see whether this balance has meaning, and whether a nation can be administered like a model farm once the farmers withdraw their cooperation. Colonialism was legitimate, in a manner of speaking, in the sense that it managed to exact the consent of the colonized people. Once this consent was disputed, all legitimacy ceased. Colonization's historical crime—if there is a crime—was not to have existed, but to have resisted the process it had set in motion and then to have betrayed the very values which, by its own admission, made it necessary for colonization to regard itself as a passing political phase.

Legitimacy is not an arbitrary value but an objective criterion that no political analysis should ever evade. A regime is only legitimate as long as it is accepted. As with authority, strength, and all the attributes of power, legitimacy rests first on the consent of the governed. But this legitimacy, in a narrow sense, rests on a broader legitimacy rooted in historical evolution. Forcing men to reject their political methods, traditionally recognized as valid, persuading them to adopt new methods that tradition decreed unacceptable and impractical, and reshaping political consensus, the evolution itself becomes the ultimate criterion of what is legitimate and what is not in political matters. Colonization in the modern sense of the term would scarcely have been possible but for the technological and sociological advantages enjoyed by Europeans over other societies. Without the changes that colonization provoked within the colonized societies, the colonial regimes would have lasted forever. Change lies at the root of colonization and is basic to its decline. In the final analysis, its legitimacy can only be judged by reference to this change.

Chapter 4

DECISION-MAKING VARIABLES

There would be no wars between states if an international organization existed that was capable of solving the problems which states, left to their own devices, tend to settle by force. Similarly, internal conflicts arise only when the decision-making centers turn out to be incapable of anticipating difficulties, or of settling them in a peaceful manner.

Political decisions are, therefore, like situations, ideologies, and collective attitudes, the essential components of the dynamics of conflict. The Franco-Moroccan conflict exploded because the local and metropolitan protectorate machinery proved incapable of making the decisions that might have anticipated its outbreak. If the conflict bore all the marks of a settling of accounts between different indigenous factions, this is because the same authorities showed themselves incapable of making the necessary decisions to restore order. The development of the crisis might have been quite different if it could have been arbitrated by international organizations endowed with adequate competence and authority. The outbreak and development of a political conflict are always the results of absence of authority, whether this authority remains absent—as is usually the case in international conflict—or whether it is too weak to intervene effectively.

In order for it to have any useful meaning, "decision" must here be understood in its broadest sense. A political authority may refuse to make certain decisions. It may make them, yet remain incapable of using its own officers to enforce them. Finally, the governed people may refuse to obey. The latter is always the case when a section of the population ignores or revolts against the decisions that concern it. Therefore, it is not the application of the decision which is being challenged, since the executive officers are presumably in favor of the proposed measure. It is the

507

productivity of the political act that is in question: its ultimate ability to produce the anticipated psychological or material effects. In practice, it makes little difference whether the decision was not made, not enforced, or ineffective. Each points to a breakdown of authority of a certain type, and it is with these breakdowns that the theory of conflicts is above all concerned.

Here it should be made quite clear that the manner in which a leader employs the decision-making capacity at his disposal is of less interest to us than the sociological mechanism that provides him with it. The set of individual, historical, and circumstantial factors governing the adoption of a particular residential decision are of secondary importance in this analysis. Our purpose is not to study the manner in which the protectorate used its authority, but to show the variations of potential authority at the protectorate's disposal.

Since the decision-making capacity effectively employed by the Residency is in many respects identical with its ability to resolve the protectorate's problems, the following remarks take the same form as those previously applied to Moroccan problems. The two analyses merely emphasize different aspects of the same phenomenon. The functionalist analysis of residential policy tended primarily to reveal the technical obstacles to peaceful decolonization of the protectorate by the regime; as far as was possible, purely political difficulties were left out of consideration. We must now throw some light on these political inadequacies in order to study them later as a function of attitudinal variables and of variables in the situation of the system. Seen from this second point of view, six types of decisions need to be considered.

1. *Decisions Promoting Development of Modern Sectors in the Moroccan Economy.* This first heading covers all decisions made to equip Morocco and supply the needs of the European community since the founding of the protectorate. We have seen that the regime had no difficulty in solving the problem in terms of political authority, which shows that all during its existence it enjoyed the full decision-making capacity required to achieve the fundamental goals of colonization. At this level there was no lack of initiative, technical means, or cooperation between the two communities.

2. *Decisions Promoting Modernization of Traditional Sectors in Muslim Society.* This second type of decision involves the postwar technical and political measures taken by the protectorate to reduce the economic and financial discriminations deplored by the nationalists; to develop education, justice, housing, and public health in the Muslim areas; and to raise the standard of living of both urban and rural workers.[1] We know that this problem only received symbolic solutions. In other words, the decision-making capacity of the regime was so weak as to be considered practically nonexistent. The protectorate began to lose interest in the development of traditional Morocco. When nationalist pressure opened its eyes to reality, the protectorate found itself paralyzed by a technical and political inability to make decisions as it lacked the means, time, and the cooperation of the Europeans and, at times, even of the Muslims. First came the refusal to make decisions and later the technical and political inability to make effective ones.

3. *Decisions Promoting Political Reform of the Regime.* The aim of this third type of decision was either to liberalize the regime in favor of the Muslims or to strengthen its colonial character by cosovereignty reforms that would favor the Europeans. In the first instance, the liberal programs developed in metropolitan France with the consent of reform-minded residents were not put into practice, either because of the opposition of the two communities (Labonne) or the opposition of the Europeans alone (Grandval). In the second case, the cosovereignty reforms in general could be instituted, but where they were not rendered ineffective by the noncooperative attitude of the Muslims (e.g. the town councils), they were sabotaged by an administration that did not intend to effect them except as they had been before (e.g. the Council of Viziers and Directors). Since, in the end, the regime was incapable either of liberalizing itself in favor of the Muslims or of organizing cosovereignty in favor of the Euro-

1. It is known that these decisions were either invalid or had only negligible effects under the First Four Year Plan (1949–1952). This tendency was reversed, to a certain extent, during the Second Four Year Plan (1954–1957) when there was an appreciable increase in social credits affecting Muslims, because of loans approved by metropolitan France. However, the protectorate never showed any sign of revising the fiscal structures and the economic privileges of the European community which made the whole colonial business worthwhile.

peans, its decision-making capacity may once again be considered as practically nonexistent. It will be noted that on this level there was no lack of political will power or technical means. The paralysis of authority was caused by a purely political incapacity: the opposition of the residential officials and the two groups of natives was sufficient to block the application of all decisions.

4. *Decisions Promoting Restoration of Residential Authority Within the Regime.* We have seen that the Residency attempted to realize this particular aim by transferring rebellious civil servants or by reorganizing the administrative divisions (Labonne, Grandval). None of these measures had any lasting effects. No sooner were they taken than they were neutralized by the resistance of those affected, or else the officials replacing them fell into their predecessor's errors, or, finally, the fall of the Resident-General responsible for the decisions was followed by a simple return to the status quo ante. Thus the decision-making capacity of the regime in relation to this fourth objective was also nonexistent. This particular failure is an example of a typical case of inability to make decisions attributable to the insubordination of executive officers. The liberal leaders did not lack political purpose. No material shortages hampered their freedom of action. The natives were not interested, because the reforms in question did not concern them. The opposition of the executive officers was sufficient to paralyze the governing power.

5. *Decisions Promoting Defeat of Political Aspects of Nationalism.* The great purge of 1952, the deposition of Mohammed V, and the clean-up operation in the Maghzen were the results of a series of decisions which tended, as the French authorities themselves admitted, to free the urban Muslims from the pressure the nationalists exerted upon them and to reestablish the traditional hold of the elite and French administration over the *bled* population. As the flow of the Muslim population toward the magnetic pole of nationalism could not be halted, and as it could not a fortiori be diverted into a stable Moroccan support of the regime, the decision-making capacity can again be considered as nonexistent. Decisions of this type were made and carried out by civil servants who judged them to be adequate. Their technical cost was not prohibitive. It was on the level of final effectiveness that

the paralysis of authority took place, the attitude of the Muslim masses being sufficient to reduce this effectiveness to nothing.

6. *Decisions Promoting Defeat of Military Aspects of Nationalism.* The collapse of Moroccan public order brought about by urban terrorists and by the Moroccan Liberation Army made the protectorate face up to a trial-by-strength and obliged it to attempt to regain control of the situation by a series of decisions which marked the origin of the police and antiguerrilla operations at the end of the conflict. The technical results of these repressive measures were not completely without significance, since they succeeded in gaining time and in slowing down the development of the armed forms of nationalism. On the other hand, their political effectiveness can be considered as nonexistent, since their unsuccessful objective was to stop the recruiting process for terrorist groups and commandos of the Moroccan Liberation Army. The situation is the same as in the previous case. Neither the will to take action, nor the material means to do so, nor the human means of putting it into practice was lacking: it was the will of the people which checked the will of their rulers in a political situation where, because of moral prohibitions, the regime could only have recourse to conventional means of repression.

With the exception of measures aimed at developing the European sector of the economy and at the marginal consolidation of Muslim social structures, the Residency failed to achieve any of the objectives it had set for itself, objectives which it had sporadically pursued between the end of the Second World War and Mohammed V's return to power in Morocco. Sometimes the Residency refused to take action or lacked the means to do so; sometimes its officers would not execute its orders; and, finally, sometimes it saw the political and technical effectiveness of the measures it had taken reduced to zero because of the attitude adopted by the Moroccan people. Even though the technical and material impotence previously examined[2] explains in part the functional impotence of the regime during the crises, it nevertheless appears that the reasons for this political inadequacy dominated those for technical inadequacy. Even if the Residency had

2. See pp. 432 ff.

had adequate technical means at its disposal, European opposition would have been strong enough to paralyze its reform policies. Therefore, it is only by a closer investigation of the decision-making capacities in terms of attitudes and social situations that light will eventually be cast upon the more specific aspects of the decolonization mechanism in Morocco.

SECTION TWO: THE METROPOLITAN ECHELON

Since the factors affecting France are described below, according to a plan which is similar in principle, if not in detail, to that employed in the preceding section concerning Morocco, the following three chapters will be devoted to an examination of the different variables of decision-making, attitude, and situation, which the conflict brought into play on the metropolitan level.[1]

1. Although extremely close to each other in concept, these two sections demonstrate certain distinctions concerning the order of presentation of facts and the plan of the analysis. To begin with, the order of presentation is reversed. This follows from the nature of the situation, since the Moroccan decision-making centers were disturbed by impulses springing from the heart of the social organism, whereas in France the governed mainly reacted to decisions made in the metropolitan political centers. The ideological level has been omitted in the analysis of metropolitan factors for two reasons: either these ideologies were not immediately relevant to the conflict, and their study would have complicated its description; or else they are immediately relevant and thus the study of ideologies made for Morocco can also be considered valid for metropolitan France. François Mauriac's arguments in Paris were no different from those offered in Rabat by liberal Frenchmen; neither was the decolonization concept advanced by Marcel Boussac or Raymond Triboulet in any way different from that recommended in Rabat by De Blesson and Boniface.

The analysis of attitudinal and situational variables in metropolitan France has been divided into two sections. Once again, this is because of the way events appeared in the Métropole. In order to be fully aware of what took place in France, it is necessary to distinguish between the attitude of the political parties and that of the population as a whole. It would be impossible to discuss these two sets of attitudes without at the same time taking into consideration the technical situation of the parties within the regime and the overall situation of the French people in the Métropole and abroad, hence the division of the last two parts of the analysis. Moreover, we decided that it would be useless to further complicate the study of the variables of decision, attitude, and situation with a functionalist analysis of the problems that Morocco produced for France, since the analyses of the problems made in the first section on Morocco are, ipso facto, applicable to France. France merely brought into play other variables of decision, attitude, and situation. It made virtually no attempt to face up to the various problems of the people with whom the representatives of France and Rabat had to deal.

Chapter 1

DECISION-MAKING VARIABLES

It would be a serious error to assert that there was any lack of French decisions concerning Morocco. Between 1944 and 1956 there was a constant flow of decisions from Paris to Rabat in the shape of ministerial instructions, direct intervention by the Council of Ministers, parliamentary votes, or legislative and administrative decrees drawn up on the initiative of the different French ministers involved in the development of a Moroccan policy. Nonetheless, it is true that France did not know how to, or could not, arbitrate the conflict; the extent of this failure should be measured before reconsideration of the different elements of situation and attitude.

Metropolitan decisions can be classified under the same headings as those examined in the protectorate discussion. Whether it is a question of developing a modern economic sector in Morocco, instituting technical and social reforms in Muslim centers, liberalizing the protectorate, taking the residential services in hand, fighting terrorists and guerrillas, or the final decolonization process, all these decisions under different headings were mixed political actions. They were both residential and French, which did not prevent some of them from showing markedly metropolitan characteristics. It is on these last decisions that this section will concentrate.

The principal themes in metropolitan politics were: the selection of new residents, the drawing up of instructions and their daily interpretation through telegrams and notes,[1] the gradual dispatch of reinforcements to help contain terrorists and guerrillas, the belated creation of a Ministry of Moroccan and Tunisian

1. On this point, the only difference between metropolitan and residential policy was that the former tried to make the Sultan accept more or less willingly the measures that the Residency was attempting to impose by threat of deposition—a principle suggested by the Métropole itself.

Affairs, and the French Parliament's final recognition of Moroccan independence. The Minister of Foreign Affairs, the Minister of Moroccan and Tunisian Affairs, the Council of Ministers, the President of the Council, and Parliament itself all played their part in the elaboration of this policy within the limits of their own constitutional powers and under pressure from political contingencies.

The balance sheet can be drawn up in the form of three observations:

1. Metropolitan decision-making centers were incapable of a peaceful arbitration of the crisis, which would have led Morocco toward internal autonomy and eventual independence according to a comprehensive plan that would have guaranteed the gradual transfer of power into Moroccan hands according to a carefully devised schedule

2. The only decisions effectively taken by the Métropole consisted of placing the men and materials the Residency needed at the protectorate's disposal in order to ensure the security of the Europeans and help with the attempts to impose the status quo on Muslims.

3. Incapable of resigning itself to the tide of independence that was sweeping the protectorate, France was contented to prop up existing structures without making any attempt to neutralize hostile forces by a massive military intervention of the Algerian type.

The final collapse of the regime instituted by the Treaty of 1912 was the inevitable consequence of this inability to evolve. Insofar as Moroccan attitudes and situations are insufficient to provide a clear picture of this failure, it can only be explained by the interplay of attitudinal variables and metropolitan situations.

Chapter 2

ATTITUDINAL VARIABLES

The description and interpretation of metropolitan attitudes toward Morocco is a delicate task. Whereas the attitudes of the individual protagonists and the opposing groups often stood out in a highly dramatic manner on Moroccan soil, the metropolitan attitudes generally appeared as half-tones. This shift from the limelight to the shadows of political life should be emphasized.

Attitudes of Metropolitan Parties [1]

The attitudes of metropolitan France toward the decolonization of her overseas empire constitute such a wide-ranging subject that we have been forced to confine ourselves to questions that are essential for a proper understanding of the Franco-Moroccan conflict. This is easier said than done. Should the attitudes of the metropolitan parties toward decolonization of Morocco be studied individually or en bloc? Does it really make sense to isolate Morocco from the rest of the North African conflict? Surely, if we confine ourselves too strictly to the period under discussion, we risk ignoring subsequent events that revealed the French attitude toward decolonization, such as the Suez crisis and May 13, 1958. Each of these alternatives involves the risk of unduly extending or restricting the analysis. It is hoped that, insofar as possible, an unsatisfactory halfway position has been avoided.

1. It should be noted here that social psychology makes a clear distinction between the concepts of opinion and motivation. Opinions are judgments made on a situation as it is or as it ought to be. A Frenchman might react to a public opinion poll on the Algerian question by declaring that Algerians should be allowed to decide their own future by secret ballot elections held under international auspices. This does not necessarily mean that he is prepared to act accordingly. When an individual or a political party expresses opinions in declarations or manifestos, the question is not to know what that individual's or the party's opinion is but to know what is done, and, no less important, what is not done, to be able to deduce from behavior the "anticipated behavior" (attitude) that determines it.

The attitude of the parties has been considered as a whole, but, whenever advisable, the different political groups have been studied separately. This study has, nevertheless, been confined to metropolitan reactions to the Moroccan crisis alone. Other colonial problems have been mentioned only when broadening the field seemed necessary to reveal the parties' attitudes to the Moroccan crisis as particular instances of a much broader reaction by the political organism to decolonization. A similar procedure has been followed with events subsequent to the declaration of Moroccan independence in 1956: references are made to Algeria, to May 13, 1958, to Suez, and to political life under the Fifth Republic whenever these events, which followed Moroccan decolonization, help to cast further light on the mechanism at the metropolitan level.

The attitudes displayed by metropolitan parties toward the Moroccan crisis appear to be reducible to the following four components: (1) the almost inevitable defense reflex of most French political groups, the Communist Party excepted, to terrorism and guerrilla warfare; (2) the second-class status given to decolonization policies by the constitutional left-wing and, to a certain extent, by the Communist extreme Left; (3) the correlative weakening of the traditional opposition in the French Left and Right; and (4) the respect for parliamentary procedure by minorities favoring decolonization.

Although these four components of attitudes are part of a composite political phenomenon, it will be useful to study them separately.

METROPOLITAN DEFENSE REFLEX

When studying the attitude of French politicians toward the North African crisis in general and the Moroccan crisis in particular, one is immediately struck by the rapidity and strength of the metropolitan defense reflex set off by nationalist aggression. With the exception of the Communists, no one in Parliament, in government, or in the parties raised any serious objections to the mobilization and dispatch of all available men and supplies to North Africa. On this point, there was almost complete moral agreement—which does not mean that the policy of keeping

North Africa under French rule by force was universally approved.

The most remarkable aspect of this defense reflex is its complete automatism. The institutional mainspring of a regime is its predisposition to quell disorder. If a colony revolts, the repressive mechanism takes immediate effect, first on the spot and later at home. It also goes into action against the colons if they provoke a secessionist movement with its accompanying violence. The maintenance of public order is a policy rooted in stereotyped attitudes. These do not necessarily presuppose the same attitudes toward decolonization as those of politicians who wish to send reinforcements overseas,[2] but they do strengthen resistance to a colony's liberation when this is linked to a hostile policy toward local nationalism, backed by powerful forces.

SECONDARY ROLE ACCORDED TO POLICY OF DECOLONIZATION IN THE HIERARCHY OF INTERESTS OF THE CENTER AND THE LEFT

Shortly after leaving the Quai d'Orsay in January 1953, Robert Schuman published a famous editorial in *La Nef* which serves as an indispensable introduction to the study of this second component of attitude. For this reason it is reproduced here almost in full.

> It has been said that France lacks a North African policy (for Morocco and Tunisia). This is true in the sense that it has not yet made a choice between several possible policies. Before describing the policy that ought to be chosen, we should ask ourselves who ought to make this decision in France's name.
>
> The two residents-general are first in the hierarchy of authority. They are on the spot and they receive and provide all information. Their influence is extensive and varied and tends to broaden when their opinions coincide with those of the French population. They interpret

2. The dispatch of assistance to colons threatened with loss of life and livelihood does not necessarily imply a wish to maintain the status quo indefinitely. The Congo crisis is a good example: after the granting of independence and under pressure from public opinion, which previously had been almost unanimous in support of decolonization, the Belgian defense reflex was extremely strong.

instructions from Paris and decide on the means of execution. The residents-general deserve credit for resisting the use of the constant temptation, the fait accompli, insofar as they themselves are not the victims of it. Moreover, they are in a similar position with those of their departments (police, information, etc.) that enjoy great independence, thus escaping any effective control, because public opinion, which elsewhere would act as a check, is nonexistent.

Above the residents-general, the minister for foreign affairs is responsible for the administration of a policy which is supposed to match the views of the former. This is one of the fictions on which a democratic regime relies. When things go well, the minister gets all the credit. When there is a turn for the worse, he is blamed for what he failed to do or for what he did badly. To begin with, this fails to take into consideration the fact I have just mentioned, that Paris has a very limited influence and control over our representatives and over events abroad. Moreover, the minister does not alone determine the policy to be followed: it is the government's affair, the business of a corporate body whose decisions are anonymous and within which the opinions of the minister do not necessarily prevail. *True, he can always resign if his own views are defeated. But is it really that easy to take such a step, perhaps even provoking a crisis, when both the government and he himself have so many other tasks at hand?* Moreover, the rules of democratic procedure require executive decisions to be the resultant of diverse opinions.

The supreme authority is Parliament, which can impose its complete will, assuming it has one, and can express it in a clear, forceful manner. In fact, a recent debate on Tunisia showed that there is more often a majority in favor of criticism than for constructive policy-making suggestions, especially when home affairs take the lead.

In conclusion, we state that to have an effective and coherent North African policy, we must start by revising the administrative and political structure of French departments in the protectorates, while stopping short of extensive constitutional reform. I have reached the conclusion that no important reform regarding relations between France and Morocco or Tunisia is possible without returning to precise concepts of responsibility and hierarchical subordination.[3]

The value of this text does not lie solely in defining how and in what order the metropolitan authorities responsible for developing French-Moroccan policy function. Nor does the text confine itself to a description of Moroccan dissidence, seen and evaluated from Paris by the holder of the most important control lever. It contains an admission which, coming from such a source, is essential: a minister of the Center, personally in favor of liberal decolonization, did not see in this objective a question of principle important enough to justify the resignation, in the case of a conflict of opinion, of the Minister for Foreign Affairs or the collapse of ministerial solidarity. Nor is this merely Robert Schuman's personal opinion; it is an attitude shared by all constitutional ministers in favor of granting independence to the North African territories. The liberal elements in the M.R.P., the S.F.I.O., or the Radical Party apparently never considered colonial problems to be politically vital. They maneuvered around them. They did not fight against the wishes of the Right. Neither Tunisia, nor Morocco, nor Algeria ruptured governmental agreements. In August 1953, immediately after the deposition of Mohammed V, Edgar Faure and François Mitterrand were content to protest to the President of the Republic.[4] In Parliament itself, not one of the Center parties—not even a faction of these parties—made decolonization a question of principle.[5] The S.F.I.O. fought for secularism in public schools and a flexible wage scale, but it hid itself on February 6, 1956 and constantly used its

3. Robert Schuman "Nécessité d'une politique," in Maroc et Tunisie, le problème du protectorat, in La Nef, No. 2 (March 1953), pp. 7–9. Italics added.

4. It is true that the latter did resign shortly after in protest against the government's Tunisian policy. This is the exception that proves the rule.

5. It should be noted that although the fall of Pierre Mendès-France came about because of the North Africa crisis, this was just a pretext and not the real cause.

theoretical opposition to the policy of force in North Africa by ceding to the Right whenever the latter was willing to make minor concessions on social matters. The M.R.P. fought for the European Defense Community and against the Left's education policy but considered it perfectly in order for a minister of foreign affairs carrying its banner to yield to the constant insubordination of colonial officials who were known to enjoy considerable support in metropolitan France. Not one constitutional party went so far as to make its participation in the government dependent on the unequivocal execution by the current cabinet of a program of decolonization. It is hardly an exaggeration to say that it did not seem worthwhile for the S.F.I.O. and the M.R.P. to instigate a ministerial crisis over the failure of a Right-sponsored policy of strength.

A different attitude is apparent on the Right and the extreme Right, and especially among the Independents and Peasants, who fought to the bitter end. It must be recognized that when they finally abandoned the struggle they yielded to the force of circumstances rather than to that of men. This phenomenon is even more pronounced when we consider the colonist blocs set up after the break-up of the R.P.F. and the Poujadists. The last shots in the Moroccan affair were fired by Gaullist ministers who preferred to be driven to resignation when Antoine Pinay and Roger Duchet had already announced their change of views.

On the whole, the extreme Left did not struggle any more intensely than the Left. The Communists never expressed their opposition to a policy of force by strikes, street demonstrations, or maneuvers within the regime. International and domestic affairs took precedence over colonial policy on the extreme Left as well as on the Left and center Left, although for very different reasons. Here again, paradoxically enough, principles gave way before tactical requirements. The Communists allied themselves with the far Right to defeat E.D.C., voted against a Radical president of the Council who was working vigorously for decolonization, and, in the last years, discussed the Algerian problem as academically as if they were a Center party. They were never seen to take a tactical risk or sacrifice their immediate interests in order to align themselves with the colonized.

In short, while the North African colons found their most

effective and passionate spokesmen on the Right and among certain protagonists of the Center, the North African nationalists had no true political allies in governmental pressure groups. They had supporters who were prepared to flout procedures whenever the rules of the game allowed. They had a few stubborn advocates, but no real champions.

WEAKENING OF LEFT-RIGHT ANTAGONISM IN FRANCE

The full significance of the previous remarks can only be grasped when they are seen as a particular instance of a more general tendency: the gradual quieting down of the opposition between the Left and Right of the French Parliament. It is understood that this easing of tension was limited to the constitutional parties, that is, the body of the French Parliament exclusive of the Communists on the one hand and the R.P.F. and the Poujadists on the other. To grasp the full significance of this third phenomenon, a distinction must be made between domestic and foreign policy.

In domestic policy, and especially on social questions, the opposition between the constitutional Left and Right, although considerably reduced, remained the mainspring of French political life. The traditional French Left could well become a reform party, lose the best part of its substance to the Communists, and compromise itself through alliances hardly compatible with its creed, but on social questions any identification of the S.F.I.O. with Independents would be absurd. The French socialist Left is an attenuated Left. It never became the Right.

The situation changes completely when we turn from domestic to foreign policy. As soon as it is a question of the cold war, European unity, or colonial policy, all opposition between Left and Right melts away, leaving a homogeneous attitude scarcely disturbed by a few psychological differences. What about the cold war, disarmament, or aid to underdeveloped nations? On these topics there was nothing to distinguish a French Socialist from a Radical or a moderate. The constitutional Center was divided within itself on the stakes, if not the rules, of the game, and it entered the cold war as a political formation with quasi-homogeneous attitudes. What about European unity? The E.D.C.

quarrel showed explicitly that the antagonism between the nationalist and European mentalities just does not apply to the French Left and Right. Except perhaps for the intensity of attitude, there is no difference between an S.F.I.O. opponent and a moderate opponent of E.D.C. The same applies to decolonization: the liberalism of any S.F.I.O. or U.D.S.R. leader was not essentially different from that of any member of the M.R.P., Radical, or moderate parties.

No one will deny that the constitutional parties were sometimes split on colonial issues. It is merely the claim that the anticolonialism of the members of the parties supporting decolonization was a leftist attitude that will be disputed. Socialist anticolonialism of 1880–1914 was a leftist attitude because it was the monopoly of one political party and was a revolutionary expression of solidarity between the proletariat and the colonized. The decolonizing humanitarianism of 1945–55 was simply a resurgence of classical liberalism. True to itself in essence, whatever political colors its current champions wore, it consisted of two opposing ways of thought found within any party and in any social class.[6] The anticolonialism of the working and revolutionary classes of the nineteenth century was replaced by a benevolent liberalism that represented a generosity of spirit rather than a political force. This liberalism recruited its adherents from every political group with the exception of the extreme Right.

RESPECT FOR MAJORITY RULE BY THE MINORITY FAVORING DECOLONIZATION

In a democracy, a political party's respect for majority rule is a vital clue to the attitude of that party toward the problem that preoccupies it and to the nature of the opponent at whose ex-

6. The weakening of the Left-Right opposition in France only seems paradoxical when one starts from the mistaken premise that anything in favor of social progress must come from the Left while anything opposing that progress is characteristic of the Right. By these standards, the industrial capitalists of the age of prosperity would have been Leftists. The workers who oppose technical innovations through fear of unemployment would have been Rightists. The paradox disappears as soon as the Left-Right struggle is returned to its proper perspective in which the Left can only be mentioned when the need for technological and economic expansion is tied to a need for emancipation of the masses whose ad hoc political groupings control all activity.

pense it is attempting to solve the problem. Playing the game, in a democracy, amounts to admitting that one is basically in agreement with one's opponent and that only marginal differences remain. Not playing the game means that the conflict which has arisen is more important than the procedure which might resolve it and that, if a choice has to be made, it will be made against the regime. Between 1946 and 1956, metropolitan partisans of Moroccan decolonization invariably respected every constitutional rule, while their extremist opponents respected the rules only when these were in their favor, eventually challenging them openly toward the end of the Moroccan conflict and at each crescendo of the Algerian crisis. This recourse to illegality is most certainly not the privilege of so-called revolutionary parties. Christian Democrats threaten to use it whenever their opponents seem to be attacking religious liberty. Social Democrats come close to using it whenever their social accomplishments are called into question. What is even more significant is the fact that these parties never found it necessary to follow this course on a question of colonial policy.

If the Left and the Right behaved in such a different manner with respect to decolonization, it is because the question of the colonial status quo was a threat to the Right, whereas a policy of immobility, sought after by the Right, was not considered a casus belli by the Left. Ultimately, it may be said that if the deeper reasons rather than the political doctrines or intellectual habits of the Left and Right are considered, both sides felt that the protection of the colons and the support of national attitudes were more important than a struggle waged alongside the colonized for the recognition of their rights. There is no common denominator between the weak leftist opposition to the policy of force and the wild, extremist antagonism to the decolonizing inclinations of their opponents. It is this profound disparity between the two attitudes that has to be established before isolating its significance.

Attitudes of the Governed

The passivity of the metropolitan population during the Moroccan crisis does not mean that its attitudes had no part to play. An attitude of passive acquiescence can have as much significance as an attitude of opposition or active approbation. When a government takes decisions involving the sacrifices of men, money, and political convictions of the leaders, then the people can adopt two extreme attitudes. They can either automatically obey or openly defy orders. In the first instance, the people consent. In the second, they object, revolt, or attempt to revolt. Between 1954 and 1956, the general attitude of the metropolitan population on colonial conflicts lay much nearer to consent than to opposition. Before proceeding further, it is essential to analyze and qualify the reaction of the French people to the Fourth Republic's decisions on Morocco.

On this level, the consensus of metropolitan opinion appears as a popular extension of the defense reflex launched among French political personnel by the Moroccan revolt. If it is normal for a community whose overseas possessions are threatened to attempt to ensure their protection through decisions made at a governmental level, then it is no less normal for the people to accept these decisions. Once again, this phenomenon is a result of political automatism. Centuries of training have conditioned western nations to accept the blood tax as the most natural of all sacrifices. The accompanying financial burdens are among the most readily accepted. The call for men and money provokes a universal, automatic reaction that is one of the factors in national unity and that tends to protect the status quo when it is threatened by a force hostile to the established order. There is little real awareness of the true nature of these sacrifices. Decolonization wars are generally fought by professional soldiers. Conscripts were brought into action in Morocco only at the end of the crisis, when they were already thoroughly committed in Algeria, and at a time when it was becoming obvious that in France there was no counter-current of opinion strong enough to restrain the national defense reflex. All these factors facilitated acceptance of the various sacrifices demanded by the government.

However, this positive reaction to orders from the top is but one component of the population's attitude. The reactions of people are not confined to governmental decisions. They have their own attitudes, which are usually shared by their leaders. If, in time of war, a soldier obeys orders sending him to his death, this is because the soldier and his officers, quite independently of any dialectic of command and obedience, hold a common attitude toward the enemy. Similarly, no country consents to sacrifices asked by its leaders to combat a colonial nationalism unless it shares, to a certain extent, the same basic attitudes as its leaders toward the whole question of decolonization. The explicit attitudes that characterize given orders and the way in which they are carried out are only terminal continuations of the basic attitudes from which they spring. These basic attitudes must now be analyzed.

The most striking characteristic is their extreme complexity. If we were to carry out an actual survey of the attitudes of a representative sample of the metropolitan population toward decolonization, we would establish that today, as before, nationalism and internationalism, pacifism and bellicosity, and racism and humanitarianism are in perpetual conflict in the minds of the French. Although we are forced to infer its exact shape, there can be no disputing the existence of such a parallelogram of attitudes. For generations, the political life of the country has been dominated by libertarian and egalitarian values, the socialist and internationalist tradition, and the idea of France's civilizing mission of bringing liberty to the rest of the world. The attitudes accompanying this tradition are today part of the national psychology. This set of noble attitudes is checked by a counter-system of attitudes made up of racism, nationalism, belligerence, and perplexed conservatism. One need only recall the Dreyfus affair, the Vichy government, and a certain postwar extreme Right movement as proof. Sometimes the two systems emerge as rival factions. More often, the battle goes on within each Frenchman's mind. The French personality, like all national personalities, is fragmented to a very marked degree. The sociology and psychology of the contemporary Frenchman is a chaos of collective situations, attitudes, and values which the history of the country has seen develop. Some of these attitudes are still very much alive. Whether they are compatible or not, they form the basic substance of metropolitan political psychology. Others exist only in the form of traces, relics, and vestiges: proletarian internationalism and France's civilizing mission, for example. Others, like anti-Semitism, are dormant like inactive germs, only to become virulent again when conditions again become favorable. All these exist in one form or another today.[7]

The dominant components of the basic system of attitudes from which the French government won the reaction of approval already described can be reduced to four principal elements: (1) adequate social cohesion; (2) marked national susceptibility; (3) a varying sense of solidarity toward Frenchmen abroad; and (4) active or latent racist feelings toward North African Muslims and Algerian workers who had settled in France.

The cohesion component[8] is the most important and at the same time the most difficult to demonstrate. The manner in which a society reacts to the sacrifices demanded of it and its attitude toward oppressed nations overseas largely depend on its cohesiveness. If in the past France was divided over the colonial wars and the Spanish Civil War, it is because revolutionary or

7. The main difficulty in using the inference method to reconstruct the parallelogram of basic French attitudes toward decolonization is the determination of the size and value of each part. How are we to estimate the mean intensity and strength of each component when the necessary statistical material is missing? However, by using the fact that social attitudes resemble mechanical forces, it is possible to tackle the problem indirectly. All attitude systems are, in fact, comparable in certain respects to a parallelogram of mechanical forces. Therefore the size and value of each component tends to emerge of its own accord whenever the system has an observable resultant. Fear and courage are inextricably involved in the psychology of a soldier. When he continues an advance, it is as if his courage were conquering his fear and in the end it is as if courage alone were responsible for his behavior. Mutatis mutandis, the same applies here to the hypothesis with which we are dealing. The problem is not so much to carry out direct observation on the French population's system of political attitudes as to infer the real structure of the system by studying its resultant.

8. It would be as well to offer a definition of this concept and to specify its relationship to political consent. *Social cohesion* is the acceptance by different groups of citizens of the collection of social relationships that unite them. Therefore, in a fully cohesive society, no social relationship would be challenged. *Political consent* is the acceptance by the people of the particular social relationship between themselves and their leaders when they acquiesce in their leader's orders. Therefore political consent is one aspect only, one constitutive element, of cohesion, since it is the acceptance of one particular social relationship, whereas cohesion is the acceptance of all such relationships. Although cohesion and political consent imply a certain mutual involvement, since any tension between the people must involve a correlative tension between the people and its leaders, this implication should not be interpreted too strictly. Consent variations can be relatively independent of cohesion variations. In a society where cohesion is superficially altered or strengthened, the degree of consent can fall extremely low. This, we believe, is what took place under the Fourth Republic.

quasi-revolutionary situations existed in France at the time. If she endured the efforts required by the policy of force in North Africa without large collective protests, it is because her improved internal cohesion had slackened the emotional bonds that, prior to 1914 and to 1941, had linked the French masses to foreign proletariats.[9] The main difficulty in this analysis stems from the fact that at first everything seems to point toward a profound alteration in the cohesion of the French political body under the Fourth Republic. The enormous gulf separating the Communist electorate from the rest of the population, and the gathering at the opposite political extreme of the pro-fascist movements, seems in retrospect to have placed the history of the Fourth Republic beneath the sign of imminent revolution. However, this only appears to be the case. It is not enough for a large section of the population to grumble about the established regime and complain about living conditions for these negative attitudes to form a revolutionary situation. Rejection of the established order is not the only basis for revolutions. They spring also from a no less fundamental disposition to overthrow this order by taking definite action against it. This aggression component is conspicuous by its absence from the spectrum of French political attitudes under the Fourth Republic. True, the consensus of popular support for the regime was consistently shrinking between 1944 and 1958. But this discontent and discouragement resulted only in a state of general apathy that is the opposite of a revolutionary attitude. Far from having produced a similar change in national cohesion, it seems that the reduction of the French consensus was accompanied by a slow but sure revival of national cohesion.

On this question, nothing is more revealing than its denouement. May 13, 1958 might have been the long-dreamed-of occa-

9. It would be an exaggeration to interpret this passage as implying that, in the course of 50 to 75 years, French workers abandoned their victorious internationalism for the insensitivity they display today toward foreign proletariats, especially those in the colonies. Unquestionably, the internationalism of the French masses has weakened over the last 75 years—with the exception of a passing renewal of interest during the Spanish Civil War—but it is nevertheless true that never, not at the beginning and not even at the most propitious moment, did it win out over the opposing attitude. For a discussion of the problem of interpretation that this retrospective point poses, see pp. 600–01.

sion for ripping everything apart in a France on the verge of social conflagration. In fact, the only indisputable conclusion to be drawn from that event was that nobody in France wanted a revolution. The general apathy at the time, and the almost unanimous acceptance of the arbitrator, leaves absolutely no room for doubt. As far as internal matters were concerned, the dominant French attitude on May 13 was refusal to fight a civil war and abdication of all responsibility into the hands of a man judged, rightly or not, to be the only person capable of satisfying the need for law and order, the result of fifteen years of parliamentary impotence. On this level, as on many others, the absence of any true revolutionary tensions in the mass of the French population is one of the characteristic aspects of the conflict.[10]

The second dominant component of the basic parallelogram of metropolitan attitudes seems to be the interference with the development of international relations and France's loss of power and prestige throughout the world. The revolt of the French colonies came at a time when national feelings were extremely sensitive due to a series of serious setbacks. The Suez crisis provides a clear demonstration of the second component, just as May 13, 1958 did of the first. The extraordinary homogeneity displayed by the French body politic in supporting an act of cold-blooded colonial aggression unleashed by French Socialists in collaboration with British Conservatives leaves not the slightest shadow of a doubt on the subject. For a short but highly reveal-

10. This was no accident; it is the most conspicuous example of the gradual erosion of revolutionary tensions that characterized French society during the second half of the nineteenth century and of their gradual replacement by a new phase of social cohesion. True, class divisions still exist in France. Undoubtedly the cohesion that has been achieved remains a fragile and tenuous quasi-cohesion. Nonetheless, its development has been fundamental. Three-quarters of a century ago and between the two wars, any challenge to the established order was usually accompanied by violence. During the 1950s it gave rise to nothing more serious than a sort of negative discontent. Like other western countries, France tends to short-circuit the phase of chronic revolutionary disturbance. After her own fashion, she works for a return to the normal, widespread support of the regime by that section of the electorate which upholds the center parties and the common values that they represent. These values are still disputed by extremist elements on the Left and Right, by the supporters of Communism, and by certain parties of the far Right. The unusual aspect of French political life in this twentieth century society is the abnormal importance of the Communist section of the French population. The French Communist Party's obvious incapacity, if not fundamental aversion, to direct action permits us to consider its political behavior as a sort of confirmatory anomaly of France's social recovery.

ing period, France gave almost unanimous support to its leaders, who were engaged in a punitive expedition that not one metropolitan political party felt capable of actively opposing.

Although no crucial political event took place to highlight the feeling of solidarity between Frenchmen at home and abroad, its existence can hardly be challenged. Moreover, this solidarity stands partially revealed by the events of February 6, 1956. When Guy Mollet yielded to the "poor whites" in Algiers, he was not merely confirming the political bankruptcy of the regime. He made a choice "for" the Algerian French and "against" the Muslims, showing that in his socialist conscience the solidarity between Europeans at home and abroad took precedence over the ideological and emotional bonds which half a century of theoretical anticolonialism was supposed to have forged between western socialism and the colonized nations. This symbolic event was not merely a stroke of sudden self-knowledge; it also demonstrated the predominance of solidarity among Europeans over proletarian internationalism.

We are now left with racism or—if this term is preferred—the sense of superiority that western man experiences when faced with social groups whom he considers to be inferior because of a distinctive phenotype. No decisive event of the first fifteen postwar years points to its importance in France. But if we remember that, ever since the Dreyfus case, the French Right has been engaged in a militant anti-Semitism, and that, at the other extreme, the working classes have been sensitized by constant exposure to North African workers in France, then it seems indisputable that the combination of circumstances created by the liquidation of France's colonial heritage provided a particularly favorable psychological climate for the rise and intensification of a certain type of racism.

The confirmation of the dominance of a given system of attitudes does not mean that the dominant system was the only one at work in a given environment. On the contrary, the dominance of an attitude implies the existence of a dominated attitude. No one will deny that residual revolutionary tensions still exist in France. Nor will any one deny that French nationalism was sometimes held in check by pacifist-inclined internationalist attitudes, that the sense of solidarity with the French abroad was partially neutralized by a sense of solidarity with the colonized, and that racism was compensated for to a certain extent by anti-racism. We merely claim that the overall result of the twofold system, formed by the two sets of component attitudes that have just been examined, shows that one of these systems predominated over the other.

Thus, the study of French political psychology under the Fourth Republic shows that a *cohesive-nationalist-racist-colonialist* attitude system generally dominated a counter system of *revolutionary-humanitarian-antiracist-internationalist* attitudes. In other words, the system of basic French attitudes toward Moroccan decolonization can be reduced to two subsystems: one dominant and supporting the colons, the other dominated and supporting the colonized. As might be expected, this twofold basic attitude system, set in action by events as they occurred, produced two complementary psychological reactions: the predominance of the attitude for the maintenance of the colonial status quo among government leaders, and the predominance of the attitude of consensual acquiescence to decisions tending to maintain the status quo within the metropolitan population.[11]

11. The intervention of leaders in the formation of political attitudes on the part of the masses undeniably complicates the problem of elucidating how these attitudes developed. Political leaders can appeal to a basic attitude system in many ways. Therefore, popular reaction depends partly on the nature of the political stimulus that affects the system. This does not mean, however, that the government can provoke any reaction at will. It is never master of the sociological conditions on the basis of which it must operate. The system of basic attitudes that determines a nation's political behavior is the outcome of its whole situation. Using appropriate stimuli, the government can only provoke the various types of reactions already present in the system. It is not in its power to provoke reactions corresponding to different social situations. The fact that the leaders of the Fourth Republic acted in a certain manner during the Moroccan crisis does not provide an adequate explanation of why the French people accepted this policy. The effect produced by the government on the attitudes of the people must remain essentially subordinate to the primary influence that the situation exercises on the attitudes of the masses. In the final analysis, governmental and popular attitudes can only be explained in the light of the overall national situation.

Chapter 3

SITUATIONAL VARIABLES

The description of the attitudes of the metropolitan political parties in relation to those of the population calls for a correlative discussion of the situation of these parties in relation to the over-all situation of the French people. The situation of political parties is determined primarily by their relationship to the social classes from which they emanate. Beyond this it is determined by the rules and methods that constitute their political scheme of reference within the parliamentary framework and, finally, by the interplay of the different forces that bind them together within the nation. In other words, the situation of the French parties under the Fourth Republic was a complex operational structure provided by a regime in crisis.[1] As for the overall situation of the French people, we will only be dealing with those components of the situation of France in the world and of Frenchmen in France that conditioned French attitudes toward decolonization. An explanation of the two attitude levels discussed in the previous chapter can a priori only be found by considering the two relevant situation levels.

Situation of the Metropolitan Parties

RELATIONSHIP AMONG THE PARTIES AND SOCIAL CLASSES

The electoral sociology of the parties under the fourth Republic can be summarized as follows:

> The opposition of the Communists and the constitutional Right was the only true partisan relationship under the Fourth Republic that embodied characteristic class antagonisms. The moderate and the Peasant parties

1. We will merely list the few characteristic anomalies that dominated French political party life during this period, without considering the crisis within the regime. For this particular point, see pp. 602 ff.

were notables who conscientiously defended class interests. The Communist Party grouped together the proletarian wage earners and rural workers who were irritated by regional underdevelopment.

All the other parties clearly more or less modified class conflicts. "Almost every party includes workers and bourgeois, townsmen and countrymen, southerners and northerners, those who yearn for the past and those who seek after the future, and rightists and leftists. Each party, in its own way, is a sort of miniature France." [2]

The S.F.I.O. gradually lost its working-class character by limiting its recruiting campaigns to the more privileged levels of the wage-earning population: white-collar workers and officials, the middle classes, and lower managerial executives.

The M.R.P. was a "reduced image of the French population," while the Radicals were the management and middle class party, and the R.P.F. included both the anticonstitutional Right and temporary fugitives from the Left and Center.

In France, the concept of the political party covers different sociological realities. "When one speaks of French political parties one is referring to groups that have only their name in common." [3] The Communist and Socialist Parties are parties in the modern sense of the term, that is, mass parties. The R.P.F. and the Poujadists were short-lived groupings formed under the pressure of special circumstances, crystallized in the personality of one man, and dissolved as rapidly as they were formed. Other political groups occupied intermediary positions between the people's party and the notables' organizations.

"French political parties are not each others' contemporaries." [4] The R.P.F., the Poujadists, the moderates, and the M.R.P. are postwar creations. The Communists and

2. Jacques Fauvet, *La France déchirée* (Paris, 1957), p. 106.
3. Ibid., p. 116.
4. "Some are still in the stone age while others are in the atomic age. There are

Socialists date back to the split in the Second International immediately after the First World War. The Radicals are survivors of the nineteenth century. All of these parties are relative newcomers. Jacques Fauvet notes quite correctly that at the beginning of the Third Republic there were no political parties in France.

PARLIAMENTARY POSITION OF THE PARTIES AND ITS DETERIORATION

It is relatively easy to identify the preconditions for the normal functioning of a democracy. Quite apart from a general consensus (a fundamental factor which we will not deal with here), the regime should be able to provide the government with large and stable majorities. These majorities should be willing and able to face up to the country's problems. There should not be too many political parties. Their programs should not be neutralized by compromise. Those playing the political game should obey both the letter and the spirit of its laws and, above all, the regime should not be confronted with too serious difficulties.[5] Not one of these preconditions was secured under the Fourth Republic.

The principal cause of the regime's ineffectuality was its lack of an adequate majority. This most obvious anomaly has been described many times.

The refusal of the extreme Left, the future, united with that of the far Right, fixed on the past. The centrifugal force of communism was thus effectively allied with that of Bonapartism. Together they deprived the government of popular support, and their ultimate effect was to swing the political axis back toward the Center.

The simultaneous existence of twin oppositions weak-

fossils which go on reproducing long after the world has abandoned them. There are vertebrates who survive the fiercest ordeals and molluscs who never react to anything." Ibid.

5. Social and political divisions can be compensated for, to a certain extent, by the use of certain well-known methods. The manipulation of the proportional system and the possibility of dissolution after two refusals of confidence in a given period of time were both used under the Fourth Republic to counteract the too-immediate consequences that social and parliamentary divisions might have had on the stability of the government. These were only palliatives which could guarantee a minimum degree of stability but not prevent the ineffectuality of the government.

ened the regime on two fronts. By weakening its popular support, it threatened it from without; by weakening its parliamentary basis, it threatened it from within. . . . Still more seriously, the twin opposition will often split the country in two, and make it more ungovernable. . . . If either the Left or Right succeeded in obtaining power, neither would have a sufficient majority to impose its will on the country or Parliament. If they both yielded to the Center parties they would find themselves in the same position and reduced to the same impotency.[6]

The ministerial crises were provoked by the coalition of the two oppositions, extremists who were thoroughly capable of overthrowing one government but thoroughly incapable of forming another.[7]

Even as we attempt to explain the regime's paralysis by this numerical inadequacy, the explanation becomes far more complex. In none of the three elected legislatures did the sum of Communist and far Right votes reduce the regime to numerical ineffectiveness. In the first legislature, Communists and fellow travelers held 183 seats out of 618. This meant that, together with the conservatives (i.e. the Gaullist Union, the Peasants, and the extreme Right), the extremist deputies still numbered no more than 254 against the 342 deputies of the Center, not counting 22 nonaligned seats.[8] In the second legislature, the sum of Communist and R.P.F. votes gave 221 seats to the anticonstitutional opposition leaving 396 seats to the Center parties with 10 nonaligned deputies.[9] In the third legislature, the anticonstitutional parties of the extreme Left and extreme Right could muster only 214 seats against 374, with 8 nonaligned.[10] In all three instances, the Center could have governed effectively had the Socialists, Radicals, M.R.P., and the constitutional Right been in permanent agreement on all issues. Since these groups rarely

6. Fauvet, pp. 81–82.
7. Jacques Fauvet, *La IVe République* (Paris, 1959), p. 9.
8. Philip Williams, *Politics in Post-War France* (London, 1958), p. 447.
9. Ibid.
10. Not counting the 42 Poujadists; ibid.

agreed on any issue, the system could only have worked if there had been within the Center itself several possible parliamentary coalitions, each assured of a stable parliamentary majority. It is precisely this technical possibility that the twofold opposition of the Left and Right eliminated. The extreme Left and the extreme Right did not paralyze the regime by making the Center parties a minority but by making a minority out of the coalitions that might have been formed within the Center parties to provide an effective government for the country. Had it been homogeneous, the Center might have been able to govern. But being the Center—i.e. "a state of reason, an imaginary concept, a pure abstraction" [11]—it could not, a priori, agree to anything other than a policy of immobility tempered by the force of circumstances. It was this policy of immobility that finally destroyed the regime.

In addition to the absence of an adequate majority, the multiplicity of parties, their lack of discipline, and their internal divisions only intensified the situation. "In France," writes Jacques Fauvet,

> there are two basic temperaments: that of the Left and that of the Right. If the Center is included, there are three main tendencies; six ideological families; ten parties (large and small), each swept by multiple cross-currents; fourteen highly undisciplined parliamentary groups; and forty million opinions. . . . [12] When the agreement made between various parties is not in any way binding, then no formal agreement, and therefore no stable majority, is possible. . . . Instability springs from this disparity between parties which bear no resemblance to each other and therefore do not share similar structures. [13]

This criticism is certainly justified, but the relative importance of the phenomenon should not be exaggerated. The constant succession of governments does not necessarily imply that there is a lack of political continuity, especially on colonial and foreign

11. Fauvet, *La France déchirée,* p. 100, citing René Rémond.
12. Ibid., p. 22.
13. Ibid., pp. 23–24.

affairs where the same ministers returned to power in the course of ten years.

In another political climate, with fewer serious problems to be faced, this kaleidoscope of groups and parties might have been molded through coalitions into more governable groups. A simple comparison between France and Belgium will demonstrate the extent and the limitations of this diversification factor. The Belgian Parliament is roughly equivalent to an enlarged Center, occupying practically every seat, and in which the S.F.I.O., the M.R.P., and the Radicals would share the electorate's favors. This absolute sovereignty of Center does not, however, prevent Belgian democracy from also demonstrating relative political ineffectiveness. Still the number of French parties and their lack of discipline remain largely responsible for establishing the commanding lead of the French Republic over neighboring democracies as an object of political pathology. Consider what might have happened had the Belgian situation existed in Paris, with Parliament dominated by the S.F.I.O., the M.R.P., and a small hinge group of Radicals. Many of the difficulties in the governmental crisis that were peculiar to the Fourth Republic might thus have been eliminated. The infinite divisions within the parliamentary structure undeniably complicated a situation already rendered difficult by the stifling of the Center, but this was only one of many different aspects of the governmental crisis. The large number of parties was an effect as well as a cause of the crisis. In a situation where the approval of practically every constitutional representative is required for the formation of a stable government, each representative has, in principle, the right to veto any government decisions. When everyone has the right of veto, the smallest group enjoys a decision-making power out of all proportion to its size: hence the multiplicity of hinge groups and other types of subgroups.

It is not enough for a majority to be large and stable; it must also be homogeneous enough to have a mind of its own. If the coalitions formed within parliaments and governments only cancel each other out instead of working in the same direction, neither numerical stature nor a stable majority can prevent the government from becoming totally ineffective. The lack of homogeneity within majorities is the curse of the modern parliamentary system and it is as evident, if not as pronounced, in western countries like Belgium where political groups are few and majorities can readily be formed as it is in nations where many parties and precarious majorities are the rule.

The stifling of the Center, the multiplicity of its groups, and the lack of homogeneity in its majorities brings us to a final aspect of French parliamentary life under the Fourth Republic: the triumph of the spirit of compromise. In limited amounts, the spirit of compromise is indispensable to democracy. Taken to extremes, it reduces democracy to a state of complete helplessness. The need for compromise demoralizes the Left, weakens the Left's opposition to the Right, and destroys its individuality by neutralizing what remains of its ideological vitality and its progressive vocation. Why does the Left so often become the hostage of the Right in these conditions? Because the Center parties do not get together to produce a positive program. The Left joins only to avoid becoming the hostage of the extreme Left, a greater evil in its opinion than ultraconservatism. The Right is satisfied because its program is ultraconservative. As for the hinge groups, their incorporation into the Center endows them with a degree of political importance out of all proportion with their size and exempts them from the necessity of having a program of their own. For many of these groups, this is close to being an ideal situation. The result of the asymmetry of the situations of the Left and Right within the Center group is that the concessions made by both sides to ensure the Center's survival were not equal. The Right hands out a few concessions but realizes the major part of its program. The Left picks up a few consolation prizes while betraying its true raison d'être.

In such a political climate, it was in nobody's interest to respect majority agreements. That was why they were always being broken. The Constitution presumed that any governmental agreement would be respected by the men and parties who had formed it. This fundamental rule was constantly being violated. "Neither the militants, nor the deputies, nor frequently the ministers themselves feel bound by the decisions of a government which they are supposed to be supporting; they see themselves as being more or less in power and in opposition at the same time." [14] The Constitution only provided for the investiture of the President of the Council appointed by Parliament. The first Prime Minister of the Fourth Republic, M. Ramadier, resumed the habits of his predecessors in the Third Republic by submitting his cabinet to the assembly and by requesting a collective investiture for his cabinet which was a duplication of the one he had received. The President of the Republic did not intervene, and this practice therefore continued until 1954. The Constitution provided that the government could only be overthrown by a motion of censure following a vote of confidence. Presidents of the Council came and went without ever being formally placed in a minority. In the end, a situation was reached which might be described as the operation of parliamentary government by way of ministerial crisis. This is the most serious and most revealing of anomalies.

> A crisis becomes a means of solving problems. No precedent was more willingly accepted by a new government. The dispute that provoked the crisis is soon settled; it is reabsorbed. People were shouting about it; now it is hardly mentioned. The same men who were incapable of solving it or of even beginning to discuss it for months on end now manage to find a solution within three weeks.[15]

This means that in a system where parliament will not tolerate an independent executive but where some action is necessary from time to time, the only means of reconciling two apparently incompatible conditions is to topple the government once it has carried out its mandate, so that decisions made by its successors seem less the result of executive initiative than the consequence of the will of a parliament whose mandate is periodically renewed. There is no more serious perversion of a parliamentary system. Such a system normally provides for the government's fall only when a fundamental disagreement exists between the legislative and executive branches. In the system of constant

14. Ibid., p. 24.
15. Ibid., p. 34.

ministerial crises, it is not fundamental disagreement that places the government in a minority but the fulfillment of a mandate by a governmental agent authorized to act once and once only. A concept of the political mandate as narrow as this could succeed if the parliament willed it. When the party issuing the mandate has no mind of its own and when the agent is deprived of the power to implement the mandate whenever it attempts to take action, the result is total paralysis.

This leaves the question of the type and the degree of gravity of the problems with which democracy has to deal. The problem posed for the Fourth Republic by the question of the fate of one and a half million Frenchmen isolated in North Africa was an exceptionally serious one. It alone would have been enough to bring down a fully operational representative regime. This aspect of the problem will be dealt with in our conclusion.[16]

CONSTANT DETERMINANTS OF THE POWER RELATIONSHIP BETWEEN
LEFT AND RIGHT ON THE NATIONAL LEVEL

The study of electoral sociology and the rules of the parliamentary game does not exhaust the situational analysis of a party. Other factors of the technical situation are involved on a national level and contribute to the strengthening or weakening of its relative position. In France, these national determinants of the interplay of political forces worked with unusual strength to the advantage of the Right. One reason is the fact that the democratic elector tends to deny an absolute majority to extremist elements and favors the compromises of the Center. The second stems from the numerical equalization of the Left and Right, which gives the Right an advantage over the Left. The third factor is that the French Left was unable to form an alliance with the extreme Left in order to radicalize its program without risking a Rightist coup d'etat which it would not have been able to control.

The hostility displayed in normal conditions by the democratic voter toward a long-term political mandate is a constant of contemporary democracy. It seems that democratic voters—whether they are English Laborites, continental Social Democrats (with

16. See p. 642 and ff.

the exception of those of the Scandinavian countries), or even American Democrats—are never willing to award a decisive majority to any of the vote-seeking parties. The benefit that the Right derives from this chronic instability in the electorate should be emphasized. It has not been sufficiently appreciated that between the Left and the Right, between progress and ultraconservatism, the balance of political forces favors the Right. To defeat the Right, the Left needs an electoral victory. To defeat the Left, the Right merely has to match the Left's strength. Therefore a greater absolute strength is needed to change the status quo than to maintain it. By refusing to give an absolute majority, the electorate maintains the Right in a dominant position. By refusing it to the Left, the electorate effectively neutralizes it. It is as if the electorate wished to preserve the balance between progressive and conservative forces by favoring the latter, occasionally backing the Left when its weakness or divisions threaten to create political tensions within the system. True, in a country like France, the Left could temporarily regain the necessary ascendancy by uniting itself. A popular front would be its technical response to the divisions within the electorate and to the advantages derived by the Right from the rules of the game. The gulf that separates the constitutional Left from the Communists is sufficient to render this hypothesis unlikely. The Right's position in the metropolitan power structure makes it impractical. In a country where the governing groups have twice, in 1871 and in 1940, formed an alliance with a foreign power to check the Left, a popular front has no chance of success as long as the Right maintains its position of strength within the regime. Today, as during the Spanish Civil War, a popular front determined to go all the way with its program would be almost certain to provoke a successful military coup d'etat. Everything points to the fact that the Left is aware of this and that this awareness of its own inferiority plays a major part in weakening its determination.

All things considered, three phenomena characterize the situation of French political parties under the Fourth Republic: the hostility of the voters on the extreme Right and extreme Left of the regime, the profound changes in parliamentary procedure, and the particularly marked ascendancy of the Right over the Left in the metropolitan power structure.

Social and International Situation of the French People

Let us now examine the situation of the metropolitan population as a whole. This brings us back to the series of factors that characterize the social, economic, demographic, and political structures of contemporary France, not counting the attitudes, ideologies, and political practices that we intend to study in relation to this situation.

This almost inexhaustible mass of statistical and sociological data goes to show that France is a western nation of the mid-twentieth century, and that its history, sociology, economy, and culture combine to give it a strong resemblance to other western countries. Certain particular characteristics and anomalies, however, distinguished France in the 1950s from what might be called the ideal prototype of western democracy. A chronic monetary instability and inflation wreaked their customary social and moral havoc among the workers and fixed income groups. When the Moroccan conflict broke out, modern economic attitudes were only beginning to take over from an economic Malthusianism that had long paralyzed a whole sector of the nation's production capacity. South of the Loire, vast areas of regional underdevelopment bore witness to the difficulties encountered in adapting the rural population to change. In industrial areas, the standard of living of the working classes seems to have been well below that of comparable classes in neighboring countries. A chronic government crisis had allowed the problems and situations awaiting solution to deteriorate. Apart from these unmistakable symptoms of sclerosis in the body politic, the characteristic difficulties that always accompany a population increase were beginning to show. Since the middle of the war the birthrate had been rising. The Fourth Republic did not quail before the task begun during the first De Gaulle administration. A massive investment program and the modernization of the country's economic system were undertaken. Any benefits would be reaped only in the future; the immediate effect was the social expenditure involved.

If our research project had involved a study in depth of a French sociological crisis rather than of a political upheaval originating in Morocco, and if the French population had shown the same tendency as the Moroccans toward sharply defined class reactions to the conflict, then it would have been necessary to repeat our Moroccan procedure and provide a detailed analysis of the situation of each of the metropolitan classes. We will proceed directly to consider the situation of the French nation as a whole, since the most active role in the development of metropolitan attitudes toward the Franco-Moroccan crisis was not played by the social and regional distinctions between different classes but by situation factors common to all Frenchmen. These are shown by five fundamental observations:

1. In one generation, France moved from the status of a major world power to that of a European power of disputed standing. In the course of thirty-five years, the survivors of the 1918 victory had seen the German recovery, the 1940 defeat, the Vichy adventures, the problems of the wartime alliance between the Free French and their Anglo-American allies, and finally the breakup of the colonial empire. More than any other Western country, France had experienced the decline of Europe as a national ordeal.

2. When the decolonization of the Maghreb began, close to one and a half million French colons were settled in North Africa. Few metropolitan families could not claim at least one relative overseas and few French villages had not seen one of the villagers setting out for the colonies.

3. A large number of Algerian workers (400,000 according to Germaine Tillion) [17] had settled in France. Whether they liked it or not, this put the French in France in a caste situation as far as this minority was concerned. It also transferred to the Métropole certain psychological problems peculiar to North African colonization.

4. The solidarity between colonial regimes and the metropolitan power structure was particularly marked in the case of France. The army and political and business circles had forged such strong links between the colons and the Métropole that

17. Germaine Tillion, *L'Algérie en 1957* (Paris, 1957), p. 84.

when a Frenchman from North Africa backed the notables, he
became one hundred percent French. It follows that the one and
a half million Frenchmen in North Africa had more of a hold
on metropolitan France than any other group of European
colons had on its mother country.

5. Finally, as has often been explained, the French people were
not actively involved in the conflict. They had no direct experience of the Moroccan problem, and it therefore touched only a
secondary political nerve among middle-class Frenchmen.

These were the main situation factors governing metropolitan
attitudes during the conflict.

PART THREE

ELABORATION OF A MODEL:
RELATIONSHIPS AMONG VARIABLES

T here is no point to studying a political system variable by variable unless this study is the first phase of a much wider undertaking in which their reciprocal influences are examined.[1] Since the variables on the Moroccan, metropolitan, and, to a certain extent, international levels have already been discussed in earlier analyses, it would now be appropriate to turn to the study of their interactions, which are the laws of the system. The Franco-Moroccan conflict brought five kinds of variables into play: time, situations, attitude, ideology, and decision-making capacity. In constructing a model of the conflict, these four main relationships must therefore be analyzed:

1. Variations in situation as a function of time
2. Attitudinal variations as a function of situations
3. Ideological variations as a function of attitudes and of situations
4. Variations in decision-making capacity as a function of attitudes

Although this schema has been considerably simplified in the case of metropolitan France and in the international context, the data used in the arguments are so complex that it seemed useful to

---

1. According to the plan described in the methodological introduction, discussions of the model should have dealt with the interrelated subjects of political functionalism and mechanism. Since such a vast undertaking would have complicated matters unduly, the functionalist correlatives in this study will not be incorporated until the final analysis. See pp. 641 ff.

provide summaries in table form which appear at the head of the
appropriate sections.[2]

2. Most of the data mentioned in Tables 1 and 2 (see pp. 547–49 and 591–92) were
introduced in Part Two of this volume. However, the data concerning the residential
authority structure and the decision-making capacity of the nationalist leaders are
taken from Part Three. Table 3 (see p. 609) summarizes the material covered more
freely than do the other two figures. Figures 1 and 2 (see pp. 630 and 635) are
incorporated in the conclusions and provide a schematization of the broader aspects
of the argument. Each of the tables synthesizes a set of data to facilitate understanding
of the corresponding sections in the exposition.

TABLE 1. THE RELATIONSHIP BETWEEN SITUATIONS, ATTITUDES, IDEOLOGIES, AND DECISION-MAKING CAPACITIES IN THE MOROCCAN POLITICAL SYSTEM, 1944-1956

Decision-Making Capacity of the Residential Regime	Decision-Making Capacity of the Nationalist Leaders
Adequate to develop modern sectors of the Moroccan economy	Adequate to organize the urban masses and to lead them toward nationalism
Inadequate to develop traditional sectors	Inadequate to realize their political objectives without recourse to terrorism and guerrilla warfare
Adequate to maintain the institutional status quo despite indigenous political opposition	Adequate to organize urban terrorism and guerrilla warfare
Inadequate to liberalize the regime in face of political opposition from the Europeans	Adequate to force the residential regime ultimately to yield to terrorism and guerrilla warfare, because of technical and political limitations preventing the utilization of its capacity to take repressive measures
Adequate to set up joint organs despite Muslim political opposition	
Inadequate to make these organs work with only European support	
Inadequate to take forceful action against the Europeans	
Adequate to organize and execute police reprisals against nationalist leaders	
Inadequate to halt the disintegration of Moroccan consent by this type of measure	
Inadequate to prevent the appearance of a clandestine nationalist leadership	
Adequate for the use of force against urban terrorists and against rural rebels	
Inadequate to ensure the effectiveness of repressive measures, because of the technical and psychological limitations on the free utilization of the potential French capacity to use force	

TABLE I (Continued)

Authority Structure of the Residential Regime

European Position in the Authority Structure of the Residential Regime	Muslim Position in the Authority Structure of the Residential Regime
Monopoly of key positions	Exclusion from key positions
Monopoly of administrative functions	Exclusion from administrative functions
Quasi-monopoly of military functions	Limited and revocable participation in subordinate military functions
Lack of political representation, notwithstanding their monopoly of political influence	Lack of political representation in a system that precluded any effective political influence on their part

Ideology of the Europeans and of the Pro-Residential Notables	Ideology of the Nationalist Muslims and of the French Liberals
Justification of attitudes and situation based on a highly distorted view of the situation	Justification of attitudes and situations based on only a slightly distorted view of the situation
Denial of the inevitability of the decolonization process	Affirmation of the inevitability of the decolonization process
Affirmation of the objectively and subjectively progressive nature of colonization	Denial of the subjectively progressive nature of colonization; a more qualified denial of its objectively progressive nature

Attitude of the Pro-Residential Europeans and of the Pro-Residential Notables Anti-Nationalism Based on:	Attitude of the Muslim Nationalists and of the Pro-Nationalist French Anti-Colonialism Based on:
Defense of the superiority factors characteristic of their situation	Progressive removal of those factors of political, socio-cultural, economic, financial, technological, and psychological inferiority affecting the situation of Muslims
The demand for political rights denied to the Europeans by the treaty of Fez and the fight against juridical inferiority factors stemming from the situation of the Europeans	Ultimate restoration of Moroccan sovereignty
Minimization of internal inequalities within the European group	Progressive transformation of initial political consent into political opposition to the conservative decisions of the regime
Conversion of initial consent into opposition whenever the Residence attempted to liberalize the protectorate	Eventual transformation of this political opposition into overt rebellion

TABLE I (*Continued*)

Situation of the Europeans, Including the Liberal French	Situation of the Pro-Residential Muslims	Situation of the Pro-Nationalist Notables	Situation of the Muslim Nationalists
De facto political superiority	Partial sharing in the superior situation of the Europeans, a factor that determined their political attitudes	Partial sharing in the inferior situation of other Muslims, a factor that determined their political attitudes	De facto political inferiority
Higher standard of living and culture			Disintegration of the traditional way of life
Economic and financial superiority			Social and cultural inferiority
Technological superiority			Economic and financial inferiority
Psychological superiority			Technological inferiority
Inferiority on the nationality issue			Psychological inferiority
			Superiority on the nationality issue

Main Time Sequences

Development of the situation, 1912–56

Evolution of urban Muslim attitudes, 1944–56

Evolution of rural Muslim attitudes, 1953–56

Period of change in European attitudes, 1944–45

SECTION ONE: THE MOROCCAN ECHELON

Chapter 1

SITUATIONAL VARIATIONS AS A
FUNCTION OF TIME

Although time as a variable has not yet been discussed, the effect of the simple passage of time on the economy and sociology of the protectorate still lies at the root of all the conditioning factors which structured the conflict. The effect of time on the system isolates its own growth factor. Between 1912 and 1943 and from 1943 to 1956, the protectorate developed along the usual lines for colonies of the same type. Colonial systems show a development curve in time whose contours are relatively independent of any political accidents. This is the basic phenomenon from which everything else follows.

The characteristic aspects of Moroccan development have been adequately described in the previous analysis of the Moroccan situation and need no further elaboration here. Since the analysis dealt with situational variables that had already been transformed by the passage of time, it will be sufficient to compare them with what they were in 1912; this will give us a general but adequate [1] idea of how the groups in question were transformed as a function of time during this period.

When the first symptoms of a decolonization crisis appeared in Morocco in 1943, the system went on evolving according to the laws governing its growth, but this basic phenomenon was

---

1. "Adequate" in the sense that the growth of underdeveloped societies has already been extensively described by other specialists. This is why it seemed unnecessary to make an explicit comparison between Moroccan situations in 1912 and those in 1951 or 1953.

complicated by a related phenomenon: the struggle between the colonists and the colonized. Undoubtedly, this struggle was rooted in locally evolving situations, but its mechanism depended primarily upon the manner in which the levels of situation, attitude, and decision influenced each other. A political component of the evolving system was now superimposed on its own growth component. There can be no doubt that these two phenomena reacted on each other. Had there been no struggle, certain aspects of Moroccan development would have been quite different. But it is not the effect of decolonization on growth which is important here; it is the reverse effect of growth upon decolonization. If Morocco had not developed, there would have been no Franco-Moroccan conflict. If the situation of both the European and the Muslim groups had not undergone irreversible transformations prior to 1943, the subsequent political crises would not have been irreversible. Post-1943 events in Morocco on the decision-making and attitudinal levels were merely adaptations in the upper strata of the political system to an evolution that had already taken place at the base. With this transformation, the cards were dealt out. All the protagonists had to do was to play their hands under conditions which did not exclude all political spontaneity but which did set insurmountable limits to it.[2]

The passage of time not only produced an irreversible transformation in Moroccan situations, it also sharply differentiated their evolutionary rhythms. Changes in the various Muslim groups did not begin at the same time or proceed at the same pace. The political distortions caused by these different evolutionary rhythms were largely responsible for the distinctive features of

2. Thus, quite naturally, the study of the conflict is linked to the study of the social consequences of technological progress. Once the first machine was constructed in the west, all the subsequent sociological development became inevitable. Obviously, this "all" includes politics. Once a certain sociological determinism is recognized, there is no need to exclude the governmental actions. In a social system that is undergoing an inevitable and irreversible process of technologically-induced transformation and within which rival political factions join with the forces of progress or inertia operating within the collectivity, the evolution of situations *necessarily* constitutes an irreversible advantage for the political movement working toward the institutional changes called for by this evolution. In our opinion, this point is such a capital one that although we have already stressed it in the introduction to this book, we are now taking this opportunity to reemphasize it.

the conflict. If the attitudes of all Moroccans had evolved over the same period of time and at the same speed, they would have achieved simultaneously and painlessly a sense of national identification. However, the attitudes within the Muslim community only evolved under political pressure brought to bear by the groups most responsive to nationalism upon those who were less responsive: pressure by the citizenry of the old towns upon the new urban proletariat, pressure by the towns upon the *bled,* and, within each group, pressure by the active minority upon the still inert masses.

Finally it will be noted that the role played by time among the Moroccans has been stressed less than among the Europeans, since the latter's political attitudes were more heavily conditioned by the Muslims' behavior than by the rhythm of their sociological development.

A statement of the effect of time on situations is only the first step. Once again, what matters is the way in which attitudinal, ideological, and decision-making levels adaped themselves to changing situations, and it is the inner determinism of this complex phenomenon that we are now going to attempt to bring out.

Chapter 2

ATTITUDINAL VARIATIONS AS A FUNCTION OF SITUATIONS

The transformation wrought upon political attitudes by a change in situation is one of the most solidly established, constantly verified laws of social psychology. The change in attitude of Central European Jewish immigrants in Israel is one striking example. There is no need for prolonged observation of a colonial struggle to see that the phenomenon applies on this level as well. None of the opposing groups on Moroccan soil adopted their attitude by chance. Each of them reacted to its own situation by adopting a characteristic attitude. This is so obvious that it is not so much a question of deciding whether the attitudes of groups were determined by their situation but of deciding just how this determinism operated. We will now examine from this angle the four attitudinal systems which have already been described.

Nationalist Muslims [1]

It is no slight task to appraise the evolution in the attitude of the great majority of the Muslim community as a consequence of its situation. The phenomenon has several component parts, which we shall attempt to isolate by considering successively the

1. By "nationalist Muslims" we mean all Moroccans who were not notables. No one will deny that this mass, dedicated to the cause of nationalism, also included until the very last minute a sizable proportion of timid, lukewarm, opportunistic, and carefree individuals who finally followed like sheep rather than through any profound conviction. But these are mere psychological accidents that can safely be ignored from a vantage point where the main lines of the decolonization process can be discerned. The lukewarm, careful, and opportunistic groups played no part. Year after year, they were either neutralized or swept along on the triumphant tide of nationalism, and in the end it was as if they had never made their presence known. The only sociologically active Muslim opponents with whom the nationalists had to deal were their declared, organized opponents in the traditional hierarchy who had been placed in a privileged situation by the regime. See pp. 566 ff.

553

abstract correlation linking attitudes to situation, the complex relationships between attitudinal factors and the corresponding situational factors, the political mechanism governing the generalization of attitudes within each group, and the mechanism governing shifts in attitude over a period of time.

ABSTRACT FORM OF THE CORRELATION BETWEEN ATTITUDES AND SITUATION

If situations and attitudes had evolved simultaneously within Muslim society, if there had been a progressive, almost mechanistic movement from an initial situation involving a high frequency of attitudes favoring the colonial regime to a final situation characterized by the high frequency of nationalist attitudes, then it would be possible to bring out the correlation index between the two phenomena simply by relating the development of Muslim attitudes to developments in the Muslim situation. For example, it might be found that whenever one hundred workers from the countryside settled in a *bidonville,* 90 per cent of them automatically abandoned their pro-residential attitude for a nationalistic one. Such a relationship would represent a statistical law, since it governed, for a significant percentage, evolving attitudes of the groups in question.

Of course, the reality bears only the most superficial resemblance to this ideal outline. Quite apart from the fact that the lack of statistics [2] makes any numerical estimate of the development of Muslim attitudes quite impossible, changes in situation and attitude are rarely simultaneous. The various groups of individuals whose situations were changing all adjusted their attitudes to the new situations at various time intervals. Another no less important factor is that changes in situation were not the

2. This lacuna reduces the strength but does not alter the nature of the argument. Saying that 90 percent of the Muslims were nationalists in 1956 or that the frequency of nationalist attitudes in Muslim society was "very high" at that time involves a shift from a precise to a general quantitative method. However, the reasoning process is the same in each case. It remains to be seen whether this type of correlation may not be fortuitous. However, this possibility seems highly unlikely, since the type of attitudes under consideration are the subjects' own attitudes to their situation. Under these circumstances, it seems reasonable to assume that the situation really did influence the attitudes or, if this is preferred, that the correlation noted between attitude and situation reveals a strong influence of the latter on the former.

only cause of changes in attitude: the political leaders, their cadres, and circumstances themselves all played an essential part. Finally, all the Muslims in the same social class were not necessarily in the same situation; some of them escaped the usual conditioning because of special privileges granted them by the regime, their religious beliefs, their age, or some other factor capable of impeding their conversion to the cause of nationalism.

Irrespective of these details, the schema demonstrates in a simplified fashion the latent determinism of the phenomenon. Moreover, it comes extremely close to reality once the concept of real attitudes is replaced by that of potential attitudes. There are in fact two possible viewpoints. One can consider the *real* influence of situation on attitude—and then it must be admitted that this real influence is but one among many. Or one can maintain that the very transformation of the situation of the Muslims tended to confer upon them potential nationalist attitudes. From this point of view, the leaders, their cadres, and the circumstances merely promoted the development of this potential nationalism at a time when it was still inhibited by sociological factors favoring the opposite tendency. Although in practice these two views amount to the same thing, the second has two advantages to recommend it. First, by linking situation changes to concomitant alterations in the potential attitude, it has the merit of bringing out the critical aspect of the conditioning of attitudes by situation. Secondly, it puts the political influence of the leaders and of the active political minorities in its correct sociological perspective by showing that the role of the leader and of political propaganda is not to impose arbitrary attitudes on the masses but to lead them to "actualize" the potential attitudes implicit in their situation. However, this choice of a potentialist theory of the evolution of political attitudes is only the argument's point of departure. Certainly the evolution of the Muslims' situation predisposed them to becoming more receptive to nationalist political influence than to that of the Residency. Before going any further, it remains to be seen how one analyzes the impact of a situation on the related attitudes. This will be the second phase in the argument.

ELUCIDATION OF THE RELATIONSHIP BETWEEN ATTITUDES AND SITUATION

Although the high frequency of one potential attitude within a group is sufficient proof that the group's attitude is determined in a specific way by its situation, this does not take the specificity itself into account. The situation of the group might very well be compared to that of a closed bag: its contents are unknown, but we do know, a priori, that it contains a large number of items related to each other in a characteristic way. Once an attitude of a certain type begins to appear with sufficient frequency within the group, it becomes certain that the homogeneity of the reactions must be explained by the contents of the bag. If more is to be known, the bag must be opened. To establish the exact nature of the correlation between the situation of the Muslim masses and their political attitudes, the two variables must be placed beside each other and the different components analyzed element by element to see how the attitudinal components are linked to the situational components. Fortunately, this correlation is simplified by the fact that the underlying attitudes in colonial revolutionary nationalism are usually linked to the demands being made, which automatically reveal the situational factors upon which they are based. If such nationalist demand reveals both an attitudinal component and a situational need, then the need in question must be the situational factor—negative in this case—which conditioned the attitude implied in the demand.

One has only to refer to the analysis of attitudinal and situational variables in the first part of this volume to see the relationship that establishes itself spontaneously between the Muslim situational and attitudinal components. The attitude of the Moroccan nationalists was based on a combination of demands relating to national sovereignty, control of natural resources, elevation of the Muslim standard of living, and the development of Muslim cultural resources. All this implied a gradually developing challenge to the political, economic, and psychological superiority of the Europeans. The link between situation and attitude thus becomes obvious. The main situational factors structuring the attitude of the colonized toward the colonizer are: the undermining of group sovereignty; the trusteeship over traditional authorities; the incorporation of Morocco's natural resources into modern economic structures independent of the local economy; the low standard of living considered from a technological, economic, sociological, or cultural point of view; and, above all, the psychological and "racial" domination of the inhabitants by the Europeans. Thus the change in attitude of the Muslim people and of the elite toward the protectorate was determined by the political, economic, cultural, and psychological inferiority of their position within the regime. The nature of the influence of situation on attitudes thus stands clearly revealed.

GENERALIZATION OF ATTITUDE WITHIN THE GROUP

In short, any change in situation as such is confined to plotting on the psychological map of the group the outline of the new attitude systems that will one day be its own. But this preliminary effect of the situation stops there. The transition from the potential to the actual, the alteration in the real attitude, is the task of the dominant groups, the active minorities, and the political leaders working within the limits of the psychological themes provided for them by the changing situation. So we must now concentrate on the role played by leaders and by the contentions which made the people susceptible to their influence.

From this point of view, three subgroups within the Muslim community need to be taken into consideration: the Muslim population in the old towns, the neo-proletariat of the western towns, and the peasantry. Each of these groups came to nationalism by a different road as a consequence of a particular experience indicative in every case of the different effect of the particular environment. The complete unity of the phenomenon is revealed precisely by these differences in the modalities of action employed by the cadres vis-à-vis the masses. Several outstanding factors help to make the mechanism more understandable.

To begin with, the *initial* structure of these three groups was vastly different. The unity of the people in the old towns had been assured from the beginning by a nationalist bourgeoisie

faced with only scattered representatives of the regime's authority. The cohesion of neo-proletariat came into existence without
any cadres; after a brief amorphous period a professional cadre
was provided by the Istiqlal and by the U.G.S.C.M. The Residency did not attempt to counter this nationalist cadre with one
of its own making. On the other hand, the initial structure in the
bled was ensured by pro-residential notables who encountered
very little opposition from the handful of militant nationalists.

Moreover, each group began by following the conservative or
innovating impulse given to it by the initial dominant segment.
The old urban population provided an almost spontaneous echo
to the nationalist agitation of the urban elite. The neo-proletariat
maintained its unionist-Istiqlal structure. The rural population
began by following the lead of the pro-residential notables. Nothing could be more natural. The leader's role is to lead and that of
the people is to follow—as long as the political grouping remains
sufficiently homogeneous. Once political attitudes become diversified and the leaders disagree, the people regain their sovereignty because they have a choice. In fact, it is evident that the population will retain its original frame of reference only when this
adapts to the attitudinal changes implied by the transformation
of the situation. Where the local leaders swam with the current,
as they did in the towns, they fulfilled their function of maintaining the group cohesion that enabled them to take over from
the tottering residential structure when the crisis came to an end.
Where, as in the *bled,* local leaders ran counter to the changing
attitudes, they were eliminated and replaced by a new rural elite
which the psychological and political evolution had produced.

The last important fact to be noted is that the stimulating or
the inhibiting influence exercised on popular attitudes by the
struggle of rival groupings for popular support was greatly
facilitated by what might be called the chain reaction factor of
political conflicts: the reaction of the urban masses to the police
measures provoked by the first manifestations of political and
terrorist activities by urban nationalists; the reaction of the rural
masses to the demands of the notables, to the deliberate establishment of nationalist guerrillas in the *bled,* and to the reprisals
inflicted by the French army in guerrilla-affected areas; the in-

citement of decisions, attitudes, and political influences in the international milieu, etc.

This evolutionary mechanism occurs to a greater or lesser extent in any group undergoing political transformation. Of course, this was nothing but the relatively static skeleton of a historical and sociological transformation in which the day-to-day vicissitudes followed the unpredictable course of historical contingency. The conflict between the Sultan and the Residency, the nature of the antinationalist measures adopted by the French government, the sequence and contingent nature of the influences of the international milieu, the thousand and one significant and insignificant vicissitudes of the conflict all resulted in one possible history of the conflict. Many other sequences of events might well have occurred. But insofar as the sociological mechanism had been built up and set in motion, they would not have modified the final outcome.

APPEARANCE OF A CHANGE IN ATTITUDE OVER TIME

The problem of discovering why Muslim attitudes should have evolved according to the norms that have just been reviewed is not necessarily the same as determining why this evolution began at any given moment rather than at another. Why did the conflict start at the end of World War II rather than at some other time? Why in 1944? Why not five years earlier? Or ten years later?

If the evolution of a system of political attitudes can be explained by the conjunction of a change in situation and a complex of circumstances skillfully exploited by leaders, then the first sign of this evolution—rightly considered as the origin of the conflict—should also be explicable by changes in the situation and by the historical circumstances which prevailed at the opening of hostilities. The problem of setting in motion a change in attitude is perhaps only a particular instance of the problem posed by its generalization.

The role played by the situational factor is just as clear in this particular instance as in the general case. The change in the situation of the Muslims was undoubtedly less pronounced in 1944 than in 1950 or in 1955. Nevertheless, it was just as definite. The first effect of the French conquest had been to force the Moroccan people to accept the fact of colonization. This resignation to defeat had gradually been consolidated by the obvious benefits to the Moroccans of the domestic peace and order imposed by a colonial regime at its peak. The enormous loss of human life during the pacification had left no indelible traumatic effect on a people who looked upon war as a natural exercise. For these people to break up the colonial arrangement and revolt once again, a new factor had to emerge: a complete change had to occur in the conditions of existence and in sociological status, transforming them into a different people, freed from the past and resensitized to their position as defeated and colonized.

This objective evolution was already apparent in 1940. The men who had been thirty in 1912 had grown old. The young urban elite had been transformed by contacts with French culture. The size of the neo-proletariat was increasing rapidly; the traditional handicraftsmen were beginning to disappear. The continued growth of the rural population together with the stagnation of traditional agriculture weighed heavily on a countryside widely exposed to political propaganda made possible by modern means of communication. The generation destined to be nationalistic was just growing up. The passage of time alone had already deprived the regime of its most obvious justification. The immaturity and underdevelopment of the colonized were no more than an ideological screen thrown up to mask an undertaking tending to perpetuate artificially—within the social framework of a situation that was undergoing a disorderly but rapid transformation—the political minority status of the indigenous inhabitants. In short, things were coming to a head.

Under other historical conditions, things might have gone no further, and colonization would have earned yet another respite. Events were precipitated by the war (a pure accident in itself) with everything that it implied in sociological, economic, psychological, and political terms. A new generation of Moroccans passed through the tough school of military life. France's military defenses collapsed. The Allied cause came under the banner of the right to self-determination. The first French colonies revolted or regained their independence. Ten years earlier, the war would probably have provoked nothing but disorganized and swiftly quelled outbreaks, but falling like a spark on the tinder of a sociological situation that had become explosive, it set off a worldwide decolonization process.

In Morocco itself, the war lies at the root of the changes in attitude that preceded the crisis and that marked its beginning. The first changes in attitude to unleash the conflict on the Moroccan side can therefore be explained in the same way as those which came later, by the interaction of sociological and historical causality. The only peculiarity intrinsic to the launching of this change in attitude is the fact that historical contingency played a much greater role at this stage than it did later on. An historical accident is almost always required to set off a sociological chain reaction. Once the reaction is under way, the accidental yields to the inevitable, and determinism pushes accidents into the background. Thus the evolution of the attitude of the Muslim masses was partly due to the situational factor which acted simultaneously as a producer of potential attitudes and as a favorable or unfavorable terrain for the political pressures which rival groups applied to the Muslim masses in an effort to gain control of them.[3] It will be seen that the same mechanism also accounts—with a few slight variations—for the psychological evolution of the other groups that are being studied.

Pro-Residential Europeans

ABSTRACT FORM OF THE CORRELATION BETWEEN ATTITUDES AND SITUATION

The evolution of political attitudes among the Europeans occurred much more easily than among the Muslims. On the one hand, antinationalist feeling spread more rapidly and more

3. As the reader will have noticed, the above analysis exceeds the limits of a study of the direct influence of the Muslim situation on the generalization of nationalist attitudes. This broadening of the argument stems from the fact that in a political system collective attitudes occupy a central position which places them under a heavy cross-fire of different influences from all the other variables: situational variables, ideological variables, or the various political pressure points that form on the decision-making level. This means that attitudes are influenced by the situation in two different ways: by direct conditioning on the one hand, and by the effect of the remaining variables in the system on the other. Therefore it would be impossible to draw up a complete balance sheet of the influence of situation on attitudes without demonstrating the relationship that exists between attitudes and the other system variables. This will be seen more clearly in the next chapter where the attitudes of French liberals in Morocco are examined, with the direct or indirect influence that the situation had upon them taken into account. See pp. 570 ff.

vigorously among the Europeans than did nationalist feelings among the Muslims. Numerically speaking, the pro-residential Muslims were not strong, but they opposed nationalism as an organized group. On the other hand, no social class proper among the Europeans supported nationalism. Only a handful of individuals fought against the current, although no sociological characteristic destined them a priori for this anomalous role. In short, of the great majority of individuals within the two communities who rallied in support of the respective dominant attitudes, the Europeans came much closer to unanimity than did the Moroccans. Instead of being spread out over a period of time, however, the change in the European attitude came suddenly during the Labonne period, as an almost immediate response to the threat posed to the colons by the Istiqlal declaration and by the Resident-General's liberal plans. Before 1943, the attitude of the Europeans toward both the Residency and the Muslims had been a positive one. A state of peaceful coexistence between the two communities had gradually been established. With the nationalist challenge to the European position, the climate changed abruptly. Residential authority was challenged on every level. Instead of peaceful coexistence there was a state of latent civil war. This time there was an almost perfect coincidence between the change of situation and the change in attitude. The two transformations developed by a process of interaction, and they were linked from the beginning.

If the true correlation between attitudes and situation among the Europeans seems so close to the abstract form to which we have tried to compare it, it is because, in this instance, time played a much more unobtrusive role than with the Muslims. Since the psychological change in the Europeans was instantaneous, there was no psychological distortion, no phase-displacement of reactions, and no time lag between the evolution of situations and the evolution of attitudes. Only the nature of the attitude continued to evolve because it never stopped growing in intensity and coherence. The die was cast for the Europeans in 1945, while the conversion of the Muslims to the nationalist cause was to take ten years.

The dependence relationship between European situations and attitudes is very similar in form to that in Muslim circles but is totally different in content. The formative group was at the same time a political minority and a privileged class, and the twofold nature of its position had a profound effect upon its attitudes.

The colonists possessed everything that the people of the colony claimed: a monopoly of power, a monopoly of force, a monopoly of wealth, a superior culture before which the traditional culture had to admit itself inferior, and, finally, a superior social standing. From the very first, in spite of inequalities that existed within the European minority itself, a class barrier had been erected between the European settlers and the people of the colony, a barrier that worked in favor of the Europeans. Therefore, all the fanatical conservatism of this minority had been sharply defined by all sorts of superiority factors characteristic of its position.

We know that this was a conservative attitude only in part. In fact, the position of the Europeans concealed factors of juridical inferiority responsible for the formulation of claims made when the privileged minority suddenly realized that it had no legal rights, that it was nothing but a foreign community in a nominally sovereign state—hence the appearance of demands designed to obtain political rights. This is possibly a unique example of a privileged class struggling bitterly to obtain political advantages which today are normally sought only by the lower classes.

To obtain a complete set of determinants for the European attitudes, one needs do no more than draw up a balance sheet of the inferiority and superiority factors that characterized their position. Rarely do two sets of factors correspond so closely, element for element, in a psychological analysis.

EVOLUTION OF ATTITUDE OVER TIME

In spite of the rapidity and force with which the change of attitude took place in European circles, political structure and circumstances played a very similar role to the one they played on the nationalist side.

The European leaders assumed, for the most part, their classic influential role. The ruling centers—both residential and extremist—structured, organized, and intensified popular passions. The one anomaly here lies in the fact that the Muslims had only one nationalist center (a diversified one, it is true, and subject to continual internal change), while the Europeans were forever oscillating between their residential directorate and an extremist directorate embodied in Présence française. This particularity is self-explanatory. The nationalist leaders remained faithful to the same ideology. The Residency was not always conservative. Hence the European swing toward the extremist organizations whenever the Residency turned liberal (Grandval) or when a conservative Resident-General was under strong reformist pressures from Paris (Boyer de Latour).

The factors governing the European response to structural influences were either analogous or identical to those revealed in the case of the Muslims. Urban terrorism and guerrilla activity played the same role in intensifying and structuring European attitudes as did arbitrary repressive acts and police brutality vis-à-vis Muslim attitudes. The outbursts of liberalism of the Residency or the Métropole had the same effect on the Europeans as the hardening of residential policies had on the Moroccans. All the other factors, whether national or international in origin, influenced the morale and consequently the attitude of the Europeans in much the same—if not in exactly the same—way as they influenced the attitudes of the Muslims: what encouraged one side discouraged or worried the other and vice versa.

It remains to be seen why the change in attitude was immediate among the Europeans but took ten years to spread through the Muslim community. First, it must be noted that in each case the threat to the situation was quite different. Muslim nationalism was linked to a progressively developing situation, involving only a slowly increasing awareness of the intolerable aspects of this evolution. On the other hand, the European defense reflex is explicable by the fact that the formation of the Istiqlal, combined with the first liberal measures of Eirik Labonne, appeared as a brutal challenge to their superior position and even to their very presence in Morocco. While no radical change proper occurred in the positions of the Muslims, the first flare-up of nationalism and the liberal reaction of the French authorities appeared to the Europeans as signs of the approaching end if not of the world, at least of their world. In a crisis of this type the threat which menaces the colonizer is more serious, more immediate, and more unacceptable than that which menaces the subject peoples. Hence the transition from initial to final attitudes was an immediate actuality among the Europeans while the Muslims made a detour through potential attitudes. Basically, it was the radical change in situation that began by being potential in the corps group, since it was still only a threat when the change in real attitudes took place. If the Muslims had seen their right to live in Morocco suddenly threatened by the Europeans, they would have reacted just as violently and just as swiftly.

Another no less essential aspect is that Muslim attitudes were one of the factors at stake in the struggle between the Residency and the nationalists, while European attitudes changed at will. The transformation of the attitudes of the colonized did not govern the evolution of the power relationship between the Residency and the nationalists by gradually narrowing the basis of the former's support to the advantage of the latter. The opposing powers used every means at their disposal in an attempt to help or hinder the psychological evolution—depending upon which way their authority seemed threatened. For ten years, the Residency struggled to forestall, slow down, or reverse the evolutionary process. The nationalists did all they could to foment and to accelerate it. If France had begun to loosen her hold during the Labonne era, the nationalist attitude would have spread among the Muslims much more rapidly because of the anticipated release of the political brake that was holding it back. On the other hand, if the Residency had operated more skillfully within the framework of its policy of defending the status quo, the spread of nationalism among the Muslims would undoubtedly have been slowed down.

These are the main observable differences between the evolution of political attitudes within the two communities. Quite apart from their sociological value, these differences do not prevent the two attitude curves from having a relationship to the situation which is based, in both cases, on a common determinism.

APPEARANCE OF A CHANGE OF ATTITUDE OVER TIME

Once again, the two collective reactions can be distinguished by peculiarities springing from an essentially similar background. While a whole combination of sociological and political circumstances were needed to set off a Muslim change of attitude, it was this very change of attitude which, because it challenged their own position, triggered the defense reflex of the Europeans. This is why, in the final analysis, the evolution of the Muslim situation lies at the root of the psychological readjustment within both communities; if it had not been for this evolution, the situation of the Europeans would not have been threatened. Chain reactions were set off among the Europeans based on changes in the position of the Muslims, each new development being explicable by reference to all its antecedents.

Pro-Residential Muslims

We will now examine the mechanism of the psychological development of the Muslims who opposed nationalism and placed their reliance on the Residency. As we have already seen, the Moroccan notables in the countryside split into three factions as the conflict progressed: an activist core which supported the Residency to the bitter end, another activist core which remained faithful to Mohammed V, and a floating mass constantly vacillating between the two opposite poles of attraction. The question now is to establish the exact proportions of this division and to see how far the particular characteristics of the group's situation explained the diversification of its political attitudes.

ABSTRACT FORM OF THE CORRELATION BETWEEN ATTITUDES
AND SITUATION

Although it is impossible to establish exact figures for those sections of this social class who were at odds with each other, it is incontrovertible that the distribution of attitudes must, once again, be linked to situation. In fact, the ambiguous nature of the situation is so clearly reflected in the attitudes that the former is constantly visible within the latter. Torn between their privileged position and their status as colonized peoples, most notables took refuge in a wait-and-see attitude, backing both sides and doing their best to end on the winning one. Since the situation brought contradictory influences to bear upon each individual, the notables most aware of their privileged position openly supported pro-residential activists like el-Glaoui, while those most aware of their status as colonized peoples rallied to the banner of young nationalist chiefs like Aherdan. Therefore, in general, the differentiation of attitudes worked as a function of each individual's particular response to the contradictory influences exercised upon him by the situation.

ELUCIDATION OF THE RELATIONSHIP BETWEEN ATTITUDE AND SITUATION

The analysis of the conditioning effect of the situation on the group's attitudes is identical in form with the preceding analyses. The notables were the only class in Muslim society whose situation embraced, without reconciliation, inferiority factors characteristic of the colonized people's situation and superiority factors characteristic of the colonists' position. Thus each notable found himself in the position of a colonist and of a colonized person at the same time. Insofar as he participated in the work of colonization, he was inclined to share European attitudes, and insofar as he shared the situation of the colonized people, he was responsive to nationalist attitudes. As we have seen, this ambivalent situation could do little but provoke a highly unstable attitude.

Given the situation-attitude relationship, what individual determinants governed the observed attitudes? Why did a given notable join the traditionalists while another joined the nationalists? It seems reasonable to assume that the individual choices were determined by age, by the varying degree of importance attached to privileges, and by a personal inclination toward conservative or progressive attitudes—in that order. The last factor could not be determined with absolute certainty by macrosociological analysis. Given the position of the notables, it was inevitable for group attitudes to become diversified more or less as they did. The reasons why a given notable rallied to one cause rather than to another remain partly undetermined. Only an individual study of the persons involved could show how far particular psychological factors determined, in each case, the psychological orientation.

EVOLUTION OF ATTITUDE OVER TIME

The determinism of the psychological evolution of the anti-nationalist notables is of the same type as that analyzed in the two previous groups, but the modalities seem to have varied significantly according to whether the attitudes of the two activist groups or those of the floating masses were under consideration. The numerical growth of the pro-residential and of the pronationalist groups seems to have been determined by the fluctuations of the conflict: in the case of the traditionalist chiefs, by the development of a modernistic nationalism increasingly linked to the Palace; and in the case of the nationalist chiefs, by the growing radicalization of the anti-sultanate policies pursued by the Residency and the traditionalist notables. The floating mass of notables, when it seemed that Mohammed V had lost, gradually drifted away from the initial hierarchy set up by the Residency and the Sultan and gave its allegiance to an intermediary hierarchy with Glaouist tendencies. This lasted until the Sultan and the nationalists regained control, at which point the dissidents came back to the Palace, but too late to avoid being purged. Once again, it was the hierarchical structure that decided the attitude. The transition from one hierarchy to another took place twice, each time under the influence of opportunist attitudes arising directly from the situation. Here as elsewhere, though in a more summary fashion, the differentiation and the evolution of attitudes took place under the combined pressures of the situation, the hierarchies, and the circumstances.

APPEARANCE OF CHANGE OF ATTITUDE OVER TIME

The beginning of the change in attitude of the pronationalist core of notables coincided in time with that of the rest of the

Muslim collectivity, while that of the pro-residential notables coincided with the change in attitude of the European community. It was evident that notables of both tendencies began to join or abandon the Sultan during the Labonne era, even though the great upheaval did not occur until later during the quarrel between Mohammed V and el-Glaoui.

Pronationalist French

The French liberals in Morocco were so few that one hesitates to speak of them as a social group in the sense in which this term is generally used in political sociology. While the Moroccan notables who supported the Residency represented a fraction of a social class, the French liberals were merely a group of individuals linked by a common ideology. Qualitatively they played a considerable role in the conflict. Their case is nevertheless a special one, stemming largely from the theory of ideologies. Hence it is impossible simply to include them in the theory of the determination of attitudes by the situation. This is why it seemed preferable to include a study of the attitudes of this group in the chapter dealing with the role of ideologies in the determination of political attitudes.[4] In order not to break the continuity of the argument, it should be made clear, however, that the attitude of the French liberals was no less a consequence of their situation than that of the French nationalists but in a different manner.

4. See below pp. 572 ff.

Chapter 3

INFLUENCE OF IDEOLOGIES
ON POLITICAL ATTITUDES

Decisions made by a political authority are not solely dependent upon the margin of flexibility allowed by the attitudes of the governed. They also depend upon the way in which the authority views the situations to be dealt with. To avoid pure empiricism, the government relies upon its knowledge of political ideology. How is this knowledge arrived at? What sort of influence does it have on the decisions it inspires? These two questions must be discussed before any attempt is made to link the decision-making activity of the protectorate to the group of variables upon which it depended.[1]

Partial Determination of Ideology by the Actual Elements of the Situation

The first determinant of the ideologies analyzed earlier is the real, objective structure of the situations in question. The dependence of ideology on situation springs from the very definition of ideological activity. If political ideology is, by definition, a concept of the situation, then this concept, like all human knowledge, must reflect the real phenomena for which it is trying to account. Whatever may be the coefficient of distortion, political ideology is essentially a concept of the situation.

---

1. All the elements in this proof are already at hand. The nature of the opposing ideologies in Morocco has already been described (see pp. 000 ff.). The impact of residential ideology on decisions taken by certain high-ranking civil servants of the protectorate has been studied indirectly in a functional analysis of the repression problem (see pp. 000 ff.). It is sufficient to make explicit the theory of Moroccan ideologies resulting from these preliminary analyses to provide a rough outline of the various reciprocal influences that were exerted by the ideological variables and the other variables of situation, attitude, and decision-making to which they were linked as the conflict evolved.

Partial Determination of Ideology by Political Attitudes

Political ideology is not determined solely by the objective structure of the situation under analysis. As a general rule, it is also strongly influenced by attitudes springing from the situation, since these condition the way in which the person responsible for the ideology visualizes his own situation.[2] At this point, the two aspects merge: either the attitudes imposed on a person by his situation prevent him from seeing the situation clearly and he can only obtain a distorted ideological version of it, or his attitudes are perfectly compatible with an accurate view of the situation and there is nothing to prevent him from working out an ideology which will conform to it. This variable degree of distortion which the political attitudes of any subject impose upon a perception of the situation must now be considered for each of the four groups that have been under study.

PRO-RESIDENTIAL EUROPEANS

Caught between the fact of an evolution implying the liquidation of their privileged situation and a defense reflex based on an attitude of strong resistance to this evolution, almost all the Europeans and their extremist leaders settled the problem by adapting their view of the Moroccan situation to their attitudes, since they were incapable of basing their attitudes on a correct view of the situation. Incapable of seeing things as they were— for this would have involved first moral and subsequently political capitulation—they were reduced to seeing things as they would have liked them to be, thus providing a formal rationalization for their will to resist. Hence the group elaborated a highly distorted idea of the situation and made decisions doomed to failure because they stemmed from this intellectual perversion.

PRO-RESIDENTIAL MUSLIMS

Since the pro-residential notables found themselves sharing the same situation and attitudes as the Europeans, their ideological

2. There are always several possible theories concerning any real phenomenon. This basic aspect of the theory of knowledge stems either from the fact that the person is not aware of every aspect of the phenomenon in question (generally the case in the development of scientific thought), or the fact that the person's own attitudes prevent him from correctly assessing certain aspects of the phenomenon although these are in fact under his eyes. This second cause of error is especially pronounced in sociology.

reaction, with a few exceptions, was the same as that of the colons. For the present purposes, therefore, there is no reason to study this particular group.

MUSLIM NATIONALISTS

Encouraged by the fact of an evolution moving toward the dissolution of their position as a colonized people and stimulated to action by the attitudes springing from this situation, the nationalist Muslims and their leaders merely had to follow the reasoning prompted by these attitudes to elaborate an ideology compatible with their position. Since there was no reason for them to distort their view of the situation, they borrowed freely from the intellectual resources of western ideological ideas, the intellectual formulations they judged most appropriate to their political ambitions and to the situation from which these ambitions sprang. Since their situation gave them in fact the means of victory, their spontaneously adopted attitudes could only encourage them to see the situation as it was and to provide it with an ideological formulation which, if not entirely valid, was at least as free from distortion and as effective as possible.

EUROPEAN LIBERALS:
THE SITUATION-ATTITUDE-IDEOLOGY RELATIONSHIP

We are now left with the apparent anomaly of the French liberals in Morocco. Why didn't their membership in the European group, which nationalism was threatening to evict, prevent them from basing their attitudes on an accurate ideological appreciation of the situation? Why, when they shared the same privileged position, did they not share the attitudes and ideology of the other Europeans? Here we are faced with a social fragment made up of a few dozen or a few hundred individuals whose attitudes, within their European environment, had not been directly conditioned by their social situation. There was no gradual conversion of a preexisting group to a dominant attitude, as was the case with the other Europeans, nor was there the refusal to adopt a prevailing attitude based on an inability to evolve, as was the case with the most conservative segment of the Muslim elite. There was merely a conscious and deliberate association of a few individuals within the European community who placed certain moral values above the spirit of European solidarity. Thus it was the attitudes which the members had in common which led to the formation of the group while in the other cases it was the group that determined the common attitudes.

This phenomenon still remains puzzling. Although no revolution exists in which certain members of the privileged class do not break with the established order, no sociological method has yet been able to reconstruct the mechanism involved. Therefore we have limited ourselves to outlining various possible explanations, offering tentative conclusions only where these are required to sustain the argument.

One hypothesis involves seeing the French liberals as individuals who succeeded in escaping from the clutches of their position as colonizers and derived their attitudes directly from moral and intellectual values which they judged superior to their immediate interests and to the demands of group solidarity.[3] A second hypothesis is that the group's ideology derived directly from its situation, bypassing attitudes, thus making this intermediate ideology directly responsible for the attitude.[4] Finally, the French liberals might be considered as people particularly sensitive not to a single attitude but to the conflict of attitudes between conservative reactions, derived from their situation as colonists, and liberal reactions, springing from the wider context of their situation as Frenchmen sensitized by the humanitarian traditions of their own culture.[5] In this third hypothesis, the only difference between the French liberal and the French extremist lies in the way in which each makes his choice between two rival forces.

The truth seems to lie somewhere between these two extremes; if the emancipation of the ideological activity of the French

3. This first explanation corresponds to the schema: moral values → political attitudes.

4. This second explanation corresponds to the schema: situation → ideology → political attitudes; in the case of the ultras the ideology-producing schema runs: situation → political attitudes → ideology.

5. The third explanation corresponds to the schema: situation (1) or (2) → political attitudes (1) or (2) → ideologies (1) or (2). These three alternatives show that in each case the individual has a choice between two contradictory reactions.

liberals presupposes the previous solution of a conflict of attitudes, this previous solution in turn implies a specially developed sensitivity among certain individuals to certain moral and intellectual values. French liberals and French extremists shared the same situation. Therefore the conflict between their ideological reactions cannot be explained a priori by differing social status. It can only be due to a difference of attitudes springing from the fact that, within a given group, only a few individuals are capable of freeing themselves sufficiently to make an objective assessment of their position.[6] This does not mean that the situation was not the main determinant of the ideology of the French liberals. The anomaly observed in their case is no exception to the rule that subordinates ideology to social status. But while the ability of other groups to form a correct image of their situation was either helped or hindered by the situation, that of the French liberals was determined by a coefficient of individual goals which had no connection with their way of life. Generally speaking, it is the overall situation which makes the subject more or less clearly aware of his own social standing. In the particular case of the French liberals, the distorting influence which the situation might have exercised on their ideological activity was neutralized by an ability to view the situation objectively, an ability which came from individual rather than social psychology.

Except in the case of the French liberals, the Moroccan crisis provides a particularly clear demonstration of the link which exists between certain ideological conflicts and the irreversible nature of certain social evolutionary processes. Experience has shown and the theory of knowledge helps us to understand that a group which finds itself threatened by an evolutionary process can only resist this evolution by denying its existence, while those groups whose chances of social advancement are improved find

6. The same applies to a group of seriously ill patients. Only a few rare individuals are capable of recognizing the gravity of their condition, while the majority console themselves with illusions for as long as they can. The problem becomes one of the distribution of higher faculties within a given group. Its solution is both psychological and sociological: on the one hand the natural superiority of a certain type of intelligence and courage, on the other the influence of sociological factors which make the person aware of certain values (family environment, childhood experiences, group traditions, etc.).

in this concord with the force of circumstances an encouragement to view the situation correctly. Therefore, in the production of political ideologies as a phase of social evolution, the decisive situational factor is the relationship that exists between each of the opposing groups and the evolution in progress. Given these relationships, the attitudes and ideologies must inevitably follow. The great majority of individuals compensate for the discouraging aspects of their situation by substituting a more satisfactory version that is more or less deliberately distorted. Only a small number of individuals manage to see the situation as it is and to adjust their attitudes accordingly. For over a century now, the connection between ideological activity, on the one hand, and situations and attitudes, on the other, has been the stock-in-trade of the theory of knowledge. Our goal in dealing with the subject at length was not so much to develop this theory as to strengthen its factual basis by applying it to a characteristic type of case.

Chapter 4

STUDY OF THE DECISION-MAKING
CAPACITY OF THE PROTECTORATE
AS A FUNCTION OF CONSENT
AND OF FORCE

The respective situations of the two Moroccan communities and those existing on the fringe were responsible for the conflict between the ideologies and attitudes already defined. These opposing attitudes—each of which implied a specific ideological reaction—obstructed the decision-making capacity of the protectorate to such an extent that it became incapable of acting as an arbitrator in the conflict.[1]

Principles of the Exposition

As we attempted to show earlier,[2] the decision-making capacity of a regime is, generally speaking, a function of the political attitudes of the population (i.e. the distribution of consent and opposition within the system) and of the amount of force at the regime's disposal for compelling obedience from its opponents, force and consent being functions of one another. We have also seen that the effect of this triple-faced relationship was strongly influenced by the authority structure of the regime under consid-

---

1. This question has already been approached from a functionalist and from a descriptive angle. We know that on the one hand the decision-making capacities of the protectorate fell well below its requirements (see supra pp. 507 ff.). We also know that the regime was incapable of solving certain problems either for technical reasons, lack of time, means, or incitement; or for political reasons: lack of time, consent and lack of strength (see supra, Part One). If one now applies to these facts the principles described in the methodological introduction, it is evident that, practical impossibilities aside, the fluctuations in the decision-making capacity of the regime were determined both by the attitude of the governed and by its own authority structure. This evidence merely makes explicit the relationship of variables which were implicitly introduced in the first two parts of this analysis.

2. See pp. 402 ff.

576

eration,[3] since the various groups do not carry the same weight in all regimes and in all authority structures. In a theoretical democracy, each group's capacity for political influence tends to be proportionate to the number of members in the group and to the intensity of their attitudes, although in practice this proportion may be modified in varying degrees by factual or legal inequalities which reduce the influence of the larger group to the advantage of privileged minorities. In authoritarian regimes the reverse tends to be the case: the political influence of the different social groups depends primarily upon the place reserved for them in the power structure by the regime and only secondarily upon their numerical strength.

In a colonial regime, these two extremes are combined in a highly distinctive manner. Such a regime is allied to authority structures of the revolutionary type in the sense that it superimposes upon a group of subjects, maintained outside the regime, a minority group whose consent is indispensable to its survival. On the other hand, it is allied to consensual-type structures of authority in the sense that even if, like a revolutionary regime, it is designed to deal with an almost total loss of consent, it does not base itself upon this assumption. Like a democracy, a colonial regime only runs smoothly when it enjoys the consent of all its subjects, indigenous inhabitants included. Even if a significant fraction of the latter join the opposition, the regime will be able to survive for a long time. It is incapable of compensating satisfactorily for permanent hostility. Thus the colonial regime is not a unique type of political organization. It has both consensual and authoritarian characteristics. What was said in the methodological introduction about these two political modes of operation thus makes it possible to study the workings of the protectorate without having to introduce new principles or new relationships. It now remains to be seen, as was done earlier for the democratic and revolutionary regimes, just what the authority structure of the protectorate consisted of and how its decision-making capacity varied as a function of consent and of force.

3. See pp. 404 ff.

Authority Structure of the Residential Regime

On analysis, the protectorate emerges as an occupation regime tempered by the consent—always liable to be withdrawn—of the colonized people and by the limits which, in its own interest, it imposed on the use of the despotism and force that are characteristic of occupation. Its authority structure can easily be reduced to five main elements: (1) a purely French political decision-making center, authoritarian but extremely sensitive to the attitude of its own officials and of its subjects of European origin; (2) a French administrative cadre whose cooperation was required for drawing up and executing any decision; (3) a privileged European minority without political powers proper, because of the nonrepresentative nature of the regime, but with a capacity for influence firmly based on the community of attitudes shared with the administration; (4) a Muslim majority group with no direct influence on the regime, because of the discrimination which excluded Muslims from the higher ranks of the authority structure, but which indirectly could weaken or destroy, by active or passive resistance, the implementation of any decision requiring their consent; and (5) two minorities of inverse political status—the pro-residential notables and the liberal Frenchmen—with varying capacity to influence the communities they had chosen to join and who strengthened this capacity to influence according to prescribed modes.

Interplay of Consent and Force Within This Particular Authority Structure

Like any political regime, a colonial regime can function during a period of social tension as well as during a period of cohesion. In the latter case, the various groups being governed accept the social relationships that unite them and consent more or less spontaneously to the decisions of their rulers. In the former case, the people regroup themselves into two main factions: one remains loyal to the regime, using it to fight the opposing faction; the other abandons the regime, thus withdrawing its support. In practice, since the indigenous inhabitants and the administrative group occupied different positions in the local authority structure, there appeared to be two residential regimes in Morocco, one governing the colons according to certain principles and a second governing the colonized people according to other principles. There were therefore four variants of the role of consent and force in the Moroccan authority structure, depending on whether the colonists or colonized were involved, and also on whether the period was one of political cohesion or of political tension.[4]

THE PROTECTORATE DURING THE PHASE OF SOCIAL
COHESION AND ADEQUATE POLITICAL CONSENT

The Authority Relationship as It Affected the Europeans

In this first instance, the effect of the authority relationship can be broken down as follows.

The principal source of the regime's authority was the consent of the European minority, insofar as this consent affected the execution and productiveness of decisions directly involving Europeans. This European consent was also partly responsible for the regime's decision-making capacity concerning the Muslims, who could only be effectively governed as long as the Europeans did not oppose residential decisions concerning the indigenous population.

Similarly, the consent of the European minority was also at the base of the force at the protectorate's disposal for putting into effect decisions concerning the two communities. To the extent that this force proceeded from the attitude of the European minority, it rested jointly on the consent of the special groups exercising it (the army, the gendarmerie, and the police) and on the consent of the European community as a whole for decisions involving the application of this force. Since, at this point, we are considering only the phase of social cohesion, this force, by definition, played a very minor role as far as the Europeans were

---

4. Since we are here studying the authority potential of the protectorate only as a function of local attitudes and situations, the following analysis ignores the fact that some of this potential was based upon means placed at the regime's disposal by metropolitan France. This simplification of the argument is not terribly important, since the final significance of men and supplies coming in from the Métropole depended upon local and not upon metropolitan attitudes. From this point of view, events took place as if the resources in question had been collected in Morocco.

concerned. The established order had not yet been challenged by the administrative group and the application of force was restricted to curbing civil law violations and to strengthening the obedience of the colonists to orders sanctioned by the law. As in all consensual regimes, the force of law was only used to affirm obligations, to bring the occasional delinquent to book, and to persuade honest folk not to stray from the straight and narrow path.

Since the regime was not representative of the European minority, there was no adaptation of protectorate decisions to the attitudes of this minority, as in a democracy, through normal electoral procedures and through the intervention of political organs that make possible either restrictive controls or a posteriori sanction of the government's actions. As in all force regimes, this adaptation took place through a direct exchange of influence between the government and the privileged minority upon which it relied. The fact that the political and economic goals of the colons and of the regime were identical largely sufficed to ensure the reciprocal adaptation of European attitudes and governmental actions. This lasted as long as the regime was not obliged to take action against the colons, thus bringing the cohesive phase to an end.

The Authority Relationship as It Affected the Muslims

The nature of the argument remains the same as in the previous case, with this one exception: even under normal conditions, the potential authority and force of the regime was much less dependent upon Muslim than upon European attitudes.

Even though Muslim consent had no direct influence on the protectorate's authority over Europeans, it played a not insignificant role in providing the foundation for the decision-making capacity of the Residency vis-à-vis the Moroccans. The regime only needed European consent in order to govern the Europeans and to draw up and execute its decisions concerning the Muslims. If these decisions were to be obeyed by the colonized people, however, without recourse to a massive use of force, then the more or less willing consent of the Moroccans was required. The colonized people stand at the base of the political pyramid.

They cannot make decisions on their own initiative, nor are they allowed to put them into execution. But within certain limits they can void their effect either actively or passively. The fact that they did not do so during the cohesive phase was one of the elements in the colonial system's strength. As long as this phase lasted, the collaboration of the traditionalist elites remained the symbol and the guarantee of the colonized nation's submission to the colonists' laws.

The link between the force potential of the regime and the attitudes of the indigenous population can be analyzed in the same way. True, this force was never actively employed during the cohesive phase, since at that time there was no declared opposition from the colonized people. Nevertheless, its very existence prevented Moroccans from yielding to the temptations of dissidence. Because they had more or less willingly consented to submit to it, they maintained this attitude as long as the pressures of the situation did not compel them to change. During the cohesive phase of the relationship between the governing and the governed, force does not create consent. It merely stabilizes certain more or less spontaneous inclinations to submit to authority. As long as the colonial agreement stood, the presence of indigenous peoples in the various armed services of the colonial administration remained, along with the cooperation of the Muslim elite, a symbol and a guarantee.

The regime was no more representative of the indigenous inhabitants than of the Europeans, but this placed the former at a much more serious disadvantage than the latter. For the colonists, the nonrepresentative character of the regime was largely compensated for by the presence in important positions of French civil servants sharing the same attitudes, prejudices, and view of the situation as the colonists; the colonized people were deprived of both political representation and of political influence. Excluded from the regime from the very first, the Muslims had no chance whatsoever of taking part in the making or execution of decisions that concerned them, except by the roundabout route of the Sultan's veto. As long as the cohesive phase lasted, however, this fundamental lack was masked by their consent to colonization.

THE PROTECTORATE DURING THE PHASE OF REVOLUTIONARY
TENSION AND INADEQUATE POLITICAL CONSENT

The transition from the phase of cohesion to that of revolutionary tensions resulted in profound modifications in the interplay of consent and force within the system.

The Authority Relationship as It Affected the Europeans

Once the conflict between the two communities had broken out, the authority relationship acquired the following characteristics.

The consent of the European minority became the sole source of authority for the protectorate, since its political base had been ipso facto reduced to this group by the move into opposition of the colonized people. Whenever the Residency attempted to take action against the will of the Europeans, it found itself deprived of all authority. When it governed according to their wishes, it was capable, as in the cohesive phase, of drawing up and executing decisions affecting the two communities. But the ultimate impact of these decisions was not the same. The consent of the Europeans, a priori, ensured the final effect of all decisions concerning them. However, it could not do so regarding decisions affecting the indigenous population, since this depended essentially upon the attitudes of the colonized people.

The consent of the European minority also became the sole source of the force available to the regime; the narrowing of the base of consent reduced the regime's potential for force in the same proportion as its potential for normal authority. Whenever the Europeans opposed the protectorate, this shift to the opposition deprived the regime of any force it might have been able to wield against them. Whenever the Moroccans strengthened their opposition, the regime was still capable of drawing up and executing decisions by the use of force, but once this opposition turned terrorist, the regime became incapable of ensuring the implementation of its decisions.

Finally, if we examine the Europeans' capacity for influencing the regime, we will see that the situation had at the same time both deteriorated and improved. It was improved in the sense that the rather turbid play of influences that had marked relations between the administration and the Europeans during the cohesive phase was now transformed into a sacred pact, once the very essence of the protectorate had been menaced by the nationalists. The surbordination of the Residency to the Europeans was now complete. Either it governed in accord with their wishes, or if it attempted to govern in the interests of the colonized people, its efforts were frustrated by civil servants with the full complicity of the colons. On the other hand, the position of the Europeans and of the regime that protected them deteriorated because the increase in the decision-making capacity of the regime, resulting from the complete integration of the colons into the authority structure, was inadequate compensation for the loss of authority and force caused by the gradual movement of the indigenous inhabitants into the opposition. Obviously, the increase in European political influence could not prevent the regime's political influence over the Muslims from deteriorating.

The Authority Relationship as It Affected the Muslims

The modalities of this second arm of the authority relationship are closely complementary to those which have just been described in the case of the European minority.

The conversion of the Muslim consent into opposition could have no effect on that fraction of authority potential which the regime derived from the attitudes of the Europeans. But Muslim opposition paralyzed the mixed institutions which the colonial administration was attempting to create despite the opposition of the inhabitants. Thus those reforms which sought to consecrate colonialism by camouflaging it behind a pseudo-democratic, pseudo-representative exterior were killed in embryo. From this point of view, the mere fact of Muslim political opposition was enough to make the Residency incapable of applying a critical series of decisions to the disadvantage of the Muslims.

A similar situation prevailed on the level of the use of force. The conversion of the Muslim consent to the nationalist cause had no effect on the force potential of the regime since this potential depended solely upon the attitude of the Europeans. However, it did reduce the effectiveness of repressive measures taken against the inhabitants so that the trial-by-strength that the Muslims had forced upon the Residency could not be resolved to the latter's advantage. Therefore, not only did Muslim opposition reduce the normal authority potential of the regime, it also reduced its ability to use force to such an extent that it could not reestablish its authority.

The Moroccan capacity for influencing the Residency remained nil as long as nationalism confined itself to the classic forms of political opposition: demonstrations, mass meetings, strikes, and so forth. Since they had no effective representation on the decision-making level, the inhabitants were obviously incapable of influencing decisions directly. They could prevent the colonial power from effectively modifying existing institutions to their disadvantage, but they could not compel it to reform or abolish itself by pure political opposition. Their only chance of emerging victorious from the struggle was to resort to insurrection, since the withdrawal of their consent had a decisive effect on the regime by neutralizing its coercive potential.

In sum, the transition from the cohesive phase to that of acute tension had four significant effects on the protectorate:

1. It created political situations that could only be dealt with by abnormal decisions.

2. By making the regime more incapable than ever of governing in opposition to the European minority, it emphasized the regime's dependence upon this minority.

3. It led relations between the Muslims and the regime into an impasse; the Residency was too strong for the nationalists to have any effective influence upon it and too weak to enforce decisions with which the nationalists disagreed.

4. Consequently, the indigenous inhabitants were compelled to move from political opposition to armed opposition; recourse to terrorism and to guerrilla warfare were their only means of exploiting decisively the loss of authority which their opposition implied for the protectorate administration.

Under these circumstances, the political attitudes of the two groups led the regime to avoid, or postpone, decisions which might alienate the Europeans and to prefer decisions which would only alienate the inhabitants, even if these would ultimately lead to irremediable disaster.

Influence of This Authority Structure on Typical Decisions Taken by the Residency During the Crisis

Once the nature of the relationship between the attitudes of the two communities and the decision-making capacity of their rulers is understood, the measures adopted by the government no longer appear fortuitous and acquire a character of inevitability. How could the Residency possibly have governed without the support of the colons when there was nobody capable of dealing with any revolt or even psychological resistance of the colons, since the political leaders, the civil servants, the police, and the armed forces were all sociologically integrated into the group structure whose attitudes and privileges they shared? How could the Moroccans hope to weaken the protectorate except by force of arms? They had no meaningful representation among the top political personnel, in the administration, among governmental advisers, or at the management level of the modern infrastructure of the economy. This regime, all-powerful when it came to refusing Moroccans an advantage it either could not or would not grant, became feebleness personified once it was forced into decisions which could not be implemented without indigenous support—whether these decisions involved establishment of joint pseudo-democratic organizations which the Moroccans refused to join, or whether they involved the restoration of public order compromised by terrorism and guerrilla warfare in a political situation where the insurgents enjoyed the support and protection of the indigenous population.

This type of authority structure of necessity provides the colonized population with the opportunity of reversing the power relationship to its own advantage by abandoning the position where it is weakest—political opposition—for one where it is relatively stronger—armed terrorist insurrection. The profile of the decision-making activity of the Residency and of the nationalist leaders was therefore quite naturally determined by these limits and this option. The Residency was strong enough to maintain the status quo despite Moroccan opposition, as long as the latter did not resort to violence. It was not strong enough to alter the status quo in favor of the inhabitants because the approval of the colons and of its own executive officers was not forthcoming. It was strong enough to organize cosovereignty groups staffed exclusively by Europeans but was incapable of making them work without Muslim cooperation. There was nothing to prevent the regime from imprisoning the nationalist leaders, but it was completely impotent when it came to halting the disintegration of the Muslim consent by such measures or preventing the population from replacing its imprisoned leaders with a new revolutionary foundation. The regime was quite capable of sending its soldiers into the field against the urban terrorists and the rural insurgents. It was incapable of attaining the military and political goals for which these measures were designed. The outlaws escaped seizure, thanks to the protection of a population that, though morally involved, was noncombatant and therefore untouchable. Under these conditions, and taking into account the conventional nature of the repressive measures applied, the failure of colonization became inevitable.

While the efficacy of residential decisions concerning the Muslims declined proportionately as Moroccan consent disintegrated, the efficacy of nationalist decisions increased as an inverse result of the same causes. Swept along by the potential or actual evolution of attitudes among the urban population, the 1944 nationalist core soon found itself invested with the authority required for organizing effective contacts with the masses and promoting their conversion to the nationalist cause. Under these conditions, the leaders' organization and propaganda efforts could not fail to bear fruit. At this stage of the struggle, when the organization was still preparing for battle, popular demonstrations, mass displays, riots, and strikes all served a supremely useful purpose as a means of mass mobilization and of developing political awareness. However, the initial leaders and cadres were inevitably victims of the success which had brought them into the limelight. They were too strong not to be of concern to the regime but too weak to overthrow it merely by mass movements. They were neither capable of nor inclined to make the shift from political opposition to armed insurrection; inevitably, they were put out of action by the police repression which their efforts provoked. Once the population in the towns had abandoned passive resistance for armed resistance, a new indigenous group was destined to emerge. It could not fail to broaden and improve, on an insurrectional level, the recruiting campaigns, the organization, and the psychological mobilization the old leaders had begun on a political level, first in the towns and then in the *bled*. As the Moroccan commandos took the field and the population supported them, the efficacy of the military and political decisions of the nationalist leaders increased at the expense of decisions in the residential camp.

Thus, when one considers the operations of the conflicting political centers on the Moroccan level, the mechanism of the crisis is essentially reduced to an inverse evolution of the decision-making capacity of both sets of leaders, linked to the growing transformation of the original Moroccan consent into an increasingly more aggressive and more effective opposition. Since it was deprived of the necessary authority to govern effectively without recourse to force and at the same time deprived of the capacity to apply repressive measures that might have enabled it to re-establish its authority, how could the Residency possibly have hoped to wage a successful battle against nationalism?

SECTION TWO: THE METROPOLITAN ECHELON

It is not enough to demonstrate that the interplay of Moroccan situations, attitudes, and ideologies deprived the Residency of the decision-making capacity required either for an orderly decolonization of Morocco in favor of the Muslims or for maintenance of the status quo through conventional measures of coercion. A conflict that may be insoluble on the local level can still be resolved by the intervention of a higher-ranking arbitrator with sufficient authority to impose a modus vivendi on the opposing factions. Like any other issue, settlement of a decolonization conflict by an authority with adequate powers of arbitration is not out of the question. The fact that the conflict had broken out on African soil meant that France, given the necessary inclination and the means, could have settled it effectively.

In a decolonization crisis, however, the intervention of a metropolitan arbitrator is subject to the same forces inducing political disability as those that paralyzed the colonial administration in Morocco. In France, as in Morocco, the government's authority stemmed from the attitudes of its subjects. The metropolitan government's ability to achieve the decision-making capacity necessary to settle the conflict depended upon its not suffering the same impotence that had paralyzed the authority of the Residency. Before embarking on this last phase of the analysis, it should be noted that although intervention by the Métropole reopens the decolonization question, it does so only partially. Paris was incapable of exercising any more authority than the Residency over the two Moroccan communities. From this point of view, the Métropole was in exactly the same predicament as the local authorities, because the latter had merely been applying the means provided by the former to combat the hostility of a society that brought the same hostility to bear upon France as it

588

had upon the protectorate.[1] France was in no better position to safeguard the protectorate than the Residency had been.

Yet the Métropole did have a choice between various methods of decolonization, assuming that this choice was not annihilated by the inadequacy of its own authority. In fact, four possible decolonization procedures were available to it: (1) allow the Moroccan situation to deteriorate until there was no choice other than abandonment of the protectorate to the triumphant nationalists; (2) steer postwar Franco-Moroccan relations through a carefully controlled decolonization process, with the support of all French political groups working together in a spirit of national unity; (3) achieve the same objective under the leadership of leftist majority strong and homogeneous enough in the Parliament to overcome all resistance; or (4) impose the decolonization of Morocco through the quasi-revolutionary pressure of a determined leftist minority enjoying enough popular support to force the decision through, making all cooperation with the Right subordinate to settlement of the colonial question.

Since it was the first of these possibilities that did in fact materialize, the time has now come to show that the interplay of situations and attitudes in the Métropole left the government no other choice, and that what has been referred to as the French governmental crisis was merely ancillary to the fundamental inability to make decisions that was evident throughout the North African conflict.

1. This point was dealt with in the first section of this study and will not be discussed here. Apart from the extent to which France was capable of transferring the conflict to the level of its own authority, its decision-making capacity as far as Moroccan affairs were concerned was no different from that of the protectorate.

Chapter 1

THE SITUATION-ATTITUDE-DECISION
RELATIONSHIP IN METROPOLITAN
FRANCE

The failure of the French as arbitrators loses any appearance of being accidental once the data in Table 2 are considered.[1] This recapitulation brings two remarkable facts to light. First, on each level of the system (situational, attitudinal, and decision-making), factors favoring a policy of force and defense of the status quo outweigh those factors which might have led to the peaceful decolonization of Morocco upon the initiative of the Métropole. The second is that the disequilibrium in the situational factors is directly responsible for the disequilibrium in the attitudinal and decision-making factors. These two aspects of the metropolitan political system must now be examined.

Predominance of Situational, Attitudinal, and Decision-Making Factors Favorable to the Colonial Right

PREDOMINANCE OF SITUATIONAL FACTORS
CREATING CONSERVATIVE ATTITUDES

Whether it is a question of the overall French situation or of the political parties alone, the disequilibrium is conspicuous.

Concerning Factors in the Overall Situation of the French

The predominance of situational factors favoring the production of nationalist or racist attitudes is so pronounced that it is

---

1. As can be seen from Table 2, certain parliamentary attitudes have been reflected in the situation of the parties under the Fourth Republic. In fact, only those attitudes which related to the situation form part of the attitudinal level as it has been defined. See p. 489 n.

TABLE 2. THE RELATIONSHIP BETWEEN SITUATIONS, ATTITUDES, AND DECISIONS IN THE POLITICAL SYSTEM OF METROPOLITAN FRANCE, IN REGARD TO THE DECOLONIZATION OF MOROCCO, 1945-1956

Decision-Making Capacity of the Regime

Adequate to take and put into effect in the Métropole political decisions to preserve the Moroccan status quo

Adequate to take and put into effect in the Métropole decisions regarding the use of military and police measures to preserve the Moroccan status quo

Inadequate to take and put into effect in the Métropole decisions regarding the genuine decolonization of the protectorate

Inadequate to take and put into effect in the Métropole decisions regarding the use of military and police measures directed at the European minority

No capacity to arbitrate between the two Moroccan communities

Ability to take action in regard to Muslim and European circles in Morocco subject to the same limitations as those affecting the Residency

Attitudes of the Political Parties

The completeness of the colonial defense reflex total on the Right and adequate on the Left

Decolonization a secondary goal of the Left, even of the extreme Left, while for the Right maintenance of the colonial status quo a fundamental objective

Correlative substantial lessening of the Left-Right opposition in regard to internal politics

Respect by the Left for governmental and parliamentary rules of the game in colonial matters; reverse attitude frequently manifested by the Right

Attitudes of the Population as a Whole to the Decolonization of Morocco

Satisfactory acquiescence in the policy of force sought by the leaders

Sporadic and indecisive popular manifestations of hostility to this policy latent in Métropole

Predominance of a cohesive system of nationalistic, colonialist, racist attitudes

To a system of revolutionary, internationalist, humanitarian, anti-racist attitudes

TABLE 2 (*Continued*)

Technical Situation of the Parties	Situation of the Population as a Whole
Elements of Electoral Sociology	Objective factors of internal cohesion dominant over residual causes of social tension but more obvious and relatively more active than in other industrial nations
The single rigid sociological barrier separating the Communist electors from the other electors	
The Communist Party, the party of the proletarian and of the revolutionary cadres	*Principal elements in the External Situation*
The S.F.I.O., the party of the deproletarized salaried class	Radical loss of international standing
The M.R.P., the limited representation of the French population	Numerical importance of the overseas colons
The Radicals, the party of the cadres and the middle classes	Numerical importance of colonial subjects in the Métropole
The Independents, the party of the rich and of the notables	Efficacy and extensiveness of colons' political channels of influence in the Métropole
The R.P.F., a meeting place of the anticonstitutional Right with temporary transfusions from the Left and Center	

Parliamentary Elements

Inadequate majorities

Multiplicity of parties

Lack of homogeneity and will within the coalitions

Triumph of the spirit of compromise

Neutralization of the Communist group by a refusal to be allied with it

Constant violation of governmental agreements and of political procedures of the regime

National Elements

Hostility of the electorate to absolute majorities

Equilibrium between the Left and Right benefitting the Right

Hostility of police and military groups toward the Left benefitting the Right determining. Almost all the factors considered under this first heading are in fact either directly or indirectly favorable to the defense of the status quo, whether it is a question of the erosion of internal revolutionary tensions in a twentieth-century western country or of the characteristics of France's international situation. True, not all the factors in the overall French situation worked in favor of the North African status quo. The abnormally low standard of living among the industrial proletariat and in certain rural communities undoubtedly helped to create fellow feelings toward the native proletariat. A modern industrial nation inherently contains situational factors favorable to decolonization. This explains in part the relative detachment with which big business circles greeted the arrival of Moroccan independence. However, we believe that these factors were heavily dominated by others that tended to produce nationalist and racist attitudes in the French leadership.

Concerning the Technical Situation of Metropolitan Political Parties

Once again, whether it is a matter of electoral sociology, of Parliament, or of the metropolitan authority structure, the forces tended to profit the Right and to disadvantage the Left.

All the electoral sociological factors that characterize the noncommunist element of the metropolitan population are homogeneous. It would be an exaggeration to assert that no sociological distinction exists between an Independent or Radical notable and an S.F.I.O. worker. However, it is still true that the noncommunist Left of the French electorate includes only social classes (salaried laymen, salaried Christians, etc.) who have more in common with the privileged members of the establishment than with the outcasts of the extreme Left. This is what counts.

All the numerical, technical, and tactical factors of the parties' parliamentary situation under the Fourth Republic worked toward downgrading the regime's decision-making ability and, consequently, in favor of the status quo. From this technical standpoint, during the whole period under discussion, the parliamentary Left was constantly and massively overwhelmed by the Right.

The distrust of the Left by the mass of the electorate, the advantages enjoyed by the partisans of inaction over the supporters of nonrevolutionary democratic progress, the strong position of key groups with rightist sympathies in the army and the police decisively reinforced on the national governmental level [2] the situational advantages which the Right already enjoyed on electoral and parliamentary levels.

PREDOMINANCE OF CONSERVATIVE ATTITUDES

OVER ATTITUDES FAVORABLE TO DECOLONIZATION

The imbalance between the two conflicting attitude systems is just as clear as that between the corresponding situational factors.

Concerning National Attitudes

On the national level, the consenting response of the population to the sacrifices demanded of it largely dominated the few sporadic outbreaks of hostility provoked by the call of conscripts. Within every group, and often within every individual, latent basic attitudes favorable to the status quo tended to outnumber humanitarian attitudes that might have militated in favor of the colonized nations.

Concerning Attitudes of the Parties

The same conservative bent applies on the level of political parties where the opposition between the attitudes of Left and

2. A detailed examination of the metropolitan governmental structure would take us too far afield. Hence, it has not been included in Table 2, while the governmental structure of the residential regime is dealt with separately in Table 1 (see p. 547). In order not to pass over the metropolitan governmental structure in complete silence, it should be noted that it was made up of two essential elements: the representative structure created by the Constitution, and the procedural devices and political practices which increased the influence of the ruling classes at the expense of the other classes, either within or without the constitutional framework. The advantages enjoyed by the Right over the Left (despite numerical equality), the position of the army and of the police in the regime, the manipulation of proportional representation at the expense of the extreme Left, the monopoly of higher administrative posts by diploma holders from the wealthier classes, the techniques and practices of a selective recruitment system which tended to eliminate opponents of the regime from its administrative, military, and police ranks—all these factors form part, in one way or another, of the true structure of authority within a democratic regime, whether they work for or against the equality of the citizen vis-à-vis the government. A study in depth of this type of authority structure would be extremely interesting. Since French reactions during the Moroccan affair were relatively homogeneous, we have limited our examination to certain elements in the metropolitan authority structure without explicitly dissociating them from their situational level.

Right were restricted to their national antagonisms. Without being fully aware of what it was doing, the Left reacted in exactly the same way as the Right or else worked in halfhearted opposition to a Right that saw the conflict as a threat to all that was essential to its values and interests and hence did not consider itself bound by majority decisions. The political parties reacted in the same way as the nation itself but in a more sharply defined manner. This lack of symmetry in the attitudes of the Right and Left needed to be brought out at each phase of the argument.

PREDOMINANCE OF METROPOLITAN DECISIONS
FAVORABLE TO THE STATUS QUO

The decision-making capacities of the two camps bear the same relationship to each other as the corresponding factors of situation and attitude. In its decision-making ability, the metropolitan Left came close to complete impotence: either it was unable to take the decisions it deemed necessary or they were sabotaged by local executive officers, who knew that the responsible ministers would be unable or unwilling to bring issues to a head. On the other hand, the decision-making potential on the Right seems to have been high, and most of the measures they deemed necessary were adopted, with or without the Left's approval. The power of the metropolitan Right was consistently greater than that of the Left. If the Left finally managed to make peace between the two communities in Morocco, this was only because the nationalists had already won the day.

Determination of Attitudes by Situation and of Decision-Making Capacities by Attitudes

We will now see how the situational factors affected attitudes and how, in turn, attitudes determined the metropolitan ability to make decisions about Morocco.

DETERMINATION OF ATTITUDES BY SITUATION

The effect of the metropolitan situation on the attitudes of the French people and of the politicians during the conflict combined two complementary influences. On the one hand, there was the influence of common situational factors on the population as a whole and on political parties. On the other hand, there was the influence of the material elements of the parties' situation on the attitude of the parties themselves and of that section of the population from which they came.

The paucity of attitudinal factors favorable to Moroccan decolonization among the French population as well as in the political parties is due in the first place to the almost total lack of factors productive of this type of attitude within the situation of the French people. A Métropole sensitized by its situation to its empire's misfortunes will of necessity, if there is no adequate counterweight, hold attitudes more favorable to the colons than to the colonized. What is true for the population as a whole is true, a fortiori, for the politicians it elects, whose role is to give a more intense and coherent expression to the reactions of the masses. The paucity of attitudinal factors favoring decolonization can be explained in the second place by the fact that the material situation of the parties worked to the decisive advantage of the Right in its struggle with the Left. A Left knowing in advance that it lacks the means to force a decision and that the struggle is in vain finds all the greater justification for not fighting. This argument is as valid for the electorate as for the parties. The metropolitan Left was demoralized by the weakness of its material position within the regime, and it was quite natural that this demoralization should spread to that part of the electorate which it represented. The Right, however, knew or believed that it ran no immediate risk in committing itself up to the hilt, and this is one reason for its aggressiveness.

The situation in France thus inhibited the anticolonialist attitudes of the parties and the masses in two different but complementary ways. It was responsible for their intrinsic weakness because it produced nothing but weak attitudes. It was also responsible for the reluctance to fight displayed by the holders of these attitudes who realized their inability to fight effectively.[3]

3. This twofold effect of the situation on attitudes is the political expression of a perfectly commonplace psychological phenomenon. A group's reluctance to fight can be explained just as easily by its lack of intrinsic interest in the struggle as by the fact that it knows itself to be outclassed by its adversary. All the indications are that this twofold cause of reluctance to fight was particularly marked in the case of the French Left.

The strength of colonialist attitudes among the parties and in the public is similarly explicable on the basis of those situational factors favorable to them. In France as in Morocco, attitudes toward the conflict were exactly what the situations required them to be.

DETERMINATION OF DECISION-MAKING CAPACITY
BY ATTITUDES

The lack of any effective arbitration of the conflict stems directly from the structure of the system of attitudes inherent in the metropolitan situation.

In reviewing the various elements comprising the attitudes of the metropolitan political parties, it is evident that each of them is closer to a decision-making factor favorable to a policy of force than to the policy of flexible decolonization that was the dream of the Left. The completeness of the metropolitan defense reflex ensured automatically the support of the Left and the Right for the forceful measures required by the nationalist revolt. The subsidiary role played by decolonization in the scale of left-wing interests meant that its colonial program was constantly sacrificed to its social or secular program. The lessening of Left-Right tension with the correlative increase in tension between the Left and the extreme Left automatically deprived the Left of its only alternative: creation of a popular front. The Left's respect for majority rule had the same effect; by resigning itself to not taking action unless it was in a majority, it virtually abandoned the struggle, since its electoral strength, its internal splits, and its views on political coalitions inevitably resulted in its being placed in a permanent minority to the advantage of the Right. In a system in which the governing bodies could only produce decisions favorable to the Moroccan status quo, decisions to which the people consented a priori because of the common attitudes linking them to their leaders, it was impossible to take decisions favorable to the colonized people and adverse to the dominant metropolitan attitudes until events had sapped the fighting spirit of the partisans of a policy of force. This in fact is exactly what happened.

Finally, it is obvious that the decolonizing decisions either made or proposed by the metropolitan French Left received insufficient support from attitudes that had no real relationship to the actual situation. The decisions, attitudes, and values of the Left were based on false premises concerning the metropolitan situation. The anticolonialist decisions and attitudes of the French Left were based solely on a residual ideology which no longer bore any relationship to the country's actual situation. Proletarian internationalism was born and bred at a time when the French proletariat was living under revolutionary conditions. Liberal humanitarianism also appeared at a time when France was playing a revolutionary role in a receptive Europe. Since these internal and external elements of the French situation had either disappeared or been drastically weakened, the ideologies flowing from them had become vestigial. Even if it is true that these elements still promoted left-wing anticolonialism, that support itself had no foundation. The Right found itself in exactly the opposite position, since attitudes favoring a defense of the colonial status quo were firmly based on current and vital elements in the situation. In both Morocco and France, although the modalities differed, the types of decisions taken were clearly determined by attitudes and by the situational factors on which these attitudes were based.

As we have already observed, there were three other possible answers to the Moroccan question: a planned emancipation of the protectorate executed by a single-minded Métropole, acting with calm deliberation even before a local nationalist movement had gone into action; liberation by a constitutional majority of the Left capable of imposing its will on a rightist minority; and revolutionary decolonization imposed on the rightist majority by a victorious popular front. The preceding analysis implicitly refutes these three hypotheses, but since a sociological impossibility is only convincing when it becomes explicit, these three unrealistic solutions of the Moroccan equation had to be included in the argument, and we had to show how and why these three alternative solutions were doomed to failure because of the metropolitan context itself.

In spite of its gratuitous appearance, the first possible solution is the least improbable of the three. It happened in West Africa, which goes to show that in principle the decolonization of an overseas French territory by decree of the Fourth Republic with the acquiescence of the Right was perfectly feasible at that time. The relationship of forces within the Métropole made it impossible for the Left to impose on a dissenting Right a decision on a vital issue. If, however, there had been agreement between Left and Right, obviously anything would have been possible, even the decolonization of a populated colony by governmental decree. The absurdity is not in imagining that a unanimous France could have decolonized Morocco under these conditions, but in imagining that the Right would ever have supported the action in a situation where its traditions, the size of the stakes, and the powerfulness of the warning system controlled by the colons would inevitably have set the metropolitan defense reflex in motion.

The nature of the objection to the second solution is more subtle. Obviously, there was little likelihood of the Left gaining a majority in any real sense of the term, because its refusal to form a popular front cut it off from the extreme Left, and it could not ally itself with the Center majorities that were too fragile and too heterogeneous to undertake any real decolonizing operations. Can one, however, go on to say that the metropolitan political system excluded the possibility of an accidental coincidence of an investiture declaration supporting a frank decolonization process and a majority vote in favor of this declaration? This would be a foolhardy claim. It is even conceivable, although improbable, that a Leftist government with the decolonization of North Africa as a plank in its platform might have been unexpectedly swept into power during the early years of the regime by a majority that included Communist votes. But this would not have altered the prospects for Moroccan decolonization. The qualification is valid only if the accidental majority is also invested with a decision-making potential that it would quite plainly not have had. The E.D.C. question was settled by a vote because the ratification of a treaty depends on a parliamentary vote and on that

vote alone.[4] On the other hand, a political procedure as complex
as the decolonization of Morocco depended upon much more
than a vote. Once in the saddle, a Leftist government attempting
the operation would have found itself incapable of putting its
policy into practice for want of that real superiority and that real
will to act without which a numerical majority is useless. These
are the very conditions for success that were excluded by the
internal situation of France.

The last solution is a decolonization process carried through by
a revolutionary minority, by a popular front, or even by the
threat of a popular front. The situation and attitudes of the constitutional Left under the Fourth Republic made this such an
unlikely eventuality that it is mentioned here only for the record.
However, this analysis of the theoretical alternative solutions to
the conflict does not obviate the necessity of examining at this
stage the historical significance of this "weakness of the Left"
which has held the center of the stage in the analysis of French
policy on Morocco. The Left's feeble reaction to the policy of
force sought by the Right on colonial issues can be interpreted in
two different ways. When emphasis is laid on the Left's weakness, does this mean that the Right's strength lay only in the fact
that the Left would not fight? Or, on the contrary, does it mean
that even if the Left had come out violently and passionately in
favor of the Moroccan nationalists—as might have happened if
the North African crisis had coincided with a social crisis similar
to that experienced by France during the Popular Front—the
Right would still have managed to defeat its opponents? In the
first instance, the relative strength of the Right is made to
depend upon attitudes adopted by the Left. In the second, the
weakness of the Left becomes the inevitable correlative of any
passionate and intransigent position on a question the Right considered vital. Both of these ways of looking at the argument are
perfectly compatible with our analysis of the combination of
circumstances dominating the metropolitan political scene, since
this depends as much upon the rigidity of rightist attitudes as on
the fickleness of leftist attitudes. The second formulation, how-

4. However, it is conceivable that if the treaty had been ratified, the ensuing crisis
in France would have made it impossible to implement.

ever, seems more comprehensive and more in line with known precedents than the first. Although it cannot be excluded a priori, it cannot be assumed that if the attitudes of the French Left had been passionately in favor of Moroccan nationalism, the ratio of forces between the Right and the Left would have been significantly modified. The least one can say is that precedents seem to favor the opposite conclusion. Two extreme suppositions can be imagined—both of them favoring the Right. First, the confrontation between Left and Right on colonial questions may occur at a time of growing, or at least adequate, social cohesion, in which case leftist attitudes are so similar to those of the Right, by the very nature of the hypothesis, that the latter has nothing to fear from its opponents. This in fact is what happened in the Moroccan case between 1946 and 1956. Second, the colonial crisis coincides with a period of acute social tensions in the Métropole, in which case the Left's intrinsic weakness may lead to the same result, since even in this case the Left cannot afford a decisive test of strength with the Right. This is a partial explanation of why the Left was incapable of effectively opposing the French take-over of Morocco in 1912 or of effectively supporting the Spanish Republican government at the time of the Popular Front. Although it was important to show that there are various historical versions of the "weakness of the Left" argument, there is no necessity for making a formal choice between them. Whether it be mechanistic or political, the evolution of a system is determinable only on the basis of a particular context. For metropolitan France, we chose 1946 as the point of departure. Our analysis of the combination of circumstances in the metropolitan political scene is thus linked to the fact that the Moroccan crisis coincided with a cohesive phase in the development of French society. To provide an answer to the question upon which our research is based, it therefore is not necessary to know what might have happened to the Franco-Moroccan conflict if the context of the French political situation in 1946 had been anything other than what the past had made it.

Chapter 2

THE GOVERNMENTAL CRISIS AND ITS
ROLE IN THE MECHANISM
OF THE CONFLICT

The Fourth Republic was born in a state of crisis. This crisis was closely linked to the revolt of the colonies, and it was no accident that the regime finally fell over the Algerian question. It would be foolhardy, however, to assume without further proof that the failure of the Métropole to arbitrate was due solely to the decay of the body politic. There is no doubt that this played a role in the decolonization of Morocco. But what type of role? A supporting role or a principal role? Did extremist strength depend only upon institutional weakness? Would the extremists have been as strong under any circumstances? These are questions which must be asked.

The analysis of the attitudes and material situation of the metropolitan political parties already suggests that the French constitutional crisis was a special case of a chronic malady from which no democracy is entirely free.[1] Neither the paralysis of the government when confronted with certain situations, nor the neutralization of coalition governments by the spirit of compromise, nor the relative advantage of Right over Left is a specifically French phenomenon. What was especially French during the 1950s was the acuteness of the malady. A full survey of this phenomenon would be irrelevant to our purpose, but some attempt must be made to determine its nature to gauge the effect it may have had on Moroccan decolonization.

If France had undergone an acute social crisis during the Fourth Republic, the governmental breakdown would be explicable as the normal distortion of the positive influences, opera-

1. See pp. 517 ff. and 539 ff.

tive in any functioning democracy, of the interaction of two basic variables: social infrastructure and political superstructure.[2] In a democracy where social cohesion has been profoundly affected by a serious threat to the social bonds uniting the various sectors of the population, it is a priori impossible for the governmental institutions to function normally. Any significant breakdown of social cohesion implies, in fact, a correlative collapse of political consent and of the authority based upon it. Quarrels within the population lead to irreducible splits vis-à-vis authority. An exchange of negative impulses begins to take place between the social infrastructure and the political superstructure. There are political as well as economic spirals; the government-society spiral is to the one what the wage-price spiral is to the other. Structural breakdowns and tensions that affect the basis of society paralyze authority. The impotence of the government aggravates structural defects and the internal conflicts on which

2. The concepts of infrastructure and superstructure are known to be of Marxist origin. Within every compartment of the social structure, they contrast the actual with the normative. In every sector of collective life, the infrastructure consists of that part of the total structure which remains when one removes theoretically the norms which obviously govern it and those social groups which proclaim and personify these norms. Superstructure, whether political, economic, or religious, always pertains to authority. Infrastructure is the remaining social element over which this authority is exercised. These two concepts are, obviously, general in character and upon analysis, they break down into a large number of subordinate variables. In his remarkable lecture series on the sociology of industrial societies (*Sociologie des sociétés industrielles,* pp. 59 ff.), Raymond Aron subdivides the democratic political superstructure into five main variables: the constitution both in theory and practice, the political parties, the operating methods of the regime (elections, parliamentary practice and relationships among the holders of power), pressure groups, and, finally, individuals themselves. To these variables must be added peripheral variables such as political morality, history, and so forth. A thorough analysis of the French governmental crisis would have to take into account the effects of all these variables on each other within the superstructure as well as within the infrastructure. Although this is not the object of the present study, we cannot fail to express our agreement with the way in which Aron poses the problem. Our sole reservation stems, once again, from the fact that there is no practical purpose in basing an analysis on variables if one refuses to examine the effect of these variables upon each other because of the complexity of the relationships involved. In fact, Aron has said that "the result of this multiplicity of variables is that one shrinks from the prospect of searching either for causal explanations or for recommended courses of action" (ibid., p. 70). One can certainly not hold this reluctance against an author who is careful to make clear in the preface to his lectures that the notes here referred to are not intended to be the expression of a fully elaborated theory. A science which restricts itself to the theory of variation without putting this theory to use is denying its own nature. More political analysts should look long and hard at the problems posed by the use of the concepts of variables and of the functional relations between variables in non-mathematical sociology.

they are based. This accentuation of the structural deterioration reduces the margin of authority required to effect an improvement in the situation, thus further aggravating the tensions within the population, and by an inverse action reducing still more the government's capacity to exert authority. Impulse by negative impulse, the march toward the abyss continues. There is nothing left for a representative government to do but to change itself into an authoritarian one while waiting for a social revolution to modify completely the traditional form of the society.

This is not always the course of events. Any lack of social cohesion inevitably involves a concomitant lack of political consent, but the reverse is not true. As has been seen, the consent upon which a regime is based can undergo profound modifications without affecting its cohesion.[3] For historical as well as sociological reasons, the attitudes of the people toward the government then become partially dissociated from their attitudes toward the social relationships which unite them. Conditioned by the traditions of their milieu, civil servants and certain categories of the population perpetuate attitudes of hostility and distrust toward the government which tend to reproduce constantly the same political anomalies when they are confronted with a set of social circumstances that are gradually becoming normalized without their being aware of it. The spiraling deterioration of authority continues, but instead of covering the whole society, it is limited to the sphere of political activity. Authority and the consent upon which it is based gradually destroy each other by means of mutual successive impulses, but this deterioration does not involve a corresponding deterioration of social cohesion. If the system fails to stabilize itself at an acceptable level of authority,[4] a

3. Consent and cohesion are defined above, p. 527. n. Also, see pp. 601 ff. for relations between the two variables.

4. The disintegration of a political regime always includes its own auto-corrective devices. A healthy administration can act as a temporary substitute for a faltering government. People gradually become accustomed to a social evil that should have been extirpated. Parisian life would certainly be improved without Les Halles (the central markets), but it has not killed the city to live with them. Such a serious disorder will generally disappear over time, unless it is settled under the pressure of economic developments that solve too late and in an anarchical situation what the government should have been able to settle earlier at a lesser cost. Political diseases develop slowly. The infected organism can immunize itself and regain control. By skillful maneuvering, the stormy headland can be rounded. When all seems lost, all can

limited constitutional crisis will eventually break out against a background of public indifference. Since the population is not split by any political tensions, the political organism stands a good chance of survival.

Both the phenomena which have just been described were in evidence in the French crisis, but the second noticeably dominated the first. To explain the crisis by a downward spiral of declining national cohesion would be to contradict the preceding analyses and the factual data upon which they are based. To attempt to account for it without giving due credit to the structural anomalies and residual social tensions that had not been entirely eliminated by the return of French national cohesion would be to err in the opposite direction. In fact, these anomalies could only have aggravated the crisis by lending support to the grudges the people might have held against their leaders. A country cannot be under-governed for two generations without leaving a mark on its structures. All the same—and this is the crux of the matter—the truth remains that deteriorations in French national cohesion were not in themselves an adequate explanation of the governmental crisis. The situation in modern Spain is an adequate explanation for modern democracy's failure to establish itself there. The internal problems of Italy partly account for the indignities suffered by representative government. The postwar social situation in France does not explain the governmental crisis. This becomes intelligible only if it is admitted that the negative attitude of the French toward their leaders was partly a result of history. Some will say that this attitude originated in political convulsions of the past and in disappearing structural anomalies. Others will call attention to the national character that is, in part, independent of the actual state of social relationships. In either case, one has to admit that in certain respects French political sociology is what history has made it, which means that one cannot hope to explain it without taking this history into account in the sociological analysis.

It remains to be seen just how much influence the governmental crisis and the decolonization process had on each other.

---

still be saved given a favorable constellation of circumstances and given a positive overall balance between deterioration and renovation.

Obviously, the North African crisis did destroy the regime. The Fourth Republic might perhaps have been able to avoid collapse by a narrow margin if the colonial revolt had not sealed its fate. From our point of view, it is just as important to decide whether a parliamentary regime working under normal conditions and enjoying the full support of public opinion would have fared any better.[5] In attempting to explain the powerlessness of France vis-à-vis Morocco entirely by the normal shortcomings of its political centers, there is a danger of explaining nothing at all. The fact that the weakness of the regime had been aggravated by the North African crisis does not eliminate the essential distinction between the two phenomena on the metropolitan level. We shall never know what the outcome might have been if the Fourth Republic had been able to tackle the decolonization of its colonial empire with its full capacity for authority intact. But it is possible to show that in Parliament as well as in the government, extremist strength rested not so much on the defects in the system as on the overall psychological and technical advantages extremism would have enjoyed in any democracy reacting to a colonial war with a sufficiently strong defense reflex. The Métropole's inadequate decision-making capacity in regard to the Moroccan crisis seems to be more explicable in terms of the vast resources of national cohesion than in terms of the residual tensions that accounted for the governmental crisis.[6]

It is paradoxical that despite their highly discrete characters, the two phenomena finally had the same consequences. To the extent that the metropolitan Left and Right displayed similar attitudes toward Morocco, it was the policy of force which benefited. To the extent that the governmental crisis neutralized the government's normal capacity for authority, it was again the

5. "If South Africa with its two million white colons had remained an integral part of Great Britain, if its inhabitants had voted like British citizens and sent their representatives to the House of Commons, can one really be sure that British democracy would have come out of the business any better than the Republic with its Algeria?" A British Labour member of Parliament, *L'Express* (June 19, 1958), p. 12.

6. Here we have only considered the governmental problem from the point of view of the interplay of variables within the infrastructure and superstructure. To adhere to our analytic scheme and to bring this point to a sharper conclusion, the problem must now be considered from the point of view of political functionalism. For this complementary aspect of the analysis, see pp. 642 ff.

North African status quo that benefited because conservative forces inevitably prevail over progressives forces under an inactive regime. The union of the two extremes in the metropolitan defense reflex and their neutralization by reason of political impotence thus operated simultaneously in a direction completely opposed to the demands of North African evolution until the day came when the force of circumstances prevailed.

SECTION THREE: INTERNATIONAL
EXTENSIONS OF THE SYSTEM

If at the international level a body had existed that was capable of firmly arbitrating in the Franco-Moroccan conflict, this body would then have represented the third authority level of the political system now being studied. Although the conflict was out of control at the residential and metropolitan echelons,[1] it might still have been resolved through a due process of arbitration by the great powers. Since this is not what actually happened, it would no doubt be better to substitute the more suggestive term "influence level" for the overambitious expression "authority level." The influence of the outside world on the development of the crisis needs to be studied from two points of view: that of international organization proper, and that of international attitudes considered in their relation to the attitudes and decision-making capacity of the Moroccan and metropolitan authorities. This complex phenomenon is outlined in Table 3.

The first aspect of this phenomenon is well known. Since a thorough study of this aspect would take too long, it will only be referred to very briefly. No one is ignorant of the reasons behind the refusal of different nations to submit to an authority created by their own consent. The community of states is objectively too differentiated and subjectively too divided to form an integrated international society. The attitudes of the various states are too contradictory to provide the consent required for creating and maintaining an effective international authority. Because a political organization of this type is nonetheless indispensable from many points of view, it has been possible to form an international organization; as yet, however, it lacks the necessary competence and the decision-making ability to enable it to settle the great conflicts of our time in an authoritative manner.[2]

1. France, of course, was a part of the international framework in the broad sense. That is why, when the problem here is one of evaluating the role played in the conflict by western moral values, no distinction will be made between the Europeans in Morocco, the French in the Métropole, and other western peoples.

2. Moreover, the situation is evolving. The nuclear arms race and the crises of the African continent have increased the need for an international authority enjoying

TABLE 3. INFLUENCE OF THE INTERNATIONAL POLITICAL SYSTEM ON THE MOROCCAN AND METROPOLITAN POLITICAL SYSTEMS

DECISION-MAKING CAPACITY OF THE UNITED NATIONS

Consent, strength and competence insufficient for arbitrating a conflict of the Franco-Moroccan type.

REGIONAL ORGANIZATIONS AND BLOCS

NATO	ARAB LEAGUE	AFRO-ASIAN BLOC	COMMUNIST BLOC

INTERNATIONAL ATTITUDES

TOWARD THE UNITED NATIONS

Too incompatible to permit even the minimum of support required to provide the UN with sufficient authority.

TOWARD THE FRANCO-MOROCCAN CONFLICT

THE INTERNATIONAL SITUATION

Too particularized and too differentiated to form a cohesive international organization.

COLD WAR	DECOLONIZATION	UNDER-DEVELOPMENT

In spite of its inadequate decision-making capacity, the United Nations exercised a demoralizing influence on the conservative groups in Morocco and France.

On the other hand, the United Nations did strengthen the morale of the nationalists and their European allies in Morocco and France.

Diplomatic action by the various power blocs had an indecisive yet negative influence on the political initiative of conservative groups in Morocco and France.

Diplomatic action by the various power blocs had an indecisive yet positive influence on the political initiative of progressive groups in Morocco and France.

International attitudes had a decisive effect by limiting French use of force against Moroccan nationalism.

On the other hand, international attitudes had very little restraining effect on Moroccan use of force against Europeans.

MOROCCO *Table I*	FRANCE *Table II*
Decision-Making Capacity	Decision-Making Capacity
(Force)	(Force)
Attitudes	Attitudes
—Consent	—Consent
—Opposition	—Opposition
Situation	Situation

The second aspect of the phenomenon calls for a detailed analysis. There can be no doubt that international attitudes had their part to play in the crisis. We have seen them weaving their way in and out of the account of every phase of the conflict. Everything leads one to believe that this role was an essential one. In a world indifferent to North African events or in a universe in which the Franco-Moroccan quarrel took place on the fringe of foreign policy, the conflict might have taken quite another course. It might not even have broken out. The Moroccan and metropolitan political systems came close to providing the substance of such an argument. But the mooring lines of the demonstration are firmly tied in the international context, and we must examine them if we are to reach a position from which conclusions can be drawn. This is what we would like to achieve by dissociating, as carefully as possible, the different components of the international factor.

---

a minimum of consent and strength. A worldwide directorate is beginning to emerge in the midst of confusion and uncertainty, as is generally true of all newly created institutions. This evolution has only just begun, but it is under way.

Chapter 1

THE INTRINSIC WEAKNESS OF INTERNATIONAL SUPPORT FOR MOROCCAN NATIONALISM

O n the international level, France encountered four main obstacles to its policy in Morocco: the United Nations, the Arab League and the Afro-Asian bloc, the anticolonialist tendencies of American diplomacy, and international communism centered in the U.S.S.R.

The inadequacy of the United Nations is glaring in the case of the Franco-Moroccan crisis. The main explanation for this was the organization's lack of competence. France alleged that, juridically speaking, the Moroccan question was a purely internal French problem. From many points of view, however, this principal argument was nothing but a façade. The deposition of Mohammed V was such a flagrant attack on Moroccan sovereignty that the United Nations, had it wished to do so, could easily have used this turn of events as an excuse for issuing a solemn condemnation of French policy in Morocco. If the United Nations made no attempt to do this, it was because the great powers that might have assured a majority on this question did not feel free to express their feelings. The shortcomings of the United Nations during the Moroccan crisis were not accidental. On the contrary, they appear as the broadest aspect of the authority crisis which had paralyzed the political forces involved on every level in the settlement of the crisis. Neither the Residency, the Métropole, nor the United Nations was capable of settling the conflict by authoritative decisions, because the authority of these three types of bodies was too heavily dependent at every level upon the attitudes of partisans of the status quo, thus making real arbitration impossible. The Residency could do

nothing without the consent of the colonists. The metropolitan
decision centers were stymied by the ferocious opposition of
partisans of the status quo and by the lack of resolution displayed
by their progressive opponents. Leaving aside all questions of
competence, the United Nations was paralyzed on a world-wide
scale by the antagonism of the two great power blocs and by the
internal requirements of the Atlantic alliance. Support in favor
of solving the problem by arbitration was not strong enough at
the Moroccan, metropolitan, or international levels. The United
Nations lacked both a consensus of its members on the issue and
the enforcement capacity that would have been required to resolve the multiple problems involved in the decolonization of the
western colonial empire. The organization thus could be little
more than a tribunal, and no great effort was made to expand its
role.

Diplomatic support from the Arab League and from the Afro-
Asian bloc to the Moroccan nationalists was no more substantial,
but the reasons for the relative impotence of this second type of
organization are very different from those which have just been
cited as an explanation of the ineffectiveness of the United
Nations Charter. The Arab League is a political and military
alliance that could only have played a decisive role by intervening, in the strongest sense of the term, in favor of the North
African nations. The weak military and political positions of its
members would not allow such a risk to be undertaken. Both
geographically and materially, armed intervention would have
been impossible. It is true that in theory the League might have
been able to initiate, throughout the Arab world, a terrorist
campaign directed against installations belonging to France and
its supporting powers. Such a dramatic gesture would definitely
have weighed heavily in the balance of decision, but politically
and morally it was quite out of the question—first, because the
members of the League could not consider breaking the thousand and one links between them and the west, and, secondly,
because a holy war is not declared dispassionately by royal
decree. Years of repression and bitter struggle would have been
required before Moroccan opinion would consider recourse to
force as a necessary evil. Also, we know that the sabotage ac-

companying guerrilla warfare in Morocco was not systematically directed against the large French companies employing native workers. How could a people who had not lived through the preliminary phases of a great colonial conflict be prepared to go to such decisive extremes as sabotage? The members of the League were not strong enough, nor independent enough, nor desperate enough, nor sufficiently united to unleash a war of solidarity in support of North Africa. Under these conditions, the only feasible weapon was a boycott of French products. The League used it. But this weapon was a dangerous one to wield, and the League was satisfied to use threats more appropriate for a propaganda campaign than for economic or military warfare.

The caution displayed by American foreign policy makers toward those who had hoped that the United States might come out against French colonial policy is no simpler to explain. Because of its preoccupation with the communist threat and its position as leader of the Atlantic alliance in which France is geographically and politically an essential partner, the United States could not lightheartedly risk a rupture of French-American relations merely to appease the Arab countries—certainly not as long as the risk of alienating the Arab world appeared less serious than the results of a quarrel with the government in Paris. Major foreign policy decisions are not arrived at in isolation but under the pressure of events. At no point during the North African crisis did this pressure become critical. The decision to be made abroad was complicated further by a decision to be made at home. The State Department was torn between two schools of thought: those who considered the Atlantic alliance as the main objective of United States foreign policy, and those who recommended a policy giving stronger support to the colonized nations. The existence of such anticolonialist opinion is beyond dispute; it merely echoed at the level of United States foreign policy an ideological tradition going back to the War of Independence and involving many internal contradictions. As for pro-French opinion, its existence can be deduced (for want of more exact data) from the actual policies pursued by the United States in matters concerning North Africa in the course of the conflict. It was hardly possible

for the United States, caught in a moderate anticolonialist position by the internal and external implications of the contradictory requirements of its foreign policy, to do more than issue
friendly warnings and undertake discreet diplomatic operations.

Everything conspired to neutralize the hostility of the communist bloc. Morocco was too far away for any direct military assistance to the nationalists to be possible. A communist offensive in
the United Nations would have been blocked by the west. The
mobilization of western communist parties, especially the French
Communist Party, in favor of the North African nationalists
would have been a slow-burning process because of the heavily
ambivalent attitudes displayed by European workers toward the
natives. Moreover, how could the Soviet Union have intervened
openly in areas covered by French sovereignty when one of the
major themes of its own foreign policy was a growing preoccupation with the defense of Afro-Asian national sovereignty? All
the same, although incapable of taking direct action, the U.S.S.R.
might have regained lost ground by conducting a rowdy anti-
French campaign on the propaganda platforms provided by the
various international organizations. It must be said that any protests made on this level by the communist powers were every bit
as restrained as those made by the French Communist Party itself. Doubtless there were sound reasons for this caution. For
want of fuller information, it would be foolish to speculate about
them. All the same, the moderation displayed by the U.S.S.R.
and its allies on decolonization problems is not lacking in importance.

Neither the United Nations, the Afro-Asian group, the United
States, nor the communist bloc was capable of arbitrating the
conflict under its own conditions; awareness of this impotence
was so pronounced that in the end no serious moves were made
toward doing so.

Chapter 2

RESTRAINING INFLUENCE OF INTERNATIONAL DIPLOMACY ON THE POLICY OF FORCE

However accurate the preceding observations may be, they are quite beside the point. No one expected the United Nations to settle the Franco-Moroccan conflict. No North African nationalist counted on seeing the Arab League, sword in hand, chase the French out of North Africa. No one really expected Soviet Russia or the United States to shorten the conflict by decisive intervention. The Moroccan nationalists did use the United Nations with the Arab states acting as intermediaries, they did entrust themselves to the Arab League as to a guiding power, and they did make constant appeals to all states in a position to speak in their favor, because they either sensed or knew that, although it might not be decisive, the backing of countries with a voice in the international forum would represent a considerable advantage in the balance of relative strength. Given these motives, the international activity of the Moroccan nationalists acquires a positive significance. The diplomatic activity of the powers in question did not put an end to the conflict, nor did it shorten it in any way, but it did help to curb possible developments. The diplomatic factor could not prevent what happened. Once again, who knows how far events might have gone, had no diplomatic moves been made and had the partisans of a policy of force felt free to do as they wished in an indifferent world? History does not consist only of events that emerged from the realm of the possible and actually took place. It must also be interpreted in the light of what might have happened if the right opportunities had arisen.

Without considering here all the limitations on the use of force

615

imposed by the international context,[1] it is obvious that the partisans of the policy of force had to contend with the attitude of the United Nations, which was constantly being alerted by the Arab League, and with the many discreet approaches made by the United States in support of a liberal solution. The anxiety of the French leaders at each mention of the North African crisis in the General Assembly or the Security Council is sufficient evidence that they were seriously embarrassed by this type of discussion, even when the powers involved were basically without competence. The counsels of moderation provided by American diplomats carried just as much weight, as France was both a receiver of financial assistance and a power heavily engaged in the western security system. It would probably be inaccurate to say that the United Nations brought real "pressure" to bear upon the French Parliament, the government, the Residency, the extremists, and the army. However, it is a justifiable conclusion that during each crisis, international intervention provided substantial support within France itself for those politicians who were working in opposition to the policy of force. In a world where it has become difficult to violate openly one's much vaunted moral values, the countries who had recourse to force in their colonies could not for the benefit of foreign opinion make periodic declarations asserting their support of the principle of future independence for their colonies without being obliged to match their words with their deeds to a certain extent. International powers had no direct influence on the conflict, but throughout they exercised a restraining influence which checked its proliferation and which was combined, in varying degree, with the efforts of supporters of a liberal solution to prevent recourse to extreme measures. By itself, this political brake would have been ineffective. But together with the other barriers thrown up by international relations in opposition to the partisans of force, its influence definitely helped to tip the scales in favor of Moroccan independence.

1. See above, pp. 619 ff.

Chapter 3

INTERNATIONAL ATTITUDES AND
IDEOLOGIES AS FACTORS
AFFECTING INDIGENOUS MORALE

A nation does not go to war without cause, but the cause itself would be nothing if there were not some hope of eventual victory. In a colonial conflict in which the subjugated cannot expect to overcome their opponents' forces, their only hope rests with outside support. Surely the international sympathy enjoyed by the Moroccan nationalists on every level eventually had the same effect on nationalist morale that the support of a regular army has on the morale of the partisans fighting with it? Would the North African nationalists have had sufficient hope and, consequently, the inclination to fight, if the whole world had not become involved in their quarrel with France? Nothing could be less certain.

If we wish to analyze further the role played by the international context in the crisis, it will be necessary to place ourselves on the planes of morale and ideology. International relations not only acted as a brake to a policy of force, but also lifted nationalist morale. The emancipation of the first ex-European colonies, the intensive propaganda put out by French and Moroccan liberal circles, the ideologies upon which they were based, the support given to the Moroccan people by millions of men belonging for the most part to the underdeveloped areas of the world, American reticence concerning the policy of force, encouragement from the U.S.S.R., and the propaganda from foreign radio stations—all combined to form a group of "signals" which must be interpreted as a group.[1] The least of these encouragements

---

1. What applies to the group of signals also applies to each one individually. The case of the Arab radio broadcasts is a good example. Perhaps they were not essential

guaranteed the Moroccans that the wheels of history were turning in their favor. Of course all this support did not excuse them from taking action, but it did give them belief in their cause, which is one of the keys to success.

Of this whole network of elements that favored nationalism, the ideological component is perhaps the most remarkable. It is nothing new for a part of the world to become enthusiastic over a people's struggle for independence. What is new is that in the case of decolonization the revolutionaries benefited because of a dominant ideology that guaranteed their success when fighting under conditions which did not permit them to make daily checks on its accuracy. Although it may not be necessary to be certain of victory before going into battle, the belief that history is on one's side is nonetheless important for men who must be fully aware of their own weakness. The proletariat in the nineteenth century enjoyed a similar advantage but under infinitely more ambiguous historical conditions. The first Marxist schema took into account only very generally the future development of the social question in the west. Serious errors distorted most of these individual predictions. The slow progress of the evolution allowed only debatable and uncertain verifications of the doctrine even when it was valid. Because of its swiftness and irresistibility, the current decolonization process provides sociological forecasting and its accompanying ideologies with an objective basis which would otherwise remain intuitive. Even if the scientific formulation of the irreversibility of the phenomenon has yet to be perfected, it has still been possible to check on its true nature over the past fifteen years. Those whose actions contributed to the acceleration of this evolution lived daily through its principal phases, as far as they were able to foresee, through their professed ideology. Never before in history have a people struggling for their independence enjoyed such massive moral support and benefited from a working doctrine that was so obviously in agreement with the facts.

---

for the psychological mobilization of the Moroccans. Inside Morocco itself, enough events and forces were at work to draw them into the struggle. The rapidity with which local news spread from mouth to mouth, the daily tribulations, and the help given to terrorists who were wanted by the police were quite enough to satisfy the population's need for information and inspiration. Powerful voices from abroad nevertheless contributed toward supporting its morale.

Chapter 4

INTERNATIONAL CONSENT
AND MORAL LIMITATIONS
ON THE USE OF FORCE

We saw above that in colonial wars, recourse to genocide by the colonial power brings it up against technical obstacles which tend to reduce considerably the effectiveness of this form of repression.[1] These practical drawbacks are not the only ones. Even if they could be overcome, genocide would inevitably come up against international opposition inspired by the western scale of political values. There are violations of its moral code which a civilization can pass over in silence. There are others which cannot possibly be ignored because they clash with the very values upon which the civilization is founded. Before a colonial power can pass from conventional means to proscribed forms of repression, international opinion and the political powers involved must first give their consent. It is evident that in the present state of international relations, this condition is not fulfilled.

Saying that the absence of an international consent[2] makes it impossible for a colonial power to resort to unlimited repressive measures means two things. The first is that the power does not have this consent at its disposal yet cannot do without it. The second is that those who need this consent cannot obtain it without first upsetting the political structure of the west.[3] These two propositions call for separate explanations.

1. See pp. 464 ff.
2. It will be noted that in this chapter the term consent has a broader meaning than it has previously been given. Since this broadening of the concept is apparent from the context, it does not seem necessary to change the terminology at this stage of the analysis.
3. As it appears here, this chapter owes a great deal to an exchange of views with Peter Paret of the Center of International Studies, Princeton University, in November 1960. In fact, at the time we were inclined to consider the opposition of international

When we say that western values and genocide are incompatible, the main implication is that those who threaten to use it risk being removed from their command posts before they have even been able to put their schemes into practice. This phenomenon applies on every level, from the combat unit to the Atlantic alliance. The partisans of genocide are not necessarily in a majority in the combat unit, the colonial army, the colony, the Métropole, or the western world. In fact, they become less and less numerous as one climbs from local to international echelons. From the reprisal of the commando to the western system, via the division, the army, the colonial and metropolitan regimes, the rule of the game is that one cannot usefully violate the strictest prohibitions of the moral code except with the consent of one's equals and superiors. The extremists in a reprisal unit are helpless without the backing of the other members of the unit and of the army. Their superiors in the colonial army are powerless without the complicity of more moderate military groups and civilian authorities in the colony. If the colonial administration did decide to adopt extreme measures, it would be powerless without metropolitan support. The latter in its turn would be unable to cover up acts of genocide without the complicity of other western powers. Unless this twofold condition is fulfilled, the violation of the international moral code by one rank alone will only lead to the removal of those guilty of the violation. The officer who covers up an act of genocide risks being cashiered. The officers who attempt to form a group for the same purpose within the army run similar or more serious risks. The colonial army that attempts a coup d'etat with the same goals in mind would find itself checked by an avalanche of

---

opinion to the use of force as a self-explanatory factor. Mr. Paret opportunely pointed out the fact that it is not enough merely to record a lack of international consent. The sociological implications of this deficiency have also to be analyzed, since the absence of consent is only the most apparent indication of the incompatibility that exists between certain ways of resorting to force and the social, political, and moral structure of the west. This correlation of the values of a civilization with its overall sociological structure was too close to our own line of research not to be immediately accepted as sound. So we went back to work on our own analysis and gave it its present shape. Not having had an opportunity to show the present text to Mr. Paret, we have no idea whether or not he would agree with the ideas expressed in it. Our conversations with him were, nonetheless, responsible for a closer investigation of this aspect of the question and for this we are extremely grateful.

measures which the metropolitan government, fully supported by public opinion, would not hesitate to release against it. The colonial power that would openly defy international morality by setting aside the prohibitions outlawing genocide would find itself facing barriers arising from international reaction to its excesses.[4] The more firmly a group or nation is integrated into the economic, political, and moral order that characterizes a civilization, the more difficult it is for it to defy openly the values upon which the civilization is based. Never in modern times has integration of the various parts into the whole been carried as far as it is today in the west. There is no need to search any further for the reasons which turn these values into an almost invincible political obstacle for anyone who might be tempted to assail them. The western moral code condones the conventional use of force. It does not condone any other, and that is all there is to say.

On the other hand, when we write that it would be hopeless to attempt to rally the west in favor of genocide without first engineering a complete revolutionary upheaval on every level, we mean to say that the attitudes and values which characterize a civilization are too closely linked to its social and political structures for us to hope to modify them radically unless the objective structures upon which these attitudes and values are based have been previously overthrown. The colonial extremists could not hope to rally the west to approve of genocide by propaganda, by the fait accompli, or even by taking over some of the political echelons. Even if the country had been at war, it would have been impossible to organize death camps in Weimar Germany. The impossible was possible ten years later because in the interval a revolution had taken place that overthrew the political structure of the country, eliminated from command posts moderates who might

4. If the U.S.S.R. was able to defy the western code of values in Budapest relatively easily, this is because it was not integrated into the political, economic, and moral structure of the west. This is also why the Afro-Asian nations judge less severely violence committed by a communist power than violence committed by the so-called "reactionary" western powers. The U.S.S.R. can commit excesses that remain prohibitive for the west because they are politically more dangerous for the west than for the U.S.S.R. These are the inequalities which, taken into consideration with all the others, finally give the forces of change the advantage over those dedicated to the protection of the status quo.

have been able to oppose this type of excess, anesthetized or terrorized the social groups from which the moderates came, and demoralized the German population by forcing down its throat a political philosophy that paved the way for the concentration camp regime.

The situation is no different today as far as the extreme use of force in the west is concerned. To be converted to genocide, the west would have to be transformed, echelon by echelon, into a concentration camp universe; the colonial army would have to be purged of all liberal elements, control of the colony would have to be seized by force, the takeover would have to be extended to the Métropole, and the entire west would have to be contaminated, because of the danger of failure at the lower echelons unless the entire system had been transformed. A venture of this sort is not inconceivable, but it would be realizable only if the presupposed factors of disintegration were sufficiently pronounced on the international level.

Therefore the point here is not to maintain that in the west it would be impossible for a state of affairs to arise in which recourse to genocide might temporarily settle actually insoluble problems,[5] but only to show that condoning genocide could never become the norm in our type of international society unless this society itself had undergone a preliminary revolutionary change similar to that we have just sketched above. Opposition to extreme forms of repression is neither completely contingent nor completely inevitable. It does not appear in a society by chance. Far from being a psychological accident, it emerges as the necessary correlative of a certain type of social and international organization. This type of social organization is not unchangeable. It can evolve in the direction of the progress of civilization and a strengthening of checks against the use of force, or it can evolve in the opposite direction, leading to the temporary or permanent elimination of these checks.

Whatever the eventuality may be, the fact remains that the international attitudes which restricted the repressive use of force

5. Something like this could very well happen if the communist powers were to bring so much pressure to bear upon the west that democracy could not survive. In a western world under totalitarian control, the new terrorist conquest of part of Europe's ancient colonial empire could become technically possible.

in the west since the last war all played an essential role in the Moroccan decolonization mechanism. Our demonstration is based essentially upon these attitudes. In a political system, the loss of consent only becomes a determining factor to the extent that the use of force is thereby sociologically, technically, or morally limited.[6] It is not therefore sufficient to show that the attitudes of the indigenous population paralyzed the potential of the conventional forces put at the protectorate's disposal by France. It must also be demonstrated that the collapse of the consent upon which the protectorate relied was only decisive to the extent that international attitudes prevented the partisans of a policy of force from resorting to unlimited repressive measures to reestablish their authority.

6. If the loss of consent is particularly serious for western regimes because of the moral and political considerations that limit the possibilities of resorting to force, it would be a mistake to assume that totalitarian, communist-type regimes are automatically in a position to neutralize the losses of consent that affect them by recourse to ad hoc forceful measures. Whatever type of regime is under consideration, there are always moral and political limits to the extremist use of force because of the general principle which makes recourse to force dependent upon the consent of the specialized groups who actually put it into practice and of the social classes from which they are recruited. From certain points of view, a totalitarian leader has more coercive power at his disposal than his Western counterpart. However, he cannot use these powers without taking into account the attitudes of the social groups with which he is linked, attitudes that can force him to extreme action as well as confine him to moderation. There is no such thing as unconditional power in politics.

Chapter 5

SIGNIFICANCE OF THE
SUCCESSION OF
COLONIAL CRISES;
DAMAGE TO THE COLONIZER'S PRESTIGE

Let us now return to the surface level of events in order to study a phenomenon that is at once extremely apparent and extremely important: the influence on the Franco-Moroccan conflict of the series of colonial conflicts in which France found herself involved after 1945. From the Levant to Indochina, from Indochina to Tunisia and Algeria, and from Tunisia and Algeria to Morocco, the decolonization of the French empire proceeded like a chain reaction. Stitch by stitch, and in a definite order, the pattern of French colonial possessions was unraveled. What does this image represent, and just how valid is it?

The essential point here is not so much the colonial nature of the conflicts as it is the damage done to French prestige by a series of international crises, the individual nature of which is unimportant. The 1940 debacle was, for France, the first shock. Next came the humiliation inflicted on Free France by the collaborationist enterprise. Subsequent to this serious, twofold attack on metropolitan prestige, the first two links to give way were Indochina under pressure from Japan and the Levant under pressure from the British. After this, the situation stabilized itself until the Dienbienphu disaster, which was the starting signal for North Africa. In Tunisia, Morocco, and Algeria, terrorism gradually began to replace political forms of nationalist activity. It is true that in each case internal factors were more effective in an immediate sense. The part played by earlier or concurrent crises should not, however, be underestimated. The French failure in Indochina fanned North African hopes. For

624

the first time, a colonial power had been defeated by a local insurrection, sustained, it is true, by a foreign power. Moreover, this foreign intervention placed the insurgents, to a certain extent, on a more equal footing with the colonists, since the North African colons were backed by the métropole, and France itself was directly or indirectly supported by its allies. The political influence exercised by the Tunisian and Algerian conflicts on the unfolding Moroccan conflict is even clearer. It was Indochina that enabled Pierre Mendès-France to solve the Tunisian crisis. It was the solution of the Tunisian crisis, reinforced by the first developments in Algeria, that persuaded the extremists to loosen their hold on Morocco.

Although the different colonial crises that affect the same métropole all act upon each other, it does not follow that they occur in an a priori order of succession, nor that the transition to the next crisis is inevitable. It was not decided in advance that the process of decolonization of the French empire would begin in the Levant and Indochina, freeing Morocco in its wake in 1956. Another combination of historical circumstances might have made one of the three North African countries act as the first link in the chain of events. This would not have prevented a defeat in those circumstances from having the same effect on other French colonies that the Indochina defeat had on North Africa in the sequence of events that actually did take place. Similarly, the transition to the next crisis is only inevitable under certain conditions. If the failure in Indochina aggravated the North African crisis, it was because French North African policy had proved incapable of extricating itself in time from the contradictions of a policy of immobility. The later events in West Africa confirm this. By changing gradually from resistance to progress, from a policy of force to one of liberal decolonization, France undoubtedly prevented the North African conflagration from spreading to its territories south of the Sahara. Thus the initial failure only determines the subsequent crisis if the métropole is incapable of effecting a change of policy between the two crises.

The flexible decolonization of French West African possessions and the abandonment of Morocco also reveal one final aspect of the reciprocal influence that colonial conflicts have upon each other; from certain points of view, these two transformations seem to be the price the extremists had to pay to make certain that the final concentration of French resistance would take place in Algeria. This does not mean that all those who fought in France for a liberal solution of the West African and Morocco problems did so in order to consolidate the French position in Algeria. It only means that the partisans of flexible decolonization would probably have failed in equatorial Africa if their opponents had not realized that if they wanted to keep Algeria they would have to abandon the struggle everywhere else. Here the question no longer has to do with the moral aspects of the international factor, but with the international incidence of a technical phenomenon, that is, the weak capacity of the military forces employed by western countries against colonial nationalism. For a certain period of time, several simultaneous colonial revolts can be contained by the so-called "small packet" method. However, once the situation has deteriorated gravely in one of the insurgent territories, the weak capacity of the métropole's repressive action forces it to concentrate all its strength in this one territory, which in turn forces it to abandon the others. The Algerian crisis showed that the forcible occupation of a colonial territory, with a surface area approximately equal to that of metropolitan France with only one fourth the population, required the concentration of all available military forces. Resistance to the last man thus becomes no more than the exception that proves the rule of forced general surrender.

The effect of other French colonial conflicts influenced the Moroccan conflict in two different ways: it administered a jolt to the morale of the two adversaries by previous successes, or defeats, in other colonies, and created the military and political vacuum that a major colonial conflict like the Algerian war can produce to the great advantage of other colonies in revolt or on the verge of revolt.

The preceding observations permit us to understand better the mechanism behind the influences that the international factor with its various components had on the Franco-Moroccan system.

Consent and force as applied on the Moroccan and French levels never ceased to be the immediate determinants of the political decisions made in the protectorate and in the métropole. International attitudes, their accompanying ideologies, western political values, and the other French colonial crises did not directly condition the decision-making capacity of the opposing political centers. They did, however, condition it indirectly by exercising positive or negative influences on Franco-Moroccan attitudes and on the force potential that these attitudes nourished. The foreign sympathy that the nationalists enjoyed had wounded their opponents in the protectorate and reduced the consent upon which the latter relied in Muslim circles while it shook colonization's faith in its own cause. French losses in other theaters of war had affected French prestige and lessened the fear of French power on the colonized nations. The need to concentrate everything in Algeria reduced military effectiveness in Morocco to below the minimum level required. The deployment of military forces was decisively limited by international attitudes forbidding the use of extreme repression. On both sides of the Mediterranean, consent and force were in direct control of the situation. What we call the international factor only acted through them.

At the same time, the role played by morale becomes much clearer. Morale cannot be included among the attitudes. It acts more as a factor governing the awareness of attitudes to the different sorts of influences being brought to bear upon them. It is a relay term, transmitting and amplifying impulses from elsewhere. The intensity of opposition or of consent varies according to whether morale is high or low, but the state of morale itself depends on the variables that condition attitudes. Emotivity intervenes in social psychology as well as in individual psychology. Although by itself it explains nothing, nothing can be fully explained without reference to it. In politics as in war, it lends warmth and color to human reactions.

Whether the international factor directly affected the attitudes of the conflicting groups or whether it only appeared by way of their morale is of little importance. What is significant is that by opposing the use of force, international opinion fixed a ceiling on the resistance capacity of the colonial authorities. As long as this intervention of attitudes and international values was not in evidence, one could still justifiably question whether recourse to the massive use of force might not have reversed the trend toward decolonization. Once it is admitted, however, that there are limits to the elasticity of international attitudes, the inquiry becomes meaningless. International attitudes become system buffers. Their description brings the analysis to an end and folds it in on itself. The limits of the phenomenon have been reached. Speculation can go no further.

CONCLUSIONS

The moment has now come to haul in our nets and to take a closer look at what they hold. The political system we have investigated consists of three main elements all fitting together in an order of increasing complexity: Moroccan, metropolitan, and international elements. This system can be viewed from two complementary aspects: that of a network of variables linked by specific influential relationships and that of a hierarchy of social groups acting as a support for a defined social function. Considered from the first perspective, the system was reduced to four types of strategic variables: situational, attitudinal, ideological, and decision-making variables. Considered from the second perspective, these variables made way for two main categories: the problems posed for the conflicting political centers by the social situations and collective attitudes with which they were at grips; and the solutions—realistic or unrealistic, adequate or inadequate—provided for these problems by the authorities whose job it was to solve or attempt to solve them. In each case, it would be useful to synthesize the results obtained.

The Mechanistic Aspect[1]

From this first point of view, the model of the conflict presents itself as a pyramid of variables, shaped at the base by the Moroccan, metropolitan, and international collective situations, at the middle echelon by the political attitudes of the groups on the lower echelon, and at the top by the decision-making capacities of the political centers in the system, in relation to the attitudes and situations of the first two echelons.[2]

1. Here the adjective "mechanistic" is not used in any pejorative sense. By definition, we will consider that a sociological theory is mechanistic to the extent that it reduces social phenomena to interactions between variables.

2. Figure 1 is merely a guide outlining for the reader's convenience the principal variables and conditioning factors involved in the analyses we are summarizing by way of conclusion. This model synthesizes both the mechanistic and the functionalist aspects of the demonstration. In order to shift from the first perspective to the second, it is sufficient to consider the situations and attitudes of the middle and lower echelons as posing political problems which the decision-making capacities of the upper echelon

FIGURE 1. THE MAIN VARIABLES AND THE MAIN CONDITIONING FACTORS BROUGHT
INTO PLAY BY THE CONFLICT

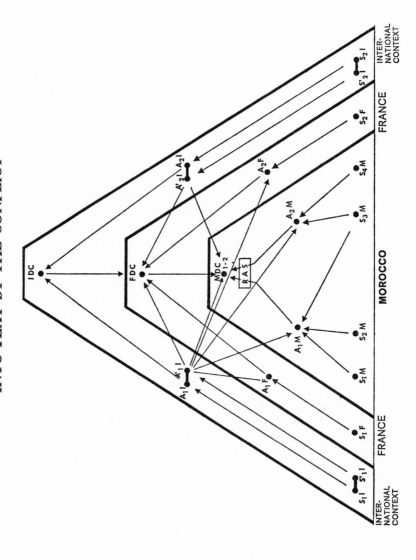

FIGURE 1 *(Continued)*

The Main Variables	The Main Conditioning Factors

(1) *Moroccan* — The Main Variables

S₁M: Situation of the nationalist Muslim masses

S₂M: Situation of the pronationalist notables

S₃M: Situation of the Europeans

S₄M: Situation of the anti-nationalist notables

A₁M: Attitude of the Muslims and of the pronationalist Europeans to political decisions made on a Moroccan level

A₂M: Attitude of the Europeans and of the anti-nationalist notables to political decisions made on a Moroccan level

RAS: Residential regime's authority structure (constant)

MDC: Moroccan decision-making capacity

MDC₁: Residential decision-making capacity

MDC₂: Decision-making capacity of nationalist leaders

(1) *Moroccan* — The Main Conditioning Factors

$S_1M \longrightarrow A_1M$
$S_2M \longrightarrow A_1M$ } Conditioning of Moroccan political attitudes by the cor-
$S_3M \longrightarrow A_2M$ responding social situations
$S_4M \longrightarrow A_2M$

$S_3M \longrightarrow A_1M$ { Partial conditioning of nationalist attitudes by Europeans sharing the privileged situation of the European group

$A_1M \longrightarrow S \longrightarrow MDC_{1\text{-}2}$
               A
$A_2M \longrightarrow R \longrightarrow MDC_{1\text{-}2}$

Conditioning of the decision-making capacity of the Moroccan leaders on the two sides by the corresponding collective attitudes working through the authority structure

FIGURE I (*Continued*)

(2) *Metropolitan*

S₁F: Factors in the overall situation of the French people in favor of the decolonization of Morocco.

S₂F: Factors in the overall situation of the French people against the decolonization of Morocco

A₁F: Metropolitan attitudes in favor of the decolonization of Morocco

A₂F: Metropolitan attitudes against the decolonization of Morocco

FDC: Metropolitan decision-making capacity concerning the conflict

(3) *International*

S₁I: Factors in the international situation in favor of the United Nations

S₂I: Factors in the international situation against the United Nations

A₁I: International attitudes in favor of the United Nations

A₂I: International attitudes against the United Nations

IDC: Decision-making capacity of the United Nations concerning the conflict

(2) *Metropolitan*

$S_1F \longrightarrow A_1F$
$S_2F \longrightarrow A_2F$
} Conditioning of metropolitan attitudes by the corresponding situation factors

$A_1F \longrightarrow FDC$
$A_2F \longrightarrow FDC$
} Conditioning of metropolitan decision-making capacity by the corresponding attitudes

(3) *International*

$S_1I \longrightarrow A_1I$
$S_2I \longrightarrow A_2I$
} Conditioning of the great powers attitudes toward the United Nations by the corresponding situation factors

$A_1I \longrightarrow IDC$
$A_2I \longrightarrow IDC$
} Conditioning of the United Nations' decision-making capacity by the attitudes of the great powers toward it

Figure 1 (*Continued*)

IDC $\longrightarrow$ FDC	Conditioning of the metropolitan decision-making capacity by the decision-making capacity of the United Nations
FDC $\longrightarrow$ MDC$_{1-2}$	Conditioning of the decision-making capacity of the Moroccan leaders on both sides in Morocco by the metropolitan decision-making capacity
$S'_1I \longrightarrow A'_1I$	Conditioning of international attitudes in favor of Moroccan nationalism by corresponding factors in the international situation
$S'_2I \longrightarrow A'_2I$	Conditioning of international attitudes against Moroccan nationalism by corresponding factors in the international situation
$A'_2I \longrightarrow$ FDC $A'_1I \longrightarrow$	Influence of both types of international attitude on the metropolitan decision-making capacity
$A'_2I \longrightarrow$ MDC$_{1-2}$ $A'_1I \longrightarrow$	Influence of both types of international attitude on the decision-making capacities of the residential and nationalist leaders
$A'_1I \longrightarrow A_2F$	Influence of international attitudes in favor of Moroccan nationalism on: —hostile metropolitan attitudes toward nationalism
$A'_1I \longrightarrow A_2M$	—the attitudes of Moroccan groups hostile to nationalism
$A'_1I \longrightarrow A_1M$	—the attitudes of Moroccan groups in favor of nationalism
$A'_1I \longrightarrow A_1F$	—the attitudes of metropolitan groups in favor of nationalism

S'_1I: Factors in the international situation in favor of Moroccan nationalism

S'_2I: Factors in the international situation against Moroccan nationalism

A'_1I: International attitudes in favor of Moroccan nationalism

A'_2I: International attitudes against Moroccan nationalism

Notes

1. The corresponding influences, with their signs reversed, exercised by international attitudes hostile to Moroccan nationalism (A'_2I) on the attitudes (A_2F, A_2M, A_1M, and A_1F) would be expressed by similar arrows.

2. The division of international situations (S_1I) (S_2I) and of international attitudes (A_1I) (A_2I) into two parts (S) (S') and (A) (A') is made in order to show the constituent components of the very complex situation or attitude elements. (S_1I) and (S'_1I) are therefore components of the same situation element. (A_1I) and (A'_1I) are components of the same attitude element. Every situation and attitude element on the metropolitan and Moroccan echelons could have been split in the same way, but the diagram would have become uselessly complicated.

In this type of model, conditioning is effected in three different ways: from bottom to top, top to bottom, and past to future. Upward conditioning is the only process that we have studied in a thorough manner. Our analysis showed that the situations in question determined the opposing attitudes which provided the conflicting political centers with unequal decision-making capacities and led to the final elimination of the protectorate by Moroccan nationalism.

Downward conditioning is closely connected to upward conditioning. When the leaders of a system in which a conflict is taking place have an adequate decision-making capacity, the situation defects that are at the root of the conflict are easily rectified. The opposing attitudes that stem from these gradually disappear. On the other hand, when the system's decision-making is inadequate, the opposing attitudes that sustain the conflict gradually spread and multiply. Situations continue to deteriorate until the lack of equilibrium between the opposing forces gives the advantage to the party that the objective evolution of the situation favors.

Temporal conditioning combines the influence of time sui generis with the two previous phenomena. The overall development of a colonial system is not only conditioned by the positive or negative incidence of governmental decisions that concern the conflicting factors linked to the situations. It is also determined by the simple passage of time; the system continues growing relatively independently of the decisions which the government is forced to make to deal with the conflicting tensions that accompany this growth.

These three conditioning processes are shown in Figure 2. Only the Moroccan aspects are covered, which means that the metropolitan and international situations remain constant enough throughout the period in question to be provisionally omitted from the argument. Let T be an axis of time on which four characteristic moments in the conflict appear: T_0, the initial temporal state corresponding to the initial situation S_0; T_4, the final temporal state corresponding to the final situation S_4; T_1,

---

try to solve. The three abbreviated pyramids superimposed on the diagram represent the system's Moroccan, metropolitan, and international echelons.

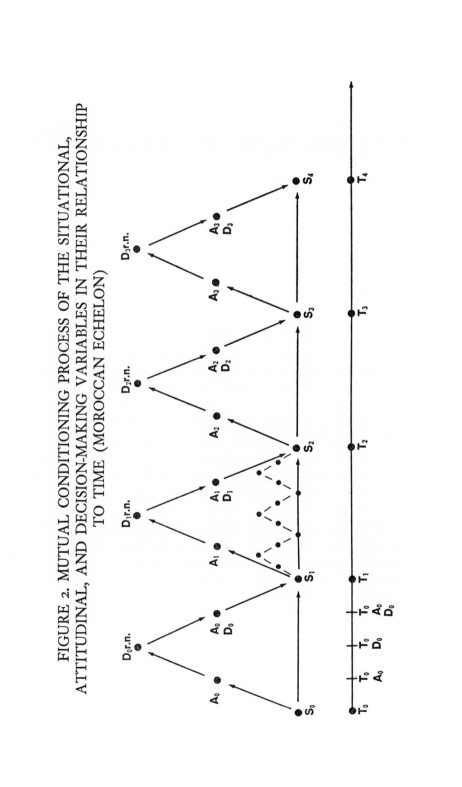

FIGURE 2. MUTUAL CONDITIONING PROCESS OF THE SITUATIONAL, ATTITUDINAL, AND DECISION-MAKING VARIABLES IN THEIR RELATIONSHIP TO TIME (MOROCCAN ECHELON)

T_2, and T_3, the intermediate temporal states corresponding to S_1, S_2, and S_3, the intermediate states of the overall situation. A_0 is the complex attitude implied by S_0; D_0r.n. represents the respective decision-making capacities of the residential and nationalist decision centers considered in their relation to the attitudes A_0 and to the situations S_0; A_0D_0 shows what happened to attitude A_0 under the effect of decisions D_0r.n. The evolution process continues in successive pyramids, following the D_1, D_2, and D_3 decisions. Each pyramid represents the transition from one system state to another and schematizes two essential phenomena.

The first is the transformation of the initial state, situation S_0 into the following state, situation S_1. This transformation itself has a tendency to occur in two complementary ways. First, S_0 tends to change into S_1 in a manner relatively independent of the conflict, simply because of the passage of time and because of the fact that the system is growing (direct conditioning $S_0 \longrightarrow S_1$). Second, S_0 is simultaneously and indirectly transformed into S_1 by the detour $S_0 \longrightarrow A_0 \longrightarrow D_0$r.n.$\longrightarrow A_0D_0 \longrightarrow S_1$, which represents the true political component of the phenomenon. S_0 is therefore definitely transformed into S_1 along two courses: the first, a direct course that shows the quasi-automatic growth component of the system, and the second, an indirect course representing the negative or positive component of the system's political evolution.

The second phenomenon is the time lag separating the variation in the upper variables in relation to the lower variables in the upward conditioning process ($S \longrightarrow A \longrightarrow D$); a reverse time lag affects the variation of the lower variables in relation to the upper variables in the downward conditioning process ($D \longrightarrow A \longrightarrow S$). This time lag phenomenon is well-known. The variation of attitude A_0 implied by situation variation S_0 does not occur at T_0, but at T_0A_0, the interval T_0—T_0A_0 being the amount of time required to actualize the virtual attitude A_0 implied by situation variation S_0. Similarly, D_0r.n. lags behind A_0; finally, A_0D_0 falls behind D_0r.n. To simplify the demonstration, all these time lags have been given equal value. This, of course, is a purely personal decision. Not only are these time lags not necessarily equal, some of them may never even have existed, for instance, when the situation change took place at the same time as the attitude variation that it implies. This was the case with the Europeans in Morocco once the political influence of Istiqlal began to make itself felt.

In spite of its relative complexity, Figure 2 is far from complete. In fact, the situational, attitudinal, and decision-making variables are considered as a whole with only their main conditionings shown by arrows. Ideology is not shown. An even more important omission is that many variables involved in the roots of situations S_0, S_1, and S_2 are not shown. The only attitudes and decisions specifically mentioned in the table are those that affected the conflict. The ordinary decisions and attitudes that affected the growth component are merely indicated by the direct process $S_1 \longrightarrow S_2$. Quite apart from the conflict, the protectorate went on making a whole series of decisions based on the political and economic situation; these decisions were rooted in collective attitudes that were scarcely affected by the crisis. To provide a complete picture, it would have been necessary to show these decisions as well as the others by removing the arrows, such as that in $S_1 \longrightarrow S_2$, and by replacing them with as many little internal pyramids as there were interactions between attitudes and this particular type of decision during the period being studied.[3]

If Figure 2 is a highly simplified model of the conflict, our analysis also falls short of the model. It did not seem possible to explore thoroughly all the conditioning processes. First, such an extensive study of the mechanism of the crisis would have involved us in lengthy developments. Second, it would only have been useful if fuller details of the system variables had been available. Finally, we decided it would be better to concentrate on the conditioning effect of the situation on attitudes and decisions. The other aspects seemed to be more concerned with the theory of political systems as such than with the discussion of the particular type of case that interests us. Nevertheless, we had to show that the situation was in fact considerably more complicated than our description might suggest and that the theory we have briefly outlined could be developed much further. Now that

3. As an example, the broken arrow $S_1 \longrightarrow S_2$ in the diagram illustrates this fact.

the model of the conflict has been shown to be intuitive, we must briefly explain the propositions that summarize its operation, after bringing the metropolitan and international extensions of the system back into the discussion.

1. In the Moroccan type of colonial structure, the passage of time effects a twofold transformation on the situation of the conflicting groups, involving, on the one hand, the subordination of the indigenous group to a colonial organizational framework that gradually grows larger, and, on the other hand, an anarchic proliferation of progressive tendencies (the positive developmental factors) and of regressive tendencies (the negative developmental factors and the disintegration of traditional culture) within the indigenous group.

2. Once the transformation of the colonial situation has gone far enough and certain historical conditions are present, this transformation of the situation sets loose a conflict of attitudes on the higher level which lines up the population against the colonial power and the colons against the demands of the population. This conflict of attitudes makes its first appearance in active minorities, but it gradually spreads and becomes more intense under the influence of leaders and groups. Only a minority of obstinate individuals on either side makes any attempt to swim against the tide: pro-colonialist notables among the indigenous population, and European liberals among the colons.

3. When, taking into account the system's authority structure, the dominant attitudes (consent or opposition) in each community become critical in numbers and in intensity, the colonial decision center finds itself incapable of finding a political solution to the conflict satisfactory to the indigenous population without at the same time losing the consent of the colonists. Because of the opposition of the indigenous population, it is also incapable of bringing about a military solution satisfactory to the colonists. This makes a decisive check on the use of the conventional measures of force by which colonial powers attempt to restore order among insurgents.

4. The métropole did not have the possibility of affecting the eventual outcome of the conflict, but it was not a priori excluded that the métropole might have commanded enough authority to

impose a program of peaceful decolonization on the two Moroccan communities. The interplay of situations and attitudes that conditioned the métropole's authority on its own level had deprived it of arbitrative powers. Everything eventually took place as if France had intervened in the conflict only in unconditional support of the Europeans.

5. Finally, it was out of the question for the United Nations to arbitrate in the conflict; international situations and attitudes and the subsequent limits to its competence reduced the decision-making capacity of the United Nations a priori to such a low level that no arbitration was possible. Since, on the other hand, international attitudes made it impossible for the protectorate to subdue Moroccan opposition by use of unlimited force, an eventual nationalist victory became the only possible outcome of the conflict provided that: (a) a revolutionary challenge to metropolitan and international values prohibiting the use of non-conventional force did not develop that would allow the Residency to restore the obedience of the population by recourse to massive or selective genocide; and/or (b) a series of historical events unconnected with the conflict (international war, a natural disaster, and so forth) did not upset the mechanism by preventing the initial states of the system from producing the ultimate states that they implied.[4]

4. This is a generalized argument that might also be applied to the Algerian conflict, but that can be considerably simplified according to the individual case. As long as international attitudes restrict the governmental use of force to its conventional application, decolonization is always inevitable. This does not mean, however, that a bitter struggle is equally inevitable. A colony with a very small European population and administrative officers who are strongly bound to metropolitan authority can be decolonized in an orderly, preventative manner by a métropole that is master of its own decisions. The size of the European population is the most important factor, but it is far from being the only one. Others are the varying degrees of consent or opposition concerning colonization within the colonized group, the density of the indigenous population and local variations of this density, the relations between colonial pressure groups and the mother country, and the condition of its political regime. These can all have a profound effect on the development of a decolonization crisis. Only a comparative survey of the various types of colonial conflicts that have broken out since the Second World War would make a general theory of decolonization possible. Besides, this theory could do little more than add variations to the basic model of the phenomenon. A colonial conflict always brings to the fore social situations, collective attitudes, and political decisions. Only the relative importance of these factors varies in individual cases. The colons are more or less numerous, the indigenous population more or less divided, the attitudes more or less coherent and intense, and the political and military decisions more or less effective. The conflicts themselves have a greater or

6. The final acquiescence to Moroccan independence by the Europeans does not pose any particular problems. The protectorate was established in 1912 when military victory forced the tribal insurrection to accept colonization. The 1956 defeat of French forces by Moroccan nationalists allowed an independent Morocco to convert European hostility into acceptance of the new political order that had emerged from the Aix-les-Bains agreements. This is no coincidence, but merely a repetition of a normal development in the mechanism of conflict. In fact, any military defeat implies the overthrow of the existing situation sui generis, adjusting the attitudes of the losing side to conform with those of the winner.[5]

---

lesser impact on international feelings. Each one of them adds another variation to the theory of decolonization, but the basis of the theory remains unaffected.

5. Although the colonial framework is doomed to defeat, there is nothing to prevent its proponents from prolonging the conflict until their means of resistance are exhausted. In the short run, an agreement between the nationalists and the métropole can give new life to the colons as well as break their spirit. Decolonization may be inevitable, but the moment when the Europeans choose to admit defeat still depends at least partially upon themselves. In other words, anticolonial terrorism may very well be replaced during the final phase of colonial-metropolitan relations by a counter-terrorism in which the indigenous population will bear the brunt. Naturally this reversal of fighting roles means that the metropolitan forces are necessarily faced with problems of maintaining public order similar to those they faced in the previous phase. Protected as they are by the Europeans, the terrorists on the inside cannot be caught. Incapable of restoring order by individual repression, the police and the army will slide irresistibly toward the use of collective repression. They will be morally and politically incapable of taking these to the limit. This, however, is an impasse in appearance only. If the situation deteriorates, a massive European exodus will put an end to the crisis. The emigration of the colonists is only one other aspect of decolonization. If the worst is to be avoided, some kind of modus vivendi must be worked out between the two communities, once the new nation's independence has been attained. Developments will continue to work against the insurgent colons. The nationalists have the whole world on their side. The Europeans have the whole world against them. The indigenous population fights in the countryside. The Europeans are trapped in the main urban centers. The local population can survive on its own resources. The colonists depend heavily on the métropole. The indigenous population is firmly entrenched. The Europeans find their local roots loosening, due to the easy escape routes open to them. Barring a political accident in the métropole, the activists' cause is lost once they lose military and police support; the colonists' dependence on the mother country makes it possible for the latter to deal with them by means of collective reprisals to which the Europeans remain extremely vulnerable, although they would be inadequate to force the local nationalists to surrender. The resistance capacity of the two communities would only be equal if their human potential and social structures were comparable. The colons remain a minority group to the end, and this lack of sociological autonomy prevents them from waging a counter-revolutionary war against their opponents.

The Functionalist Aspect

To convert the mechanistic model whose transformation has just been schematized into a functionalist model, we have identified the situations and attitudes on the lower and middle echelons of the system with social problems, and have considered the decisions taken on the upper echelon as solutions to these problems provided by the decision-making centers whose social function was to solve them.

From 1912 to 1956, a continuous flow of problems swept the Franco-Moroccan system. As the solution of a political problem tends to be determined by its enunciation and as each adopted solution tends to produce new problems, the different terms in the series succeeded themselves in a definite order. By solving the problem of the establishment of a European economic sector, the Residency raised that of the development of traditional sectors. Inasmuch as this could not be resolved so as to neutralize local nationalism, the Moroccan elite in turn found itself faced with the problem of the regime. The problem could only have been met if the French authorities had been in a position to neutralize the opposition of the nationalist leaders and the Muslim masses supporting them with normal police measures. Because the difficulty was insoluble, the simple removal of the first nationalist directorate inevitably left the protectorate facing one final problem, the most bitter and serious one: the control of a political and military insurrection supported by the local population under direction of underground leaders.

When the protectorate is judged from the point of view of social problems, its inability to resolve the structural, political, and military problems provoked by its own actions condemns it. A regime that becomes incapable of maintaining public order is doomed to disappear; there is no reason why a colonial government should be an exception to the rule.

Functional analysis of this perfectly commonplace truth shows that the functional impotence of a regime can be caused by the nature of the problems it faces as well as by a deterioration of the political organism. A regime weakened by a prolonged authority crisis becomes incapable of handling the problems it was designed to solve. Conversely, a regime otherwise operating smoothly can be suddenly thrown off the track by a crisis that it was not intended to solve. In the first place, the functional short-coming in the system is due to a functional disorder. In the second, it is the result of the destructive influence that an unusual problem has on the political organism.

Clearly, Moroccan events are covered by the second supposition. In 1945, the protectorate possessed enough functional integrity to undertake the solution of the economic and political problems that normally fall within the sphere of competence of a colonial regime. It might have grappled with them better than it did, but it is nevertheless true that until the very end it proved itself sufficiently capable to avoid any difficulties at that level in the regime. When the regime finally did collapse, it was because the solutions it had provided for this type of problem had created other problems that proved insoluble.

The operational capacity of any regime has its limits. Democracy is designed to solve marginal problems on the basis of a general consent. Revolutionary regimes are equipped to handle the necessary institutional readaptation and structural development because they rely on the support of one half of the population to dominate the other. The protectorate was designed to ensure the development of a modern economic sector in an under-developed area, to ensure the political and sociological superiority of the colonist group over the indigenous group, and, under certain conditions and within certain limits, to ensure the obedience of the latter group. It was not designed—nor is any regime—to undertake the dissolution of those social groups upon which it depends nor to maintain order among a population allied with the terrorists and guerrillas who had come from this milieu. Political regimes should govern with the support of the social groups from which they recruit their administrative personnel and executive officers; they should not govern against the will of these groups.

Even if we do not doubt that the protectorate was destroyed by some unusual problems, we might still be tempted to believe that the métropole was paralyzed only because an accidental governmental crisis rendered it temporarily incapable of arbitrating the conflict, a decision that normally would have been within its powers. The unnatural character of the decision to abandon Morocco made by Paris is, in fact, less flagrant than the decision made in Rabat to dissolve the European group there. Moreover, the phenomenon was masked by the traditional impotence of the regime. A careful examination of the record still leads one to believe that the decisions required of France by the conflict were scarcely less extraordinary in the métropole than in the Residency.

Except in the case of wartime defeat, no regime is designed to adopt uncompromising measures toward the population to the advantage of a foreign group. Paris could never have ordered the cold-blooded evacuation of all Francophiles from an Alsace supposedly divided and eager to become German, nor could it have maintained order in a revolting province where the population would have sheltered the outlaws. Political situations of this type soon destroy the representative regime that challenges them. It might then be asserted that a colonial group is not a metropolitan group, and that the mother country's political choice over the threatened colons would not be the same as that applied to its own countrymen confronted with a similar crisis at home. The whole problem is precisely to decide whether or not the colons have the same sociological and political "value" for the métropole as a metropolitan group of the same size. When there are relatively few colons, the métropole may decide that their defense is not worth the costs involved; in this case, the problems posed by local nationalism remain quite normal and the metropolitan regime eventually employs drastic measures without bringing its own integrity into question. When, on the other hand, there is a sufficiently large number of colons whose bonds with the métropole are strong enough to make the political and emotional reactions to nationalist attacks similar, if not identical, to those which would be provoked by a foreign act of aggression against a metropolitan province, then the problem of decolonization may eventually destroy any regime that attempts to solve it. The Algerian crisis was the only one corresponding to this extreme type, but the Moroccan and Tunisian crises were close enough to make the argument applicable. Algeria finally destroyed the Fourth Republic. Morocco and Tunisia were content

to cripple it. A decolonization crisis may pose problems of varying degrees of gravity to the métropole. Once the North African
Frenchman assimilates the attributes of a metropolitan Frenchman, a justifiable conclusion would be that French institutions
are no better designed to decolonize North Africa than the
French-instituted regimes in the Maghreb were to decolonize
themselves.

Seen in this way, the governmental crisis becomes less important. True, the Fourth Republic suffered from a congenital authority defect which made it incapable of dealing with certain
normal problems. Everything indicates, however, that it was
finally destroyed by the effect on its institutions of a highly
unusual problem which it was not designed to solve. The relative
independence of these two phenomena leads us at least to believe
that it was preferable to minimize the role played in the conflict
by this governmental crisis than to attempt to explain everything
by it. Under present conditions and for want of more precise
mechanistic and explanatory schemas, the separation of the problems which a regime can solve from those which it cannot solve
remains the most effective method of distinguishing between
political phenomena that are basically different but run the risk
of remaining obscure at first glance. This essential distinction
would alone have provided sufficient justification for the use of
the functionalist method in the study of decolonization.

Return to the Theory and Integration of Both Aspects of the Model

Both aspects of the demonstration have, on the whole, conformed with the theoretical outline discussed in the methodological introduction. At each stage of the analysis, the study of the
conflict has intermingled with that of a social structure viewed
simultaneously as a mechanism and as a political organism.

Considered from the mechanistic point of view, the decolonization of Morocco was identified with the transformation of a
political system under the control of an exclusively residential
decision center into another system under the control of
a nationalist decision center. The passage from the initial
to the terminal state in this transformation was achieved

by means of a series of intermediate states involving increasing polarization of the political structure. In Morocco itself, the attitudes and situations on the lower echelons were thus linked to the two competing decision centers whose authority potential was sharply differentiated. In the residential part of the system, consent tended to drop off, whereas in the nationalist part of the system, it increased; this inverse evolution of the two consensual potentials was reflected by a symmetrical evolution of the decision-making and force-using capacities of the conflicting decision centers. Eventually the normal decision-making capacity of the Residency fell too low to be rescued by the conventional use of force. On the other hand, the decision-making and force-using capacities of the nationalist leaders were raised to the level required for them to maintain effectively their hold over the Muslim masses. While the authority potential of the Residency decreased, that of the nationalists increased. The elimination of the residential operations center by the nationalists was inevitable, once the Métropole was bound by the political mechanism that determined the relations of the forces on the Moroccan level, and once international attitudes prevented the colonial power from regaining control of the situation by means of unrestricted repressive measures.

Considered from the functionalist point of view, the decolonization of Morocco was also identified with the transformation of a political quasi-organization of the residential type into a political quasi-organization of the nationalist type. The initial and final terms of the transformation were separated by transitory phases that brought the two types of organizations into competition with each other. This transformation took place under the influence of a gradual decline in the Residency's ability to solve problems connected with its environment, together with a correlative increase in the nationalist directorate's ability to solve its problems. This functional ability or disability was due to either the technical or the political nature of the problems. Since the functional impotence of the Residency was reflected on the metropolitan and international echelons, the problem was finally settled in Morocco itself by a clash between the two factions. When the decision centers of a society are paralyzed, the people have no other choice. The communities could not be blamed for the deterioration of their political organs. In extreme cases, this deterioration is the result, with no possible alternative on the internal level, of the problems set for the leaders by the evolving social structure and by the defense and aggression reflexes that are tied to this evolution. Barring the intervention of a third party capable of arbitrating and solving the problems of the system on the basis of its own authority, the crisis-ridden organization has no other choice but to restore its shattered authority potential by renewing its faltering decision centers by revolutionary means.

This close association between the mechanism and political functionalism would never have been possible if the political systems had not shared the same ambivalence that characterizes the entire social structure. The structural elements in the Franco-Moroccan system were not only mechanically interdependent, they were also almost organically correlated, and this participation by each explanatory factor in the two complementary aspects of the structure under examination is the key to this structural-functional analysis. Once one loses sight of this structural ambivalence, the interplay of political variables dissociates itself from the functional activity of the system and the theory then ceases to be a full reflection of reality. The sociologist then becomes like a biologist who is incapable of linking physico-chemical analysis to the main organic functions.

Finally, whatever the analytic method adopted, it seems to us that the arguments have largely corroborated the sociological law that subordinates political authority to consent, to force, and to the social situations within the framework of a given authority structure.[6] The demonstration thus remains subject to the principles from which this law is derived and especially to the principles of the inequality of actions and of a reaction's dependence on action. This cannot be overemphasized. If the Residency had had the same influence on the attitudes within the system that

6. This law applies to the mechanistic as well as to the functionalist aspects of the model. Saying that situations, consent, and force determine the decision-making capacity of a system or that the enunciation of a problem integrating situation and attitude variables determines the solutions that the leaders provide amounts, once again, to saying the same thing in two different ways.

these attitudes exercised on its own decision-making capacity, and if the Residency had been able *arbitrarily* to reestablish its authority by forcing the Moroccans to accept the status quo or by persuading international opinion to condone genocide, then the Franco-Moroccan conflict would never have occurred. The inequality of actions and the reaction's dependence on action were in fact confirmed. The full circle of the demonstration closes as its conclusions meet the principles upon which they are based.

Is this concept of the decolonization mechanism in Morocco open to debate? On the contrary, it would seem that even the supporters of the policy of force implicitly admitted it, if at least one can go by their constant attempts to escape from the grips of those political attitudes and structures that were preventing them from realizing their objectives.

Agreement on the theory was sometimes even explicit. "One day," Robert Lacoste said to a writer for *L'Express,* "Mendès-France told me, 'When Napoleon was in Spain, the Spaniards didn't want anything to do with him and he had to pack his bags.' I replied, 'You are absolutely right. If the Algerians didn't want us, we would have to leave. But, don't you see, it is just not true that the majority does not want us.' " [7] This exchange tends to confirm that the conflict between the leaders of the two sides took place more on a factual than on a theoretical plane. Agreement on theoretical principles does not necessarily put an end to the discussion. Although settled in principle, the controversy would inevitable break out again on the factual level. Whatever attitude may be adopted in theory, it is always possible to say, in the absence of exact statistics, that a colonial revolt is less popular than is claimed, that an increase in military supplies coupled with the help of exceptional circumstances could easily reverse the relative strength, and that a marginal increase in the pressure applied to the population would soon bring them to heel.

In the field where the facts upon which the theories are based will remain controversial until the question is finally settled, no amount of analysis will convince those who do not wish to be convinced. This is why it would be futile to hope that knowledge of the mechanism of conflict alone can help mankind overcome

7. *L'Express* (May 2, 1958), p. 16.

the strife that divides it. A complete knowledge of the mechanism of war would not prevent war. Conversely, war might very well vanish from a world in which men were ignorant of its mechanism. Modern conflicts are not born through ignorance. They stem from defective social situations. Even if these defects were understood and reforms feasible, nothing would be settled. To reform a social situation, it must be possible to take action on it, and this ad hoc decision-making capacity is under continuous attack by the conflicting groups. To persuade men, it is not enough to know what has to be done. One must be capable of doing it. Political science has no magic formula for manufacturing more authority than the situations to be reformed normally provide. The more involved one becomes in politics, the more difficult it is to pass directly from knowledge to action. Medical discoveries have put an end to the great epidemics. No amount of progress in political analysis alone could ever put an end to the era of social and international conflicts. Universal peace is not a utopian concept. But it is utopian to believe that a radical reform of social attitudes can come from anything other than a transformation of civilization caused by factors powerful enough to take traditional forms of collective existence and shake them from top to bottom. Nothing is more certain than that the voice of knowledge must be heard but only in its own place, a place that will remain a humble one as long as human societies lack sufficient power to make their leaders put political knowledge to work in the service of humanity.

BIBLIOGRAPHY

OFFICIAL SOURCES

Official Texts

FRANCE

Journal officiel de la République française, Débats parlementaires, Assemblée consultative provisoire, August 2, 1945.
———, *Débats parlementaires, Conseil de la République*, August 4, 1955.
———, *Débats parlementaires, Assemblée nationale*, 1951–56.
———, *Ordonnances et décrets*, September 16, 1955.
———, *Lois et décrets*, April 7, 1955.
Commission des affaires étrangères de l'Assemblée nationale, *Note du 4 Septembre 1953*, Paris, 1953.

MOROCCO

Protectorat de la République française (empire chérifien), *Bulletin officiel*, Rabat, 1930, 1946, 1947, 1949, 1951–54.
Résidence générale de la République française au Maroc, *Bulletin d'information du Maroc*, Rabat, nos. 7, 9, 10, 1946; supplement to no. 2, 1947; nos. 6, 7, 1947; nos. 8, 9, 1950; no. 6, 1951; nos. 38, 43, 45, 46, 48, 1954.
Bulletin de renseignements de la direction de l'intérieur de la Résidence générale (section politique), Rabat, no. 2, February 1953.
Plan de réformes, Rabat 1945, Rabat, Imprimerie officielle, 1945.

UNITED NATIONS

General Assembly, *Official Records,* 7th Session, 392d Plenary Meeting, November 10, 1952, paras. 76–158; 10th Session, 528th Plenary Meeting, September 29, 1955, paras. 51–54.
———, 11th Session, Supplement no. 17 (A/3572), Resolution 1111 (XI), November 12, 1956.
Security Council, *Official Records,* 11th Session, Supplement for July, August, and September 1956 (S/3617 and S/3619).

649

Minutes, Memoranda

Istiqlal Party (Morocco), *Documents 1944–1946,* English ed. Paris, Documentation and Information Office of the Istiqlal Party, September 1946.

Centre d'études et de documentation, *Un Processus d'évolution du Maroc* (Maroc A6), Paris 1954.

———, *Urgence d'une politique française au Maroc* (Maroc A8), Paris, 1954.

Comité national pour la solution du problème franco-marocain, *Compte rendu de la conférence nationale pour la solution du problème franco-marocain; Paris les 7 et 8 mai 1955,* Paris, 1955.

La Documentation française

Notes documentaires et études (later, *Notes et études documentaires*), no. 357, "Textes et documents, Discours d'ouverture prononcé par M. Eirik Labonne, ambassadeur de France, commissaire résident général de la République française au Maroc au Conseil du gouvernement le 22 juillet 1946 à Rabat," July 22, 1946.

———, no 2,026, "Chronologie internationale du 16 au 31 mai 1955," May 31, 1955.

Articles et documents, Textes du jour, no. 088, "Déclaration de M. Mendès-France au Bey de Tunis," August 3, 1954.

———, no. 0335, "Protocole franco-tunisien," March 22, 1956.

NEWSPAPERS AND WEEKLIES

Belgium

Le Peuple, Brussels.

Egypt

Al Goumhourya, Cairo.

France

L'Aurore, Paris.
Combat, Paris.
L'Express, Paris.
Le Figaro, Paris.
Franc-Tireur, Paris.
France-Soir, Paris.
L'Humanité, Paris.
Jours de France, Paris.

Maghreb, Paris.
Le Monde, Paris.
Paris-Match, Paris.
Paris-Presse-L'Intransigeant, Paris.
Le Populaire de Paris, Paris.

Italy

Corriere della sera, Milan.
Il Giornale d'Italia, Rome.

Morocco

L'Action du peuple, Fez.
Al Alam, Casablanca.
El Azima, Casablanca.
Echo du Maroc, Rabat.
Al Istiqlal, Casablanca.
Libération, Rabat.
Liberté, Casablanca.
Maroc-Presse, Casablanca.
Al Oummah, Tetuán.
Le Petit Marocain, Casablanca.
La Vigie marocaine, Casablanca.

Spain

A.B.C., Madrid.

United Kingdom

The New Statesman and Nation, London.

United States

The New York Times, New York.

BOOKS AND ARTICLES

Almond, G. A., and Coleman, James, eds., *The Politics of the Developing Areas,* Princeton, Princeton University Press, 1960.
L'Année politique 1953, Paris, Presses universitaires de France, 1954.
L'Année politique 1955, Paris, Presses universitaires de France, 1956.
Aron, Raymond, *Sociologie des sociétés industrielles: esquisse d'une théorie des régimes politiques,* Paris, 1958.
Ayache, Albert, *Le Maroc,* Paris, Ed. sociales, 1956.
Barrat, Robert, *Justice pour le Maroc,* Paris, Ed. du Seuil, 1953.

Bernard, Stéphane, "Note sur la théorie des conflits internationaux," mimeo., Le Congrès de l'association internationale de science politique, 1959.

Bonnet, Gabriel, *Les Guerres insurrectionnelles et révolutionnaires de l'antiquité à nos jours*, Paris, 1958.

Boyer de Latour, Pierre, *Vérités sur l'Afrique du Nord*, Paris, Plon, 1956.

Bulletin marocain d'information et de documentation, 5th year, 101, 102, 104, 105, Casablanca, 1955.

Carnap, Rudolph, *Logical Foundations of Probability*, 2d ed. Chicago, University of Chicago Press, 1962.

Corval, Pierre, *Le Maroc en révolution*, Paris, Bibliothèque de l'homme d'action, 1956.

Davis, Kingsley, "The Myth of Functional Analysis as a Special Method in Sociology and Anthropology," *American Sociological Review*, 24 (1959), 757–72.

Le Drame marocain devant la conscience chrétienne: les événements de Casablanca à travers la presse française du Maroc, Cahiers du témoignage chrétien, Paris, 1953.

Duverger, Maurice, *Méthodes de la science politique*, Paris, Presses universitaire de France, 1959.

Encyclopaedia Britannica, 9 (1953).

"Evolution de la question tunisienne," *Chronique de politique étrangère* (Brussels), 9 (July 1956), 506–28.

Fauvet, Jacques, *La IVᵉ République*, Paris, A. Fayard, 1959.

——, *La France déchirée*, Paris, 1957.

France-Maghreb (Paris), no. 1 (1956).

Garas, Félix, *Bourguiba et la naissance d'une nation*, Paris, R. Julliard, 1956.

Le General Raymond Duval, preface by Marshal Juin, Paris, Ed. Berger-Levrault, 1957.

Girod, Roger, *Attitudes collectives et relations humaines*, Paris, 1953.

Grandval, Gilbert, *Ma mission au Maroc*, Paris, Plon, 1956.

Hogard, J., "Guerre révolutionnaire et pacification," *Revue militaire d'information* (Paris), *280* (January 1957).

Izard, Georges, "Le 'Secret' d'Antsirabé," *Etudes méditerranéenes* (Paris), no. 4 (1958), pp. 61–75.

Janne, Henri, "Fonction et finalité en sociologie," *Cahiers internationaux de sociologie* (Paris), *14* (1954).

Juin, Alphonse, *Le Maghreb en feu*, Paris, Plon, 1957.

——, *Mémoires*, *1* (1959), 2 (1960), Paris, A. Fayard.

Julien, Charles-Andre, *L'Afrique du Nord en marche; nationalismes musulmans et souveraineté française*, Paris, R. Julliard, 1952.

Lacheroy, Charles, *Action Viet-Minh et communiste ou une leçon de "guerre révolutionnaire"*, Centre militaire d'information et de specialisation pour l'outre-mer, Section de documentation militaire de l'outre-mer, Paris, 1955 (mimeographed).

Lacouture, Jean et Simonne, *Le Maroc a l'épreuve*, Paris, Ed. du Seuil, 1958.

Lawrence, T. E., *Seven Pillars of Wisdom*, New York, Doubleday, 1938.

Lipkowski, Jean de, "Comment le 30 septembre 1955 le sultan ben Arafa renonça au trône chérifien," *La Nef* (Paris), n.s., 14th year, *4* (1957), 34–41.

Merton, Robert K., *Social Theory and Social Structure*, rev. ed. Glencoe, Ill., Free Press, 1957.

Meynaud, Jean, *Introduction à la science politique*, Cahiers de la Fondation nationale des sciences politiques, 100, Paris, A. Colin, 1959.

Mitterrand, François, *Présence française et abandon*, Tribune libre, 12, Paris, Plon, 1957.

Modelski, George, *The International War*, Research Monograph No. 11, Princeton, Princeton University Press, 1961.

Montagne, Robert, *Révolution au Maroc*, Paris, Ed. France-Empire, 1953.

Monteil, Vincent, *Les officiers*, Paris, Ed. du Seuil, 1958.

Nagel, Ernest, *Logic Without Metaphysics*, Glencoe, Ill., Free Press, 1956.

Pareto, Vilfredo, *Mind and Society*, trans. Andrew Bongiorno and Arthur Livingston, New York, Dover, 1958.

Parsons, Talcott, *The Social System*, Glencoe, Ill., Free Press, 1951.

Pinner, Frank A., *Notes on Method in Social and Political Research*, Bureau of Social and Political Research, College of Business and Public Service, Michigan State University, 1960.

"Le Problème algérien," *Chronique de politique étrangère* (Brussels), *8* (November 1955), 677–740.

Rezette, Robert, *Les partis politiques marocains*, Cahiers de la Fondation nationale des sciences politiques, 70, Paris, A. Colin, 1955.

Roosevelt, Elliott, *As He Saw It*, New York, Duell, Sloan and Pearce, 1946.

Schuman, Robert, "Nécessité d'une politique," Maroc et Tunisie, le problème du protectorat, *La Nef* (Paris), n.s., 10th year, *2* (1953), 7–9.

Souyris, A., "Les Conditions de la parade et de la riposte à la guerre révolutionnaire," *Revue militaire d'information* (Paris), *281* (February–March 1957).

Tillion, Germaine, *L'Algérie en 1957*, Paris, 1957.

Williams, Philip, *Politics in Post-War France*, London, 1958.

Ximenès, "La Guerre révolutionnaire et ses données fondamentales," *Revue militaire d'information* (Paris), *281* (February–March 1957).

ANNEX I

PROTECTORATE TREATY BETWEEN FRANCE AND MOROCCO [1]

Signed at Fez, March 30, 1912

The Government of the French Republic and the Government of His Majesty the Sultan, desirous of inaugurating a regular régime in Morocco based upon internal order and general security, making it possible to introduce reforms and to insure the economic development of the country, have agreed upon the following:

ARTICLE I

The Government of the French Republic and His Majesty the Sultan have agreed to establish in Morocco a new régime admitting of the administrative, juridical, educational, economic, financial and military reforms which the French Government may deem useful to be introduced within the Moroccan territory.

This régime shall safeguard the religious status, the respect and traditional prestige of the Sultan, the exercise of the Mohammedan religion and of the religious institutions and in particular those of the *habous*. It shall admit of the organization of a reformed Shereefian makhzen.

The Government of the Republic will come to an understanding with the Spanish Government regarding the interests which this government has in virtue of its geographical position and territorial possessions on the Moroccan coast.

In like manner, the City of Tangiers shall retain the distinctive characteristic for which it has been known and which will determine its municipal organization.

ARTICLE II

His Majesty the Sultan consents that henceforth the French Government, after it shall have notified the makhzen, may proceed to such military occupation of the Moroccan territory as it might deem necessary for the maintenance of good order and the security of commercial transactions, and to exercise every police supervision on land and within the Moroccan waters.

ARTICLE III

The Government of the Republic pledges itself to lend constant support to His Shereefian Majesty against all dangers which might threaten his person or throne, or endanger the tranquillity of his states. The same support shall be given the heir to the throne and his successors.

ARTICLE IV

Such measures as the new régime of the protectorate may require shall be edicted, upon the proposal of the French Government, by His Shereefian Majesty or the authorities to whom he may have delegated his power. The same process shall be observed in the matter of new regulations and of modifications to the existing regulations.

ARTICLE V

The French Government shall be represented near His Shereefian Majesty by a resident commissioner general, representative of all the powers of the republic in Morocco, who shall attend to the execution of the present agreement.

The resident commissioner general shall be the sole intermediary of the Sultan near foreign representatives and in the relations which these representatives maintain with the Moroccan Government. In particular, he shall have charge of all matters relating to foreigners in the Shereefian Empire.

1. *Le Memorial Diplomatique*, April 7, 1912, p. 214. Reproduced in *Supplement to the American Journal of International Law*, 6 (1912), 207–09.

He shall have the power to approve and promulgate, in the name of the French Government, all the decrees issued by His Shereefian Majesty.

ARTICLE VI

The diplomatic and consular agents of France shall be charged with the representation and protection of Moroccan subjects and interests abroad.

His Majesty the Sultan pledges himself not to conclude any act of an international nature without the previous approval of the French Republic.

ARTICLE VII

The Government of the French Republic and the Government of His Shereefian Majesty reserve unto themselves to determine by mutual agreement the bases for a financial reorganization which, while respecting the rights conferred upon bondholders of the Moroccan public loans, shall make it possible to guarantee the engagements of the Shereefian treasury and to collect regularly the revenues of the empire.

ARTICLE VIII

His Shereefian Majesty declares that in future, he will refrain from contracting, directly or indirectly, any public or private loan, and from granting in any form whatever any concession without the authorization of the French Government.

Signed Regnault
Moulay Abd El Hafid

ANNEX II

CHRONOLOGICAL TABLE OF THE GOVERNMENTS AND MINISTRIES PERTAINING TO MOROCCO

I. The French Committee for National Liberation (C.F.L.N.) and the Provisional Governments

Dates [1]	Premiers	Foreign Affairs
C.F.L.N. June 3, 1943–June 2, 1944	Charles de GAULLE Henri GIRAUD	René MASSIGLI
First provisional government June 3, 1944–Nov. 9, 1945	Charles de GAULLE	René MASSIGLI later Georges BIDAULT (M.R.P.)
Second provisional government Nov. 13, 1945–Jan. 20, 1946	Charles de GAULLE resigned on Jan. 20, 1946	Georges BIDAULT (M.R.P.)
Third provisional government Jan. 23–June 11, 1946	Félix GOUIN (S.F.I.O.)	Georges BIDAULT (M.R.P.)
Fourth provisional government June 19–Nov. 28, 1946	Georges BIDAULT (M.R.P.)	Georges BIDAULT (M.R.P.)
Fifth provisional government Dec. 12, 1946–Jan. 16, 1947	Léon BLUM (S.F.I.O.)	Léon BLUM (S.F.I.O.)

FIRST LEGISLATURE

1. This table gives the dates of inauguration and fall of the governments.

II. The Fourth Republic [2]

Dates	Premiers	Foreign Affairs	North Africa [3]
Jan. 21–Nov. 19, 1947 + 2 cabinet reshuffles (May and October 1947)	Paul RAMADIER (S.F.I.O.)	Georges BIDAULT (M.R.P.)	
Nov. 22, 1947–July 19, 1948	Robert SCHUMAN (M.R.P.)	Georges BIDAULT (M.R.P.)	
July 24–Aug. 28, 1948	André MARIE (Rad.)	Robert SCHUMAN (M.R.P.)	
Sept. 10, 1948–Oct. 6, 1949	Henri QUEUILLE (Rad.)	Robert SCHUMAN (M.R.P.)	
Oct. 27, 1949–June 24, 1950	Georges BIDAULT (M.R.P.)	Robert SCHUMAN (M.R.P.)	
July 11, 1950–Feb. 28, 1951	René PLEVEN (U.D.S.R.)	Robert SCHUMAN (M.R.P.)	
Mar. 9–July 10, 1951	Henri QUEUILLE (Rad.)	Robert SCHUMAN (M.R.P.)	

FIRST LEGISLATURE

2. Only those cabinet changes directly relevant to the crisis are indicated. The two caretaker governments of Schuman (Sept. 5–7, 1948) and Queuille (July 1–4, 1950) have not been included.

3. As far as North Africa is concerned, only the two Ministers of Moroccan and Tunisian Affairs and their direct successors have been included. The Under-Secretaries of State before June 19 are not mentioned.

Dates	Premiers	Foreign Affairs	North Africa
Aug. 8, 1951–Jan. 7, 1952	René PLEVEN (U.D.S.R.)	Robert SCHUMAN (M.R.P.)	
Jan. 18–Feb. 29, 1952	Edgar FAURE (Rad.)	Robert SCHUMAN (M.R.P.)	
Mar. 6–Dec. 23, 1952	Antoine PINAY (Ind.)	Robert SCHUMAN (M.R.P.)	
Jan. 7–May 21, 1953	René MAYER (Rad.)	Georges BIDAULT (M.R.P.)	
June 26, 1953–June 12, 1954	Joseph LANIEL (Ind.)	Georges BIDAULT (M.R.P.)	
June 18, 1954–Feb. 5, 1955	Pierre MENDÈS-FRANCE (Rad.)	Pierre MENDÈS-FRANCE (Rad.) Edgar FAURE (Rad.)	Christian FOUCHET (Soc. Rep.), *Minister for Moroccan and Tunisian Affairs.*[4]
Feb. 23, 1955–Jan. 24, 1956 + 1 cabinet reshuffle (Oct. 6, 1955)	Edgar FAURE (Rad.)	Antoine PINAY (Ind.)	Pierre JULY (A.R.S. then R.G.R.), *Minister for Moroccan and Tunisian Affairs.*[5]
Jan. 31, 1956–May 21, 1957	Guy MOLLET (S.F.I.O.)	Christian PINEAU (S.F.I.O.)	Alain SAVARY (S.F.I.O.), *Secretary of State for Foreign Affairs in Charge of Moroccan and Tunisian Affairs.* Maurice FAURE (Rad.), *until then Secretary of State for Foreign Affairs; took over the functions of Alain SAVARY on Nov. 4, 1956 after the latter resigned.*

SECOND LEGISLATURE

THIRD LEGISLATURE

4. The Ministry for Moroccan and Tunisian Affairs was created on June 19, 1954.

5. After the dissolution of the Ministry for Moroccan and Tunisian Affairs on October 20, 1955, its powers were once again assumed by the Quai d'Orsay. Pierre July became Assistant to the Premier, Jean Chamant (Independent) became Secretary of State for Foreign Affairs and was given special charge of the affairs of Morocco, Tunisia, and associated states.

ANNEX III

THE ASSEMBLIES OF THE INTERMEDIARY PERIOD AND THE COMPOSITION OF THE SUCCESSIVE NATIONAL ASSEMBLIES

I. The Assemblies of the Intermediary Period

First provisional Consultative Assembly (Algiers)	November 1943 (first session) July 1944 (last session)
Second provisional Consultative Assembly (Paris)	November 1944 (first session) July 1945 (dissolution)
First Constituent Assembly	October 1945 (election) April 1946 (dissolution)
Second Constituent Assembly	June 1946 (election) October 1946 (dissolution)

II. Composition of the Successive National Assemblies [1]

(France and overseas)

Election date	Com.	S.F.I.O.	M.R.P.	Rad.	U.D.S.R.	Cons.	R.P.F.	Others	Total Seats
First legislature Nov. 10, 1946	183	105	167	43	27	71	—	22	618
Second legislature June 17, 1951	101	107	96	76	19	98	120	10	627
Third legislature Jan. 2, 1956	150	99	84	75	19	97	22	50	596

1. This table is based on that of Philip Williams, *Politics in Post-War France* (London, 1958), p. 447. The information is taken from the official lists of parliamentary groups. The figures given for 1946 show the situation that existed several months after the election. Those for 1951 are from the first official list, modified by two by-elections and by the Assembly's decision on the representation of Seine-Maritime. Those for 1956 are from the first official list, modified by one by-election and by the invalidation of ten Poujadist members. The Radical total includes the R.G.R. members; "Conservatives" takes in the Moderates, Independents, and Peasants as well as other groups of the Right; and "Others" includes the 42 Poujadist members of 1956. No elections were held for the 30 Algerian seats or for the territories ceded to India (1 seat).

659

ANNEX IV

MAPS

Map 1

Map 2

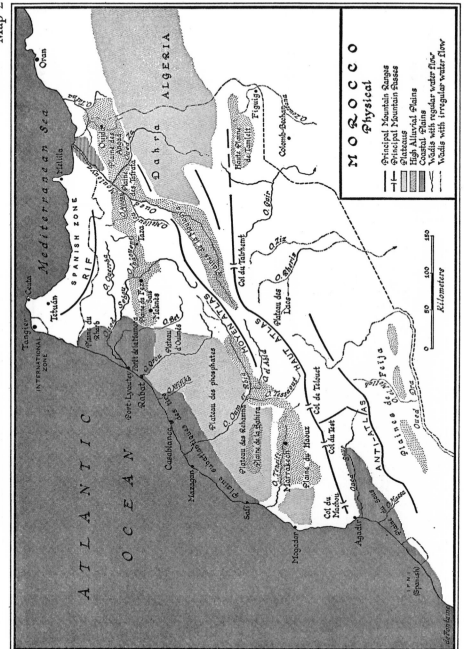

MOROCCO
Physical

Principal Mountain Ranges
Principal Mountain Passes
Plateaus
High Alluvial Plains
Coastal Plains
Wadis with regular water flow
Wadis with irregular water flow

ATLANTIC OCEAN

Mediterranean Sea

ALGERIA

Dahra

SPANISH ZONE

RIF

INTERNATIONAL ZONE

Oran

Melilla

Tangier
Ceuta
Tetuán

Col du Touahar
Oued Moulouya
Oued Inaouene
Taza
Plaine des Triffa

O. Guerba

O. Sebou

O. Inaouene

Plaine du Rharb

Plaine du Saïs
Meknès

MOYEN ATLAS

HAUT ATLAS

Colomb-Bechar

Figuig

Hauts Plaines de Tamlelt

O. Gair

O. Ziz

O. Rheris

Col du Tahremt

Plateau des Lacs

Port-Lyautey
Rabat
O. Oron
O. Bet

Plateau d'Oulmès

Forêt de Mamora

Casablanca

Mazagan

Safi

Mogador

Plateau des phosphates

Plaine de la Bahira

Plateau des Rehamna

Plaine du Haouz

Marrakech

Col du Test

Col du Telouet

ANTI-ATLAS

Plaines de l'Oued Fetja

Oued Dra

Col du Machou

Agadir

IFNI
(Spanish)

0   50   100   150
Kilometers

Map 3

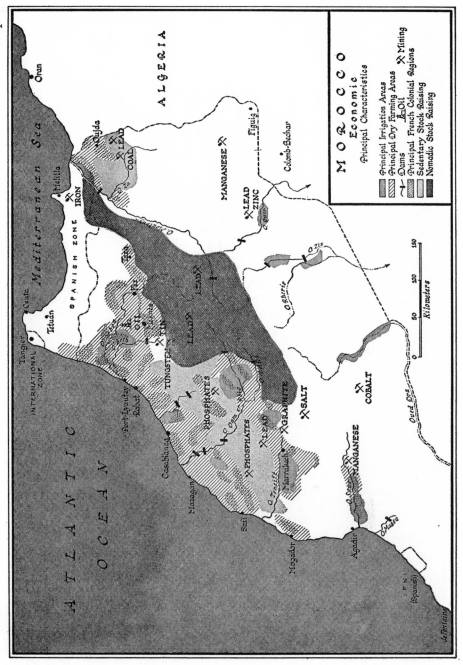

ATLANTIC OCEAN

Mediterranean Sea

SPANISH ZONE

ALGERIA

Oran

Melilla

Ceuta

Tangier

INTERNATIONAL ZONE

Tetuán

Oujda

IRON ✕

✕ LEAD

COAL

MANGANESE ✕

Figuig

Colomb-Béchar

LEAD ✕
ZINC

Fez

OIL ✕

LEAD ✕

Port-Lyautey

Rabat

TUNGSTEN ✕

Casablanca

Mazagan

PHOSPHATES

✕ PHOSPHATES

✕ LEAD

✕ GRAPHITE

✕ SALT

COBALT ✕

Marrakech

MANGANESE ✕

Safi

Mogador

Agadir

(IFNI)
(Spanish)

O. Dra

O. Ziz

O. Rheris

O. Ouarga

O. Oum er-Rbia

O. Tensift

MOROCCO
Economic
Principal Characteristics

Principal Irrigation Areas
Principal Dry Farming Areas
Dams
Oil ✕ Mining
Principal French Colonial Regions
Sedentary Stock Raising
Nomadic Stock Raising

0   50   100   150
Kilometers

Map 4

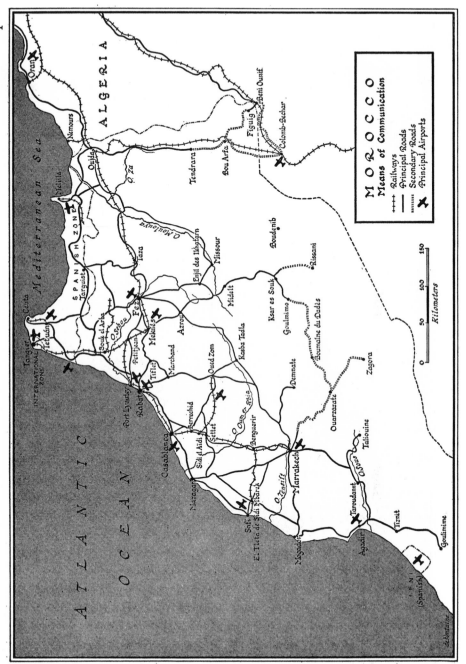

Map 5

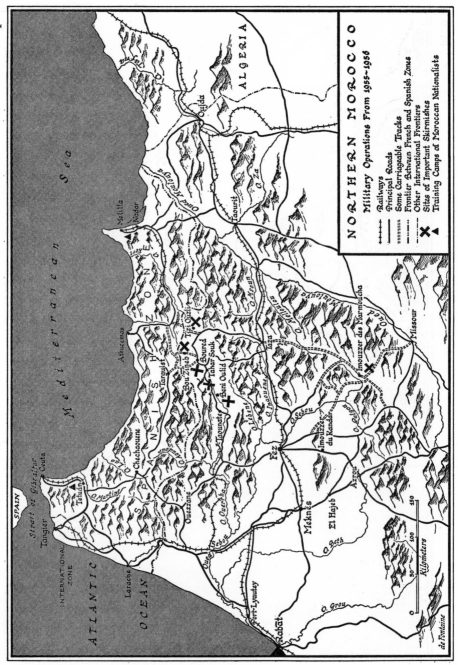

INDEX